P9-CQX-548

Fodor's

VENICE & THE BEST
OF NORTHERN ITALY

1st Edition

Fodor's Travel Publications   New York, Toronto, London, Sydney, Auckland
www.fodors.com

Be a Fodor's Correspondent

Your opinion matters. It matters to us. It matters to your fellow Fodor's travelers, too. And we'd like to hear it. In fact, we need to hear it.

When you share your experiences and opinions, you become an active member of the Fodor's community. That means we'll not only use your feedback to make our books better, but we'll publish your names and comments whenever possible. Throughout our guides, look for "Word of Mouth," excerpts of your unvarnished feedback.

Here's how you can help improve Fodor's for all of us.

Tell us when we're right. We rely on local writers to give you an insider's perspective. But our writers and staff editors—who are the best in the business—depend on you. Your positive feedback is a vote to renew our recommendations for the next edition.

Tell us when we're wrong. We're proud that we update most of our guides every year. But we're not perfect. Things change. Hotels cut services. Museums change hours. Charming cafés lose charm. If our writer didn't quite capture the essence of a place, tell us how you'd do it differently. If any of our descriptions are inaccurate or inadequate, we'll incorporate your changes in the next edition and will correct factual errors at fodors.com immediately.

Tell us what to include. You probably have had fantastic travel experiences that aren't yet in Fodor's. Why not share them with a community of like-minded travelers? Maybe you chanced upon a beach or bistro or B&B that you don't want to keep to yourself. Tell us why we should include it. And share your discoveries and experiences with everyone directly at fodors.com. Your input may lead us to add a new listing or highlight a place we cover with a "Highly Recommended" star or with our highest rating, "Fodor's Choice."

Give us your opinion instantly at our feedback center at fodors.com/contact-us. You may also e-mail editors@fodors.com with the subject line "Venice Editor." Or send your nominations, comments, and complaints by mail to Venice Editor, Fodor's, 1745 Broadway, New York, NY 10019.

You and travelers like you are the heart of the Fodor's community. Make our community richer by sharing your experiences. Be a Fodor's correspondent.

Buon viaggio! (Or simply: Happy traveling!)

Tim Jarrell, Publisher

FODOR'S VENICE & THE BEST OF NORTHERN ITALY

Editor: Matthew Lombardi

Writers: Peter Blackman, Bruce Leimsidor, Megan McCaffrey-Guerrera, Nan McElroy, Sara Rosso

Production Editor: Jennifer DePrima

Maps & Illustrations: Mark Stroud and David Lindroth, *cartographers;* Bob Blake, Rebecca Baer, *map editors;* William Wu, *information graphics*

Design: Fabrizio La Rocca, *creative director*; Guido Caroti, Siobhan O'Hare, *art directors*; Tina Malaney, Nora Rosansky, Chie Ushio, Jessica Walsh, Ann McBride, *designers*; Melanie Marin, *senior picture editor*

Cover Photo: (Church of San Giovanni in Bragora, Rio della Pieta, Venice) SIME/eStock Photo

Production Manager: Angela L. McLean

SPECIAL SALES

This book is available at special discounts for bulk purchases for sales promotions or premiums. Special editions, including personalized covers, excerpts of existing books, and corporate imprints, can be created in large quantities for special needs. For more information, write to Special Markets/Premium Sales, 1745 Broadway, MD 6-2, New York, New York 10019, or e-mail specialmarkets@randomhouse.com.

AN IMPORTANT TIP & AN INVITATION

Although all prices, opening times, and other details in this book are based on information supplied to us at press time, changes occur all the time in the travel world, and Fodor's cannot accept responsibility for facts that become outdated or for inadvertent errors or omissions. So **always confirm information when it matters,** especially if you're making a detour to visit a specific place. Your experiences—positive and negative—matter to us. If we have missed or misstated something, **please write to us.** Share your opinion instantly through our online feedback center @ fodors.com/contact-us.

PRINTED IN SINGAPORE

10 9 8 7 6 5 4 3 2 1

CONTENTS

Fodor's Features

CONTENTS

MAPS

ABOUT
THIS BOOK

Our Ratings

Sometimes you find terrific travel experiences and sometimes they just find you. But usually the burden is on you to select the right combination of experiences. That's where our ratings come in.

As travelers we've all discovered a place so wonderful that its worthiness is obvious. And sometimes that place is so unique that superlatives don't do it justice: you just have to be there to know. These sights, properties, and experiences get our highest rating, **Fodor's Choice**, indicated by orange stars throughout this book.

Black stars highlight sights and properties we deem **Highly Recommended**, places that our writers, editors, and readers praise again and again for consistency and excellence.

By default, there's another category: any place we include in this book is by definition worth your time, unless we say otherwise. And we will.

Disagree with any of our choices? Care to nominate a place or suggest that we rate one more highly? Visit our feedback center at www.fodors.com/feedback.

Budget Well

Hotel and restaurant price categories from ¢ to $$$$ are defined in the opening pages of each chapter. For attractions, we always give standard adult admission fees; reductions are usually available for children, students, and senior citizens. Want to pay with plastic? **AE, D, DC, MC, V** following restaurant and hotel listings indicate whether American Express, Discover, Diners Club, MasterCard, and Visa are accepted.

Restaurants

Unless we state otherwise, restaurants are open for lunch and dinner daily. We mention dress only when there's a specific requirement and reservations only when they're essential or not accepted—it's always best to book ahead.

Hotels

Hotels have private bath, phone, TV, and air-conditioning unless we indicate otherwise. Hotels with the designation **BP** (for Breakfast Plan) at the end of their listing include breakfast in the rate; offerings can vary from coffee and a roll to an elaborate buffet. Those designated **EP** (European Plan) have no meals included; **MAP** (Modified American Plan) means you get breakfast and dinner; **FAP** (Full American Plan) includes all meals. We always list facilities but not whether you'll be charged an extra fee to use them, so when pricing accommodations, find out what's included.

Listings

★	Fodor's Choice
★	Highly recommended
⊠	Physical address
⊕	Directions or Map coordinates
⌂	Mailing address
☎	Telephone
🖷	Fax
⊕	On the Web
✎	E-mail
🖅	Admission fee
⊙	Open/closed times
Ⓜ	Metro stations
▭	Credit cards

Hotels & Restaurants

🏨	Hotel
➡	Number of rooms
⌂	Facilities
❑	Meal plans
✕	Restaurant
⌂	Reservations
🜛	Dress code
⌇	Smoking
⸙	BYOB

Outdoors

🏌	Golf
⛺	Camping

Other

☾	Family-friendly
⇨	See also
⊠	Branch address
☞	Take note

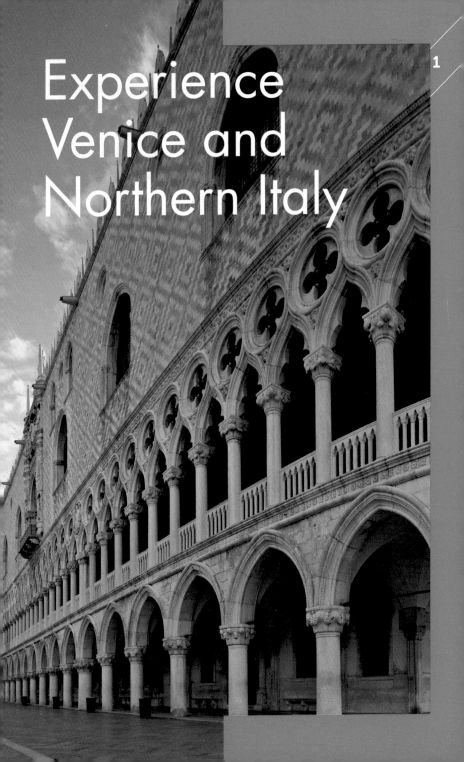

Experience
Venice and
Northern Italy

WHAT'S WHERE

1 Venice. One of the world's most novel cities—and one of the most beautiful—Venice has canals where the streets should be and an atmosphere of faded splendor that practically defines the word *decadent*.

2 The Veneto and Friuli-Venezia Giulia. The green plains stretching west of Venice hold three of northern Italy's most artistically significant midsize cities: Padua, Vicenza, and Verona. Farther north and east, Alpine foothills are dotted with small, welcoming towns and some of Italy's most distinguished vineyards.

3 The Dolomites. Along Italy's northeast border, the Dolomites are the country's finest mountain playground, with gorgeous cliffs, curiously shaped peaks, lush meadows, and crystal-clear lakes. The skiing is good, and the scenery is different from what you find in the Austrian, Swiss, or French Alps.

4 Milan, Lombardy, and the Lakes. The deep-blue lakes of the Lombardy region—Como, Garda, and Maggiore—have been attracting vacationers since the days of ancient Rome. At the center of Lombardy is Milan, Italy's second-largest city and its business capital. It holds

Italy's most renowned opera house, and as the epicenter of Italian fashion and design, it's a shopper's paradise.

5 Piedmont and Valle d'Aosta. A step off the usual tourist circuit, these regions in Italy's northwest corner have attractions that are well worth a visit. You'll find here great Alpine peaks along the French and Swiss borders, a highly esteemed food-and-wine culture, and an elegant regional capital in Turin.

6 The Italian Riviera. Northern Italy's most attractive coastline runs along the Italian Riviera in the region of Liguria. The best beaches lie west of Genoa, but the main appeal lies to the east of the city, in the beauty of the seaside cliffs and coves, and the villages interspersed among them.

AUSTRIA

ALPI

TRENTINO-
ALTO ADIGE

Cortina
d'Ampezzo

Bolzano

FRIULI-VENEZIA
GIULIA

Lugano

Lake
Como

Trento

Belluno

Udine

Como

Bergamo

Lake
Garda

VENETO

Treviso

Trieste

Brescia

Vicenza

Milan

Verona

2

4 LOMBARDY

Padua

1 Venice

Pavia

Mantua

Adige

Gulf of
Venice

Po

Parma

Ferrara

Modena

LIGURIA

Bologna

Ravenna

Genoa

Rapallo

6

Adriatic Sea

Gulf of
Genoa

La Spezia

Rimini

SAN MARINO

Pistoia

SAN MARINO

Lucca

Florence

Pisa

Arno

THE
MARCHES

Ancona

Livorno

TUSCANY

Arezzo

Macerata

Sea

Siena

Perugia

Assisi

UMBRIA

CORSICA

ELBA

FRANCE

Grosseto

Orvieto

VENICE AND NORTHERN ITALY PLANNER

Speaking the Language

People who interact regularly with tourists—such as hotel, restaurant, museum, and transportation personnel—generally speak some English. However, even in the cosmopolitan north, although knowledge of foreign languages is increasing, often highly educated Italians speak only Italian. Many are slightly offended if a foreigner assumes they speak English without first asking politely, "*Parla lei inglese?*" If you do ask, most Italians, even those with no English, will try to be helpful. Perhaps because of their own linguistic limitations, Italians are very tolerant of foreigners who try to speak their language and do wonders in understanding fractured Italian.

Even if you speak Italian, don't be surprised if you can't understand conversations going on around you, which may be in local dialect. Because of television and mass education, now almost everyone speaks standard Italian, and in cities such as Milan dialect has almost died out, but it still thrives in the Veneto and in areas that have not had a large influx of residents from other parts of Italy. Among friends, at home, and in moments of high emotion, standard Italian gives way to the local language.

Getting Here

Aeroporto Malpensa, 50 km (31 mi) northwest of Milan, is the major northern Italian hub for intercontinental flights and also sees substantial European and domestic traffic. Venice's **Aeroporto Marco Polo** also serves international destinations.

There are regional airports in Turin, Genoa, Bologna, Verona, Trieste, Treviso, Bolzano, and Parma, and Milan has a secondary airport, Linate. You can reach all of these on connecting flights from within Italy and from other European cities. If you fly into Malpensa, but Milan isn't your final destination, you can also get where you're going by train, using the Italian national rail system, **Ferrovie dello Stato** (☎ 892021 *toll-free within Italy* ⊕ *www.trenitalia.com*). Shuttle buses run three times an hour (less often after 10 PM) between Malpensa and Milan's main train station, Stazione Centrale; the trip takes about 75 minutes, depending on traffic. The Malpensa Express Train, which leaves twice an hour, takes 40 minutes and delivers you to Cadorna station in central Milan.

Typical Travel Times

	Hours by Car	Hours by Train
Venice–Milan	3:30	2:35
Venice–Turin	5:00	4:20
Venice–Genoa	4:45	4:30
Venice–Como	4:00	3:30
Venice–Bolzano	3:15	3:10
Milan–Turin	2:00	2:00
Milan–Genoa	2:00	1:45
Milan–Verona	1:45	1:20
Genoa–Turin	2:00	2:00
Milan–Bolzano	3:00	3:30
Genoa–Como	2:45	3:20

Restaurants: The Basics

A full meal in Italy has traditionally consisted of five courses, and every menu you encounter will still be organized along some version of this five-course plan:

First up is the *antipasto* (appetizer), often consisting of cured meats or marinated vegetables. Next to appear is the *primo*, usually pasta or soup, and after that the *secondo*, a meat or fish course with, perhaps, a *contorno* (vegetable dish) on the side. A simple *dolce* (dessert) rounds out the meal.

This, you've probably noticed, is a lot of food. Italians have noticed as well—a full, five-course meal is an indulgence usually reserved for special occasions. Instead, restaurant meals are a mix-and-match affair: you might order a primo and a secondo, or an antipasto and a primo, or a secondo and a contorno.

The crucial rule of restaurant dining is that you should **order at least two courses.** It's a common mistake for tourists to order only a secondo, thinking they're getting a "main course" complete with side dishes. What they wind up with is one lonely piece of meat.

Hotels: The Basics

Hotels in Italy are usually well maintained (especially if they've earned our recommendation in this book), but in some respects they won't match what you find at comparably priced U.S. lodgings. Keep the following points in mind as you set your expectations, and you're likely to have a good experience:

■ First and foremost, rooms are usually smaller, particularly in cities. If you're truly cramped, ask for another room, but don't expect things to be spacious.

■ A "double bed" is commonly two singles pushed together.

■ In the bathroom, tubs are not a given—request one if it's essential. In budget places, showers sometimes use a drain in the middle of the bathroom floor. And washcloths are a rarity.

■ Most hotels have satellite TV, but there are fewer channels than in the United States, and only one or two will be in English.

■ Don't expect wall-to-wall carpeting. Particularly outside the cities, tile floors are the norm.

When to Go

Spring: Late April through early June is an ideal time to tour northern Italy: the weather is mild, and the volume of tourists isn't as large as in summer. By May the coastal towns of Liguria are coming to life, but mountain hiking trails can stay icy into June.

Summer: Away from the mountains, summers are warm and humid; bring sunscreen. Summer is prime hiking season in the Alps, and the lakes and the Riviera are in full swing (meaning lodging reservations are a must).

Fall: Autumn, like spring, is an ideal time for touring most of the region. In much of northern Italy it's usually pleasant and sunny well into October, and it doesn't really begin to get cold until mid-November—except in the mountains, where temperatures drop sharply in September. Many mountain tourist facilities close until ski season.

Winter: Venetian winters are relatively mild, with fewer tourists, but there are frequent rainy spells, and early and late in the season there's the threat of *acqua alta,* the brief flooding of low-lying areas. In the Dolomites most ski resorts are open from mid-December through April, but snowfall in early winter is unreliable; the best skiing often isn't until February. Likewise, in Piedmont and Valle d'Aosta, snow conditions vary from year to year. Resort towns of the Lake District and the Riviera are all but shut down.

VENICE AND NORTHERN ITALY TOP ATTRACTIONS

Venice's Piazza San Marco

(A) Perhaps nowhere else in the world gathers together so many of man's noblest artistic creations. The centerpiece of the piazza is the Basilica di San Marco, arguably the most beautiful Byzantine church in the West, with not only its shimmering Byzantine Romanesque facade, but also its jewel-like mosaic-encrusted interior. Right next door is the Venetian Gothic Palazzo Ducale, which was so beloved by the Venetians that when it burned down in the 16th century, they rejected projects by the greatest architects of the Renaissance and had their palace rebuilt *come era, dove era*—exactly how and where it was. (⇨ *Chapter 2.*)

Venice's Grand Canal

(B) No one ever forgets a first trip down the Grand Canal. The sight of its magnificent palaces, with the light reflected from the canal's waters shimmering across their facades, is one of Italy's great experiences. (⇨ *Chapter 2.*)

Venice's Gallerie dell'Accademia

(C) The greatest museum in northern Italy is a treasure trove of Venetian masters; Titian, Veronese, Tintoretto, Tiepollo, Bellini, Giorgione, and Carpaccio are all represented by some of their finest work. After a few hours here, you'll understand why art historians are so enamored of the way Venice's great painters used color. (⇨ *Chapter 2.*)

The Villas and Palazzi of Palladio

(D) The great 16th-century architect Palladio created harmoniously beautiful buildings that were influential in spreading the neoclassical style to northern Europe, England, and, later, America. He did most of his work in and around his native city of Vicenza. If a visit to Vicenza simply whets your appetite for Palladio, you can see another wonderful

Palladian villa outside Venice (La Malcontenta) and his famous collaboration with Veronese outside Treviso (Villa Barbaro). (⇨ *Chapter 7.*)

Lake Como

(E) Just a short drive or train ride north of Milan, Lake Como combines spectacular mountain scenery with the elegance of baroque and neoclassical villas and gardens and the charm of picturesque villages. It's great any time of year, but best in the spring, when the azaleas are in bloom in the gardens of Villa Carlotta. (⇨ *Chapter 9.*)

Giotto's Frescoes in the Scrovegni Chapel, Padua

(F) Dante's contemporary Giotto decorated this chapel with an eloquent and beautiful fresco cycle. Its convincing human dimension helped to change the course of Western art. (⇨ *Chapter 7.*)

Mantua

(G) This charming town, slightly off the beaten track in Lombardy, contains a highpoint of 15th-century painting: Mantegna's frescoes in the wedding chamber of the Palazzo Ducale, a masterpiece of spatial illusion. On the outskirts of town, Giulio Romano's Palazzo Te is an elegant pleasure palace, frescoed with illusionistic painting carrying the tradition established by Mantegna several steps further. (⇨ *Chapter 9.*)

Leonardo's *Last Supper*

(H) On the refectory wall of Santa Maria della Grazia in Milan, one of the world's most famous paintings still evokes wonder, not at all trivialized by millions of reproductions or dulled by its poor state of conservation. (⇨ *Chapter 9.*)

TOP EXPERIENCES

Churchgoing

Few images are more identifiable with Italy than the country's great churches, amazing works of architecture that often took centuries to build. The name *Duomo* (derived from the Latin for "house," *domus,* and the root of the English "dome") is used to refer to the principal church of a town or city. Generally speaking, the bigger the city, the more splendid its duomo, though impressive churches can sometimes inhabit unlikely places.

In Venice, there are more spectacular churches than you can count on two hands, but the Byzantine-influenced **Basilica di San Marco** (⇨ *Chapter 2)* holds pride of place. **Milan's Duomo** (⇨ *Chapter 9)* is the largest Gothic cathedral in Italy. To the west of Turin, the **Sacra di San Michele** (⇨ *Chapter 10)* is a remarkably imposing medieval abbey.

Discovering the Cinque Terre

Along the Italian Riviera east of Genoa are five tiny, remote fishing villages known collectively as the **Cinque Terre** (⇨ *Chapter 11)*. The beauty of the landscape—with steep, vine-covered hills pushing smack-dab against an azure sea—and the charm of the villages have turned the area into one of Italy's top destinations. The number-one activity is hiking the trails that run between the villages—the views are once-in-a-lifetime gorgeous—but if hiking isn't your thing, you can still have fun lounging about in cafés, admiring the water, and wandering through the medieval streets of the villages.

Taking Part in Venice's Festivals

Few people love a good party as much as the Venetians. The biggest is, of course, **Carnevale,** culminating on Fat Tuesday, the day before Lent, but with revelry beginning about 10 days earlier. Visitors from the world over join the Venetians in a period of institutionalized fantasy, dressing in sometimes exquisitely elaborate costumes. The program changes each year and includes public, mostly free cultural events in all the districts of the city.

The **Redentore,** on the third weekend in July, is a festival essentially for Venetians, but guests are always welcome. The Venetians pack a picnic dinner and eat in boats decorated with paper lanterns in the Bacino di San Marco. Just before midnight, there's a magnificent fireworks display. The next day (Sunday), everyone crosses a temporary bridge spanning the Canale della Giudecca to Palladio's Redentore church to light a candle.

Venice Biennale is a cutting-edge international art exposition held in odd numbered years from June to November in special exhibition halls in the Venice Public Gardens (Giardini) and in the 14th-century industrial complex (Le corderie) in the Arsenale. It's the most important exhibition of contemporary art in Italy and one of the three most important in Europe.

Hiking in the Dolomites

Even if you don't fancy yourself a disciple of Reinhold Messner (the local hero and the first man to reach the peak of Everest without oxygen), you'll find great summer hiking aplenty in the **Dolomites** (⇨ *Chapter 8)*. There are appealing trails for all levels of hikers; the scenery is uniquely beautiful, with massive slabs of rock towering over alpine meadows; and the culture is a pleasing mix of Austrian efficiency and Italian charm. The ultimate Dolomites experience is to stay in a *rifugio,* a mountain lodge accessible only by foot, where

accommodations are usually modest but food is usually delicious.

Getting Fashionable in Milan

Italian clothing and furniture design are world famous, and the center of the Italian design industry is **Milan** (⇨ *Chapter 9*). The best way to see what's happening in the world of fashion is to browse the designer showrooms and boutiques of the fabled *quadrilatero della moda*, along and around Via Montenapoleone. The central event in the world of furniture design is Milan's annual Salone Internazionale del Mobile, held at the Milan fairgrounds for a week in April. Admission is generally restricted to the trade, but the Salone is open to the general public for one day, generally on a Sunday, during the week of the show.

Tasting the Wine

When it comes to wine making, the Italian Renaissance is happening right now: throughout the country, vintners are challenging themselves to produce wines of ever-higher quality. You can taste the fruits of their labor at wine bars and restaurants, and in many areas you can visit the vineyards as well. For touring guidance in the northeastern region of the Veneto, see **Traveling the Wine Roads** (⇨ *Chapter 7*). For the lowdown on Italy's "King of Wines," see **On the Trail of Barolo** (⇨ *Chapter 10*).

Driving the Back Roads

If you associate Italian roads with unruly motorists and endless traffic snarls, you're only partly right. Along the rural back roads, things are more relaxed. You might stop on a lark to take a picture of a crumbling farmhouse, have a coffee in a time-frozen hill town, or enjoy an epic lunch at a rustic *agriturismo* inaccessible to public transportation. Driving, in short, is the best way to see Italy.

Among the countless beautiful drives, these are three of the most memorable: the legendary mountain ascent on **SS48, the Grande Strada delle Dolomiti** (⇨ *Chapter 8*), takes you through the heart of the Dolomites, the famous Passo di Sella, and into the Val Gardena, passing unforgettable, craggy-peaked views. Every time the A1 autostrada tunnels through the mountains, this smaller **SS1, Via Aurelia** (⇨ *Chapter 11*), stays out on the jagged coastline of the Italian Riviera, passing terraced vineyards, cliff-hanging villages, and shimmering seas.

Il Dolce Far Niente

"The sweetness of doing nothing" has long been an art form in Italy. This is a country in which life's pleasures are warmly celebrated, not guiltily indulged.

Of course, doing "nothing" doesn't really mean nothing. It means doing things differently: lingering over a glass of wine for the better part of an evening as you watch the sun slowly set; savoring a slow and flirtatious evening *passeggiata* along the main street of a little town; and making a commitment—however temporary—to thinking that there is nowhere that you have to be next, and no other time than the magical present.

It's easy to achieve such a state of mind in **Bellagio**, on Lake Como (⇨ *Chapter 9*), where you can meander through stately gardens, dance on the wharf, or just watch the boats float by in the shadow of the Alps. And there's still nothing more romantic than a **gondola ride** along Venice's canals (⇨ *Chapter 2*), your escorted trip to nowhere, watched over by Gothic palaces with delicately arched eyebrows.

QUINTESSENTIAL VENICE AND NORTHERN ITALY

Il Caffè (Coffee)

The Italian day begins and ends with coffee, and more cups of coffee punctuate the time in between. To live like the Italians do, drink as they drink, standing at the counter or sitting at an outdoor table of the corner bar. (In Italy, a "bar" is a coffee bar.) A primer: *caffè* means coffee, and Italian standard issue is what Americans call espresso—short, strong, and usually taken very sweet. *Cappuccino* is a foamy half-and-half of espresso and steamed milk; cocoa powder *(cacao)* on top is acceptable, cinnamon is not. If you're thinking of having a cappuccino for dessert, think again—Italians drink only caffè or caffè *macchiato* (with a spot of steamed milk) after lunchtime. Confused? Homesick? Order caffè *americano* for a reasonable facsimile of good-old filtered joe. Note that you usually pay for your coffee first, then take your receipt to the counter and tell the barista your order.

Il Calcio (Soccer)

Imagine the most rabid American football fans—the ones who paint their faces on game day and sleep in pajamas emblazoned with the logo of their favorite team. Throw in a dose of melodrama along the lines of a tear-jerking soap opera. Ratchet up the intensity by a factor of 10, and you'll start to get a sense of how Italians feel about their national game, soccer—known in the mother tongue as *calcio*. On Sunday afternoons throughout the long September-to-May season, stadiums are packed throughout Italy. Those who don't get to games in person tend to congregate around television sets in restaurants and bars, rooting for the home team with a passion that feels like a last vestige of the days when the country was a series of warring medieval city-states. How calcio mania affects your stay in Italy depends on how eager you are to get involved. At the very least, you may notice an eerie

If you want to get a sense of contemporary Italian culture and indulge in some of its pleasures, start by familiarizing yourself with the rituals of daily life. These are a few highlights—things you can take part in with relative ease.

Sunday-afternoon quiet on the city streets, or erratic restaurant service around the same time, accompanied by cheers and groans from a neighboring room. If you want a memorable, truly Italian experience, attend a game yourself. Availability of tickets may depend on the current fortunes of the local team, but they often can be acquired with help from your hotel concierge.

Il Gelato (Ice Cream)

During warmer months, *gelato*—the Italian equivalent of ice cream—is a national obsession. It's considered a snack rather than a dessert, bought at stands and shops in piazzas and on street corners, and consumed on foot, usually at a leisurely stroll *(see La Passeggiata, below)*. Gelato is softer, less creamy, and more intensely flavored than its American counterpart. It comes in simple flavors that capture the essence of the main ingredient. (You won't find Chunky Monkey or Cookies

'n' Cream.) Standard choices include pistachio, *nocciola* (hazelnut), caffè, and numerous fresh-fruit varieties. Quality varies; the surest sign that you've hit on a good spot is a line at the counter.

La Passeggiata (Strolling)

A favorite Italian pastime is the *passeggiata* (literally, the promenade). In the late afternoon and early evening, especially on weekends, couples, families, and packs of teenagers stroll the main streets and piazzas of Italy's towns. It's a ritual of exchanged news and gossip, window-shopping, flirting, and gelato-eating that adds up to a uniquely Italian experience. To join in, simply hit the streets for a bit of wandering. You may feel more like an observer than a participant, until you realize that observing is what la passeggiata is all about.

NORTHERN ITALY TODAY

...feels the influence of immigration

The population of northern Italy, especially the western regions, has undergone a substantial transformation due to immigration. Beginning during the economic boom of the 1960s and continuing to the 1980s, Italians from the south moved to the great industrial centers of Turin and Milan, changing the face of those cities. The southerners, or at least their children, adopted most northern customs—few now go home for a nap at midday—but their presence has had a clear influence on the culture of the north. Especially in the cities, local dialects died out, and at the dinner table, the traditional polenta and risotto now share the scene with spaghetti and other pastas, and southern dishes often appear on menus.

Prosperity, and immigration, came later to the northeast. Venetians still enjoy the 18th-century dialect comedies of Goldoni, and it's not uncommon to hear dialect spoken by elegant operagoers at La Fenice. Emilia-Romagna, an essentially agricultural region that attracted few Italian immigrants, has kept its great culinary culture intact.

Northern Italy, like the rest of the country, has recently experienced an influx of foreign immigrants, although their numbers are smaller relative to the local population than in many other European countries. Their welcome has varied widely: proudly cosmopolitan Venice is fairly open to the newcomers, while in cities where government is controlled by the overtly xenophobic Northern League, integration has been contentious. But despite fears stemming from cultural differences, and perhaps because labor is sorely needed by local industry, northern Italians tend to accept new arrivals.

...is eating well

Italy is home of one of the world's greatest cuisines, so it may seem disingenuous to claim that it's improving—but it clearly is. Ingredients that in the past were available only to the wealthy can now be found even in the remotest parts of the country at reasonable prices. Dishes originally conceived to make the most of inferior cuts of meat or the least flavorful part of vegetables are now made with the best.

The same is true of Italian wine. A generation ago, the omnipresent straw-basket Chianti was a mainstay of pizzerias around the world, but the wine inside was often watery and insipid. Today, through investment and experimentation, Italy's winemakers are figuring out how to get the most from their gorgeous vineyards. It's fair to say that Italy now produces more types of high-quality wine from more different grape varieties than any other country in the world.

Italian restaurateurs are keeping up with the changes. Though quaint family-run trattorias with checkered tablecloths, traditional dishes, and informal atmosphere are still common, there's no doubt that they are on the decline. And nearly every town has a newer eatery with matching flatware, a proper wine list, and an innovative menu.

...struggles with the global economy

Parts of northern Italy are among the most prosperous areas in Europe. But recently, even these economic powerhouses have run into trouble. The industrial base consists mainly of small and midsize businesses, many of which have had either to close or outsource to Eastern Europe or Central Asia because of a lack of unskilled and semiskilled labor at home. And many of those businesses, such as those in the

textile sector, have had difficulty dealing with competition from China.

. . . is passionate about soccer

Soccer stands without rival as the national sport of Italy, but recently there have been some changes to the beautiful game. On the positive side, Italy won its fourth World Cup in 2006. But in subsequent years there were unwelcome developments involving alleged match fixing, backroom deals for television contracts, drug scandals among players, increased violence between rival fans—and an uninspired performance in the 2010 Cup.

Italian professional soccer leagues are trying to put those issues behind them and focus on on-the-field play, where the Italian leagues rank with England and Spain as the best in Europe. One emerging positive trend is geographic parity. After several years of the top *Serie A* league being dominated by northern teams, success recently has been spread more evenly around, much to the joy of soccer-mad fans from the south.

. . . remains influenced by the Church

Despite Italy's being officially a secular state, most Italians, whether pious or pagan, would agree that it is difficult to separate Italian politics from the Roman Catholic Church. The Church's influence is greatest when it acts in support of the political right and conservative social policies. So, divorce is complicated, and gays and lesbians enjoy fewer rights than in most other European countries. The Church's power is more limited if it tries to espouse liberal causes: it treads lightly when condemning corruption and scandalous behavior on the part of powerful politicians, and recent attempts to foster the rights of immigrants and ethnic minorities have fallen on deaf ears.

The Veneto has been the stronghold of the socially conservative successors to the Church-oriented Christian Democratic Party. Emilia-Romagna, on the other hand, has had a strong socialist, and even communist, tradition, but the Church still is a powerful force there also. The dichotomy has been raised to the level of a folk legend by the novels and films featuring disputes between Don Camillo and Peppone, a priest and the communist mayor of Brescello, a town in Emilia.

. . . is getting older

Italy is the oldest country in Europe (worldwide, only Japan is older)—the result of its low birth rate, relatively strict immigration standards, and one of the highest life expectancy rates in the world. As of 2010, the average Italian was 42.9 years old, and the number keeps rising.

The result is a remarkably stable population: the total number of Italian residents barely rises most years, and, according to the most recent estimates, is projected to start contracting by 2020. But the situation is putting a strain on the country's pension system and on families, since elderly family members are likely to live with their children or grandchildren in a country where nursing homes are rare.

The trend also has an impact on other areas, including politics (where older politicians are eager to promote policies aimed at older voters), the popular culture (where everything from fashion to television programming takes older consumers into consideration), and a kind of far-reaching nostalgia; thanks to a long collective memory, it's common to hear even younger Italians celebrate or rue something that happened 50 or 60 years earlier as if it had just taken place.

A GREAT ITINERARY

Day 1: Bellagio

If you're flying to northern Italy from overseas, there's no better way to rest up after a long flight than a day on Lake Como, combining some of Italy's most beautiful scenery with elegant historic villas and gardens. At the center of it all is Bellagio, a pretty village with world-class restaurants and hotels, as well as more-economical options. From Bellagio you can ferry to other points along the lake, take walking tours, go hiking, or just sit on a terrace watching the light play on the sapphire water and the snowcapped mountains in the distance.

Logistics: There are inexpensive bus-train combinations from Milan's Malpensa airport. A limousine service, Fly to Lake (☎ *0341/286887* ⊕ *www.flytolake.com*), leaves Malpensa four times per day (€35–€70 per person depending on the number of travelers, no service Sunday, late fall, or winter). The trip takes a little over two hours. In Bellagio you won't need a car, since most of your touring will be on foot, by ferry, or by bus.

Day 2: Milan

After a leisurely breakfast in Bellagio, take the ferry to Varenna (15 minutes) and then the train (1 hour, 15 minutes) to Milan's Central Station. Milan is a leading center of fashion and design, and many visitors keep to the area of elegant shops around Via Montenapoleone. But the city also houses some of Europe's great art treasures in the Brera Gallery and has two churches by Bramante, perhaps the most refined of the Italian High Renaissance architects. And then, of course, there's Leonardo's *Last Supper.* You may want to spend your evening taking in an opera at Italy's most illustrious opera house, La Scala.

Logistics: Central Milan is compact, with excellent public transportation. Milan does have its share of crime; keep an eye on your possessions around the train station and avoid hotels in that area.

Days 3 to 5: Verona/Mantua/Vicenza

Take an early express train to Verona (1½ hours from Milan) and settle into your hotel, where you'll stay for three nights; you'll be using this stately medieval city as your base to see three of the most important art cities in northern Italy. Verona, with its ancient Roman arena, theater, and city gates, its brooding medieval palaces and castle, and its graceful bridge spanning the Adige, is probably the most immediately impressive of the three, and you'll want to spend the first day exploring its attractions. But the real artistic treasures are in the two smaller cities you'll see on day trips out of Verona.

The next day, take a short train trip to Mantua (30–45 minutes). Be sure to arrive in time for lunch, because Mantua has one of the most interesting local cuisines in northern Italy. The great local specialty is *tortelli di zucca* (pumpkin-, cheese-, and almond-paste-filled ravioli), served with sage butter and Parmesan cheese. The top artistic attractions are the Mantegna frescoes in the Palazzo Ducale, and you should also pay a visit to Giulio Romano's Palazzo Te, a 16th-century pleasure palace, on the outskirts of town. Take the train back to Verona in time for dinner, and perhaps catch an opera performance in Verona's Roman amphitheater.

The day after, take a short train trip to Vicenza (30 minutes) to see the palaces, villas, and public buildings of the lion of late 16th-century architecture, Andrea Palladio. Don't miss his Teatro Olimpico

and his most famous villa, La Rotonda, slightly out of town. For lunch, try the *baccalà alla vicentina*, the local version of dried salt cod, which is surprisingly good. Also be sure to see the frescoes by Gianbattista and Giandomenico Tiepolo in the Villa dei Nani, near the Rotonda. In spring and summer there are musical performances in the Teatro Olimpico; if you want to attend, you will have to book a hotel in Vicenza for the night, since you will miss the last train back to Verona.

Day 6: Padua

Most people visit this important art and university center on a day trip out of Venice, but then they miss one of Padua's main attractions, the nightlife that goes on in the city's wine bars and cafés from evening until quite late. Most cities in northern Italy, even Venice and Milan, have surprisingly little to offer after dinner or the theater, but in Padua, going out for a nightcap or coffee with friends is a tradition, not only for students but also for older folks. Arrive early enough to see at least the Giotto frescoes in the Cappella degli Scrovegni and the Basilica di San Antonio before lunch, then spend a relaxing afternoon at the Villa Pisani, enjoying its gardens and important Tiepolo fresco.

Logistics: Trains are frequent to Padua from Verona (1 hour) and Vicenza (30 minutes); you don't really have to schedule ahead.

Day 7: Venice

Three days are hardly enough to see one of the world's most beautiful cities and one of the cradles of modern Western civilization. But running from museum to museum, church to church would be a mistake, since Venice is a wonderful place to stroll or "hang out," taking in some of the atmosphere that inspired such great art.

The first things you will probably want to do in Venice are to take a vaporetto ride down the Grand Canal and see the Piazza San Marco. These are best done in the morning; before 8:30 you'll avoid rush hour on the vaporetto, and while there's likely to be a line at San Marco when it opens, you'll be better off then than later in the day. Move on to the adjacent Palazzo Ducale and Sansovino's Biblioteca Marciana, facing it in the Piazzetta.

For lunch, take vaporetto 1 to the Ca' Rezzonico stop and have a sandwich and a spritz in the Campo Santa Margherita, where you can mingle with the university students in one of Venice's most lively squares. From there, make your way to

the Galleria dell'Accademia and spend a few hours taking in its wonderful collection of Venetian painting. In the evening, take a walk up the Zattere and have a drink at one of the cafés overlooking the Canale della Giudecca.

Logistics: Be careful selecting your early train from Padua to Venice; some can be very slow. The 7:38 is one of the fastest (34 minutes), and will get you into Venice in time to beat rush hour on the Grand Canal vaporetto. To get an early start, unless your hotel is very near San Marco, deposit your luggage at the station, and pick it up later, after you've seen the piazza. Seeing the Grand Canal and Piazza San Marco in relative tranquility will be your reward for getting up at the crack of dawn and a little extra planning.

Day 8: Venice

If the Accademia has just whet your appetite for Venetian painting, start out the day by visiting churches and institutions where you can see more of it. For Titian, go to Santa Maria Gloriosa dei Frari church and Santa Maria della Salute; for Tintoretto, Scuola Grande di San Rocco; for Bellini, the Frari and San Giovanni e Paolo; for Tiepolo, Ca' Rezzonico, Scuola Grande dei Carmini, and the Gesuati; for Carpaccio, Scuola di San Giorgio; and for Veronese, San Sebastiano. If your taste runs to more modern art, there is the Guggenheim Collection and, down the street from it, the Pinault collection in the refashioned Punta della Dogana.

In the afternoon, head for the Fondamenta Nuova station to catch a vaporetto to one or more of the outer islands: Murano, where you can shop for Venetian glass and visit the glass museum and workshops; Burano, known for lace-making and colorful houses; and Torcello, Venice's first inhabited island, home to a beautiful cathedral.

Day 9: Venice

Venice is more than a museum—it's a lively city, and the best way to see that aspect of La Serenissima is to pay a visit to the Rialto Market, where the Venetians buy their fruits and vegetables and, most important, their fish, at one of Europe's largest and most varied fish markets. Have lunch in one of the excellent restaurants in the market area.

On your last afternoon in Venice, allow time to sit and enjoy a coffee or spritz in one of the city's lively squares or in a café along the Fondamenta della Misericordia in Cannaregio, simply watching the Venetians go about their daily lives. There's certainly a good deal more art and architecture to see in the city, and if you can't resist squeezing in another few churches, you may want to see Palladio's masterpiece of ecclesiastical architecture, the Redentore church on the Giudecca, or Tullio Lombardo's lyrical Miracoli, a short walk from the San Marco end of the Rialto Bridge.

Day 10: Venice/Departure

Take one last vaporetto trip up the Grand Canal to Piazzale Roma and, after saying good-bye to Venice, catch city bus 5 to the airport.

Exploring Venice

WORD OF MOUTH

"There's no way to adequately describe the uniqueness, the beauty, and the charm of Venice. It's like the Grand Canyon. It doesn't matter how many pictures you've seen, until you've come face to face with her, you can't begin to imagine her splendor."

—dcd

WELCOME TO VENICE

TOP REASONS TO GO

★ **Basilica di San Marco:** Don't miss the gorgeous mosaics inside. They're worth standing on line for.

★ **Santa Maria Gloriosa dei Frari:** Its austere, cavernous interior houses some of the most beautiful and significant art works in Venice.

★ **Gallerie dell'Accademia:** The world's most extensive collection of Venetian painting is on display at this world-class museum.

★ **Cruising the Grand Canal:** The beauty of its palaces, enhanced by plays of light on the water, make a trip down Venice's main street unforgettable.

★ **Snacking at a bacaro:** For a sample of tasty local cuisine in a uniquely Venetian setting, head for one the city's many wine bars.

1 The Grand Canal. Venice's major thoroughfare is lined with grand palazzi that once housed the city's most prosperous and prominent families.

2 San Marco. The neighborhood at the center of Venice streets is filled with fashion boutiques, art galleries, and grand hotels. Its Piazza San Marco—which Napoléon is said to have called "the drawing room of Europe"—is one of the world most beautiful and elegant urban spaces.

3 Dorsoduro. This elegant residential area is home to the Santa Maria della Salute, the Gallerie dell'Accademia, and the Peggy Guggenheim Collection. The Zattere promenade is one of the best spots to stroll with a gelato or linger at an outdoor café.

4 Santa Croce and San Polo. These bustling *sestieri* (districts) are both residential and commercial, with all sorts of shops and artisan studios, several major sights, and the Rialto fish and produce markets.

Stazione
Ferrovia
Santa Luca

S
Glorios

Canal Della Giudecca

LA G

5 **Cannaregio.** Brimming with residential Venetian life, this sestiere provides some of the sunniest open-air canal-side walks in town. The Fondamenta della Misericordia is a hub of restaurants and cafés, and the Jewish Ghetto has a fascinating history and tradition all its own.

6 **Castello.** Along with Cannaregio, this area is home to most of the locals. With its gardens, park, and narrow, winding walkways, it's the sestiere least influenced by Venice's tourist culture—except when the Biennale art festival is on.

GETTING ORIENTED

Venice proper is divided into six *sestieri,* or districts (the word *sestiere* means, appropriately, "sixth"): Cannaregio, Santa Croce, San Polo, Dorsoduro, San Marco, and Castello. More-sedate outer islands float around them—San Giorgio Maggiore and the Giudecca just to the south, beyond them the Lido, the barrier island; to the north, Murano, Burano, and Torcello.

THE JEWISH GHETTO

Misericordia

5

CANNAREGIO

Fond d

Grande

1

Canal

Canal Grande

Ca' d'Oro

SANTA CROCE

4

SAN POLO

anta Maria a dei Frari

2

SAN MARCO

Piazza San Marco

Basilica di San Marco

Palazzo Ducale

6 CASTELLO

Gallerie dell' Accademia

Canal Grande

Peggy Guggenheim Collection

3

Santa Maria della Salute

DORSODURO

Zatterre Promenade

SAN GIORGIO MAGGIORE

IUDECCA

0   1/4 mi

0   1/4 km

VENICE PLANNER

Festivals to Build a Trip Around

Venice's most famous festival is **Carnevale**, drawing revelers from all over the world. For 10 days leading up to Ash Wednesday there are concerts and other cultural events throughout the city, and costume balls are held in Venice's glorious palazzi. The prestigious **Biennale** is a century-old international contemporary art festival held from June through early November of odd-number years. It has spawned other festivals, including the **Biennale Danza, Biennale Musica**, and, most famously, **Biennale Cinema**, also known as the Venice Film Festival, held yearly at the end of August.

The **Festa della Redentore** (Feast of the Redeemer), on the third weekend in July, is the biggest celebration of the year among locals. It starts Saturday evening, when revelers eat dinner in lantern-bedecked boats in the Bacino San Marco, then watch the late-night fireworks display.

There are three main annual contests of Venetian rowing: the **Regata delle Bafane**, on January 6; **Vogalonga** (long row), on a Sunday in May, in which any boat can participate; and the splendidly costumed **Regata Storica**, on the first Sunday in September.

Making the Most of Your Time

The hoards of tourists visiting Venice are legendary, especially in spring and fall, but during other seasons, too—there is really no "off-season" in Venice. Unfortunately, tales of impassible, tourist-packed streets and endless queues to get into the Basilica di San Marco are not exaggerated. A little bit of planning, however, will help you avoid the worst of the crowds.

The majority of tourists do little more than take the *vaporetto* (water bus) down the Grand Canal to Piazza San Marco, see the piazza and the basilica, and walk up to the Rialto and back to the station. You will want to visit these areas, too, but do so in the early morning, before most tourists have finished their breakfast cappuccinos. You can further decrease your competition with other tourists for Venice's pleasures by choosing weekdays, instead of weekends, to visit the city.

Away from San Marco and the Rialto, the streets and quays of Venice's beautiful medieval and Renaissance residential districts receive only a moderate amount of traffic. Besides the Grand Canal and the Piazza San Marco, and perhaps Torcello, the other historically and artistically important sites are seldom overcrowded. Even on weekends you probably won't have to queue up to get into the Accademia museum.

Venice proper is quite compact, and you should be able to walk across it in a couple of hours, counting even a few minutes for getting lost. The water buses will save wear and tear on tired feet, but won't always save you much time.

Tourist Offices

The multilingual staff of the **Venice tourism office**
(☎ 041/5298711 ⊕ www.turismovenezia.it) can provide
directions and up-to-the-minute information. Its free, quar-
terly *Show and Events Calendar* lists current happenings
and venue hours. Tourist office branches are at Marco
Polo Airport; the Venezia Santa Lucia train station; Garage
Comunale, on Piazzale Roma; at Piazza San Marco near
Museo Correr at the southwest corner; the Venice Pavilion
(including a Venice-centered bookstore), on the *riva (canal-
front street)* between the San Marco vaporetto stop and
the Royal Gardens; and on the Lido at the main vaporetto
stop. The train-station branch is open daily 8–6:30; other
branches generally open at 9:30.

Passes and Discounts

Avoid lines and save money by booking services and
venue entry online with **Venice Connected** (⊕ venicecon-
nected.com). The service was introduced in 2009 and
continues to evolve. Currently, you must book at least seven
days in advance; discounts depend on arrival dates. For
example, during the "medium/low" season, a weeklong
vaporetto transit pass is €37.50 instead of €50. Venice
Connected guarantees the lowest prices on parking, public
transit passes, toilet service, museum passes, Wi-Fi access,
and airport transfers. Venice Connected may replace the
VENICEcard (☎ 041/2424 ⊕ www.hellovenezia.com), a
pass that provides more-comprehensive discounted access
to sights and transportation.

Sixteen of Venice's most significant churches are part
of the **Chorus Foundation** (☎ 041/2750462 ⊕ www.
chorusvenezia.org) umbrella group, which coordinates their
administration, hours, and admission fees. Churches in the
group are open to visitors all day except Sunday morning.
Single church entry costs €3; you have a year to visit all 16
with the €10 Chorus Pass. Family and student discounts are
also available. Get a pass at any church or online.

The **Museum Pass** (€18) from **Musei Civici**
(☎ 041/2715911 ⊕ www.museicivicivenezia.it) includes
one-time entry to 12 Venice museums. The **Museums of
San Marco Pass Plus** (€13; April–October) is good for the
museums on the piazza, plus another civic museum of your
choice. The **Museums of San Marco Pass** (€12; November–March) is good only for the piazza's museums. All
these passes are discounted at ⊕ VeniceConnected.com.

Going by Gondola

An enchanting diversion rather
than a practical way to get
around, *un giro in gondola* is
a round-trip ride. Some consider these trips tourist traps;
others wouldn't miss them. To
make the most of it, request to
go through more-remote side
canals, where you'll get an intimate glimpse of the city that
can't be seen any other way.

San Marco is loaded with gondola stations, so the waters
are crowded with gondolas.
Instead, try the San Tomà or
Santa Sofia (near Ca' d'Oro) station. The price of a 40-minute
ride is supposed to be €80 for
up to six passengers, increasing
to €100 between 7:30 PM and
8 AM. (Never pay a per-person
rate.) Agree on cost and duration of the ride beforehand,
and make it clear you want
to see the more serene areas
of the city. Feel free to bring
prosecco—your gondolier may
even supply glasses.

GETTING HERE AND AROUND

Getting Here by Car

Venice is at the end of SR11, just off the east–west A4 auto-strada. There are on cars in Venice; if possible, return your rental when you arrive.

A warning: don't be waylaid by illegal touts, often wearing fake uniforms, who try to flag you down and offer to arrange parking and hotels; use one of the established garages. Consider reserving a space in advance. The **Autorimessa Comunale** (☎ 041/2727211 ⊕ www.asmvenezia.it) costs €24 for 24 hours, less if you book with Venice Connected (⊕ www.veniceconnected. com). The **Garage San Marco** (☎ 041/5232213 ⊕ www. garagesanmarco.it) costs €24 for up to 12 hours and €30 for 12 to 24 hours with online reservations. On its own island, **Tronchetto** (☎ 041/5207555) charges €21 for 6 to 24 hours. Watch for signs coming over the bridge—you turn right just before Piazzale Roma. Many hotels and the casino have guest discounts with San Marco or Tronchetto garages. A cheaper alternative is to park in Mestre, on the mainland, and take a train (10 minutes, €1) or bus into Venice. The garage across from the station and the Bus 2 stop costs €8–€10 for 24 hours.

Getting Here by Air

Venice's **Aeroporto Marco Polo** (☎ 041/2609260 ⊕ www. veniceairport.it) is 10 km (6 mi) north of the city on the mainland. It's served by domestic and international flights, including connections from 21 European cities, plus direct flights from New York's JFK.

Water transfer: From Marco Polo terminal it's a mostly covered seven-minute walk to the dock where boats depart for Venice's historic center. **Alilaguna** (☎ 041/2401701 ⊕ www.alilaguna.it) has regular ferry service from pre-dawn until nearly midnight. The charge is €13, including bags, and it takes about 1½ hours to reach the landing near Piazza San Marco; some ferries also stop at Fonda-mente Nove, Murano, Lido, the Cannaregio Canal, and the Rialto. For €25 you can take the one-hour Oro line direct to San Marco. A *motoscafo* (water taxi) carries up to four people and four bags to the city center in a power-boat—with a base cost of €95 for the 25-minute trip. Each additional person, bag, and stop costs extra; it's essential to agree on a fare before boarding.

Land transfer: Buses run by **ATVO** (☎ 0421/383672 ⊕ www.atvo.it) make a quick (20-minute) and cheap (€3) trip from the airport to Piazzale Roma, from where you can get a vaporetto to the stop nearest your hotel. Tickets are sold from machines and at the airport booth in Ground Transportation (open daily 9–7:30), and on the bus when tickets are otherwise unavailable. The public ACTV Bus 5 also runs to the Piazzale Roma in about the same time. Tickets (€ 2.50) are available at the airport ground trans-portation booth. A taxi to Piazzale Roma costs about €35.

Getting Here by Train

Venice has rail connections with many major cities in Italy and Europe. Note that Venice's train station is **Venezia Santa Lucia,** not to be confused with Venezia-Mestre, which is the mainland stop prior to arriving in the historic center. Some trains do not continue beyond the Mestre station; in such cases you can catch the next Venice-bound train. Get a €1 ticket from the newsstand on the platform and vali-date it (in the yellow time-stamp machine) to avoid a fine.

Getting Around by Vaporetto

Venice's primary public transportation is the *vaporetto* (water bus). The **ACTV** (☏ *041/2424* ⊕ *www.hellovenezia. com*) operates *vaporetti* on routes throughout the city. Beginning at about 11:30 PM there is limited, but fairly frequent, night service. Although most landings are well marked, the system takes some getting used to; check before boarding to make sure the boat is going in your desired direction. Line 1 is the Grand Canal local, making all stops and continuing via San Marco to the Lido. The trip takes about 35 minutes from Ferrovia to San Marco. Line 2 travels up the Grand Canal (with fewer stops), down the Giudecca Canal to San Zaccaria, and back again (continuing to Lido in summer).

A single ticket for all lines costs €6.50, and is good for 60 minutes one-way. A better option is a Travel Pass: €16 for 12 hours, €18 for 24 hours, €33 for 72 hours, and €50 for a week of unlimited travel. Travelers ages 14–29 can opt for the €4 Rolling Venice card (available from the HelloVenezia booth at principal vaporetto stops), which allows 72 hours of travel for €18. A ticket to take the vaporetto one stop across the Grand Canal is €2. ■**TIP➔** The best discounts are available in advance through ⊕ *Venice-Connected.com.*

Line information is posted at each landing, and complete timetables are available at ACTV ticket booths, at most major stops, and are free for download at ⊕ *HelloVenezia. com.* ■**TIP➔** If you board without a valid ticket, ask immediately to buy one on board to avoid a €35 fine. The law says you must buy tickets for bags more than 28 inches long (the charge is waived if you have a Travel Pass), but this is generally enforced only for very bulky bags. If you are sitting in the open-air front seats, do not stand up while in transit, as this blocks the driver's view.

Getting Around by Traghetto

Many tourists are unaware of these two-man gondola ferries that cross the Grand Canal at or near many gondola stations. At €0.50, they're the cheapest and shortest gondola ride in Venice—and can also save a lot of walking. Look for TRAGHETTO signs and hand your fare to the gondolier when you board; they're marked on many maps. Stand up in these gondolas, straddling the width to keep your balance, unless the gondolier tells you otherwise. Most traghetti operate only in the morning.

Getting Around by Foot

Finding one's way around Venice is complicated. Addresses are given not by street but by sestiere. The numbering starts at 1 and ends in the thousands for each sestiere, and doesn't always follow a logical pattern. The street names are so insignificant that many Venetians don't know the name of the street where they live. So don't be put off if you are greeted with a shrug and an embarrassed smile when you ask a Venetian for directions to an address. Find out first which landmark your destination is near and seek directions to that point. From there you should be able to find where you're going by searching out the house number.

Getting Around by Water Taxi

A *motoscafo* (water taxi) isn't cheap: you'll spend about €60 for a short trip in town, €75 to the Lido, and €90 per hour to visit the outer islands. The fare system is convoluted, with luggage handling, waiting time, early or late hours, and even ordering a taxi from your hotel adding expense. However, a water taxi can carry up to 14 passengers, so if you're traveling in a group, it may not that much more expensive than a vaporetto. Always agree on the price before departing.

Updated
by Bruce
Leimsidor

It's called La Serenissima, "the most serene," a reference to the majesty, wisdom, and impressive power of this city that was for centuries the unrivaled leader in trade between Europe and the Orient, and a major center of European culture. Built entirely on water by a people who saw the sea as a defense and ally, Venice is unlike any other town.

No matter how often you've seen it in photos and films, the real thing is more dreamlike than you could ever imagine. Its landmarks, the Basilica di San Marco and the Palazzo Ducale, are hardly what we normally think of as Italian: fascinatingly idiosyncratic, they are exotic mixes of Byzantine, Romanesque, Gothic, and Renaissance styles. Shimmering sunlight and silvery mist soften every perspective here; it's easy to understand how the city became renowned in the Renaissance for its artists' use of color. It's full of secrets, inexpressibly romantic, and at times given over to sensuous enjoyment.

You'll see Venetians going about their daily affairs in *vaporetti* (water buses), aboard the *traghetti* (gondola ferries) that carry them across the Grand Canal, in the *campi* (squares), and along the *calli* (narrow streets). They are nothing if not skilled—and remarkably tolerant—in dealing with the veritable armies of tourists from all over the world who fill the city's streets.

PIAZZA SAN MARCO

One of the world's most beautiful squares, Piazza San Marco (Saint Mark's Square) is spiritual and artistic heart of Venice, a vast open space bordered by an orderly procession of arcades marching toward the fairy-tale cupolas and marble lacework of the Basilica di San Marco. From mid-morning on, it is generally packed with tourists. (If Venetians have business in the piazza, they try to conduct it in the early morning, before the crowds swell.) At night it can be magical, especially in winter, when mists swirl around the lampposts and the campanile.

If you face the basilica from in front of the Correr Museum, you'll notice that rather than being a strict rectangle, the square is wider at the basilica end, creating the illusion that it's even larger than it is.

On your left, the long, arcaded building is the Procuratie Vecchie, renovated to their present form in 1514 as offices and residences for the powerful procurators (magistrates).

On your right is the Procuratie Nuove, built half a century later in a more imposing, classical style. It was originally planned by Venice's great Renaissance architect, Jacopo Sansovino (1486–1570), to carry on the look of his Libreria Sansoviniana (Sansovinian Library), but he died before construction on the Nuove had begun. Vincenzo Scamozzi (circa 1552–1616), a pupil of Andrea Palladio (1508–80), completed the design and construction. Still later, the Procuratie Nuove was modified by architect Baldassare Longhena (1598–1682), one of Venice's baroque masters.

When Napoléon (1769–1821) entered Venice with his troops in 1797, he called Piazza San Marco "the drawing room of Europe"—and promptly gave orders to alter it. His architects demolished a church with a Sansovino facade in order to build the Ala Napoleonica (Napoleonic Wing), or Fabbrica Nuova (New Building), which linked the two 16th-century *procuratie* (procurators' offices) and effectively enclosed the piazza.

Piazzetta San Marco is the "little square" leading from Piazza San Marco to the waters of Bacino San Marco (Saint Mark's Basin); its *molo* (landing) once served as the grand entrance to the Republic.

Two imposing columns tower above the waterfront. One is topped by the winged lion, a traditional emblem of Saint Mark that became the symbol of Venice itself; the other supports Saint Theodore, the city's first patron, along with his dragon. (A third column fell off its barge and ended up in the bacino before it could be placed alongside the others.) Though the columns are a glorious vision today, the Republic traditionally executed convicts between them. Even today, some superstitious Venetians avoid walking between the two columns.

TIMING

You can easily spend several days seeing the historical and artistic monuments in and around the Piazza San Marco, but at a bare minimum plan on at least an hour for the basilica, with its wonderful mosaics. Add on another half hour if you want to see its Pala d'Oro, Galleria, and Museo di San Marco.

You'll want at least an hour to appreciate the Palazzo Ducale. Leave another hour for the Museo Correr, through which you enter also the archaeological museum and the Libreria Sansoviniana. If you choose to take in the piazza itself from a café table with an orchestra, keep in mind there will be an additional charge for the music.

Continued on page 41

THE BASILICA DI SAN MARCO
Venice's Cultural Mosaic

Above, 11th century stamp of the winged lion, symbol of Venice.

Below, facade of Basilica di San Marco with Palazzo Ducale in the background.

Standing at the heart of Venice, the spectacular Basilica di San Marco has been, for about a millennium, the city's religious center. Like other great churches—and even more so—it's also an expression of worldly accomplishments and aspirations. As you take in the shimmering mosaics and elaborate ornamentation, you begin to grasp the pivotal role Venice has played for centuries in European culture.

ORIGINS. The basilica began as a political statement. The original church, consecrated in 832, was built to house the body of St. Mark. According to legend, the saint's body had been stolen from Alexandria by two Venetians in 828. The whole enterprise was intended to establish Venice's prominence over neighboring Aquileia, a city with a glorious Roman past that claimed to have been founded by St. Mark.

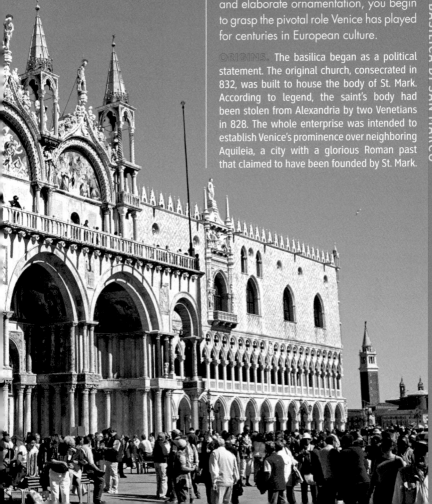

THE BASILICA'S FACADES

St. Mark and lion, main portal

VENICE'S TROPHY CASE. When the present church was built in the 11th century, Venice was still officially under the rule of the Byzantium, and the basilica was patterned after the Byzantine Church of the Twelve Apostles in Constantinople. The external appearance was initially rather simple, bearing an unadorned brick facade. But the 12th and 13th centuries were a period of intense military and economic expansion, and by the early 13th century the wealth and power of Venice were on display: the facades of the basilica were being adorned with precious marbles and art that were trophies from the military city's triumphs—most notably the conquest and sacking ot its former ruler, Constantinople, in 1204.

PORTAL OF SANT ALIPIO. Be sure to take a look at the apse of the portal of Sant Alipio, the farthest north of the five west facade portals. It bears a 13th-century mosaic showing how the church looked at that time. Note how the facade is already decorated with marble columns and the famous gilt bronze ancient Roman horses, taken by the Venetians during the sack of Constantinople.

Main portal entrance

The portal of Sant Alipio is typical of many parts of the basilica in that it contains elements that far predate the construction of the church. The base of the pointed arch beneath the mosaic, for example, dates from the 5th century, and the Byzantine capitals of the precious marble columns, as well as the window screens, are mostly from the 7th century. The use of these elements, most of them pillaged from raids and conquests, testifies to Venetian daring and power, and they create the illusion of an ancient heritage that Venice itself lacked and looked upon with envy.

Detail of bas-relief

Portal of Sant Alipio with 13th-century mosaic of the basilica

Bronze horses, facade

Detail of lunette in West facade

THE MAIN PORTAL. By the time these ancient trophies were put into place, Venice had both the wealth and the talent to create its own, new decoration. On the inner arches of the main portal, look for the beautiful and fascinating Romanesque and early Gothic allegorical, biblical, and zodiac bas-reliefs.

THE TETRARCHS. The Christian relevance of some of the trophies on the basilica is scant. For a fine example of pride over piety, take a look at the fourth-century group of four soldiers in red porphyry on the corner of the south facade. It's certain that this was taken from Constantinople, because a missing fragment of one of the figures' feet can still be found attached to a building in Istanbul. The current interpretation is that they are the Tetrarchs, colleagues of the Emperor Diocletian, having little if any religious significance.

The incorporation of art from many different cultures into Venice's most important building is a sign of imperial triumph, but it also indicates an embrace of other cultures that's a fundamental part of Venetian character. (Think of Marco Polo, who was on his way to China only a few years after the first phase of decoration of the facade of the basilica began.) Venice remains, even today, arguably the most tolerant and cosmopolitan city in Italy.

Statues of Tetrarchs

TREASURES INSIDE THE BASILICA

THE MOSAICS. The glory of the basilica is its brilliant, floor-to-ceiling mosaics, especially those dating from the medieval period.

The mosaics of the atrium, or porch, represent the Old Testament, while those of the interior show the stories of the Gospel and saints, ending with the image of Christ in Glory (a Renaissance copy) in the apse. Many of the mosaics of the New Testament scenes are actually somewhat earlier (mid-12th century), or contemporaneous with the 13th-century mosaics of the atrium. You wouldn't know it from the style: the figures of the atrium still bear the late classical character of the early Christian manuscript, brought to Venice after the sack of Constantinople, that inspired them. In the mosaics of the church proper, notice the flowing lines, elongated figures, and stern expressions, all characteristics of high Byzantine art. Look especially for the beautiful 12th-century mosaics in the dome of the Pentecost, the first dome in the nave of the basilica as you enter the main part of the church, and for the 12th-century mosaics in the dome of the Ascension, considered the masterpiece of the Venetian school.

The choir

Above, detail of the nave
Below, detail of mosaic

The centerpiece of the basilica is, naturally, ❶ **THE SANTUARIO (SANCTUARY)**, the main altar built over the tomb of St. Mark. Its green marble canopy, lifted high on carved alabaster columns, is another trophy dating from the fourth century. Perhaps even more impressive is the ❷ **PALA D'ORO**, a dazzling gilt silver screen encrusted with 1,927 precious gems and 255 enameled panels. Originally commissioned (976–978) in Constantinople, it was enlarged and embellished over four centuries by master craftsmen and wealthy merchants.

❸ **THE TESORO (TREASURY)**, entered from the right transept, contains treasures carried home from conquests abroad. Climb the stairway to the Galleria and the Museo di San Marco for the best overview of the basilica's interior. From here you can step out for a sweeping panorama of Piazza San Marco and across the lagoon to San Giorgio. The highlight is a close-up view of the original gilt bronze horses that were once on the outer gallery.

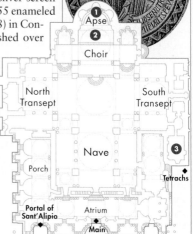

Opposite, detail of ceiling mosaics of the atrium

DID YOU KNOW?

The mosaics of the basilica are illuminated one hour a day, from 11:30 to 12:30. Visit then to see them at their most magnificent.

PLANNING YOUR VISIT

Be aware that guards at the basilica door turn away anyone with bare shoulders, midriff, or knees: no shorts, short skirts, or tank tops are allowed. Volunteers offer free guided tours in English from April to October—look for the calendar to the right of the center entrance, or get more information by calling the phone number below.

■ TIP➔ To skip the line at the basilica entrance, reserve your arrival—at no extra cost—on the basilica Web site (choose "Reservations" under "Plan your visit"). You can also skip the line if you check a bag at the nearby bag-check facility (find it on the map at the basilica entrance)—just show your bag-check ticket to the entrance guard and he'll wave you in.

✉ Piazza San Marco

☎ 041/2708311 basilica, 041/2413817 (10–noon weekdays) tour info

⊕ www.basilicasanmarco.it

🎟 Basilica free, Tesoro €2, Santuario and Pala d'Oro €1.50, Galleria and Museo di San Marco €3

🕐 May–Sept., Mon.–Sat. 9:45–5, Sun. 2–5; Oct.–Apr., Mon.–Sat. 9:45–5, Sun. 2–4. Last entry 1 hr before closing. Interior illuminated Mon.–Sat. 11:30–12:30, Sat. 2–5.

Above, Piazza San Marco.

Left, Crowds gather around the basilica.

TOP ATTRACTIONS

Fodor's Choice   **Palazzo Ducale** *(Doge's Palace)*. Rising above the Piazzetta San Marco,
★   this Gothic fantasia of pink-and-white marble is a majestic expression of Venetian prosperity and power. While the site was the doge's residence from the 10th century, the building began to take its present form around 1340; what you seen now is essentially a product of the first half of the 15th century. It served not only as the doge's residence, it was also the central administrative center of the Venetian Republic.

The Palazzo Ducale took so long to finish that by the time it was completed, around 1450, it was already a bit out of fashion. It barely predates the main gate of the Arsenale, built in 1460 in fully conceived Renaissance classical style. The Venetians, however, even later on, were not disturbed by their palazzo's dated look. In the 1570s the upper floors were destroyed by fire and Palladio submitted an up-to-date design for its reconstruction, but the Venetians refused his offer and insisted on reconstruction *"come era, dove era"* (as it was, where it was).

Unlike other medieval seats of authority, the Palazzo Ducale is free of any military defenses—a sign of the Republic's self-confidence. The position of the loggias below instead of above the retaining wall, and the use of pink marble to emphasize the decorative function of that wall, gave the palazzo a light and airy aspect, one that could impress visitors—and even intimidate them, though through opulence and grace rather than fortresslike bulk.

Near the basilica you'll see Giovanni and Bartolomeo Bon's Gothic **Porta della Carta** (Gate of the Paper), built between 1438 and 1442, where official decrees were traditionally posted, but you enter the palazzo under the portico facing the water. You'll find yourself in an immense courtyard that holds Antonio Rizzo's **Scala dei Giganti** (Stairway of the Giants), erected between 1483 and 1491, directly ahead, guarded by Sansovino's huge statues of Mars and Neptune, added in 1567.

The palace's sumptuous chambers have walls and ceilings covered with works by Venice's greatest artists. Visit the **Anticollegio,** a waiting room outside the Collegio's chamber, where you can see the *Rape of Europa* by Veronese and Tintoretto's *Bacchus and Ariadne Crowned by Venus.* The ceiling of the **Sala del Senato** (Senate Chamber), featuring *The Triumph of Venice* by Tintoretto, is magnificent, but it's dwarfed by his masterpiece *Paradise* in the **Sala del Maggiore Consiglio** (Great Council Hall). A vast work commissioned for a vast hall, this dark, dynamic piece is the world's largest oil painting (23 by 75 feet). The room's carved gilt ceiling is breathtaking, especially with Veronese's majestic *Apotheosis of Venice* filling one of the center panels. Around the upper walls, study the portraits of the first 76 doges, and you'll notice one picture is missing near the left corner of the wall opposite *Paradise.* A black painted curtain, rather than a portrait, marks Doge Marin Falier's fall from grace; he was beheaded for treason in 1355, which the Latin inscription bluntly explains.

A narrow canal separates the palace's east side from the cramped cell blocks of the **Prigioni Nuove** (New Prisons). High above the water arches the enclosed marble **Ponte dei Sospiri** (Bridge of Sighs), which earned its name in the 19th century, from Lord Byron's *Childe Harold's Pilgrimage.*" ■ TIP➔ Reserve your spot for the palazzo's popular Secret Itineraries tour well in advance. You'll visit the doge's private apartments, through hidden passageways to the interrogation (torture) chambers, and into the rooftop *piombi* (lead) prison, named for its lead roofing. Venetian-born writer and libertine Giacomo Casanova (1725–98), along with an accomplice, managed to escape from the piombi in 1756; they were the only men ever to do so. ✉ *Piazzetta San Marco* ☎ *041/2715911, 041/5209070 Secret Itineraries tour* ⊕ *www. museiciviciveneziani.it* 🎫 *Museums of San Marco Pass €12 (Nov.–Mar.) or €13 (Apr.–Oct.), Musei Civici Pass €18, Secret Itineraries tour €18* ☉ *Apr.–Oct., daily 9–7; Nov.–Mar., daily 9–5. Last entry 1 hr before closing* Ⓥ *San Zaccaria, Vallaresso.*

QUICK BITES

Caffè Florian (☎ *041/5205641*), in the piazza's Procuratie Nuove, has served coffee to the likes Goldoni, Wagner, Casanova, Charles Dickens, and Marcel Proust. It's Venice's oldest café, continuously in business since 1720 (though you'll find it closed Wednesday in winter). Counter seating is less expensive than taking a table, especially when there's live music. In the Procuratie Vecchie, **Caffè Quadri** (☎ *041/5289299*) exudes almost as much history as Florian across the way, and is similarly pricey. It was shunned by 19th-century Venetians when the occupying Austrians made it their gathering place. In winter it closes on Monday.

WORTH NOTING

Biblioteca Marciana *(Marciana Library).* There's a wondrous collection of centuries-old books and illuminated manuscripts at this library, located across the piazzetta from Palazzo Ducale in two buildings designed by Renaissance architect Sansovino, **Libreria Sansoviniana** and the adjacent **Zecca** (**mint**). The complex was begun in 1537, and the Zecca was finished in 1545. Facing the Bacino, the Zecca forms, along with the Palazzo Ducale, across the piazzetta, Venice's front door. It differs from its earlier Gothic pendent not only in style, but also in effect. The Palazzo Ducale, built during a period of Venetian ascendance and self-confident power, is light and decidedly unmenacing. The Zecca, built in a time when the Republic had received some serious defeats and was economically strapped, is purposefully heavy and stresses a fictitious connection with the classical world. The library is, again, much more graceful and was finished according to his design only after Sansovino's death. Palladio was so impressed by the Biblioteca that he called it "beyond envy." The books can only be viewed by written request and are primarily the domain of scholars. But the **Gilded Hall** in the Sansoviniana is worth visiting for the works of Veronese, Tintoretto, and Titian that decorate its walls. You reach the Gilded Hall, which often hosts special exhibits relating to Venetian history, through Museo Correr. ✉ *Piazza San Marco, enter through Museo Correr* ☎ *041/2405211* 🎫 *Piazza San Marco museums €13, Musei Civici Pass €18* ☉ *Apr.–Oct., daily 9–7; Nov.–Mar., daily 9–6. Last tickets sold 1 hr before closing* Ⓥ *Vallaresso, San Zaccaria.*

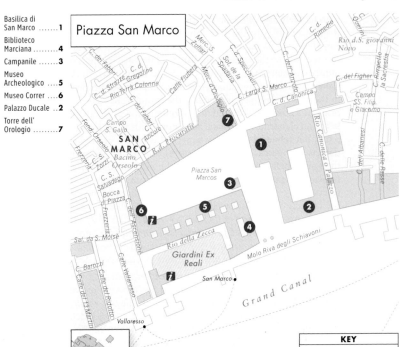

Piazza San Marco

2

🕙 **Campanile.** Venice's famous brick bell tower (325 feet tall, plus the angel) had been standing nearly 1,000 years when in 1902, practically without warning, it collapsed, taking with it Jacopo Sansovino's 16th-century marble loggia at the base (the largest original bell, called the *marangona*, remains). The crushed loggia was promptly restored, and the new tower, rebuilt to the old plan, reopened in 1912. In the 15th century, clerics found guilty of immoral behavior were suspended in wooden cages from the tower, some forced to subsist on bread and water for as long as a year, others left to starve. The stunning view from the tower on a clear day includes the Lido, the lagoon, and the mainland as far as the Alps, but, strangely enough, none of the myriad canals that snake through the city. ⊠ *Piazza San Marco* ☎ *041/5224064* 🎟 *€8* 🕙 *Easter–June, Oct., and Nov., daily 9–7; July–Sept., daily 9–9; Nov.–Easter, daily 9–3:45. Last entry 1 hr before closing* Ⓥ *Vallaresso, San Zaccaria.*

Museo Archeologico. Venice is the only major Italian city without an ancient past, and this perceived shortcoming was the source of an inferiority complex that determined many of the Republic's decisions during the centuries of her rise to power. This also explains why Venice hosts a collection of ancient art second in Italy only to those in Rome and Naples. This museum housing this collection was first established in 1596, when the heirs of Cardinal Domenico Grimani, a noted humanist, who had left his collection of original Greek (5th–1st centuries BC) and Roman marbles to the Republic, inaugurated the Public Statuary in Sansovino's then recently completed library in Piazza San Marco. You can see part of the collection, displayed just as Grimani, or at least his immediate heirs, had conceived it, in the vestibule of the **Libreria Sansoviniana**, which the museum shares with the **Biblioteca Marciana**. Highlights in the rest of the museum include the statue of Kore (420 BC), an Attic original known as Abbondanza Grimani; the 1st-century BC *Ara Grimani*, an elaborate Hellenistic altar stone with a bacchanalian scene; and a tiny but refined 1st-century BC crystal woman's head, which some say depicts Cleopatra. The very beautiful original venue of the collection, the family palazzo built and designed by Domenico Grimani's nephew, Giovanni, near Campo Santa Maria Formosa, is open to the public (by reservation only, call ☎ *0415200345*). Even though it no longer contains the collection, it is still well worth a visit. ⊠ *Piazza San Marco, enter through Museo Correr* ☎ *041/5225978* ☏ *Piazza San Marco museums €13, Musei Civici Pass €18. Contact the museum for information about free guided tours in English* ☉ *Apr.–Oct., daily 9–7; Nov.–Mar., daily 9–5; last tickets sold 1 hr before closing* Ⓥ *Vallaresso, San Zaccaria.*

Museo Correr. Exhibits in this museum of Venetian art and history range from the absurdly high-sole shoes worn by 16th-century Venetian ladies (who walked with the aid of a servant) to the huge *Grande Pianta Prospettica* by Jacopo de' Barbari (circa 1440–1515), which details in carved wood every nook and cranny of 16th-century Venice. The city's proud naval history is evoked in several rooms through highly descriptive paintings and numerous maritime objects, including ships' cannons and some surprisingly large iron mast-top navigation lights. The Correr has a room devoted entirely to antique games, and its second-floor **Quadreria** (Picture Gallery) has works by Venetian, Greek, and Flemish painters. The Correr exhibition rooms lead directly into the **Museo Archeologico** and the **Stanza del Sansovino,** the only part of the **Biblioteca Nazionale Marciana** open to visitors. ⊠ *Piazza San Marco, Ala Napoleonica (opposite the basilica)* ☎ *041/2405211* ⊕ *www.museicivicivenezani.it* ☏ *Museums of San Marco Pass €12 (Nov.–Mar.) or €13 (Apr.–Oct.), Musei Civici Pass €18* ☉ *Apr.–Oct., daily 9–7; Nov.–Mar., daily 9–5. Last entry 1 hr before closing* Ⓥ *Vallaresso, San Zaccaria.*

Torre dell'Orologio. Five hundred years ago, when this enameled clock was built, twin Moor figures would strike the hour, and three wise men with an angel would walk out and bow to the Virgin Mary on Epiphany (January 6) and during Ascension Week (40 days after Easter). An inscription on the tower reads HORAS NON NUMERO NISI SERENAS ("I only count happy hours"). After years of painstaking work, the clock tower has been reassembled and returned to its former glory. Visits in English are offered daily and must be booked in advance at the Museo Correr or online. ⊠ *North side of Piazza San Marco at the Mercería* ☎ *041/5209070* ⊕ *www.museicivicivenezani.it* ☏ *€12* ☉ *Tours in English Mon.–Wed. at 10 and 11; Thurs.–Sun. at 2 and 3* Ⓥ *Vallaresso, San Zaccaria.*

Continued on page 52

CRUISING THE GRAND CANAL

THE BEST INTRODUCTION TO VENICE IS A TRIP DOWN MAIN STREET

Venice's Grand Canal is one of the world's great thoroughfares. It winds its way in the shape of a backward "S" from Ferrovia (the train station) to Piazza San Marco, passing 200 palazzos born of a culture obsessed with opulence and fantasy. There's a theatrical quality to a boat ride on the canal: it's as if each pink- or gold-tinted facade is trying to steal your attention from its rival across the way.

The palaces were built from the 12th to 18th centuries by the city's richest families. A handful are still private residences, but many have been converted to other uses, including museums, hotels, government offices, university buildings, a post office, a casino, and even a television station.

It's romantic to see the canal from a gondola, but the next best thing, at a fraction of the cost, is to take the Line 1 *vaporetto* (water bus) from Ferrovia to San Marco. The ride costs €6 and takes about 35 minutes. Invest in a Travel Card (€15 buys 24 hours of unlimited passage) and you can spend the better part of a day hopping on and off at the vaporetto's 16 stops, visiting the sights along the banks.

Either way, keep your eyes open for the highlights listed here; the major sites also have fuller descriptions later in this chapter.

FROM FERROVIA TO RIALTO

Palazzo Labia
On September 3, 1951, during the Venice Film Festival, the Palazzo Labia hosted what's been dubbed "the party of the century." The Aga Khan, Winston Churchill, Orson Welles, and Salvador Dalì were among those who donned 18th-century costume and danced in the Tiepolo-frescoed ballroom.

Santa Maria di Nazareth

Ponte di Scalzi

R. DI BIASIO

Stazione Ferrovia Santa Lucia

FERROVIA

SANTA CROCE

As you head out from Ferrovia, the baroque church immediately to your left is **Santa Maria di Nazareth**. Its shoeless friars earned it the nickname Chiesa degli Scalzi (Church of the Barefoot).

One of the four bridges over the Grand Canal is the **Ponte di Scalzi**. The original version was built of iron in 1858; the existing stone bridge dates from 1934.

After passing beneath the Ponte di Scalzi, ahead to the left you'll spy **Palazzo Labia**, one of the most imposing buildings in Venice, looming over the bell tower of the church of San Geremia.

A hundred yards or so further along on the left bank, the uncompleted façade of the church of **San Marcuola** gives you an idea of what's behind the marble decorations of similar 18th-century churches in Venice.

Across the canal, flanked by two *torricelle* (side wings in the shape of small towers) and a triangular *merlatura* (crenellation), is the **Fondaco dei Turchi,** one of the oldest Byzantine palaces in Venice; it's now a natural history museum. Next comes the plain brick **Depositi del Megio,** a 15th-century granary—note the lion marking it as Serenissima property—and beyond it the obelisk-topped **Ca' Belloni-Battagia**. Both are upstaged by the **Palazzo Vendramin-Calergi** on the opposite bank: this Renaissance gem was built in the 1480s, at a time when late-Gothic was still the prevailing style. A gilded banner identifies the palazzo as site of Venice's casino.

CANNAREGGIO

Palazzo Vendramin-Calergi
The German composer Richard Wagner died in Palazzo Vendramin-Calergi in 1883, soon after the success of his opera Parsifal. His room has been preserved—you can visit it on Saturday mornings by appointment.

Church of San Marcuola

G H E T T O

S. MARCUOLA

Ca' Belloni-Battagia

Ca' d'Oro
Ca' d'Oro means "house of gold," but the gold is long gone—the gilding that once accentuated the marble carvings of the facade has worn away over time.

S. STAE

Ca' Pesaro

Fondaco dei Turchi

Depositi del Megio

San Stae Church

CA' D'ORO

SAN POLO

Ca' Corner della Regina

Pescheria
The pescheria has been in operation for over 1,000 years. Stop by in the morning to see the exotic fish for sale—one of which may wind up on your dinner plate. Produce stalls fill the adjacent fondamenta, and butchers and cheesemongers occupy the surrounding shops.

Rialto Mercato

Fondaco dei Tedeschi

Ca' dei Camerlenghi

RIALTO

SAN MARCO

The white, whimsically baroque church of **San Stae** on the right bank is distinguished by a host of marble saints on its facade. Further along the bank is another baroque showpiece, **Ca' Pesaro**, followed by the tall, balconied **Ca' Corner della Regina**. Next up on the left is the flamboyant pink-and-white **Ca' d'Oro**, arguably the finest example of Venetian Gothic design.

Across from Ca' d'Oro is the loggia-like, neo-Gothic **pescheria**, Venice's fish market, where boats dock in the morning to deliver their catch.

The canal narrows as you approach the impressive Rialto Bridge. To the left, just before the bridge, is the **Fondaco dei Tedeschi**. This was once the busiest trading center of the republic—German, Austrian, and Hungarian merchants kept warehouses and offices here; today it's the city's main post office. Across the canal stands

the curiously angled **Ca' dei Camerlenghi**. Built in 1525 to accommodate the State Treasury, it had a jail for tax evaders on the ground floor.

FROM RIALTO TO THE PONTE DELL' ACCADEMIA

S A N   P O L O

Ponte di Rialto

RIALTO

Ca' Foscari
Positioned at one of the busiest junctures along the Grand Canal, Ca' Foscari was recently restored after suffering severe foundation damage as a result of the relentless wake from passing boats.

Palazzo Barzizza

S. SILVESTRO

Ca' Loredan

Ca' Farsetti

Palazzo Pisani Moretta

Ca' Grimani

S. ANGELO

TOMA

Ca' Corner-Spinelli
If Ca' Corner-Spinelli has a familiar look, that's because it became a prototype for later Grand Canal buildings—and because its architect, Mauro Codussi, himself copied the windows from Palazzo Vendramin-Calergi.

Ca' Garzoni

Palazzo Grassi

Palazzo Falier
Palazzo Falier is said to have been the home of Doge Martin Fallier, who was beheaded for treason in 1355.

S A N   M A R C O

Ca' Rezzonico

REZZONICO

ACCADEMIA

Gallerie dell'Accademia

D O R S O D U R O

Until the 19th century, the shop-lined **Ponte di Rialto** was the only bridge across the Grand Canal.

Rialto is the only point along the Grand Canal where buildings don't have their primary entrances directly on the water, a consequence of the two spacious *rive* (waterside paths) once used for unloading two Venetian staples: coal and wine. On your left along Riva del Carbon stand **Ca' Loredan** and **Ca' Farsetti**, 13th-century Byzantine palaces that today make up Venice's city hall. Just past the San Silvestro vaporetto landing on Riva del Vin is the 12th- and 13th-century facade of **Palazzo Barzizza**, an elegant example of Veneto-Byzantine architecture that managed to survive a complete renovation in the 17th century. Across the water, the sternly

Renaissance **Ca' Grimani** has an intimidating presence that seems appropriate for today's Court of Appeals. At the Sant'Angelo landing, the vaporetto passes close to another massive Renaissance palazzo, **Ca' Corner-Spinelli**.

Back on the right bank, in a salmon color that seems to vary with the time of day, is elegant **Palazzo Pisani Moretta**, with twin water entrances. To your left, four-storied **Ca' Garzoni**, part of the Universita di Venezia Ca' Foscari, stands beside the San Toma *traghetto* (gondola ferry), which has operated since 1354. The boat makes a sharp turn and, on the right, passes one of the city's tallest Gothic palaces, **Ca' Foscari**.

The vaporetto passes baroque **Ca' Rezzonico** so closely that

you get to look inside one of the most fabulous entrances along the canal. Opposite stands the Grand Canal's youngest palace, **Palazzo Grassi**, commissioned in 1749. Just beyond Grassi and Campo San Samuele, the first house past the garden was once Titian's studio. It's followed by **Palazzo Falier**, identifiable by its twin loggias (windowed porches).

Approaching the canal's fourth and final bridge, the vaporetto stops at a former church and monastery complex that houses the world-renowned **Gallerie dell'Accademia**.

The wooden pilings on which Venice was built (you can see them at the bases of the buildings along the Grand Canal) have gradually hardened into mineral form.

ARCHITECTURAL STYLES ALONG THE GRAND CANAL

BYZANTINE: 12th and 13th centuries. **Distinguishing characteristics:** high, rounded arches, relief panels, multicolored marble. **Examples:** Fondaco dei Turchi, Ca' Loredan, Ca' Farsetti, Palazzo Barzizza (and, off the canal, Basilica di San Marco).

GOTHIC: 14th and 15th centuries. **Distinguishing characteristics:** Pointed arches, high ceilings, and many windows. **Examples:** Ca' d'Oro, Ca' Foscari, Ca' Franchetti, Palazzo Falier (and, off the canal, Palazzo Ducale).

RENAISSANCE: 16th century. **Distinguishing characteristics:** classically influenced emphasis on order, achieved

through symmetry and balanced proportions. **Examples:** Palazzo Vendramin-Calergi, Ca' Grimani, Ca' Corner-Spinelli, Ca' dei Camerlenghi (and, off the canal, Libreria Sansoviniana on Piazza San Marco and the church of San Giorgio Maggiore).

BAROQUE: 17th century. **Distinguishing characteristics:** Renaissance order wedded with a more dynamic style, achieved through curving lines and complex decoration. **Examples:** churches of Santa Maria di Nazareth and San Stae, Ca' Pesaro, Ca' Rezzonico (and, off the canal, the church of Santa Maria della Salute).

FROM THE PONTE DELL'ACCADEMIA TO SAN ZACCARIA

Ca' Franchetti
Until the late 19th century, Ca' Franchetti was a *squero* (gondola workshop). A few active *squeri* remain, though none are on the Grand Canal. The most easily spotted is Squero di San Trovaso, in Dorsoduro on a small canal near the Zattere boat landing.

Ca' Barbaro
Monet, Henry James, and Cole Porter are among the guests who have stayed at Ca' Barbaro. Porter later lived aboard a boat in Giudecca Canal.

SAN MARCO

Ponte dell' Accademia

Casetta Rossa

Ca' Pisani-Gritti

ACCADEMIA

S. M. DEL GIGLIO

DORSODURO

Ca' Barbarigo

SALUTE

Palazzo Venier dei Leoni
When she was in residence at Palazzo Venier dei Leoni, Peggy Guggenheim kept her private gondola parked at the door and left her dogs standing guard (in place of Venetian lions).

Palazzo Salviati

S. Maria della Salute

Ca' Dario
However tilted Dario might be, it has outlasted its many owners, who seem plagued by misfortune. They include the Italian industrialist Raul Gardini, whose 1992 suicide followed charges of corruption and an unsuccessful bid to win the America's Cup.

The wooden **Ponte dell' Accademia**, like the Eiffel Tower (with which it shares a certain structural grace), wasn't intended to be permanent. Erected in 1933 as a quick replacement for a rusting iron bridge built by the Austrian military in 1854, it was so well liked by Venetians that they kept it. (A perfect replica, with steel bracing, was installed 1986.)

You're only three stops from the end of the Grand Canal, but this last stretch is packed with sights. The lovely **Ca' Franchetti**, with a central balcony made in the style of Palazzo Ducale's loggia, dates from the late Gothic period, but its gardens are no older than the cedar tree standing at their center.

Ca' Barbaro, next door to Ca' Franchetti, was the residence of the illustrious family who rebuilt the church of Santa Maria del Giglio.

Farther along on the left bank, a garden, vibrant with flowers in summer, surrounds **Casetta Rossa** (small red house) as if it were the centerpiece of its bouquet. Across the canal, bright 19th-century mosaics on

Ca' Barbarigo give you some idea how the frescoed facades of many Venetian palaces must have looked in their heyday. A few doors down are the lush gardens within the walls of the unfinished **Palazzo Venier dei Leoni**, which holds the **Peggy Guggenheim Collection** of contemporary art.

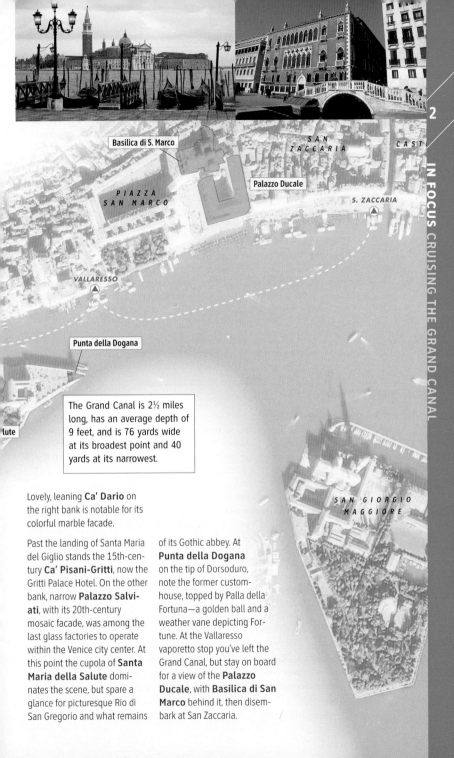

Basilica di S. Marco

SAN ZACCARIA

CAST

Palazzo Ducale

PIAZZA SAN MARCO

S. ZACCARIA

VALLARESSO

Punta della Dogana

lute

The Grand Canal is 2½ miles long, has an average depth of 9 feet, and is 76 yards wide at its broadest point and 40 yards at its narrowest.

SAN GIORGIO MAGGIORE

Lovely, leaning **Ca' Dario** on the right bank is notable for its colorful marble facade.

Past the landing of Santa Maria del Giglio stands the 15th-century **Ca' Pisani-Gritti**, now the Gritti Palace Hotel. On the other bank, narrow **Palazzo Salviati**, with its 20th-century mosaic facade, was among the last glass factories to operate within the Venice city center. At this point the cupola of **Santa Maria della Salute** dominates the scene, but spare a glance for picturesque Rio di San Gregorio and what remains of its Gothic abbey. At **Punta della Dogana** on the tip of Dorsoduro, note the former custom-house, topped by Palla della Fortuna—a golden ball and a weather vane depicting Fortune. At the Vallaresso vaporetto stop you've left the Grand Canal, but stay on board for a view of the **Palazzo Ducale**, with **Basilica di San Marco** behind it, then disembark at San Zaccaria.

SAN MARCO AND DORSODURO

The sestiere Dorsoduro (named for its "hard back" solid clay foundation) is across the Grand Canal to the south of San Marco. It is a place of monumental churches, meandering canals, modern art galleries, the city's finest art museums, and a promenade called the Zattere, where on sunny days you'll swear half the city is out for a *passeggiata*, or stroll. The eastern tip of the peninsula, the Punta della Dogana, was once the city's customs point; it became accessible to the public in 2009 when the old customs house was reopened as a contemporary art museum. At the western end of the sestiere is the Stazione Marittima, where in summer cruise ships line the dock. Midway between these two points, just off the Zattere, is the Squero di San Trovaso, one of the three remaining workshops where gondolas have been built and repaired for centuries. It is not open to the public.

Dorsoduro is also home to the Gallerie dell'Accademia, which has an unparalleled collection of Venetian painting, and gloriously restored Ca' Rezzonico, which houses the Museo del Settecento Veneziano. Another of its landmark sites, the Peggy Guggenheim Collection, has a fine selection of 20th-century art.

TIMING

The Gallerie dell'Accademia demands a few hours, but if time is short an audio guide can help you cover the highlights in about an hour. Ca' Rezzonico deserves at least an hour.

TOP ATTRACTIONS

★   **Ca' Rezzonico.** Designed by Baldassare Longhena in the 17th century, this palace was completed nearly 100 years later by Giorgio Massari and became the last home of English poet Robert Browning (1812–89). Stand on the bridge by the Grand Canal entrance to spot the plaque with Browning's poetic excerpt, "*Open my heart and you will see graved inside of it, Italy . . .*" on the left side of the palace. Today Ca' Rezzonico is the home of the **Museo del Settecento** (Museum of Venice in the 1700s). Its main floor successfully retains the appearance of a magnificent Venetian palazzo, decorated with period furniture and tapestries in gilded salons, as well as Tiepolo ceiling frescoes and oil paintings. Upper floors contain a fine collection of paintings by 18th-century Venetian artists, including the famous genre and Pucinella frescoes by Giabattista Tiepolo's son, Giandomenico, moved here from the Villa di Zianigo. There's even a restored apothecary, complete with powders and potions. ⊠ *Fondamenta Rezzonico, Dorsoduro 3136* ☎ *041/2410100* ⊕ *www.museiciviciveneziani.it* 🎟 *€6.50, Musei Civici Pass €18* ☉ *Apr.–Oct., Wed.–Mon. 10–6; Nov.–Mar., Wed.–Mon. 10–5. Last entry 1 hr before closing* Ⓥ *Ca' Rezzonico.*

Fodor's Choice
★   **Gallerie dell'Accademia.** Napoléon founded these galleries in 1807 on the site of a religious complex he had suppressed. They were carefully and subtly restructured between 1945 and 1959 by the renowned architect Carlo Scarpa. In them you'll find the world's most extensive collection of Venetian paintings.

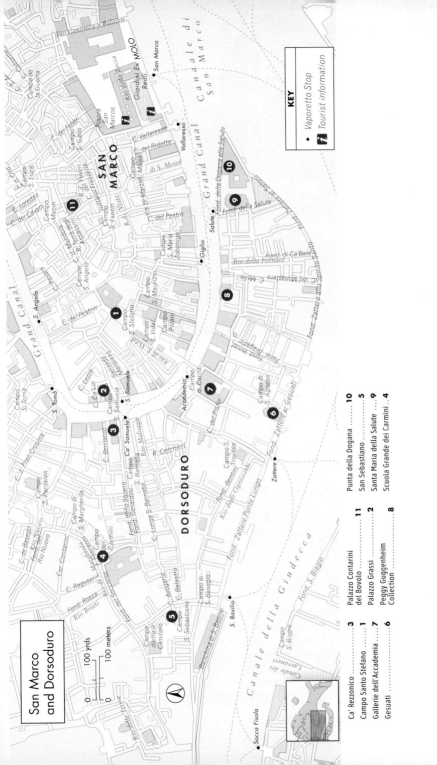

San Marco and Dorsoduro

| 0 | 100 yds |
| 0 | 100 meters |

KEY

• Vaporetto Stop

i Tourist Information

Gentile Bellini's *Miracle of the Cross at the Bridge of San Lorenzo* in the Gallerie dell'Accademia presents a view of Venice at the end of the 15th century.

Jacopo Bellini is considered the father of the Venetian Renaissance, and in Room 2 you can compare his *Madonna and Child with Saints* with such later works as *Madonna of the Orange Tree* by Cima da Conegliano (circa 1459–1517) and *Ten Thousand Martyrs of Mt. Ararat* by Vittore Carpaccio (circa 1455–1525). Jacopo's more-accomplished son Giovanni (circa 1430–1516) attracts your eye not only with his subjects but also with his rich color. Rooms 4 and 5 have a good selection of his Madonnas. Room 5 contains *Tempest* by Giorgione (1477–1510), a revolutionary work that has continued to intrigue viewers and critics over the centuries. It is unified not only by physical design elements, as was usual, but more importantly by a mysterious, somewhat threatening atmosphere. In Room 10, *Feast in the House of Levi,* commissioned as a Last Supper, got Veronese summoned to the Inquisition over its depiction of dogs, jesters, and other extraneous figures. The artist responded with the famous retort, *"Noi pittori ci prendiamo le stesse libertà dei poeti e dei pazzi."* ("We painters permit ourselves the same liberties that poets and madmen do." He resolved the problem by simply changing the title, so that the painting represented a different, less-solemn biblical feast.

Room 10 also houses several of Tintoretto's finest works, including three paintings from the life of St. Mark. Titian's *Presentation of the Virgin* (Room 24) is the collection's only work originally created for the building in which it hangs. Don't miss rooms 20 and 21, with views of 15th- and 16th-century Venice by Carpaccio and Gentile Bellini (1429–1507), Giovanni's brother—you'll see how little the city has changed.

VENICE THROUGH THE AGES

BEGINNINGS

Venice was founded in the 5th century when the Veneti, inhabitants of the mainland region roughly corresponding to today's lower Veneto, fled their homes to escape invading Lombards. The unlikely city, built on islands in the lagoon and atop wooden posts driven into the marshes, would evolve into a maritime republic lasting over a thousand years.

After liberating the Adriatic from marauding pirates, its early fortunes grew as a result of its active role in the Crusades, beginning in 1095 and culminating in the Venetian-led sacking of Constantinople in 1204. The defeat of rival Genoa in the Battle of Chioggia (1380) established Venice as the dominant sea power in Europe.

EARLY DEMOCRACY

As early as the 7th century, Venice was governed by a participatory democracy, with a ruler, the doge, elected to a lifetime term. Beginning in the 12th century, the doge's power was increasingly subsumed by a growing number of councils, commissions, and magistrates. In 1268 a complicated procedure for the doge's election was established to prevent nepotism, but by that point power rested foremost with the Great Council, which at times numbered as many as 2,000 members.

Laws were passed by the Senate, a group of 200 elected from the Great Council; executive powers belonged to the College, a committee of 25. In 1310 the Council of Ten was formed to protect state security. When circumstances dictated, the doge could expedite decision making by consulting only the Council of Ten. To avoid too great a concentration of power, these 10 served only one year and belonged to different families.

A LONG DECLINE

Venice reached the height of its wealth and territorial expansion in the early 15th century, during which time its domain included all of the Veneto region and part of Lombardy, but the seeds of its decline were soon to be sown, with the fall of Constantinople to the Turks in 1453.

By the beginning of the 16th century, the pope, threatened by Venice's mainland expansion, organized the League of Cambrai, defeated Venice in 1505, and effectively put a stop to the Republic's mainland territorial designs. The Ottoman Empire blocked Venice's Mediterranean trade routes, and newly emerging sea powers such as Britain and the Netherlands ended Venice's monopoly by opening oceanic trading routes.

When Napoléon arrived in 1797, he took the city without a fight, gave it briefly to the Austrians, and then got it back in 1805. With his defeat Venice was ceded again to the Austrians at the Council of Vienna in 1815, and they ruled until 1848. In that tumultuous year throughout Europe, the Venetians rebelled, but the rebellion was defeated the following year. Venice remained in Austrian hands until the formation of the Italian Republic in 1866.

2

The dome of Santa Maria della Salute dramatically caps the eastern end of Dorsoduro.

Booking tickets in advance isn't essential but helps during busy seasons and costs only an additional €1. Booking is necessary to see the **Quadreria,** where additional works cover every inch of a wide hallway. A free map names art and artists, and the bookshop sells a more-informative English-language booklet. In the main galleries a €4 audio guide saves reading but adds little to each room's excellent annotation. ⊠ *Campo della Carità just off the Accademia Bridge, Dorsoduro 1050* ☎ *041/5222247, 041/5200345 reservations* ⊕ *www.gallerieaccademia. org* ✉*€6.50, €11 includes Ca' d'Oro and Museo Orientale* ⊗ *Galleria: Tues.–Sun. 8:15 AM–7:15 PM, Mon. 8:15–2. Quadreria: Fri. 11 AM–1 PM, Sat. 11–noon* Ⓥ *Accademia.*

QUICK BITES

There's no sunnier spot in Venice than **Fondamenta delle Zattere,** along the southern edge of Dorsoduro. It's the city's gigantic public terrace, with bustling bars and gelato shops; come here to stroll, read in the open air, and play hooky from sightseeing. Enjoy the Zattere's most decadent treat at **Gelateria Nico** (⊠ *Dorsoduro 922* ☎ *041/5225293*)—their famous *gianduiotto,* a slab of chocolate-hazelnut ice cream floating on a cloud of whipped cream—and relax on the big, welcoming deck. Saunter up to **El Chioschetto** (⊠ *Dorsoduro 1406* ☎ *041/5225293*) for a fine sandwich or *bibita* (soft drink).

🕓 **Peggy Guggenheim Collection.** A small selection of 20th-century painting and sculpture is on display at this gallery in the late heiress Peggy Guggenheim's Grand Canal home. The collection represents the eccentric lady's generally excellent taste. Through wealth and social connections,

CLOSE UP

Speaking Venetian

Venice is one of the few Italian cities where the local dialect is still alive and well. Much of the language you will hear in Venice is not Italian, but rather Venetian, or Italian heavily laced with Venetian. Venetian has its own rich and widely respected literature. The Venetian dialect comedies of Goldoni, the great 18th-century playwright, are regularly performed in the city.

Even when speaking Italian, Venetians will use dialect terms to refer to certain common objects. Sometimes the term means something totally different in standard Italian.

Here are a few frequently used words:

sestiere: One of six neighborhoods in central Venice.

rio: A canal. Only the Grand Canal and a few other major waterways are called "canali." Everything else is a "rio."

fondamenta: A quay, a street running along a canal or a "rio."

calle: A street, what is elsewhere in Italy called a "via." "Via" is used in Venice, but it means "boulevard."

campo: A square—what is elsewhere in Italy called a piazza. (The only piazza in Venice is Piazza San Marco.)

bacaro: A traditional wine bar.

cicheto (pronounced chee-*kay*-toh): An hors d'oeuvre—roughly the Venetian equivalent of tapas, Generally served at a bacaro and in many cafés.

ombra: A small glass of wine.

focaccia: A traditional Venetian raised sweet cake, similar to a panettone, but much lighter and without candied fruit or raisins. (Very different from the better-known Genoese focaccia, a dense slightly raised bread sometimes flavored with herbs or cheese.)

Venetians tend to use the informal second person form, "tu," much more readily than people do in other parts of Italy. Venetians also frequently address each other with the term *amore* (love), as is done sometimes in England. But in Venice it is used even between members of the same sex, without any romantic connotation.

Guggenheim (1898–1979) became an important art dealer and collector from the 1930s through the 1950s, and her personal collection here in Palazzo Venier dei Leoni includes works by Picasso, Kandinsky, Pollock, Motherwell, and Ernst (at one time her husband). The museum serves beverages, snacks, and light meals in its refreshingly shady, artistically sophisticated garden. On Sunday at 3 PM the museum offers a free tour and art workshop for children 12 and under. ⊠ *Fondamenta Venier dei Leoni, Dorsoduro 701* ☎ *041/2405411* ⊕ *www.guggenheim-venice.it* ☏ *€10* ☽ *Wed.–Mon. 10–6* Ⓥ *Accademia.*

★ **Santa Maria della Salute.** The view of La Salute (as this church is commonly called) from the Riva degli Schiavoni at sunset or from the Accademia Bridge by moonlight is unforgettable. Baldassare Longhena was 32 years old when he won a competition in 1631 to design a shrine honoring the Virgin Mary for saving Venice from a plague that in the

In warm weather, restaurants and cafés of Campo Santa Margherita spill out onto the square, providing numerous options for al fresco dining.

space of two years (1629–30) killed 47,000 residents, or one-third the population of the city. Outside, this ornate white Istrian stone octagon is topped by a colossal cupola with snail-like ornamental buttresses and a baroque facade; inside are a polychrome marble floor and six chapels. The Byzantine icon above the main altar has been venerated as the Madonna della Salute (Madonna of Health) since 1670, when Francesco Morosini brought it here from Crete. Above it is a sculpture showing Venice on her knees to the Madonna as she drives the wretched plague from the city.

Do not leave the church without a visit to the **Sacrestia Maggiore,** which contains a dozen works by Titian, including his *San Marco Enthroned with Saints* altarpiece. You'll also see Tintoretto's *The Wedding at Cana.* For the Festa della Salute, held November 21, a votive bridge is constructed across the Grand Canal, and Venetians make pilgrimages here to light candles in prayer for another year's health. ⊠ *Punta della Dogana, Dorsoduro* ☎ *041/2743928* 🖅 *Church free, sacristy €2* ☉ *Apr.–Sept., daily 9–noon and 3–6:30; Oct.–Mar., daily 9–noon and 3–5:30* Ⓥ *Salute.*

CLOSE UP

Wading Through the Acqua Alta

There are two ways to get anywhere in Venice: walking and by water. Occasionally you walk *through* water, when falling barometers, southeasterly winds, and even a full moon may exacerbate normally higher fall and spring tides. The result is *acqua alta*—flooding in the lowest parts of town, especially Piazza San Marco. It generally occurs in late fall and, to a lesser extent, in spring, and lasts a few hours until the tide recedes.

Contending with *acqua alta*.

Venetians handle the high waters with aplomb, donning waders and erecting temporary walkways, but they're well aware of the damage caused by the flooding and the threat it poses to their city. The Moses Project, underwater gates that would close off the lagoon when high tides threaten, is still in progress. The expensive works have altered the lagoon-scape, and still represent a much-debated response to an emotionally charged problem, particularly after the historic tide in December 2008. How to protect Venice from high tides—aggravated by the deep channels dug to accommodate oil tankers and cruise ships, as well as the lagoon-altering wave action caused by powerboats—is among the city's most contentious issues.

WORTH NOTING

Campo Santo Stefano. In Venice's most prestigious residential neighborhood, you'll find one of the city's busiest crossroads just over the Accademia Bridge; it's hard to believe this square once hosted bullfights, with bulls or oxen tied to a stake and baited by dogs. For centuries the *campo* was grass except for a stone avenue called the *liston*. It was so popular for strolling that in Venetian dialect *"andare al liston"* still means "to go for a walk." A sunny meeting spot popular with Venetians and visitors alike, the campo also hosts outdoor fairs during Christmas and Carnevale seasons. Check out the 14th-century **Chiesa di Santo Stefano.** The pride of the church is its very fine Gothic portal, created in 1442 by Bartomomeo Bon. Inside, you'll see works by Tintoretto. ✉ *Campo Santo Stefano, San Marco* ☏ *041/2750462 Chorus Foundation* ⊕ *www.chorusvenezia.org* ✆ *€3, Chorus Pass €10* ⊙ *Mon.–Sat. 10–5, Sun. 1–5* Ⓥ *Accademia.*

Gesuati. When the Dominicans took over the church of Santa Maria della Visitazione from the suppressed order of Gesuati laymen in 1668, Giorgio Massari was commissioned to build this structure. It has an important Tiepolo illusionistic ceiling and several other works by Giambattista Tiepolo (1696–1770), Giambattista Piazzetta (1683–1754), and Sebastiano Ricci (1659–1734). ✉ *Zattere, Dorsoduro* ☏ *041/2750462*

CLOSE UP

Touring Venice

If you want some expert guidance around Venice, you may opt for private tours, semiprivate tours, or large group tours. Any may include a boat tour as a portion of a longer walking tour. For private tours, make sure to choose an authorized guide.

PRIVATE TOURS
Walks Inside Venice (⊕ *www.walksinsidevenice.com*) offers a host of particularly creative private tours from historic to artistic to gastronomic. Luisella Romeo of **See Venice** (⊕ *www.seevenice.it*) is a delightful guide capable of bringing to life even the most convoluted aspects of Venice's art and history. **A Guide in Venice** (⊕ *www.aguideinvenice.com*) offers a wide variety of innovative, entertaining, and informative themed tours for groups of up to 10 people. **Venice Events** (⊠ *Frezzaria, San Marco 1827* ☎ *041/5239979* ⊕ *www.tours-venice-italy.com*) offers a daily, 10-person-max canal tour, along with many other group and private tour options.

SEMIPRIVATE TOURS
Venice Cultural Tours (⊕ *venice-cultural-tours.com*) is group of

collaborating guides who offer regularly scheduled, semiprivate group tours with a maximum of only eight participants, making a nice alternative to more costly private tours.

LARGE GROUP TOURS
Visit any **Venice tourism office** (☎ *041/5298711* ⊕ *www.turismovenezia.it*) to book walking tours of the San Marco area (€38), which ends with a glassblowing demonstration daily (no Sunday tour in winter). From April to October there's also an afternoon walking tour that ends with a gondola ride (€40), and a daily serenaded gondola ride (€40). Other options can be purchased at local travel agencies. Check the tourist office or Web site for scheduled offerings. The **Cooperativa Guide Turistiche Autorizzate** (⊠ *San Marco 750, near San Zulian* ☎ *041/5209038* ⊕ *www.guidevenezia.it*) has a list of more than 100 licensed guides. Two-hour tours with an English-speaking guide start at €133 for up to 30 people. Agree on a total price before you begin, as there can be additional administrative and pickup fees. Guides are of variable quality.

⊕ *www.chorusvenezia.org* ⌦ *€3, Chorus Pass €10* ☉ *Mon.–Sat. 10–5, Sun. 1–5* Ⓥ *Zattere.*

Palazzo Contarini del Bovolo. Easy to miss despite its vicinity to Piazza San Marco, this Renaissance-Gothic palace is accessible only through a narrow backstreet that connects Campo Manin with Calle dei Fuseri. Built around 1500 for the renowned Contarini family, it is indefinitely closed for repairs, but its striking six-floor spiral staircase (*bovolo* means "snail" in Venetian dialect), the most interesting aspect of the palazzo, can be seen from the street. ⊠ *Corte del Bovolo, San Marco 4299* ☎ *041/924933* Ⓥ *Rialto.*

Palazzo Grassi. Built between 1748 and 1772 by Giorgio Massari for a Bolognese family, this palace is one of the last of the great noble residences on the Grand Canal. Once owned by auto magnate Giovanni

Agnelli, it was bought by French businessman François Pinaut in 2005 to house his very important collection of modern and contemporary art. Pinaut brought in Japanese architect Tadao Ando to remodel the interior. Check online for a schedule of temporary exhibitions. ⊠ *Campo San Samuele, San Marco* ☎ *041/5231680* ⊕ *www.palazzograssi.it* ⊠*€15, €20 includes the Punta della Dogana* ⊗ *Daily 9–6* Ⓥ *San Samuele.*

Punta della Dogana. The François Pinault Foundation had Japanese architect Tadao Ando redesign this former customs house, now home to works from Pinault's collection of contemporary art. The streaming light, polished surfaces, and clean lines of Ando's design contrast beautifully with the brick, massive columns, and sturdy beams of the original Dogana. Even if you don't visit the museum, walk down to the *punta* (point) for a maginficent view of the Venetian basin. Check online for a schedule of temporary exhibitions. ⊠ *Punta della Dogana, Dorsoduro* ☎ *041/5231680* ⊕ *www.palazzograssi.it* ⊠*€15, €20 includes the Palazzo Grassi* ⊗ *Wed.–Mon. 10–7. Last entry 1 hr before closing. Closed Dec. 24–Jan. 1* Ⓥ *Salute.*

San Sebastiano. Paolo Veronese (1528–88), although still in his twenties, was already the official painter of the Republic when he began the oil panels and frescoes at this, his parish church, in 1555. For decades he continued to embellish the church with very beautiful illusionistic scenes. The cycles of panels in San Sebastiano are considered to be his supreme accomplishment. Veronese is buried beneath his bust near the organ. ⊠ *Campo San Sebastiano, Dorsoduro* ☎ *041/2750462* ⊕ *www. chorusvenezia.org* ⊠*€3, Chorus Pass €10* ⊗ *Mon.–Sat. 10–5, Sun. 1–5* Ⓥ *San Basilio.*

Scuola Grande dei Carmini. When the order of Santa Maria del Carmelo commissioned Baldassare Longhena to build Scuola Grande dei Carmini in the late 1600s, their brotherhood of 75,000 members was the largest in Venice and one of the wealthiest. Little expense was spared in the decorating of stuccoed ceilings and carved ebony paneling, and the artwork was choice, even before 1739, when Tiepolo painted the **Sala Capitolare.** In what many consider his best work, Tiepolo's nine great canvases vividly transform some rather conventional religious themes into dynamic displays of color and movement. ⊠ *Campo dei Carmini, Dorsoduro 2617* ☎ *041/5289420* ⊠*€5* ⊗ *Daily 10–5* Ⓥ *Ca' Rezzonico.*

SAN POLO AND SANTA CROCE

The two smallest of Venice's six *sestieri* (districts), San Polo and Santa Croce, were named after their main churches, though the Chiesa di Santa Croce was demolished in 1810. The city's most famous bridge, the Ponte di Rialto, unites sestiere San Marco (east) with San Polo (west). The Rialto takes its name from Rivoaltus, the high ground on which it was built.

San Polo has two other major sites, Santa Maria Gloriosa dei Frari and the Scuola Grande di San Rocco, as well as some worthwhile but lesser-known churches.

The iconic Ponte di Rialto spans the Grand Canal between the sestieri of San Polo and San Marco.

Shops abound in the area surrounding the Rialto Bridge. On the San Marco side you'll find fashions, on the San Polo side, food. Chiesa di San Giacometto, where you see the first fruit vendors as you come off the bridge on the San Polo side, was probably built in the 11th and 12th centuries, about the time the surrounding market came into being. Public announcements were traditionally read in the church's campo; its 24-hour clock, though lovely, has rarely worked.

TIMING

To do the area justice requires at least half a day. If you want to take part in the food shopping, come early to beat the crowds. Campo San Giacomo dell'Orio, west of the main thoroughfare that takes you from the Ponte di Rialto to Santa Maria Gloriosa dei Frari, is a peaceful place for a drink and a rest. The museums of Ca' Pesaro are a time commitment—you'll want at least two hours to see them both.

TOP ATTRACTIONS

Ponte di Rialto *(Rialto Bridge)*. The competition to design a stone bridge across the Grand Canal (replacing earlier wooden versions) attracted the late-16th-century's best architects, including Michelangelo, Palladio, and Sansovino, but the job went to the less-famous but appropriately named Antonio da Ponte (1512–95). His pragmatic design featured shop space and was high enough for galleys to pass beneath; it kept decoration and cost to a minimum at a time when the Republic's coffers were low due to continual wars against the Turks and the competition brought about by the Spanish and Portuguese opening of oceanic trade routes. Along the railing you'll enjoy one of the city's most famous views: the Grand Canal vibrant with boat traffic. [v] *Rialto.*

Fodor's Choice ★ **Santa Maria Gloriosa dei Frari.** This immense Gothic church of russet-color brick was completed in the 1400s after more than a century of work. *I Frari* (as it's known locally) contains some of the most brilliant paintings in any Venetian church. Visit the sacristy first, to see Giovanni Bellini's 1488 triptych *Madonna and Child with Saints* in all its mellow luminosity, painted for precisely this spot. The Corner Chapel on the other side of the chancel is graced by Bartolomeo Vivarini's (1415–84) 1474 altarpiece *St. Mark Enthroned and Saints John the Baptist, Jerome, Peter, and Nicholas*, which is much more conservative, displaying attention to detail generally associated with late medieval painting. In the first south chapel of the chorus, there is a fine sculpture of Saint John the Baptist by Donatello, done in the 1450s and displaying a psychological intensity rare for early Renaissance sculpture. You can see the rapid development of Venetian Renaissance painting by contrasting Bellini with the heroic energy of Titian's *Assumption*, over the main altar, painted only 30 years later. Unveiled in 1518, it was the artist's first public commission and did much to establish his reputation.

Titian's beautiful *Madonna di Ca' Pesaro* is in the left aisle. The painting took almost 10 years to complete, and in it Titian disregarded the conventions of his time by moving the Virgin out of center and making the saints active participants. The composition, built on diagonals, anticipates structural principals of the baroque painting of the following century. ⊠ *Campo dei Frari, San Polo* ☎ *041/2728618, 041/2750462 Chorus Foundation* ⊕ *www.chorusvenezia.org* ⊠ *€3, Chorus Pass €10* ☉ *Mon.–Sat. 9–6, Sun. 1–6* [v] *San Tomà.*

★ **Scuola Grande di San Rocco.** Saint Rocco's popularity stemmed from his miraculous recovery from the plague and his care for fellow sufferers. Throughout the plague-filled Middle Ages, followers and donations abounded, and this elegant example of Venetian Renaissance architecture, built between 1517 and 1560 and including the work of at least four architects, was the result. Although it is bold and dramatic outside, its contents are even more stunning—a series of more than 60 paintings by Tintoretto. In 1564 Tintoretto edged out competition for a commission to decorate a ceiling by submitting not a sketch, but a finished work, which he moreover offered free of charge. *Moses Striking Water from the Rock, The Brazen Serpent,* and *The Fall of Manna* represent three afflictions—thirst, disease, and hunger—that San Rocco and later his brotherhood sought to relieve. ⊠ *Campo San Rocco, San Polo 3052* ☎ *041/5234864* ⊕ *www.scuolagrandesanrocco.it* ⊠ *€7 (includes audio guide)* ☉ *Daily 9:30–5:30. Last entry ½ hr before closing* [v] *San Tomà.*

QUICK BITES Just over the bridge in front of the Frari church is **Caffè dei Frari** (⊠ *Fondamenta dei Frari, San Polo* ☎ *041/5241877*), where you'll find a delightful assortment of sandwiches and snacks. Established in 1870, it's one of the last Venetian tearooms with its original decor. **Pasticceria Tonolo** (⊠ *Calle Crosera, Dorsoduro 3764* ☎ *041/5237209*) in operation since 1886, is widely considered among Venice's premier confectionaries. During

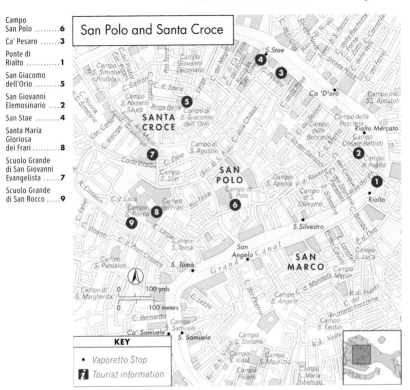

San Polo and Santa Croce

KEY

• *Vaporetto Stop*

🛈 *Tourist information*

Carnevale it's still the best place in town for *fritelle*, fried doughnuts (traditional raisin or cream-filled), and before Christmas and Easter, Venetians order their *focaccia*, the traditional raised cake eaten especially at holidays, from here well in advance. Closed Monday, and there's no seating any time.

WORTH NOTING

Campo San Polo. Only Piazza San Marco is larger than this square, and the echo of children's voices bouncing off the surrounding palaces makes the space seem even bigger. Campo San Polo once hosted bull races, fairs, military parades, and packed markets, and now comes especially alive on summer nights, when it's home to the city's outdoor cinema. The **Chiesa di San Polo** has been restored so many times that little remains of the original 9th-century church, and sadly, 19th-century alterations were so costly that the friars sold off many great paintings to pay bills. Though Giambattista Tiepolo is represented here, his work is outdone by 16 paintings by his son Giandomenico (1727–1804), including the *Stations of the Cross* in the oratory to the left of the entrance. The younger Tiepolo also created a series of expressive and theatrical renderings of the saints. Look for altarpieces by Tintoretto and Veronese that managed to escape auction. San Polo's bell tower

Behind its redbrick facade, Santa Maria Gloriosa dei Frari holds some of the most brilliant artwork of any church in Venice.

remained unchanged through the centuries—don't miss the two lions guarding it, playing with a disembodied human head and a serpent. ⊠ *Campo San Polo* ☎ *041/2750462 Chorus Foundation* ⊕ *www. chorusvenezia.org* ✉ *€3, Chorus Pass €10* ⏱ *Mon.–Sat. 10–5, Sun. 1–5* Ⓥ *San Silvestro, San Tomà.*

Ca' Pesaro. Baldassare Longhena's grand baroque palace is the beautifully restored home of two impressive collections. The **Galleria Internazionale d'Arte Moderna** has works by 19th- and 20th-century artists such as Klimt, Kandinsky, Matisse, and Miró. It also has a collection of representative works from Venice's Biennale art show that amounts to a panorama of 20th-century art. The pride of the **Museo Orientale** is its collection of Japanese art, and especially armor and weapons, of the Edo period (1603–1868). It also has a small but striking collection of Chinese and Indonesian porcelains and musical instruments. ⊠ *San Stae, Santa Croce 2076* ☎ *041/721127 Galleria, 041/5241173 Museo Orientale* ⊕ *www.museicivicivenezian.it* ✉ *€7 includes both museums, Museums of San Marco Plus Pass €13 (Apr.–Oct.), Musei Civici Pass €18* ⏱ *Apr.–Oct., daily 10–6; Nov.–Mar., daily 10–5. Last entry 1 hr before closing* Ⓥ *San Stae.*

San Giacomo dell'Orio. It was named after a laurel tree *(orio)*, and today trees give character to this square. Add benches and a fountain (with a drinking bowl for dogs), and the pleasant, oddly shaped campo becomes a welcoming place for friendly conversation and neighborhood kids at play. Legend has it the **Chiesa di San Giacomo dell'Orio** was founded in the 9th century on an island still populated by wolves. The current church dates from 1225; its short unmatched Byzantine columns

Venice's Scuola Days

An institution you'll inevitably encounter from Venice's glory days is the *scuola*. These weren't schools, as the word today translates, but important fraternal institutions. The smaller ones (*scuole piccole*) were established by different social groups—enclaves of foreigners, tradesmen, followers of a particular saint, and parishioners. The *scuole grandi*, however, were open to all citizens and included people of different occupations and ethnicities. They formed a more democratic power base than the Venetian governmental Grand Council, which was limited to nobles.

For the most part secular, despite their devotional activities, the scuole concentrated on charitable work, either helping their own membership or assisting the city's neediest citizens. The tradesmen's and servants' scuole formed social security nets for elderly and disabled members. Wealthier scuole assisted orphans or provided dowries so poor girls could marry. By 1500 there were more than 200 minor scuole in Venice, but only six scuole grandi, some of which contributed substantially to the arts. The Republic encouraged their existence— the scuole kept strict records of the names and professions of contributors to the brotherhood, which helped when it came time to collect taxes.

---

survived renovation during the Renaissance, and the church never lost the feel of an ancient temple sheltering beneath its 15th-century ship's-keel roof. In the sanctuary, large marble crosses are surrounded by a group of small medieval Madonnas. The altarpiece is *Madonna with Child and Saints* (1546) by Lorenzo Lotto (1480–1556), and the sacristies contain works by Palma il Giovane (circa 1544–1628). ⊠ *Campo San Giacomo dell'Orio, Santa Croce* ☎ *041/2750462 Chorus Foundation* ⊕ *www.chorusvenezia.org* ⊠ *€3, Chorus Pass €10* ☉ *Mon.–Sat. 10–5, Sun. 1–5* Ⓥ *San Stae.*

San Giovanni Elemosinario. Storefronts make up the facade, and the altars were built by market guilds—poulterers, messengers, and fodder merchants—at this church intimately bound to the Rialto Market. The original church was completely destroyed by a fire in 1514 and rebuilt in 1531 by Antonio Abbondi, who had also worked on the Scuola di san Rocco. During a recent restoration, workers stumbled upon a frescoed cupola by Pordenone (1484–1539) that had been painted over centuries earlier. Don't miss Titian's *St. John the Almsgiver* and Pordenone's *Sts. Catherine, Sebastian, and Roch*, which in 2002 were returned after 30 years by the Gallerie dell'Accademia. ⊠ *Rialto Ruga Vecchia San Giovanni, Santa Croce* ☎ *041/2750462 Chorus Foundation* ⊕ *www.chorusvenezia.org* ⊠ *€3, Chorus Pass €10* ☉ *Mon.–Sat. 10–5. Last entry ¼ hr before closing* Ⓥ *San Silvestro, Rialto.*

San Stae. The most renowned Venetian painters and sculptors of the early 18th century decorated this church around 1717 with the legacy left by Doge Alvise Mocenigo II, who's buried in the center aisle. Stae affords a good opportunity to see the early works of Tiepolo, Ricci, and Piazzetta, as well as those of the previous generation of

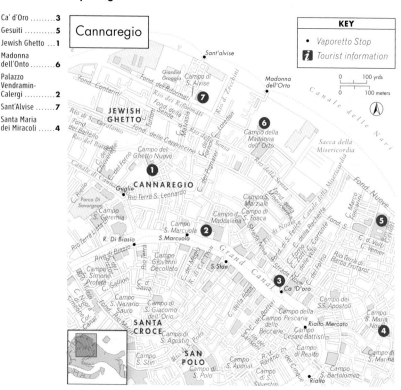

Venetian painters. ⊠ *Campo San Stae, Santa Croce* ☎ *041/2750462 Chorus Foundation* ⊕ *www.chorusvenezia.org* ⊒ *€3, Chorus Pass €10* ☉ *Mon.–Sat. 9–5* Ⓥ *San Stae.*

Scuola Grande di San Giovanni Evangelista. This scuola was founded in the 13th century, but the actual building is the work of various Venetian Renaissance architects and dates from the 15th century. In the 1480s the architect Pietro Lombardo finished the school's most beautiful and important architectural feature, the outdoor atrium and gateway that separate the complex from the campo adjoining it. Shortly after, in 1498, the architect Mauro Codussi finished work on a double staircase connecting the upper and lower halls. It is illuminated by a mullioned window on the landing between the two flights of stairs, an architectural device much used by Codussi. Carpaccio and Gentile Bellini painted their cycle of the miracle of the holy cross, now in the Accademia museum, originally for the Scuola di San Giovanni. ⊠ *Campiello della Scuola, San Polo 2454* ☎ *041/718234* ☉ *Atrium screen is visible from the street; scuola open to the public by appointment* Ⓥ *Ferrovia.*

CANNAREGIO

Cannaregio's main drag, which is also the longest street in Venice, runs parallel to the Grand Canal, and was once a canal itself. Lined with fruit and vegetable stalls near Ponte delle Guglie, quiet shops, gelaterias, and bakeries, the Strada Nova (literally, "New Street," as it was opened in 1871) serves as a pedestrian expressway from the train station to Ca' d'Oro. A number of nightspots, including Venice's only disco, have cropped up along this paved ribbon, which, although bereft of sights itself, is a convenient point of reference while exploring Cannaregio. Seen from above, this part of town seems like a wide field plowed by several long, straight canals that are linked by intersecting straight streets—not typical of Venice, where the shape of the islands usually defines the shape of the canals. But these canals were cut through a vast bed of reeds (hence the name Cannaregio, which may mean "Reed Place"), and not even the Venetians could overlook such an opportunity to make long, straight thoroughfares. The daylight reflected off the bright-green canals, wooden boats painted vivid red or blue, and the big sky visible from the fondamente make this a particularly luminous area of town. It's no surprise, perhaps, that Titian and Tintoretto had houses nearby.

Though Cannaregio has noble palaces built along the Grand Canal, the northern part of the sestiere was, and still is, a typical working-class neighborhood, where many *bacari* (wine bars) fill up with old card players every afternoon. The Jewish Ghetto, with its rooftop synagogues, and several striking churches are architectural highlights, while the Ca' d'Oro and the churches of Madonna dell'Orto and the Miracoli are among the most beautiful and interesting buildings in the city.

TOP ATTRACTIONS

★ **Ca' d'Oro.** This exquisite Venetian Gothic palace was once literally a "Golden House," when its marble traceries and ornaments were embellished with gold. It was created by Giovanni and Bartolomeo Bon between 1428 and 1430 for the patrician Marino Contarini as a present to his wife. The last proprietor, Baron Giorgio Franchetti, left Ca' d'Oro to the city, after having had it carefully restored and furnished with antiquities, sculptures, and paintings that today make up the **Galleria Franchetti.** Besides Andrea Mantegna's *St. Sebastian* and other Venetian works, the Galleria Franchetti contains the type of fresco that once adorned the exteriors of Venetian buildings (commissioned by those who could not afford a marble facade). One such detached fresco displayed here was made by the young Titian for the facade of the Fondaco dei Tedeschi, now the main post office near the Rialto. ⊠ *Calle Ca' d'Oro, Cannaregio 3933* ☏ *041/5238790* ⊕ *www.cadoro. org* 🎫*€5, plus €1 to reserve; €11 includes Gallerie dell'Accademia and Museo Orientale* ⊗ *Tues.–Sun. 8:15–7, Mon. 8:15–2. Last entry ½ hr before closing* Ⓥ *Ca' d'Oro.*

★ **Jewish Ghetto.** The neighborhood that gave the world the word *ghetto* is today a quiet neighborhood surrounding a large campo. It is home to Jewish institutions, two kosher restaurants, a rabbinical school, and five synagogues. Present-day Venetian Jews live all over the city, and the contemporary Jewish life of the ghetto, with the exception of the Jewish museum and the synagogues, is an enterprise conducted almost exclusively by American Hassidic Jews of Eastern European descent and tradition.

Though Jews may have arrived earlier, the first synagogues weren't built and a cemetery (on the Lido) wasn't founded until the Askenazim, or Northern European Jews, came in the late 1300s. Dwindling coffers may have prompted the Republic to sell temporary visas to Jews, who were over the centuries alternately tolerated and expelled. The Rialto commercial district, as mentioned in Shakespeare's *The Merchant of Venice*, depended on Jewish moneylenders for trade, and to help cover ever-increasing war expenses.

In 1516 relentless local opposition forced the Senate to confine Jews to an island in Cannaregio, then on the outer reaches of the city, named for its *geto* (foundry). The term "ghetto" also may come from the Hebrew "ghet" meaning separation or divorce. Gates at the entrance were locked at night, and boats patrolled the surrounding canals. Jews were allowed only to lend money at low interest, operate pawnshops controlled by the government, trade in textiles, or practice medicine. Jewish doctors were highly respected and could leave the ghetto at any hour when on duty. Though ostracized, Jews were nonetheless safe in Venice, and in the 16th century the community grew considerably, primarily with refugees from the Inquisition, which persecuted Jews in southern and central Italy, Spain, and Portugal. The ghetto was allowed to expand twice, but it still had the city's densest population and consequently ended up with the city's tallest buildings. Although the gates were pulled down after Napoléon's 1797 arrival, during the Austrian occupation the ghetto was reinstated. The Jews realized full freedom only in 1866 with the founding of the Italian state. Many Jews fled Italy as a result of Mussolini's 1938 racial laws, and on the eve of World War II, there were about 1,500 Jews left in the ghetto. Jews continued to flee, and the remaining 247 were deported by the Nazis; 8 returned.

The area has Europe's highest density of Renaissance-era synagogues, and visiting them is interesting not only culturally, but also aesthetically. Though each is marked by the tastes of its individual builders, Venetian influence is evident throughout. Women's galleries resemble those of theaters from the same era, and some synagogues were decorated by artists who were simultaneously active in local churches; Longhena, the architect of Santa Maria della Salute, renovated the Spanish synagogue in 1635.

The small but well-arranged **Museo Ebraico** highlights centuries of Jewish culture with splendid silver Hanukkah lamps and Torahs, and handwritten, beautifully decorated wedding contracts in Hebrew. Hourly tours (on the half hour) of the ghetto in Italian and English leave from the museum. ⊠ *Campo del Ghetto Nuovo, Cannaregio 2902/B* ☎ *041/715359* ⊕ *www. museoebraico.it* ⊡ *Museum €3; guided tour, museum, and synagogues €8.50* ☉ *June–Sept., Sun.–Fri. 10–7; Oct.–May, Sun.–Fri. 10–6. Tours hourly starting at 10:30* Ⓥ *San Marcuola, Guglie.*

The main entryways to many Venetian homes on side canals are accessible only by water.

You might complete your circuit of Jewish Venice with a visit to the **Antico Cimitero Ebraico** *(Ancient Jewish Cemetery)* on the Lido, full of fascinating old tombstones half hidden by ivy and grass. The earliest grave dates from 1389; the cemetery remained in use until the late 18th century. ⊠ *Via Cipro at San Nicolo, Lido* ☎ *041/715359* 🎫 *€8.50* ⊗ *Tours Apr.–Oct., Sun. at 2:30, by appointment other days; call to reserve* Ⓥ *Lido, San Nicolo.*

Madonna dell'Orto. Though built toward the middle of the 14th century, this church takes its character from its beautiful late Gothic facade, added between 1460 and 1464; it's one of the most beautiful Gothic churches in Venice. Tintoretto lived nearby, and this, his parish church, contains some of his most powerful work. Lining the chancel are two huge (45 feet by 20 feet) canvases, *Adoration of the Golden Calf* and *Last Judgment.* In glowing contrast to this awesome spectacle is Tintoretto's *Presentation of the Virgin at the Temple* and the simple chapel where Tintoretto and his children, Marietta and Domenico, are buried. Paintings by Domenico, Cima da Conegliano, Palma il Giovane, Palma il Vecchio, and Tiziano also hang in the church. A chapel displays a photographic reproduction of a precious *Madonna with Child* by Giovanni Bellini. The original was stolen one night in 1993. ⊠ *Campo della Madonna dell'Orto, Cannaregio* ☎ *041/2750462 Chorus Foundation* ⊕ *www.chorusvenezia.org* 🎫 *€3, Chorus Pass €10* ⊗ *Mon.–Sat. 10–5, Sun. 1–5* Ⓥ *Orto.*

★ **Santa Maria dei Miracoli.** Tiny yet harmoniously proportioned, this early-Renaissance gem built between 1481 and 1489 is sheathed in marble and decorated inside with exquisite marble reliefs. Architect Pietro

Let's Get Lost

Getting around Venice presents some unusual problems: the city's layout has few straight lines; house numbering seems nonsensical; and the six sestieri of San Marco, Cannaregio, Castello, Dorsoduro, Santa Croce, and San Polo all duplicate each other's street names. The numerous vaporetto lines can be bewildering, and often the only option for getting where you want to go is to walk. Yellow signs, posted on many busy corners, point toward the major landmarks—San Marco, Rialto, Accademia, and so forth—but don't count on finding such markers once you're deep into residential neighborhoods. Even buying a good map at a newsstand—the kind showing all street names and vaporetto routes—won't necessarily keep you from getting lost.

Fortunately, as long as you maintain your patience, getting lost in Venice can be a pleasure. For one thing, being lost is a sign that you've escaped the tourist throngs. And although you might not find the Titian masterpiece you'd set out to see, instead you could wind up coming across an ageless bacaro or a quirky shop that turns out to be the highlight of your afternoon. Opportunities for such serendipity abound. Keep in mind that the city is nothing if not self-contained: sooner or later, perhaps with the help of a patient native, you can rest assured you'll regain your bearings.

Lombardo (circa 1435–1515) miraculously compressed the building into its confined space, then created the illusion of greater size by varying the color of the exterior, adding extra pilasters on the building's canal side, and offsetting the arcade windows to make the arches appear deeper. The church was built in the 1480s to house *I Miracoli*, an image of the Virgin Mary that is said to perform miracles—look for it on the high altar. ⊠ *Campo Santa Maria Nova, Cannaregio* ☎ *041/2750462 Chorus Foundation* ⊕ *www.chorusvenezia.org* ✉ *€3, Chorus Pass €10* ⊙ *Mon.–Sat. 10–5* Ⓥ *Rialto.*

WORTH NOTING

Gesuiti. Extravagantly baroque, this 18th-century church completely abandons classical Renaissance straight lines in favor of flowing, twisting forms. Its interior walls resemble brocade drapery, and only touching them will convince skeptics that rather than paint, the green-and-white walls are inlaid marble. Over the first altar on the left, the *Martyrdom of St. Lawrence* is a dramatic example of Titian's feeling for light and movement. ⊠ *Campo dei Gesuiti, Cannaregio* ☎ *041/5286579* ⊙ *Daily 10–noon and 4–6* Ⓥ *Fondamente Nove.*

Palazzo Vendramin-Calergi. This Renaissance classic on the Grand Canal is the work of Mauro Codussi (1440–1504). You can see some of its interior by dropping into the **Casinò di Venezia.** Fans of Richard Wagner (1813–83) might enjoy visiting the **Sala di Wagner,** the room (separate from the casino) in which the composer died. Though rather plain, it's loaded with music memorabilia. To visit the Sala call the dedicated

tour line by noon the day before a scheduled tour, or book a private tour. ✉ *Cannaregio 2040* ☏ *041/5297111, 338/4164174 Sala di Wagner tours* ⊕ *www.casinovenezia.it* ✆ *Casinò €10, Sala di Wagner tour €5 suggested donation* ⊙ *Casinò Sun.–Thurs. 3:30 PM–2:30 AM, Fri. and Sat. 3:30 PM–3 AM; slot machines open daily at 3 PM. Sala di Wagner tours Tues. and Sat. at 10:30, Thurs. at 2:30 (call until noon the day before to reserve)* Ⓥ *San Marcuola.*

Sant'Alvise. For Tiepolo fans, trekking to the outer reaches of a pleasant residential section of Cannaregio to visit the unassuming Gothic church of Sant'Alvise is well worth the trouble. The little church holds Gianbattista Tiepolo's three panels of the Passion of Christ. He painted these panels, which display a new interest in dramatic intensity, and perhaps the influence of Tintoretto and Titian, for the church during his middle period, between 1737 and 1740. ✉ *Campo Sant'Alvise, Cannaregio* ☏ *041/2750462 Chorus Foundation* ✆ *€3, Chorus Pass €10* ⊙ *Mon.–Sat. 10–5, Sun. 1–5* Ⓥ *Sant'Alvise.*

CASTELLO

Castello, Venice's largest sestiere, includes all of the land from east of Piazza San Marco to the city's easternmost tip. Its name probably comes from a fortress that once stood on one of the eastern islands.

Not every well-off Venetian family could afford to build a palazzo on the Grand Canal. Many that couldn't instead settled in western Castello, taking advantage of its proximity to the Rialto and San Marco, and built the noble palazzos that today distinguish this area from the fishermen's enclave in the more easterly streets of the sestiere.

Castello isn't lacking in colorful history. In the early 15th century, large Greek and Dalmatian communities moved into the area along the Riva degli Schiavoni, where many of them sold dried fish and meat; the Confraternity of San Marco, based in what is now the hospital on Campo Santi Giovanni e Paolo, was patronized by Venetian high society in the 16th to 18th century; and nearby Campo Santa Maria Formosa served as a popular open-air theater for shows of various kinds (some including livestock among the cast members).

There is a lot to see here. Carpaccio's paintings at the Scuola di San Giorgio degli Schiavoni are worth a long look. San Francesco della Vigna, with a Palladio facade and Sansovino interior, certainly deserves a stop. The churches of Santi Giovanni e Paolo, San Zaccaria, and Santa Maria dei Miracoli are major attractions, as is the Querini-Stampalia museum.

TOP ATTRACTIONS

☺ **Arsenale.** Visible from the street, the Arsenale's impressive Renaissance gateway, the **Porta Magna** (1460), was the first classical revival structure to be built in Venice. It is guarded by four lions, war booty of Francesco Morosini, who took the Peloponnese from the Turks in 1687. The 10-foot-tall lion on the left stood sentinel more than 2,000 years ago near Athens, and experts say its mysterious inscription is runic "graffiti"

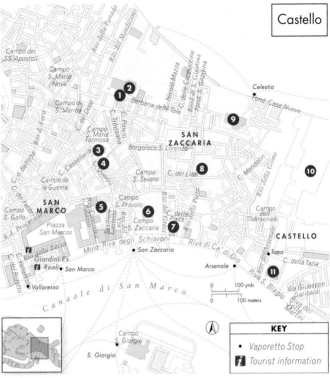

left by Viking mercenaries hired to suppress 11th-century revolts in Piraeus. If you look at the winged lion above the doorway, you'll notice that the Gospel at his paws is open but lacks the customary *Pax* inscription; praying for peace perhaps seemed inappropriate above a factory that manufactured weapons. The interior is not regularly open to the public, since it belongs to the Italian Navy, but it opens for the Biennale and for Venice's festival of traditional boats, **Mare Maggio** (⊕ *www. maremaggio.it*), held every May. If you're here during those times, don't miss the chance for a look inside, even entering from the back via a northern-side walkway leading from the Ospedale vaporetto stop.

The Arsenale is said to have been founded in 1104 on twin islands. The immense facility that evolved—it was the largest industrial complex in Europe built prior to the Industrial Revolution—was given the old Venetian dialect name *arzanà*, borrowed from the Arabic *darsina'a*, meaning "workshop." At times it employed as many as 16,000 *arsenalotti*, workers who were among the most respected shipbuilders in the world. (Dante immortalized these sweating men armed with pitch and boiling tar in his *Inferno*.) Their diligence was confirmed time and again—whether building 100 ships in 60 days to battle the Turks in Cyprus (1597) or completing one perfectly armed warship—start to finish—while King Henry III of France attended a banquet. ⊠ *Campo dell'Arsenale, Castello* ▾ *Arsenale.*

Fodor'sChoice
★
Santi Giovanni e Paolo. This massive Dominican church, commonly called San Zanipolo, contains a wealth of art. The 15th-century stained-glass window near the side entrance is breathtaking for its brilliant colors and beautiful figures, made from drawings by Bartolomeo Vivarini and Gerolamo Mocetto (circa 1458–1531). The second official church of the Republic after San Marco, San Zanipolo is the Venetian equivalent of London's Westminster Abbey, with a great number of important people, including 25 doges, buried here. Artistic highlights include an outstanding polyptych by Giovanni Bellini (right aisle, second altar), Alvise Vivarini's *Christ Carrying the Cross* (sacristy), and Lorenzo Lotto's *Charity of St. Antonino* (right transept). Don't miss the *Cappella del Rosario* (Rosary Chapel), off the left transept, built in the 16th century to commemorate the 1571 victory of Lepanto, in western Greece, when Venice led a combined European fleet to defeat the Turkish Navy. The chapel was devastated by a fire in 1867 and restored in the early years of the 20th century with works from other churches, among them the sumptuous Veronese ceiling paintings. However quick your visit, don't miss the Pietro Mocenigo tomb to the right of the main entrance, by Pietro Lombardo and his sons. ⊠ *Campo dei Santi Giovanni e Paolo, Castello* ☎ *041/5235913* ⌨ *€2.50* ☉ *Mon.–Sat. 9–6, Sun. noon–6* ▾ *Fondamente Nove, Rialto.*

QUICK BITES
To satisfy your sweet tooth, head for Campo Santa Marina and the family-owned and -operated **Didovich Pastry Shop** (⊠ *Campo Santa Marina, Castello* ☎ *041/5230017*). It's a local favorite, especially for Carnevale-time *fritelle* (fried doughnuts). There is limited seating inside, but in the warmer months you can sit outside. **Un Mondo di Vino** (⊠ *Salizzada San Cancian, Cannaregio* ☎ *041/5211093*), below Campo Santa Maria Nova on Calle San Canciano, is a friendly place to recharge with a *cicchetto* (snack) or two and some wine. It's closed Sunday.

WORTH NOTING

Campo Santi Giovanni e Paolo. This large, attractive square is the site of two city landmarks: the imposing namesake Gothic church and the Scuola Grande di San Marco, with one of the loveliest Renaissance facades in Italy. The scoula's exterior is the combined work of Venice's most prominent renaissance architects. The facade was begun by Pietro Lombardo in the 1480s, then in 1490 the work was given over to Mauro Codussi, who also added a grand stairway in the interior. In the 16th century, Sansovino designed the facade facing the Rio dei Mendicanti. The campo also contains the only equestrian monument ever erected by La Serenissima. The rider, Bartolomeo Colleoni, served Venice well as a *condottiere*, or mercenary commander—the Venetians preferred to pay others to fight for them on land. When he died in 1475, he left his fortune to the city on the condition that a statue be erected in his honor "in the piazza before San Marco." The Republic's

The Campo Santi Giovanni e Paolo is bordered by its mammoth namesake church and the Scuola Grande di San Marco, which has Venice's finest Renaissance facade.

shrewd administrators coveted Colleoni's ducats but had no intention of honoring anyone, no matter how valorous, with a statue in Piazza San Marco. So they collected the money, commissioned a statue by Florentine sculptor Andrea del Verrocchio (1435–88), and put it up before the Scuola Grande di San Marco.

Chiesa della Pietà. Unwanted babies were left on the steps of this religious institute, founded by a Franciscan friar in 1346. The girls were immediately taken in at the adjoining orphanage, which provided the children with a musical education. The quality of the performances here reached Continental fame—the in-house conductor was none other than Antonio Vivaldi (1675–1745), who wrote some of his best compositions here for the hospice. The present church was designed in the 18th century by Giorgio Massari, but the facade was completed only in the early 20th century. The main reason for a visit is to view the magnificent ceiling fresco by Gianbattista Tiepolo. In a room to the left of the entrance is a tiny collection of baroque instruments, including the violin played by Vivaldi. ⊠ *Riva degli Schiavoni, Castello* ☎ *041/5222171* 🌐 *€3* 🕙 *Thurs–Sun. 10–5* Ⓥ *San Zaccaria.*

Chiostro di Sant'Apollonia. Behind the basilica and over a bridge, a short fondamenta leads right toward the unassuming entrance of the **Museo Diocesano** (upstairs), housed in a former Benedictine monastery. Its peacefully shady 12th-century cloister has been modified over the centuries, but it remains the only surviving example of a Romanesque cloister in Venice. The brick pavement is original, and the many inscriptions and fragments on display (some from the 9th century) are all that remain of the first Basilica di San Marco. The museum contains an array of

sacred vestments, reliquaries, crucifixes, ex-votos, and paintings from various Venetian churches. ⊠ *Ponte della Canonica, Castello 4312* ☎ *041/5229166* 🖭 *Museum €4, cloister €1* ⊘ *Daily 10–6* Ⓥ *Vallaresso, San Zaccaria.*

Ⓒ **Museo Storico Navale** (*Museum of Naval History*). The boat collection here includes scale models such as the doges' ceremonial *Bucintoro*, and full-size boats such as Peggy Guggenheim's private gondola complete with romantic *felze* (cabin). There's a range of old galley and military pieces, and also a large collection of seashells. ⊠ *Campo San Biagio, Castello 2148* ☎ *041/2441399* ⊕ *www. marina.difesa.it/venezia/museo.asp* 🖭 *€1.55* ⊘ *Weekdays 8:45–1:30, Sat. 8:45–1* Ⓥ *Arsenale.*

Querini-Stampalia. The art collection at this Renaissance palace includes Giovanni Bellini's *Presentation in the Temple* and Sebastiano Ricci's triptych *Dawn, Afternoon, and Evening*. Portraits of newlyweds Francesco Querini and Paola Priuli were left unfinished on the death of Giacomo Palma il Vecchio (1480–1528); note the groom's hand and the bride's dress. Original 18th-century furniture and stuccowork are a fitting background for Pietro Longhi's portraits. Nearly 70 works by Gabriele Bella (1730–99) capture scenes of Venetian street life; downstairs is a café. ⊠ *Campo Santa Maria Formosa, Castello 5252* ☎ *041/2711411* ⊕ *www.querinistampalia.it* 🖭 *€8* ⊘ *Tues.–Sat. 10–8, Sun. 10–7. Last entry 1 hr before closing* Ⓥ *San Zaccaria.*

San Francesco della Vigna. Although this church contains some interesting and beautiful painting, it's the architecture that makes it worth the hike through a lively middle-class Venetian residential neighborhood to get here. The Franciscan church was enlarged and rebuilt by Sansovino in 1534, and its facade was added in 1562 by Palladio. It represents, therefore, a unique collaboration of the two great stars of Veneto 16th-century architecture. Antonio Vivarini's (circa 1415–84) triptych of Saints Girolamo, Bernardino da Siena, and Ludovico hangs to your right as you enter the main door. Giovanni Bellini's *Madonna with Saints* is down some steps to the left, inside the Cappella Santa. ⊠ *Campo di San Francesco della Vigna, Castello* ☎ *041/5206102* 🖭 *Free* ⊘ *Daily 8–12:30 and 3–7* Ⓥ *Celestia.*

San Zaccaria. A striking Renaissance facade, with central and upper portions representing some of Mauro Codussi's best work, is attached to this 14th-century Gothic church. The facade was completed in 1515, some years after Codussi's death in 1504, and retains the proportions of the rest of the essentially Gothic structure. Giovanni Bellini's celebrated altarpiece, *La Sacra Conversazione*, is easily recognizable in the left nave. Completed in 1505, when the artist was 75, it shows Bellini's ability to incorporate the esthetics of the High Renaissance into his work. It bears a closer resemblance to the contemporary works of Leonardo (it dates from approximately the same time as the *Mona Lisa*) than it does to much of Bellini's early work. The **Cappella di San Tarasio** displays frescoes by Tuscan Renaissance artists Andrea del Castagno (1423–57) and Francesco da Faenza (circa 1400–1451). Castagno's frescoes (1442) are considered the earliest examples of Renaissance painting in Venice. The three outstanding Gothic polyptychs attributed to Antonio Vivarini earned it the nickname "Golden Chapel." ⊠ *Campo San Zaccaria, 4693 Castello* ☎ *041/5221257* ⌑ *Church free, chapels and crypt €1* ⊙ *Mon.–Sat. 10–noon and 4–6, Sun. 4–6* Ⓥ *San Zaccaria.*

Santa Maria Formosa. Guided by his vision of a beautiful Madonna, 7th-century Saint Magno is said to have followed a small white cloud and built a church where it settled. Gracefully white, the marble building you see today dates from 1492, built by Mauro Codussi on an older foundation. Codussi's harmonious Renaissance design is best understood by visiting the interior; the Renaissance facade facing the canal was added later, in 1542, and the baroque facade facing the campo was added in 1604. Of interest are three fine paintings: *Our Lady of Mercy* by Bartolomeo Vivarini, *Santa Barbara* by Palma il Vecchio, and *Madonna with St. Domenic* by Gianbattista Tiepolo. The surrounding square bustles with sidewalk cafés and a produce market on weekday mornings. ⊠ *Campo Santa Maria Formosa, Castello* ☎ *041/2750462 Chorus Foundation* ⊕ *www.chorusvenezia.org* ⌑ *€3, Chorus Pass €10* ⊙ *Mon.–Sat. 10–5* Ⓥ *Rialto.*

Scuola di San Giorgio degli Schiavoni. Founded in 1451 by the Dalmatian community, this small scuola was, and still is, a social and cultural center for migrants from what is now Croatia. It's dominated by one of Italy's most beautiful rooms, lavishly yet harmoniously decorated with the *teleri* (large canvases) of Vittore Carpaccio. A lifelong Venice resident, Carpaccio painted legendary and religious figures against backgrounds of Venetian architecture. Here he focused on saints especially venerated in Dalmatia: Saints George, Tryphone, and Jerome. He combined keen empirical observation with fantasy, a sense of warm color, and late medieval realism. (Note the priests fleeing Saint Jerome's lion, or the body parts in the dragon's lair.) ⊠ *Calle dei Furlani, Castello 3259/A* ☎ *041/5228828* ⌑ *€4* ⊙ *Tues.–Sat. 9:15–1 and 2:45–6, Sun. 10–12:30. Last entry 1 hr before closing* Ⓥ *Arsenale, San Zaccaria.*

SAN GIORGIO MAGGIORE AND THE GIUDECCA

Beckoning travelers across Saint Mark's Basin, sparkling white through the mist, is the island of San Giorgio Maggiore, separated by a small channel from the Giudecca. A tall brick campanile on that distant bank perfectly complements the Campanile of San Marco. Beneath it looms the stately dome of one of Venice's greatest churches, San Giorgio Maggiore, the creation of Andrea Palladio.

You can reach San Giorgio Maggiore via vaporetto Line 2 from San Zaccaria. The next three stops on the line take you to the Giudecca. The island's past may be shrouded in mystery, but today it's about

San Giorgio Maggiore, as seen from across the Bacino di San Marco.

as down to earth as you can get and one of the city's few remaining neighborhoods that feels truly Venetian.

TIMING

A half day should be plenty of time to visit the area. Allow about a half hour to see each of the churches and an hour or two to look around the Giudecca.

TOP ATTRACTIONS

San Giorgio Maggiore. There's been a church on this island since the 8th century, with a Benedictine monastery added in the 10th century (closed to the public). Today's refreshingly airy and simply decorated church of brick and white marble was begun in 1566 by Palladio and displays his architectural hallmarks of mathematical harmony and classical influence. *The Last Supper* and the *Gathering of Manna,* two of Tintoretto's later works, line the chancel. To the right of the entrance hangs *The Adoration of the Shepherds* by Jacopo Bassano (1517–92); his affection for his foothills home, Bassano del Grappa, is evident in the bucolic subjects and terra-firma colors he chooses. The monks are happy to show Carpaccio's *St. George and the Dragon,* hanging in a private room, if they have time. The campanile dates from 1791, the previous structures having collapsed twice. ✉ *Isola di San Giorgio Maggiore* ☎ *041/5227827* 🖃 *Church free, campanile €3* ☉ *Daily 9–12:30 and 2:30–6* Ⓥ *San Giorgio.*

Santissimo Redentore. After a 16th-century plague claimed some 50,000 people, nearly one-third of the city's population, Andrea Palladio was

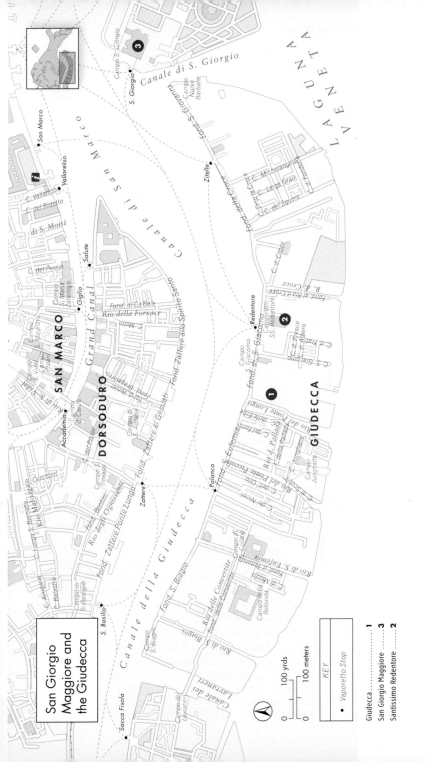

San Giorgio Maggiore and the Giudecca

LAGUNA VENETA

Canale di S. Giorgio

S. Giorgio

San Marco

Vallaresso

C. Vallaresso
C. del Ridotto
di S. Moisè

C. del Pestin

Campo N.ple Barbaro

Fond. S. Giovanni

Zitelle

Fond. delle Croce

C. Michelangelo

Fra'n Croce

C. Larga Gran

C. del Squero

C. d. Croce

C. d. Croce

R. d. Croce

Fond. al Rio d. Croce

Redentore

SS. Redentore

Campo S. Cosmo

C.d. Prescc

C. d. Fratti

C.d. Albero

Campo S. Giacomo

C. S. Giacomo

Fond. di S. Giacomo

Campo Giacomo

Rio d. Ponte Longo

Rio d. Palladio

Rio dell'Erbe

C. delle Erbe

Fond. delle Convertite

C. Ferrando

C. d. Michel Pasina

Campo Junghans

GIUDECCA

JUNGHANS

Salute

Maria
Torcello

Giglio

Fond. di Ca'Bala

Rio della Fornace

C. Molini

Fond. Zattere allo Spirito Santo

Grand Canal

Canale di San Marco

SAN MARCO

Campo
S. Maurizio

Campo
S. Vidal

Rio di S. Vidal

Accademia

C. del Fior

Campo S.
Trovaso

Fond. Bonlini

Fond. Zattere Ponte Lungo

Campo Venier

Fond. Venier

Fond. Eremite

Campo di
S. Agnese

DORSODURO

Fond. Zattere ai Gesuati

Palanca

Fond. delle Zattere

Fond. S. Biagio

Zattere

Rio degli Ognissanti

R. Cerchieri

R. Malpaga

C. Lunga S. Barnaba

C. Avogaria

C. Barastro

Campo di
S. Basegio

S. Basilio

Canale della Giudecca

C. dei Nicoli

C. dell'Olio

Rio del Ponte Piccolo

Fond. S. Eufemia

Rio di S. Eufemia

C. di Mezzo

Fond. d. Redentore

Fond. delle Convertite

Campo della
Rotonda

Rio delle Convertite

Rio di S. Biagio

Campo
S. Biagio

Sacca Fisola

Canale dei
Lavraneri

Campo dei
Lavraneri

N

0   100 yrds
0   100 meters

KEY

• Vaporetto Stop

Giudecca **1**
San Giorgio Maggiore **3**
Santissimo Redentore **2**

asked to design a commemorative church. Giudecca's Capucin friars offered land and their services, provided the building was in keeping with the simplicity of their hermitage. Consecrated in 1592, Palladio's creation, which is considered his supreme achievement in ecclesiastical design, is dominated by a dome and a pair of slim, almost minaret-like bell towers. Its deceptively simple, stately facade leads to a bright, airy interior.

For hundreds of years, on the third weekend in July the doge would make a pilgrimage here to give thanks to the Redeemer for ending a 16th-century plague. The event has become the Festa del Redentore, a favorite Venetian festival featuring boats, fireworks, and outdoor feasting. It's the one time of year you can walk to Giudecca—across a temporary pontoon bridge connecting Redentore with the Zattere. ✉ *Fondamenta San Giacomo, Giudecca* ☎ *041/5231415, 041/2750462 Chorus Foundation* 🎟️ *€3, Chorus Pass €10* ⊙ *Mon.–Sat. 10–5, Sun. 1–5* Ⓥ *Redentore.*

WORTH NOTING

Giudecca. The island's name is something of a mystery. It may come from a possible 14th-century Jewish settlement, or because 9th-century nobles condemned to *giudicato* (exile) were sent here. It became a plea-sure garden for wealthy Venetians during the Republic's long and luxurious decline, but today, like Cannaregio, it's largely working class. The Giudecca provides spectacular views of Venice and is becoming increasingly gentrified. Thanks to several bridges, you can walk the entire length of the Giudecca's promenade, relaxing at one of several restaurants or just taking in the lively atmosphere. Accommodations run the gamut from youth hostels to the city's most exclusive hotel, Cipriani. ✉ *Fondamenta San Giacomo, Giudecca* ☎ *041/2750462 Chorus Foundation* ⊕ *www.chorusvenezia.org* 🎟️ *€3, Chorus Pass €10* ⊙ *Mon.–Sat. 10–5* Ⓥ *Redentore.*

ISLANDS OF THE LAGOON

The perfect vacation from your Venetian vacation is an escape to Murano, Burano, and sleepy Torcello, the islands of the northern lagoon. Torcello offers ancient mosaics, greenery, breathing space, and picnic opportunities (remember to pack lunch). Burano is an island of fishing traditions and houses painted in a riot of colors—blue, yellow, pink, ocher, and dark red. Visitors still love to shop here for "Venetian" lace, even though the vast majority of it is machine-made in Taiwan; visit the island's Museo del Merletto (Lace Museum) to discover the undeniable difference between the two.

Murano is renowned for its glass, plenty of which you can find in Venice itself. It's also notorious for high-pressure sales on factory tours, even those organized by top hotels. Vaporetto connections to Murano aren't difficult, and for the price of a boat ticket (included in any vaporetto pass), you'll buy your freedom and more time to explore. The Murano "guides" herding new arrivals follow a rotation so that factories take

The view of Burano and the surrounding wetlands from the campanile on Torcello.

turns giving tours, but you can avoid the hustle by just walking away.
■ TIP→ Refuse the "free" taxi to Murano: it only means that should you
choose to buy (and you will be strongly encouraged), your taxi fare and
commission will be included in the price you pay.

TIMING

Hitting all the sights on all the islands takes a busy, full day. If you
limit yourself to Murano and San Michele, you can easily explore for
an ample half day; the same goes for Burano and Torcello. In summer, the express vaporetto Line 5 will take you to Murano from San
Zaccaria (the Jolanda landing) in 25 minutes; otherwise, local Line 41
makes a 45-minute trip from San Zaccaria every 20 minutes, circling
the east end of Venice, stopping at Fondamente Nove and San Michele
island cemetery on the way. To see glassblowing, get off at Colonna;
the Museo stop will put you near the Museo del Vetro.

Line LN goes from Fondamente Nove direct to Murano and Burano
every 30 minutes (Torcello is a 5-minute ferry from there); the full
trip takes 45 minutes each way. To get to Burano and Torcello from
Murano, pick up Line LN at the Faro stop (Murano's lighthouse).

TOP ATTRACTIONS

★ **Burano.** Cheerfully painted houses line the canals of this quiet village
where lace making rescued a faltering fishing-based economy centuries
ago. As you walk the 100 yards from the dock to Piazza Galuppi, the
main square, you pass stall after stall of lace vendors. These good-
natured ladies won't press you with a hard sell, but don't expect precise

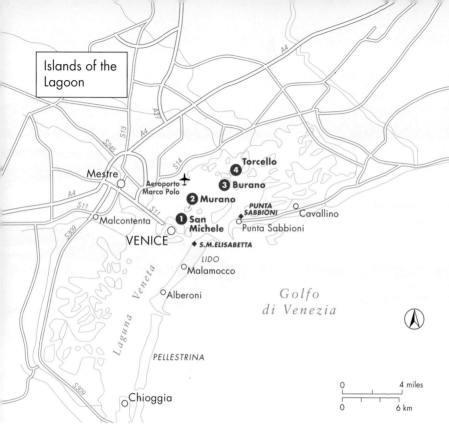

Islands of the Lagoon

Mestre

Aeroporto
Marco Polo

Malcontenta

VENICE

Murano

Torcello 4

3 **Burano**

2 **Murano**

1 **San**
Michele

PUNTA
SABBIONI Cavallino

Punta Sabbioni

◆ **S.M.ELISABETTA**

LIDO

Malamocco

Alberoni

Golfo
di Venezia

Laguna Veneta

PELLESTRINA

Chioggia

| 0 | | 4 miles |
| 0 | | 6 km |

product information or great bargains—authentic, handmade Burano lace costs $1,000 to $2,000 for a 10-inch doily.

The **Museo del Merletto** (Lace Museum) lets you marvel at the intricacies of Burano's lace making. At this writing, the museum is closed for renovations, with plans to reopen in 2011. The museum will likely continue to host a "sewing circle" of sorts, where on most weekdays you can watch local women carrying on the lace-making tradition. They may have authentic pieces for sale privately. ⊠ *Piazza Galuppi 187* ☎ *041/730034* ⊠ *€4.50, Museums of San Marco Plus Pass €13 (Apr.–Oct.), Musei Civici Pass €18* ⊙ *Apr.–Oct., daily 10–5; Nov.–Mar., daily 10–4* Ⓥ *Burano.*

☾ **Murano.** As in Venice, bridges here link a number of small islands, which are dotted with houses that once were workmen's cottages. In the 13th century the Republic, concerned about fire hazard and anxious to maintain control of its artisans' expertise, moved its glassworks to Murano, and today you can visit the factories and watch glass being made. Many of them line the Fondamenta dei Vetrai, the canal-side walkway leading from the Colonna vaporetto landing.

Before you reach Murano's Grand Canal (a little more than 800 feet from the landing), you'll pass **Chiesa di San Pietro Martire.** Reconstructed in the 16th century, it houses Giovanni Bellini's Madonna and Child

Burano is famous for its colorfully painted houses.

and Veronese's St. Jerome. ✉ *Fondamenta dei Vetrai* ☎ *041/739704* ⏱ *Weekdays 9–6, Sat. 2–6, Sun. 11:30–5* Ⓥ *Colonna.*

The collection at the **Museo del Vetro** *(Glass Museum)* ranges from priceless antiques to only slightly less-precious modern pieces. You can see an exhibition on the history of glass, along with a chance to review authentic Venetian styles, patterns, and works by the most famous glassmakers. Don't miss the famous Barovier wedding cup (1470–80). ✉ *Fondamenta Giustinian 8* ☎ *041/739586* ⊕ *www.museicivicivenezianini.it* ▭ *€6.50, Museums of San Marco Plus Pass €13 (Apr.–Oct.), Musei Civici Pass €18* ⏱ *Apr.–Oct., Thurs.–Tues. 10–6; Nov.–Mar., Thurs.– Tues. 10–5. Last entry 1 hr before closing* Ⓥ *Museo.*

The **Basilica dei Santi Maria e Donato,** just past the glass museum, is among the first churches founded by the lagoon's original inhabitants. The elaborate mosaic pavement includes the date 1140; its ship's-keel roof and Veneto-Byzantine columns add to the semblance of an ancient temple. ✉ *Fondamenta Giustinian* ☎ *041/739056* ⏱ *Mon.–Sat. 8–6, Sun. 2–6* Ⓥ *Museo.*

★ **Torcello.** In their flight from barbarians 1,500 years ago, the first Venetians landed here, prospering even after many left to found the city of Venice. By the 10th century, Torcello had a population of 10,000 and was more powerful than Venice. From the 12th century on, the lagoon around the island began silting up, and a malarial swamp developed. As malaria took its toll, Torcello was gradually abandoned and its palaces and houses were dismantled, their stones used for building materials in Venice. **Santa Maria Assunta** was built in the 11th century, and Torcello's wealth at the time is evident in the church's high-quality mosaics.

The mosaics show the gradually increasing cultural independence of Venice from Byzantium. The magnificent late-12th-century mosaic of the Last Judgment shows the transition from the stiffer Byzantine style on the left to the more-fluid Venetian style on the right. The virgin in the main apse dates possibly from about 1185, and is of a distinctly Byzantine type, with her right hand pointing to the Christ child held with her left arm. The 12 apostles below her are possibly the oldest mosaics in the church and date from the early 12th century. The adjacent **Santa Fosca** church, built when the body of the saint arrived in 1011, is still used for religious services. The bell tower is undergoing renovation (completion date is unknown at this writing). It is not accessible to visitors. ⊠ *Isola di Torcello* ☎ *041/2960630* ✉*Santa Maria Assunta €5, audio guide €1* ⊗ *Basilica: Mar.–Oct., daily 10:30–6; Nov.–Feb., daily 10–5. Campanile: Mar.–Oct., daily 10:30–5:30; Nov.–Feb., daily 10–4:30. Last entry ½ hr before closing* Ⓥ *Torcello.*

QUICK
BITES

Locanda Cipriani (⊠ *Piazza Santa Fosca 29, Isola di Torcello* ☎ *041/730150*), closed Tuesday and January, is famous for good food and its connection to Ernest Hemingway, who often came to Torcello seeking solitude. Today the restaurant (still in the Cipriani family, along with Harry's Bar in Venice) is busy with well-heeled customers speeding in for lunch (dinner also on weekends). Dining is pricey, but you can relax in the garden with just a glass of prosecco.

WORTH NOTING

San Michele. Tiny, cypress-lined San Michele is home to the pretty **San Michele in Isola** Renaissance church—and to some of Venice's most illustrious deceased—and nothing else. The church was designed by Codussi; the graves include those of poet Ezra Pound (1885–1972), impresario and art critic Sergey Diaghilev (1872–1929), and composer Igor Stravinsky (1882–1971). Surrounded by the living sounds of Venice's lagoon, this would seem the perfect final resting place. However, these days newcomers are exhumed after 10 years and transferred to a less-grandiose location. ⊠ *Isola di San Michele* ☎ *041/7292811* ⊗ *Apr.–Sept., daily 7:30–6; Oct.–Mar., daily 7:30–4* Ⓥ *Cimitero.*

Where to Eat in Venice

WORD OF MOUTH

"A few general rules that I have found work for 'tourist-intensive' cities in Italy. . . . If it has a hand-written menu that's different from when you passed the same restaurant yesterday: probably a good choice. And only for Venice: If it has a sign saying 'Osteria' or 'Bacaro' and looks dark and mysterious (almost foreboding), and outside only has a list of wines by the glass, mostly under €3.00: Bingo!"

—I_Heart_Venice

EATING AND DRINKING WELL IN VENICE

The catchword in Venetian restaurants is fish, often at its tastiest when it looks like nothing you've seen before. Even if you're not normally a fish fan, it's worth trying here—there's nothing quite like an expertly prepared fish that was, as the vendors like to say, swimming with its brothers only a few hours before. The best restaurants won't even give you a lemon, believing that it masks the pure, fresh flavor.

How do you learn about the catch of the day? A visit to the Rialto's *pescheria* (fish market) is more instructive than any book. And when you're dining at a well-regarded restaurant (such as one you've found in this chapter), don't be reluctant to ask your waiter for a recommendation, either: that's what a local would do.

GOING BACARO

You can sample regional wines and scrumptious *cicchetti* (bite-size snacks) in *bacari* (traditional wine bars), a great Venetian tradition. For centuries, locals have gathered at these neighborhood spots to chat over a glass of *sfuso* (wine on tap) or the ubiquitous spritz: an iridescent red cocktail of white wine, seltzer, and either Aperol, Select, or Bitter liqueur. *Crostini* (toast with toppings) and *polpette* (meat, fish, or vegetable croquettes) are popular cicchetti, as are small sandwiches, seafood salads, baccalà mantecato, and toothpick-speared items such as roasted peppers, marinated artichokes, and mozzarella balls.

3

SEAFOOD

Granseola (crab), *moeche* (soft-shell crab), sweet *canoce* (mantis shrimp), *capelunghe* (razor clams), calamari, and *seppie* or *seppioline* (cuttlefish) are all prominently featured, as well as *rombo* (turbot), *branzino* (sea bass), *San Pietro* (John Dory), *sogliola* (sole), *orate* (gilthead), *triglia* (mullet)—to name but a few of the options. Trademark dishes include *sarde in saor* (panfried sardines with olive oil, vinegar, onions, pine nuts, and raisins), *la frittura mista* (tempura-like fried fish and vegetables), and *baccalà mantecato* (creamed cod with olive oil). When prepared whole, fish is usually priced by the *etto* (100 grams, about 4 ounces) and can be expensive; but once you try it that way, you'll never want filleted fish again.

RISOTTO, PASTA, POLENTA

As a first course, Venetians favor the creamy rice dish risotto *al onda* ("undulating," as opposed to firm), prepared with vegetables or shellfish. Pasta is accompanied by seafood sauces, too: *pasticcio di pesce* is lasagna-type pasta baked with fish, usually *baccalà* (salt cod), and *bigoli* is a strictly local pasta shaped like short, thick spaghetti, usually served *in salsa* (an anchovy sauce), or with *nero di seppia* (squid-ink sauce). A classic first course is pasta *e fagioli* (bean soup with pasta). Polenta (creamy cornmeal) is another staple; it's often served with *fegato alla veneziana*

(calves' liver and onions) or *schie* (lagoon shrimp).

VEGETABLES

The larger islands of the lagoon are legendary for fine vegetables, such as the Sant'Erasmo *castraure* artichokes that herald spring. Just a few stalls at the Rialto Market sell local crops, but most feature high-quality produce from the surrounding regions. Spring treats are fat white asparagus, and artichoke bottoms (*fondi*), usually sautéed with olive oil, parsley, and garlic. From December to March, the prized *radicchio di Treviso* is grilled and used in salads and risottos. Fall brings small wild mushrooms called *chiodini*, and *zucca barucca*, a bumpy squash used in soups and to stuff ravioli.

SWEETS

Tiramisu lovers will have ample opportunity to sample this creamy concoction made from ladyfingers soaked in espresso and covered with sweetened mascarpone cheese—a dessert invented in the Veneto. In addition to sorbets and *semifreddi* (ice cream and cake desserts), other sweets frequently seen on Venetian menus are almond cakes and strudels, as well as dry cookies served with dessert wine. Gelato (ice cream) is sold all over; the best is homemade, labeled *produzione propria* or *fatto in casa.*

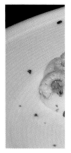

Updated by
Nan McElroy

Dining options in Venice range from the ultra high-end, where jackets and ties are a must, to the very casual. Once staunchly traditional, many restaurants have renovated their menus along with their dining rooms, creating dishes that blend classic Venetian elements with ingredients less common to the lagoon environs.

Mid-range restaurants are often more willing to make the break, offering innovative options while keeping dishes like *sarde in saor* and *fegato alla veneziana* available as mainstays. Restaurants are often quite small with limited seating, so make sure to reserve ahead. It's not uncommon for restaurants to have two seatings a night, one at 7 and one at 9.

There's no getting around the fact that Venice has more than its share of overpriced, mediocre eateries that prey on tourists. Avoid places with cajoling waiters standing outside, and beware of restaurants that don't display their prices. At the other end of the spectrum, showy *menu turistico* (tourist menu) boards make offerings clear in a dozen languages, but for the same €15–€20 you'd spend at such places you could do better at a *bacaro* making a meal of *cichetti* (savory snacks).

Budget-conscious travelers might want to take their main meal at lunch, when restaurant prices tend to be lower. Also keep an eye out for cafés and trattorias that offer meals prepared for *operai* (workers); they'll have daily specials designed for those who have to eat and run, which anyone is welcome to partake in. Bacari offer lighter fare, usually eaten at the bar (prices are higher if you sit at a table) and wine lists that offer myriad choices by the glass.

Although pizzerias are not hard to find, Venice is not much of a pizza town—standards aren't what they are elsewhere in Italy, and local laws impede the use of wood-burning ovens. Seek out recommended pizzerias, or opt for a bacaro snack instead of a soggy slice of pizza *al volo*, which is too commonly precooked and reheated. *Tramezzini*, the triangular white-bread sandwiches served in bars all over Italy, however, are almost an art form in Venice. The bread is white but doesn't at all

BEST BETS FOR VENICE DINING

With hundreds of restaurants to choose from, how will you decide where to eat? Fodor's writers and editors have selected their favorite restaurants by price and experience in the Best Bets lists below. In the first column, Fodor's Choice properties represent the "best of the best."

3

Fodor'sChoice ★

Al Paradiso, $$$, p. 105

Antiche Carampane, $$$, p. 105

La Zucca, $, p. 108

Osteria Orto dei Mori, $$, p. 97

Vini da Gigio, $$, p. 98

By Price

¢

Cantinone già Schiavi, p. 112

$

Al Prosecco, p. 107

Antico Panificio, p. 106

Botteghe di Promessi Sposi, p. 96

La Cantina, p. 96

La Zucca, p. 108

Muro Pizzeria con Cucina, p. 108

Ostaria al Garanghelo, p. 106

$$

Anice Stellato, p. 94

La Bitta, p. 102

Osteria Orto dei Mori, p. 97

Vini da Gigio, p. 98

$$$

Al Fontego dei Pescatori, p. 94

Al Paradiso, p. 105

Antiche Carampane, p. 105

$$$$

De Pisis, p. 104

Fiaschetteria Toscana, p. 96

Il Ridotto, p. 99

Best by Experience

OUTDOOR DINING

Al Fontego dei Pescatori, $$$, p. 94

Algiubagiò, $$, p. 94

La Cantina, $, p. 96

Muro Pizzeria con Cucina, $, p. 108

Osteria Orto dei Mori, $$, p. 97

Ristorante Riviera, $$$, p. 103

ROMANTIC

Al Fontego dei Pescatori, $$$, p. 94

Al Paradiso, $$$, p. 105

Anice Stellato, $$, p. 94

De Pisis, $$$$, p. 104

Osteria Orto dei Mori, $$, p. 97

Ristorante Riviera, $$$, p. 103

GOOD FOR KIDS

Antico Panificio, $, p. 106

La Trattoria ai Tosi, $, p. 99

Ostaria al Garanghelo, $, p. 106

IF YOU DON'T WANT FISH

La Bitta, $$, p. 102

La Zucca, $, p. 108

Muro Pizzeria con Cucina (Frari location), $, p. 108

Vini da Gigio, $$, p. 98

GREAT VIEWS

Algiubagiò, $$, p. 94

De Pisis, $$$$, p. 104

Ristorante Riviera, $$$, p. 103

EXCEPTIONAL WINE LIST

Antiche Carampane, $$$, p. 105

La Cantina, $, p. 96

Osteria Orto dei Mori, $$, p. 97

Ristoteca Oniga, $$, p. 103

Vini da Gigio, $$, p. 98

GOOD FOR LUNCH

Al Prosecco, $, p. 107

El Rèfolo, $, p. 98

La Cantina, $, p. 96

La Zucca, $, p. 108

Muro Pizzeria con Cucina, $, p. 108

Ostaria al Garanghelo, $, p. 106

CUCINA ALTA (SOPHISTICATED CUISINE)

De Pisis, $$$$, p. 104

Il Ridotto, $$$$, p. 99

CASALINGA (HOME COOKING)

Antico Panificio, $, p. 106

La Trattoria ai Tosi, $, p. 99

Ostaria al Garanghelo, $, p. 106

resemble the "Wonder" of your youth; many bars here still make their own mayonnaise, and few skimp on the fillings.

Use the coordinate (✛ B2) at the end of each listing to locate a restaurant on the Where to Eat in Venice map.

WHAT IT COSTS IN EUROS					
	¢	$	$$	$$$	$$$$
AT DINNER	under €20	€20–€30	€30–€45	€45–€65	over €65

Prices are for a first course (primo), second course (secondo), and dessert (dolce).

CANNAREGIO

$$$ ✕ **Al Fontego dei Pescatori.** Having had a stall at the Rialto fish market
VENETIAN for more than 25 years, and being the president of the area fishmongers association for 10, proprietor "Lolo" knows his fish. The seafood served here might just be the freshest in Venice. Antipasti include Orologio, a "clock" of raw selections; Poker, four different *tartars* of seafood and fresh fruit; and succulent grilled *capelunghe* (razor clams). The pasta is served al dente, the risotto *al onda* (undulating, as opposed to firm). Chef Massimo prepares entrées simply but always with a twist, such as *branzino* (sea bass) topped with its own crispy skin or a frizzle of zucchini. The wine list includes excellent regional choices that pair well with fish. There's meat for non–fish eaters, too. The dining rooms are spacious and the garden is enchanting in temperate weather. ⊠ *Calle Priuli, Cannaregio 3711* ☎ *041/5200538* ═ *MC, V* ☉ *Closed Mon., 3 wks in Jan., 2 wks in Aug. No lunch in July and Aug.* Ⓥ *Ca' d'Oro* ✛ *D2.*

$$ ✕ **Algiubagiò.** A waterfront table is still relatively affordable at lunch-
ITALIAN time here on Venice's northern Fondamente Nove, where you can gaze out toward San Michele and Murano—on a clear day you can even see the Dolomites. Algiubagiò has a dual personality: pizzas and big salads at lunch; at dinner, creative *primi* (first courses) like ravioli stuffed with *pecorino di fossa* (a hard sheep's-milk cheese) are followed by elegant *secondi* (second courses) such as Angus fillets with vodka and Gorgonzola. The young, friendly staff also serves ice cream, drinks, and sandwiches all day. A lunch table here is worth the walk for the view; the price rises considerably at dinner. ⊠ *Fondamente Nove, Cannaregio 5039* ☎ *041/5236084* ⊕ *www.algiubagio.net* ✍ *Reservations essential-for dinner* ═ *MC, V* Ⓥ *Fondamente Nove* ✛ *E2.*

$–$$ ✕ **Anice Stellato.** Off the main concourse, on one of the most romantic
VENETIAN *fondamente* (canal-side streets) of Cannaregio, this family-run bacaro-trattoria is the place to stop for fairly priced, satisfying fare, though service can feel indifferent. The space has plenty of character: narrow columns rise from the colorful tile floor, dividing the room into cozy sections. Venetian classics are enriched with such offerings as *carpacci di pesce* (thin slices of raw tuna, swordfish, or salmon dressed with olive oil and fragrant herbs), tagliatelle with king prawns and zucchini flowers, and several tasty fish stews. They also serve several meat dishes, including a tender beef fillet stewed in Barolo wine with potatoes. Book

THE LOGISTICS OF A MEAL IN VENICE

The standard procedures of a restaurant meal in Venice and throughout Italy are different from those in the United States (and many other places). When you sit down in a *ristorante or trattoria* you're expected to order two courses at a minimum, such as a *primo* (first course) and a *secondo* (second course), or an antipasto (starter) followed by a primo or secondo. A secondo is not a "main course" that can serve as a full meal.

The handiest places for a snack between sights are bars, cafés, and the quintessentially Venetian bacari (wine bars). Bars are small cafés that can serve any sort of drink from coffee to grappa, along with a quick *panino* (sandwich, often warmed on a griddle) or *tramezzino* (sandwich on untoasted white bread, usually with a mayonnaise-based filling). A café is like a bar but usually with more seating, and it may serve a few additional food items. If you place your order at the counter, ask if you can sit down: many places charge considerably more for table service. In some cases you'll pay a cashier first, then give your *scontrino* (receipt) to the person at the counter who fills your order.

MEALTIMES AND CLOSURES

Breakfast (*la colazione*) is usually served from 7 to 10:30, and it usually consists of little more than coffee and a roll; the only place you may find meat or eggs is at your hotel. Lunch (*il pranzo*) is served from 12:30 to 2, dinner (*la cena*) from 7:30 to 10. Many bacari open as early as 8 AM, but they do not serve typical breakfast items or coffee; some Venetians partake of cichetti for their morning meal.

RESERVATIONS AND DRESS

Reservations are always recommended in restaurants, especially Friday through Sunday. We mention them in reviews only when they are essential or not accepted. We mention dress only when men are required to wear a jacket or a jacket and tie. Keep in mind that Italian men never wear shorts or running shoes in a restaurant or bacaro, no matter how humble. The same "rules" apply to ladies' casual shorts, running shoes, and plastic sandals. Shorts are acceptable in pizzerias and cafés.

PRICES AND TIPPING

All prices include tax. Prices include service *(servizio)*, unless indicated otherwise on the menu. It's customary to leave a small tip (from a euro to 10% of the bill) in appreciation of good service. Tips are always given in cash. Most restaurants have a "cover" charge, usually listed on the menu as *pane e coperto*. It should be modest (€1–€2.50 per person) except at the most expensive restaurants. Some instead charge for bread, which should be brought to you (and paid for) only if you order it. When in doubt, ask about the policy upon ordering.

The price of fish dishes is often given by weight (before cooking); the price on the menu will be for 100 grams (4 ounces); a typical fish portion will come to 350 grams (14 ounces). Keep some cash on hand, because many osterie, bacari, and pizzerias don't take credit cards.

early to grab one of the outdoor waterside tables on summer evenings. ⊠ *Fondamenta de la Sensa, Cannaregio 3272* ☎ *041/720744* ▤ *MC, V* ⊙ *Closed Mon. and Tues., 1 wk in Feb., and 3 wks in Aug.* Ⓥ *San Alvise or San Marcuola* ⊹ *C1.*

$–$$ ✕ **Botteghe di Promessi Sposi.** The former Promessi Sposi eatery was reju-
ITALIAN   venated when three *fioi* (guys) with decades of restaurant experience
★   joined forces to open this restaurant. Claudio mans the kitchen, while Nicola and Cristiano will serve you either an *ombra* (small glass of wine) and cicchetto at the *banco* (counter), or a delightful meal in the dining room or the intimate courtyard. A season-centered menu includes standards like Venetian calves' liver and grilled *canestrelli* (tiny Venetian scallops) along with more-adventurous creations, like home-made ravioli stuffed with *rapi rossi* (red turnip) and topped with the Sardinian ricotta *salata* (a firm, medium-aged ricotta), or a steak tartar served with bean sprouts and spoonfuls of capers, paprika, mustard, and minced red onions. It's the best of many worlds: a comfy trat-toria where there's something for everyone. ⊠ *Calle de l'Oca (just off Campo Santi Apostoli), Cannaregio 4367* ☎ *041/2412747* ⊜ *Reservations essential* ▤ *No credit cards* ⊙ *Closed Wed.* Ⓥ *Ca' d'Oro* ⊹ *E2.*

$$ ✕ **Dalla Marisa.** It doesn't get any more Venetian than this. At Marisa, a
VENETIAN   beloved Cannaregio institution, don't expect a menu, tourist or other-wise: what Marisa cooks—whether meat, wild game, or fish—you eat. Expect is an abundant, five-course meal of expertly prepared Venetian comfort food. The pasta and gnocchi are always *fatto in casa* (home-made). Primi might include tagliatelle with *sugo del masaro* (duck sauce), risotto *di caroman* (with mutton), or perhaps a *zuppa di funghi,* soup made with fresh mushrooms. *Salmì di cervo* (stewed venison), or *fagiano ripieno arrosto* (stuffed roast pheasant) are possibilities for *secondi di carne,* and on fish nights, *frittura mista.* In temperate weather ask to eat canal-side—but be on time or lose your table. ⊠ *Calle de la Canne (near the Tre Archi bridge, Fondamenta San Giobbe), Cannare-gio 652/B* ☎ *041/720211* ⊜ *Reservations essential* ▤ *No credit cards* ⊙ *Closed Tues.* Ⓥ *Crea or Tre Archi* ⊹ *B1.*

$$$$ ✕ **Fiaschetteria Toscana.** Contrary to what the name suggests, there's noth-
ITALIAN   ing Tuscan about this restaurant's menu. It was formerly a Tuscan wine-and-oil storehouse, and it's worth a visit for its cheerful and courteous service, fine *cucina* (cooking), and noteworthy cellar. The owners, Albino and Mariuccia Busatto, make their presence felt as they walk among the well-appointed tables, opening special bottles of wine and discuss-ing the menu. Gastronomic highlights include a light *tagliolini neri al ragù di astice* (thin spaghetti served with squid ink and mixed with a delicate lobster sauce), and zabaglione. ⊠ *Campo San Giovanni Crisos-tomo, Cannaregio 5719* ☎ *041/5285281* ⊕ *www.fiaschetteriatoscana.it* ⊜ *Reservations essential* ▤ *AE, DC, MC, V* ⊙ *Closed Tues. and 4 wks in July and Aug. No lunch Wed.* Ⓥ *Rialto* ⊹ *E3.*

$ ✕ **La Cantina.** With its understated facade, you'd never guess that La
CONTEMPORARY   Cantina offered anything more than a nice sandwich and an acceptable pinot grigio. Perhaps if you spotted the fresh raw oysters, a whole tuna patiently waiting to be filleted, or the sign for today's *zuppa di lenticchie* (lentil soup), you might begin to understand how satisfying a meal here

Vini da Gigio's refined cuisine is one of the best values in the city.

can be. Co-owner and chef Francesco chooses from only the choicest meats and cheeses, the freshest vegetables, seasonings, and fish to create his inspired meals. There's effectively no menu: tell co-owner Andrea or wine expert Giovanni your preferences and your budget, then sit back and wait to be satisfied. One caveat: Service can be slow on busier evenings, especially after 8 PM. ⊠ *Campo San Felice, Cannaregio 3689* ☎ *041/5228258* ⊲ *Reservations essential* ▤ *AE, MC, V* ⊗ *Closed Sun. and Mon.* Ⓥ *Ca' d'Oro* ✛ *D2.*

$$
ITALIAN
Fodor's Choice
★
✕ **Osteria Orto dei Mori.** "Pure pleasure" might be the best way to describe the dining experience here: from the fanciful, tasteful interior decor, to romantic candlelit tables dotting the Campo dei Mori, to the inspired cucina. The attentive expertise of chef and co-owner Lorenzo is evident in every dish: try the *fagotti* (bundles of beef marinated in Chianti with goat cheese) or a seafood version with prawns, zucchini, and ricotta. Risotto with scampi and savory *fenferli* mushrooms won't disappoint, nor will the signature parchment-baked monkfish. Co-owner Micael has artfully constructed the wine list—ask about periodic tastings. The osteria is just under the nose of the campo's corner statue. ⊠ *Campo dei Mori, Fondamenta dei Mori, Cannaregio 3386* ☎ *041/5235544* ▤ *AE, DC, MC, V* ⊗ *Closed Tues.* Ⓥ *Orto, Ca d'Oro, or San Marcuola* ✛ *D1.*

¢
CAFÉ
✕ **Tiziano.** A staggering array of *tramezzini* (sandwiches) lines the display cases at this *tavola calda* (roughly the Italian equivalent of a cafeteria) on the main drag from the Rialto to Santi Apostoli; inexpensive salad plates and daily pasta specials are also served. Whether you choose to sit or stand, it's a handy—and popular—spot for a quick meal or a snack at very modest prices. Vegetarians delight in Tiziano's version of the classic Italian toast, in this case a grilled-cheese sandwich with eggplant

slices and roasted zucchini. ⊠ *Salizzada San Giovanni Crisostomo, Cannaregio 5747* ☎ *041/5235544* ▭ *No credit cards* Ⓥ *Rialto* ✛ *E3*.

$$ ✕ **Vini da Gigio.** Paolo and Laura, a brother-sister team, run this refined
VENETIAN   trattoria as if they've invited you to dinner in their home, while keeping
Fodor'sChoice   the service professional. Deservedly popular with Venetians and visitors
★   alike, it's one of the best values in the city. Indulge in homemade pastas such as rigatoni with duck sauce and arugula-stuffed ravioli. Fish is well represented—try the sesame-encrusted tuna—but the meat dishes steal the show. The *anatra* (duck) is a flavorful fricassee; the steak with red-pepper sauce and the *tagliata di agnello* (sautéed lamb fillet with a light, crusty coating) are both superb, and you'll never enjoy a better *fegato alla veneziana* (Venetian-style liver with onions). It's a shame to order the house wine here: just let Paolo know your budget and he'll choose for you from his more than 3,000 labels. ⊠ *Fondamenta San Felice, Cannaregio 3628/A* ☎ *041/5285140* ⊕ *www.vinidagigio.com* 🍴 *Reservations essential* ▭ *MC, V* ⊗ *Closed Mon. and Tues., 2 wks in Jan., and 3 wks in Aug.* Ⓥ *Ca' d'Oro* ✛ *D2*.

CASTELLO

$$$ ✕ **Alle Testiere.** A strong local following can make it tough to get one of
SEAFOOD   the 22 seats at this tiny trattoria near Campo Santa Maria Formosa. With its decidedly unglamorous ceiling fans, the place feels as informal as a bistro (or a saloon); the food, however, is much more sophisticated. Chef Bruno Gavagnin's dishes stand out for lightness and balance: try the *gnocchetti con moscardini* (little gnocchi with tender baby octopus) or the linguine with *coda di rospo* (monkfish), or inquire about the carpaccio of the day. The well-assembled wine list is particularly strong on local whites. ⊠ *Calle del Mondo Novo, Castello 5801* ☎ *041/5227220* ⊕ *www.osterialletestiere.it* 🍴 *Reservations essential* ▭ *MC, V* ⊗ *Closed Sun. and Mon., 3 wks in Jan. and Feb., and 4 wks in July and Aug.* Ⓥ *Rialto or San Zaccaria* ✛ *E3*.

$ ✕ **Al Mascaron.** At the convivial, crowded Al Mascaron, with its paper
VENETIAN   tablecloths and informal atmosphere, you'll likely find locals who drop in to gossip, drink, play cards, and eat cicchetti at the bar—but there are also plenty of travelers who return again and again to take advantage of the food and the hospitality. You can count on delicious fish, pasta, risotto, and seafood salads. Locals complain that the prices have become somewhat inflated, but grudgingly admit that the food is good. ⊠ *Calle Lunga Santa Maria Formosa, Castello 522530122* ☎ *041/5225995* ⊕ *www.osteriamascaron.it* ▭ *No credit cards* ⊗ *Closed Sun. and mid-Dec.–mid-Jan.* Ⓥ *Rialto or San Marco* ✛ *F3*.

$ ✕ **El Rèfolo.** This hip hangout is named after a play by turn-of-the-20th-
WINE BAR   century emancipated lady Amalia Rosselli—look for the framed title
★   page inside. El Rèfolo (The Breeze, in Venetian) is a contemporary cantina in a very Venetian neighborhood, and is more for lunch, *un aperitivo* (an aperitif), or supper than formal dinner. Owner Massimiliano pairs great wines with select meats, savory cheese, and seasonal vegetable combos. In temperate weather, this niche-size *enoteca*'s exuberance effervesces out onto the city's broadest street. It's open every day but Sunday from 9:30 AM to 12:30 AM. ⊠ *Via Garibaldi 1580,*

Castello ☎ *No phone* ▭ *MC, V* ⊙ *Closed Sun., hrs limited in winter* Ⓥ *Arsenale* ✛ *H5.*

$$$$ ✕ **Il Ridotto.** Longtime restaurateur Gianni Bonaccorsi of nearby Aci-
VENETIAN ugheta fame has succeeded in opening a locale that is the pure expression of the best he has to offer. Ridotto, "reduced" in Italian, may
refer to the size of this tiny, gracious restaurant. The dimensions allow
Gianni to spoil you, should you manage to snag one of the five tables
(easier at lunch). The artful menu is revised daily, a luxury only such a
personalized restaurant can afford; you may find fettuccine with Piedmont Fassona beef ragout or scampi with crustacean sauce, and, for
dessert, pistachio flan. The tasting menu never fails to impress. Have
Gianni choose a wine for you from his excellent cantina. ⊠ *Campo SS
Filippo e Giacomo, Castello 4509* ☎ *041/5208280* ⊕ *www.ilridotto.
com* ⚑ *Reservations essential* ▭ *AE, DC, MC, V* ⊙ *Closed Wed. No
lunch Thurs.* Ⓥ *San Zaccaria* ✛ *F4.*

$ ✕ **La Trattoria ai Tosi.** Getting off the beaten track to find good, basic
ITALIAN local cuisine isn't easy in Venice, but La Trattoria ai Tosi (aka Ai Tosi
Piccoli) fills the bill with its remote (but not too), tranquil location,
homey atmosphere, and variety of fine traditional fare at prices that
make it worth the walk from anywhere in the city. The baccalà mantecato "sanwicini" are excellent, as are the classic frittura mista and the
spaghetti with scallops and zucchini (a bargain at €10). You'll also find
a grilled steak and ribs platter that should fulfill any meat cravings. The
fixed-price lunch menu, created for local workers with limited time, is
another good deal, and there's even decemt pizza. (Note: make sure you
end up at this smaller, locally owned Tosi, rather than the Tosi Grande
across the way that's no longer family owned.) ⊠ *Seco Marina 738,
Castello* ☎ *041/5237102* ▭ *MC, V* ⊙ *Closed Mon.* Ⓥ *Giardini* ✛ *H5.*

$$$ ✕ **Osteria di Santa Marina.** The romantic, candlelit tables in the campo are
VENETIAN inviting enough, but it's this intimate restaurant's imaginative kitchen
creations that are likely to win you over. Star dishes include *tortino di
baccalà mantecato* (cod torte) with baby arugula and fried polenta;
passatina di piselli (fresh pea puree with scallops and tiny calamari);
scampi *in saor,* a turn on a Venetian classic with leeks and ginger; and
fresh ravioli stuffed with mussels and turbot in a creamed celery sauce.
You can also opt for the rewarding tasting menu, in either a meat or
fish version, for €55. The wine list is ample and well thought out. Ser-
vice is gracious and cordial—just don't be in a terrible rush, or expect
the server to be your new best friend. ⊠ *Campo Santa Marina, Cas-
tello 5911* ☎ *041/5285239* ⚑ *Reservations essential* ▭ *MC, V* ⊙ *Closed
Sun., no lunch Mon.* Ⓥ *Rialto* ✛ *E3.*

DORSODURO

$$ ✕ **Ai 4 Feri.** The paper tablecloths and cozy, laid-back ambience are part
VENETIAN of this small restaurant's charm. The menu varies according to what's
fresh that day; imaginative combinations of ingredients in the primi—
herring and sweet peppers, salmon and radicchio, giant shrimp and
broccoli with pumpkin gnocchi—are the norm. A meal here followed
by after-dinner gelato at Il Doge or drinks in Campo Santa Margherita,
a five-minute walk away, makes for a lovely evening. The kitchen is

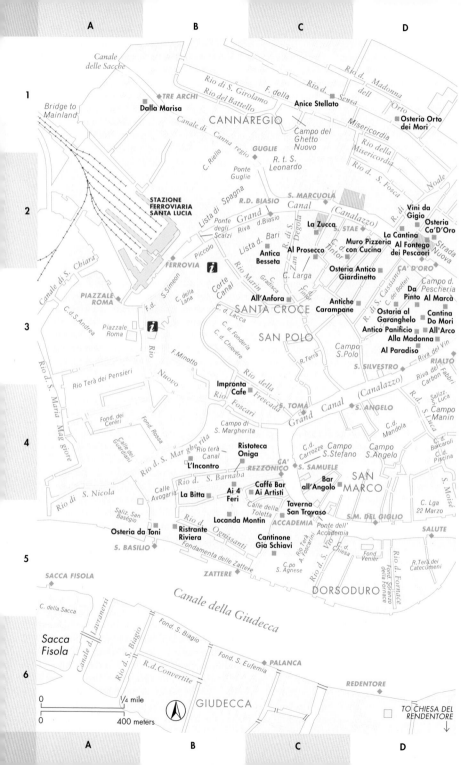

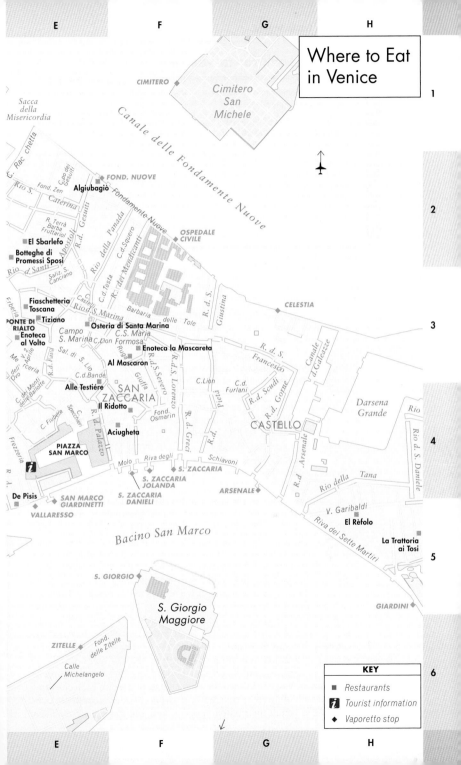

Where to Eat in Venice

E F G H

1

CIMITERO

Cimitero San Michele

Sacca della Misericordia

Canale delle Fondamente Nuove

2

FOND. NUOVE
■ Algiubagiò

Fondamente Nuove

OSPEDALE CIVILE

■ El Sbarlefo
■ Botteghe di Promessi Sposi

CELESTIA

3

PONTE DI RIALTO
■ Fiaschetteria Toscana
■ Tiziano
■ Enoteca al Volto

■ Osteria di Santa Marina

Campo S. Marina
C.S. Maria Formosa

■ Enoteca la Mascareta
■ Al Mascaron

SAN ZACCARIA

■ Alle Testiére
■ Il Ridotto

CASTELLO

Darsena Grande

■ Aciugheta

Rio

4

PIAZZA SAN MARCO

Molo *Riva degli*
S. ZACCARIA

■ De Pisis
SAN MARCO GIARDINETTI

S. ZACCARIA JOLANDA
S. ZACCARIA DANIELI

Schiavoni

ARSENALE

Rio della Tana

V. Garibaldi
■ El Rèfolo

5

VALLARESSO

Bacino San Marco

Riva dei Sette Martiri

■ La Trattoria ai Tosi

S. GIORGIO

S. Giorgio Maggiore

GIARDINI

ZITELLE
Fond. delle Zitelle

Calle Michelangelo

KEY	
■	*Restaurants*
🛈	*Tourist information*
◆	*Vaporetto stop*

6

E F G H

Wines to Look for in Venice

Tre Venezie regional wines (from the Veneto, Trentino–Alto Adige, and Friuli–Venezia Giulia) go far beyond the famous Amarone, and include some spectacular whites like the crisp Malvasia and Tocai, the smooth Garganega (Soave) and Ribolla Pialla, along with the versitile, just-dry-enough bubbly, prosecco.

Reds are dry and flavorful but relatively low in alchohol, making

them the perfect accompaniment to regional cuisine: look for Cabernet Franc, Corvina (Valpolicella, Bardolino), Marzemino, Lagrein, Refosco, Raboso, or Teroldego Rotaliano.

If this all seems a little confusing, the best (and definitely the most pleasurable) course of action is to head to a bacaro for some expert guidance.

---

open until 10:30 PM. ⊠ *Calle Lunga San Barnaba, Dorsoduro 2754/A* ☎ *041/5206978* ⊟ *No credit cards* ✆ *Closed Sun. and 2 wks in June* Ⓥ *Ca' Rezzonico* ✛ *B4.*

¢ ✕ **Caffè Bar Ai Artisti.** Sitting on a campo made famous in film by Katharine Hepburn and Indiana Jones, Ai Artisti gives locals, students, and travelers alike good reason to pause and refuel. The location is central, pleasant, and sunny—perfect for people-watching and taking a break before the next destination—and the hours are long: you can come here for a morning cappuccino, or drop by as late as midnight for an after-dinner spritz. The *panini are* composed on-site from fresh, seasonal ingredients, their names scribbled in front of each on the glass case; ask about the day's pasta and other primi. There's a varied selection of wines by the glass, as well as herbal teas, and even caffè with ginseng. ⊠ *Campo San Barnaba, Dorsoduro 2771* ☎ *041/5238994* ⊟ *No credit cards* Ⓥ *Ca' Rezzonico* ✛ *C4.*

VENETIAN

$ ✕ **Impronta Cafe.** This lively spot is a bar-osteria-enoteca-bacaro-ristorante all in one. You might call it Venice reenvisioned: the minimalist decor contrasts with ample gastronomic offerings that change according the hour of the day; the *orario continuato* (continuous open hours) from 7 AM until 2 AM are unheard of. Stop in at breakfast for a caffè and brioche. At lunch there are fresh cichetti and panini, a fine selection of sliced meats and cheeses, and a daily hot primo. In the afternoon take a tea or chocolate break. At aperitivo hour, have a spritz or glass of wine from the abundant selection. Full dinner is served until midnight, snacks until 2 AM. Whenever you stop in, you'll always find company. The desire to attract students from the nearby university keeps prices in line; on occasion you'll even find live music. ⊠ *Crosera San Pantalon, Dorsoduro 3815* ☎ *041/2750386* ⊟ *AE, MC, V* ✆ *Closed Sun.* Ⓥ *San Tomà* ✛ *C4.*

ITALIAN

$$ ✕ **La Bitta.** The decor is more discreet, the dining hours longer, and the service friendlier and more efficient here than in many small restaurants in Venice—and the creative non-fish menu is a temptation at every course. You can start with a light salad of Treviso radicchio and crispy bacon, followed by smoked-beef carpaccio or *gnocchetti ubriachi al Montasio* (small, marinated gnocchi with Montasio cheese). Then

ITALIAN

choose a secondo such as lamb chops with thyme, *anatra in pevarada* (duck in a pepper sauce), or Irish Angus fillet steak. Secondi are served with vegetables, which helps bring down the price. The restaurant is open only for dinner, but serves much earlier and later than most, continuously from 6:30 to 11. ⊠ *Calle Lunga San Barnaba, Dorsoduro 2753/A* ☎ *041/5230531* ⌂ *Reservations essential* ▭ *No credit cards* ☾ *Closed Sun. and July. No lunch* Ⓥ *Ca' Rezzonico* ✛ *B4.*

$ ✕ **L'Incontro.** This trattoria between San Barnaba and Campo Santa
ITALIAN Margherita has a faithful clientele of Venetians and visitors, attracted
★ by flavorful Sardinian food, sociable service, and reasonable prices. Starters include Sardinian sausages, but you might skip to the delicious traditional primi, such as *culingiones* (large ravioli filled with pecorino, saffron, and orange peel). The selection of secondi is heavy on herb-crusted meat dishes such as *coniglio al mirto* (rabbit baked on a bed of myrtle sprigs) and the *costine d'agnello con rosmarino e mentuccia* (baby lamb ribs with rosemary and wild mint). ⊠ *Rio Terà Canal (just off Campo Santa Margherita), Dorsoduro 3062/A* ☎ *041/5222404* ▭ *AE, DC, MC, V* ☾ *Closed Mon., Jan., and 2 wks in Aug. No lunch Tues.* Ⓥ *Ca' Rezzonico* ✛ *B4.*

$$$ ✕ **Locanda Montin.** Peggy Guggenheim used to take famous painters—
ITALIAN including Jackson Pollock and Mark Rothko—to this archetypal Venetian inn not far from her Palazzo Venier dei Leoni. The walls are still covered with modern art, but it's far from the haute bohemian hangout it used to be (except for when the Biennale crowd takes over). Outside, you can dine under an elongated arched arbor on such specialties as rigatoni *ai quattro formaggi* (with four cheeses), spaghetti Adriatica (with fish sauce), and antipasto Montin (seafood antipasto). ⊠ *Fondamenta Eremite, Dorsoduro 1147* ☎ *041/5227151* ▭ *MC, V* ☾ *Closed Aug.; Jan. to Carnevale, closed Wed., no dinner Tues.* Ⓥ *Accademia* ✛ *B5.*

$$$ ✕ **Ristorante Riviera.** Two lovely dining rooms and a canal-side terrace
NORTHERN with an exquisite view, combined with truly inspired cuisine, make a
ITALIAN visit to Riviera one to remember. Chef Monica Scarpa brings her creative touch to both traditional and contemporary dishes. Fish lovers will enjoy the tuna tartare, seafood risotto, or a mixed-fish platter, while carnivores can dig into prosciutto with figs and pecorino cheese followed by a plate of succulent lamb chops with blueberry sauce. Host Luca excels at selecting the perfect wine for any combination of foods. A simple but appealing children's menu is offered. ⊠ *Zattere, Dorsoduro 1473* ☎ *041/5227621* ⊕ *www.ristoranteriviera.it* ⌂ *Reservations essential* ▭ *MC, V* ☾ *Closed Mon. and 4 wks in Jan. and Feb. No lunch Wed.* Ⓥ *San Basilio* ✛ *B5.*

$$ ✕ **Ristoteca Oniga.** Marino Oniga and his wife, Annika, successfully com-
VENETIAN bine classic Venetian elements in an out-of-the-ordinary way, adding a touch of personality and imagination to both creation and presentation. Delectably roasted duck is one of several meat alternatives to the fresh fish; the wine list is ample, and Annika's desserts are all fatto in casa (homemade). The outdoor seating in Campo San Barnaba makes a charming setting for a delightful meal. ⊠ *Campo San Barnaba, Dorsoduro 2852* ☎ *041/0997534* ⊕ *www.oniga.it* ⌂ *Reservations essential* ▭ *AE, MC, V* ☾ *Closed Tues.* Ⓥ *Ca' Rezzonico* ✛ *B4.*

¢   ✕ **Taverna San Trovaso.** A wide choice of Venetian dishes served in
ITALIAN   robust portions, economical fixed-price menus, pizzas, and house
wine by the glass or pitcher keep this two-floor, no-nonsense tavern
abuzz with young locals and budget-conscious visitors in the know.
It's always packed, and table turnover is fast. Not far from the Gallerie
dell'Accademia, this is a good place to slip into while sightseeing in
Dorsoduro. ⊠ *Fondamenta Priuli, Dorsoduro 1016* ☎ *041/5203703*
⊕ *www.tavernasantrovaso.it* ⊟ *AE, MC, V* ⊗ *Closed Mon. and 1 wk
Dec.–Jan.* Ⓥ *Accademia, Zattere* ✛ *C5.*

SAN MARCO

¢   ✕ **Bar all'Angolo.** This corner of Campo Santo Stefano is one of the most
VENETIAN   pleasing locations to sit and watch the Venetian world go by. The constant motion of the café staff assures you'll receive your coffee, spritz,
panino, or *tramezzino* (sandwich on untoasted white bread, usually
with a mayonnaise-based filling) in short order; consume it at your
leisure either at one of the outdoor tables, at the bar, or take refuge at
the tables in the back. They'll whip you up a fresh salad or a hot primo,
and they offer a delectable tiramisu for dessert—homemade, just like the
sandwiches. Closing time is 9 PM, making the Angolo a good alternative
to a more-elaborate evening meal. ⊠ *Campo Santo Stefano (just in front
of the Santo Stefano church), San Marco 3464* ☎ *041/5220710* ⊟ *AE,
MC, V* ⊗ *Closed Sun. and Jan.* Ⓥ *Sant'Angelo* ✛ *C4.*

$$$$ ✕ **De Pisis.** Romance and elegance pervade the interior and luminous
MODERN ITALIAN   terrace here, which has a Grand Canal panorama that includes the
radiant Santa Maria della Salute. The service is impeccable, as is Chef
Giovanni Ciresa's cuisine, where you'll find Venetian, Asian, and Mediterranean influences synthesized to create inspired, delectable works of
art. If you're feeling adventurous, do try one of the chef's experimental
dishes for which he is quite famous and let your sommelier suggest a
wine from their masterful list. This formal restaurant attracts well-
dressed clientele and is a fine choice for a splurge. ⊠ *Calle San Moise,
San Marco 1459* ☎ *041/5207022* ⊿ *Reservations essential* ⊟ *AE, DC,
MC, V* Ⓥ *Valaresso or Santa Maria del Giglio* ✛ *E5.*

$–$$ ✕ **Enoteca al Volto.** A short walk from the Rialto Bridge, this bar has
WINE BAR   been around since 1936; the fine cicchetti and primi have a lot to do
with its staying power. Two small, dark rooms with a ceiling plastered
with wine labels provide a classic backdrop for simple fare. The place
prides itself on its considerable wine list of both Italian and foreign vintages, as you might reckon from the decoration. If you stick to panini
(sandwiches) and a cicchetto or two, you'll eat well for relatively little.
If you opt for one of the primi of the day, the price category goes up
a notch. ⊠ *Calle Cavalli, San Marco 4081* ☎ *041/5228945* ⊕ *www.
alvoltoenoteca.it* ⊿ *Reservations essential* ⊟ *No credit cards* ⊗ *Closed
Sun.* Ⓥ *Rialto* ✛ *E3.*

SAN POLO

$$$
VENETIAN

⊁**Alla Madonna.** Locals relax at Alla Madonna, which prides itself on the freshness, abundance, and quality of their fish. In business since 1954 (Rado Fluvio still runs the place), it is a classic in service, atmosphere, and cuisine. The *materia prima* (the principal ingredients) are of paramount importance here, and impeccable preparation ensures its characteristics are always accentuated, never overwhelmed. Get

your server's recommendation for the day. There are a variety of meat dishes, a fine wine list, and space for groups. It's a popular spot, so expect a lively and bustling atmosphere. ⊠ *Calle della Madonna, San Polo 594* ☎ *041/5223824* ⊕ *www.ristoranteallamadonna.com* ⊜ *Reservations essential* ⊟ *AE, MC, V* ⊙ *Closed Sun., Jan., and 2 wks in Aug.* Ⓥ *San Silvestro* ⊕ *D3.*

¢
VENETIAN

⊁**All'Arco.** Just because it's noon and you only have time between sights for a sandwich doesn't mean that it can't be a satisfying, even awe-inspiring one. There's no menu at All'Arco, but a scan of what's behind the glass counter is all you need. Order what entices you, or have Roberto or Matteo (father and son) suggest a cichetto or panino. Options here are broad enough to satisfy both conservative and adventurous eaters. Wine choices are well suited to the food. Arrive early or at the tail end of lunchtime to snag one of the few tables in the calle. ⊠ *Calle Arco, San Polo 436* ☎ *041/5220619* ⊟ *AE, MC, V* ⊙ *Closed Sun.* Ⓥ *San Silvestro* ⊕ *D3.*

$$$
MODERN ITALIAN
Fodor's Choice
★

⊁**Al Paradiso.** In a small dining room made warm and cozy by its pleasing and unpretentious decor, proprietor Giordano makes all diners feel like honored guests. Pappardelle "al Paradiso" takes pasta with seafood sauce to new heights, while risotto with shrimp, champagne, and grapefruit puts a delectable twist on a traditional dish. The inspired and original array of entrées includes meat and fish selections such as a salmon with honey and balsamic vinegar in a stunning presentation. Desserts include a perfect panna cotta. ⊠ *Calle del Paradiso, San Polo 767* ☎ *041/5234910* ⊜ *Reservations essential* ⊟ *AE, MC, V* ⊙ *Closed Mon. and 3 wks in Jan. and Feb.* Ⓥ *San Silvestro* ⊕ *D3.*

$$$
VENETIAN
Fodor's Choice
★

⊁**Antiche Carampane.** Since its appearance in the first of Donna Leon's *Inspector Brunetti* mysteries, Piera Bortoluzzi Librai's trattoria has lost none of its charm but gained considerably in elegance. You'll find all the classic Venetian fish dishes ranging from a mixed seafood antipasto to fish soups, pasta, and perfectly grilled fish. Updated plates such as seafood and fruit salads for starters and entrées like turbot with citrus sauce also delight diners. Chocolate mousse, panna cotta, and sweet wine with biscotti make delectable desserts. Francesco, the son of Franco and Piera, whose family recipes elevate many of the classics, is responsible for some of the new presentations. ⊠ *Rio Terà della Carampane, San Polo 1911* ☎ *041/5240165* ⊕ *www.antichecarampane.*

3

Fresh scallops—part of Venice's bounty of seafood.

com ⚭ *Reservations essential* ▭ *AE, MC, V* ☺ *Closed Sun. and Mon.,*
10 days in Jan., and 3 wks in July and Aug. Ⓥ *San Silvestro* ✛ *D3.*

$ ✗ **Antico Panificio.** Tasty, economical fare in a friendly atmosphere *senza*

ITALIAN *pretesa* (without pretense) can be a tall order in Venice, but the Antico
Panificio succeeds in offering just that: traditional, satisfying dishes,
from pizza in every form conceivable to pasta with meat sauce, to a
grilled pork chop or fillet of sole—all at a handy location just down
from the Rialto. It's apparent from the mix of locals and travelers chat-
tering away that the Panificio is no secret, so arrive on the early side
for lunch, and be sure to reserve in the evening. Service can be a bit
slow when the place is full, so it's best not to come here in a rush.
⊠ *Campiello del Sole, San Polo 945/A–B* ☎ *041/2770967* ▭ *AE, MC,*
V ☺ *Closed Tues.* Ⓥ *San Silvestro* ✛ *D3.*

$ ✗ **Ostaria al Garanghelo.** Superior quality, competitive prices, and great

ITALIAN ambience mean this place is often packed with Venetians, especially for
★ lunch and an after-work ombra (glass of wine) and cicchetti (snack).
Chef Renato takes full advantage of the fresh ingredients from the
Rialto Market, a few steps away, bakes his own bread daily, and prefers
cooking many dishes *al vapore* (steamed). The spicy *fagioli al uciletto*
(literally "bird-style beans," prepared with a light marinara sauce) has
an unusual name and Tuscan origins; it's a perfect companion to a plate
of fresh pasta. Don't confuse this restaurant with one of the same name
in Via Garibaldi. ⊠ *Calle dei Boteri, San Polo 1570* ☎ *041/721721*
▭ *MC, V* ☺ *Closed Sun.* Ⓥ *Rialto* ✛ *D3.*

At charming little La Zucca, the menu's strength is its vegetarian dishes.

SANTA CROCE

¢ ✕ **All'Anfora.** This lively, informal trattoria-pizzeria offers more than 50

ITALIAN different pizzas, described by owners Claudio and Mariano as *buone e gigante* (good and gigantic). The pizza is indeed a main attraction, but you'll also find fresh salads (which are good and gigantic as well), and a full menu of trattoria fare: *baccalà* with polenta, risotto *con rucola e* scampi (with arugula and scampi), and *branzino al forno* (baked sea bass) with roast potatoes. There are two dining rooms, but when the weather's fine try for a table in the garden courtyard, or if it's full, on the calle out front. ⊠ *Lista dei Bari, Santa Croce 1223* ☏ *041/5240325* ⊕ *www.pizzeriaallanfora.com* ▭ *MC, V* ☉ *Closed Wed.* Ⓥ *Riva de Biasio* ✛ *C3.*

$ ✕ **Al Prosecco.** Locals stream into this friendly wine bar, down a "spritz"

WINE BAR (a combination of white wine, Campari or Aperol, and seltzer water), and continue on their way. Al Prosecco is the perfect place to explore wines from the region—or from anywhere in the county for that matter. They accompany a carefully chosen selection of meats, cheeses, and other food from small, artisanal producers, used in tasty panini like the *porchetta romane verdure* (roast pork with greens). Proprietors Davide and Stefano preside over a young and friendly staff who reel off the day's specials with ease. There are a few tables in the intimate back room, and when the weather cooperates you can sit outdoors on the lively campo, watching the Venetian world go by. It's open 9 to 9, and later if the mood strikes. ⊠ *Campo San Giacomo dell'Orio, Santa Croce 1503* ☏ *041/5240222* ⊕ *www.alprosecco.com* ▭ *No credit cards* ☉ *Closed Sun.* Ⓥ *San Stae* ✛ *C2.*

$$ ✕**Antica Besseta.** Tucked away in a quiet corner of Santa Croce, with
SEAFOOD a few tables under an ivy shelter, the Antica Besseta dates from the
18th century, and it retains some of its old feel. The menu focuses
on vegetables and fish, according to what's at the market: spaghetti
with *caparozzoli* or cuttlefish ink, *schie* (tiny shrimp) with polenta,
and plenty of grilled fish. ⊠ *Salizzada de Ca' Zusto, Santa Croce 1395*
☏ *041/5240428* ⊕ *www.anticabesseta.it* ▭ *AE, MC, V* ☻ *Closed Mon.
and Tues. No lunch Wed.* Ⓥ *Rive di Biasio* ✛ *C2.*

$ ✕**La Zucca.** The simple place settings, lattice-wood walls, canal win-
ITALIAN dow, and mélange of languages make La Zucca (the pumpkin) feel as
Fodor's Choice much like a typical vegetarian restaurant as you could expect to find
★ in Venice. Though the menu does have superb meat dishes such as the
piccata di pollo ai caperi e limone con riso (sliced chicken with capers
and lemon served with rice), more attention is paid to dishes from the
garden: try the radicchio *di Treviso con funghi e scaglie di Monta-
sio* (with mushrooms and shavings of Montasio cheese) or the *finoc-
chi piccanti con olive* (fennel in a spicy tomato-olive sauce). In good
weather, dining at outdoor table couldn't be more pleasant. Reserve
several days in advance to book one of two dinner seatings, at 7–7:30
or 9–9:30. ⊠ *Calle del Tintor (at Ponte de Megio), Santa Croce 1762*
☏ *041/5241570* ⊕ *www.lazucca.it* ⟐ *Reservations essential.* ▭ *AE, DC,
MC, V* ☻ *Closed Sun. and 1 wk in Dec.* Ⓥ *San Stae* ✛ *C2.*

$ ✕**Muro Pizzeria con Cucina.** Don't let the moniker *pizzeria con cucina*
ITALIAN fool you: Muro offers a varied menu and uses high-quality ingredients,
taking its cue from its more refined sister restaurant, Muro Rialto. Select
from excellent Venetian fare and pizza in classic and innovative forms—
try the *arrotolata amoretesoro* (a rolled pizza) with *bresaola* (thinly
sliced salt-cured beef), *scamorza* (mozzarella-like cow's-milk cheese),
and radicchio. Chef Francesco adds dimension to the menu with classic
Italian selections, along with the *piatti unici,* a single course fancifully
combining elements of first and second courses. A wide selection of beer
is on tap. ⊠ *Campiello dello Spezier, Santa Croce 2048* ☏ *041/5241628*
⊕ *www.murovenezia.com* ⟐ *Reservations essential* ▭ *MC, V* ☻ *Closed
Tues.* Ⓥ *San Stae* ✛ *C2.*

$ ✕**Osteria Antico Giardinetto.** The name refers to the intimate garden
ITALIAN where co-owner Larisa will welcome you warmly, once you've wound
your way from the Rialto or San Stae down the narrow calle to this
romantic locale. (There's an indoor dining room as well, but the garden
is covered and heated in winter.) Larisa's husband, Virgilio, mans the
kitchen, where he prepares such dishes as sea bass in salt crust and a
grilled fish platter. Be sure to try the homemade gnocchi or pasta—per-
haps the *tagliolini* (thin spaghetti) with scallops and artichokes. You'll
also find some fine meat options here. Desserts, like the chocolate
mousse or crème caramel, are homemade as well. The wine list features
some excellent regional selections. ⊠ *Calle dei Morti, Santa Croce 2953*
☏ *041/5240325* ⊕ *www.anticogiardinetto.it* ▭ *MC, V* ☻ *Closed Mon.
and Jan. 4–31* Ⓥ *San Stae* ✛ *D3.*

LIDO

$$ ✗ **Al Vecio Cantier.** The wild scenery, with intersecting canals and reeds,
ITALIAN contributes to the appeal of one of the liveliest places on the Lido,
always filled to the gills during the film festival. There's efficient cichetti
service, but the restaurant deserves a longer visit for a relaxing meal
in the best Venetian tradition: try whipped baccalà with polenta, or
tagliolini *con gamberetti e carciofi* (with shrimp and artichokes) in
spring. Homemade desserts include lemon and almond tarts, or you
can dip cookies in a glass of *vino passito*, a dessert wine. Outside dining
is in a pretty garden. ✉ *Via della Droma 76, The Lido* ☎ *041/5268130*
⊕ *www.alveciocantier.com* ▭ *AE, DC, MC, V* ☉ *Closed Mon. No lunch
Tues., Nov., or Jan.* Ⓥ *Lido.*

$ ✗ **Bar Trento.** This neat, old-style osteria 10 minutes from Piazzale Santa
VENETIAN Maria Elisabetta has a soft spot for meat and innards (one of the own-
ers was a *bechèr,* or butcher). Lunch is the only meal served, but *ombre*
(the Venetian term for a glass of wine) and cichetti are available from
8 to 8. Many of the tasty snacks are made from organ meats (and thus
not for squeamish eaters), but there are more familiar options as well,
including baccalà *alla vicentina* (stewed with onion, milk, and Parme-
san); pasta with seafood; and several seasonal risottos. As a secondo,
fish can be cooked any way you want. ✉ *Via Sandro Gallo 82, The Lido*
☎ *041/5265960* ▭ *No credit cards* ☉ *Closed Sun. No dinner except
during Biennale* Ⓥ *Lido.*

MURANO

$$ ✗ **Antica Trattoria.** This lunch-only trattoria can be easily spotted by the
VENETIAN bright red walls close to the Grand Canal on the island of Murano. For
company you'll probably find local glass workers with a *caffè corretto
con grappa* (espresso with grappa liqueur) in front of them. If it's more
solid nourishment you're after, go for the freshly grilled fish or the *seppie in tecia* (cuttlefish in squid ink), served in the rear garden. ✉ *Riva
Longa 20, Murano* ☎ *041/739610* ▭ *AE, DC, MC, V* ☉ *Closed Sat.
and Feb. No dinner* Ⓥ *Murano.*

$$ ✗ **Busa alla Torre da Lele.** A pretty square with olive trees and a well
VENETIAN sets the stage for Da Lele, a favorite of the Muranese and returning
travelers. On the ground floor of a dark-red building with a loggia, the
restaurant stretches out on the campo, where you eat in the shade of
large umbrellas. Check the blackboard for such daily specials as anti-
pasto Busa, with granseola and *garusol* (sea snails); *bavette alla busara*
(flat spaghetti with a hot, spicy shrimp and tomato sauce); and baked
rombo or branzino with potatoes. Homemade cookies are served with
fragolino, a sweet, sparkling wine redolent of strawberries. ✉ *Campo
Santo Stefano 3, Murano* ☎ *041/739662* ▭ *AE, DC, MC, V* ☉ *Closed
Mon. No dinner* Ⓥ *Faro.*

$ ✗ **La Perla—Ai Bisatei.** There is nothing unusual about the food served
VENETIAN here; almost any eatery in the city will offer the *frittura* (fried seafood
platter). You won't find better one, though—and certainly not at a better
price. So if you're visiting the island of Murano and looking for a lunch
spot, wind your way to La Perla. You'll find a relaxed, local atmosphere

and lots of Venetian standard fare, from the frittura to *bigoli in salsa* (spaghetti with onions and anchovies) to other fresh catch from the lagoon, served grilled or fried. ⊠ *Campo San Bernardo 6, Murano* ☎ *041/739528* ▭ *No credit cards* ⊗ *Closed Wed. and Aug.* Ⓥ *San Stae* ✛ *C3*.

$$$ ✕ **Valmarana.** The most upscale restaurant on Murano is housed in a
SEAFOOD palace on the *fondamenta* (street) across from the Museo del Vetro. Stucco walls and glass chandeliers complement well-appointed tables, and although the menu contains no surprises, the cuisine is more refined than at other places here. Try the baked sea scallops, the crab with fresh herbs, or the rich risotto *alla pescatora*, containing all kinds of fish. In warm weather, reserve a table in the back garden or on the terrace overlooking the canal. ⊠ *Fondamenta Navagero 31, Murano* ☎ *041/739313* ▭ *AE, DC, MC, V* ⊗ *Closed 3 wks in Jan. No dinner* Ⓥ *Navagero*.

BURANO

¢–$ ✕ **Al Gatto Nero da Ruggero.** Even cats know that this restaurant dedi-
SEAFOOD cated to one of their own offers the best fish on Burano. It's only been around since 1965, when Ruggero Bovo took it over from its owners of the prior 19 years. "Each day our fisherman return with the best the lagoon has to offer," says the owner, who decided, upon understanding he could not pursue his dream of being a musician, deciding instead to make the kitchen sing. The fish is top quality and couldn't get any fresher; all pastas and desserts are made in-house; the *fritto misto* (fish fry) is outstanding for its lightness and variety of fish. No matter what you order though, you'll savor the pride Ruggero and his family have in their lagoon, their island, and the quality of their cucina (maybe even more so when enjoying it on the picturesque fondamenta). ⊠ *Fondamenta della Giudecca 88, Burano* ☎ *041/730120* ⊕ *www.gattonero.com* ▭ *AE, DC, MC, V* ⊗ *Closed Mon. and 3 wks in Nov.* Ⓥ *LN*.

TORCELLO

$$$ ✕ **Locanda Cipriani.** Owned by a nephew of Arrigo Cipriani—the founder
SEAFOOD of Harry's Bar—this inn profits from its idyllic location on the island of Torcello. Hemingway, who loved the silence of the lagoon, came here often to eat, drink, and brood under the green veranda. The food is not exceptional, especially considering the high-end prices, but dining here is more about getting lost in Venetian magic. The menu features pastas, *vitello tonnato* (chilled poached veal in a tuna and caper sauce), baked *orata* (gilthead) with potatoes, and lots of other seafood. A vaporetto service runs until 11:30 PM, and then upon request; service is sporadic. ⊠ *Piazza Santa Fosca 29, Torcello* ☎ *041/730150* ⌂ *Reservations essential* ▭ *AE, DC, MC, V* ⊗ *Closed Tues. and early Jan.–early Feb.* Ⓥ *Torcello*.

BACARI (WINE BARS)

While the list below covers some of the best of Venice's bacari, it's by no means exhaustive. Venetians themselves don't know how many bacari thrive in their hometown, and often the perfect one is the one you happen upon when hunger strikes.

The ice cream treat *tartufo* is a delicious way to finish up a Venetian meal.

¢ ✕ **Aciugheta.** Though the "tiny anchovy" (as the name translates) doubles as a pizzeria, stick to the tasty cicchetti offered at the bar, like the eponymous anchovy minipizzas. The selection of wines by the glass changes daily, but there are always the ubiquitous local whites on hand, as well as some Tuscan and Piedmontese choices thrown in for good measure. Don't miss the *tonno con polenta* (tuna with polenta) if it's offered, but scan the banco and choose whatever appeals. ✉ *Campo SS. Filippo e Giacomo, Castello 4357* ☎ *041/5224292* ▭ *MC, V* Ⓥ *San Zaccaria* ⊹ *F4.*

¢ ✕ **Al Marcà.** It's easy to spot this tiny bacaro shoved into corner of the campo just beyond the Rialto Market: it's the one mobbed with chatty patrons—dressed in suits, jeans, or travel wear, shouldering messenger bags or backpacks, with strollers or carts loaded with market acquisitions—each with a glowing spritz or glass of wine in hand. Step up to the banco, scan the chalkboards for the lists of wines (whites on the left, reds are on the right), then choose from the myriad cicchetti (meat, tuna, or eggplant croquettes; crostini and panini with imaginative combos of radicchio, artichokes, fish, *soppressa, ossocollo,* and more) in the glass case. ✉ *Campo Cesare Battista, San Polo 213* ☎ *347/1002583* ▭ *MC, V* Ⓥ *Rialto Mercato* ⊹ *D3.*

¢ ✕ **Cantina Do Mori.** This bacaro par excellence—cramped but warm

Fodor'sChoice and cozy under hanging antique copper pots—has been catering to
★ the workers of the Rialto Market since before Columbus discovered America. In addition to young, local whites and reds, the well-stocked cellar offers about 600 more-refined labels, many available by the glass. Between sips you can munch on crunchy *grissini* (breadsticks) draped with prosciutto or a few well-stuffed, tiny tramezzini, appropriately

Cantina Do Mori is one of Venice's classic wine bars.

called *francobolli* (postage stamps). Don't leave without tasting the delicious baccalà mantecato. Come here a second time and you'll be received like an old friend. ✉ *Calle dei Do Mori, San Polo 429* ☎ *041/5225401* ▭ *No credit cards* ⏱ *Closed Sun., 3 wks in Aug., and 1 wk in Jan.* Ⓥ *Rialto Mercato* ✛ *D3.*

¢ ✕ **Cantinone già Schiavi.** This beautiful 19th-century bacaro opposite

Fodor's Choice the *squero* (gondola repair shop) of San Trovaso has original furnish-

★ ings and one of the best wine cellars in town—the walls are covered floor to ceiling by bottles for purchase. Cicchetti here are some of the most inventive in Venice—try the crostini-style layers of bread, smoked swordfish, and slivers of raw zucchini, or pungent slices of *parmeggiano* (Parmesan cheese), fig, and toast. They also have a creamy version of baccalà mantecato spiced with herbs, and there are nearly a dozen open bottles of wine for experimenting at the bar. ✉ *Fondamenta Nani, Dorsoduro 992* ☎ *041/5230034* ▭ *No credit cards* ⏱ *Closed 2 wks in Aug. and most Sun. after 2 PM* Ⓥ *Zattere, Accademia* ✛ *C5.*

¢ ✕ **Da Pinto.** In the heart of the Rialto Market just behind the Pescheria, Da Pinto is serving up cicchetti by 10:30 in the morning to curious visitors, fish vendors, and clerks of the nearby Tribunale (Court of Justice). There's tons of outdoor seating, but it's just as functional for a quick bite. The cicchetti at the bar are better than the blander primi ordered from the tables. The wine selection is broader than most in the area. ✉ *Campo delle Becarie, San Polo 367* ☎ *041/5224599* ▭ *AE, DC, MC, V* ⏱ *Closed Mon. and 2 wks in Nov.* Ⓥ *San Marco* ✛ *D3.*

¢ ✕ **El Sbarlefo.** This odd name is Venetian for "smirk," although you'd be hard pressed to find one of those around here. A recent entry onto the bacaro scene, Sbarlefo has arrived with aplomb. Making the most of their limited space, owners Alessandro and Andrea have installed counters and stools inside, tables outside, and external banco-access for ordering a second round. And order you will, selecting from a spread of delectable cicchetti to suit every taste. They've paid equal attention to their wine list—ask for to recommendation and you're likely to make a new discovery. ⊠ *Salizzada del Pistor (off Campo Santi Apostoli), Cannaregio 4556/C* ☎ *041/5233084* ▭ *No credit cards* Ⓥ *Ca d'Oro* ✢ *E2.*

ᙅ ✕**Enoteca la Mascareta.** As long as you're not looking for a secondo, Mascareta is one of the last, best bets for a late-night bite. An offspring of the popular casual restaurant Al Mascaron just down the calle, the Mascareta offers mostly cold plates: refined cicchetti and a selection of cured pork and cheeses, and the occasional soup. What it might lack in food choice, la Mascareta more than makes up for in wine selection; the list entirely handpicked by the owner, brilliant Friuli madman Mauro Lorenzon (you'll know him by his bow tie). The place doesn't open until 6 PM, but doesn't close until past midnight—sometimes, way past. ⊠ *Calle Lunga Santa Maria Formosa, Castello 5183* ☎ *041/5230744* ▭ *MC, V* ☉ *Closed Sun., 4 wks over Christmas. No lunch* Ⓥ *Rialto or San Zaccaria* ✢ *F3.*

ᙅ ✕**Osteria Ca' D'Oro (alla Vedova).** "The best *polpette* in town," you'll hear fans of the venerable Vedova say, and that explains why it's an obligatory stop on any *giro d'ombra* (bacaro tour). The Vedova is a full-fledged restaurant as well, but it's appreciated far more for its cicchetti than for its sit-down meals. It's one of the few places that still serves house wine in tiny, traditional *palline* glasses. ⊠ *Calle del Pistor (off the Strada Nova), Cannaregio 3912* ☎ *041/5285324* ▭ *No credit cards* ☉ *Closed Aug.* Ⓥ *Ca d'Oro* ✢ *D2.*

ᙅ ✕**Osteria da Toni.** This unpretentious bar-bacaro sits on the western edge of the Zattere promenade, near a pretty, breezy side canal. It caters mainly to workers from the harbor over the bridge; there's a raw and real atmosphere full of dialect, rounds on the house, and jokes from the young owners Matteo and Silvano. The classic cicchetti are available, and lunch features a good-value set menu, with dishes such as pasta with shrimp and zucchini. ⊠ *Fondamenta San Basilio, Dorsoduro 1642* ☎ *041/5238272* ▭ *No credit cards* ☉ *Closed Mon. and 3 wks Aug.–Sept.* Ⓥ *San Basilio* ✢ *B5.*

PASTICCERIE (PASTRY SHOPS)

Venetians have always loved pastry, not so much as dessert at the end of a meal, but rather as a nibble that could go well with a glass of sweet wine or a cup of hot milk. Traditional cookies are sold in *pasticcerie* (pastry shops) throughout town, either by weight or by the piece, and often come in attractive gift packages. Search for *zaeleti* (cookies made with yellow corn flour and raisins), *buranelli* (S-shaped cookies from Burano, which also come in heavy, fat rings), and *baicoli* (crunchy cookies made with yeast). Many bakeries also sell pastry by the portion: from apple strudel to *crostate* (jam tarts) and *torta di mandorle* (almond cake)—just point out what you want. After Christmas and through Carnevale, a great deal of frying takes place behind the counter to prepare the tons of pastries annually devoured by Venetians and tourists alike in the weeks preceding Lent: specialties are *frittole* (doughnuts with pine nuts, raisins, and candied orange peel, rolled in sugar), best eaten warm; the ribbonlike *galani* (crunchy, fried pastries sprinkled with confectioners' sugar); and walnut-shaped *castagnole* (fried pastry dumplings rolled in sugar).

Dal Col. This is a good spot near Piazza San Marco for coffee and pastry on the run, with bar (coffee and beverage) service at the counter. Open every day. ⊠ *Calle dei Fabbri, San Marco 1035* ☎ *041/5205529* ▭ *AE, MC, V* ⊗ *Closed Aug. 5–20* Ⓥ *San Marco.*

Dal Mas. Crisp croissants, pastries such as *kranz* (a braided pastry filled with almond paste and raisins) and strudel from the Friuli region, and bar service make this a great place for breakfast. ⊠ *Lista di Spagna, Cannaregio 150/A* ☎ *041/715101* ▭ *MC, V* ⊗ *Closed Tues.* Ⓥ *Stazione.*

Didovich. Here you'll find all the usual amenities of a pasticceria, and also some sublime vegetable tortes. ⊠ *Campo di Santa Marina, Castello 5909* ☎ *041/5230017* ▭ *No credit cards* ⊗ *Closed Sun. June–Sept.; closed Sun. afternoon Oct.–May* Ⓥ *Rialto.*

Giovanni Volpe. This is the only place in town that all year round still bakes traditional Venetian-Jewish pastry and delicious *pane azimo* (matzo bread), although the days of operation give away that the shop is not kosher. ⊠ *Calle del Ghetto Vecchio, Cannaregio 1143* ☎ *041/715178* ▭ *No credit cards* ⊗ *Closed Sun.* Ⓥ *Guglie.*

Harry's Dolci. With tables outside in warm weather and an elegant room inside, Harry's makes for a perfect break while exploring the Giudecca, or you can fill your bag to go. ⊠ *Fondamenta San Biagio 773, Giudecca* ☎ *041/5204844* ▭ *AE, MC, V* ⊗ *Closed Tues. and Nov.–Mar.* Ⓥ *Palanca.*

Maggion. It's worth the trip to the Lido even in bad weather for celebrated, custom-made fruit tarts (to be ordered one day ahead; no bar service). ⊠ *Via Dardanelli 46, The Lido* ☎ *041/5260836* ▭ *No credit cards* ⊗ *Closed Mon. and Tues.* Ⓥ *Lido.*

Marchini. The best-known and most expensive pasticceria in town has a fantastic display of tarts and gifts (no bar service at the main shop, though there is at another branch in Castello). ⊠ *Spadaria, San Marco 676* ☎ *041/5229109* ▭ *AE, MC, V* Ⓥ *San Marco.*

Rizzardini. This is the tiniest and prettiest pastry shop in Venice, with a counter dating from the late 18th century. Try the Zurigo (light, flakey apple pastry) and *pastine di riso* (pastry with a creamy rice filling); you'll also find *salatine* (pastry with ham or cheese and vegetables) by 10 AM. ⊠ *Calle Papadopoli, San Polo 1415* ☎ *041/5223835* ▭ *No credit cards* ⊗ *Closed Tues.* Ⓥ *San Silvestro.*

Rosa Salva. There are several branches to this venerable pasticceria in town; the headquarters is a small shop on Calle Fiubera in San Marco with a wide selection of pastry and savory snacks as well as bar service at the counter. ⊠ *Calle Fiubera, San Marco 951* ☎ *041/5210544* ⊠ *Campo San Luca, San Marco 4589* ☎ *041/5225385* ▭ *AE, DC, MC, V* ⊗ *Closed Sun.* Ⓥ *Rialto.*

Tonolo. Students from the nearby Università di Ca' Foscari crowd the counter at Tonolo, which makes for a nice break while visiting the

Sweets for sale in the Jewish Ghetto.

Frari district. In operation for over 120 years. ✉ *Calle San Pantalon, Dorsoduro 3764* ☎ *041/5237209* ▭ *No credit cards* ⏲ *Closed Mon. and Aug.* 🅥 *San Tomà.*

Vio. Besides the usual selection of small pastries and drinks, here you can get a piece of *crostata di marroni* (chestnut tart) or a bag of spicy cookies made with chili. ✉ *Fondamenta Rio Marin, Santa Croce 784* ☎ *041/718523* ▭ *No credit cards* ⏲ *Closed Wed.* 🅥 *Stazione.*

GELATERIE (ICE-CREAM SHOPS)

According to Venetians, Marco Polo imported from China a dessert called *panna in ghiaccio* (literally, "cream in ice"), a brick of frozen cream between wafers. There's no documentation to support the claim, but the myth lives on. Several local *gelaterie* (gelato shops) sell panna in ghiaccio, the supposed "ancestor" of gelato, but you'll have to ask around for it, because it's almost never kept on display. On a hot summer day, nothing is better than a cup of fruit-flavor gelato to restore your energy: light and refreshing, it will help you go that extra mile before you call it a day.

Newer gelato enterprises, including some chains, are popping up almost daily, many right next to the less-flamboyant artisan operations that have been producing their own gelato for decades. The new stuff may or may not be better—but you can almost guarantee it will cost more. Most gelaterie are open nonstop from mid-morning to late evening; some keep longer business hours in summer.

Alaska Gelateria-Sorbetteria. Carlo Pistacchi whips up delicious gelato and is endlessly experimenting with imaginative flavors. Combine a tried-and-true favorite with, say, asparagus or fennel. ⊠ *Calle Larga dei Bari, Santa Croce 1159* 🕾 *041/715211* ⊻ *Riva de Biasio.*

Boutique del Gelato. Even though you'll find newer, shinier gelaterie all up and down this calle, good value and marvelous flavors give this artisanal enterprise a dedicated following. ⊠ *Salizzada San Lio, Castello 5727* 🕾 *041/5223283* ☺ *Closed Jan.* ⊻ *Rialto.*

Caffè Paolin. The morning sun draws crowds of all ages and nationalities to take a seat on busy Campo Santo Stefano and enjoy a little cup at this favorite bar-gelateria. A scoop of *limone* (lemon) gelato is particularly refreshing on a hot summer day. ⊠ *Campo Santo Stefano, San Marco 3464* 🕾 *041/5220710* ☺ *Closed Sat.* ⊻ *San Samuele or Sant'Angelo.*

Da Titta. On the Lido, strategically located on the main drag between the vaporetto stop and the most central beaches, Titta is one of the oldest gelaterie in Venice. Get your receipt at the *cassa* (register) for a cone to go, or enjoy one of the special combinations while lolling in a swinging chair under the trees that line the Gran Viale. There's also bar service. ⊠ *Gran Viale Santa Maria Elisabetta 61, The Lido* 🕾 *041/5260359* ☺ *Closed Nov.–early Mar.* ⊻ *Lido.*

Gelateria Ca' d'Oro. Here you'll find the usual array of flavors, a few more-inventive ones, plus granita, panna in ghiaccio, and some chocolate-covered specialties in the freezer to the side of the counter. ⊠ *Strada Nova near Campo Santi Apostoli, Cannaregio 4273/B* 🕾 *041/5228982* ⊻ *Ca' d'Oro.*

Gelateria Il Doge. This popular take-away gelateria, just off Campo Santa Margherita, offers a wide selection of flavors, from a few low-calorie options including yogurt, to the extra-rich *strabon* (Venetian for "more than good," which in this case means made with cocoa, espresso, and chocolate-covered almonds), as well as granitas in summer. It's worth a detour, and it's open late most of the year. ⊠ *Campo Santa Margherita, Dorsoduro 3058/A* 🕾 *041/5234607* ☺ *Closed Nov.–Feb.*

Gelatone. Devoted locals wouldn't think of consuming gelato from any other vendor. The flavors are inspired and the servings ample. ⊠ *Rio Terà della Maddalena, Cannaregio 2063* 🕾 *041/720631* ⊻ *San Marcuola.*

Le Café. On Campo Santo Stefano across from Paolin, Le Café has see-and-be-seen tables outside year-round. It also has bar service and afternoon tea and offers a variety of hot chocolate drinks and desserts. ⊠ *Campo Santo Stefano, San Marco 2797* 🕾 *041/5237201* ⊻ *San Samuele or Sant'Angelo.*

Millevoglie. The creamy, homemade gelato here satisfies the ad-hoc *voglie* (yearnings) of *mille* (thousands) passersby as they crisscross between the Frari, Scuola di San Rocco, and San Tomà vaporetto. ⊠ *Campo Santo Stefano, San Marco 2797* 🕾 *041/5237201* ⊻ *San Samuele or Sant'Angelo.*

Nico. With an enviable terrace on the Zattere, Nico is the city's gelateria with a view. The house specialty is the *gianduiotto*, a brick of dark chocolate ice cream flung into a tall glass filled with freshly whipped cream. There's also bar service. ⊠ *Zattere, Dorsoduro 922* 🕾 *041/5225293* ☺ *Closed Thurs. and Dec. 21–Jan. 8* ⊻ *Zattere.*

Where to Stay
in Venice

WORD OF MOUTH

"I really enjoyed the peace and quiet in Cannaregio. Each day I went to other sestieri, but my walks back to Cannaregio forced me to explore hidden paths I would have never seen had I stayed closer to the action."

—fardolce

Updated by
Nan McElroy

Venetian magic can still linger when you retire for the night, whether you're staying in a grand hotel or budget find. Some of the finest Venetian hotel rooms are lighted with Murano chandeliers and swathed in famed fabrics of Rubelli and Bevilacqua, with gilded mirrors and furnishing styles from baroque to Biedermeier and even art deco.

Though more-contemporary decor is working its way into renovation schemes, you still may find the prized Venetian terrazzo flooring, tufted walls, Oriental carpets, and canal views in more-modest *pensioni*. Your window will open, sometimes on a balcony, so you may enjoy gondoliers' serenades, watch the ebb and flow of city life in the *campo* (square) below . . . or simply contemplate what the lack of motor traffic permits you to hear.

WHAT TO EXPECT FROM VENETIAN HOTELS

Even if well renovated, most hotels occupy very old buildings. Preservation laws prohibit elevators in some, so if an elevator is essential, confirm before you book. In the ¢–$$ price categories, hotels may not have lounge areas, and rooms may be cramped (this is also true for standard rooms even in more expensive hotels). En suite bathrooms have become the norm; they're usually well equipped but can on the small side (tubs are considered a luxury) in less expensive lodging. Carpeted floors are rare. Windows open; air-conditioning doesn't usually become a necessity until mid-June. A few of the budget hotels make do with fans. Mosquitoes can begin to pester in midsummer; turn lights off in the evening if you leave windows open, and ask the hotel staff for a Vape, an anti-mosquito device.

Before choosing a hotel, decide in advance what's important to you and don't be reluctant to ask detailed questions. The staff members at most Venetian hotels will be able to converse with you in English. Space is at a premium, and even exclusive hotels have carved out small, dowdy, Cinderella-type rooms in the "standard" category. It's not at all unusual for each room to be different even on the same floor: windows overlooking charming canals and bleak alleyways are both common. Confirm your preferences on booking and even again prior to arrival; if you're not happy with the room you've been given, ask to be moved or upgraded.

CHOOSING YOUR SESTIERE

"Only a stone's throw from Saint Mark's square . . ." is the standard hotel claim. Whether or not that's the case, it's not necessarily an advantage. In Venice, you can't go terribly wrong in terms of "good" areas to stay, and once you get your bearings, you'll find you're never far from anything.

The area in and around San Marco is always the most crowded, touristy, and almost always more expensive: even two- and three-star hotels cost more here than in other parts of town. If you want to stay in less-trafficked surroundings, consider still-convenient but more-tranquil locations in Dorsoduro, Santa Croce, and east Cannaregio (hotels near the train station in Cannaregio can have their own crowd issues), or even Castello in the area beyond the Pietà church. A stay on the Lido in shoulder season offers serenity, but it also includes about a half-hour boat ride to the historic center, and in summer it's crowded with beachgoers.

MAKING RESERVATIONS

You should book your room as far in advance as possible. Planning your trip four to five months (or even further) ahead will give you a much greater selection. Double-booking is not uncommon, unfortunately, so make sure you take your reservation confirmation along with you, including any special requests you've made (tub or shower, first or top floor, and so on). Almost all hotels can be booked online, either via e-mail or using the booking system on the individual hotel's Web site—where they often guarantee the lowest rates. You can also try larger booking sites such as ⊕ *venere.com or* ⊕ *veniceby.com.*

Venezia Sì (☏ *041/5222264* ⊕ *www.veneziasi.it*), the public relations arm of **AVA** (Venetian Hoteliers Association), also offers online booking for almost all hotels in town, and you can make reservations through them by phone daily from 8 AM to11 PM. If you're in Venice without a room booked, try making same-day reservations at one of the AVA booths, which are at **Piazzale Roma** (☏ *041/5231397* ⊙ *Daily 9* AM*–10* PM), **Santa Lucia train station** (☏ *041/715288 or 041/715016* ⊙ *Daily 8* AM*–9* PM), and **Marco Polo Airport** (☏ *041/5415133* ⊙ *Daily 9* AM*–10* PM). They also have counters at the San Marco and A.S.M. Parking Garages in Piazzale Roma.

FINDING YOUR HOTEL

If you'll be arriving by any means except a pricey water taxi (which deposits you at the hotel's entrance), it is *essential* to have detailed arrival directions along with the complete address (street name as well as the sestiere). Nothing is obvious on Venice's streets (even if you have GPS). Turn-by-turn directions can help you avoid wandering back and forth along side streets and across bridges, luggage in tow.

WHAT IT COSTS IN EUROS					
	¢	$	$$	$$$	$$$$
HOTELS	under €75	€75–€125	€125–€200	€200–€300	over €300

Prices are for a standard double room in high season.

CANNAREGIO

$–$$ ⊞ **3749 Ponte Chiodo.** This cheery, homey bed-and-breakfast takes its name from the bridge leading to its entrance (one of only two left in the lagoon without hand railings). Attentively appointed rooms with geranium-filled window boxes overlook either the bridge and expansive canals below or the spacious enclosed garden. It's a family-owned operation, and service is accommodating and friendly; you can get lots of suggestions for dining and sightseeing. The private garden and patio are perfect for a relaxing breakfast or scribbling postcards. Some bathrooms are smallish, but overall it's an excellent value. The location is also handy to the Ca' d'Oro vaporetto. **Pros:** highly attentive service; warm, relaxed atmosphere; private garden; canal or garden views. **Cons:** no elevator could be a problem for some. ⊠ *Calle Racchetta, Cannaregio 3749* ☎ *041/2413935* ⊕ *www.pontechiodo.it* ⤢ *6 rooms* ⌂ *In-room: no phone, safe, refrigerator, Wi-Fi. In-hotel: room service, bar, Wi-Fi hotspot, Internet terminal* ☲ *MC, V* ⓧⓞⓘ *BP* Ⓥ *Ca' d'Oro* ⊕ *D2.*

$–$$ ⊞ **Al Palazzetto.** Understated yet gracious Venetian decor, original ★ open-beam ceilings and terrazzo flooring, spotless marble baths, and friendly, attentive service are the hallmarks of this intimate, family-owned *locanda* (inn). Rooms overlooking tranquil side canals are the best in terms of size as well as view. The spacious common salon overlooks the Rio San Sofia. The location is serene, but only a short *calle* (street) away from the Strada Nova, the Ca' d'Oro stop, the traghetto across to the Rialto Market, and the San Marco area. Al Palazzetto is also good for small groups or families, as there are triple and quad rooms; some are connecting. Spring for the attic suite if it's available. **Pros:** standout service; owner on-site; quiet, side canal views from some rooms; free Wi-Fi. **Cons:** not for amenity-seekers or lovers of ultramodern decor. ⊠ *Calle delle Vele, Cannaregio 4057* ☎ *041/2750897* ⊕ *www.guesthouse.it* ⤢ *6 rooms, 1 suite* ⌂ *In-room: safe, refrigerator, Internet, Wi-Fi. In-hotel: Wi-Fi hotspot, laundry facilities* ☲ *AE, DC, MC, V* ⓧⓞⓘ *BP* Ⓥ *Ca' d'Oro* ⊕ *E2.*

$$$–$$$$ ⊞ **Al Ponte Antico.** The Peruch family, proprietors of this 16th-century **Fodor's Choice** palace inn (as well as Locanda Orseolo), has lined its Gothic windows ★ with tiny white lights, creating an inviting glow that's emblematic of the hospitality and sumptuous surroundings that await you inside. Rich brocade-tufted walls, period furniture, and hand-decorated beamed ceilings all contribute to a luxurious, distinctively Venetian warmth in both rooms and common areas. One of the most enjoyable features, whether for a morning caffè or evening *aperitivo* (aperitif), is the intimate, upstairs terrace, from which you can observe the Rialto bridge in

BEST BETS FOR VENICE LODGING

Fodor's provides a selective listing of hotels in every price range, from comfortable, well-maintained bargain finds to luxury pleasure palaces. Here's we've compiled our top recommendations, by price category and type of experience. The best of the best earn our Fodor's Choice logo.

Fodor'sChoice ★

Al Ponte Antico, $$$–$$$$, p. 120

Bauer Il Palazzo, $$$$, p. 136

Ca' dei Dogi, $$, p. 136

Hotel al Ponte Mocenigo, $$, p. 142

Hotel American-Dinesen, $$$–$$$$, p. 131

Hotel Bucintoro, $$$–$$$$, p. 129

La Calcina, $$–$$$, p. 133

Locanda Orseolo, $$$, p. 136

Oltre il Giardino-Casaifrari, $$–$$$, p. 141

Pensione Accademia Villa Maravege, $$–$$$, p. 135

Ruzzini Palace Hotel, $$$–$$$$, p. 130

$

Casa del Melograno, p. 124

Santa Maria della Pietà, p. 130

$$

Al Palazzetto, p. 120

Hotel UNA Venezia, p. 126

La Villeggiatura, p. 140

Locanda San Barnaba, p. 134

Pensione Guerrato, p. 141

$$$

Acqua Palace, p. 127

Ca' Sagredo Hotel, p. 124

Hotel Antico Doge, p. 125

Novecento, p. 137

$$$$

Metropole, p. 129

Palazzo Abadessa, p. 126

Palazzo Barbarigo, p. 141

Palazzo Stern, p. 134

Best by Experience

CANAL VIEWS

3749 Ponte Chiodo, $–$$, p. 120

Hotel American-Dinesen, $$$–$$$$, p. 131

La Calcina, $$–$$$, p. 133

Palazzo Sant'Angelo, $$$$, p. 137

ROMANTIC

Ca' dei Dogi, $$, p. 136

La Calcina, $$–$$$, p. 133

Oltre il Giardino-Casaifrari, $$–$$$, p. 141

Palazzo Barbarigo, $$$$, p. 141

Ruzzini Palace Hotel, $$$–$$$$, p. 130

GOOD FOR FAMILIES

Al Palazzetto, $–$$, p. 120

Al Teatro, $$, p. 136

Casa Rezzonico, $$, p. 131

Locanda Ca' Zose, $$, p. 133

Pensione Guerrato, $$, p. 141

AWAY FROM THE CROWDS

3749 Ponte Chiodo, $–$$, p. 120

Ca' Maria Adele, $$$$, p. 131

Ca' San Rocco, $$, p. 139

Casa Rezzonico, $$, p. 131

Hotel al Ponte Mocenigo, $$, p. 142

PERSONAL SERVICE

Al Ponte Antico, $$$–$$$$, p. 120

Al Teatro, $$, p. 136

Ca' dei Dogi, $$, p. 136

Hotel American-Dinesen, $$$–$$$$, p. 131

Locanda Orseolo, $$$, p. 136

CLASSIC VENETIAN DESIGN

Al Ponte Antico, $$$–$$$$, p. 120

Ca' Sagredo Hotel, $$$–$$$$, p. 124

Palazzo Abadessa, $$$–$$$$, p. 126

CONTEMPORARY DESIGN

Acqua Palace, $$$, p. 127

Hotel UNA Venezia, $$–$$$, p. 126

4

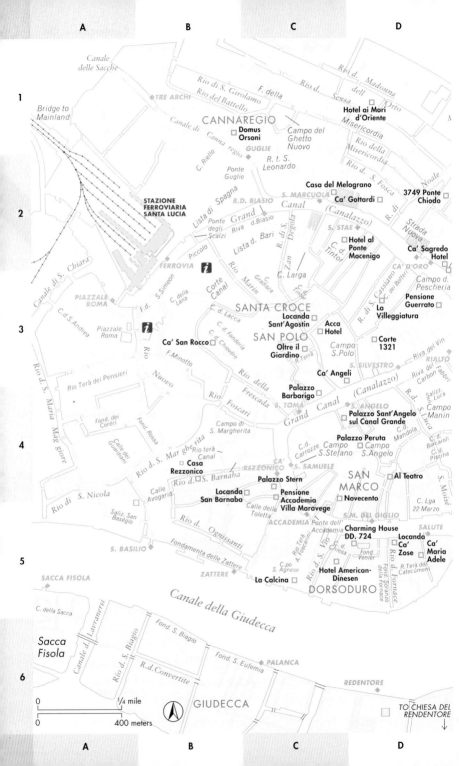

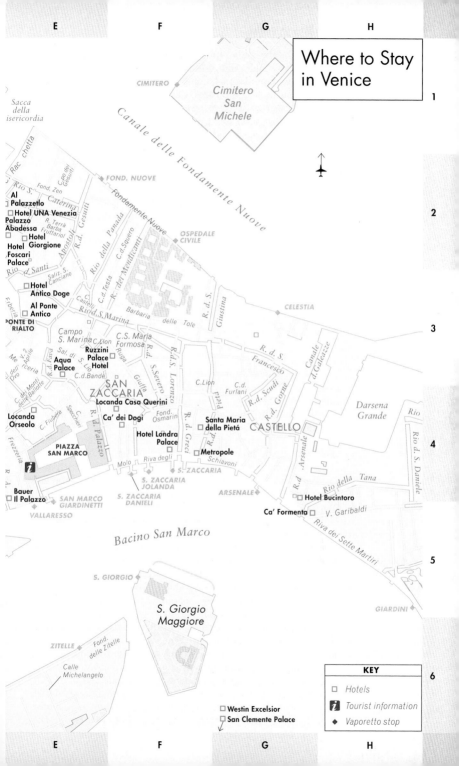

one direction and the famous fish and produce markets in the other. The deluxe rooms have high ceilings and sweeping views. **Pros:** upper-level terrace overlooks Grand Canal; family run; superior service; Internet is free. **Cons:** in one of the busiest areas of the city. ⊠ *Calle dell'Aseo, Cannaregio 5768* ☎ *041/2411944* ⊕ *www.alponteantico.com* ↴ *12 rooms, 1 junior suite* ♿ *In-room: safe, refrigerator, Internet, Wi-Fi. In-hotel: room service, bar, laundry service, Internet terminal, Wi-Fi hotspot* ⊟ *AE, DC, MC, V* ⊚| *BP* Ⓥ *Rialto* ✛ *E3*.

$$$–$$$$ 🏨 **Ca' Gottardi.** Ca' Gottardi is part of a new generation of small hotels that mix traditional Venetian style with contemporary design. The clean white-marble entrance leading up to the luminous *piano nobile* (main floor) of the 15th-century palace gracefully contrasts with the opulent Murano chandeliers and rich wall brocades in the guest rooms. Some rooms have canal views, bathrooms are large and modern, and a rich breakfast is served in a bright salon that overlooks a wide canal. The location, just off the Grand Canal near the Ca' d'Oro and a variety of good restaurants, is another plus. Confirm the type of room (suite or standard, with or without a view) and its location (in the annex or the main hotel) when booking. **Pros:** great location; mix of old and new styles; canal views. **Cons:** no outdoor garden or terrace; standard rooms are quite small. ⊠ *Strada Nova, Cannaregio 2283* ☎ *041/2759333* ⊕ *www.cagottardi.com* ↴ *23 rooms, 2 junior suites, 3 suites* ♿ *In-room: safe, refrigerator, Internet, Wi-Fi. In-hotel: bar* ⊟ *DC, MC, V* ⊚| *BP* Ⓥ *Ca' d'Oro* ✛ *D2*.

$–$$ 🏨 **Casa del Melograno.** This renovated classic Venetian residence is modestly appointed, but you'll still find features like Venetian terrazzo flooring, frescoed ceilings, and tiled baths. Rooms are pristinely and functionally furnished; they vary in size and view (garden or canal). Staff is welcoming, helpful—and available; not always the case with smaller locandas. The Melograno (pomegranate) sometimes offers discounts for cash and prepaid booking; check their Web site or ask when you inquire. Relax with a good book or take breakfast in the airy, ample garden. **Pros:** simple; pristine; gracious; handy to vaporetto stop and the train station for day trips. **Cons:** not opulent; may be too far from San Marco for some. ⊠ *Fondamenta del Ponte Storto, Cannaregio 2023* ☎ *041/5208807* ⊕ *www.locandadelmelograno.it* ↴ *6 rooms* ♿ *In-room: safe, refrigerator, Internet, Wi-Fi. In-hotel: Internet terminal, Wi-Fi hotspot, some pets allowed* ⊟ *MC, V* ⊚| *BP* Ⓥ *San Marcuola* ✛ *C2*.

$$$–$$$$ 🏨 **Ca' Sagredo Hotel.** This expansive palace, the Sagredo family resi-
★   dence since the mid-1600s, is a study in Venetian opulence: the massive staircase has Longhi frescoes soaring above it; the large common areas are adorned with original art by Tiepolo, Longhi, and Ricci, among others. Rooms are traditional Venetian style, some retaining important original art and architectural elements, many with full or partial canal and rooftop views; flooring might be Venetian terrazzo, wood parquet, or plush carpeting. One suite even offers a private rooftop balcony. **Pros:** excellent location; authentic yet comfortable renovation of Venice's patrician past. **Cons:** more opulent than intimate. ⊠ *Campo San Sofia, Cannaregio 4198/99* ☎ *041/2413111* ⊕ *www.casagredohotel. com* ↴ *42 rooms, 2 junior suites, 3 suites* ♿ *In-room: safe, refrigerator, Internet, Wi-Fi. In-hotel: bar* ⊟ *DC, MC, V* ⊚| *BP* Ⓥ *Ca' d'Oro* ✛ *D2*.

$–$$$ **Domus Orsoni.** Glass mosaics have been an integral element of Venetian decor almost from its inception. Not only will you find this element in abundance in the rooms at Domus Orsoni, you can also discover how they're produced: the Domus is located on the grounds of the famous Orsoni Mosaics factory. Each of the five rooms has been uniquely decorated by individual Italian designer, with color and gold mosaics accenting furniture, fixtures, and baths. As a guest, you are also entitled to a free tour of the mosaic factory. All the rooms are on ground level (and if you come by vaporetto, there are no bridges to cross). There's a terrace for relaxing or taking breakfast in temperate weather. On-site service is limited to mornings and afternoons, but there is 24-hour assistance by phone. **Pros:** a fine option for anyone looking for a unique experience in lodging; no bridges and few steps to deal with. **Cons:** although handy to a vaporetto stop, it's not on the Grand Canal; no sweeping views. ⊠ *Calle dei Vedei, Cannaregio 1045* ☎ *041/2759538* ⊕ *www. DomusOrsoni.it* ⤳ *5 rooms* ♿ *In-room: safe, refrigerator, Internet, Wi-Fi. In-hotel: Wi-Fi hotspot* ☰ *AE, DC, MC, V* ⦵ *BP* ⓥ *Guglie, Tre Archi, or Crea* ✛ *B1.*

$$–$$$ **Hotel ai Mori d'Oriente.** The theme here, reflected in the decor, is Venice's connection with the exotic East. Some rooms and suites overlook the expansive canal along the Fondamenta della Sensa, one of the bright, broad byways typical of the upper Cannaregio district. In good weather, you can also take breakfast or a Venetian spritz cocktail at a sunny table along the canal. Though the atmosphere harkens back to Venice's past, facilities and amenities are everything you'd expect from a 21st-century establishment, and the staff is accommodating. Ask about the type and location of room you're reserving when booking; rooms overlooking the canal are especially pleasant. **Pros:** quiet area; modern structure; nice for families; canal-side bar for breakfast or cocktails. **Cons:** a bit remote from San Marco; fee for Wi-Fi. ⊠ *Fondamenta della Sensa, Cannaregio 3319* ☎ *041/711001* ⊕ *www.morihotel.com* ⤳ *19 rooms, 2 junior suites* ♿ *In-room: safe, refrigerator, DVD, Internet, Wi-Fi. In-hotel: bar, laundry facilities, laundry service, Internet terminal, Wi-Fi hotspot* ☰ *AE, DC, MC, V* ⦵ *BP* ⓥ *San Marcuola or Madonna dell'Orto* ✛ *D1.*

$$$–$$$$ **Hotel Antico Doge.** Once the home of Doge Marino Falier, this palazzo
★ has been attentively modernized in elegant Venetian style, with some fine, original furnishings—quite rare in many newer hotels. Some rooms have *baldacchini* (canopied beds) and courtyard views, the suite and two superior room have canal views; all are adorned with brocades, damask tufted walls, gilt mirrors, and parquet floors. The location, on the main thoroughfare from the station to San Marco, is handy but can stay quite lively well into the night, especially during festivals. An ample buffet breakfast is served in a room with a frescoed ceiling and a Murano chandelier. **Pros:** meticulous renovation in true Venetian style, convenient to the Rialto and beyond. **Cons:** on a busy thoroughfare; no outdoor garden or terrace; no elevator. ⊠ *Campo Santi Apostoli, Cannaregio 5643* ☎ *041/2411570* ⊕ *www.anticodoge.com* ⤳ *19 rooms, 1 suite* ♿ *In-room: safe, Wi-Fi, In-hotel: bar, laundry service, Wi-Fi hotspot, Internet terminal* ☰ *MC, V* ⦵ *BP* ⓥ *Ca' d'Oro or Rialto* ✛ *E3.*

$$$$ ⊞ **Hotel Foscari Palace.** According to the hotel's historical accounts, Mantua's Gonzaga Dukes called this 14th-century palazzo home when staying in Venice in 1521. The extensively renovated palace sits on the Grand Canal; rooms overlook the canal or the busy campo, a square that's handy for sightseeing in any direction by foot, gondola ferry, or vaporetto. Plush, traditional furnishings and extensive use of marble and blond wood trim contribute to a relaxed yet gracious ambience. Rooms 302 and 303 have balconies overlooking the campo, and a rooftop terrace offers truly spectacular views. The top-floor junior suite has its own terrace. All rooms have hydro-massage bathtubs. **Pros:** lovely view over the rooftops and Grand Canal from the terrace; handy for walking, vaporetto, and gondola traghetto. **Cons:** on a busy square; has a less distinctively Venetian feel than some other options. ⊠ *Campo Santo Sofia, Cannaregio 4200/1/2* ☎ *041/5297611* ⊕ *www. hotelfoscaripalace.com* ↴ *23 rooms, 1 junior suite, 2 suites* ⛆ *In-room: safe, Internet, Wi-Fi. In-hotel: room service, bar, laundry service, Wi-Fi hotspot, Internet terminal* ▭ *MC, V* ⓘ⊙ⓘ *BP* ⓥ *Ca' d'Oro* ✛ *D2.*

$$$ ⊞ **Hotel Giorgione.** Family owned and operated, this quietly elegant hotel charms guests with its original terrazzo flooring, gracious courtyard and marble fountain, and billiard salon. The staff is professional and helpful, and the location is convenient for exploring in any direction. Rooms are decorated with traditional Venetian fabric and furniture, are comfortably appointed, and have either rooftop or courtyard views. Room sizes vary considerably, so book early and ask about the size and view. Seasonal refreshments are offered each afternoon. **Pros:** family run; unique ambience; elegant garden. **Cons:** no canal views. ⊠ *Off Campo Santi Apostoli, Cannaregio 4587* ☎ *041/5225810* ⊕ *www. hotelgiorgione.com* ↴ *76 rooms* ⛆ *In-room: safe, refrigerator, Internet. In-hotel: bar, laundry service, Internet terminal* ▭ *AE, DC, MC, V* ⓘ⊙ⓘ *BP* ⓥ *Ca' d'Oro or Fondamente Nove* ✛ *E2.*

$$–$$$ ⊞ **Hotel UNA Venezia.** Up a narrow calle and across the bridge from the
   ★   bustling Strada Nova, this 15th-century palazzo lingers silently over a tranquil canal and an evocative corner campo named for its two cisterns, or *pozzi*. Inside you'll find the results of a 2008 renovation that maintains a traditional Venetian decor of creams, burgundies, and elegant sages. Rooms feature silk striped and swirling damasks tufted onto multi-windowed walls. Ask for the suite with a columned balcony overlooking the Priuli Canal, or hide away in the attic *mansarda*, with sloping ceilings and a rooftop view from all of its seven windows. Another option unique to UNA's guests: a menu of pillows in a variety of shapes and sizes. **Pros:** an intimate, boutique hideaway still handy for exploring the city. **Cons:** classic rooms are on the smallish side; no Internet in the attic room. ⊠ *Ruga Do Pozzi, Cannaregio 4173* ☎ *041/2442711* ⊕ *www.unahotels.com* ↴ *28 rooms, 3 junior suites, 3 suites* ⛆ *In-room: safe, refrigerator, Internet, Wi-Fi. In-hotel: room service, bar, laundry facilities, laundry service, Internet terminal, Wi-Fi hotspot, some pets allowed* ▭ *AE, DC, MC, V* ⓘ⊙ⓘ *BP* ⓥ *Ca' d'Oro* ✛ *E2.*

$$$–$$$$ ⊞ **Palazzo Abadessa.** At this elegant late-16th-century palazzo, you can
   ★   experience gracious hospitality and a luxurious atmosphere in keeping with Venice's patrician heritage. You'll feel like nobility yourself as you

ascend the majestic staircase and enter the expansive piano nobile, which overlooks a picturesque side canal. Unusually spacious rooms are well appointed with antique furniture, frescoed ceilings, and fine silk fabrics. The location is remote enough to escape the San Marco masses while still within striking

distance of major sights, and there's a private dock for taxi arrival. In summer, breakfast is served in a walled garden complete with sculptures and marble benches. **Pros:** a unique, historic lodging; spacious rooms and garden; superb guest service. **Cons:** not best for families with young children, who may have difficulty dodging the antique accessories. ⊠ *Calle Priuli off Strada Nova, Cannaregio 4011* ☎ *041/2413784* ⊕ *www.abadessa.com* ⤴ *10 rooms, 5 suites* ⏶ *In-room: safe, refrigerator, Wi-Fi. In-hotel: room service, bar, Wi-Fi hotspot, laundry service, some pets allowed* ▭ *AE, DC, MC, V* ⵏⵑ *BP* Ⅴ *Ca' d'Oro* ✛ *E2.*

CASTELLO

$$$ 🏨 **Acqua Palace.** The Caputo family wanted to name its accommodation
★ to recall Venice's perpetual relationship with water, particularly since the five-story former Scalfarotto residence hovers over one of the most gondola-traversed canals in the city. Silk rope trims period furnishings and ties back richly toned damask drapes from tall windows to create an opulent, yet intimate atmosphere in guest rooms and common areas. Massive floor mirrors reflect natural light to help keep spaces feeling airy. A few of the marble tiled baths even have bathtubs; all are spacious. Some suites have balconies overlooking the canal; the highest ones add rooftop views. **Pros:** family-run; thoughtful renovation; lots of canal views; Wi-Fi is free. **Cons:** no outdoor breakfast area or bar. ⊠ *Calle della Malvasia, Castello 1083* ☎ *041/2960442* ⊕ *www. aquapalace.it* ⤴ *12 rooms, 5 junior suites, 6 suites* ⏶ *In-room: safe, refrigerator, Internet, Wi-Fi. In-hotel: room service, laundry service, Internet terminal, Wi-Fi hotspot, some pets allowed* ▭ *AE, DC, MC, V* ⵏ *Closed Jan.* ⵏⵑ *BP* Ⅴ *Rialto* ✛ *E3.*

$$$ 🏨 **Ca' Formenta.** In a residential rather than tourist area of Venice, Ca' Formenta offers high-quality services in a thoroughly removated 15th-century building. Front rooms have a wonderful view of the lagoon. The 15-minute stroll along the waterfront between Piazzo San Marco and the hotel is through a genuinely "local" part of the city, with plenty of cafés and restaurants. One of the rear rooms has direct access to a pleasant rooftop terrace with tables. **Pros:** Castello area still feels like authentic Venice; convenient to the piazza, the Lido, and the north lagoon islands. **Cons:** not as convenient to San Polo or upper Dorsoduro. ⊠ *Via Garibaldi, Castello 1650* ☎ *041/5285494* ⊕ *www.hotelcaformenta.it* ⤴ *12 rooms, 2 junior suites* ⏶ *In-room: safe, refrigerator, Internet, Wi-Fi (some). In-hotel: room service, bar, laundry service, Wi-Fi hotspot, some pets allowed* ▭ *AE, DC, MC, V* ⵏⵑ *BP* Ⅴ *Arsenale or Giardini* ✛ *G5.*

4

Hotel Bucintoro

Ruzzini Palace Hotel

$$$–$$$$
Fodor's Choice
★

Hotel Bucintoro. "All rooms with a view" touts this pensione-turned-four-star-hotel. And the views are indeed expansive: from the hotel's waterfront location near lively Via Garibaldi (and so removed from San Marco throngs), your windows swing open to a panorama that sweeps from the Lido across the basin to San Giorgio and San Marco; upper-floor vistas are particularly inspiring. Decor could be termed "gracious maritime," meaning deep mahogany wood tones, brass accents, and nautical appliqué abound, from railings to reading lamps to hallway lighting. Enjoy breakfast, a sunset aperitivo, or nightcap on the quay-side terrace. **Pros:** recent renovation; lagoon views from all rooms, waterfront without the San Marco crowds. **Cons:** yachts sometimes dock outside the hotel, partially blocking lagoon views on lower floors. ⊠ *Riva degli Schiavoni, Castello 2135/A* ☎ *041/5209909* ⊕ *www.hotelbucintoro.com* ⤳ *20 rooms, 6 junior suites* ⌂ *In-room: safe, refrigerator, Wi-Fi. In-hotel: bar, laundry service, Internet terminal, Wi-Fi hotspot, some pets allowed* ▭ *AE, DC, MC, V* ⏐◯⏐ *BP* ⊻ *Arsenale* ⊹ *G4.*

$$$$

Hotel Londra Palace. A wall of windows makes this the hotel of choice for soaking up extraordinary, sweeping views of the lagoon and the island of San Giorgio. The downstairs restaurant is all glass, light, and water views, and the superior rooms and junior suites offer the same spectacle. The vista must have been pleasing to Tchaikovsky, who wrote his Fourth Symphony here in 1877. Neoclassical public rooms, with splashes of blue-and-green glass suggesting the sea, play nicely off individually decorated guest rooms, which have fine fabric, damask drapes, Biedermeier furniture, and Venetian glass. The staff is top-notch, as are the restaurant and the bar. **Pros:** superlative views; professional service. **Cons:** area is one of the most touristy in Venice, and the Riva's liveliness can extend late into the evening. ⊠ *Riva degli Schiavoni, Castello 4171* ☎ *041/5200533* ⊕ *www.londrapalace.com* ⤳ *35 rooms, 18 junior suites* ⌂ *In-room: safe, refrigerator, Wi-Fi. In-hotel: restaurant, room service, bars, laundry service, Internet terminal, Wi-Fi hotspot* ▭ *AE, DC, MC, V* ⏐◯⏐ *BP* ⊻ *San Zaccaria* ⊹ *F4.*

$–$$

Locanda Casa Querini. This traditional locanda is located on a quiet campo along a principal route from San Zaccaria to Campo Santa Maria Formosa. You'll easily spot the canopied entrance, flanked by two topiaries and umbrella-topped café tables where you can take your breakfast or sip a late afternoon prosecco, weather permitting. Pastel, lacquered room furnishings pay tribute to the 18th-century Venetian style; deep blue carpeting helps keep rooms quiet. Each of the 16 modestly appointed rooms is named after a flower; ask for one that overlooks the front square. Service is reserved but accommodating. **Pros:** strategic location on a quiet campo. **Cons:** no elevator. ⊠ *Campo San Giovanni Novo, Castello 4388* ☎ *041/2411294* ⊕ *www.locandaquerini.com* ⤳ *6 rooms* ⌂ *In-room: safe, refrigerator, Wi-Fi. In-hotel: Internet terminal, Wi-Fi hotspot* ▭ *MC, V* ⏐◯⏐ *BP* ⊻ *San Zaccaria* ⊹ *F4.*

$$$$
★

Metropole. Eccentrics, eclectics, and fans of Antonio Vivaldi (who taught music here) love the Metropole, a labyrinth of intimate, opulent spaces featuring exotic Eastern influences and jammed with cabinets displaying collections of ivory-adorned cigarette cases, antique corkscrews, beaded bags, and more. The owner, a lifelong collector of unusual objects, fills common areas and the sumptuously appointed guest rooms with endless antiques. The best rooms are up on the roof, where there are also two spacious rooftop terraces. Only six of the standard double rooms offer lagoon views. Suites feature sparkling mosaic sunken baths, Fortuny fabrics, and other notable architectural details. Their Met restaurant has one of Venice's most acclaimed chefs, Corado Fasolato. **Pros:** owner has exquisite taste and collections; hotel harkens back to a gracious Venice of times past. **Cons:** one of the most densely touristed locations in the city. ⊠ *Riva degli Schiavoni, Castello 4149* ☎ *041/5205044* ⊕ *www.hotelmetropole.com* ↘ *67 rooms, 13 junior suites, 9 suites* ⚴ *In-room: safe, refrigerator, Internet. In-hotel: restaurant, room service, bar, laundry service, Wi-Fi hotspot, some pets allowed* ⊟ *AE, DC, MC, V* ⓞ *BP* ▼ *San Zaccaria* ✛ *F4.*

$$$–$$$$
Fodor's Choice
★

🏨 **Ruzzini Palace Hotel.** After a painstaking renovation, the historic Ruzzini Palace once again graces the northern end of the lively Campo Santa Maria Formosa. The palace design encompasses Renaissance and baroque. Its soaring spaces feature Venetian terrazzo flooring, frescoed and open-beamed ceilings, and Murano chandeliers, integrated seamlessly with contemporary furnishings and appointments. Even the smaller rooms are quite comfortable, and the larger doubles and suites showcase paintings by Tiepolo's maestro, Gregorio Lazzarini. The location is handy no matter where you're headed for the day's explorations, and the attentive staff will satisfy your every request. Suites are supplied with coffeemakers, bathrobes, and DVD players. **Pros:** excellent service; a luminous, pristine, aristocratic ambience. **Cons:** the walk from San Zaccaria or Rialto includes two bridges and can be cumbersome for those with mobility issues or significant amounts of luggage. ⊠ *Campo Santa Maria Formosa, Castello 5866* ☎ *041/2410447* ⊕ *www.ruzzinipalace.com* ↘ *19 rooms, 6 junior suites, 3 suites.* ⚴ *In-room: safe, refrigerator, Wi-Fi (free), DVD (some). In-hotel: room service, bar, laundry service, Wi-Fi hotspot* ⊟ *MC, V* ⓞ *BP* ▼ *San Zaccaria or Rialto* ✛ *F3.*

$

🏨 **Santa Maria della Pietà.** Though this *casa per ferie* (vacation house) is more spartan than sumptuous, there's more light and space here than in many of Venice's four-star lodgings. The hotel, which occupies the upper floors of two historic palaces, has large windows, restored Venetian terrazzo floors, and a huge rooftop terrace with a coffee shop, a bar, and unobstructed lagoon views. On top of these advantages, it's well situated—just 100 yards from the main waterfront and about a 10-minute walk from Saint Mark's. The shared bathrooms are plentiful, spacious, and scrupulously clean. Some rooms have en suite baths, and family rooms with up to six beds are available. **Pros:** space, light, and views at a bargain price. **Cons:** not luxurious; few amenities. ⊠ *Calle della Pietà, Castello 3701* ☎ *041/2443639* ⊕ *www.pietavenezia.org/casaferie.htm* ↘ *15 rooms with shared bath* ⚴ *In-room: no phone, no TV. In-hotel: bar* ⊟ *No credit cards* ⓞ *BP* ▼ *Arsenale or San Zaccaria* ✛ *F4.*

DORSODURO

$$$$ ⛌ **Ca' Maria Adele.** One of Venice's most elegant small hotels is a mix of classic style—terrazzo floors, dramatic Murano chandeliers, antique furnishings—and touches of the contemporary, found in the African-wood reception area and breakfast room. Five dramatic "concept rooms" take on themes from Venetian history; the Doge's Room is draped in deep-red brocades, while the Oriental Room is inspired by the travels of Marco Polo. Ca' Maria Adele's location is a tranquil yet convenient spot near the church of Santa Maria della Salute. **Pros:** quiet and romantic; imaginative contemporary decor; free Wi-Fi. **Cons:** more-formal atmosphere may not suit young children. ⊠ *Campo Santa Maria della Salute, Dorsoduro 111* ☎ *041/5203078* ⊕ *www.camariaadele. it* ⏎ *12 rooms, 4 suites* △ *In-room: safe, refrigerator, Wi-Fi. In-hotel: room service, bar, laundry service, Wi-Fi hotspot, some pets allowed* ⊟ *AE, DC, MC, V* ⍥*BP* Ⓥ *Salute* ⊕ *D5.*

$$ ⛌ **Casa Rezzonico.** Rooms here are the rarest occurrence in Venice: an
★ excellent value. A sunny fondamenta and canal front the hotel entrance; a private garden beckons you to enjoy the inner courtyard for breakfast or after a long day of sightseeing. Rooms vary in size but are pleasant and comfortable, with traditional furnishings that complement the Venetian terrazzo or parquet flooring. Rooms overlook either the garden or the canal. Young owners Matteo and Mattia are attentive and helpful, and the location is around the corner from campos San Margherita and San Barnaba, convenient for exploring the sights from San Marco to the Zattere, with easy vaporetto access, too. **Pros:** spacious garden for relaxing; canal views at a reasonable rate; two lively squares nearby. **Cons:** must reserve well in advance. ⊠ *Fondamenta Gherardini, Dorsoduro 2813* ☎ *041/2770653* ⊕ *www. casarezzonico.it* ⏎ *6 rooms* △ *In-room: safe, Internet, Wi-Fi. In-hotel: Wi-Fi hotspot* ⊟ *AE, MC, V* ⍥*BP* Ⓥ *Ca' Rezzonico* ⊕ *B4.*

$$$$ ⛌ **Charming House DD 724.** This ultramodern boutique hotel abandons all things traditionally Venetian, opting instead to create the air of a stylish residence. With impeccable, minimalist decor, Charming House has a contemporary, warmly romantic, and occasionally even dramatic atmosphere. Some rooms overlook small canals and side calli; apartment options with kitchenettes are available. The location is convenient to the Guggenheim, Accademia, Zattere, and San Marco. Art borrowed from neighboring museums is on display in common areas. The Web site lists additional locations with similar ambience in Castello. **Pros:** unique decor; variety of lodging options. **Cons:** not traditional Venetian style. ⊠ *Ramo da Mula off Campo San Vio, Dorsoduro 724* ☎ *041/2770262* ⊕ *www.thecharminghouse.com* ⏎ *5 rooms, 2 junior suites, 2 suites* △ *In-room: safe, refrigerator (some), Wi-Fi. In-hotel: room service, laundry service, Internet terminal, some pets allowed* ⊟ *AE, DC, MC, V* ⍥*BP* Ⓥ *Accademia* ⊕ *D5.*

$$$–$$$$ ⛌ **Hotel American–Dinesen.** This quiet, family-run hotel has a yellow
Fodor's Choice stucco facade typical of Venetian houses. A hall decorated with repro-
★ duction antiques and Oriental rugs leads to a breakfast room reminiscent of a theater foyer, with red velvet chairs and gilt wall lamps. Guest rooms are spacious and tastefully furnished in sage-green and delicate

4

La Calcina

Pensione Accademia Villa Maravege

pink fabrics with lacquered Venetian-style furniture throughout. Some front rooms have terraces with canal views. Although the four-story building has no elevator, you'll have assistance with your luggage, if needed. The exceptional service will help you feel at home. Three adjacent apartments are also available. **Pros:** high degree of personal service; on a bright, quiet, exceptionally picturesque canal; free Wi-Fi. **Cons:** no elevator. ⊠ *San Vio, Dorsoduro 628* ☎ *041/5204733* ⊕ *www. hotelamerican.com* ↝ *28 rooms, 2 suites* ♿ *In-room: safe, refrigerator, Wi-Fi. In-hotel: room service, bar, laundry service, Wi-Fi hotspot, some pets allowed* ⊟ *AE, MC, V* ⍩⍥⍥ *BP* Ⓥ *Accademia or Salute* ✛ *C5.*

$$-$$$
Fodor's Choice
★

🔲 **La Calcina.** The elegant, eclectic La Calcina sits in an enviable position along the sunny Zattere, with front rooms offering heady vistas across the expansive Giudecca Canal. You can reserve the rooftop *altana* (wooden terrace) for sunbathing or a private retreat, or enjoy an afternoon tea in one of the lounge's quiet corners with flickering candlelight and barely perceptible classical music. A stone staircase leads to the rooms upstairs, which have parquet floors, original art deco furniture, and firm beds; some have truly inspirational views. A penchant for the floral is evidenced in the wall drawings and the live and silk flower arrangements that dot the hallways and common areas. A few rooms have private terraces, and when windows are open in corner rooms, you'll never think to turn on the air-conditioning. Besides full meals at lunch and dinner, the Piscina bar and restaurant offers drinks and snacks all day in the elegant dining room or on the waterside terrace. A variety of apartments is also available. One single room does not have an en suite bath. **Pros:** rooftop altana; panoramic views from some rooms; elegant, historic atmosphere. **Cons:** quite eclectic; not for travelers who prefer ultramodern surroundings; no elevator. ⊠ *Dorsoduro 780* ☎ *041/5206466* ⊕ *www.lacalcina.com* ↝ *27 rooms, 26 with bath; 5 suites* ♿ *In-room: safe, refrigerator, Internet, Wi-Fi. In-hotel: restaurant, room service, bar, laundry service, Wi-Fi hotspot* ⊟ *AE, DC, MC, V* ⍩⍥⍥ *BP* Ⓥ *Zattere* ✛ *C5.*

$$

🔲 **Locanda Ca' Zose.** The idea that the Campanati sisters named the 15 rooms in their locanda after the stars and constellations of the highest magnitude in the northern hemisphere says something about how personally this place is run. Located on one of the brightest, most tranquil canals in the Dorsoduro area, Ca' Zose is two minutes from the Salute (both the church and the vaporetto stop) and the Guggenheim Museum, but is also handy to the Zattere promenade, the Accademia, and San Marco. The 17th-century building was completely renovated in 2003, but original beamed ceilings and use of pastel enameled furnishings recall times past. Guest rooms are carpeted in deep blues and rich reds (save one, which is tiled). The cheeriest rooms are on the top floor overlooking the canal. The sisters go out of their way to assist guests; the Wi-Fi and Internet point in the common area is free. **Pros:** quiet but convenient location; efficient, personal service. **Cons:** no outdoor garden or terrace; no Wi-Fi in rooms (at this writing). ⊠ *Calle del Bastion, Dorsoduro 193/B* ☎ *041/5226635* ⊕ *www.hotelcazose. com* ↝ *10 rooms, 1 junior suite, 1 suite* ♿ *In-room: safe, refrigerator.*

4

The garden at Pensione Accademia Villa Maravege is a rare feature for a Venice hotel.

In-hotel: Wi-Fi hotspot, Internet terminal, some pets allowed ⊟ *MC, V* ⫲◎⫳ *BP* Ⓥ *Salute* ✛ *D5.*

$$ ⚏ **Locanda San Barnaba.** This family-run establishment, housed in a 16th-century palazzo, is handily located just off the Ca' Rezzonico vaporetto

★ stop. The arched openings in the private garden wall peek through to the side canal; head upstairs to relax on the tiled, rooftop terrace. There's no elevator, but the accommodating staff will happily assist with your luggage (a ground-level room is available, too). Two superior rooms and one double have original 18th-century frescoes; one junior suite has two small balconies and is exceptionally luminous. All rooms are spacious, with traditional furnishings that make them attractive and welcoming. **Pros:** garden and terrace; close to vaporetto stop. **Cons:** no elevator, minibar, or Internet access. ⊠ *Calle del Traghetto, Dorsoduro 2785–2786* ☎ *041/2411233* ⊕ *www.locanda-sanbarnaba.com* ⤵ *11 rooms, 2 junior suites* ⚱ *In-room: safe. In-hotel: room service, bar, some pets allowed* ⊟ *AE, MC, V* ⫲◎⫳ *BP* Ⓥ *Ca' Rezzonico* ✛ *C4.*

$$$–$$$$ ⚏ **Palazzo Stern.** The gracious terrace that eases onto the Grand Canal

★ is almost reason alone to stay here. An opulent refurbishment of this early-15th-century neo-Gothic palace, carried out by the Stern family in the early 20th century, incorporated marble-columned arches, terrazzo floors, frescoed ceilings, mosaics, and a majestic carved staircase (copied from the Ca' d'Oro). It's also one of a limited number of palaces in the city that have not one, but two exposed sides decorated, one facing the Canal Grand, the other Rio Malpaga. Inside, some rooms have tufted walls, parquet flooring, and 42-inch, flat-screen TVs. From the rooftop terrace—which has a Jacuzzi—you get a classic Venetian view: over the city's roofs to the Campanile, and even to the Dolomites on a clear day. Lodgings range from standard rooms to junior suites to an eclectic attic suite. **Pros:** excellent service; lovely views from many rooms; modern renovation retains historic ambience; steps from vaporetto stop. **Cons:** multiple renovations over centuries may turn off some Venetian architectural purists. ⊠ *Calle del Traghetto, Dorsoduro 2792* ☎ *041/2770869* ⊕ *www.palazzostern.com* ➯ *18 rooms, 5 junior suites, 1 suite* ⚒ *In-room: safe, refrigerator, Internet, Wi-Fi. In-hotel: room service, bar, laundry service, Wi-Fi hotspot, some pets allowed* ▭ *AE, DC, MC, V* ⍟ *BP* ⍌ *Ca' Rezzonico* ⊹ *C4.*

$$–$$$ ⊡ **Pensione Accademia Villa Maravege.** Though the Salmaso family is
Fodor's Choice not originally Venetian, they have created and maintained one of the
★ most quintessentially Venetian accommodations in the city for over 40 years. Aptly nicknamed "Villa of the Wonders," this patrician retreat once served as the Russian embassy and was the residence of Katharine Hepburn's character in the film *Summertime*. Outside, a garden awaits just beyond an iron gate, complete with a mini Palladian-style villa, flower beds, stone cupids, and verdant trees—all rarities in Venice. The spacious terrace sits on a promontory where two side canals converge with the Grand Canal. The traditionally decorated rooms are outfitted with Venetian-style antiques and fine tapestry, and overlook either the picturesque Rio San Trovaso or the lush gardens. Inlaid designs or mosaics decorate marble or ceramic tiled baths. Book well in advance. **Pros:** a historic, classic Venetian property. **Cons:** formal setting with antiques not well suited to children; standard rooms are on the small side. ⊠ *Fondamenta Bollani, Dorsoduro 1058* ☎ *041/5210188* ⊕ *www. pensioneaccademia.it* ➯ *27 rooms, 2 suites* ⚒ *In-room: safe, Internet, Wi-Fi. In-hotel: bar, laundry service, Wi-Fi hotspot* ▭ *AE, DC, MC, V* ⍟ *BP* ⍌ *Accademia* ⊹ *C4.*

LAGOON

$$$$ ⊡ **San Clemente Palace.** If you prefer wide-open spaces to the intimacy of Venice, this is your hotel. This massive complex occupies an entire island, about 15 minutes from Piazza San Marco by (free) shuttle launch, with acres of parkland, a swimming pool, tennis courts, a wellness center, and four restaurants. The 19th-century buildings are on the site of a 12th-century monastery, of which only the chapel remains. They form a large quadrangle and contain spacious, modern, well-appointed rooms done in a variety of Venetian themes: nobles, doges, merchants, and navigators. Standard rooms are sumptuous and bright, but only some superiors and suites offer lagoon views; on a clear day, the view back to Venice with the Dolomites looming behind is stunning. You get all the five-star comforts here—and even three holes of golf. **Pros:** true five-star service and amenities. **Cons:** a shuttle is required to visit the rest of the city. ⊠ *Isola di San Clemente 1* ☎ *041/2445001* ⊕ *www.sanclementepalacevenice.com* ➯ *119 rooms, 53 junior suites, 28 suites* ⚒ *In-room: safe, refrigerator, Wi-Fi. In-hotel: 4 restaurants, bars, golf course, tennis courts, pool, gym, spa, laundry service, some pets allowed* ▭ *AE, DC, MC, V* ⍟ *BP* ⊹ *G6.*

SAN MARCO

$$ ⊡ **Al Teatro.** Behind the Fenice Theater, just off the Maria Callas Bridge, this small B&B is the renovated home of owners Fabio and Eleonora—in fact, it's where Eleanora was born. There are three spacious, comfortable, and conscientiously appointed rooms with private baths, each overlooking a gondola-filled canal; the largest room has a broad balcony. An ample breakfast (served at a common table) and exceptional service make Al Teatro an excellent value and a relaxing choice in the sometimes-frenetic San Marco atmosphere. Book well in advance. **Pros:** airy rooms; convenient San Marco location; good for families. **Cons:** the intimacy of a family B&B is not for everyone. ⊠ *Fondamenta della Fenice, San Marco 2554* ☎ *041/5204271* ⊕ *www. bedandbreakfastalteatro.com* ⌘ *3 rooms* ⌂ *In-room: safe, refrigerator, Wi-Fi. In-hotel: room service, Internet terminal, Wi-Fi hotspot* ⊟ *AE, MC, V* ⏏⊙⏐ *BP* ⊻ *Santa Maria del Giglio* ✛ *D4.*

$$$$ ⊡ **Bauer Il Palazzo.** This is the ultimate word in luxury, Venetian-style.
Fodor'sChoice Surroundings are spacious yet intimate, with high ceilings, tufted walls
★ of Bevilacqua and Rubelli fabrics, Murano glass, marble bathrooms, and damask drapes; no two rooms are decorated the same. Many rooms have sweeping views over the Grand Canal and beyond. Breakfast is served on Venice's highest rooftop terrace, appropriately named Il Settimo Cielo (Seventh Heaven). The highly lauded De Pisis restaurant overlooks the Grand Canal. The outdoor hot tub, also on the rooftop, offers views of La Serenissima that will leave you breathless, and personable, professional staff will accommodate your every whim. **Pros:** pampering service; high-end luxury. **Cons:** in one of the busiest areas of the city. ⊠ *Campo San Moisè, San Marco 1413/D* ☎ *041/5207022* ⊕ *www.ilpalazzovenezia.com* ⌘ *44 rooms, 38 suites* ⌂ *In-room: safe, refrigerator, DVD, Wi-Fi. In-hotel: restaurant, room service, bars, gym, laundry service, Internet terminal, some pets allowed* ⊟ *AE, DC, MC, V* ⏏⊙⏐ *EP* ⊻ *San Marco or Vallaresso* ✛ *E4.*

$$ ⊡ **Ca' dei Dogi.** Amid the crush of mediocre hotels around Piazza San
Fodor'sChoice Marco, this delightful choice, in a 15th-century palace and in a quiet
★ courtyard secluded from the melee, stands out. The thoughtful, personal touches added by owners Stefano and Susanna are evident everywhere, from the six individually decorated rooms (some with private terraces), to the carefully chosen contemporary furnishings and accessories, to classic Venetian elements such as the marble stairway, beamed ceilings, wall tapestries, and mosaic tiles. Service is highly personal: guests are often welcomed by one of the owners. There's a courtyard where you can enjoy breakfast or an evening interlude. One room has a Jacuzzi. One attic apartment is available. **Pros:** offers respite from San Marco crowds; terraces with views of the Doge's Palace. **Cons:** rooms are not expansive; nearby dining selection is limited. ⊠ *Corte Santa Scolastica, Castello 4242* ☎ *041/2413751* ⊕ *www.cadeidogi.it* ⌘ *6 rooms* ⌂ *In-room: safe, refrigerator. In-hotel: room service, Internet terminal, some pets allowed* ⊟ *AE, DC, MC, V* ⏏⊙⏐ *BP* ⊻ *San Zaccaria* ✛ *F4.*

$$$ ⊡ **Locanda Orseolo.** This cozy, elegant hotel offers a welcome respite
Fodor'sChoice from the throngs churning around Piazza San Marco. Family owned,
★ it has an attentive staff and comfortable, well-appointed rooms.

Traditional Venetian decor takes on a Carnevale theme, with each room design inspired by a particular mask; many rooms have fanciful wall murals. Common areas have warm mahogany paneling, tufted leather furniture, beamed ceilings, and tapestries. A relaxed atmosphere pervades at breakfast, where it's common to get engrossed in conversation with the other guests as gondolas glide lazily by the water-level windows. **Pros:** intimate and romantic; friendly staff; Wi-Fi is free. **Cons:** in the one of the busiest and most commercial areas of the city. ⊠ *Corte Zorzi off Campo San Gallo, San Marco 1083* ☎ *041/5204827* ⊕ *www.locandaorseolo.com* ➵ *12 rooms* ♿ *In-room: safe, refrigerator, Wi-Fi. In-hotel: room service, laundry facilities, laundry service, Internet terminal, Wi-Fi hotspot* ▤ *AE, DC, MC, V* ☉ *Closed Jan.* ⧉ *BP* Ⓥ *Rialto or Vallaresso* ✛ *E4.*

$$$ 🏨 **Novecento.** This small, family-run hotel is on a quiet street a 10-min-
★   ute walk from the Piazza San Marco. Inspired by the style of Mariano Fortuny, the early-1900s Spanish artist and fashion designer who made Venice his home, the intimate rooms are a surprisingly elegant mélange of multiethnic and exotic furnishings. The Mediterranean, Indian, and Venetian fabrics, silverware, chandeliers, and furniture create a sensual turn-of-the-20th-century atmosphere. In fine weather, breakfast is served in the inner courtyard. **Pros:** intimate, romantic atmosphere; free Wi-Fi. **Cons:** a bit of a walk to vaporetto stop. ⊠ *Calle del Dose, Campo San Maurizio, San Marco 2683/84* ☎ *041/2413765* ⊕ *www.novecento.biz* ➵ *9 rooms* ♿ *In-room: safe, refrigerator, Internet, Wi-Fi. In-hotel: bar, laundry service, Internet terminal, Wi-Fi hotspot, some pets allowed* ▤ *AE, DC, MC, V* ⧉ *BP* Ⓥ *Santa Maria del Giglio* ✛ *C4.*

$$$–$$$$ 🏨 **Palazzo Paruta.** This palace is one of the most extraordinary hotel renovations in the city. Many earlier architectural features have been maintained, including ornate frescoes, pastel bas-reliefs, 19th-century doors, and splendid coffered and carved beamed ceilings; what is not original is reproduced to seem so. Carrara marble lines bathroom walls hung with Venetian-style mirrors. After crossing the private bridge that leads to the hotel, guests are greeted with a glass of prosecco in a green, open courtyard. Many of the common areas, including the spectacular breakfast area, overlook the courtyard. Junior suites are palatial; superior rooms comfortably sized, bright, and well appointed. Ask for rooms with views over a quiet side canal. Check the Web site for specials. Pros: steeped in lavish Venetian ambience; there are few boutique lodgings that compare. **Cons:** standard rooms are quite small; not handy to the best values for dining; no Wi-Fi in rooms (at this writing). ⊠ *Campo Sant'Angelo, San Marco 3824* ☎ *041/2410835* ⊕ *www.palazzoparuta.com* ➵ *8 rooms, 5 junior suites* ♿ *In-room: safe, refrigerator, Internet. In-hotel: bar, laundry service, Wi-Fi hotspot* ▤ *AE, DC, MC, V* ⧉ *EP* Ⓥ *Sant'Angelo* ✛ *D4.*

$$$$ 🏨 **Palazzo Sant'Angelo sul Canal Grande.** There's a distinguished yet comfortable feel to this elegant palazzo, which is large enough to deliver expected facilities and services but small enough to pamper its guests. Rooms have tapestry-adorned walls and Carrara and Alpine marble in the bath; those facing the Grand Canal have balconies that practically bring the canal to you. Common areas include an entrance hall

4

Bauer Il Palazzo

Hotel American-Dinesen

Hotel al Ponte Mocenigo

Locanda Orseolo

Oltre il Giardino-Casaifrari

with original Palladian flooring, a bright front lounge, and an intimate bar that puts the canal almost at arm's length. Ask ahead for a room with a view. **Pros:** convenient to vaporetto stop. **Cons:** some rooms have no special view; fee for Wi-Fi. ⊠ *Campo Sant'Angelo, San Marco 3488* ☎ *041/2411452* ⊕ *www.palazzosantangelo.com* ⇄ *14 rooms* ⌂ *In-room: safe, refrigerator, Internet, Wi-Fi. In-hotel: bar, laundry service, Wi-Fi hotspot, some pets allowed* ⊟ *AE, DC, MC, V* ⊠ *EP* ⊻ *Sant'Angelo* ⊹ *D4.*

SAN POLO

$ ⊞ **Acca Hotel.** This small, newish hotel of modern construction is one of Venice's more economical options, with bright, well-appointed rooms and attentive service. Most rooms are spacious by Venetian standards; furnishings recall traditional Venetian style and feature damask fabrics and even tufted walls. Floors are carpeted; the suite has a Jacuzzi. There's no staff on hand in the evening, but you get your own key. Breakfast is served in the courtyard, weather permitting. Make sure you get good directions for arriving. **Pros:** lots of amenities for its category; excellent value. **Cons:** no views; not terribly handy to a vaporetto stop. ⊠ *Calle Pezzana, San Polo 2160* ☎ *041/2440126* ⊕ *www.accahotel.com* ⇄ *8 rooms, 1 suite* ⌂ *In-room: safe, refrigerator, Wi-Fi (free). In-hotel: room service (breakfast), laundry service, Internet terminal, Wi-Fi hotspot* ⊟ *MC, V* ⊠ *BP* ⊻ *San Silvestro* ⊹ *C3.*

$$–$$$ ⊞ **Ca' Angeli.** The heirs of an important Venetian architect have transformed his former residence, on the third and top floors of a palace along the Grand Canal, into an elegant B&B. It retains a traditional yet innovative style instilled by the former owner—most of the furniture was his, including an 18th-century briar-wood bureau, and there's a private library accessible to guests. The five rooms and two suites have views of either the Grand Canal or a side canal—or in the case of the smallish Room 6, rooftops from a terrace twice the size of the room. A rich breakfast, including select cheeses and meats from local producers, is served in a salon overlooking the Grand Canal. There's also an attic apartment option. **Pros:** historic residence with Grand Canal and rooftop views; helpful staff. **Cons:** a bit of a walk from the vaporetto stop; credit cards accepted only for stays of two or more nights. ⊠ *Calle del Traghetto de la Madoneta, San Polo 1434* ☎ *041/5232480* ⊕ *www.caangeli.it* ⇄ *6 rooms, 1 suite, 1 apartment* ⌂ *In-room: safe, refrigerator, Wi-Fi. In-hotel: Wi-Fi hotspot* ⊟ *MC, V* ⊠ *BP* ⊻ *San Silvestro* ⊹ *D3.*

$$ ⊞ **Ca' San Rocco.** Through an iron gate on a calle just off the main thoroughfare from Piazzale Roma to the San Tomà vaporetto stop, you'll spy the small, inviting garden terrace of the Ca' San Rocco. The Cuogo sisters updated a former doctor's residence to create a green, exceptionally quiet oasis. Though rooms are modestly decorated, they're spacious and bright. The upper trellised terrace (available for breakfast or relaxing) overlooks a marvelous private garden; one of the double rooms has doors that open onto a balcony above it. Location is handy to both Piazzale Roma and the train station for day trips, and there are lots of eateries and shops nearby. **Pros:** lots of greenery and outdoors areas; extraordinarily quiet. **Cons:** a bit of a walk from the vaporetto stops.

✉ *Ramo Cimesin, San Polo 3078* ☎ *041/716744* ⊕ *www.casanrocco.it*
↪ *6 rooms* ♿ *In-room: safe, refrigerator, Wi-Fi. In-hotel: Wi-Fi hotspot*
▭ *MC, V* ☉ *BP* Ⓥ *Piazzale Roma or San Tomà* ♧ *B3.*

$$ 🛏 **Corte 1321.** If you're looking to escape the 18th-century-style decor that predominates Venetian lodging, try Corte 1321, nestled off the main drag between Campo Sant'Aponal and San Polo. Here you'll find spacious, carefully renovated rooms where ceramic lamps, tapestries, and carved platform beds are combined with standard Venetian features such as beamed ceilings and parquet flooring. Unwind in an intimate, interior courtyard and garden after a day of exploring, sharing discoveries with other guests or checking e-mail using the free Wi-Fi. Mother-daughter owners Deborah and Amelia (of Italian-American descent) provide efficient, personal service. Make sure you get detailed directions and cross-check on a good map before arriving. **Pros:** contemporary decor; convivial, eclectic atmosphere. **Cons:** all rooms but one open onto the courtyard—and the occasionally lively conversations of its guests. ✉ *Campiello Ca' Bernardi, San Polo 1321* ☎ *041/5224923* ⊕ *www.corte1321.com* ↪ *4 rooms, 1 apartment* ♿ *In-room: safe, Internet, Wi-Fi. In-hotel: bar, laundry service, Internet terminal, Wi-Fi hotspot* ▭ *MC, V* ☉ *Closed Jan.* ☉ *BP* Ⓥ *San Silvestro* ♧ *D3.*

$$–$$$ 🛏 **La Villeggiatura.** If eclectic Venetian charm is what you seek, don't be
★ dismayed by La Villeggiatura's unprepossessing entrance or the number of stairs (36) you'll climb to reach this lofty attic lodging. Your reward is a luminous residence and six individually decorated rooms, each with its own original, theatrically themed fresco by a local artist. There's traditional period furniture, but the amenities are all contemporary: signature linens, free Wi-Fi throughout, and a kettle in every room. Tiled baths may or may not have a tub, but all have complementary kimonos; every bed is king size. You'll find Venetian parquet flooring in the larger rooms. The two upstairs garrets have electronically controlled skylights. **Pros:** relaxed atmosphere; meticulously maintained; well located. **Cons:** positioned high over a popular and busy thoroughfare; no elevator; modest breakfast. ✉ *Calle dei Botteri, San Polo 1569* ☎ *041/5244673* ⊕ *www.lavilleggiatura.it* ↪ *6 rooms* ♿ *In-room: safe, refrigerator, Wi-Fi (free). In-hotel: Wi-Fi hotspot (free)* ▭ *MC, V* ☉ *BP* Ⓥ *Rialto Mercato* ♧ *D3.*

$$ 🛏 **Locanda Sant'Agostin.** In this meticulously restored boutique hotel you'll find enough classic Venetian characteristics to remind of you where you are, but not so many as to be stuffy or ostentatious. The homey yet elegant feel is accentuated by period furniture, parquet and Venetian terrazzo flooring, and tall windows, some of which open onto small balconies (ask for a room with a canal view). While you're not "steps from San Marco," you are handy to the Frari and the Scuola di San Rocco, the Campo San Polo and the Rialto, and all the characteristic shopping, eateries, and residential ambience of San Polo and Santa Croce. Service is personal, thorough, and thoughtful. There's no elevator, but all rooms are on one level, one flight up. **Pros:** tranquil atmosphere; attentive service; authentic period renovation. **Cons:** a bit of a walk from the vaporetto stop; no Wi-Fi in rooms. ✉ *Campo Sant'Agostin, San Polo 2344* ☎ *041/2759414* ⊕ *www.locandasantagostin.com* ↪ *9*

rooms, 1 junior suite ♿ In-room: safe, refrigerator. In-hotel: Wi-Fi hot-spot ⊟MC, V ⏏⦿¦BP ☑ San Stae, San Silvestro, or San Tomà ⊹ C3.

$$–$$$
Fodor's Choice
★

□ **Oltre il Giardino–Casaifrari.** It's easy to overlook—and it can be a challenge to find—this secluded palazzo, sheltered behind a brick wall just over the bridge from the Frari church. Especially in high season, the eight-room hotel with airy, individually decorated rooms and an expansive garden is an oasis of peace. The prevalent white-and-pastel color scheme (in fact, each room is named for its predominant hue) and elegant, understated decor contribute to a relaxed, high-country ambience not found anywhere else in the city. Antiques and period pieces complement the contemporary furnishings. The house was once the residence of Alma Mahler, widow of composer Gustav Mahler and a fascinating woman in her own right; it still conveys her style and charm today. The owner's service and professional attention is as con-scientious as the renovation. **Pros:** a peaceful, gracious, and conve-nient setting; walled garden. **Cons:** no Grand Canal views. ⊠ *San Polo 2542* ☎ *041/2750015* ⊕ *www.oltreilgiardino-venezia.com* ⤸ *4 rooms, 4 suites* ♿ *In-room: safe, refrigerator, Internet, Wi-Fi. In-hotel: room service, bar, Internet terminal, some pets allowed* ⊟ *AE, DC, MC, V* ⏏⦿¦ *BP* ☑ *San Tomà* ⊹ *C3.*

$$$$
★

□ **Palazzo Barbarigo.** It is not unusual to find an opulent hotel along the Grand Canal; it is unusual to discover black marble, matte lacquer, indirect lighting, and decidedly art deco contours ensconced in a 16th-century Venetian palace. Massive mirrors soar floor to ceiling to accent the spaciousness, and the minimalist decor draws your attention to every detail. Each of the 18 rooms, whether suite or standard, feels like a refuge; all have Grande Canal or side-canal views and 42-inch flat-panel TVs. The expansive, ultrachic bar runs the length of the soaring piano nobile to a balcony above the canal, just large enough for a table and two chairs. There's a front water entrance; a narrow calle leads you in from the back, right past the entrance to the Palazzo Pisani Moretta. **Pros:** small; lavish; an uncommon ambience. **Cons:** no outdoor terrace. ⊠ *San Polo 3765* ☎ *041/74072* ⊕ *www.palazzobarbarigo.it* ⤸ *8 rooms, 6 junior suites* ♿ *In-room: safe, refrigerator, Internet, Wi-Fi. In-hotel: bar, laundry service* ⊟ *AE, DC, MC, V* ⏏⦿¦ *BP* ☑ *San Tomà* ⊹ *C4.*

$$

□ **Pensione Guerrato.** This welcoming, rambling pensione is housed in one of oldest palaces located in one of the oldest parts of the city. A moment's walk from the Rialto Bridge, it's surrounded by markets, cafés, and an energetic atmosphere of vendors, shoppers, and occa-sional revelers (there are rooms with guaranteed quiet, but you may not have a view). It's family owned and run, and the staff goes out of its way to assist you, with lots of recommendations for sightsee-ing, eating, and shopping. Period furnishings are Early Flea Market, rooms are comfortable, attentively maintained, and spacious enough to easily hold an extra bed or two if you need them. Top floor rooms have air-conditioning. **Pros:** economic lodging; friendly, efficient service; spacious accommodations. **Cons:** no elevator; reception is one flight up; rooms are on upper floors. ⊠ *Campiello Calle Drio le Scimia, San Polo 240/A* ☎ *041/5285927* ⊕ *www.pensioneguerrato.it* ⤸ *14 rooms*

⚲ *In-room: safe, a/c (some), Wi-Fi (some). In-hotel: no elevator, Wi-Fi hotspot (free)* ⊟ *AE, MC, V* ⍐⎮ *BP* ⍰ *Rialto Mercato* ✛ *D3.*

SANTA CROCE

$$ ⊡ **Hotel al Ponte Mocenigo.** A columned courtyard welcomes you to this
Fodor's Choice   elegant, charming palazzo, former home of the Santa Croce branch of
★   the Mocenigo family (which has a few doges in its past). The meticu-
lously renovated interior has an updated 18th-century Venetian feel,
incorporating a number of distinctive architectural elements such as
open-beam ceilings, fireplaces transformed into writing nooks, and
Murano chandeliers. Canopied beds, striped damask fabrics, lustrous
terrazzo flooring, and gilt-accented furnishings keep the sense of Ven-
ice's past strong. The courtyard offers an ideal ambience for break-
fast or an aperitivo, and there's a Turkish sauna for unwinding after
a day of seeing sights. The hotel is located on a side canal convenient
to any number of sights, eateries, and shops. **Pros:** enchanting court-
yard; water access; friendly staff; free Wi-Fi. **Cons:** rooms do not over-
look a canal (although the courtyard and foyer do). ⊠ *Fondamento de
Rimpeto a Ca' Mocenigo, Santa Croce 2063* ☎ *041/5244797* ⊕ *www.
alpontemocenigo.com* ⮌ *10 rooms, 1 junior suite* ⚲ *In-room: safe,
refrigerator, Wi-Fi. In-hotel: room service, bar, Internet terminal, Wi-Fi
hotspot* ⊟ *AE, DC, MC, V* ⍐⎮ *BP* ⍰ *San Stae* ✛ *D2.*

LIDO

$$$$ ⊡ **Westin Excelsior.** The Excelsior's imposing, Moorish-style building
with its green cupolas and inner courtyard comes complete with pot-
ted lemon trees and a reflecting pool; the feel is decidedly southern
Mediterranean. No longer a haunt of the noble and famous of the dolce
vita days (except during the Biennale), the hotel nonetheless offers the
same panache, luxury, and space as ever. Rooms are spacious and taste-
fully modern, done in bright colors, and face either the inner garden
or the beach below; there are all the services you might expect from a
five-star hotel, including a pool, fitness center, tennis, and restaurants
and bars in the hotel and on the beach. A shuttle boat between the
hotel and San Zaccaria runs every half hour. **Pros:** private beach with
classic European beach facilities; pool June–September; superb service.
Cons: removed from Venice proper; no Wi-Fi in rooms. ⊠ *Lungomare
Marconi 17, The Lido* ☎ *041/5260201* ⊕ *www.hotelexcelsiorvenezia.
com* ⮌ *178 rooms, 19 suites* ⚲ *In-room: safe, refrigerator, Internet. In-
hotel: room service, bar, restaurants, laundry service, tennis, pool, gym,
spa, beachfront, Wi-Fi hotspot, some pets allowed* ⊟ *AE, DC, MC, V*
⊙ *Closed Nov.–Mar.* ⍐⎮ *BP* ⍰ *Lido* ✛ *D5.*

Nightlife and the Arts in Venice

WORD OF MOUTH

"Venice doesn't have much of a nightlife. There are only a couple of dance clubs, and they are fairly bizarre. After midnight, open bars are few and far between. Bringing a bottle of wine and some plastic cups to Piazza San Marco is always fun, especially at 2 AM, when you have the place to yourself."

—rialtogrl

Updated by
Nan McElroy

Your first impression may well be that Venice doesn't have a nightlife. As the last rays of daylight slip away, so, too, do most signs of a bustling town. Boat traffic drops to the occasional vaporetto, shutters roll down, and signs go dark.

Even though *bacari* (wine bars) would seem to be natural after-hours gathering spots, most close around 9 PM. Yet sprinkled judiciously around the city's residential-looking *calli* and *campi* (streets and squares), you'll stumble upon *locali* (nightspots) that stay open until 1 or 2 AM. Some even offer live music, though rarely past midnight—a city noise ordinance prohibits too much wildness except during Carnevale. Though there are no suitable venues for rock shows, Piazza San Marco has hosted some less-rambunctious concerts on summer evenings. Except for a few lounge bars with dancing, nightlife tends to be student oriented.

Both private and city museums regularly host major traveling art exhibits, from ancient to contemporary. From mid-June to early November in odd-numbered years, the Biennale dell'Arte attracts several hundred contemporary artists from around the world. Classical music buffs can rely on a rich season of concerts, opera, chamber music, and some ballet. Smaller venues and churches offer lower-priced, occasionally free performances that often highlight Venetian and Italian composers. Though the city has no English-language theater, during Carnevale you'll find foreign companies that perform in their mother tongue. All films screened at the Venice Film Festival (some in an ad-hoc amphitheater constructed in Campo San Polo) in late summer are shown in the original language, with subtitles in English, Italian, or both.

There is a variety of resources for finding what's on in Venice. Both the city and the province have tourism offices and associated Web sites with English versions, ⊕ *turismovenezia.com* and ⊕ *comune.venezia.it*, respectively. (For the second, click on the "Tourism" tab.) Be sure to ask for the "Shows and Events" calendar at the APT tourist offices: it provides extensive, current information on museums, churches, exhibitions, events day-by-day, useful phone numbers, gondola and taxi fares, opening hours, and more. *A Guest in Venice*, a monthly bilingual booklet, free at hotels, also includes information about pharmacies, vaporetto and bus lines, and main trains and flights; ⊕ *aguestinvenice. com* lists musical, artistic, and sporting events, as does Agenda Venezia (⊕ *agendavenezia.org*). *Venezia News,* available at newsstands, has similar information but also includes in-depth articles about noteworthy events; listings are bilingual, but most articles are in Italian. *Venezia da Vivere* is a bilingual guide that comes out seasonally listing nightspots and live music. Try ⊕ *venicexplorer.com* for a fantastic map function to find any address in Venice, and ⊕ *venicebanana.com* and the ⊕ *2night.it* listings for lots of insider restaurant and entertainment goings-on. Look to ⊕ *musicinvenice.com* for a comprehensive calendar of musical events that you can also reserve (they even have a 24-hour phone service). Last but not least, don't ignore the posters you see everywhere in the streets; they're often as current as you can get.

THE ARTS

5

Art has been a way of life in Venice for so many centuries that it seems you need only inhale to enjoy it. While the Biennale is a whirlwind of contemporary arts, Carnevale masks and costumes let revelers dance with history. Costumed musicians will entice you to performances in the finest churches, palaces and *scuole grande,* but don't ignore the bel canto wafting through the canals or the opera issuing from open windows of conservatory practice halls.

CONCERTS

The band Pink Floyd made rock history with a 1989 concert staged aboard a pontoon floating near Piazza San Marco. Fans made such a mess of the piazza and loud music stirred up such antipathy that the show was destined to become the city's first and last rock happening. Nearby Parco San Giuliano, Mestre, Padua, Verona, Trieste, and Treviso sometimes host artists on their European tours. Though the Biennale Musica and some clubs in Venice do spotlight contemporary music, the vast majority of the city's concerts are classical. Consult the local resources listed above for up-to-date information.

HelloVenezia (⊠ *Isola nova del Tronchetto 21* ☎ *041/2424* ⊕ *www. hellovenezia.it* ⊠ *Piazzale Roma*), which handles public transit ticket sales, also sells tickets for events at the Fenice and Malibran theaters. Purchase tickets by phone, on their Web site, at the Fenice, or at sales kiosks at Piazzale Roma and the train station.

CLASSICAL
Numerous orchestras perform pricey "greatest hits" programs marketed toward tourists—you'll easily spot ticket vendors in period costume. Groups may have a semipermanent venue, such as an ex-church or *scuola,* although they can change frequently. You'll find these promoted at your hotel, in tourist offices, in travel agencies, and in many of the previously mentioned Web sites and local publications. It's not usually necessary to book in advance, however, as these performances rarely sell out.

The Biennale, an Arts Feast

A Venice institution, the Biennale (as the name suggests) started as an art festival held every two years, but during the century-plus of its existence it has outgrown the name, becoming one of the world's major interdisciplinary art expositions. "Biennale" now refers to the group that coordinates festivals of art, film, music, dance, theater, and architecture. For information on all events, contact **La Biennale di Venezia** (✉ *Ca' Giustinian, San Marco 1364/A* ☎ *041/5218711* ⊕ *www. labiennale.org*).

The **Biennale dell'Arte** was originated in 1894 and, except for World War interruptions, has taken place every two years since. In 1910 Klimt and Renoir had their own exhibition rooms, while Picasso was removed from the Spanish salon over concern his paintings were too shocking. Picasso's work was finally shown in 1948, the same year Peggy Guggenheim brought her collection to Venice at the Biennale's invitation.

The Biennale dell'Arte currently takes place from mid-June to early November in odd-numbered years. The Giardini della Biennale, located in the Castello sestiere, was developed specifically for the event. In this park-like setting overlooking the lagoon, 30 countries have permanent pavilions to exhibit works by their native artists. In the neighboring Arsenale's Corderie, a long, beautiful building otherwise off-limits to visitors, works by artists from smaller nations, as well as some more avant-garde installations, are shown. Numerous palaces, warehouses, and churches all over town also hold exhibits, often allowing you to visit buildings not normally open to the public.

The **Biennale del Cinema** (also known as the Mostra Internazionale d'Arte Cinematografica, or Venice Film Festival) was first held in 1932 and soon turned into an annual event. Films are shown in several theaters at the **Palazzo del Cinema** (✉ *Lungomare Guglielmo Marconi 90, The Lido* ☎ *041/2726511* Ⓥ *Lido Casinò or S.M. Elizabetta*), which is closed most of the year but comes to life in August with bright lights, movie stars, and thousands of fans.

Ten days of 9 AM to 2 AM screenings include films vying for awards as well as retrospectives and debuts of mainstream releases. Advance tickets are recommended for the most eagerly awaited films (the tourist office has details). The night after films play the Palazzo del Cinema, they're shown at Campo San Polo's open-air cinema and at the Giorgione Movie d'essai. San Polo screens the winner of the Leone d'Oro (Golden Lion) prize the night following the awards ceremony.

Since its launch in 1930, the **Biennale Musica** has attracted world-famous composers and performers. Igor Stravinsky premiered his *Rake's Progress* during the 1951 festival, and four years later it was George Gershwin's turn with *Porgy and Bess.* The annual event stretches over several months, with performances in some of the city's smaller venues. Scheduling is similar for the **Biennale Danza** and **Biennale Teatro,** both of which stage some performances in the city's campi. The Theatro Verde, an outdoor amphitheater on the island of San Giorgio, was restored for Biennale use, and you can't beat its lagoon backdrop. The **Biennale of Architecture** began in 1980 but has yet to develop a regular schedule.

The Biennale gives a contemporary look to its classic Venetian setting.

In addition to these commercial groups, there are professional orchestras that perform less regularly, usually in museums or palazzi. Churches, scuole, palazzi, and museums sometimes sponsor concerts of their own, especially around the holidays, often featuring touring musicians. Keep an eye out for notices plastered on walls along walkways for last-minute, often free concerts offered by local musicians, choirs, and city-sponsored groups.

Museo Querini-Stampalia stays open late Friday and Saturday evenings to host *musica antica*, short concerts featuring centuries-old music played on antique instruments. Your museum ticket includes the concert, and the Florian Art e Caffè on the premises has food and drink available. ⊠ *Campo Santa Maria Formosa, Castello 5252* ☎ *041/2711411* ✉ *€6.*

Cini Foundation, located on the island of San Giorgio, often has concerts, which are generally free. It's well worth attending, even if only to visit the lovely Benedictine monastery, which is normally closed to the public. ⊠ *Isola di San Giorgio* ☎ *041/5289900* ⊕ *www.cini.it.*

CONTEMPORARY
Contemporary music options are at their richest during Biennale Musica (⇨ *Biennale close-up box)*, when concerts are held throughout Venice and advertised on their Web site, with materials available in tourist offices, and on billboards in all principal campi.

OPERA AND BALLET

The magnificent **Teatro La Fenice,** located between Piazza San Marco and Campo San Stefano, is one of Italy's oldest opera houses and a shrine for opera lovers. It has witnessed many memorable operatic premieres, including, in 1853, the dismal first-night flop of Verdi's *La Traviata*. It has also witnessed its share of disasters. The most recent was a horrific fire that burned it to the ground, deliberately set in January 1996, followed by endless delays in a complicated reconstruction. In keeping with its name (which translates as The Phoenix, coined when it was built over the ashes of its predecessor in 1792), La Fenice rose again, luxuriously restored and reopened to great fanfare in 2004, once again hosting seasons of symphony, opera, and dance. ⊠ *Campo San Fantin, San Marco 1965* Ⓥ *Sant'Angelo, Giglio.*

La Fenice's more intimate sister venue is the **Teatro Malibran** (⊠ *Campiello del Teatro Malibran, Cannaregio 5870* Ⓥ *Rialto*). When built by the powerful Grimani family in 1677, it was one of Europe's most famous opera houses. It was converted into a movie theater in 1927 and then reopened for live performances in 2001 after lengthy restoration.

You can review the calendar and by tickets for both the theaters at ⊕ *www.teatrolafenice.it*, or *contact* **HelloVenezia** (☎ *041/2424* ⊕ *hellovenezia.com* ◔ *8* AM–8 PM), or visit one of their **sales offices** (⊠ *Piazzale Roma or Ferrovia*). It's even worth a try to head for the theater box office an hour before showtime.

FESTIVALS

FESTA DELLA MADONNA DELLA SALUTE

This thanksgiving festival celebrates not a harvest, but survival. Every November 21, Venetians make a pilgrimage to the church of Madonna della Salute, where they light candles to thank the Virgin Mary for liberating the city from the plague of 1630–31 and to pray for health in the year to come. It was while the plague was raging that the church was commissioned, but before the saint could intervene, nearly one third of the city's 145,000 inhabitants were dead. To make the pilgrims' progress more expedient, a temporary bridge is erected across the Grand Canal between Campo Santa Maria del Giglio (near the Gritti Palace hotel) and the sestiere of Dorsoduro. The weather is usually cold and foggy, and the winter season is traditionally ushered in with a traditional stew called *castradina*. Outside and to the back of the church is a carnival-like atmosphere, with *frittelle* (fritters), *palloncini* (balloons on strings), clowns, and votive candles.

FESTA DELLA SENSA

The oldest Venetian festival, the Festival of the Ascension, was initiated by Doge Pietro Orseolo II in the year 1000, after he led the Venetian fleet to victory over the Slavic pirates (who had invaded the Istrian-Dalamatian coast) on Ascension Day. Originally the Ascension was a very simple ceremony in which the doge led a procession of boats to the entrance of the port of San Nicolò di Lido to meet the religious leader of the period, the bishop of San Pietro di Castello, who blessed the waters as a sign of peace and gratitude.

In 1177, with the famous "Peace of Venice" between Emperor Frederick Barbarossa and Pope Alexander III, the festival was transformed into the so-called "wedding with the sea." The story goes that following the occupation of Rome by Barbarossa's troops, Alexander III escaped to Venice disguised as a pilgrim, and after having passed the first night in the open air on the Sottoportego della Madonna near the Church of Sant'Aponal (now marked by a wooden plaque), he found work in the kitchens of the Convento della Carità (today home of the Gallerie dell'Accademia). Some time later, Alexander III was recognized by a Roman high prelate who was visiting the monastery. When the doge Sebastiano Ziani heard of this, he immediately began peace talks with the emperor. But Barbarossa did not want to make peace, so the doge armed a strong fleet and with the blessing of Alexander III set off from Piazzetta di San Marco to attack the imperial ships in the Istrian waters. The Venetians won and captured Barbarossa's son, thereby forcing the emperor to negotiate. In gratitude the pope gave a gold ring to the doge, with which he could remarry Venice with the sea every year.

In the days of the Republic, the Ascension began with a series of performances and celebrations that went on for 15 days and culminated with a large fair in Piazza San Marco. Today the Ascension is held on the Sunday following Ascension Day, the Thursday that falls 40 days after Easter, and begins at about 9 AM with a procession of Venetian-oared boats led by the mayor in the Serenissima, who tosses a ring into the water and pronounces the ritual phrase *"In segno di eterno dominio, noi, Doge di Venezia, ti sposiamo o mare!"* (As a symbol of our eternal dominion, we wed you, o sea!). Masses in the Chiesa di San Nicolò and boat races follow later in the afternoon. In the Sala del Maggior Consiglio in Palazzo Ducale, you can see several objects that are part of the ceremony, such as the thick candle, the umbrella, the gilded throne, and the eight white, red, blue, and yellow banners. The Museo Storico Navale has an 18-foot-long scale model of the gilded boat once used by the doge.

FESTA DEL REDENTORE

Fodor's Choice ★ On the third Sunday of July, crowds of pilgrims cross the Canale della Giudecca by means of a pontoon bridge, which is traditionally built every year to commemorate the doge's annual visit to Palladio's Chiesa del Redentore to offer thanks to the Redeemer for the end of a 16th-century plague. Over the course of the Saturday before, neighbors mark off picnic turf with tables and chairs along the fondamenta on Giudecca and Zattere, and even off in Sant'Elena park. As evening falls, thousands take to the streets and tables, and thousands more take to the water. Boats decorated with colored lanterns, well provisioned with wine, watermelon, and snacks, jockey for position to watch the grand event. Half an hour before midnight, from a barge floating in the Bacino di San Marco, Venice kicks off a fireworks display right over the top of the boat fleet, moored so densely across the bacino that you could almost walk from San Marco and San Giorgio. Any hotel and restaurant with a view of the bacino will organize expensive terrace dinners and parties (reserve well ahead), and many tourist boats host evening excursions. Anywhere along Piazza San Marco, Riva degli Schiavoni, or Giardini you'll find good viewing, or try Zattere, as close to Punta Dogana as you can get. Anywhere along the Giudecca is good, but the Zitelle end is the most popular. The show is not held in the rain, but

The highlight of the Festa del Redentore, held on the third Sunday on July, is a spectacular fireworks display over the Bacino di San Marco.

no one can recall the last time it rained for Festa del Redentore. After the fireworks you can join the young folks staying out all night and greeting sunrise on the Lido beach, or rest up and make the procession to Mass Sunday morning.

FESTA DI SAN MARCO

The festival honoring the evangelist who for 1,000 years protected his city is somewhat eclipsed by the fact that April 25 is also Italian Liberation Day, a national holiday. On St. Mark's Day men traditionally buy *boccoli* (red roses) for ladies in their lives (wives, mothers, sisters, cousins, friends)—the longer the stem the deeper the token of love. Legend tells of a soldier enamored of the doge's daughter who was mortally wounded in a far-off battle. As it spilled, his blood was transformed into red roses, which he entrusted his companion to bring to the girl. The story doesn't say if the flowers arrived on the saint's day, but by tradition Venetians celebrate the miracle on this date.

NIGHTLIFE

Nightspots in and around Venice can be difficult to categorize. Pubs, of the English or Irish variety, with beer on tap and occasional live music, are easy enough to identify and are especially popular with local and traveling youth. When you're looking to dance, things get murkier: lounge-type piano bars generally have small dance floors, while dance clubs are scarce but may serve snacks and even late-night meals. Bars and cafés are even harder to classify, as availability of snacks, meals, beverages, and music varies with the time of day and the season. Many also decorate their walls with works by local artists, whose paintings are for sale.

The proximity to the university makes Campo Santa Margherita and the surrounding area one of the livelier gathering places in town after dark.

BARS

Al Chioschetto is among Venice's "nonbars," consisting only of a kiosk set up to serve some outdoor tables. Located on the Zattere, it's popular in nice weather for late-night *panini* (sandwiches) or a sunny breakfast. Live funk, reggae, jazz, or soul is on tap once a week in summer, usually Friday or Saturday. ⊠ *Near Ponte Lungo, Dorsoduro 1406/A* ☎ *338/1174077* Ⓥ *Zattere.*

Bácaro Jazz has hot jazz on the sound system and hot meals until 2 AM. It also has a very interactive owner and staff, so you're not likely to feel lonely even if you arrive alone. ⊠ *Across from Rialto Post Office, San Marco 5546/A* ☎ *041/5285249* ⊕ *www.bacarojazz.com.*

Comfortably warm **Bagolo,** with its contemporary Murano glass sconces that are never too bright, welcomes clientele of all ages and all lifestyles. It's open daily, except Monday, from 7 AM until midnight or later. ⊠ *Campo San Giacomo dell'Orio, Santa Croce 1584* ☎ *041/717584* Ⓥ *San Stae.*

Caffè Blue is a very popular bar for students from nearby Ca' Foscari, with a top-shelf whiskey selection, absinthe for the adventurous, and free Internet. Sandwiches are available from noon until 2 AM. There are frequent art openings and occasional live music performances. ⊠ *Calle dei Preti near San Pantalon, Dorsoduro 3778* ☎ *041/710227* Ⓥ *San Tomà.*

★ It's tiny dimensions notwithstanding, **El Refolo** is inviting to anyone on their way up or down Via Garibaldi, owing to its savory snacks, wine selection, and live music on most Friday nights when the weather's fine. There's no set closing hour—they'll tell you when it's time to leave. ⊠ *Via Garibaldi, Castello 1580* Ⓥ *Arsenale.*

Il Caffè, commonly called "Bar Rosso" for its bright-red exterior, hosts occasional summer jazz concerts and has far more tables outside than in. A favorite with students, it's famous for strong *spritz,* the preferred Venetian aperitif, of white wine, Campari or Aperol, soda water, and a twist of lemon. ⊠ *Campo Santa Margherita, Dorsoduro 2963* ☎ *041/5287998.*

Modern, hip, and complemented by a nice internal garden, **Orange** anchors the south end of Campo Santa Margherita, the liveliest campo in Venice. You can have *piadine* sandwiches and drinks while watching soccer games on a massive screen inside, or sit at the tables in the campo. ⊠ *Campo Santa Margherita, Dorsoduro 3054/A* ☎ *041/5234740.*

Paradiso Perduto has been catering to night owls since the '70s with drinks, wine, and slightly overpriced fish dishes (a better option is the *cicchetti*). It often serves up live music on weekends, mainly jazz and ethnic music. With closely placed tables, this huge room is full of conviviality; in temperate weather, patrons fill the fondamenta until they're

CLOSE UP

Unfettered Feting at Carnevale

What Mardi Gras is to New Orleans and Carnaval to Rio, Carnevale is to Venice. For the 12 days leading up to *quaresima* (Lent), the city is given over to feasting and celebration, with more than half a million people attending masquerade balls, historical processions, concerts, plays, street performances, fashion shows, and all other manner of revelry.

The first record of Carnevale dates back to 1097, but it was in the 18th century that Venice earned its international reputation as the "city of Carnevale." During that era the partying began after Epiphany (January 6) and transformed the city for over a month into one ongoing, decadent masquerade. After the Republic's fall in 1797, the tradition of Carnevale was abandoned.

Festivities were revived in the 1970s, when locals began taking to the calli and campi for impromptu celebrations as a way to beat the winter doldrums. It wasn't long before events became more elaborate, emulating their 18th-century predecessors (with encouragement from the tourism industry). The trademark feature of present-day Carnevale is the bauta costume, worn by would-be Casanovas (and their would-be conquests).

Many of Carnevale's costume balls are open to the public—but they come with an extravagant price tag, and the most popular of them need to be booked in advance. Balls start at roughly €295 per person, dinner included, and though you can rent a standard costume for €200–€400 (not including shoes or mask), the most elaborate attire can cost much more. *(See "Costumes and Accessories" in the Shopping chapter for resources.)*

Ballo del Doge (☎ 041/5233851 🖷 041/5287543 ⊕ www.ballodeldoge. com) is one of the most exclusive (and expensive) events, held at Palazzo Pisani-Moretta the last Saturday of Carnevale.

See ⊕ www.meetingeurope.com for the **Ballo Tiepolo** (☎ 041/524668 🖷 041/722285), which also takes place in the Tiepolo-frescoed ballroom of Pisani-Moretta—along with many more held in a variety of the city's more lavish palaces.

You don't have to blow the bank on a masquerade ball in order to take part in Carnevale—many people go simply for the exuberant street life. Be aware, though, that the crowds are enormous, and ball or no ball, prices for everything absolutely skyrocket.

Carnevale events and schedules change from year to year. If you want to attend, first check out these resources:

Consorzio Comitato per il Carnevale di Venezia (☎ 041/717065, 041/2510811 during Carnevale ⊕ www.meetingeurope.com) is one of the primary event organizers.

Venezia Marketing & Eventi (⊕ www.carnevale.venezia.it) hosts the official Web site for Carnevale and other events.

The **tourist office** (☎ 041/5298711 ⊕ www.turismovenezia.it) has detailed information about daily events.

A Guest in Venice (⊕ www. aguestinvenice.com) gives free advertising to public and private events, and as a result it's one of the most complete—if potentially overwhelming—Carnevale guides.

shooed away. It's open Thursday through Monday. ⊠ *Fondamenta della Misericordia, Cannaregio 2540* ☎ *041/720581.*

★ At **Teamo** (*te amo* is Italian for "I love you"), owner Gianni has brought a passion for his native region of Friuli and a contemporary aesthetic sense to a San Marco locale. This is today's Venice: young (but not too), sophisticated, and friendly. You can indulge in inventive cicchetti here until 10 PM daily—and even get breakfast starting at 8 AM. Teamo is closed all of August. ⊠ *Rio Terà de la Mandola, San Marco 3795* ☎ *347/3665016* ⊕ *www.teaamo.it* V *Sant'Angelo.*

Nothing special by day, **Torino@notte** is a lively nightspot, often spilling out into the campo in summer. Cocktails, served until 2 AM, include the popular *cubino* (rum and Coke). Snacks are available until 7 PM. ⊠ *Campo San Luca, San Marco 459* ☎ *041/5223914* V *Rialto.*

★ **Venice Jazz Club** hosts the only live jazz concerts in town; €20 gets you a concert, a table, and your first drink. They also serve cold cuts and sandwiches before the music begins at 9 PM. It's best to reserve a table—you can book through the Web site. The club is closed in August. ⊠ *Near Ponte dei Pugni, Dorsoduro 3102* ☎ *041/5232056 or 340/1504985* ⊕ *www.venicejazzclub.com* V *Ca' Rezzonico.*

Zanzibar is a kiosk bar that's very popular on warm summer evenings, especially Friday, when there's live music. Food available is limited to sandwiches and ice cream, but the location along the canal near Chiesa di Santa Maria Formosa makes it a pleasant place to sip a drink. ⊠ *Campo Santa Maria Formosa, Castello 5840* ☎ *347/1460107* V *San Zaccaria.*

PUBS

Fiddler's Elbow, a typical Irish pub (of the Italian variety), serves plenty of Guinness and gab from 5 PM to 1 AM. There are four Irish brews, plus cider, on tap, as well as sports on TV and occasional live music, either Irish or rock. ⊠ *Corte dei Pali off Strada Nova, Cannaregio 3847* ☎ *041/5239930* V *Ca' d'Oro.*

The popular Italo-Irish pub **Innishark,** located midway between San Marco and Rialto, is known for its variety of international beers. It's open until 1:30 AM. ⊠ *Calle Mondo Novo near San Lio, Castello 5787* ☎ *051/5235300* ☉ *Closed Mon.* V *Rialto.*

Senso Unico is a popular neighborhood hangout, decorated in wood and brick with a couple of tables that have a great view of the canal. There are brews on tap and plenty of wine and sandwich choices from 10 AM to 1 AM. ⊠ *Past Campo San Vio before the Guggenheim, Dorsoduro 684* ☎ *348/3720847* ☉ *Closed Tues.* V *Accademia.*

Thirsty sailors can find night moorage at **Sotto Sopra,** a roomy watering hole on two floors decked out like an old ship, with wooden benches, ropes, and brass lamps. Thirty different beers, 20 aged whiskeys, and an assortment of wine should slake the thirst of even the briniest deckhand. It opens at 10 AM weekdays, 5 PM Saturday, and the galley whips up yummy salads, sandwiches, and pasta until 1:30 AM every night. You have to be alert to find the place—there's no sign out front. ⊠ *San Pantalon, Dorsoduro 3740* ☎ *041/5242177* V *San Tomà.*

MIDNIGHT SNACKS

Venice may be a sleepy city, but there are a number of places where you can answer the call of late-night hunger.

Karaoke on weekends and six specialty brews on tap set **Brasserie Vecchia Bruxelles** apart from other late-night eateries. There's no cover charge for table seating or live music; you can get pizza and light entrées until midnight and sandwiches until 2 A.M. ⊠ *Near San Pantalon, Santa Croce 81* ☎ *041/710636.*

For the late-night, chilled-out crowd, **Centrale** is in a former movie theater, with a clientele that looks more Hollywood than Venice. You'll find classic (if overpriced) wines and mojitos and other mixed drinks; black leather couches, dim lighting, and a DJ set the lounge mood. There's occasional live music. ⊠ *Piscina Frezzeria, San Marco 1659/B* ☎ *041/2960664*

★ **Gelateria il Doge** has more than 30 flavors of gelato and several lighter varieties of milk-free sorbet. Try their decadently rich chocolate or the unique *strabon* (Venetian for extra good) made with vanilla, chocolate, and almond brittle. In summer you'll also find refreshing granita that isn't pumped out of a machine. Il Doge stays open until 2 A.M. ⊠ *Campo Santa Margherita, Dorsoduro 3058/A* ☎ *041/5234607* ☸ *Closed Nov.–Feb.*

Tables along a canal and a great atmosphere for catching Italian football matches make **Gibo Bar** a dependable address all year round. Board games and an Internet corner don't encourage fast turnover, but if tables are full you can sit Venetian style on the canal wall while dining on *cicchetti* and sandwiches, served from lunchtime to late at night. ⊠ *Ponte della Donna Onesta, San Polo 2925* ☎ *041/5229969* ☸ *Closed Sun.* ▼ *San Tomà.*

Artsy and upscale **Imagina** keeps well-dressed hipsters happy with aperitifs past midnight. DJs often spin in the back-room art gallery. ⊠ *Campo Santa Margherita, Dorsoduro 3126* ☎ *041/2410625* ▼ *Ca' Rezzonico.*

Impronta is one of the rare locales that has kitchen serving until midnight, and the bar menu is available until 2. It's also a good spot for nightcap—you can expect a fairly lively atmosphere right up until closing time. ⊠ *Calle Crosera, Dorsoduro 3815* ☎ *041/2750386* ▼ *San Tomà.*

The French-sounding name **Margaret Duchamp** befits this café-brasserie with an artfully minimalist decor. Warm sandwiches and light salads take the place of cicchetti, but you won't pay more for the "designer touch." It's open until 2 A.M. ⊠ *Campo Santa Margherita, Dorsoduro 3019* ☎ *041/5286255* ▼ *Ca' Rezzonico.*

NIGHTCAPS

During Carnevale, many ordinary bars, which close around dinnertime the rest of the year, stay open around the clock.

★ **Caffè Florian** opened up in 1720 as Venezia Trionfante (Triumphant Venice) but was soon renamed after its founder, Floriano Francesconi. The café started as a fashionable spot for a hot chocolate, but during the

Austrian domination of Venice it became the favorite meeting place of Italian patriots and intellectuals who boycotted the rival Caffè Quadri across the piazza because of its Austrian military clientele. Stucco, mirrors, wooden carvings, and intimate booths date back to 1859, but the historical atmosphere comes at a price: though an espresso at the bar costs €2, sitting doubles that price, and live music will double it again. Afternoon tea can end up costing as much as a meal. Unlike most cafés, they do take credit cards. ⊠ *Piazza San Marco 56, Procuratie Nuove* ☎ *041/5205641* Ⓥ *Vallaresso.*

Just outside Piazza San Marco (near Museo Correr), Hotel Luna Baglioni's **Caffè Baglioni** is perfect for an intimate chat in the cold winter months. There's live piano (or guitar) music from 6 until midnight Thursday, Friday, and Saturday. ⊠ *Calle Larga de l'Ascension, San Marco 1243* ☎ *041/5289840* Ⓥ *Vallaresso.*

Wander the long calle from Santa Maria Formosa to find the **Enoiteca Mascareta** where you're sure to find the light on. Choose from one of the best wine selections in the city, and even opt for a late-night snack if you prefer. They're closed Wednesday and Thursday, but open until 2 AM other nights. ⊠ *Calle Lurga Santa Maria Formosa, Castello 5138* ☎ *041/5230744* Ⓥ *San Zaccaria.*

DANCE CLUBS

With only one good disco in the historic center, Venice's club scene is rather skimpy. Dedicated dancers are often willing to face long and dangerous drives to reach the celebrated seaside clubs in Rimini and Riccione, south of Venice. On the mainland around Venice, clubs come and go frequently, and their opening hours are often seasonal and unpredictable. If you go to a club in Mestre or Jesolo, you can plan your night so your return to Venice coincides with sunrise over the lagoon, but make sure you check public transportation details before you leave town.

Metallic walls, red leather couches, and theme nights at **Casanova** attract a young and often wild clientele. By day they serve up meals and Internet access; by night, it's dancing and soccer matches on a large-screen TV. ⊠ *Lista di Spagna, Cannaregio 158/A* ☎ *041/2750199.*

CASINOS

The city-run gambling casino in splendid **Palazzo Vendramin-Calergi** is a classic scene of well-dressed high rollers playing French roulette, Caribbean poker, chemin de fer, 30–40, and slots. You must be at least 18 to enter, and men must wear jackets. ⊠ *Cannaregio 2040* ☎ *041/5297111* 🎫 *€10 entry includes €10 in chips* ☉ *Slots daily 2:45 PM–2:30 AM, tables daily 3:30 PM–2:30 AM* Ⓥ *San Marcuola.*

Mestre's **Ca' Noghera** casino, near the airport, has slots, blackjack, craps, poker, and roulette. The minimum age is 18, and there's no dress code. ⊠ *Via Triestina 222, Tessera, Mestre* ☎ *041/5297111* 🎫 *€10 entry includes €10 in chips* ☉ *Slots daily 11 AM–3:30 AM, tables daily 3:30 PM–3:30 AM.*

Shopping in Venice

WORD OF MOUTH

"I walked the length and breadth of Venice, and I found that as one got farther away from San Marco the shopping choices seemed more affordable, more interesting, and less touristy."

—elaine

"We quickly learned if you find something you like somewhere buy it, as you may never find the place again."

—wanderer

Updated by
Nan McElroy

It's no secret that Venice offers some excellent shopping opportunities—but the best of them are often not the most conspicuous. Look beyond the ubiquitous street vendors and the hundreds of virtually indistinguishable purse, glass, and lace shops that line the calli, and you'll discover a bounty of unique and delightful treasures—from kitschy to one-of-a-kind—to fit any budget.

Alluring shops abound. You'll find countless vendors of trademark Venetian wares such as Murano glass and Burano lace; the authenticity of some goods can be suspect, but they're often pleasing to the eye regardless of their heritage. For more sophisticated tastes (and deeper pockets), there are jewelers, antiques dealers, and high-fashion boutiques on a par with those in Italy's larger cities but often maintaining a uniquely Venetian flair. Don't ignore the contemporary, either: Venice's artisan heritage lives on in the hand and eye of the today's designers—no matter where they hail from.

While the labyrinthine city center can seem filled with imposing high-fashion, art-glass, and antiques emporiums, it is the individual craftsmen in quieter parts of town who produce much of what is worth taking home from Venice. In their workshops artful stationery is printed with antique plates; individual pairs of shoes are adroitly constructed; jewelry is handcrafted; fine fabrics are skillfully woven; paper is glued, pressed, and shaped into masks; and gilded cherubs are born from the hands of wood-carvers.

VENICE'S SHOPPING DISTRICTS
PIAZZA SAN MARCO
The rule here is simple: the closer you are to Piazza San Marco, the higher the prices. The serious jewelry and glasswork in the windows of the shops of the Procuratie Vecchie and Nuove make for a pleasant browse; in summer your stroll will be accompanied by the music from the bands that set up in front of Caffè Quadri and Florian. In the shade of the arcades you'll also find an art gallery, old-fashioned shops

selling kitschy souvenirs, and an assortment of lace, linen blouses, silk ties, and scarves.

MERCERIE

The network of streets between the tower clock in Piazza San Marco and Campo San Salvador near Rialto is called the *Mercerie*—from *merce* (goods). For centuries this was where Venetians came to shop, but unfortunately only a few of the more refined, locally operated shops survive. The rest have either closed or abandoned the high rents for other areas of the center—and a run of anonymous clothing stores and souvenir boutiques has taken their place.

Cartier remains on Campo San Zulian, which is always worth a look. One of the three Gucci shops in town is on Merceria dell'Orologio, but its flagship store, which rivals sister shops in Florence and Milan, is on Calle XXII Marzo. For a sweet treat, try Marchini, Venice's most famous chocolate shop, on Calle Spadaria, just parallel to Merceria dell'Orologio. Duca d'Aosta, on Merceria del Capitello, has designer labels for both men and women. Up ahead on Campo San Salvador is La Perla, with lingerie so elegant it could be mistaken for evening wear; the irresistible Max Mara; and Fratelli Rossetti, carrying high-quality leather for your feet.

CAMPO SAN BARTOLOMEO AND RIALTO

The Rialto district is the mecca for buyers of traditional, inexpensive souvenirs: *pantofole del gondoliere,* velvety slippers with rubber soles that resemble the traditional gondoliers' shoes; 18th-century-style wooden trays and coasters that look better after a little wear; and glass "candies," which make a nice, inexpensive (if inedible) gift. Clothing and shoe shops are concentrated between the Rialto Bridge and San Polo, along Ruga Vecchia San Giovanni and Ruga Ravano, and around Campo Sant'Aponal. From the Rialto heading toward Campo Santi Apostoli, you'll find the department store Coin is just past the central post office (they don't close for lunch).

WEST OF PIAZZA SAN MARCO

The area of San Marco sestiere west of the piazza (in the Frezzeria and beyond the Fenice) has a concentration of boutiques, jewelry shops, antiques dealers, and the most important art galleries in the city, including Bugno.

STORE HOURS

Regular store hours are usually 9–12:30 and 3:30 or 4–7:30 PM; some stores are closed Saturday afternoon or Monday morning. Food shops are open 8–1 and 5–7:30, and are closed all day Sunday and Wednesday afternoon. However, many tourist-oriented shops are open all day, every day, especially those in the San Marco area. Some privately owned shops close for both a summer and a winter vacation.

It's always a good idea to mark the location of a shop that interests you on your map; otherwise, you may not be able to find it again in the maze of tiny streets.

TAX REFUNDS

If you make a major purchase, take advantage of tax-free shopping with the value-added tax (V.A.T., or IVA in Italian) refund. On clothing and luxury-goods purchases totaling more than €155 made at a single store, non-EU residents are entitled to get back the up to 20% tax included in the purchase price. *(For details, see "Taxes" in the Travel Smart chapter at the end of this book.)*

ANTIQUES AND ART DEALERS

You probably won't ship home a 19th-century bed from Venice, and even a relatively common item like an art deco chest of drawers is more easily found in Rome, Florence, or Naples. But if you have a taste for odd accessories from another age, Victorian silver plate, prints, or portable antiques with a *je ne sais quoi* to fill an empty corner, you might just find what you weren't even looking for.

DORSODURO

Antichità Pietro Scarpa, next to the Gallerie dell'Accademia, sells old master paintings—originals, not copies—with accordingly rarified prices. ⊠ *Campo della Carità, Dorsoduro 1023/A* ☎ *041/5239700* ⊕ *www. scarpa1953.com* Ⓥ *Accademia.*

Claudia Canestrelli is a tasteful shop with a limited choice of antiques, small paintings, and plenty of interesting-looking bric-a-brac, including silver ex-votos and period souvenirs such as brass ashtrays in the shape of lions' heads. ⊠ *Campiello Barbaro, near the Peggy Guggenheim Collection, Dorsoduro 364/A* ☎ *041/5227072 or 340/5776089* Ⓥ *Accademia or Salute.*

SAN MARCO

Antiquus, a cozy shop from another era, sells a bit of everything, from old master paintings to jewelry. Among the hottest items are the lovely earrings and brooches in the shape of Moors' heads. ⊠ *Calle delle Botteghe, San Marco 3131* ☎ *041/5206395* ⊕ *antiquusvenezia.com* Ⓥ *San Samuele.*

Kleine Galerie is a good address for antique books and prints, majolica, and other ceramics. ⊠ *Calle delle Botteghe, San Marco 2972* ☎ *041/5222177* Ⓥ *San Samuele.*

Luisa Semenzato offers a good selection of furniture, a few paintings by minor masters, and European ceramics, as well as a miscellanea of more-affordable objets d'art, as well as furs. ⊠ *Mercerie San Zulian, San Marco 732* ☎ *041/5231412* ⊕ *luisasemenzato.com* Ⓥ *San Marco.*

ART GALLERIES

Art galleries have become a burgeoning business in Venice. After centuries of commercial slumber, the city seems on its way to finally catching up with the world's contemporary art scene.

CANNAREGIO

Melori & Rosenberg shows established and young Italian artists on their way up, including Luigi Rocca (hyper-realist scenes of modern life), Miria Malandri (views of Venice, portraits, still lifes), and Norberto Moretti (glass designer). ✉ *Campo del Ghetto Nuovo, Cannaregio 2919* ☎ *041/2750039* ⊕ *www.melori-rosenberg.com* Ⓥ *San Marcuola.*

GIUDECCA

Galleria del Leone is run by Pierre Higonnet, a French art dealer specializing in contemporary etching, sculpture, and works on paper. Artists represented include Joan FitzGerald, Mauro Corda, and Serge d'Urach. ✉ *Fondamenta Sant'Eufemia, Giudecca 597* ☎ *041/5288001 or 339/6886954* ⊕ *www.galleriadelleone.com* Ⓥ *Palanca.*

SAN MARCO

Bugno, a retailer of modern and contemporary art along with photography, puts together windows representative of the whole gallery. ✉ *Campo San Fantin, San Marco 1996/D* ☎ *041/5229315* ⊕ *www. bugnoartgallery.it* Ⓥ *Sant'Angelo or San Giglio.*

Caterina Tognon Arte Contemporanea features contemporary visual artists who employ glass as their medium. ✉ *Calle del Dose, San Marco 2746* ☎ *041/5207859* ⊕ *www.caterinatognon.com* Ⓥ *San Giglio.*

Contini shows only 20th-century artists, including such household names as Picasso, Chagall, Magritte, and Giacometti. It's also Italy's only dealer for Botero, Navarro Vires, Zoran Music, and the marble and bronze sculptures by Mitorag. They have another location at Calle Larga XXII Marzo 2288. ✉ *Campo Santo Stefano, San Marco 2765* ☎ *041/5207525 or 041/5204942* ⊕ *www.continiarte.com* Ⓥ *San Marco Valleresso.*

Galleria Ravagnan has been the exclusive dealer since 1967 of some of the most famous living artists on the Italian scene, including Venetian surrealist Ludovico de Luigi and metaphysical painter Andrea Vizzini. You also find glass sculptures by Primo Formenti and collages by Piero Princip. ✉ *Procuratie Nuove, Piazza San Marco 50/A* ☎ *041/5203021* ⊕ *www.ravagnangallery.com* Ⓥ *San Marco.*

Holly Snapp Gallery focuses on the works by the eclectic English-born artist Geoffrey Humphries, including paintings, drawings, and etchings ranging from landscapes to portraits; he also produces watercolors of Venetian vistas. ✉ *Calle delle Botteghe, San Marco 3133* ☎ *328/4592526* ⊕ *www.hollysnappgallery.it* Ⓥ *San Samuele.*

At **Le Sculture di Livio de Marchi,** Signor De Marchi's swift hands turn wood into outstanding full-scale sculptures that perfectly reproduce everyday objects such as hats, laundry hung out to dry, telephones, jackets, books, fruit, lace—even underwear. Prices start at about €80 but can reach four figures. The shop is closed weekends. ✉ *Salizzada San Samuele near Palazzo Grassi, San Marco 3157/A* ☎ *041/5285694* ⊕ *www.liviodemarchi.com* Ⓥ *San Samuele.*

SAN POLO

Scriba, run by a delightful husband-and-wife team, sells exclusive Italian-made crafts, along with maps, fine prints, and paintings by Italian and international artists. ⊠ *Campo dei Frari, San Polo 3030* ☎ *041/5236728* Ⓥ *San Tomà.*

CERAMICS

With so much attention concentrated on Venetian glass, it's not surprising that the city has never been known for its pottery. You can find replicas of 19th-century chocolate cups, usually cream-white and delicately gilded (not for daily use); pottery from Bassano, typically decorated with reliefs of fruit and vegetables; and some modern, handmade plates and mugs.

DORSODURO

★ **Fustat** is the workshop and showroom of Cinzia Cingolani, who creates exquisite handmade pottery. Her keen sense of color and unique forms make each piece a work of art. Raku demonstrations and ceramics courses are also offered. ⊠ *Campo Santa Margherita, Dorsoduro 2904* ☎ *041/5238504* Ⓥ *Ca' Rezzonico.*

SAN MARCO

Angela Greco, a must for lovers of antique ceramics, has affordable items such as replicas of 19th-century Venetian chocolate cups. ⊠ *Campo Santa Maria del Giglio, San Marco 2433* ☎ *041/5234573* Ⓥ *Santa Maria del Giglio.*

SANTA CROCE

Margherita Rossetto creates deliciously appealing faience-style majolica on a white background, with figures of animals, flowers, and fruit designed in oxidized copper. ⊠ *Sotoportego della Siora Bettina off Campo San Cassiano, Santa Croce 2345* ☎ *041/723120* ⊕ *www.lamargheritavenezia.com* Ⓥ *San Stae or Rialto.*

CLOTHING

Venice's streets are lined with so many designer stores and tiny, pricey boutiques that you may wonder how Venetians can afford to keep themselves clothed. (They head to markets and the mainland for the bulk of their shopping, that's how.) The best prices are to be had during the semiannual sale periods, January 7 until mid-February and July to early September.

SAN MARCO

Fodor's Choice ★ At **Araba Fenice Venezia** you'll find impeccable, original, classic day and evening wear along with stylish, novel jewelry; making a purchase here means you'll be going home with something unique. Even if you're not looking to buy, at least stop by to take in the shop window display. ⊠ *Calle de le Barcaroli (Frezzeria), San Marco 1822* ☎ *041/5200664* Ⓥ *San Marco Vallaresso.*

Camiceria San Marco is the town's top custom shirtmaker, counting Hemmingway and the Duke of Windsor among its former customers. Only the finest fabrics are used (they can also be bought by the meter). As

Colorful fabrics are among Venice's trademark wares.

well as elegant, made-to-measure shirts, they also make blouses, pajamas, gowns, and ladies' dresses. ⊠ *Calle Vallaresso, San Marco 1340* ☎ *041/5221432* ⊕ *www.camiceriasanmarco.it* Ⓥ *San Marco.*

Fiorella Mancini Gallery is your best bet for original creations and the craziest looks in town. ⊠ *Campo Santo Stefano, San Marco 2806* ☎ *041/5209228* Ⓥ *Accademia or San Samuele.*

La Coupole, with three shops a stone's throw from one another, offers an excellent selection of name-brand *alta moda* (high fashion) for men, women, and children. ⊠ *Calle Larga XXII Marzo, San Marco 2366* ☎ *041/5224243* ⊠ *Calle Larga XXII Marzo, San Marco 2414* ☎ *041/2960555* ⊠ *Calle Larga XXII Marzo, San Marco 2254* ☎ *041/5231273* Ⓥ *San Marco.*

SAN POLO
Kirikù is the place for trendy children's wear, with all the latest names for boys and girls, from infants to early teens. It may make you wish you were still a kid. ⊠ *Calle de la Madoneta, San Polo 1465* ☎ *041/2960619* Ⓥ *San Silvestro.*

MEN'S FASHIONS
CASTELLO
Ceriello is the only place in town selling Brioni suits. ⊠ *Campo SS. Filippo e Giacomo, Castello 4275* ☎ *041/5222062* Ⓥ *San Zaccaria.*

Élite is the source for not-so-casual Italian outdoor wear as well as the quintessentially English Aquascutum coats that so many Italians favor. Silk ties and cashmere scarves complete the English country look. ⊠ *Calle Larga San Marco, San Marco 284* ☎ *041/5230145* Ⓥ *San Marco.*

WOMEN'S FASHIONS

CANNAREGIO

Le Ragazze di Cima carries the best Italian brands of lingerie, from glossy silk to cotton lace. ⊠ *Strada Nova near Ponte San Felice, Cannaregio 3683* ☏ *041/5234988* ⊕ *www.cimaboutique.it* Ⓥ *Ca' d'Oro.*

CASTELLO

Fodor's Choice
★ **Barbieri-Arabesque** has scarves and shawls for women in myriad colors and textures; you can also pick up fine men's ties while you're here. They've been in business since 1945. ⊠ *Ponte dei Greci, Castello 3403* ☏ *041/5228177* Ⓥ *San Zaccaria.*

DORSODURO

Arras sells exclusive scarves as well as a few blouses and jackets, all hand woven in wool or silk. It also occasionally organizes weaving workshops. ⊠ *Campiello Squellini, Dorsoduro 3234* ☏ *041/5226460* Ⓥ *Ca' Rezzonico.*

SAN MARCO

You need only step off the vaporetto to find tiny **Boutique Marly's,** which has a highly appealing collections of classic Italian women's wear. ⊠ *Calle Vallaresso, San Marco 1321* ☏ *041/5203851* Ⓥ *San Marco.*

Caberlotto has cornered the market on fabulous fur coats and hats. They sell interesting wool blazers and pashmina shawls by Rosenda Arcioni Meer, along with a complete line of luxurious cashmere clothing. ⊠ *Larga Mazzini, San Marco 5114* ☏ *041/5229242* ⊕ *www.caberfurs.com* Ⓥ *Rialto.*

At **Godi Fiorenza,** Patrizia Fiorenza's designs in silk chiffon appear more sculpted than sewn—they're highly tailored pieces that both conceal and expose. Her sister Samatha is a jewelry designer and silversmith whose unique pieces compliment any outfit. ⊠ *Rio Terà San Paternian, San Marco 4261* ☏ *041/2410866* ⊕ *www.fiorenzadesign.com* Ⓥ *Rialto.*

La Perla specializes in extremely elegant lingerie that's comfortable, too. ⊠ *Campo San Salvador, San Marco 4828* ☏ *041/5226459* Ⓥ *Rialto.*

Malo is recognized as one of Italy's highest-quality producers of cashmere garments. Its styles are tasteful and refined, designed and made to be worn for many years. ⊠ *Calle de le Ostreghe, San Marco 2359* ☏ *041/5232162* Ⓥ *San Marco or Santa Maria del Giglio.*

SAN POLO

★ **Hibiscus** is an explosion of colors and textures. The clothing here is ethnic-chic and definitely original. Accessories are eye-catching as well. ⊠ *Calle dell'Olio near the Rialto Market, San Polo 1060* ☏ *041/5208989* Ⓥ *Rialto.*

Valeria Bellinaso designs expensive, attractive straw hats, perfect for a romantic spring gondola ride. The store also features shawls full of character and foldable silk bags that are light as a feather yet large enough to pack for the weekend. ⊠ *Campo Sant'Aponal, San Polo 1226* ☏ *041/5223351* Ⓥ *San Silvestro.*

Zazù clothing and accessories have a definite Eastern feel. Owner Federica Zamboni is also a jewelry expert; ask to see her collection of

6

antique Indian necklaces and earrings. ⊠ *Calle dei Saoneri, San Polo 2750* ☏ *041/715426* Ⓥ *San Tomà.*

COSTUMES AND ACCESSORIES

CANNAREGIO

At **Laboratorio Parrucche Carlotta,** wig maker Carlotta Carisi believes that at Carnevale details count, and her sensational creations are the ideal way to top off an elegant costume. The quality comes at a price (€230–€500), and credit cards are not accepted. ⊠ *Campo Widman, Cannaregio 5415* ☏ *041/5207571* Ⓥ *Ca' d'Oro.*

Nicolao Atelier has outfitted many a period film (including *Casanova*), and is the largest costume-rental showroom in town. They have nearly 7,000 choices ranging from the historical to the fantastic, including thematic costumes ideal for group masquerades. By appointment only. ⊠ *Fondamenta Misericordia, Cannaregio 2590* ☏ *041/5207051* ⊕ *www.nicolao.com* Ⓥ *Ca d'Oro.*

CASTELLO

Flavia is a good address for historical costumes, either made-to-order or for rent; you can also rent tuxedos all year round. When you walk into the shop, ask for either Adriano or Susan, both of whom speak flawless English, to take you to the atelier nearby. ⊠ *Near Campo San Lio, Castello 6010* ☏ *041/2413200 or 041/5287429* ⊕ *www.veniceatelier. com* Ⓥ *Rialto.*

SAN MARCO

At **Venetia** the colorful, fanciful display window of 18th-century Venetian outfits often makes passersby stop to admire the mannequins. Less-glamorous medieval-style garments, masks, and accessories are kept behind the curtains inside. ⊠ *Frezzeria, San Marco 1286* ☏ *041/5224426* Ⓥ *San Marco.*

SAN POLO

Atelier Pietro Longhi rents and sells costumes inspired by 18th- and 19th-century models, with masks (for sale only) to match. Large sizes are available for both sexes. ⊠ *Campiello Zen (near the Frari), San Polo 2580* ☏ *041/714478* ⊕ *www.pietrolonghi.com* Ⓥ *San Tomà.*

If you are making your own costume, Monica Daniele at **Laboratorio Arte & Costume** can offer you professional sartorial assistance while you browse hundreds of hats, bags, and vintage clothing. ⊠ *Calle del Scaleter near Campo San Polo, San Polo 2235* ☏ *041/5246242* Ⓥ *San Tomà.*

DEPARTMENT STORES

The upscale chain department store **Coin** has managed to settle into one of Venice's largest storefronts. ⊠ *Salizzada San Crisostomo near Campo San Bartolomio, Cannaregio 5787* ☏ *041/5203581* Ⓥ *Rialto.*

ENGLISH-LANGUAGE BOOKS

Venice, unlike Rome or Florence, does not have an English-language bookstore. However, some places carry small selections of books in English. For newspapers and magazines in English, the best-stocked newsstands are in San Marco near the Museo Correr or at the foot of the Accademia bridge.

DORSODURO

Ca' Foscarina, the bookstore of Università di Venezia Ca' Foscari, has a reasonable selection of books in English. Shelves teem with literature and history, but there's also a handful of travel books, as well as the latest best sellers. ⊠ *Campiello Squellini, Dorsoduro 3259* ☎ *041/5229602* Ⓥ *Ca' Rezzonico.*

Libreria San Pantalon sells children's books (some in English), small arts and crafts, and books on music and opera (in Italian). ⊠ *Crosera, also known as Calle Lunga San Pantalon, Dorsoduro 3950* ☎ *041/5224436* Ⓥ *San Tomà.*

SAN MARCO

Fantoni specializes in coffee-table books on art, architecture, photography, and design, mostly in Italian, but the beautiful illustrations speak for themselves. You'll find books in English on Venice and Italian food. ⊠ *Off Campo San Luca, San Marco 4119* ☎ *041/5220700* Ⓥ *Rialto or Sant'Angelo.*

Libreria Mondadori, Venice's answer to Barnes & Noble, is the biggest bookstore in town, with three floors of reading material. There is a large selection of English-language titles. ⊠ *Salizada San Mois, San Marco 1345* ☎ *041/5222193* ⊕ *www.libreriamondadorivenezia. it* Ⓥ *San Marco.*

Studium is a good stop for books in English, especially guidebooks and books on Venetian culture and food. It's also particularly strong on English-language fiction with Italian, mostly Venetian, settings and themes; in addition, it has a small but worthy collection of recent hardcover fiction. ⊠ *Calle della Canonica, San Marco 337/C* ☎ *041/5222382* Ⓥ *San Marco.*

GIFTS

CANNAREGIO

Fusetti Diego Baruch has all manner of handmade Jewish handicrafts, including copies of antique menorahs, in glass, bronze, gold, silver, and mosaic. It's closed Saturday. ⊠ *Ghetto Vecchio, Cannaregio 1218* ☎ *041/720092* ⊕ *www.shalomvenice.com* Ⓥ *Guglie.*

La Stamperia del Ghetto sells black-and-white prints of the old Ghetto. It's closed Saturday. ⊠ *Calle del Ghetto Vecchio, Cannaregio 1185/A* ☎ *041/2750200* Ⓥ *San Marcuola or Guglie.*

CASTELLO

You'll want to peruse every pleasing piece in tiny **Mionsu** to decide which necklace, earring, purse, or sculpture might be just the thing. Proprietor Susanna Mion promotes works of a small group of contemporary

artists, much of it in glass. ⊠ *Fondamenta dei Preti, Castello 5844* ☏ *041/2410827* Ⓥ *Rialto or San Zaccaria.*

DORSODURO

At **Madera**, craftswoman and architect Francesca Meratti and a team of local and international artisans combine traditional and contemporary design to create a mix of most appealing objects, including dishware, carved wooden bowls, jewelry, and ceramic pieces. ⊠ *Campo San Barnaba, Dorsoduro 2762* ☏ *041/5224181* ⊕ *www.maderavenezia.it* Ⓥ *Ca'Rezzonico.*

Signor Blum makes solid, large-piece jigsaw puzzles (painted or in natural wood colors) depicting animals, views of Venice, and trompe l'oeil scenes. Ideal for toddlers, the puzzles also look nice hanging on a wall. ⊠ *Fondamenta Gherardini off Campo San Barnaba, Dorsoduro 2840* ☏ *041/5226367* ⊕ *www.signorblum.com* Ⓥ *Ca' Rezzonico.*

SAN MARCO

Giuliana Longo is a hat shop that's been around since 1901; it even has a special corner dedicated to accessories for antique cars. You could also use the leather goggles and helmets for skiing. ⊠ *Calle del Lovo, San Marco 4813* ☏ *041/5226454* ⊕ *www.giulianalongo.com* Ⓥ *San Marco.*

Artists Maddalena Venier and Alessandro Salvadori of **Materialmente** envision "balancing the precious with the everyday." They succeed with a fascinating collection of fanciful, light-as-air sculpture, lamps, jewelry, and house wares. ⊠ *Mercerie San Salvador, San Marco 5844* ☏ *041/5286881* ⊕ *www.materialmente.it* Ⓥ *Rialto.*

Perle Veneziane, two minutes from Piazza San Marco, fits the bill when you've got last-minute gifts to buy. There's an assortment of necklaces, faux-period Venetian glass jewelry, and loose modern beads, along with *murrine* (pour tops for olive oil bottles), and an assortment of other glass curios. ⊠ *Ponte della Canonica, San Marco 4308* ☏ *041/5289059* Ⓥ *San Marco.*

SAN POLO

Il Baule Blu specializes in *orsi artistici,* teddy bears to collect and treat with great care. Painstakingly handmade in many sizes and colors with articulated paws and glass eyes, when squeezed they can either grumble or play a carillon tune. Some are stark naked; others are dressed in old baby garments trimmed with lace and ribbons. ⊠ *Calle Prima off Campo San Tomà, San Polo 2916/A* ☏ *041/719448* Ⓥ *San Tomà.*

The Japanese aesthetic is quite apparent at **Sabbie e Nebbie** in artist-owner Maria Theresa Laghi and her collaborators' ceramic and porcelain bowls, plates, vases, and teapots with inviting clean, natural lines and muted colors. Her silk scarves are just as appealing. ⊠ *Calle de le Nomboli, San Polo 2768/A* ☏ *041/719073* Ⓥ *San Tomà.*

GLASS

Glass, most of it made in Murano, is Venice's trademark product: you can't avoid encountering a mind-boggling variety of it in shop windows, often in kitschy displays. Take your time and be selective. If you want to make an investment, the important producers to remember are Barovier,

Pauly, Poli, Seguso, Toso, and Venini. Freelance designers create pieces for more than just a single glasshouse: look for signatures and certificates of authentication. Bear in mind that the value of any piece—signature and shape apart—is also based on the number and quality of colors, the presence of gold, and, in the case of goblets, the thinness of the glass. Prices are about the same all over, but be warned that some shops sell glass made in Taiwan. All shops will arrange for shipping.

CANNAREGIO

Do Maghi means "two magicians," but in fact there's only one at work here, Hans Peter Neidhardt, who despite his name is a native Venetian and has been making glass since 1982. Though he's clearly cognizant of the Murano tradition, he injects humor and whimsy into his creations, from his goldfish in bowls to single long-stemmed red roses. ⊠ *Calle Dolfin, Cannaregio 5621* ☎ *041/5208535* ⊕ *www.domaghi. com* Ⓥ *Ca' d'Oro.*

Gianfranco Penzo decorates Jewish ritual vessels in glass and makes commemorative plates. He takes special orders. ⊠ *Campo del Ghetto Nuovo, Cannaregio 2895* ☎ *No phone* Ⓥ *Ferrovia Santa Lucia.*

CASTELLO

Al Campanil specializes in replicas of antique Murano pieces and jewelry made with tiny glass Venetian beads. The jewelry designer here, Sabina, is a teacher at the International School of Glass on Murano. ⊠ *Calle Lunga Santa Maria Formosa, Castello 5184* ☎ *041/5235734* Ⓥ *Rialto.*

DORSODURO

Antichità Zaggia displays fascinating period objects made with the tiniest Murano glass beads "woven" on linen threads, as well as more-modern creations, all crafted with the same antique beads. You can also purchase small quantities of antique beads for making your own jewelry. ⊠ *Calle della Toletta, Dorsoduro 1195* ☎ *041/5223159* Ⓥ *Accademia.*

Genninger Studio is the retail outlet for Leslie Ann Genninger, an American from Ohio who was the first woman to enter the male-dominated world of Murano master bead makers. She established her own line of jewelry, called Murano Class Act, in 1994 using period glass beads, and when she could no longer find antique beads she started designing her own. ⊠ *Campiello Barbaro, Dorsoduro 364* ☎ *041/5225565* Ⓥ *Accademia.*

★ **Marina and Susanna Sent** have had their glass jewelry featured in *Vogue.* Vases and design pieces are also exceptional. ⊠ *Campo San Vio, Dorsoduro 669* ☎ *041/5208136* Ⓥ *Accademia.*

MURANO

Berengo Studio sells contemporary fine-art glass and is a rare high-end manufacturer that gives tours of its Murano factory. ⊠ *Fondamenta Vetrai, Murano 109/A* ☎ *041/739453* ⊕ *www.berengo.com.*

Domus has a selection of smaller objects and jewelry from the best glassworks. ⊠ *Fondamenta dei Vetrai, Murano 82* ☎ *041/739215.*

Venice's Signature Crafts: Glass

A furnace in Murano.

Perhaps it's a matter of character that Venice, a city whose beauty depends so much upon the effects of shimmering, reflected light, also developed glass—a material that seems to capture light in solid form—as an artistic and expressive medium. There's not much in the way of a practical explanation for the affinity, since the materials used to make glass, even from earliest days, have not been found in the Venetian lagoon. They've had to be imported, frequently with great difficulty and expense.

Glass production in the city dates back to the earliest days of the Republic; evidence of a seventh- or eighth-century glass factory has been found on Torcello. Glass was already used as an artistic medium, employing techniques imported from Byzantine and Islamic glassmakers, by the 11th century. You can see surviving examples of early Venetian glass in the tiles of the mosaics of San Marco.

By 1295 the secrets of Venetian glassmaking were so highly prized that glassmakers were forbidden to leave the city. Venice succeeded in keeping the formulas of Venetian glass secret until the late 16th century, when some renegades started production in Bohemia. In 1291, to counter the risk of fire in Venice proper, Venetian glass furnaces were moved to the then underpopulated island of Murano, which has remained the center of Venetian glassmaking up to the present day.

The fall of Damascus in 1400 and of Constantinople in 1435 sent waves of artisans to Venice, who added new techniques and styles to the repertoire of Venetian glass factories, but the most important innovation was developed by a native Venetian, Angelo Barovier. In the mid-15th century he discovered a way of making pure, transparent glass, *cristallo veneziano.* This allowed for the development of further decorative techniques, such as filigree glass, which became mainstays of Venetian glass production.

Angelo Barovier's company, now called Barovier e Toso, still exists today—it is among the oldest continually operating firms in the world. It

Glass candies, a unique (and inedible) Venetian treat.

6

and such "newcomers" as Cenadese, Venini, Seguso, Pauly, Salviati, Moretti, and Berengo make up the premium line of Venetian glass production. These firms all have factories and showrooms on Murano, but they also have showrooms in Venice. While their more elaborate pieces can cost thousands of dollars, you can take home a modest but lovely piece baring one of their prestigious signatures for about $100, or even less.

Venice and Murano are full of shops selling glass, of varying taste and quality. Some of it is made on the Venetian mainland, or even in Eastern Europe or China. Many minor producers on Murano now have formed a consortium and identify their pieces with a sticker, which guarantees that the piece was made on Murano. The premium glass manufacturers, however, do not belong to the consortium—so the sticker guarantees only where the piece was made, not necessarily its quality or value.

On Murano you can visit a factory and watch Venetian glass being made, but among the premium manufacturers only Berengo allows visitors to its factory. If you go to a minor factory, you'll generally get an adequate demonstration of Venetian glassmaking, but expect a high-pressure sales pitch at the end. Berengo, on the other hand, is quite dedicated to educating the public about glass, and their excellent demonstrations of glass making are not part of a sales promotion.

The major Venetian glass producers are now distributed worldwide, and the prices you will pay at home is about what you will pay in Venice. But in Venice the selection is much greater. Also, some showrooms offer discontinued models that you won't find elsewhere at a substantial discount—but you have to ask. Because glass is a Venetian passion and central to Venetian culture, antique pieces and even vintage pieces from the 1920s to the '60s by the major producers are quickly bought up by locals, and the prices are actually higher for them in Venice than elsewhere.

SAN MARCO

L'Isola has chic, contemporary glassware signed by Carlo Moretti. ⊠ *Campo San Moisè, San Marco 1468* ☎ *041/5231973* ⊕ *www. carlomoretti.com*

★ **Ma.Re** sells Salviati glass, as well as other blown and solid glass. It also sells one-of-a-kind objects by leading glass artists. ⊠ *Via XXII Marzo, San Marco 2088* ☎ *041/5231191* ⎙ *041/5285745* ⊕ *www.mareglass. com* Ⓥ *San Marco.*

Marina Barovier's Gallery has an excellent selection of collectible contemporary glass. She's the exclusive Venice dealer of famous glass artists such as Lino Tagliapietra, Dale Chihuly, and Ettore Sottsass. ⊠ *Calle delle Botteghe off Campo Santo Stefano, San Marco 3216* ☎ *041/5236748* ⎙ *041/2447042* ⊕ *www.barovier.it* Ⓥ *San Samuele.*

Paropàmiso sells stunning Venetian glass beads and jewelry from all over the world. ⊠ *Frezzeria, San Marco 1701* ☎ *041/5227120.*

★ **Pauly & C,** established in 1866, features a truly impressive selection of authentic Murano art glass (both traditional and contemporary styles) by the most accomplished masters—and at better prices than on the island. The showroom at No. 73 houses the more traditional collection; at No. 77 you can find works by artists and designers. ⊠ *Piazza San Marco 73 and 77, San Marco* ☎ *041/5235484 or 041/2770279* ⊕ *www.pauly.it.*

Tre Erre is a reliable and respected firm for both traditional and contemporary glass designs. ⊠ *Piazza San Marco 79/B* ☎ *041/5201715* Ⓥ *San Marco.*

Venini has been an institution since the 1930s, attracting some of the foremost names in glass design. Visit their Web site to see a series of glass artisans in action. For a more refined experience and to see some of their best offerings, visit the **Venini Showroom** (⊠ *Fondamenta Vetrai 47* ☎ *041/2737211*). ⊠ *Piazzetta dei Leoncini 314* ☎ *041/5224045* ⊕ *www.venini.com.*

SAN POLO

★ At **Angolo del Passato,** Giordana Naccari collects 20th-century glassware and produces her own intriguing cups, plates, and pitchers at prices that are quite accessible. ⊠ *Campiello dei Squelini, Dorsoduro 3276* ☎ *041/5287896.*

GOLD, WOOD, AND METALWORK

Venice's passion for glittering golden objects, which began with the decoration in the Basilica di San Marco and later spread into the finest noble homes, kept specialized gold artisans (called *doradori*) busy throughout the city's history. They still produce lovely cabinets, shelves, wall lamps, lanterns, candleholders, banisters, headboards, frames, and the like by applying gold leaf to wrought iron and carved wood. Numerous skilled silversmiths still cater to the faithful; in their workshops you'll find silver devotional icons of the Madonna della Salute and of the Madonna Nicopeia, traditionally hung in Venetian bedrooms.

Le Forcole de Saviero Pastor preserves the Venetian craft of handmade gondola oars and oarlocks.

Most foundries have long since closed their doors, but you can still find top-quality brass pieces at Valese Fonditore.

CANNAREGIO

Giora is a workshop and showroom for lamp shades, handmade ornaments, and gilded mirrors. ⊠ *Campo Santa Maria Nova, Cannaregio 6043/B* ☎ *041/5286098* Ⓥ *Rialto.*

CASTELLO

Jonathan Ceolin makes traditional wrought-iron chandeliers, wall lamps, and Venetian lanterns, either plain black or gilded (like in the old days), in his tiny workshop near Campo Santa Maria Formosa. ⊠ *Ponte Marcello off Campo Santa Marina, Castello 6106* ☎ *041/5200609* ⊕ *www. ceolinjonathan.com* Ⓥ *Rialto.*

Luca Sumiti carries on the work of his father, Maurizio; traditional wrought-iron chandeliers and lamps come unadorned, gilded, or tastefully enameled in bright colors. Here you'll also find conspicuous, 5-foot-tall wooden sculptures of *mori veneziani* (Venetian Moors). ⊠ *Calle delle Bande, Castello 5274* ☎ *041/5205621* Ⓥ *Rialto or San Marco.*

DORSODURO

Cornici Trevisanello has Byzantine and rich Renaissance handcrafted frames, made of gold-leafed wood and inset with antique glass beads, mosaic tesserae, and small ceramic tiles. More-elaborate pieces are at their best when used to frame an old mirror. ⊠ *Fondamenta Bragadin off Campo San Vio, Dorsoduro 662* ☎ *041/5207779* Ⓥ *Accademia.*

Fodor'sChoice ★ **Le Forcole di Saverio Pastor** sells the sculpted walnut-wood oarlocks *(forcole)* used exclusively by Venetian rowers. Though utilitarian, forcole are beautiful, custom-made objects that make for uniquely Venetian gifts or souvenirs. Saverio Pastor (along with Paolo Brandolisio) is one of the few remaining oar and *forcola* makers left in Venice. ⊠ *Fondamenta Soranzo, Dorsoduro 341* ☎ *041/5225699* ⊕ *www.forcole.com* Ⓥ *Salute.*

SAN MARCO

Valese Fonditore has been casting brass, bronze, copper, and pewter into artistic handles, menorahs, Carnevale masks, and real gondola decorations (which make great paperweights, bookends, or shelf pieces) since 1913. The coups de grâce are the brass chandeliers, exactly like those that hang in the Oval Office in the White House. Open daily, but call to arrange a visit for when they pour. ⊠ *Shop: Calle Fiubera, San Marco 793* ☎ *041/5227282* Ⓥ *San Marco* ⊠ *Foundry: near Madonna dell'Orto, Cannaregio 3535* ☎ *041/720234* Ⓥ *San Marcuola.*

SAN POLO

Gilberto Penzo is the gondola and lagoon boat expert in Venice. He creates scale models and real gondola *forcole* in his *laboratorio* (workshop) nearby. (If the retail shop is closed, a sign posted on the door will explain how to find Signor Penzo.) When he's not busy sawing and sanding, Mr. Penzo writes historical and technical books about gondola building. Here you'll also find gondola model kits, a great gift for the boatbuilder in your life. ⊠ *Calle Seconda dei Saoneri, San Polo 2681* ☎ *041/719372* ⊕ *www.veniceboats.com* Ⓥ *San Tomà.*

JEWELRY

Venetians have always liked gold, and the city is packed with top-of-the-line jewelry stores, as well as more-modest shops found outside the San Marco area, most notably around the Rialto district. One of the most typical pieces of inexpensive jewelry that you can buy is a *murrina*, a thin, round slice of colored glass (imagine a bunch of colored spaghetti firmly held together and sliced) encircled with gold and sold as pendants or earrings. The Museo del Vetro at Murano does a good job of explaining how they're made.

DORSODURO

Gualti makes creative earrings, broaches, and necklaces in colored resin that looks as fragile as glass but is as strong and soft as rubber. Silk shoes can be custom "garnished" with jewelry. ⊠ *Rio Terà Canal near Campo Santa Margherita, Dorsoduro 3111* ☎ *041/5201731* ⊕ *www.gualti.it* Ⓥ *Ca' Rezzonico.*

SAN MARCO

Bastianello has classic jewelry as well as pieces made with semiprecious stones. ⊠ *Via Due Aprile off Campo San Bartolomio, San Marco 5042* ☎ *041/5226751* Ⓥ *Rialto.*

Missiaglia is a landmark in Piazza San Marco, selling fabulous jewelry and a few silver accessories. ⊠ *Procuratie Vecchie, San Marco 125* ☎ *041/5224464* Ⓥ *San Marco.*

Nardi sells exquisite *moretti*—earrings and brooches in the shape of Moors' heads—studded with diamonds, rubies, or emeralds. ⊠ *Under*

Procuratie Nuove, San Marco 69 ☏ *041/5225733* ⊕ *www.nardi-venezia.com* Ⓥ *San Marco.*

Pomellato is a leading Italian designer, with shops also in Rome and Milan. ⊠ *Calle Seconda dell'Ascensione, San Marco 1298* ☏ *041/5201048* Ⓥ *San Marco.*

Salvadori specializes in watches but also has sparkling diamonds and other precious stones set in its own designs. ⊠ *Merceria San Salvador, San Marco 5022* ☏ *041/5230609* ⊕ *www.salvadori-venezia.com* Ⓥ *Rialto.*

SAN POLO

At **Attrombi**, celebrated brothers Daniele and Stefano blend and weave copper and silver wire with Murano glass beads to render stylish, contemporary pieces with a timeless feel. There's a second location in San Marco. ⊠ *Sottoportego degli Oresi, San Polo 74* ☏ *041/5212524* ⊕ *www.attombri.com* Ⓥ *Rialto Mercato or Rialto* ⊠ *Campo San Maurizio, San Marco 2668/A* ☏ *041/5210789.*

Laberintho is a tiny *bottega* near Campo San Polo run by a team of young goldsmiths and jewelry designers specializing in inlaid stones. The work on display in their shop is exceptional, and they also create customized pieces. ⊠ *Calle del Scaleter, San Polo 2236* ☏ *041/710017* ⊕ *www.laberintho.it* Ⓥ *San Stae or San Tomà.*

LACE, LINEN, AND PRECIOUS FABRICS

CASTELLO

G. Scarpa is an old-fashioned shop with no dressing room: you'll have to make do in a tiny corner behind a folding screen. Its top-of-the-line silk lace shirts, from €40 to €50, are well worth the trouble, as are the lace cooking aprons. ⊠ *Campo San Zaccaria, Castello 4683* ☏ *041/5287883* Ⓥ *San Zaccaria.*

DORSODURO

Annelie has a lovely selection of everything from tablecloths to baby clothing along with shirts, nightgowns, and towels—from Venice and beyond. Ask to see antique lace. ⊠ *Calle Lunga San Barnaba, Dorsoduro 2748* ☏ *041/5203277* Ⓥ *Ca' Rezzonico.*

★ **Capricci e Vanità,** a small shop near the Church of San Pantalon, is where owner and lace-lover Signora Giovanna Gamba sells her wonderful authentic Burano lace. She specializes in tablecloths and lingerie made on the bobbin as well as more rare and precious pieces made with a needle in the extra-light Burano stitch. ⊠ *Calle San Pantalon, Dorsoduro 3744* ☏ *041/5231504* Ⓥ *San Tomà.*

GIUDECCA

Fortuny Tessuti Artistici is the original Fortuny textile factory, now converted into a showroom. Prices are over-the-top at €150 a meter, but it's worth a trip to see the extraordinary colors and textures of their hand-printed silks and velvets. ⊠ *Fondamenta San Biagio, Giudecca 805* ☏ *041/5224078* Ⓥ *Palanca.*

Venice's Signature Crafts: Lace

A piece of delicate Burano lace.

The craft of weaving brocades, damasks, and velvets is still very much alive in Venice, with top manufacturers catering to royal courts, theaters, and the movie industry. At the time of the tourist boom in the 1980s, the descendants of underpaid embroiderers opened up fine lace and handicraft boutiques. Prices range from €120 per meter for old-style fabrics woven on power looms to €1,500 per meter for handmade silk velvets of unparalleled softness and beauty.

On the lower end of the price range are striking lampas, brocades, and damasks, which come in different floral and striped patterns as well as solid colors. Sometimes the fabrics are hand dyed after they've been woven to obtain mellow watercolor effects. It's always worth inquiring about sales for discontinued designs—you might want to give a Venetian look to your favorite reading chair.

Although most of the lace sold in town is machine made in China or Taiwan, you can still find something that more closely resembles the real thing in the best shops. Surprisingly, period lace (made between 1900 and 1940) is easier to find and less expensive than contemporary lace, even though the former is a finer product, made *ad ago* (with the needle), while the latter is made with thicker threads or *a fusello* (with the bobbin).

At the Museo del Merletto (Lace-Making Museum) in Burano you get an idea of how lace once looked. Despite the reopening of the Scuola del Merletto (Lace-Making School), lace makers no longer sell their creations in shops, but older ones might accept jobs on commission. The best way to contact them is to ask around in Burano (they object to having their names advertised), but consider that a 10-inch doily takes about 400 hours to make, and the price will show it.

SAN MARCO

★ **Bevilacqua** has kept the weaving tradition alive in Venice since 1875, using 18th-century hand looms for its most precious creations. Its repertoire of 3,500 different patterns and designs yields a ready-to-sell selection of hundreds of brocades, Gobelins, damasks, velvets, taffetas, and satins. You'll also find tapestry, cushions, and braiding. Fabrics made by this prestigious firm have been used to decorate the Vatican, the Royal Palace of Stockholm, and the White House. ⊠ *Campo di Santa Maria del Giglio, San Marco 2520* ☎ *041/2410662* Ⓥ *Giglio* ✉ *Fondamenta della Canonica, San Marco 337/B* ☎ *041/5287581* ⊕ *www.luigi-bevilacqua.com* Ⓥ *San Marco* ⊠ *Factory: Campiello della Comare, Santa Croce 1320* ☎ *041/721576* ☾ *Visits by appointment only* Ⓥ *Riva di Biasio.*

Frette sells high-quality sheets and bath towels—lace and embroidery are machine-made, but the general effect is nonetheless luxurious and elegant. ⊠ *Calle Larga XXII Marzo, San Marco 2070/A* ☎ *041/5224914* ⊕ *www.frette.com* Ⓥ *San Marco.*

You need to ring the bell to be admitted inside **Gaggio,** one of Venice's most prestigious fabric shops. Bedcovers, cushions, tapestry, and the like are available, plus a line of delightful small bags made in silk velvet with dark wooden frames. The colors of the fabric are never garish—they tend toward mellow autumn tones. ⊠ *Calle delle Botteghe near Campo Santo Stefano, San Marco 3451* ☎ *041/5228574* ⊟ *041/5228958* ⊕ *www.gaggio.it* Ⓥ *Sant'Angelo or San Samuele.*

The best of Burano's renowned lace-making tradition is rarely represented by the examples you'll see on display. However, at **Il Merletto,** you can ask for the authentic, handmade lace safeguarded in drawers behind the counter. This is the only place in Venice connected with the students of the Scuola del Merletto in Burano, who, officially, do not sell to the public. Hours of operation are daily 10 to 5. ⊠ *Sotoportego del Cavalletto under the Procuratie Vecchie, Piazza San Marco 95* ☎ *041/5208406.*

Jesurum, Venice's top name for lace and embroidered linen for over 130 years, has a flagship store in San Marco. Dreamy gowns and nightshirts, sheets, bedcovers, and towels are ready to buy or custom made-to-order. ⊠ *Calle Larga XXII Marzo, San Marco 2401* ☎ *041/5238969* ⊕ *www.jesurum.it.*

La Fenice Atelier sells attractive lace nightdresses and handwoven bath towels at affordable prices. ⊠ *Calle dei Frati, down the bridge on Campo Sant'Angelo, San Marco 3537* ☎ *041/5230578* Ⓥ *Sant'Angelo.*

Lorenzo Rubelli, founded in 1858, offers the same sumptuous brocades, damasks, and cut velvets used by the world's most prestigious decorators. ⊠ *Palazzo Corner Spinelli, San Marco 3877* ☎ *041/5236110* ⊕ *www.rubelli.com.*

Pina Bonzio offers lace souvenirs from handkerchiefs and baggy blouses to lovely bookmarks at, despite the proximity to Piazza San Marco, prices that can't be beat. ⊠ *Merceria dell'Orologio, San Marco 298* ☎ *041/5226791* Ⓥ *San Marco.*

6

Trois is one of those humble little treasures often overlooked by passersby. It stocks original "Tessuti Artistici Fortuny," the intoxicating handwoven and hand-dyed fabrics "invented" by Mariano Fortuny, which are great for curtains, bedspreads, cushions, and more. The stunningly vibrant colors are all obtained from natural pigments. ⊠ *Campo San Maurizio, San Marco 2666* ☎ *041/5222905* Ⓥ *San Marco.*

Fodor'sChoice
★
Venetia Studium creates exclusive velvet fabrics in a splendid array of colors and turns them into scarves, bags, stoles, and pillows of various sizes. They also make the famous pleated Fortuny dress and Fortuny lamps. ⊠ *Calle Larga XXII Marzo, San Marco 2403* ☎ *041/5229281*⊠ *Calle Larga XXII Marzo, San Marco 723* ☎ *041/5229859* ⊕ *www. venetiastudium.com.*

SAN POLO

Fodor'sChoice
★
La Bottega di Cenerentola, or "Cinderella's Workshop," creates unique handmade lamp shades out of silk, old lace, and real parchment, embroidered and decorated with gold braids and cotton or silk trim. The pieces on display are a perfect match for country- and antique-style furniture. The owner, Lidiana Vallongo, and her daughter will be happy to discuss special orders. ⊠ *Calle dei Saoneri, San Polo 2718/A* ☎ *041/5232006* ⊕ *www.cenerentola.eu* Ⓥ *San Tomà.*

LEATHER GOODS

In Venice you'll find a good assortment of leather goods, especially shoes and ladies' bags. All shoe shops listed below are for both men and women. Unless stated otherwise, these shops tend to carry upmarket designer articles. For less fancy items, explore the areas of Rialto and Campo San Polo.

CANNAREGIO

Glamour is a tiny neighborhood shop with a sign proudly stating CHAUSSURE DE TENDENCE (trendy shoes). The owner-designers make attractive, reasonably priced footwear. ⊠ *Ponte delle Guglie, Cannaregio 1298* ☎ *041/716246* Ⓥ *San Marcuola.*

CASTELLO

Fodor'sChoice
★
Cobbler-designer **Giovanna Zanella Caeghera** creates whimsical contemporary footwear in a variety styles and colors. She was a student of the famous Venetian master cobbler Rolando Segalin. ⊠ *Calle Carminati, Castello 5641* ☎ *041/5235500* Ⓥ *Rialto.*

Kalimala should not be missed if you are looking for soft leather bags, a perfect match for almost any outfit, or very pretty, inexpensive copper jewelry. ⊠ *Salizzada San Lio near Campo Santa Maria Formosa, Castello 5387* ☎ *041/5283596* ⊕ *www.kalimala.it* Ⓥ *Rialto.*

SAN MARCO

Bottega Veneta is a prestigious Italian chain selling bags typically made with intertwined strips of leather, plus smooth bags and elegant low-heeled shoes (for women only). ⊠ *Calle Vallaresso, San Marco 1337* ☎ *041/5228489* Ⓥ *San Marco.*

Daniela Ghezzo, Segalin a Venezia makes custom shoes, following in the footsteps of the shop's founder, Rolando Segalin. This artisan team can

The Rialto market shows off exceptional produce from the Lido and the surrounding region.

give life to your wildest shoe fantasy as well as make the most classic designs. ✉ *Calle dei Fuseri, San Marco 4365* ☎ *041/5222115.*

Emporium has traveling bags and suitcases by Alviero Martini, typically decorated with maps in light colors, and Trussardi accessories. ✉ *Spadaria, San Marco 670* ☎ *041/5235911* Ⓥ *San Marco.*

Fratelli Rossetti has bags, boots, leather jackets, and shoes of the Rossetti brothers—for once, the selection here is better than in the Rome shop. ✉ *Campo San Salvador, San Marco 4800* ☎ *041/5230571* Ⓥ *San Marco.*

La Parigina is a Venetian institution, with five large windows in two neighboring shops. You'll find the house collection plus a dozen lesser-known designers. ✉ *Merceria San Zulian, San Marco 727* ☎ *041/5226743* ✉ *Merceria San Zulian, San Marco 733* ☎ *041/523155* Ⓥ *San Marco.*

★ The evening shoes at **Macri** are so glamorous and over-the-top that you might feel compelled to buy a pair and then create an occasion to wear them. René Caovilla's shoes are meant for showing off, not walking around town (especially in Venice). Prices start at €350. ✉ *Calle dell'Ascensione, San Marco 1296* ☎ *041/5231221* Ⓥ *San Marco.*

Mariani is one of Venice's best shoe shops, with reasonable prices. They have another location at Castello 4313 on the Ponte de la Canonica. ✉ *Calle del Teatro off Campo San Luca, San Marco 4775* ☎ *041/5222967* Ⓥ *Rialto or Sant'Angelo.*

SAN POLO

Fanny, run by a family of market stall sellers, combines good value, friendly service, and cheerful design. Come here for leather and suede bags and soft leather gloves. ⊠ *Calle dei Saoneri, San Polo 2723* ☎ *041/5228266* Ⓥ *San Tomà.*

Francis Model is a tiny workshop specializing in handmade leather bags in all shapes and sizes. The craftsmanship is exceptional; get Bottega Veneta look-alikes at half the price. ⊠ *Ruga Rialto, San Polo 773/A* ☎ *041/5212889* Ⓥ *San Silvestro.*

MARKETS

The itinerant flea markets operating on the mainland periodically include Venice in their tours, but the majority of markets left in town trade in food. The morning open-air **Rialto Fruit and Vegetable Market,** on the Santa Croce side of the Rialto Bridge (open Monday through Saturday, roughly 8–1), has been in business since the 11th century. It offers animated local color and gorgeous produce that's tantalizing to browse through even if you have no plans to buy. The same holds true for the adjacent **Rialto Fish Market,** or *pescheria,* where you're almost certain to find species you've never seen before. It's in operation Tuesday through Saturday, roughly 8–1.

Smaller but still lively morning food markets are located on Via Garibaldi, near the Giardini della Biennale, in Campo Santa Margherita, along the Cannaregio Canal, and on Strada Nova at San Leonardo, just below the Ponte delle Guglie bridge (open all day, Monday through Saturday). Every Tuesday morning there's a big open-air market on the Lido where you can find housewares and clothing as well as fruit and vegetables.

MASKS

The boom in Venetian mask shops started only in the early 1980s when the Carnevale tradition was resurrected. Now almost every shop and street vendor offers some version of the mask, in countless sizes, colors, designs, and materials, from cheap, mass-produced ceramics to the original papier-mâché and handcrafted leather. Prices go up dramatically for leather and gilded masks, and you might come across expensive *pezzi da collezione* (collectors' items)—unique pieces whose casts are destroyed. You'll get better value direct from producers, so make a point to visit several of the largest workshops.

CASTELLO

Il Canovaccio is a treasure trove of papier-mâché objects, panels, and masks designed for the theater stage. Mask-making classes are offered by appointment. ⊠ *Calle delle Bande, Castello 5369* ☎ *041/5210393* ⊕ *www.ilcanovaccio.com* Ⓥ *Rialto or San Marco.*

What distinguishes family-owned and operated **Scheggi di Arlecchino** is that many of their masks are inspired by the works of famous painters, including Picasso, Klimt, and de Chirico, to name but a few. ⊠ *Calle Longa Santa Maria Formosa, Castello 6185* ☎ *041/5225789* Ⓥ *Rialto.*

DORSODURO

Ca' Macana, a large workshop offering lots of gilded creations, both traditional and new, is a must-see. ⊠ *Calle delle Botteghe off Campo San Barnaba, Dorsoduro 3172* ☎ *041/2776142* ⊕ *www.camacana.com* Ⓥ *San Tomà.*

Fodor's Choice ★ **Mondonovo** is the "new world" of master craftsman Guerrino Lovato. His masks have appeared in films by Stanley Kubrick, Kenneth Branagh, and Franco Zeffirelli. You can also admire his papier-mâché ceiling figures in the restored Fenice theater. ⊠ *Rio Terà Canal, Dorsoduro 3063* ☎ *041/5287344* ⊕ *www.mondonovomaschere.it.*

SAN POLO

Tragicomica has a good mask selection, and is a useful information resource for Carnevale parties. It also turns out a limited number of costumes made from hand-printed cotton fabric. ⊠ *Calle dei Nomboli off Campo San Tomà, San Polo 2800* ☎ *041/721102* ⊕ *www.tragicomica. it* Ⓥ *San Tomà.*

PAPER GOODS

Though in 1482 Venice was the printing capital of the world, 20 years ago there was only one *legatoria* (bookbindery) in town. Nowadays you find dozens of them, often next door to a mask shop. Hand-printed paper and ornate leather-bound diaries make great souvenirs, and the young artisans come out with new ideas all the time, the latest invention being a glass pen to dip into colored ink (with a matching ink bottle, of course)—the ideal accompaniment to your handmade writing paper, wax, and seals.

DORSODURO

Il Pavone, whose name aptly translates as "The Peacock," offers a great selection of *coda di pavone*, a kind of paper with colors and patterns resembling peacock feathers. The artisans here are particularly proud of their hand-painted paper. ⊠ *Fondamenta Venier, Dorsoduro 721* ☎ *041/5234517* Ⓥ *Zattere.*

SAN MARCO

Antica Legatoria Piazzesi is the oldest bookbindery in Venice. Its historic *stampi*—hand-printed paper using carved wood plates, which artisans carefully filled with colored inks—are on exhibit in the shop, and slowly being sold off. Due to the high production costs, this kind of paper is now only made to order. ⊠ *Campo della Feltrina near Campo Santa Maria del Giglio, San Marco 2511* ☎ *041/5221202* ⊕ *www.legatoria-piazzesi.it* Ⓥ *Santa Maria del Giglio.*

Ebrû, a Turkish word meaning "cloudy," refers to the technique that Alberto Valese uses to decorate paper, as well as silk ties and paperweights. ⊠ *Campo Santo Stefano, San Marco 3471* ☎ *041/5238830* ⊕ *www.albertovalese-ebru.it* Ⓥ *Accademia.*

La Ricerca is the biggest bookbindery in town. It has a broad assortment of writing materials, and even a medieval writing kit, complete with personalized wax seal. ⊠ *Ponte delle Ostreghe near Campo Santa Maria*

Venice's Signature Crafts: Masks

Venetian mask making has experienced a rebirth. In the time of the Republic, the mask trade was vibrant—Venetians used masks all year long to go about town incognito—but it was suppressed by Napoléon, a by-product of his effort to end Carnevale and other Venetian holidays. When Carnevale was revived in the late 1970s, mask making returned as well. Though many workshops stick to centuries-old techniques, none has been in business for more than 40 years.

A key date in the history of Venetian masks is 1436, when the *mascareri* (mask makers) founded their guild. By then the techniques were well established: a mask is first modeled in clay, then a chalk cast is made from it and lined with papier-mâché, glue, gauze, and wax.

Masks were popular well before the mascareri's guild was established. Local laws regulating their use appeared as early as 1268, often intended to prevent people from carrying weapons when masked or in an attempt to prohibit the then-common practice of masked men disguised as women entering convents to seduce nuns. Even on religious holidays—when masks were theoretically prohibited—they were used by Venetians going to the theater or attempting to avoid identification at the city's brothels and gaming tables.

In the 18th century actors started using masks for the traditional roles of the commedia dell'arte. Arlecchino, Pantalone, Pulcinella, and company would wear leather masks designed to amplify or change their voices. It's easy to spot these masks in stores today: Arlecchino (Harlequin) has the round face and surprised expression, Pantalone has the curved nose and long mustache, and Pulcinella has the protruding nose.

The least expensive mask is the white *larva*, smooth and plain with a long upper lip and no chin, allowing the wearer to eat and drink without having to remove it. In the 18th century it was an integral part of the *Bauta* costume, composed of the *larva*, a black tricornered hat, and a black mantled cloak. The *Moretta* is the *Bauta's* female counterpart; she kept her oval mask on by biting down on a button inside it, thus rendering her mute.

The pretty Gnaga, which resembles a cat's face, was used by gay men to "meow" compliments and proposals to good-looking boys. The most interesting of the traditional masks is perhaps the Medico della Peste (the Plague Doctor), with glasses and an enormous nose shaped like a bird's beak. During the plague of 1630 and 1631, doctors took protective measures against infection: as well as wearing masks, they examined patients with a rod to avoid touching them and wore waxed coats that didn't "absorb" the disease. Inside the nose of the mask they put medical herbs and fragrances thought to filter the infected air, while the glasses protected the eyes.

Following the boom of mask shops, numerous costume rental stores opened in the 1990s. Here you'll find masks and simplified versions of 18th-century costumes. If you plan to rent a costume during Carnevale, it's a good idea to reserve several months in advance.

DID YOU KNOW?

Venice's iconic masks, used for centuries by residents wishing to travel incognito, were banned by Napoléon when he occupied the city. Masks didn't return until the revival of Carnevale in the 1970s.

del Giglio, San Marco 2431 ☏ *041/5212606* ⊕ *venicemarbledpaper. com* ⓥ *Santa Maria del Giglio.*

SAN POLO

Legatoria Polliero has beautiful leather-bound blank books, desk accessories, and picture frames, at some of Venice's most reasonable prices. ✉ *Campo dei Frari, San Polo 2995* ☏ *041/5285130* ⓥ *San Tomà.*

SANTA CROCE

At **Cartavenezia**, Fernando and Zelda will furnish you with gloves to browse their all-white, handmade cotton writing paper, bas-relief cards, and other pleasurable paper objects. ✉ *Off Campo Santa Maria Mater Domini, Santa Croce 2125* ☏ *041/5241283* ⊕ *www.cartavenezia.it* ⓥ *San Stae.*

WINE

Once you've identified some favorite wines at your chosen bacaro, you may want to take some home with you. The shops listed below are owner-operated; all bring abundant experience to their trade, and know each wine they stock personally.

CASTELLO

Bottiglieria Colonna specializes in handpicked regional wines from small producers and also stocks an ample selection of unusual wines from central Italy. You'll find sparkling wines and liquor, too. ✉ *Calle de la Fava, Castello 5595* ☏ *041/5285137* ⓥ *Rialto.*

Vino e . . . Vini carries an extensive selection of local wines, but their in-store experts will happily help you choose international wines as well. ✉ *Salizzada del Pignater, Castello 3566* ☏ *041/5210184* ⓥ *Rialto.*

DORSODURO

Cantinone Già Schiavi, one of Venice's finest wine bars, is just as popular for the ample choice of excellent wines sold to go. ✉ *Ponte San Trovaso, Dorsoduro 992* ☏ *041/5285137* ⓥ *Accademia.*

SAN MARCO

Fodor's Choice ★ At **Millevini**, Lorenzo will be more than happy to assist you in exploring the broad selection of wines from across the Italian landscape. They also carry liquors and brandies, lovely bubblies, and even a few microbrews. ✉ *Ramo del Fontego dei Turchi, San Marco 5362* ☏ *041/5206090* ⓥ *Rialto.*

The Veneto and Friuli–Venezia Giulia

WORD OF MOUTH

"Verona is a wonderful walking town. We took the first of what were many walks down the upscale Via Mazzini to the Piazza Erbe. Piazza Erbe appears to be the heart of the city and is filled with stalls selling all sorts of things, from foodstuffs to tacky things for tourists. We shared a cone of hot chestnuts as we walked."

—basingstoke2

WELCOME TO THE VENETO AND FRIULI–VENEZIA GIULIA

TOP REASONS TO GO

★ **Giotto's frescoes in the Cappella degli Scrovegni:** In this Padua chapel, Giotto's expressive and innovative frescos foreshadowed the painting techniques of the Renaissance.

★ **Villa Barbaro in Maser:** Master architect Palladio's graceful creation meets Veronese's splendid paintings in a one-time-only collaboration.

★ **Opera in Verona's ancient arena:** The performances may not be top-notch, but even serious opera fans can't resist the almost campy spectacle of these shows.

★ **Roman and early Christian ruins at Aquileia** Aquileia's ruins offer an image of the transition from pagan to Christian Rome, and are almost entirely free of tourists.

★ **The wine roads north of Treviso:** A series of routes takes you through beautiful hillsides to some of Italy's finest wines.

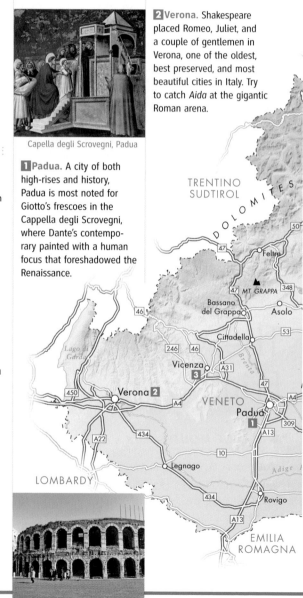

Capella degli Scrovegni, Padua

1 Padua. A city of both high-rises and history, Padua is most noted for Giotto's frescoes in the Cappella degli Scrovegni, where Dante's contemporary painted with a human focus that foreshadowed the Renaissance.

2 Verona. Shakespeare placed Romeo, Juliet, and a couple of gentlemen in Verona, one of the oldest, best preserved, and most beautiful cities in Italy. Try to catch *Aida* at the gigantic Roman arena.

Arena, Verona

3 **Vicenza.** This elegant art city, on the green plain reaching inland from Venice's lagoon, bears the signature of the great 16th-century architect Andrea Palladio, including several palazzi and other important buildings.

4 **Treviso and the Hillside Towns.** Treviso is a busy town with a touch of Venetian style. Asolo (the City of a Hundred Horizons) is the most popular destination in a series of charming towns that dot the wine-producing hills north of Treviso.

GETTING ORIENTED

The Venetian Arc is the sweep of land curving north and east from the River Adige to the Slovenian border. It's made up of two Italian regions—the Veneto and Friuli–Venezia Giulia—that were once controlled by Venice, and the culture is a mix of Venetian, Alpine, and central European sensibilities.

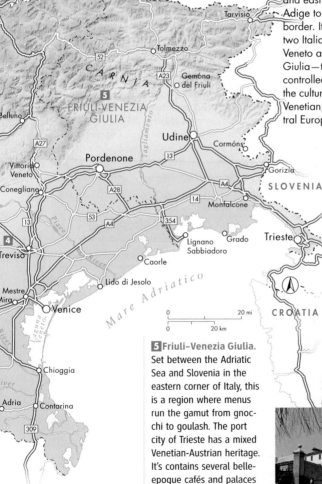

5 **Friuli–Venezia Giulia.** Set between the Adriatic Sea and Slovenia in the eastern corner of Italy, this is a region where menus run the gamut from gnocchi to goulash. The port city of Trieste has a mixed Venetian-Austrian heritage. It's contains several belle-epoque cafés and palaces built for Habsburg nobility.

Treviso

THE VENETO AND FRIULI– VENEZIA GIULIA PLANNER

Planning Ahead

Three of the top sights in the region demand advance planning:

Reservations are required to see the Giotto frescoes in Padua's Cappella degli Scrovegni—though if there's space, you can "reserve" on the spot.

On the outskirts of Vicenza, Villa della Rotonda, one of star architect Palladio's masterpieces, is open to the public only on Wednesday from mid-March through October. (Hours for visiting the grounds are less restrictive.)

Another important Palladian villa, Villa Barbaro near Maser, is open weekends and several days during the week March to October. From November to February, it's open only on weekends. *For details about Cappella degli Scrovegni, look in this chapter under "Top Attractions" in Padua. For the villas, see "Top Attractions" in Vicenza and Palladio Country.*

Making the Most of Your Time

Lined up in a row west of Venice are Padua, Vicenza, and Verona—three prosperous small cities, each worth at least a day on a northern Italy itinerary. Verona has the greatest charm, and it's probably the best choice for a base in the area (though Verona also draws the most tourists). The hills north of Venice make for good drives, with appealing villages set amid a visitor-friendly wine country.

East of the Veneto, the region of Friuli–Venezia Giulia is off the main tourist circuit. You probably won't go here on a first trip to Italy, but by your second or third visit you may be drawn by its caves and castles, its battle-worn hills, and its mix of Italian and central European culture. The port city of Trieste, famous for its elegant cafés, has quiet character that some people find dull and others find alluring. (Famed travel writer Jan Morris's book in praise of the city is tellingly titled *Trieste and the Meaning of Nowhere*.)

Finding a Place to Stay

There's a full range of accommodations throughout the region. Hotels often renovate and raise their prices, but good low-cost options can still be found. Ask about weekend discounts, often available at hotels catering to business clients. Rates tend to be higher in Padua and Verona; in Verona especially, seasonal rates vary widely and soar during trade fairs and the opera season. There are fewer good lodging choices in Vicenza, perhaps because more overnighters are drawn to the better restaurant scene in Verona and Padua. *Agriturismo* (farm stay) information is available at tourist offices and sometimes on their Web sites.

WHAT IT COSTS IN EUROS

	¢	$	$$	$$$	$$$$
Restaurants	under €20	€20–€30	€30–€45	€45–€65	over €65
Hotels	under €75	€75–€125	€125–€200	€200–€300	over €300

Restaurant prices are for a first course (primo), second course (secondo), and dessert (dolce). Hotel prices are for two people in a standard double room in high season, including tax and service.

Getting Around by Car

Padua, Vicenza, and Verona are on the highway and train line between Venice and Milan. Seeing them without a car isn't a problem; in fact, having a car can complicate matters. The cities sometimes limit access, permitting only cars with plates ending in an even number on even days, odd on odd, or prohibiting cars altogether on weekends. There's no central source for information about these sporadic traffic restrictions; the best strategy is to check with your hotel before arrival for an update. On the other hand, you'll need a car to get the most out of the hill country that makes up much of the Venetian Arc.

The two main access roads to the Venetian Arc from southern Italy are both linked to the A1 (Autostrada del Sole), which connects Bologna, Florence, and Rome. They are the A13, which culminates in Padua, and the A22, which passes through Verona running north–south. Linking the region from east to west is the A4, the primary route from Milan to Trieste, skirting Verona, Padua, and Venice along the way. The distance from Verona to Trieste via A4 is 263 km (163 mi, 2½ hours), with one break in the autostrada near Venice/Mestre. Branches link the A4 with Treviso (A27), Pordenone (A28), and Udine (A23).

Getting Around by Bus

There are interurban and interregional connections throughout the Veneto and Friuli, handled by nearly a dozen private bus lines. To figure out which line will get you where, the best strategy is to get assistance from local tourist offices *(listed throughout this chapter)*.

Getting Around by Train

Trains on the main routes from the south stop almost hourly in Verona, Padua, and Venice. From northern Italy and the rest of Europe, trains usually enter via Milan or through Porta Nuova station in Verona. Treviso and Udine both lie on the main line from Venice to Tarvisio. Unfortunately, there are no daytime express trains between Venice and Tarvisio, only the slower interregional and regional service.

To the west of Venice, the main line running across the north of Italy stops at Padua (30 minutes from Venice), Vicenza (1 hour), and Verona (1½ hours); to the east is Trieste (2 hours). Local trains link Venice to Bassano del Grappa (1 hour), Padua to Bassano del Grappa (1 hour), Vicenza to Treviso (1 hour), and Udine to Trieste (1 hour).

Be sure to take express trains whenever possible—a local "milk run" that stops in every village along the way can take considerably longer. The fastest trains are the Eurostars, but reservations are obligatory and fares are higher than on regular express trains. You can check schedules at the Web site of the Italian national railway, **FS** (☎ *892021* ⊕ *www.trenitalia.com*).

7

EATING AND DRINKING WELL IN THE VENETO AND FRIULI–VENEZIA GIULIA

With the decisive seasonal changes of the Venetian Arc, it's little wonder that many restaurants shun printed menus. Elements from field and forest define much of the region's cuisine, including white asparagus, wild herbs, chestnuts, radicchio, and mushrooms.

Restaurants of the Venetian Arc tend to cling to tradition, not only in the food they serve but how they serve it. This means that from 3 in the afternoon until 8 in the evening most places are closed tight (though you can pick up a snack at a bar during these hours), and on Sunday afternoon restaurants are packed with Italian families and friends indulging in a weekly ritual of lunching out.

Meals are still a sacred ritual for most Italians, so don't be surprised if you get disapproving looks when you gobble down a sandwich or a slice of pizza while seated on the church steps or a park bench. In many places it is actually illegal to do so. If you want to fit in with the locals, eat while standing at the bar and they may not even notice that you are a tourist.

THE BEST IN BEANS

Pasta e fagioli, a thick bean soup with pasta, served slightly warm or at room temperature, is made all over Italy. Folks in Veneto, though, take a special pride in their version. It features particularly fine beans that are grown around the village of Lamon, near Belluno.

Even when bought in the Veneto, the beans from Lamon cost more than double the next most expensive variety, but their rich and delicate taste is considered to be well worth the added expense. You never knew bean soup could taste so good.

PASTA, RISOTTO, POLENTA

For *primi* (first courses), the Veneto dines on *bigoli* (thick whole-wheat pasta) generally served with an anchovy-onion sauce, and risotto—saturated with red wine in Verona and prosecco in Conegliano. Polenta is everywhere, varying from a stiff porridge topped with Gorgonzola or stew, to a patty grilled alongside meat or fish, as in the photo below.

FISH

The catch of the day is always a good bet, whether sweet and succulent Adriatic shellfish, sea bream, bass, or John Dory, or freshwater fish from Lake Garda near Verona. But be sure to note whether the fish is wild or farmed—the taste, texture, and price difference are considerable.

A staple in the Veneto is *baccalà*, dried salt cod, soaked in water or milk, and then prepared in a different way in each city. In Vicenza, *baccalà alla vicentina,* pictured at left, is cooked with onions, milk, and cheese, and is generally served with polenta. Locals consider it as central to their city's identity as Palladio.

MEAT

Inland, meat prevails: pork and veal are standards, while goose, duck, and guinea fowl are common poultry options. Lamb is best in spring, when it's young and delicate. In Friuli–Venezia Giulia, menus show the influences

of Austria-Hungary: you may find deer and hare on the menu, as well as Eastern European–style goulash. Throughout the Veneto an unusual treat is *nervetti*—cubes of gelatin from a cow's knee with onions, parsley, olive oil, and lemon.

RADICCHIO DI TREVISO

In fall and winter be sure to try the radicchio di Treviso, pictured above, a red endive grown near that town but popular all over the region. It's best in a stew with chicken or veal, in a risotto, or just grilled or baked with a drizzle of olive oil and perhaps a bit of taleggio cheese from neighboring Lombardy.

WINE

Wine is excellent here: the Veneto produces more D.O.C. (Denominazione di Origine Controllata) wines than any other region in Italy. Amarone, the region's crowning achievement, is a robust and powerful red with an alcohol content as high as 16%. Valpolicella and Bardolino are other notable appellations.

The best of the whites are Soave, sparkling prosecco, and pinot bianco (pinot blanc). In Friuli–Venezia Giulia, the local wines par excellence are Tocai Friulano, a dry, lively white made from Tocai grapes that has attained international stature, and piccolit, perhaps Italy's most highly prized dessert wine.

Updated by Bruce Leimsidor

The arc around Venice—stretching from Verona to Trieste, encompassing the Veneto and Friuli–Venezia Giulia regions—has, in recent centuries, fallen under the cultural influence of its namesake city. Whether coastal or inland, the emblem of Venice, Saint Mark's winged lion, is emblazoned on palazzi or poised on pedestals, and the art, architecture, and way of life all reflect, since the 16th century, Venetian splendor. But in the Middle Ages Padua and Verona were independent cities that developed substantial cultural traditions of their own, leaving behind many artistic treasures. And 16th-century Vicenza, even while under Venetian political domination, contributed more to the cultural heritage of La Serenissima than it took from her.

The area is primarily flat green farmland. As you move inland, though, you encounter low hills, which swell and rise in a succession of plateaus and high meadows, culminating in the snowcapped Dolomite Alps. Much of the pleasure of exploring here comes from discovering the variations on the Venetian theme that give a unique character to each of the towns. Some, such as Verona, Treviso, and Udine, have a solid medieval look; Asolo, dubbed "the town of a hundred horizons," has an idyllic setting; Bassano del Grappa combines a bit of both of these qualities. Padua, with its narrow arcaded streets, is romantic. Vicenza, ennobled by the architecture of Palladio, is elegant. In Friuli–Venezia Giulia, Udine is a genteel, intricately sculpted city that's home to the first important frescoes by Giambattista Tiepolo. In Trieste, its past as a port of the Austro-Hungarian Empire is still alive in its Viennese-inspired coffeehouses.

PADUA

A romantic warren of arcaded streets, Padua has long been one of the major cultural centers of northern Italy. It's home to Italy's second-oldest university, founded in 1222, which attracted such cultural icons as Dante (1265–1321), Petrarch (1304–74), and Galileo Galilei (1564–1642), thus earning the city the sobriquet *La Dotta* (The Learned). Padua's Basilica di Sant'Antonio, begun around 1238, is dedicated to Saint Anthony, and it attracts droves of pilgrims, especially on his feast day, June 13. Three great artists—Giotto (1266–1337), Donatello (circa 1386–1466), and Mantegna (1431–1506)—left significant works in Padua, with Giotto's Scrovegni Chapel one of the best-known, and most meticulously preserved, works of art in the country. Today, a cycle-happy student body—some 50,000 strong—flavors every aspect of local culture. Don't be surprised if you spot a *laurea* (graduation) ceremony marked by laurel leaves, mocking lullabies, and X-rated caricatures.

GETTING HERE

Many people visit Padua from Venice: the train trip between the cities is short, and regular bus service originates from Venice's Piazzale Roma. By car from Milan or Venice, Padua is on the Autostrada Torino–Trieste A4/E70. Take the San Carlo exit and follow Via Guido Reni to Via Tiziano Aspetti into town. From the south, take the Autostrada Bologna Padova A13 to its Padua terminus at Via Ballaglia. Regular bus service connects Venice's Marco Polo airport with downtown Padua.

Padua is a pedestrian's city. If you arrive by car, leave your vehicle in one of the parking lots on the outskirts, or at your hotel. Unlimited bus service is included with the Padova Card (€15 or €20, valid for 48 or 72 hours), which allows entry to all the city's principal sights. It is available at tourist information offices and at some museums and hotels.

VISITOR INFORMATION

Padua tourism office (✉ *Padova Railway Station* ☎ *049/8752077* ✉ *Galleria Pedrocchi* ☎ *049/8767927* ⊕ *www.turismopadova.it*).

EXPLORING PADUA

TOP ATTRACTIONS

★ **Basilica di Sant'Antonio** *(Basilica del Santo)*. Thousands of faithful make the pilgrimage here each year to pray at the tomb of Saint Anthony. The huge church, which combines elements of Byzantine, Romanesque, and Gothic styles, was probably begun around 1238, seven years after the death of the Portuguese-born saint. It was completed in 1310, with structural modifications added from the end of the 14th century into the mid-15th century. The imposing interior contains works by the 15th-century Florentine master Donatello. He sculpted the series of bronze reliefs illustrating the miracles of Saint Anthony, as well as the bronze statues of the Madonna and saints, on the high altar. But because of the site's popularity with pilgrims, Masses are held in the basilica almost constantly, which makes it difficult to see these works. More accessible is the recently restored **Cappella del Santo** housing the tomb of the saint, which dates from the 16th century. Its walls are covered

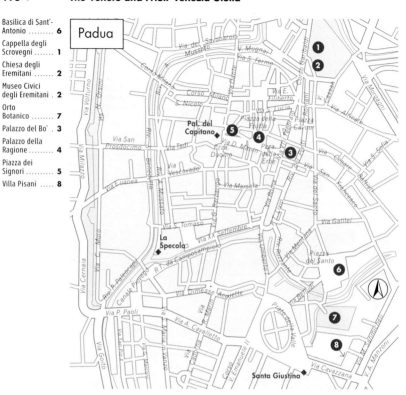

with impressive reliefs by various important Renaissance sculptors, including Jacopo Sansovino (1486–1570), the architect of the library in Venice's Piazza San Marco, and Tullio Lombardo (1455–1532), the greatest in a family of sculptors who decorated many churches in the area, among them Venice's Santa Maria dei Miracoli. In front of the church is an undisputed masterpiece of Italian Renaissance sculpture, Donatello's equestrian statue (1453) of the *condottiere* (mercenary general) Erasmo da Narni, known as Gattamelata. Inspired by the ancient statue of Marcus Aurelius in Rome's Campidoglio, it is the first in a series of Italian Renaissance monumental equestrian statues. ⊠ *Piazza del Santo* ☎ *049/8789722* ⊕ *www.santantonio.org* ⊗ *Oct.–Apr., daily 6:20 AM–7 PM; May–Sept., daily 6:20 AM–7:45 PM.*

Fodor's Choice **Cappella degli Scrovegni** *(The Arena Chapel).* This world-famous cha-
★ pel and its frescoes were commissioned by Enrico Scrovegno to atone for the sins of his deceased father, Reginaldo, the usurer encountered by Dante in the Seventh Circle of the Inferno in his *Divine Comedy.* Giotto and his assistants decorated the interior from 1303 to 1305 with a universally acclaimed fresco cycle illustrating the lives of Mary and Jesus. The 38 panels are arranged in tiers and are to be read from left to right. The spatial depth, emotional intensity, and naturalism of these frescoes—note the use of blue sky instead of the conventional,

depth-destroying gold background of medieval painting—broke new ground in Western art. Opposite the altar is a *Last Judgment*, most likely designed and painted by Giotto's assistants, where Enrico offers his chapel to the Virgin, celebrating her role in human salvation—particularly appropriate, given the penitential purpose of the chapel.

Mandatory reservations are for a specific time and are nonrefundable. They can be made well in advance at the ticket office, online, or by phone. Payments online or by phone by credit card must be made one day in advance; payments by bank transfer (possible by phone only) should be made four days in advance. Reservations are necessary even if you have a Padova Card. In order to preserve the artwork, doors are opened only every 15 minutes. A maximum of 25 visitors at a time must spend 15 minutes in an acclimatization room before making a 15-minute (20-minute in winter, late June, and July) chapel visit. Punctuality is essential; tickets should be picked up at least one hour before your reservation time. If you don't have a reservation, it's sometimes possible to buy your chapel admission on the spot—but you might have to wait a while until there's a group with an opening. You can see fresco details as part of a virtual tour at Musei Civici degli Eremitani. A good place to get some background before visiting the chapel is the multimedia room, which offers films and interactive computer presentations. ⊠ *Piazza Eremitani 8* ☎ *049/2010020 for reservations* ⊕ *www.cappelladegliscrovegni.it* 🎫 *€13 includes Musei Civici, or €1 with Padova Card* ☉ *Early Nov.–early Mar. and mid-June–early Aug., daily 9–7; early Mar.–mid-June and early Aug.–early Nov., Mon. 9–7, Tues.–Sun. 9* AM*–10* PM*; entry by reservation only.*

★ **Palazzo della Ragione.** Also known as Il Salone, this spectacular arcaded reception hall, which divides the Piazza delle Frutta from the Piazza delle Erbe, was built between 1303 and 1309, with later 15th-century additions. Giotto painted the original frescoes, which were destroyed in a fire in 1420. In the Middle Ages, as its name implies, the building housed Padua's law courts; today, its street-level arcades shelter shops and cafés. Art shows are often held upstairs in the frescoed **Salone**, at 85 feet high one of the largest and most architecturally pleasing halls in Italy. In the Salone there's an enormous wooden horse, crafted for a 15th-century public tournament, with a head and tail later remodeled to replicate the steed from Donatello's *Gattamelata*. In the piazza surrounding the building are Padua's colorful open-air fruit and vegetable markets. ⊠ *Piazza della Ragione* ☎ *049/8205006* 🎫 *Salone €4, free with Padova Card* ☉ *Feb.–Oct., Tues.–Sun. 9–7; Nov.–Jan., Tues.–Sun. 9–6.*

Piazza dei Signori. Some fine examples of 15th- and 16th-century buildings line this square. On the west side, the **Palazzo del Capitanio** (facade constructed 1598–1605) has an impressive **Torre dell'Orologio,** with an astronomical clock dating from 1344 and a portal made by Falconetto

THE VENETIAN ARC, PAST AND PRESENT

Long before Venetians made their presence felt on the mainland in the 15th century, Ezzelino III da Romano (1194–1259), a larger-than-life scourge who was excommunicated by Pope Innocent IV, laid claim to Verona, Padua, and the surrounding lands and towns. After he was ousted, powerful families such as Padua's Carrara and Verona's della Scala (Scaligeri) vied throughout the 14th century to dominate these territories. With the rise of Venetian rule came a time of relative peace, when noble families from the lagoon and the mainland commissioned Palladio and other accomplished architects to design their palazzi and villas. This rich classical legacy, superimposed upon medieval castles and fortifications, is central to the identities of present-day Padua, Vicenza, and Verona. The region remained under Venetian control until the Napoleonic invasion and the fall of the Venetian Republic in 1797. The Council of Vienna ceded it, along with Lombardy, to Austria in 1815. The region revolted against Austrian rule and joined the Italian Republic in 1866.

Friuli–Venezia Giulia has a diverse cultural history that's reflected in its architecture, language, and cuisine. It's been marched through, fought over, hymned by patriots, and romanticized by writers James Joyce, Rainer Maria Rilke, and Jan Morris. Trieste was also vividly depicted in the novels of the towering figure of early-20th-century Italian letters, Italo Svevo. The region has seen Fascists and Communists, Romans, Habsburgs, and Huns. It survived by forging sheltering alliances—Udine beneath the wings of San Marco (1420), Trieste choosing Duke Leopold of Austria (1382) over Venetian domination.

Some of World War I's fiercest fighting took place in Friuli–Venezia Giulia, where memorials and cemeteries commemorate hundreds of thousands who died before the arrival of Italian troops in 1918 finally liberated Trieste from Austrian rule. Trieste, along with the whole of Venezia Giulia, was annexed to Italy in 1920. During World War II, the Germans occupied the area and placed Trieste in an administrative zone along with parts of Slovenia. One of Italy's two concentration camps was near Trieste. After the war, during a period of Cold War dispute, Trieste was governed by an allied military administration; it was officially reannexed to Italy in 1954, when Italy ceded the Istrian peninsula to the south to Yugoslavia. These arrangements, long de facto in effect, were ratified by Italy and Yugoslavia in 1975.

in 1532 in the form of a Roman triumphal arch. The 12th-century **Battistero del Duomo** (Cathedral Baptistry), with frescoes by Giusto de Menabuoi (1374–78), is just a few steps away. ⊠ *Piazza del Duomo* ☎ *049/656914* 🖂 *€2.80, free with Padova Card* ☾ *Daily 10–6.*

Ↄ   **Villa Pisani.** Extensive grounds with rare trees, ornamental fountains, and garden follies surround this extraordinary palace built in 1721 for the Venetian doge Alvise Pisani in Stra, 13 km (8 mi) southeast of Padua. Recalling Versailles more than a Veneto villa, it was one of the last and grandest of many stately residences constructed along the Brenta River from the 16th to 18th century by wealthy Venetians for their *villeggiatura*—vacation and escape from the midsummer humidity. Gianbattista

The Giotto frescoes at Padua's Cappella degli Scrovegni are some of northern Italy's greatest art treasures.

Tiepolo's (1696–1770) spectacular frescoes on the ballroom ceiling alone are worth the visit. For a relaxing afternoon, explore the gorgeous park and maze. To get here from Venice, take Bus 53 from Piazzale Roma. The villa is a five-minute walk from the bus stop in Stra. ✉ *Via Doge Pisani 7, Stra* ☎ *049/502074* ⊕ *www.villapisani.beniculturali.it* 🎟 *Villa, maze, and park €10; maze and park only €7.50* ⏱ *Villa and park: Apr. and May, Tues.–Sun. 9–8; June–Sept., Tues.–Sun. 8:30–8; Oct.–Mar., Tues.–Sun. 9–5. Last entry 1 hr before closing. Maze: Apr.–Sept. 9–1:30 and 2:15–7:15.*

WORTH NOTING

Chiesa degli Eremitani. This 13th-century church houses substantial fragments of Andrea Mantegna's frescoes (1448–50), damaged by allied bombing in World War II. Despite their fragmentary condition, Mantegna's still beautiful and historically important frescoes depicting the martyrdom of Saint James and Saint Christopher show the young artist's mastery of extremely complex problems of perspective. ✉ *Piazza degli Eremitani* ☎ *049/8756410* ⏱ *Nov.–Mar., weekdays 7:30–12:30 and 3:30–7, weekends 9–12:30 and 3:30–7; Apr.–Oct., weekdays 8–12:30 and 4–7, weekends 9–12:30 and 4–7.*

Musei Civici degli Eremitani *(Civic Museum).* What was formerly a monastery now houses works of Venetian masters, as well as fine collections of archaeological pieces and ancient coins. Notable are the Giotto Crucifix, which once hung in the Scrovegni Chapel, and the *Portrait of a Young Senator* by Giovanni Bellini (1430–1516). ✉ *Piazza Eremitani 10* ☎ *049/8204551* 🎟 *€10, €12 with Scrovegni Chapel, free with Padova Card* ⏱ *Tues.–Sun. 9–7.*

Orto Botanico *(Botanical Garden).* The Venetian Republic ordered the creation of Padua's botanical garden in 1545 to supply the university with medicinal plants. You can stroll the arboretum and wander through hothouses and beds of plants that were first introduced to Italy in this late-Renaissance garden, which still maintains its original layout. A St. Peter's palm, planted in 1585, inspired Goethe to write his 1790 essay called "The Metamorphosis of Plants." ⊠ *Via Orto Botanico 15* ☏ *049/8272119* ⊕ *www.ortobotanico.unipd.it* ☑ *€4, free with Padova Card* ☉ *Apr.–Oct., daily 9–1 and 3–7; Nov.–Mar., Mon.–Sat. 9–1.*

Palazzo del Bo'. The University of Padua, founded in 1222, centers around this 16th-century palazzo with an 18th-century facade. It's named after the Osteria del Bo' (*bo'* means "ox"), an inn that once stood on the site. It's worth a visit to see the exquisite and perfectly proportioned anatomy theater (1594), the beautiful "Old Courtyard," and a hall with a lectern used by Galileo. You can enter only as part of a guided tour. Most guides speak English, but it is worth checking ahead by phone. ⊠ *Via VIII Febbraio* ☏ *049/8273044* ⊕ *www.unipd.it* ☑ *€5* ☉ *Nov.–Feb., Mon., Wed., and Fri. at 3:15 and 4:15, Tues., Thurs., and Sat. at 10:15 and 11:15; Mar.–Oct., Mon., Wed., and Fri. at 3:15, 4:15, and 5:15, Tues., Thurs., and Sat. at 9:15, 10:15, and 11:15.*

WHERE TO EAT

$$$
MODERN ITALIAN

✕ **La Finestra.** Perhaps the trendiest restaurant in Padua, cozy yet elegant La Finestra richly deserves its reputation. The carefully prepared and creatively presented dishes may not always stick to the traditional recipes, but no one can contest that owners Carlo Vidali and Hélène Dao know what they're doing in the kitchen. Their version of the regional classic *pasta e fagioli,* for example, uses the most exquisite beans in the region, leaves out the pasta, and substitutes croutons and a dollop of foie gras. This is not grandma's bean soup, but it's heavenly. ⊠ *Via dei Tadi 15* ☏ *049/650313* ⊕ *www.ristorantefinestra.it* ⊟ *AE, MC, V* ☉ *Closed Mon. and 3 wks in Aug. No lunch Tues.–Thurs., no dinner Sun.*

$
WINE BAR
★

✕ **L'Anfora.** This mix between a traditional *bacaro* (wine bar) and an *osteria* (tavernlike restaurant) is a local institution. Stand at the bar shoulder to shoulder with a cross section of Padovano society, from construction workers to professors, and let the friendly and knowledgeable proprietors help you choose a wine. The reasonably priced menu offers simple *casalinga* (home-cooked dishes), plus salads and a selection of cheeses. Portions are ample, and no one will look askance if you don't order the full meal. The place is packed with loyal regulars at lunchtime, so come early or expect a wait; if you come alone, you'll probably end up with a table of friends before you leave. ⊠ *Via Soncin 13* ☏ *049/656629* ⊟ *AE, V* ☉ *Closed Sun. (except in Dec.), 1 wk in Jan., and 1 wk in Aug.*

$$$$
MODERN ITALIAN

✕ **Le Calandre.** If you are willing to shell out €400 to €500 for a dinner for two, Le Calandre should definitely be on your itinerary. The quietly elegant restaurant is consistently judged by major critics as one of the two or three best restaurants in the country. The food, based on traditional Veneto recipes, is given a highly sophisticated and creative treatment. The traditional squid in its ink, for example, is served as a "cappuccino," in a glass with a crust of potato foam. The menu changes seasonally, with owner-chef Massimiliano Alajmo's creative impulses. Alajmo considers food to be an art form, not nourishment, so be prepared for minuscule portions. Make reservations well in advance. Le Calandre is in the village of Sarmeola di Rubano, a few kilometers west of Padua and easily reached by taxi. ⊠ *Via Liguria 1, Sarmeola di Rubano* ☎ *049/630303* ⊕ *www.calandre.com* ⚐ *Reservations essential* ▭ *MC, V* ☼ *Closed Sun. and Mon., late Dec.–early Jan., and mid-Aug.–early Sept.*

$$$
ITALIAN

✗ **Nerodiseppia.** Behind the Basilica di San Antonio, Nerodiseppia has a cool atmosphere and unadorned decor. Don't be put off, as this is one of the finest fish restaurants in a region noted for its seafood. Patrizia and Eugenia Rubin, its friendly Padovane owners, serve up simply but carefully prepared dishes using the freshest fish from the catch of the day. The reasonably priced menu varies according to the season and what local fishermen brought in that day. In fall, locals flock here to try the *moeche,* baby soft-shell crabs dipped in eggs and flour and fried to a crispy, golden brown. The weekday set lunch, ranging from €16.50 to €18, is one of the city's gastronomic bargains. ⊠ *Via San Francesco 161* ☎ *049/8364049* ⊕ *www. ristorantenerodiseppia.it* ▭ *DC, MC, V* ☼ *Closed Sun. and Mon., Dec. 26–Jan. 7, and Aug.*

$$
VENETIAN
★

✗ **Osteria Dal Capo.** A friendly trattoria in the heart of what used to be Padua's Jewish ghetto, Osteria Dal Capo serves almost exclusively traditional Veneto dishes and does so with refinement and care. The liver and onions is extraordinarily tender. Even the accompanying polenta is grilled to perfection—slightly crisp on the outside and moist on the inside. And the desserts are nothing to scoff at, either. Word is out among locals about this hidden gem, and the tiny place fills up quickly, so reservations are necessary. ⊠ *Via degli Oblizzi 2* ☎ *049/663105* ⚐ *Reservations essential* ▭ *AE, DC, MC, V* ☼ *Closed Sun., 2 wks in early Jan., and 3 wks in Aug. No lunch Mon.*

WHERE TO STAY

$

🏠 **Al Fagiano.** This delightfully funky budget hotel sits near Basilica di Sant'Antonio, and some rooms have views of the church's spires and cupolas. The decor includes sponge-painted walls, brush-painted chandeliers, and an elevator where self-proclaimed artists can add graffiti to their heart's content. An amiable staff and relatively central location make Al Fagiano pleasant and convenient. Breakfast is available for €7. **Pros:** large rooms; relaxed atmosphere; convenient location. **Cons:** no room service or help with baggage; some find the eccentric decor a bit much. ✉ *Via Locatelli 45* ☎ *049/8750073* ⊕ *www.alfagiano.com* ⤴ *40 rooms* ⚒ *In room: a/c, Wi-Fi (some). In-hotel: room service, bar, Wi-Fi hotspot, some pets allowed, parking (paid)* ▭ *AE, DC, MC, V* ⦿ *EP.*

$ 🏨 **Albergo Verdi.** Located close to the Piazza dei Signori, this is one of
★ the best-situated hotels in the city. The tastefully renovated rooms tend toward the minimalist, without being severe. For rooms in the center of a crowded city with narrow medieval streets, they have the rare virtue of being absolutely quiet. **Pros:** excellent location; attentive staff; pleasant and warm atmosphere; quiet. **Cons:** rooms, while ample, are not large; few views; charge for Wi-Fi access; hefty parking fee (€15). ✉ *Via Dondi dell'Orologio 7* ☎ *049/8364163* ⊕ *www.albergoverdipadova.it* ⤴ *14 rooms* ⚒ *In-room: safe, Wi-Fi. In-hotel: bar, Internet terminal, parking (paid), some pets allowed* ▭ *AE, DC, MC, V* ⦿ *BP.*

$ 🏨 **Methis.** The strikingly modern Methis takes its name from the Greek
★ word for style and spirit. Four floors of sleekly designed guest rooms reflect the elements: gentle earth tones, fiery red, watery cool blue, and airy white in the top-floor suites. Rooms have Japanese-style tubs, and four are equipped for guests with disabilities. The lobby has one lounge and a quieter reading room. There's a pleasant view from the front rooms, which face the canal. **Pros:** attractive rooms; helpful and attentive staff; pleasant little extras like umbrellas. **Cons:** a 15-minute walk from major sights and restaurants; public spaces are cold and uninviting. ✉ *Riviera Paleocapa 70* ☎ *049/8725555* ⊕ *www.methishotel.com* ⤴ *52 rooms, 7 suites* ⚒ *In-room: safe, refrigerator, Wi-Fi. In-hotel: bar, gym, Internet terminal, parking (free)* ▭ *AE, DC, MC, V* ⦿ *BP.*

CAFÉS AND WINE BARS

No visit to Padua is complete without a trip to **Caffè Pedrocchi** (✉ *Piazzetta Pedrocchi* ☎ *049/8781231* ⊕ *www.caffepedrocchi.it*). You can still sit here, as the French writer Stendahl did shortly after the café was established in 1831, and observe a good slice of Veneto life, especially, as he noted, the elegant ladies sipping their coffee. The massive café, built in a style reflecting the fashion set by Napoléon's expeditions in Egypt, has long been central to the city's social life. It also serves lunch and dinner, and is proud of its innovative menu. Open 9 AM to midnight daily from mid-June to mid-September; hours for the rest of the year are Sunday to Wednesday 9 to 9, Thursday to Saturday 9 AM to midnight.

Hostaria Ai Do Archi (✉ *Via Nazario Sauro 23* ☎ *049/652335*) is the most popular Padovano version of the bacari that are so typical of the Veneto: wine bars where people sip wine, sample local treats, and talk politics. The Ai Do Archi is as famous for its impressive platters of sliced meats as it is for its selections of wine. Besides attracting students and locals, it is also a meeting place for many of Padova's reggae fans.

VICENZA

Vicenza bears the distinctive signature of the 16th-century architect Andrea Palladio, whose name has been given to the "Palladian" style of architecture. He effectively emphasized the principles of order and harmony in the classical style of architecture established by Renaissance architects such as Brunelleschi, Alberti, and Sansovino. He used these principles and classical motifs not only for public buildings but also for private dwellings. His elegant villas and palaces were influential in propagating classical architecture in Europe, especially Britain, and later in America—most notably at Thomas Jefferson's Monticello.

In the mid-16th century Palladio was commissioned to rebuild much of Vicenza, which had been greatly damaged during wars waged against Venice by the League of Cambrai, an alliance of the papacy, France, the Holy Roman Empire, and several neighboring city-states. He made his name with the basilica, begun in 1549 in the heart of Vicenza, and then embarked on a series of lordly buildings, all of which adhere to the same classicism and principles of harmony.

GETTING HERE

Vicenza is midway between Padua and Verona, and several trains leave from both cities every hour. By car, take the Autostrada Brescia–Padova/Torino–Trieste A4/E70 to SP247 North directly into Vicenza.

VISITOR INFORMATION

Vicenza tourism office (✉ *Piazza Giacomo Matteotti 12* ☎ *0444/320854* ⊕ *www.vicenzae.org*).

EXPLORING VICENZA

Many of Palladio's works are interspersed among the Venetian Gothic and baroque palaces that line Corso Palladio, an elegant shopping thoroughfare where Vicenza's status as one of Italy's wealthiest cities is evident. Part of this wealth stems from Vicenza's being a world center for gold jewelry.

TOP ATTRACTIONS

Fodor's Choice ★ **Teatro Olimpico.** Palladio's last, and perhaps most spectacular work, was completed after his death by Vincenzo Scamozzi (1552–1616). Based closely on the model of ancient Roman theaters, it represents an important development in theater and stage design and is noteworthy for its acoustics and the cunning use of perspective in Scamozzi's permanent backdrop. The anterooms are frescoed with images of important figures in Venetian history. ✉ *Piazza Matteotti* ☎ *0444/222800* 🎟 *€8 includes admission to Palazzo Chiericati* ⊙ *Sept.–June, Tues.–Sun. 9–5; July and Aug., Tues.–Sun. 9–7; times may vary depending on performance schedule.*

Villa della Rotonda (Villa Almerico Capra). This beautiful Palladian villa, commissioned in 1556 as a suburban residence for Paolo Almerico, is undoubtedly the purest expression of Palladio's architectural theory and aesthetic. Although it seems more of a pavilion showplace, it was in fact commissioned as a residence, and as such demonstrates the priority

Palladio gave to architectural symbolism of celestial harmony over practical considerations. It's more a villa-temple than a house to live in, and in this respect, it goes beyond the rational utilitarianism of Renaissance architecture. Although a visit to the interior of the building may be difficult to schedule (it's still privately owned), it is well worth the effort in order to get an idea of how the people who commissioned the residence actually lived. Viewing the exterior and the grounds is a must for any visit to Vicenza. The villa is a 20-minute walk from town or a short ride on Bus 8 from Piazza Roma. ⊠ *Via della Rotonda* ☎ *0444/321793* ⊡ *Grounds and interior €10, grounds €5* ⊙ *Mar. 15–Nov. 10: grounds Tues.–Sun. 10–noon and 3–6; interior Wed. and Sat. 10–noon and 3–6.*

Villa Valmarana ai Nani. Inside this 17th- to 18th-century country house, named for the statues of dwarfs adorning the garden, is a series of frescoes executed in 1757 by Gianbattista Tiepolo depicting scenes from classical mythology, *The Illiad*, Tasso's *Gerusalemme Liberata*, and Ariosto's *Orlando Furioso*. They include his *Sacrifice of Iphigenia*, unanimously acclaimed by critics as a major masterpiece of 18th-century painting. The neighboring *foresteria* (guest house) is also part of the museum; it contains frescoes showing 18th-century life at its most charming, and scenes of chinoiserie popular in the 18th century, by Tiepolo's son Giandomenico (1727–1804). The garden dwarves are probably taken from designs by Giandomenico. You can reach the villa on foot by following the same path that leads to Palladio's Villa della Rotonda. ⊠ *Via dei Nani 2/8* ☎ *0444/321803* ⊡ *€8* ⊙ *Mid-Mar.–Oct., Tues.–Sun. 10–noon and 3–6; Nov.–mid-Mar., weekends 10–noon and 2–4.*

WORTH NOTING

Palazzo Chiericati. This imposing Palladian palazzo (1550) would be worthy of a visit even if it didn't house Vicenza's **Museo Civico.** Because of the ample space surrounding the building site, Palladio combined here elements of an urban palazzo with those he used in his country villas. The museum's important Venetian collection includes significant paintings by Cima, Tiepolo, Piazzetta, and Tintoretto, but its main attraction is an extensive collection of highly interesting and rarely found painters from the Vicenza area, such as Jacopo Bassano (1515–92) and the eccentric and innovative Francesco Maffei (1605–60), whose work foreshadowed important currents of Venetian painting of subsequent generations. ⊠ *Piazza Matteotti* ☎ *0444/325071* ⊡ *€8 includes admission to Teatro Olimpico* ⊙ *Sept.–June, Tues.–Sun. 9–5; July and Aug., Tues.–Sun. 9–5.*

Piazza dei Signori. At the heart of Vicenza sits this square, which contains the **Palazzo della Ragione** (1549), commonly known as Palladio's basilica, a courthouse, and public meeting hall (the original Roman meaning of the term "basilica"). The previously almost-unknown Palladio made his name by successfully modernizing the medieval building, grafting a graceful two-story exterior loggia onto the existing Gothic structure. Take a look also at the **Loggia del Capitaniato,** opposite, which Palladio designed but never completed. The palazzo and the loggia are open to the public only when there's an exhibition; ask at

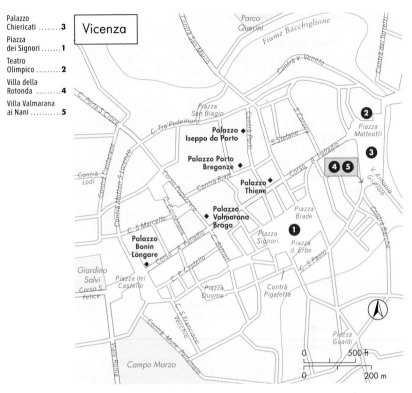

Vicenza

the tourist office. The interior of the basilica is closed for restorations projected to continue into 2012.

WHERE TO EAT

$$
NORTHERN
ITALIAN
✕ **Antico Ristorante agli Schioppi.** When they want to eat well, Vicenza's natives generally travel to the neighboring countryside—Antico Ristorante agli Schioppi is one of the few in the city frequented by Vicentino families and businessmen. Veneto country-style decor, with enormous murals, matches simple, well-prepared regional cuisine at this family-run restaurant. The risotto, delicately flavored with wild mushrooms and zucchini flowers, is creamy and—a rarity in restaurant risottos—beautifully textured. This is also an excellent place to try baccalà, a cod dish that is a Vicenza specialty. ⊠ *Contrà Piazza del Castello 26* ☎ *0444/543701* ⊕ *www.ristoranteaglischioppi.com* ▭ *AE, DC, MC, V* ⊙ *Closed Sun., last wk of July–late Aug., and Jan. 1–6. No lunch Mon.*

¢
PIZZERIA
✕ **Da Vittorio.** It has little in the way of atmosphere or decor, but Vicentini flock to this small eatery for what is perhaps the best pizza north of Naples. There's an incredible array of toppings, from the traditional to the exotic (mangoes), but the pies are all so authentic that they will make you think you are sitting by the Bay of Naples. The service is friendly and efficient. This is a great place to stop for lunch if you're

walking to Palladio's Rotonda or the Villa Valmarana. ⊠ *Borgo Berga 52* ☎ *0444/525059* ▭ *No credit cards* ⊙ *Closed Tues. and 2 wks in July.*

$ ✕ **Ponte delle Bele**. Vicenza lies at the foot of the Alps, and many residents spend at least a part of summer in the mountains to escape the heat. Alpine cuisine has been incorporated into the local culture and can be enjoyed at this popular and friendly Veneto trattoria. The house specialty, *stinco di maiale al forno* (roast port shank), is wonderfully fragrant with herbs and aromatic vegetables. Also try such game as venison with blueberries or guinea fowl roasted with white grapes. The rather kitschy decor doesn't detract from the good, hearty food. ⊠ *Contrà Ponte delle Bele 5* ☎ *0444/320647* ⊕ *www.pontedellebele.it* ▭ *AE, DC, MC, V* ⊙ *Closed Sun. and 2 wks in mid-Aug.*

NORTHERN
ITALIAN
★

¢ ✕ **Righetti**. For a city of its size, Vicenza has few distinguished restaurants. That's why many people gravitate to this popular cafeteria, which serves classic dishes without putting a dent in your wallet. There's frequently a hearty soup such as *orzo e fagioli* (barley and bean) on the menu. The classic *baccalà alla vicentina*, a cod dish, is a great reason to stop by on Friday. ⊠ *Piazza Duomo 3* ☎ *0444/543135* ▭ *No credit cards* ⊙ *Closed weekends, 1st wk in Jan., and Aug.*

ITALIAN

WHERE TO STAY

During annual gold fairs in January, May, and September, it may be quite difficult to find lodging. Be sure to reserve well in advance and expect to pay higher rates.

$$ ☷ **Campo Marzio**. A five-minute walk from the railway station, this comfortable hotel is right in front of the city walls. You can borrow a bicycle to explore the town. Rooms are ample and furnished in a pleasant modern style, but don't expect anything spectacular or romantic. This is the only full-service hotel in Vicenza, so it fills up quickly during the gold fairs—when rates nearly double. **Pros:** central location; more amenities than its competitors; set back from the street, so it's quiet and bright. **Cons:** public spaces are uninspiring; incredibly expensive during fairs. ⊠ *Viale Roma 21* ☎ *0444/5457000* ⊕ *www.hotelcampomarzio. com* ⇜ *36 rooms* ⚐ *In-room: safe, refrigerator, Internet, Wi-Fi. In-hotel: bar, parking (free), some pets allowed* ▭ *AE, DC, MC, V* ⍾ *BP.*

$ ☷ **Due Mori**. Authentic turn-of-the-20th-century antiques fill the rooms at this 1883 hotel, one of the oldest in the city. Regulars favor the place because the high ceilings in the main building make it feel light and airy. This comfortable hotel, just off the Piazza dei Signori, has a great location. It's also a true bargain—rates stay the same throughout the year, with no high-season price hikes. Breakfast is available for €5. **Pros:** tastefully furnished rooms; friendly staff; central location. **Cons:** no air-conditioning (although ceiling fans minimize the need for it); no one to help with baggage. ⊠ *Contrà Do Rode 24* ☎ *0444/321886* ⊕ *www. hotelduemori.com* ⇜ *53 rooms* ⚐ *In-room: no a/c, no TV, Wi-Fi (some). In-hotel: bar, parking (free), some pets allowed* ▭ *MC, V* ⊙ *Closed 1st 2 wks of Aug. and 2 wks in late Dec.* ⍾ *EP.*

★

Continued on page 214

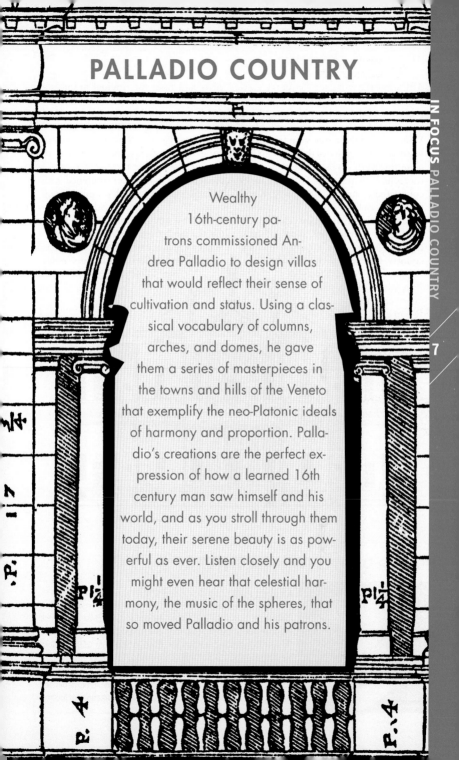

Wealthy 16th-century patrons commissioned Andrea Palladio to design villas that would reflect their sense of cultivation and status. Using a classical vocabulary of columns, arches, and domes, he gave them a series of masterpieces in the towns and hills of the Veneto that exemplify the neo-Platonic ideals of harmony and proportion. Palladio's creations are the perfect expression of how a learned 16th century man saw himself and his world, and as you stroll through them today, their serene beauty is as powerful as ever. Listen closely and you might even hear that celestial harmony, the music of the spheres, that so moved Palladio and his patrons.

TOWN & COUNTRY

Although the villa, or "country residence," was still a relatively new phenomenon in the 16th century, it quickly became all the rage once the great lords of Venice turned their eyes from the sea toward the fertile plains of the Veneto. They were forced to do this once their trade routes had faltered when Ottoman Turks conquered Constantinople in 1456 and Columbus opened a path to the riches of America in 1492. In no time, canals were built, farms were laid out, and the fashion for *villeggiatura*—the attraction of idyllic country retreats for the nobility— became a favored lifestyle. As a means of escaping an overheated Rome,

villas had been the original brainchild of the ancient emperors and it was no accident that the Venetian lords wished to emulate this palatial style of country residence. Palladio's method of evaluating the standards, and standbys, of ancient Roman life through the eye of the Italian Renaissance, combined with Palladio's innate sense of proportion and symmetry, became the lasting foundation of his art. In turn, Palladio threw out the jambalaya of styles prevalent in Venetian architecture—Oriental, Gothic, and Renaissance—for the pure, noble lines found in the buildings of the Caesars.

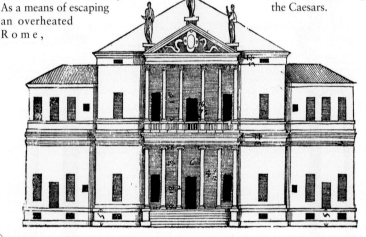

PALLADIO, STAR ARCHITECT

Andrea Palladio (1508–1580)

"Face dark, eyes fiery. Dress rich. His appearance that of a genius." So was Palladio described by his wealthy mentor, Count Trissino. Trissino encouraged the young student to trade in his birth name, Andrea di Pietro della Gondola,

for the elegant Palladio. He did, and it proved a wise move indeed. Born in Padua in 1508, Andrea moved to nearby Vicenza in 1524 and was quickly taken up by the city's power elite. He experienced a profound revelation on his first

THE OLD BECOMES NEW

La Malcontenta

Studying ancient Rome with the eyes of an explorer, Palladio employed a style that linked old with new—but often did so in unexpected ways. Just take a look at Villa Foscari, nicknamed **"La Malcontenta"** (Mira, 041/5470012, www.lamalcontenta.com €8. Open May–Oct., Tues. and Sat. 9–noon; from Venice, take an ACTV bus from Piazzale Roma to Mira or opt for a boat ride up on the Burchiello). Shaded by weeping willows and mirrored by the Brenta Canal, "The Sad Lady" was built for Nicolò and Alvise Foscari and is the quintessence of Palladian poetry. Inspired by the grandeur of Roman public buildings, Palladio applied the ancient motif of a temple facade to a domestic dwelling, topped off by a pediment, a construct most associated with religious structures. Inside, he used the technique of vaulting seen in ancient Roman baths, with giant windows and immense white walls ready-made for the colorful frescoes painted by Zelotti. No one knows for certain the origin of the villa's nickname—some say it came from a Venetian owner's wife who was exiled there due to her scandalous behavior. Regardless of the name, it's hard today to associate such a beautiful, graceful villa with anything but harmony and contentment.

trip, in 1541, to Rome, where he sensed the harmony of the ancient ruins and saw the elements of classicism that were working their way into contemporary architecture. This experience led to his spectacular conversion of the Vicenza's Palazzo della Ragione (1545) into a basilica recalling the great meeting halls of antiquity. In years to come, after relocating to Venice, he created some memorable churches, such as S. Giorgio Maggiore (1564). Despite these varied projects, Palladio's unassailable position as one of the world's greatest architects is tied to the countryside villas, which he spread across the Veneto plains like a firmament of stars. Nothing else in the Veneto illuminates more clearly the idyllic beauty of the region than these elegant residences, their stonework now nicely mellowed and suntanned after five centuries.

VICENZA, CITY OF PALLADIO

Palazzo della Ragione

La Rotonda

To see Palladio's pageant of palaces, head for Vicenza. His **Palazzo della Ragione**, or "Basilica," marks the city's heart, the Piazza dei Signori. This building rocketed young Palladio from an unknown to an architectural star. Across the way is his redbrick **Loggia dei Capitaniato**.

One block past the Loggia is Vicenza's main street, appropriately named Corso Andrea Palladio. Just off this street is the Contrà Porti, where you'll find the **Palazzo Barbaran da Porto** (1570) at No. 11, with its fabulously rich facade erupting with Ionic and Corinthian pillars. Today, this is the Centro Internazionale di Studi di Architettura Andrea Palladio (0444/323014, www.cisapalladio.org), a study center which mounts impressive temporary exhibitions. A few steps away, on the Contrà San Gaetano Thiene, is the Palazzo Thiene (1542-58), designed by Giulio Romano and completed by Palladio.

Doubling back to Contrà Porti 21, you find the **Palazzo Iseppo da Porto** (1544), the first palazzo where you can see the neoclassical effects of young Palladio's trip to Rome. Following the Contrà Reale, you come to Corso Fogazzaro 16 and the **Palazzo Valmarana Braga** (1565). Its gigantic pilasters were a first for domestic architecture.

Returning to the Corso Palladio, head left to the opposite end of the Corso, about five blocks, to the Piazza Mattoti and **Palazzo Chiericati** (1550). This was practically a suburban area in the 16th century, and for the palazzo Palladio combined elements of urban and rural design. The pedestal raising the building and the steps leading to the entrance—unknown in urban palaces—were to protect from floods and to keep cows from wandering in the front door. (For opening times and details, see the main text).

Across the Corso Palladio is Palladio's last and one of his most spectacular works, the **Teatro Olimpico** (1580). By careful study of ancient ruins and architectural texts, he reconstructed a Roman theater with archaeological precision. Palladio died before it was completed, but he left clear plans for the project. (For opening times and details, see the main text.)

Although it's on the outskirts of town, the **Villa Almerico Capra**, better known as **La Rotonda** (1566), is an indispensable part of any visit to Vicenza. It's the iconic Palladian building, the purest expression of his aesthetic. (For opening times, details, and a discussion of the villa, see the main text.)

A MAGNIFICENT COLLABORATION

Villa Barbaro

At the **Villa Barbaro** (1554) near the town of Maser in the province of Treviso, 48 km (30 miles) northeast of Vicenza, you can see the results of a one-time collaboration between two of the greatest artists of their age.

Palladio was the architect, and Paolo Veronese decorated the interior with an amazing cycle of trompe l'oeil frescoes—walls dissolve into landscapes, and illusions of courtiers and servants enter rooms and smile down from balustrades.

Legend has it a feud developed between Palladio and Veronese, with Palladio feeling the illusionistic frescoes detracted from his architecture; but there is practically nothing to support the idea of such a rift.

It's also noteworthy that Palladio for the first time connected the two lateral granaries to the main villa. This was a working farm, and Palladio thus created an architectural unity by connecting with graceful arcades the working parts of the estate to the living quarters, bringing together the Renaissance dichotomy of the active and the contemplative life. *Via Cornuda 7, Maser, 0432/923004 www. villadimaser.it, €5 Open April–October Tues. and weekends 3-6; Nov.–March, weekends 2:30–5, or by reservation; Closed 24 Dec.–6 Jan.*

ALONG THE BRENTA CANAL

During the 16th century the Brenta was transformed into a landlocked version of Venice's Grand Canal with the building of nearly 50 waterside villas. Back then, boating parties viewed them in *"burchielli"*—beautiful boats. Today, the Burchiello excursion boat (Via Orlandini 3, Padua, 049/8206910, www.ilburchiello. it) makes full- and half-day tours along the Brenta, from March to November, departing from Padua on Wednesday, Friday, and Sunday and from Venice on Tuesday, Thursday, and Saturday; tickets are €40–€71 and can also be bought at American Express at Salizzada San Moisè in Venice. You visit three houses, including the Villas Pisani and Foscari, with a lunchtime break in Oriago. Another canal excursion is run by the Battelli del Brenta (www.battellidel brenta.it). Note that most houses are on the left side coming from Venice, or the right from Padua.

VERONA

On the banks of the fast-flowing River Adige, 60 km (37 mi) west of Vicenza, enchanting Verona has timeless monuments, a picturesque town center, and a romantic reputation as the setting (in fiction only) of Shakespeare's *Romeo and Juliet*. With its lively Venetian air and proximity to Lake Garda, it attracts hordes of tourists, especially Germans and Austrians. Tourism peaks during summer's renowned season of open-air opera in the arena and during spring's **Vinitaly** (⊠ *Fiera di Verona, Viale del Lavoro 8* ☎ *045/8298170* ⊕ *www.vinitaly.com*), one of the world's most important wine expos. For five days you can sample the wines of more than 3,000 wineries from dozens of countries.

Verona grew to power and prosperity within the Roman Empire as a result of its key commercial and military position in northern Italy. With its Roman arena, theater, and city gates, it has the most significant monuments of Roman antiquity north of Rome. After the fall of the empire, the city continued to flourish under the guidance of barbarian kings such as Theodoric, Alboin, Pepin, and Berenger I, reaching its cultural and artistic peak in the 13th and 14th centuries under the della Scala (Scaligero) dynasty. (Look for the *scala*, or ladder, emblem all over town.) In 1404 Verona traded its independence for security and placed itself under the control of Venice. (The other recurring architectural motif is the lion of Saint Mark, a symbol of Venetian rule.)

GETTING HERE

Verona is midway between Venice and Milan. It is served by a small airport, Aeroporto Valerio Catullo, which accommodates domestic and European flights; however, many travelers still prefer to fly into Venice or Milan and drive or take the train to Verona. Several trains per hour depart from any point on the Milan–Venice line. By car, from the east or west, take the Autostrada Trieste–Torino A4/E70 to the SS12 and follow it north into town. From the north or south, take the Autostrada del Brennero A22/E45 to the SR11 East (initially, called the Strada Bresciana) directly into town.

VISITOR INFORMATION

Verona tourism office (⊠ *Piazza Brà* ☎ *045/8068680* ⊠ *Porta Nuova railway station* ☎ *045/8000861* ⊕ *www.tourism.verona.it*).

EXPLORING VERONA

If you're going to visit more than one or two sights, it's worthwhile to purchase a VeronaCard, available at museums, churches, and tobacconists for €10 (one day) or €15 (three days). It buys a single admission to most of the city's significant museums and churches, plus you can ride free on city buses. If you are mostly interested in churches, a €5 Chiese Vive Card is sold at Verona's major houses of worship and gains you entry to the Duomo, San Fermo Maggiore, San Zeno Maggiore, Sant'Anastasia, and San Lorenzo. Do note that Verona's churches strictly enforce their dress code: no sleeveless shirts, shorts, or short skirts.

The skyline of central Verona.

TOP ATTRACTIONS

Ancient City Gates/Triumphal Arch. In addition to its famous arena and Roman theater, two of ancient Verona's city gates and a beautiful triumphal arch have survived from antiquity. These graceful and elegant portals give us an idea of the high aesthetic standards of ancient Verona. The oldest, the Porta dei Leoni (on Via Leoni, just a few steps from Piazza delle Erbe), dates from the 1st century BC, but its original earth-and-brick structure was sheathed in local marble during early Imperial times. The Porta dei Borsari (at the beginning of Corso Porta Borsari, just a few steps from the opposite side of Piazza della Erbe), as its elegant decoration suggests, was the main entrance to ancient Verona, and, in its present state, dates from the 1st century AD. Continuing down Corso Cavour, which starts on the other (front) side of Porta dei Borsari, you can find the beautiful Arco dei Gavi, which is simpler and less imposing, but certainly more graceful, than the triumphal arches in Rome. It was built in the 1st century AD by the architect Lucius Vitruvius Cerdo to celebrate the accomplishments of the patrician Gavia family. It was highly esteemed by several Renaissance architects, including Palladio.

Fodor's Choice
★

Arena di Verona. Only Rome's Colosseum and Capua's arena would dwarf this amphitheater. Though four arches are all that remain of the arena's outer arcade, the main structure is complete. It dates from the early Imperial age, and was used for gymnastic competitions, choreographed sacrificial rites, and games involving hunts, fights, battles, and wild animals. Unlike at Rome's Colosseum, there is no evidence that Christians were ever put to death here. Today you can visit the arena year-round; in summer, you can join up to 16,000 people packing the

Fodor's Choice
★

stands for one of Verona's spectacular opera productions. Even those who aren't crazy about opera can sit in the stands and enjoy Italians enjoying themselves—including, at times, singing along with their favorite hits. ⊠ *Arena di Verona, Piazza Brà 5* ☎ *045/8003204* ⊕ *www.arena. it* ⛱ *€6, free with Chiese Vive and VeronaCard* ⊙ *Mon. 1:30–7:30, Tues.–Sun. 8:30–7:30 (8–4:30 on performance days). Last entry 45 mins before closing.*

Castelvecchio *(Old Castle).* This crenellated, russet brick building with massive walls, towers, turrets, and a vast courtyard was built for Cangrande II della Scala in 1354. It presides over a street lined with attractive old buildings and palaces of the nobility. Only by going inside the **Museo di Castelvecchio** can you really appreciate this massive castle complex with its vaulted halls. You also get a look at a significant collection of Venetian art, medieval weapons, and jewelry. The interior of the castle was restored and redesigned as a museum between 1958 and 1975 by one of the most important architects of the 20th century, Carlo Scarpa. Behind the castle is the Ponte Scaligero (1355), which spans the River Adige. ⊠ *Corso Castelvecchio 2* ☎ *045/8062611* ⛱ *€6, free with Chiese Vive and VeronaCard* ⊙ *Mon. 1:30–7:30, Tues.–Sun. 8:30–7:30. Last entry 6:45.*

Duomo. The present church was begun in the 12th century in the Romanesque style; its later additions are mostly Gothic. On pilasters guarding the main entrance are 12th-century carvings thought to represent Oliver and Roland, two of Charlemagne's knights and heroes of several medieval epic poems. Inside, Titian's *Assumption* (1532) graces the first chapel on the left. ⊠ *Via Duomo* ☎ *045/592813* ⊕ *www.chieseverona.it* ⛱ *€2.50, free with Chiese Vive and VeronaCard* ⊙ *Nov.–Feb., Tues.–Sat. 10–1 and 1:30–5, Sun. 1–5; Mar.–Oct., Mon.–Sat. 10–5:30, Sun. 1:30–5:30.*

Piazza delle Erbe. Frescoed buildings surround this medieval square, on a site where a Roman forum once bustled. During the week it's still bustling, as vendors hawk produce and trinkets. Relax at one of the cafés and take in the chaos.

★ **San Zeno Maggiore.** San Zeno is one of Italy's finest Romanesque churches. The rose window by the 13th-century sculptor Brioloto represents a wheel of fortune, with six of the spokes formed by statues depicting the rising and falling fortunes of mankind. The 12th-century porch is the work of Maestro Niccolò. Eighteen 12th-century marble reliefs flanking the porch by Niccolò and Maestro Guglielmo depict scenes from the Old and New Testaments and scenes from the legend of Theodoric. The bronze doors are from the 11th and 12th centuries; some were probably imported from Saxony and some are from Veronese workshops. They combine allegorical representations with scenes from the lives of saints. Inside, look for the 12th-century statue of San Zeno to the left of the main altar. In modern times it has been dubbed the "Laughing San Zeno" because of a misinterpretation of its conventional Romanesque grin. A justly famous *Madonna and Saints* triptych by Andrea Mantegna (1431–1506) hangs over the main altar, and a peaceful cloister (1120–38) lies to the left of the nave. The detached bell tower was begun in 1045, before the construction of much of the

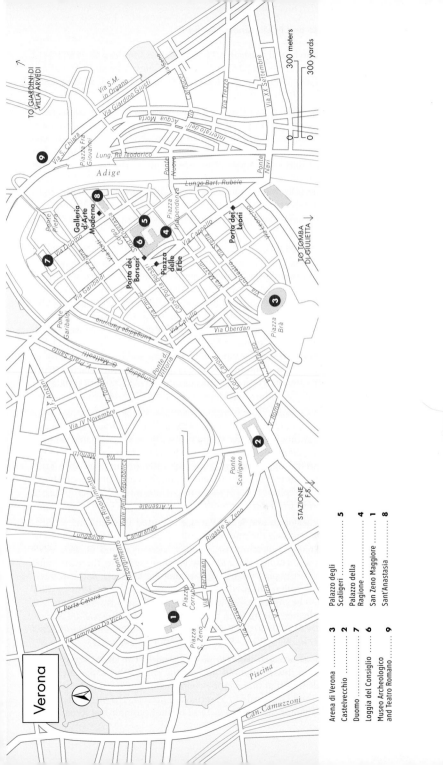

Verona

Arena di Verona	**3**
Castelvecchio	**2**
Duomo	**7**
Loggia del Consiglio	**6**
Museo Archeologico and Teatro Romano	**9**
Palazzo degli Scaligeri	**5**
Palazzo della Ragione	**4**
San Zeno Maggiore	**1**
Sant'Anastasia	**8**

TO GIARDINI +DI VILLA ARVEDI

Via S.M. in Organo
Via Giardino Giusti
Via S. Chiata
Piazza Fra Giovanni
Lung. Re Teodorico
Interrato dell' Acqua Morta
Adige
Ponte Navi
Lungo Bart. Rubele
Ponte Pietra
Galleria d'Arte Moderna
Via Duomo
Via Garibaldi
Porta dei Borsari
Piazza delle Erbe
Piazza Independenza
Via Cappello
Porta dei Leoni
TO TOMBA DI GIULIETTA
Piazza Brà
Via Oberdan
Via Catullo
Ponte d. Vittoria
Via IV Novembre
Via Mazzini
Ponte Scaligero
V. Arsenale
STAZIONE F.S.
Corso Porta Nuova
Corso Cavour
Via Roma
V. Pallone
Via Pallone
Lungadige Panvinio
Ponte Garibaldi
V. Prato Santo
V.F. Anzani
Ponte Risorgimento
Corso Cangrande
Lungadige Re-Teodorico
Viale della Repubblica
V. Barbarani
Piazza Corrubio
Rigaste S. Zeno
Lungadige
Piscina
V. Porta Catena
Via Tommaso Da Vico
Piazza S. Zeno
V.S. Polo
V. Scarsellini
Can. Camuzzoni
Piazza Corrubio
Via Menti
V. Mercanti

300 meters
300 yards
0

present church, and finished in 1173. ✉ *Piazza San Zeno* ☎ *045/592813* ⊕ *www.chieseverona.it* 💰 *€2.50, free with Chiese Vive and VeronaCard* ⊙ *Nov.–Feb., Tues.–Sat. 10–1 and 1:30–5, Sun. noon–5; Mar.–Oct., Mon.–Sat. 8:30–6, Sun. noon–6.*

Sant'Anastasia. Verona's largest church, begun in 1290 but consecrated in 1471, is a fine example of Gothic brickwork and has a grand doorway with elaborately carved biblical scenes. The main reason for visiting this church, however, is *St. George and the Princess* (1434, but perhaps earlier) by Pisanello (1377–1455) above the Pellegrini Chapel off the main altar. As you come in, look also for the *gobbi* (hunchbacks) supporting holy-water stoups. ✉ *Vicolo Sotto Riva 4* ☎ *045/592813* ⊕ *www.chieseverona.it* 💰 *€2.50, free with Chiese Vive and VeronaCard* ⊙ *Nov.–Feb., Tues.–Sat. 10–1 and 1:30–5, Sun. 1–5; Mar.–Oct., Mon.–Sat. 9–6, Sun. 1–6.*

WORTH NOTING

Arche Scaligere. On a little square adjacent to the Piazza dei Signori are the fantastically sculpted Gothic tombs of the della Scalas, who ruled Verona during the late Middle Ages. The 19th-century English traveler and critic John Ruskin described the tombs as graceful places where people who have fallen asleep live. The tomb of Cangrande I hangs over the portal of the adjacent church and is the work of the Maestro di Sant'Anastasia. The tomb of Mastino II, begun in 1345, has an elaborate baldachin, originally painted and gilded, and is surrounded by an iron grillwork fence and topped by an equestrian statue. The latest and most elaborate tomb is that of Cansignorio (1375), the work principally of Bonino di Campione. The major tombs are all visible from the street.

Loggia del Consiglio. This graceful structure on the north flank of the Piazza dei Signori was finished in 1492 and built to house city council meetings. Although the city was already under Venetian rule, Verona still had a certain degree of autonomy, which was expressed by the splendor of the loggia. Very strangely for a Renaissance building of this quality, its architect remains unknown, but it is undoubtedly the finest surviving example of late-15th-century architecture in Verona. ✉ *Piazza dei Signori* ⊙ *Closed to the public.*

Museo Archeologico and Teatro Romano. Housed in what was a 15th-century monastery, the museum's collections were formed largely out of the donated collections of Veronese citizens proud of their city's classical past. Though there are few blockbusters here, there are some very noteworthy pieces (especially among the bronzes), and it is interesting to see what cultured Veronese from the 17th to 19th century collected. The museum sits high above the Teatro Romano, ancient Verona's theater, dating from the 1st century AD. ✉ *Rigaste del Redentore 2* ☎ *045/8000360* 💰 *€4.50, free with Chiese Vive and VeronaCard* ⊙ *Mon. 1:30–7:30, Tues.–Sun. 8:30–7:30. Last entry 6:45.*

Palazzo degli Scaligeri (Palazzo di Cangrande). The della Scalas ruled Verona from this stronghold built at the end of the 13th century by Cangrande I. At that time Verona controlled the mainland Veneto as far as Treviso and Lombardy to Mantua and Brescia. The portal facing the Piazza dei Signori was added in 1533 by the accomplished Renaissance architect Michele Sanmicheli. You have to admire the palazzo from the outside, as it's not open to the public. ⊠ *Piazza dei Signori* ☺ *Closed to the public.*

Palazzo della Ragione. An elegant pink marble staircase leads up from the *mercato vecchio* (old market) courtyard to the magistrates' chambers in the 12th-century palace, built at the intersection of the main streets of the ancient Roman city. The building is now used for art exhibitions. You can get the highest view in town from atop the attached 270-foot-tall **Torre dei Lamberti,** which attained its present height through a modification in 1452. ⊠ *Piazza dei Signori* ☎ *045/8032726* €6, free with Chiese Vive and VeronaCard ☺ *Daily 8:30–7:30. Last entry 6:45.*

WHERE TO EAT

$ ✕ **Antica Osteria al Duomo.** This friendly side-street eatery, lined with
NORTHERN old wood paneling and decked out with musical instruments, serves
ITALIAN Veronese food to a Veronese crowd; they come to quaff the local wine
★ (€1 to €3 per glass) to savor excellent versions of local dishes like *bigoli con sugo di asino* (thick whole-wheat spaghetti with sauce made from donkey meat) and *pastissada con polenta* (horse-meat stew with polenta). Don't be put off by the dishes featuring unconventional meats; they're tender and delicious, and this is probably the best place in town to sample them. First-rate Veronese home cooking comes at very reasonable prices here and is served by helpful, efficient staff. This is a popular place, so arrive early. Reservations are not possible on weekends. ⊠ *Via Duomo 7/A* ☎ *045/8007333* ☐ *AE, MC, V* ☺ *Closed Sun. (except in Dec. and during wine fair).*

$$$$ ✕ **Dodici Apostoli.** In a city where many high-end restaurants tend toward
NORTHERN nouvelle cuisine, this highly esteemed restaurant is an exceptional place
ITALIAN to enjoy classic dishes made with elegant variations on traditional recipes. Near Piazza delle Erbe, it stands on the foundations of a Roman temple. Specialties include gnocchi *di zucca e ricotta* (with squash and ricotta cheese) and *vitello alla Lessinia* (veal with mushrooms, cheese, and truffles). ⊠ *Vicolo Corticella San Marco 3* ☎ *045/596999* ⊕ *www.12apostoli.it* ☐ *AE, DC, MC, V* ☺ *Closed Mon., Jan. 1–10, and June 15–30. No dinner Sun.*

$$$$ ✕ **Il Desco.** *Cucina dell'anima,* meaning food of the soul, is how Chef
MODERN ITALIAN Elia Rizzo describes his cuisine. True to Italian culinary traditions, his technique preserves natural flavors through quick cooking and limiting the number of ingredients. But there is little tradition in the inventive and even daring way in which he combines those few ingredients in dishes such as duck breast with grappa, grapes, and eggplant puree, or beef cheeks with goose liver and caramelized pears. For a gastronomic adventure, order the tasting menu (€130), which includes appetizers, two first courses, two second courses, and dessert. The decor is elegant, if overdone, with tapestries, paintings, and an impressive 16th-century lacunar ceiling. The service is efficient, if not exactly friendly. ⊠ *Via Dietro San Sebastiano 7* ☎ *045/595358* ⌂ *Reservations essential* ☐ *AE, DC, MC, V* ☺ *Closed Sun. and Mon. (open for dinner Mon. in July, Aug., and Dec.), Dec. 25–Jan. 10, and 1st 2 wks in June.*

7

$$$$
MODERN ITALIAN
★

✕**Ostaria La Fontanina.** Veronese go to La Fontanina to enjoy a sumptuous meal under vine-covered balconies on a quiet street in one of the oldest sections of town. The Tapparini family takes great pride in the kitchen's modern versions of traditional dishes. Particularly successful is the risotto made with Verona's famed sweet wine, riciotto di Soave, accompanied with a slice of foie gras. There are also such standards as *risotto al Amarone* made with Verona's treasured red wine, *pastissada* (horse-meat stew) with polenta, and, of course, an excellent version of assorted baccalà preparations. There are several reasonably priced set menus. ⊠ *Portichiette fontanelle S. Stefano 3* ☎ *045/913305* ⊕ *www.ristorantelafontanina.com* ⚍ *Reservations essential* ⊟ *AE, DC, MC, V* ☺ *Closed Sun., 1 wk in Jan., and 2 wks in Aug. No lunch Mon.*

WHERE TO STAY

Book hotels months in advance for spring's Vinitaly, usually the second week in April, and for opera season. Verona hotels are also very busy during the January, May, and September gold fairs in neighboring Vicenza. Hotels jack up prices considerably during trade fairs and the opera season.

$$–$$$
★

🏨 **Hotel Accademia.** The columns and arches of Hotel Accademia's stately facade are a good indication of what you can discover inside: an elegant, full-service historic hotel in the center of old Verona. Despite the location, the traditionally furnished rooms are reasonably quiet. The staff is friendly and helpful. The buffet breakfast, included in the rate, is sumptuous. **Pros:** central location; Old World charm; up-to-date services. **Cons:** expensive parking; few standard rooms. ⊠ *Via Scala 12* ☎ *045/596222* ⊕ *www.accademiavr.it* ⤳ *93 rooms* ⚷ *In-room: safe, refrigerator, Wi-Fi. In-hotel: restaurant, bars, parking (paid)* ⊟ *AE, DC, MC, V* ⅋ *BP.*

$$$

🏨 **Hotel Victoria.** Busy business executives and tourists demanding a bit of pampering frequent this full-service hotel located near the Piazza delle Erbe. The Victoria offers a modern, sleek entryway and traditionally decorated, comfortable rooms. As is the case with many Verona hotels, lower rates are available depending on the season. Standard rooms are attractive and well proportioned, but the "superior" rooms (€335) are really quite lavish (some have hydromassage showers). **Pros:** quiet and tasteful rooms; central location; good business center. **Cons:** no views; expensive parking; staff not particularly helpful. ⊠ *Via Adua 8* ☎ *045/5905664* ⊕ *www.hotelvictoria.it* ⤳ *66 rooms* ⚷ *In-room: safe, refrigerator, Wi-Fi. In-hotel: bar, gym, laundry service, parking (paid)* ⊟ *AE, DC, MC, V* ⅋ *EP.*

Opera productions at the Arena di Verona often include larger-than-life sets.

$ ⊞ **Torcolo.** At this budget hotel you can count on a warm welcome from the owners and the courteous, helpful service; pleasant rooms decorated tastefully with late-19th-century furniture; and a central location close to Piazza Brà. Breakfast, which costs an extra €8 to €15, is quite generous and is served on the front terrace in summer. Note that during opera season and during the wine fair, the price for a double jumps to €160 (though breakfast is included). **Pros:** tastefully decorated rooms; staff gives reliable advice. **Cons:** some street noise; no help with baggage; pricey parking. ⊠ *Vicolo Listone 3* ☎ *045/8007512* ⊕ *www. hoteltorcolo.it* ↯ *19 rooms* ⚐ *In-room: safe, refrigerator. In-hotel: bar, parking (paid), some pets allowed* ▭ *AE, DC, MC, V* ☉ *Closed Dec. 21–27 and 2 wks in Jan. and Feb.* ⑩*EP.*

OPERA

Fodor's Choice
★ Milan's La Scala, Venice's La Fenice, and Parma's Teatro Regio offer performances more likely to satisfy serious opera fans, but none offers a greater spectacle than the **Arena di Verona** (*Box office* ⊠ *Via Dietro Anfiteatro 6/b* ☎ *045/8005151* ⊕ *www.arena.it* ✉ *Tickets start at €22* ☉ *Box office Sept.–June 20, weekdays 9–noon and 3:15–5:45, Sat. 9–noon; June 21–Aug., daily noon–9*). Many Italian opera lovers claim their enthusiasm was initiated when they were taken as children to a production at the arena. During its summer season (July–September) audiences of as many as 16,000 sit on the original stone terraces or in modern cushioned stalls. Most of the operas presented are the big, splashy ones, like *Aïda* or *Turandot,* which demand huge choruses, lots of color and movement, and, if possible, camels, horses, or elephants.

Order tickets by phone or online: if you book a spot on the cheaper terraces, be sure to take or rent a cushion—four hours on a 2,000-year-old stone bench can be an ordeal.

TREVISO AND THE HILLSIDE TOWNS

North of Venice, the Dolomites spawn rivers and streams that flow through market towns dotting the foothills. Villa Barbaro, one of Palladio's most graceful country villas (*see the "Palladio Country" feature*), is nearby, as are the arcaded streets and romantic canals of undiscovered Treviso and the graceful Venetian Gothic structures of smaller hill towns.

MAROSTICA

26 km (16 mi) northeast of Vicenza, 93 km (58 mi) northwest of Venice.

GETTING HERE

There is no train station in Marostica. The closest rail connection is Bassano del Grappa, about 8 km (5 mi) away. There are regular bus connections from Vicenza's main station on FTV Bus 5; the trip takes about 45 minutes. By car, take SP248 northeast from Vicenza, or southwest from Bassano.

VISITOR INFORMATION

Marostica tourism office (⊠ *Piazza Castello 1* ☎ *0424/72127* ⊕ *www. marosticaschacci.it*).

EXPLORING

From the 14th-century Castello Inferiore, where the town council still meets, an ancient stone wall snakes up the hill to enclose the Castello Superiore, with its commanding views. Marostica's most celebrated feature is the checkerboard-like square made with colored stone, Piazza Castello.

☾ A human-scale chess game known as **Partita a Scacchi** is acted out in Piazza Castello by players in medieval costume on the second weekend in September in even-number years. The game dates from 1454 and originated as a peaceful way of settling a love dispute for the hand of the daughter of the Lord of Marostica Castle. The orders are still given in the local Veneto dialect. There's a game presented Friday–Sunday evenings and there are Sunday-afternoon shows. If you book an evening show and do not have a hotel reservation in Marostica, be sure you have a way of reaching your lodgings afterward. Buses do not run late in the evening, and taxis, if you can find one, may hike up their prices. Tickets (€10 to €80) go on sale in February; the tourist office can help with bookings.

WHERE TO STAY

$$ 🏨 **Due Mori.** Although this inn dates from the 18th century, the decor is severely minimalist. Some windows look out onto the city walls or olive tree–filled terraces, but rooms 7, 8, 11, and 12 have picture-perfect views of the upper castle. There's a restaurant downstairs. Rates vary according to season, and considerable advance booking is required for the weekend of the chess game. **Pros:** one of very few hotels in town;

central location; train station transfers available; great views of castle from some rooms. **Cons:** parking fee (unheard of for rural hotels); only one hour free Wi-Fi; rather bland decor. ⊠ *Corso Mazzini 73* ☎ *0424/471777* ⊕ *www.duemori.com* ⇆ *10 rooms* ⚬ *In-room: refrigerator, Wi-Fi. In-hotel: restaurant, Internet terminal, parking (paid), some pets allowed* ⊟ *AE, DC, MC, V* ⊗ *Some yrs closed 1st wk in Jan. and 2 wks in mid-Aug.* ⦿ *BP.*

BASSANO DEL GRAPPA

7 km (4½ mi) east of Marostica, 37 km (23 mi) northwest of Venice by local roads, 85 km (53 mi) by highway.

GETTING HERE

Several trains leave every hour from Venice's Santa Lucia station. The trip takes a little over an hour. By car, take the A13 from Venice, via Padua, to Bassano (1 hour, 20 minutes).

VISITOR INFORMATION

Bassano del Grappa tourism office (⊠ *Largo Corona d'Italia 35* ☎ *0424/524351* ⊕ *www.vicenzae.org*).

EXPLORING

Nestled at the base of the Mt. Grappa massif (5,880 feet), with the mountain-fresh Brenta River sluicing through, this town seems to be higher in the mountains than it actually is. Bassano has old streets lined with low-slung buildings adorned with wooden balconies and colorful flowerpots. Bright ceramic wares produced in the area are displayed in shops along byways that curve uphill toward a centuries-old square and, even higher, to a belvedere with a good view of Mt. Grappa and the beginning of the Val Sugana.

★ Bassano's most famous landmark is the **Ponte degli Alpini**, a covered bridge named for Italy's Alpine soldiers. There's been a bridge across the Brenta here since 1209, but floods and wars have necessitated repeated rebuilding. Following World War II, soldiers constructed the present version using a variation on Andrea Palladio's 16th-century design. (At the insistence of the town fathers, they went against Palladio's plan to build a classical stone bridge, essentially reproducing the original 13th-century structure with some technical changes.)

Almost as famous as Bassano's bridge is the adjacent **Grapperia Nardini** (⊠ *Ponte Vecchio 2* ☎ *0424/527741*). The Nardini family was one of the first to distill grappa on a commercial scale. The site of this family's first grappa distillery, opened in 1779, and its original still is open to the public. Grappa Nardini continues to be a major producer of a standard, commercial grade grappa; visit for the history, not the middling brandy. You can schedule a visit to the current distillery, 2 km (1 mi) out of town, and take in *Le Bolle*, striking architectural "Bubbles" (futuristic constructions housing a research center and reception halls designed by Massimilliano Fuksas), as well.

Grappa, once a working man's drink, has developed into a drink of considerable delicacy and refinement, with great care given to selection of ingredients and distillation techniques. A few steps uphill from Ponte

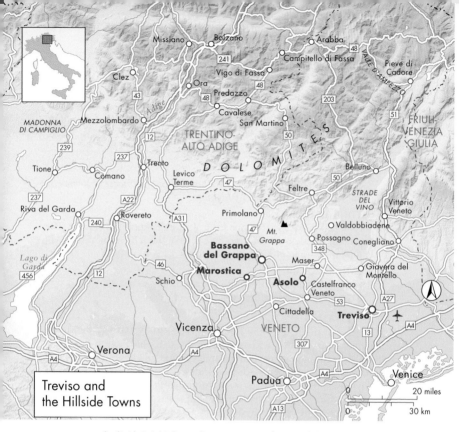

Treviso and
the Hillside Towns

degli Alpini, high-quality grappa producer Poli has set up the **Poli Grappa Museum** (✉ *Ponte Vecchio* ☎ *0424/524426* ✉ *Free* ☉ *Daily 9* AM–*7:30* PM). Most interesting are the old grappa stills, their glass tubes twisting into improbably shaped coils. You can taste many of Poli's numerous grappas (for free) and purchase a bottle or two.

★ The most significant cultural monument in the area is the **Museo Canova (Gypsoteca)**, dedicated to the work of the Italian neoclassical sculptor Antonio Canova (1757–1822). Set up shortly after the sculptor's death in his hometown, the village of Possagno, a short ride from Bassano, the gypsoteca houses most of the original plaster casts, models, and drawings made by the artist in preparation for his marble sculptures. In 1957 the museum was extended by the world famous Italian architect Carlo Scarpa. Buses leave regularly for Possagno from the Bassano railroad station. By car follow SP26 out to Bassano to Possagno. Allow 40 minutes for the 17½-km (11-mi) drive. ✉ *Via Canova 74, Possagno* ☎ *0423544323* ⊕ *www.museocanova.it* ✉ €7 ☉ *Tues.–Sun. 9:30–6.*

In Possagno is also the Tempio Canoviano, a church designed by Canova in 1819 and finished in 1830, which combines motifs from the rotunda of the Roman Pantheon and the *pronaos* (inner portico) of the Parthenon. It contains several works by Canova, including his tomb, along with paintings by Luca Giordano, Palma il Giovane, and il Pordenone. ⊠ *Piazza Canova, Possagno* ☎ *0423544323* ☉ *Winter, Tues.–Sun. 9–oon and 2–5; summer, Tues.–Sun. 9–noon and 3–6.*

WHERE TO EAT AND STAY

$$ ╳ **Trattoria del Borgo.** This well-established trattoria a few steps from
NORTHERN the center of town features regional dishes prepared with the freshest
ITALIAN seasonal ingredients. This is the place to try Bassano's famous white asparagus in spring, or hearty bean and chickpea soup in winter. There's also always a good selection of homemade pastas. For a main dish, try the braised veal cheeks or baccalà *alla vicentina* (cooked with onions, milk, and cheese). There is also a good selection of wines and, of course, grappas. ⊠ *Via Margnan 7* ☎ *0424/522155* ▭ *DC, MC, V* ☉ *Closed 2 wks in Jan., Wed. in winter, and Sun. in summer. No lunch Sat.*

$ ▥ **Al Castello.** In a restored town house at the foot of the medieval Torre Civica, the Cattapan family's Castello is a reasonably priced, attractive choice. The simply furnished rooms all differ in shape and size, some have wood-beam ceilings. Request a room at the front for a small balcony with a view of the charming square below. **Pros:** central location; some rooms have views; attentive and helpful staff. **Cons:** pricey breakfast. ⊠ *Piazza Terraglio 19* ☎ *0424/228665* ⊕ *www.hotelalcastello.it* ⬐ *11 rooms* △ *In-room: Wi-Fi (some). In-hotel: bar, parking (free), some pets allowed* ▭ *AE, MC, V* ☉ *Closed 1 wk in Aug, 1st wk in Feb.* ⦿ *EP.*

$$ ▥ **Ca' Sette.** The main building is in an 18th-century villa that has been
★ tastefully modernized; there are also rooms available in the former granary, which dates from the 16th century and has rustic beamed ceilings. The furnishings of the rooms are modern, but do not intrude upon the historic atmosphere. The restaurant is generally considered the best in the area. Chef Alex Lorenzon's seasonal selection includes a wide variety of salt- and freshwater fish, as well as meat and game. Creatively updated versions of regional specialties are served by an attentive and helpful waitstaff. **Pros:** very atmospheric; great restaurant; helpful staff. **Cons:** outside city's historic center; a 20-minute scenic walk to town. ⊠ *Via Cunizza da Romano 4* ☎ *0424/383350* ⊕ *www.ca-sette. it* ⬐ *17 rooms, 2 suites* △ *In-room: safe, refrigerator, Wi-Fi. In-hotel: restaurant, bicycles, parking (free), some pets allowed* ▭ *AE, DC, MC, V* ☉ *Restaurant closed Mon., 1st wk in Jan., and 3 wks in mid-Aug. No dinner Sun.* ⦿ *BP.*

ASOLO

16 km (10 mi) east of Bassano del Grappa, 33 km (20½ mi) northwest of Treviso.

GETTING HERE

There is no train station in Asolo; the closest one is in Montebelluna, 12 km (7½ mi) away. Bus connections are infrequent and buses are not coordinated with trains, making it about a 2½-hour trip from Venice via public transportation. Therefore, it is recommended that you drive.

By car from Treviso take Via Feltrina and continue onto Via Padre Agostino Gemelli (SR348). Follow SR348 about 16 km (10 mi), then turn left on SP667, which you follow for almost 4 km (2½ mi). At the roundabout, take the first exit, Via Monte Grappa (SP284) and follow

The Ponte degli Alpini, spanning the Brenta River at Bassano del Grappa.

it for 6½ km (4 mi) to Via Loredan, where you turn right and then left onto Via Bordo Vecchio. Asolo is less than 7 km (4½ mi) away from the Palladian Villa Barbaro at Maser.

VISITOR INFORMATION

Asolo tourism office (✉ *Piazza Garibaldi* ☎ *0423/529046* ⊕ *www.asolo.it*).

EXPLORING

A pleasant place to stop for lunch on a visit to the Palladian villa of Maser, or to use as a base for touring the surrounding countryside, the visually striking hillside hamlet of Asolo was the consolation prize of an exiled queen. At the end of the 15th century, Venetian-born Caterina Cornaro was sent here by Venice's doge to keep her from interfering with Venetian administration of her former kingdom of Cyprus, which she had inherited from her husband. To soothe the pain of exile she established a lively and brilliant court in Asolo. It was in this court that the Renaissance poet-essayist Pietro Bembo set his famous "Gli asolani" (1505), in which six Venetian courtiers discuss the pros and cons of love. Through the centuries, Veneto aristocrats continued to build elegant villas on the hillside, and in the 19th-century Asolo once again became the idyllic haunt of musicians, poets, and painters. And it's no wonder why—this is one of Italy's most strikingly situated villages, with views across miles of hilly countryside. Here, you can stroll past villas once inhabited by Robert Browning and actress Eleonora Duse, the mistress of the poet Gabriele D'Annunzio. Be warned that the town's charm vaporizes on holiday weekends when the crowds pour in. Even on weekdays, the village, given over to tourism and vacation residences, has almost no local population. Asolo hosts a modest antiques market on the second Sunday of every month except July and August.

One of the major monuments of contemporary Italian architecture, the **Brion family tomb** (⊠ *SP6, Via Castellan, about 7 km [4½ mi] south of Asolo, near village of San Vito* ☎ *No phone* 🎟 *Free* ☉ *Apr.–Sept., daily 8–7; Oct.–Mar., daily 9–3:30*) was designed and built by the highly celebrated architect Carlo Scarpa (1906–78) between 1970 and 1972. Combining Western rationalism with Eastern spirituality, Scarpa avoids the gloom and bombast of conventional commemorative monuments, creating, in his words, a secluded Eden.

Renaissance palaces and antique cafés grace **Piazza Maggiore**, Asolo's town center. In the piazza, the frescoed 15th-century Loggia del Capitano contains the **Museo Civico**, which displays memorabilia—Eleonora Duse's correspondence, Robert Browning's spinet, and portraits of Caterina Cornaro. ⊠ *Piazza Maggiore* ☎ *0423/952313* 🎟 *€4* ☉ *Weekends 10–noon and 3–7 and by reservation.*

QUICK BITES While away some idle moments at **Caffè Centrale** (⊠ *Via Roma 72* ☎ *0423/952141* ⊕ *www.caffecentrale.com* ☉ *Closed Tues.*), which has overlooked the fountain in Piazza Maggiore and the Duomo since about 1700. Now half café and half tourist shop, it's open until 1 AM.

WHERE TO EAT

$ ✕ **Al Bacaro.** This family-style restaurant offers affordable home-style food. Take the leap and try a dish with stewed game, tripe, or snails. NORTHERN ITALIAN Less-adventurous diners can go for goulash, polenta with cheese and mushrooms, or one of Bacaro's open-face sandwiches generously topped with fresh salami, speck, or other cold cuts. ⊠ *Via Browning 165* ☎ *0423/55150* 🟰 *AE, DC, MC, V* ☉ *Closed Wed.*

$$$ ✕ **Locanda Baggio.** Here you can choose between the formality of the NORTHERN Locanda's white-lace tablecloths or the rustic tables (with simpler dishes ITALIAN and lower prices) of its adjacent enoteca. Chef Nino Baggio specializes ★ in elegant versions of traditional cuisine—the rabbit stuffed with sausage, for example, is deboned and served with a crust of grana cheese—and takes pride in his homemade pasta, bread, and desserts. This is one of the best restaurants in Asolo, and the €35 prix-fixe menu is one of the best values in the region. ⊠ *Via Bassane 1* ☎ *0423/529648* ⊕ *www.caderton.com* 🟰 *AE, DC, MC, V* ☉ *Closed 2 wks in Aug. No dinner Sun. or Mon. No lunch Mon. in summer.*

WHERE TO STAY

$$-$$$ 🏨 **Al Sole.** This elegant pink-washed hotel in a 16th-century building ★ overlooks the main square. This was once actress Eleonora Duse's preferred haunt, and you can choose to stay in the room where she regularly entertained the poet Gabriele D'Annunzio. All the rooms are large and furnished with well-maintained turn-of-the-last-century antiques. The more-expensive superior rooms enjoy great views over the town, while the back rooms have leafy, rural views. Decoratively tiled, the bathrooms come equipped with massage showers, which might come in handy for legs that have climbed up the hill for a view. Less-demanding vistas are available from the hotel's pleasant terrace, where you can

gaze upon picturesque Asolo as you have a sunset drink or dinner in summer. **Pros:** central location; beautiful views; attentive service. **Cons:** restaurant open only in summer; substantial difference between low- and high-season rates. ⊠ *Via Collegio 33* 🖷 *0423/951332* ⊕ *www. albergoalsole.com* ⌐⊃ *22 rooms, 1 suite* ⚷ *In-room: safe, refrigerator, Wi-Fi. In-hotel: restaurant, bar, gym, parking (free), some pets allowed* ▭ *AE, MC, V* ¶◯¶ *BP.*

$$ 🖾 **Duse.** A spiral staircase winds its way up this narrow, centrally located building to rooms with a view of the main square. The scene gets lively on antiques fair weekends, but if the sights don't make up for the sounds, ask for the larger and quieter attic room—skylights instead of windows mean your only view is of the stars. Some rooms are smallish, but for Asolo, the price is a real deal. **Pros:** simple but tasteful rooms; central location. **Cons:** some street noise; not as much of a bargain when you add fees for breakfast and parking. ⊠ *Via Browning 190* 🖷 *0423/55241* ⊕ *www.hotelduse.com* ⌐⊃ *14 rooms* ⚷ *In-room: refrigerator, Wi-Fi. In-hotel: bar, parking (paid)* ▭ *AE, MC, V* ☻ *Closed 3 wks in Jan. and Feb.* ¶◯¶ *EP.*

$$$$ 🖾 **Villa Cipriani.** A romantic garden surrounded by gracious country homes is the setting for this 16th-century villa, which once belonged to the famous Venice restaurateur and hotelier Harry Cipriani. From 19th-century furnishings to a 21st-century spa, the hotel strives for opulence. Superior-class rooms have views; the two suites with private terraces are significantly more expensive but the view is absolutely stunning. The restaurant has its own terrace overlooking the garden and hills, a perfect place to sip an aperitif. Book online, as prices are about half the official rate. **Pros:** incomparable views; truly elegant grounds; good spa services. **Cons:** small bathrooms; furnishings are old but not always tasteful; restaurant is pricey. ⊠ *Via Canova 298* 🖷 *0423/523411* ⊕ *www.villaciprianiasolo.com* ⌐⊃ *31 rooms* ⚷ *In-room: safe, refrigerator, Wi-Fi. In-hotel: restaurant, bar, spa, parking (paid), some pets allowed* ▭ *AE, DC, MC, V* ¶◯¶ *BP.*

TREVISO

35 km (22 mi) southeast of Maser, 30 km (19 mi) north of Venice.

GETTING HERE

Treviso is only 30 minutes by train from Venice; there are frequent daily departures. By car from Venice, pick up the SS13 in Mestre (Via Terraglio) and follow it all the way to Treviso; the trip takes about 45 minutes.

VISITOR INFORMATION

Treviso tourism office (⊠ *Piazza Monte di Pietà 8* 🖷 *0422/547632* ⊕ *turismo. provincia.treviso.it*).

EXPLORING

Treviso has been dubbed "Little Venice" because of its meandering, moss-banked canals. They can't really compare with Venice's spectacular waterways, but on the whole, Treviso's historic center, with its medieval arcaded streets, has a great deal of charm. It's a fine place to stop for a few hours on the way from Venice to the wine country to the north or to the Palladian villas in the hinterland.

Treviso is one of the wealthiest small cities in the country, with fashionable shops and boutiques at every turn in the busy city center. Though a World War II Allied bombing on Good Friday 1944 destroyed half the city, Treviso meticulously preserved what remained of its old town's narrow streets while simultaneously introducing modernity far more gently than in many other parts of Italy.

Inside Treviso's **Duomo**, which was modified during the 19th century, the Malchiostro Chapel contains an *Annunciation* by Titian and frescoes by Pordenone (1484–1539), including an *Adoration of the Magi*. The crypt has 12th-century columns. Bring a handful of 10- and 20-cent coins for the coin-operated lights that illuminate the artwork. To the left of the Duomo is the Romanesque Battistero di San Giovanni (11th to 12th century), which is probably quite similar in style to the medieval Duomo. It's open only for special exhibitions. ⊠ *Piazza del Duomo* ☎ *0422/545720* ⊙ *Mon.–Sat. 8–noon and 3:30–6, Sun. 8–1 and 3:30–6.*

The **Piazza dei Signori** is the center of medieval Treviso and still the town's social hub, with outdoor cafés and some impressive public buildings. The most important of these, the Palazzo dei Trecento (1185–1268), was the seat of the city government, composed of the Council of 300, during the Middle Ages. Behind it is a small alley that leads to the *pescheria* (fish market), on an island in one of the small canals that flow through town.

While strolling the city, take in the restored **Quartiere Latino**, an area between Riviera Garibaldi and Piazza Santa Maria Battuti. It's the site of university buildings, upscale apartments, and a number of bustling restaurants and shops. If you walk along the northern part of the historic city wall, you'll look down on the island home of a number of ducks, geese, and goats. Their little farm occupies some of the city's prettiest real estate.

The most important church in Treviso is **San Nicolò**, a huge Venetian Gothic structure of the early 14th century, with an ornate vaulted ceiling and frescoes (circa 1350) of saints by Tommaso da Modena (circa 1325–79) on the columns; the depiction of *St. Agnes* on the north side is particularly interesting. Also worth examining are Tommaso's realistic portraits of 40 Dominican friars, found in the seminary next door. They include the earliest-known painting of a subject wearing glasses, an Italian invention (circa 1280–1300). ⊠ *Seminario Vescovile, Via San Nicolò* ☎ *0422/3247* ⊙ *Daily 8–noon and 3:30–6.*

OFF THE BEATEN PATH

Conegliano. The town of Conegliano, 23 km (14 mi) north of Treviso, is in wine-producing country. The town itself is attractive, with Venetian-style villas, arcaded streets, and an elegant 14th-century Duomo, housing an altarpiece (1492) by Gianbattista Cima (called Cima di Conegliano). Along with prosecco, Cima's work is the town's main claim to fame. Alongside Giovanni Bellini, Cima is one of the greatest painters of the early Venetian Renaissance. The front of the Duomo is formed by the frescoed late medieval facade and Gothic arcade of the Scuola dei Battuti. If you stop in town, be sure to taste the prosecco, sold in local wine bars and shops.

Traveling the Wine Roads

You'd be hard-pressed to find a more stimulating and varied wine region than northeastern Italy. From the Valpolicella, Bardolino, and Soave produced near Verona to the superlative whites of the Collio region, wines from the Veneto and Friuli–Venezia Giulia earn more Denominazione di Origine Controllata seals for uniqueness and quality than those of any other area of Italy.

You can travel on foot, by car, or by bicycle over hillsides covered with vineyards, each field nurturing subtly different grape varieties. On a casual trip through the countryside you're likely to come across wineries that will welcome you for a visit; for a more-organized tour, check local tourist information offices, which have maps of roads, wineries, and vendors. Be advised that Italy has become more stringent about its driving regulations; seat belts and designated drivers can save fines, embarrassment, or worse.

One of the most hospitable areas in the Veneto for wine enthusiasts is the stretch of country north of Treviso, where you can follow designated wine roads—tours that blend a beautiful rural setting with the delights of the grape. Authorized wineshops where you can stop and sample are marked with a sign showing a triangular arrangement of red and yellow grapes. There are three routes to choose from, and they're manageable enough that you can do them all comfortably over the course of a day or two.

MONTELLO AND ASOLO HILLS
This route provides a good balance of vineyards and nonwine sights. It winds from Nervesa della Battaglia,

18 km (10 mi) north of Treviso, past two prime destinations in the area, the lovely village of Asolo and the Villa Barbaro at Maser. Asolo produces good prosecco, whereas Montello favors merlot and cabernet. Both areas also yield pinot and chardonnay.

PIAVE RIVER
The circular route follows the Piave River and runs through orchards, woods, and hills. Among the area's gems are the Torchiato di Fregona and Refrontolo Passito, both made according to traditional methods.

Raboso del Piave, renowned since Roman times, ages well and complements local dishes such as beans and pasta or goose stuffed with chestnuts. Other reds are cabernet, merlot, and cabernet sauvignon. As an accompaniment to fish, try a Verduzzo del Piave or, for an aperitif, the warm-yellow Pinot Grigio del Piave.

PROSECCO
This route runs for 47 km (29 mi) between Valdobbiadene and Conegliano, home of Italy's first wine institute, winding between knobby hills covered in grapevines. These hang in festoons on row after row of pergolas to create a thick mantle of green.

Turn off the main route to explore the narrower country lanes, most of which eventually join up. They meander through tiny hamlets and past numerous family wineries where you can taste and purchase the wines. Spring is an excellent time to visit, with no fewer than 15 local wine festivals held between March and early June.

The Collio region produces exceptional white wines.

WHERE TO EAT

$$$
NORTHERN
ITALIAN
★

✕ **Beccherie.** The name means butcher shop, and in fact this area behind Treviso's Palazzo Trecento is where people bought and sold meat for centuries. It is only fitting that Beccherie should specialize in *bollito*, a celebrated dish of assorted boiled meats and sauces, which originated in Piedmont but is now so much a part of Veneto cooking that most Veneti regard it as their own. The varied menu, based on the local cuisine, changes according to the season, offering hearty fare in winter and lighter choices in summer. The owner's mother, Depillo Alba Campeol, invented the famous dessert tiramisu in the 1960s, and the Beccharie still serves it according to the original, featherlight recipe. Locals have been keeping this family-owned restaurant busy since 1939. Reservations are recommended for dinner. ⊠ *Piazza Ancilotto 10* ☎ *0422/540871* ▭ *AE, DC, MC, V* ✆ *Closed Mon. and last 2 wks in July. No dinner Sun.*

$$
NORTHERN
ITALIAN

✕ **Toni del Spin.** Wood paneled and styled with 1930s decor, this friendly, bustling place oozes old-fashioned character. The reasonably priced, wholesome menu, chalked on a hanging wooden board, is based on local Veneto cooking. The "Spin" in the restaurant's name is the spine of the baccalà, one of the restaurant's specialties. In autumn and winter, don't miss trying Treviso's hallmark product, radicchio, in risotto or pasta. The chef-owner, Alfredo Sturlese, is also justly proud of his *sopa coada* (pigeon-and-bread soup). ⊠ *Via Inferiore 7* ☎ *0422/543829* ⊕ *www.ristorantetonidelspin.com* ✍ *Reservations essential* ▭ *AE, MC, V* ✆ *Closed Sun. and 3 wks in July and Aug. No lunch Mon.*

$$
NORTHERN
ITALIAN

✕ **Vineria.** One of the first tenants in Treviso's restored Quartiere Latino, Vineria specializes in food with local ingredients and has a €30 three-course prix-fixe meal with ingredients strictly from the province.

Chef Alberto Toè follows a cardinal rule of classic Italian cooking: use the best, freshest ingredients and prepare them simply, seasoning just enough to enhance their flavor. ⊠ *Largo Umanesimo Latino 2* ☎ *0422/419787* ▭ *AE, DC, MC, V.*

WHERE TO STAY

$$ ⊞ **Carlton Hotel.** Pass the river flowing outside, walk through the lobby, and seek out the huge terrace right on top of the old city wall. Even the parking lot has a view from here. The hotel is fresh, clean, and comfortable. Five minutes on foot from the train station and the heart of Treviso, it is convenient for touring—that is, if you're not too busy tasting wine in the vineyards nearby, or taking advantage of the hotel's discount at Asolo Golf Course. **Pros:** central location. **Cons:** decor is not always tasteful. ⊠ *Largo di Porta Altinia 15* ☎ *0422/411661* ⊕ *www.hotelcarlton.it* ☞ *93 rooms* ⌂ *In-room: safe, refrigerator, Wi-Fi. In-hotel: restaurant, bar, bicycles, parking (paid), some pets allowed* ▭ *AE, DC, MC, V* ⦿ *BP.*

FRIULI–VENEZIA GIULIA

The peripheral location of the Friuli–Venezia Giulia region in Italy's northeastern corner makes it easy to overlook, but with its mix of Italian, Slavic, and central European cultures, along with a legendary wine tradition, it's a fascinating area to explore. Venetian culture crept northward until it merged with northern European into the Veneto-Byzantine style evident in places like the medieval city of Udine. The Cividale del Friuli and the Collio wine regions are a short hop away from Udine, and the old Austrian port of Trieste was, in the late 19th and early 20th centuries, an important center of Italian literature.

UDINE

94 km (58 mi) northeast of Treviso, 127 km (79 mi) northeast of Venice.

GETTING HERE

There is frequent train service from both Venice and Trieste; the trip takes about two hours from Venice, and a little over an hour from Trieste. By car from Venice, take the SR11 to the E55 and head east. Take the E55 (it eventually becomes the Autostrada Alpe Adria) to SS13 (Viale Venezia) east into Udine. Driving from Trieste, take the SS202 to the E70, which becomes the A4. Turn off onto the E55 north, which is the same road you would take coming from Venice. Driving times are 1½ hours from Venice and 1 hour from Trieste.

VISITOR INFORMATION

Udine tourism office (⊠ *Piazza I Maggio 7* ☎ *0432/295972* ⊕ *www.turismo.fvg.it*).

EXPLORING

Udine, the largest city on the Friuli side of the region, has a provincial, genteel atmosphere and lots of charm. The city sometimes seems completely unaffected by tourism, and things are still done the way they were decades ago. In the medieval and Renaissance historical center of town, you'll find unevenly spaced streets with appealing little wine bars and open-air cafés. Friulani are proud of their local culture, with many restaurants featuring Friulano cuisine, and street signs and announcements written in both Italian and Friulano dialect. But the main reason for devoting some time to Udine is to see the largest assembly outside Venice of works by the last of the great Italian painters, Gianbattista Tiepolo (1696–1770), distributed in several palaces and churches around town. Udine calls itself, in fact, *la città di Tiepolo*.

Commanding a view from the Alpine foothills to the Adriatic Sea, Udine stands on a mound that, according to legend, was erected so Attila the Hun could watch the burning of Aquileia, an important Roman center to the south. Although the legend is a bit dubious (Attila burned Aquileia about 500 years before the first historical mention of Udine), the view from Udine's castle across the alluvial plane down to the sea is impressive. In the Middle Ages Udine flourished, thanks to its favorable trade location and the right granted by the local patriarch to hold regular markets.

Udine was conquered by the Venetians in 1420, so there is a distinctly Venetian stamp on the architecture of the historic center, most noticeably in the large main square, the **Piazza della Libertà**. The Loggia del Leonello, begun in 1428, dominates the square and houses the municipal government. Its similarity to the facade of Venice's Palazzo Ducale (finished in 1424) is clear, but there is no evidence that it is an imitation of that palace. It's more likely a product of the same architectural fashion. Opposite stands the Renaissance Porticato di San Giovanni (1533–35) and the Torre dell'Orologio, a 1527 clock tower complete with naked *mori* (the Moors who strike the hours) on the top.

★ The **Palazzo Arcivescovile** (also known as Palazzo Patriarcale) contains several rooms of frescoes by the young Gianbattista Tiepolo, painted from 1726 to 1732. They comprise the most important collection of early works by Italy's most brilliant 18th-century painter. The Galleria del Tiepolo (1727) contains superlative Tiepolo frescoes depicting the stories of Abraham, Isaac, and Jacob. The *Judgment of Solomon* (1729) graces the Pink Room. There are also beautiful and important Tiepolo frescoes in the staircase, throne room, and palatine chapel of this palazzo. Even in these early works we can see the Venetian master's skill in creating an illusion of depth, not only through linear perspective, but also through subtle gradations in the intensity of the colors, with the stronger colors coming forward and the paler ones receding into space. Tiepolo was one of the first artists to use this method of representing space and depth, which reflected the scientific discoveries of perception and optics in the 17th century. In the same building, the **Museo Diocesano** features a collection of sculptures from Friuli churches from the 13th through the 18th century. ⊠ *Piazza Patriarcato 1* ☎ *0432/25003* ⊕ *www.museiprovinciaud.it* 🖅 *€5, includes Museo Diocesano* ⊗ *Wed.– Sun. 10–noon and 3:30–6:30.*

From the hilltop **Castello** (construction began 1517) panoramic views extend to Monte Nero (7,360 feet) in neighboring Slovenia. Here Udine's civic museums of art and archaeology are centralized under one roof. Particularly worth seeing is the national and regional art

collection in the **Galleria d'Arte Antica,** which has canvases by Venetians Vittore Carpaccio (circa 1460–1525) and Giambattista Tiepolo, an excellent Caravaggio, and a carefully selected collection of works by lesser known but still interesting Veneto and Friuli artists. The museum also has a small but wonderful collection of drawings, containing several by Tiepolo; some find his drawings even more moving than his paintings. ✉ *Castello di Udine* ☎ *0432/271591* ⊕ *www.comune.udine. it* 🎟 *€5 (€8 during special exhibits)* 🕓 *Tues.–Sun. 10:30–7.*

Just a few steps from the Piazza della Libertà is Udine's 1335 **Duomo.** Its Cappella del Santissimo has important early frescoes by Tiepolo and the Cappella della Trinità sports a Tiepolo altarpiece. There is also a beautiful late Tiepolo *Resurrection* (1751) in an altar by the sculptor Giuseppi Toretti. Ask the Duomo's attendant to let you into the adjacent **Chiesa della Purita** to see more important late paintings by Tiepolo. ✉ *Piazza del Duomo 1* ☎ *0432/506830* 🕓 *Mon.–Sat. 9–noon and 4–6, Sun. 4–6.*

WHERE TO EAT

$$ ✕ **Hostaria alla Tavernetta.** One of Udine's most trusted food addresses
FRIULIAN since 1954, this restaurant has rustic fireside dining downstairs and smaller, more elegantly decorated rooms upstairs, where there's even a small terrace. Steps from the Piazza Duomo, it serves regional specialties such as *orzotto* (barley prepared like risotto), delicious *cjalzòns*

(ravioli stuffed with ricotta, apples, raisins, and spices and topped with smoked ricotta, butter, and cinnamon), and perhaps the most tender suckling pig you have ever eaten. The restaurant offers a reasonably priced prix-fixe menu. The service is pleasant and attentive, and there's a fine selection of Friuli's celebrated wines and grappas. ⊠ *Via di Prampero 2* ☎ *0432/501066* ⊟ *AE, MC, V* ⊘ *Closed Sun. and Mon., 1 wk in June, 2 wks in mid-Aug., and 2nd wk in Jan.*

$ ✕ **Osteria Al Vecchio Stallo.** This former stable bursts with character, its
FRIULIAN   beautiful courtyard shaded by grape arbors. The menu includes a wide
★   choice of traditional Friuli home cooking. As an appetizer, try the prized prosciutto from the neighboring village of San Daniele, which some regard even more highly than the famous prosciutto from Parma. For the first course try cjalzòns (the region's answer to ravioli), or the excellent *mignàculis con luagne* (pasta with local sausage). Friuli classics such as *frico con patate* (hash-brown potatoes with Montasio cheese) or goulash with polenta are good second courses. On Friday there are also fish dishes. There's a great selection of wines by the glass, and the gregarious chef-owner is a gracious host. ⊠ *Via Viola 7* ☎ *0432/21296* ⊟ *No credit cards* ⊘ *Closed Wed. Sept.–June, Sun. in July and Aug., 3 wks in Aug., and Dec. 25–Jan. 7.*

WHERE TO STAY

$$ 🏨 **Hostaria Hotel Allegria.** In this 15th-century building, a humble osteria has grown into a modern, comfortable family-run hotel. Design includes plenty of wood, polished into finely crafted furnishings and wall treatments. Lighting is done to dramatic effect. The attractive cantina hosts private dinner parties. **Pros:** well-appointed rooms; great staff; discounted weekend rates. **Cons:** rooms may be too minimalist for some; fee for parking. ⊠ *Via Grazzano 18* ☎ *0432/201116* ⊕ *www.hotelallegria.it* ⤴ *20 rooms* ⚹ *In-room: safe, refrigerator, Internet. In-hotel: restaurant, bar, parking (paid), Wi-Fi hotspot* ⊟ *AE, MC, V* ⊘ *No dinner Sun. No lunch Mon.* ⦿ *BP.*

$$ 🏨 **Hotel Clocchiatti.** You have two choices here: stay in the restored
★   19th-century villa, where large double doors open onto canopy beds and Alpine-style wood ceilings and paneling, or opt for the rich colors and spare furnishings of the starkly angular rooms in the ultramodern (and slightly more expensive) "Next" wing. Some suites have sunken Japanese baths and gardens. Centuries-old trees shade the terrace, and high-design chaises surround the pool that's painted entirely black. **Pros:** individually decorated rooms; quiet surroundings; swimming pool. **Cons:** 10-minute drive from town center; small bathrooms. ⊠ *Via Cividale 29* ☎ *0432/505047* ⊕ *www.hotelclocchiatti.it* ⤴ *27 rooms* ⚹ *In-room: safe, refrigerator, Wi-Fi. In-hotel: bar, pool, bicycles, laundry service, parking (free), some pets allowed* ⊟ *AE, DC, MC, V* ⦿ *BP.*

7

CIVIDALE DEL FRIULI

17 km (11 mi) east of Udine, 144 km (89 mi) northeast of Venice.

GETTING HERE

There is hourly train service from Udine. Since the Udine-Cividale train line is not part of the Italian national rail system, you have to buy the tickets from the tobacconist or other retailers within the Udine station. You cannot buy a ticket through to Cividale from another city.

By car from Udine, take Via Cividale, which turns into SS54; follow SS54 into Cividale.

VISITOR INFORMATION

Cividale tourism office (✉ *Corso Poalino d'Aquileria 10* ☎ *0432/731398*).

EXPLORING

Cividale is the best place to see the art of the Lombards, a Germanic people who entered Italy in 568 and ruled until the late 8th century. The city was founded in AD 53 by Julius Caesar, then commander of Roman legions in the area. Here you can also find Celtic, Roman, and medieval Jewish ruins alongside Venetian Gothic buildings, including the Palazzo Comunale. Strolling through the part of the city that now occupies the former gastaldia, the Lombard ducal palace, affords spectacular views of the medieval city and the river.

Cividale's Renaissance **Duomo** is largely the work of Pietro Lombardo, principal architect of Venice's justly famous Santa Maria dei Miracoli. It contains a magnificent 12th-century silver gilt altarpiece. ✉ *Piazza Duomo* ☎ *0432/731144* ☼ *Daily 7:30–7:30.*

The **Museo Cristiano e Tesoro del Duomo,** which you enter in a courtyard off to the right of the Duomo, contains two interesting and important monuments of Lombard art: the Altar of Duke Ratchis (737–744) and the Baptistry of Patriarch Callisto (731–776). Both were found under the floor of the present Duomo in the early 20th century. The museum also has two fine paintings by Veronese, one by Pordenone, and a small but fine collection of medieval and Renaissance vestments. ✉ *Via Candotti 1* ☎ *0432/730403* ✉ *Combined ticket with Tempietto Longobardo €4* ☼ *Wed.–Sun. 10–1 and 3–6.*

★ Seeing the beautiful and historically important **Tempietto Longobardo** *(Lombard church)* from the 8th century is more than sufficient reason to visit Cividale. Now within the Monastery of Santa Maria in Valle (16th century), the Tempietto was originally the chapel of the ducal palace, or the gastaldia. The west wall is the best-preserved example of the art and architecture of the Lombards, a Germanic people who entered Italy in 568. It has an archway with an exquisitely rendered vine motif, guarded by an 8th-century procession of female figures, showing the Lombard interpretation of classical forms that resembles the style of the much earlier Byzantine mosaics in Ravenna, which had passed briefly to Lombard rule in 737. This procession of female figures had originally extended to the side walls of the Tempietto, but were destroyed by the earthquake of 1222. The post-Lombard frescoes decorating the vaults and the east wall date from the 13th and 14th centuries, and the fine carved wooden stalls also date from the 14th century. The Tempietto has been nominated to be a UNESCO world heritage site. ✉ *Via Monastero Maggiore* ☎ *0432/700867* ⊕ *www.museiprovinciaud.it* 🎫*€3; combined ticket with Tempietto Longobardo €4* ☉ *Apr.–Sept., Mon.–Sat. 9:30–12:30 and 3–6:30, Sun. 9:30–1 and 3–7:30; Oct.–Mar., Mon.–Sat. 9:30–12:30 and 3–5, Sun. 9:30–12:30 and 2:30–6.*

WHERE TO STAY

$$ 🏨 **Locanda Al Castello**. Set on a peaceful hillside a few minutes' drive out of town, this creeper-covered hotel was once a monastery. Rooms are spacious and furnished in varying styles, some antique, some modern, but all with large bathrooms. Locals gather here for Sunday lunch outdoors on the terrace, or indoors beside the large open fireplace. The most popular special is *maltagliata alla lungobarda*, thinly sliced beef, marinated and grilled. **Pros:** quiet area; discounts possible, depending on availability. **Cons:** need a car to get around. ✉ *Via del Castello 12* ☎ *0432/733242* ⊕ *www.alcastello.net* 🛏 *25 rooms, 2 suites* 🛁 *In-room: a/c, safe, refrigerator, Wi-Fi. In-hotel: restaurant, bar, tennis courts, spa, parking (free), some pets allowed* ☰ *AE, DC, MC, V* ⊗*BP.*

AQUILEIA

77 km (48 mi) west of Trieste, 163 km (101 mi) east of Venice.

GETTING HERE

Getting to Aquileia by public transport is difficult, but not impossible. There is frequent train service from Venice and Trieste to Cervignano di Friuli, which is 8 km (5 mi) away by taxi (about €20) or infrequent bus service. (Ask the newsstand attendant or the railroad ticket teller for assistance.) By car from Venice or Trieste, take Autostrada A4 (Venezia–Trieste) to the Palmanova exit and continue 17 km (11 mi) to Aquileia. From Udine, take Autostrada A23 to the Palmanova exit.

VISITOR INFORMATION

Aquileia tourism office (✉ *Piazza Capitolo* ☎ *0431/919491*).

EXPLORING

This sleepy little town was, in the time of Emperor Augustus, Italy's fourth most important city (after Rome, Milan, and Capua). It was the principal northern Adriatic port of Italy and the beginning of Roman routes north. Its prominence continued into the Christian era. The patriarchate (bishopric) of Aquileia was founded here around 314, just after the Edict of Milan halted the persecution of Christians and about the time that the Emperor Constantine officially declared his conversion. After several centuries of decline and frequent pillaging, including a sacking by Attila the Hun in 452, the town regained its stature in the 11th century, which it held onto until the end of the 14th century. Aquileia's Roman and early Christian remains offer an image of the transition from pagan to Christian Rome. Aquileia is also refreshingly free of the mass tourism that you might expect at such a culturally historic place.

★ Aquileia's **Basilica** was founded by Theodore, its first patriarch, who built two parallel basilicas, now the north and the south halls, on the site of a 3rd-century Gnostic chapel. These were joined by a third hall, forming a U, with the baptismal font in the middle. The complex was rebuilt between 1021 and 1031, and later accumulated different elements including the Romanesque portico and the Gothic bell tower, producing the church you see today. The highlight of this monument is the spectacular 3rd- to 4th-century mosaic covering the entire floor of the basilica and the adjacent crypt, comprising one of the most beautiful and important early Christian monuments. The mosaic floor of the present-day basilica is essentially the remains of the floor of Theodore's south hall, while those of the Cripta degli Scavi are those of his north hall, along with the remains of the mosaic floor of a pre-Christian Roman house and warehouse.

The mosaics of the basilica are important not only because of their beauty, but also because they provide a window into Gnostic symbolism and the conflict between Gnosticism and the early Christian church. In his north hall, Theodore retained much of the floor of the earlier Gnostic chapel, whose mosaics, done largely in the 3rd century, represent the ascent of the soul, through the realm of the planets and constellations, to God, who is represented as a ram. (The ram, at the head of the zodiac, is the Gnostic generative force.) Libra is not the scales, but rather a battle between good (the rooster) and evil (the tortoise); the constellation Cancer is represented as a shrimp on a tree. The basis for the representation in Aquileia is the Pistis Sophia, a 2nd-century Gnostic tract written in Alexandria.

This integration of Gnosticism into a Christian church is particularly interesting, since Gnosticism had already been branded a heresy by influential early Church fathers. In retaining these mosaics, Theodore may have been making a rather daring political gesture, publicly expressing a leaning toward Gnosticism. Alternatively, the area of the north hall may have been Theodore's private residence, where the retention of Gnostic symbolism may have been more acceptable.

The 4th-century mosaics of the south hall (the present-day nave of the basilica) are somewhat more doctrinally conventional, and represent the story of Jonah as prefiguring the salvation offered by the Church.

Down a flight of steps, the **Cripta degli Affreschi** contains beautiful 12th-century frescoes, among them Saint Peter sending Saint Mark to Aquileia and the beheading of Saints Hermagoras and Fortunatus, to whom the basilica is dedicated. ⊠ *Piazza Capitolo* ☎ *0431/91067* 📩 *Basilica free, both crypts €3, campanile €1.20* ◷ *Apr.–Oct., daily 9–7; Nov.–Mar., weekdays 9–4:30, weekends 9–5.*

Beyond the basilica and across the road, the **archaeological site** among the cypresses reveals Roman remains of the forum, houses, cemetery, and port. The little stream was once an important waterway extending to Grado. The area is well signposted. Unfortunately, many of the excavations of Roman Aquileia could not be left exposed because of the extremely high water table under the site. Much of Roman Aquileia had to be reburied after archaeological studies had been conducted; nevertheless, what remains aboveground, along with the monuments in the archaeological museum, is sufficient to give an idea of the grandeur of this ancient city. ⊕ *www.museoarcheo-aquileia.it* 📩 *Free* ◷ *Daily 8:15–7.*

The **Museo Archeologico** is rewarding, containing a wealth of material from the Roman era. Notable are the portrait busts from Republican times, semiprecious gems, amber and gold work—including preserved flies—a fine glass collection, and beautiful pre-Christian mosaics from the floors of Roman houses and palaces. ⊠ *Via Roma 1* 🕾 *0431/91096* ⊕ *www.museoarcheo-aquileia.it* 💶 *€4* 🕙 *Tues.–Sun. 8:30–7:30.*

The **Museo Paleocristiano** is not simply a museum, it is rather an early-Christian 4th-century suburban basilica that was transformed in the 9th century into a monastery and then, lastly, into a farmhouse. Some of the fragments of 4th-century mosaics preserved here are even more delicate than those in the main basilica. ⊠ *Località Monastero* 🕾 *0431/91035* ⊕ *www.museoarcheo-aquileia.it* 💶 *Free* 🕙 *Tues.–Sun. 8:30–1:45.*

TRIESTE

77 km (48 mi) east of Aquileia, 163 km (101 mi) east of Venice.

GETTING HERE

Trains to Trieste depart regularly from Venice, Udine, and other major Italian cities. By car, it is the eastern terminus of the Autostrada Torino–Trieste (E70). Trieste is served by Ronchi dei Ligioneri Airport, which receives flights from major Italian airports and some European cities. The airport is 33 km (20½ mi) from the city; transportation into Trieste is by taxi or Bus 51.

VISITOR INFORMATION

Trieste tourism office (⊠ *Piazza dell'Unità d'Italia 4/b* 🕾 *040/3478312* ⊕ *www.triesteturismo.com*).

EXPLORING

Trieste is built along a fringe of coastline where a rugged karst plateau tumbles abruptly into the beautiful Adriatic. It was, up until the end of World War I, the only port of the Austro-Hungarian Empire and therefore a major industrial and financial center. In the early years of the 20th century, Trieste and its surroundings also became famous by their association with some of the most important names of Italian literature, such as Italo Svevo, and English and German letters. James Joyce drew inspiration from the city's multiethnic population, and Rainer Maria Rilke was inspired by the seacoast west of the city.

Trieste has lost its importance as a port and a center of finance, but perhaps because of its multicultural nature at the juncture of Latin, Slavic, and Germanic Europe, it has never fully lost its role as an intellectual center. In recent years, the city has become a center for science and the computer industry. The streets hold a mix of monumental, neoclassical, and art nouveau architecture built by the Austrians during Trieste's days of glory, granting an air of melancholy stateliness to a city that lives as much in the past as the present.

Italian revolutionaries of the 1800s rallied their battle cry around Trieste, because of what they believed was foreign occupation of their motherland. After World War II, the sliver of land including Trieste and a small part of Istria became an independent, neutral state that was officially recognized in a 1947 peace treaty. Although it was actually

Trieste's Canal Grande.

occupied by British and American troops for its nine years of existence, the Free Territory of Trieste issued its own currency and stamps. In 1954 a Memorandum of Understanding was signed in London, giving civil administration of Trieste to Italy.

★ The sidewalk cafés on the vast seaside **Piazza dell'Unità d'Italia** are popular meeting places in the summer months. The imposing square, ringed by grandiose facades, was set out as a plaza open to the sea, like Venice's Piazza San Marco, in the late Middle Ages. It underwent countless changes through the centuries and its present size and architecture are essentially products of late-19th- and early-20th-century Austria. The huge square was named and renamed, according to the political fortunes of the city; it was given its current name in 1955, when Trieste was finally given to Italy. On the inland side of the piazza note the facade of the **Palazzo Comunale** (Town Hall) designed by the Triestino architect Giuseppi Bruni in 1875. Sadly, it was from this building's balcony in 1938 that Mussolini proclaimed the infamous racial laws, depriving Italian Jews of most of their rights.

A statue of Habsburg emperor Leopold I looks out over **Piazza della Borsa**, which contains Trieste's original stock exchange, the **Borsa Vecchia** (1805), an attractive neoclassical building now serving as the chamber of commerce. It sits at the end of the Canal Grande, a canal dug in the 18th century by the Austrian empress Maria Theresia as a first step in the expansion of what was then a small fishing village of 7,000 into the port of her empire.

The ruins of a 1st century AD amphitheater, **Teatro Romano**, near the Via Giuseppi Mazzini opposite the city's *questura* (police station), were

Trieste's Caffè Culture

Trieste is justly famous for its coffee. The elegant civility of Trieste plays out beautifully in a *caffè* culture combining the refinement of Vienna with the passion of Italy. In Trieste, as elsewhere in Italy, ask for a caffè and you'll get a thimbleful of high-octane espresso. Your cappuccino here will also come in an espresso cup, with only half as much frothy milk as you'll find elsewhere and, in the Viennese fashion, a dollop of whipped cream. Many cafés are part of a *torrefazione* (roasting shop), so you can sample a cup and then buy beans to take with you.

Few cafés in Italy can rival **Antico Caffè San Marco** (⊠ *Via Battisti 18* ☎ *040/363538* ⊙ *Closed Mon.*) for its bohemian atmosphere. After being destroyed in World War I, it was rebuilt in the 1920s, and then restored several more times, but some of the original art nouveau decor remains. It became a meeting place for local intellectuals and was the haunt of the Triestino writers Italo Svevo and Umberto Saba. For a great view of the great piazza, you couldn't do better than **Caffè Degli Specchi** (⊠ *Piazza dell'Unità d'Italia 7* ☎ *040/365777*), where the many mirrors heighten the opportunities for people-watching. Originally opened in 1839, it was taken over by the British Navy after World War II, and Triestini were not allowed in unless accompanied by an Englishman. Because of its location, it is the café most frequented by tourists; it's open daily until midnight. Founded in 1830, classic **Caffè Tommaseo** (⊠ *Piazza Tommaseo 4/C* ☎ *040/362666*) is a comfortable place to linger, especially on weekend evenings and Sunday morning (11–1:30), when there's live music. It's open daily until 12:30 AM. **Cremcaffè** (⊠ *Piazza Carlo Goldoni 10* ☎ *040/636555* ⊙ *Closed Sun.*) isn't the ideal place to sit and read the paper, but its downtown location and selection of 20 coffee blends make it one of the busiest cafés in town. The atmosphere is more modern than Old World at **I Paesi del Caffè** (⊠ *Via Einaudi 1* ☎ *040/633897* ⊙ *Closed Sun.*), which brews coffee and sells beans of most of the top varieties, including Jamaica Blue Mountain.

7

discovered during 1938 demolition work. Its statues are now displayed at the Museo Civico, and the space is used for summer plays and concerts. ⊠ *Via del Teatro Romano*.

The 14th-century **Cattedrale di San Giusto,** built on the site of an ancient Roman forum, contains remnants of at least three previous buildings built on the same ground, the earliest a hall dating from the 5th century. A section of the original floor mosaic still remains, incorporated into the floor of the present church. In the 9th and 11th centuries two adjacent churches were built on the same site, the Church of the Assumption and the Church of San Giusto. The beautiful apse mosaics of these churches, done in the 12th and 13th centuries by a Venetian artist, still remain in the apses of the side aisles of the present church. In the 14th century the two churches were joined and a Romanesque-Gothic facade was attached, ornamented with fragments of Roman monuments taken from the forum. The jambs of the main doorway are the most conspicuous Roman element. ✉ *Piazza della Cattedrale 2* ☎ *040/309666* ⊗ *Apr.–Oct., Mon.–Sun. 7:30–7:30; Nov.–Mar., Mon.–Sat. 7:30–noon and 3–6:30, Sun. 7:30–1 and 3:30–7.*

The hilltop **Castello di San Giusto** (built 1470–1630) was constructed on the ruins of the Roman town of Tergeste. Given the excellent view, it's no surprise that 15th-century Venetians turned the castle into a shipping observation point; the structure was further enlarged by Trieste's subsequent rulers, the Habsburgs. ✉ *Piazza della Cattedrale 3* ☎ *040/309362* 💶 *€4* ⊗ *Nov.–Mar., daily 9–5; Apr.–Oct., daily 9–7.*

On the hill near the Castello is the **Civico Museo di Storia ed Arte**, an eclectic history and art museum with statues from the Roman theater and artifacts from Egypt, Greece, and Rome. There's also an assortment of glass and manuscripts. The **Orto Lapidario** (Lapidary Garden) has classical statuary, pottery, and a small Corinthian temple. ✉ *Via Cattedrale 15* ☎ *040/310500* 💶 *€4* ⊗ *Tues.–Sun. 9–1.*

The **Civico Museo Revoltella e Galleria d'Arte Moderna** was founded in 1872, when the city inherited the palazzo, library, and art collection of shipping magnate Baron Pasquale Revoltella. The collection holds almost exclusively 19th- and 20th-century Italian art, much of which was collected by Revoltella himself. Along with the palace, the museum presents a good picture of the tastes of a Triestino captain of industry during the city's days of glory. Call for hours during special exhibits. The museum's rooftop café, where the view rivals the artwork, is open some evenings in summer. ✉ *Via Armando Diaz 27* ☎ *040/6754350* 💶 *€6.50* ⊗ *Wed.–Mon. 10–7.*

OFF THE BEATEN PATH

Castello Di Duino. The 14th-century Castle of Duino, where in 1912 Rainer Maria Rilke was inspired to write his masterpiece, the *Duino Elegies*, is just 12 km (7½ mi) from Trieste. Take Bus 44 or 51 from the Trieste railway station. The easy path along the seacoast from the castle toward Trieste has gorgeous views that rival the Amalfi Coast and the Cinque Terre. The castle itself, still the property of the Princes of Thurn and Taxis, is open to the public; it contains a fine collection of antique furnishings and an amazing Palladian circular staircase. ✉ *Frazione Duino 32, Duino-Ausina* ☎ *040/208120* ⊕ *www.castellodiduino.it* 💶 *€7* ⊗ *Apr.–Sept., Wed.–Mon. 9:30–5:30; Oct.–Mar., weekends and holidays 9:30–4.*

WHERE TO EAT

¢
SEAFOOD
★

✕ **Antipastoteca di Mare.** Hidden halfway up the hill to the Castello di San Giusto, in what the Triestini call the old city, this little informal restaurant specializes in traditional preparations from the *cucina povera*. The inexpensive fish—bluefish, sardines, mackerel, mussels, and squid—are accompanied by salad, potatoes, polenta, and house wine. The consistently tasty and fresh dishes, especially the fish soup and the *sardoni in savor* (large sardines with raisins, pine nuts, and caramelized onions; "savor" is the Triestino-dialect equivalent of the Venetian "saor"), show what a talented chef can do on a limited budget. ✉ *Via della Fornace 1* ☎ *040/309606* ▬ *No credit cards* ⊗ *Closed Mon. No dinner Sun.*

¢ ✕ **Da Pepi.** A Triestino institution, Da Pepi is the oldest and most
NORTHERN esteemed of the many "buffet" restaurants around town. It specializes
ITALIAN in *bollito di maiale*, a dish of boiled pork and pork sausages accompanied by delicately flavored sauerkraut, mustard, and grated horserad-
ish. This hole-in-the-wall eatery with few tables and simple decor, and
others like it, are as much a part of the Triestino scene as the cafés.
Unlike other Italian restaurants, buffets don't close between lunch and
dinner, and tap beer is the drink of choice. ⊠ *Via Cassa di Risparmio
3* ☎ *040/366858* ═ *AE, MC, V* ⊘ *Closed Sun. and last 2 wks in July.*

$$ ✕ **Suban.** An easy trip slightly outside town, this landmark trattoria
NORTHERN operated by the hospitable Suban family has been in business since
ITALIAN 1865. Sit by the dining room fire or relax on a huge terrace and watch
the sunset. This is Italian food with a Slovene, Hungarian, and Austrian
accent. Start with *jota carsolina* (a rich soup of cabbage, potatoes, and
beans), and then you might order a steak grilled and sliced at your table.
Lighter fare includes *insalatine tiepide* (warm salads with smoked pork
or duck) and a smoked beef that is truly special. To get here you can
take Bus 35 from Piazza Oberdan. ⊠ *Via Comici 2* ☎ *040/54368* ═ *AE,
DC, MC, V* ⊘ *Closed Tues., 1st 3 wks in Aug., and 2 wks in early Jan.
No lunch weekdays.*

WHERE TO STAY

$ ▥ **Filoxenia.** The location on the city waterfront, and the reasonable
prices, make this small hotel a good choice for travelers on a tight
budget. Members of Trieste's Greek community run the Filoxenia,
and there's a Greek restaurant on-site, offering basic fare. The staff
is friendly and helpful and rooms are simple and fresh. **Pros:** central
location; friendly staff; budget price. **Cons:** some very small, spar-
tan rooms; some street noise; showers are cramped. ⊠ *Via Mazzini
3* ☎ *040/3481644* ⊕ *www.filoxenia.it* ⤴ *20 rooms* ♿ *In-room: Wi-Fi.
In-hotel: restaurant, bar, parking (paid), some pets allowed* ═ *DC, MC,
V* ◉ *BP.*

$$ ▥ **L'Albero Nascosto Hotel Residence.** Though hardly noticeable on its
★ busy, narrow street, this hotel residence is one of the best values in
Trieste. Each room is decorated with paintings by a local artist and furnished with antiques. The lobby boasts an old Roman column, recycled
when the 18th-century building was constructed, and the smoking patio
is enclosed by Trieste's 15th-century city walls. All rooms have kitch-
enettes, and though they lack phones, the kindly owners offer loaner
cell phones. **Pros:** very central location; clean and spacious rooms.
Cons: steps to climb; no staff on-site after 8 PM (though late arrivals
can be arranged). ⊠ *Via Felice Venezian 18* ☎ *040/300188* ⊕ *www.
alberonascosto.it* ⤴ *10 rooms* ♿ *In-room: no phone, kitchen, Wi-Fi.
In-hotel: bar, parking (paid), some pets allowed* ═ *AE, MC, V* ◉ *BP.*

$$ ▥ **Riviera & Maximilian's.** Seven kilometers (4½ mi) north of Trieste,
★ this lovely hotel commands views across the Golfo di Trieste, includ-
ing nearby Castello di Miramare; dining areas, the bar, and all guest
rooms enjoy this stunning panorama. There's no sand on this stretch
of coast, but an elevator leads to the hotel's own private bathing quay
below, as well as to a children's area. Some rooms have balconies and
kitchenettes. The restaurant has indoor trompe l'oeil decor and an

outdoor terrace. **Pros:** great views; gorgeous grounds. **Cons:** far from town; some rooms are cramped. ⊠ *Strada Costiera 22* ☎ *040/224551* ⊕ *www.hotelrivieraemaximilian.com* ⟿ *56 rooms, 2 suites, 9 apartments* ⚲ *In-room: safe, refrigerator, Wi-Fi. In-hotel: restaurant, bar, pool, beachfront, Internet terminal, parking (free), some pets allowed* ☰ *AE, DC, MC, V* ⎮⊙⎮ *BP.*

CASTELLO DI MIRAMARE

7 km (4½ mi) northwest of Trieste.

GETTING HERE
Bus 36 from Piazza Oberdan in Trieste runs here every half hour.

EXPLORING

☾ ★ Archduke Maximilian of Habsburg, brother of Emperor Franz Josef and retired commander of the Austrian Navy, built this seafront extravaganza from 1856 to 1860. The throne room has a ship's-keel wooden ceiling; in accordance with late 19th-century taste, the rooms are generally furnished with very elaborate somewhat ponderous versions of medieval, Renaissance, and French period furniture, and the walls are covered in red damask. Maximilian's retirement was interrupted in 1864, when he became emperor of Mexico at the initiative of Napoléon III. He was executed three years later by a Mexican firing squad. His wife, Charlotte of Belgium, went mad and returned to Miramar, and later to her native country. During the last years of the Habsburg reign, Miramar became one of the favorite residences of the wife of Franz Josef, the Empress Elizabeth (Sissi). The castle was later owned by Duke Amadeo of Aosta, who renovated some rooms in the rationalist style and installed modern plumbing in his art deco bathroom. Tours in English are available by reservation. Surrounding the castle is a 54-acre park, partly wooded and partly sculpted into attractive gardens. ⊠ *Viale Miramare off SS14, Trieste* ☎ *040/224143* ⊕ *www.castello-miramare.it* ⛬ *Castle €4 (€6 during some special exhibits), guided tour €4, park free* ☉ *Castle: daily 9–7. Last entry ½ hr before closing. Park: Apr.–Sept., daily 8–7; Nov.–Feb., daily 8–5; Mar. and Oct., daily 8–6.*

The Dolomites

TRENTINO–ALTO ADIGE

WORD OF MOUTH

". . . an unearthly experience. Bare rock towers, boulders the size of cars strewn all about . . . quite bleak, quite surreal and quite amazing . . . The Dolomites truly need to be seen to be appreciated, as pictures don't do them justice."

—pjal

WELCOME TO THE DOLOMITES

Dolomites

TOP REASONS TO GO

★ **Museo Archeologico dell'Alto Adige, Bolzano:** The impossibly well-preserved body of the iceman Ötzi, the star attraction here, provokes countless questions about the meaning of life 5,000 years ago.

★ **Hiking:** No matter your fitness level, there's an unforgettable walk in store for you here.

★ **Trento:** A graceful fusion of Austrian and Italian styles, this breezy, frescoed town is famed for its imposing castle.

★ **Grande Strada delle Dolomiti (Great Dolomites Road):** Your rental Fiat will think it's a Ferrari as it wends its way along this gorgeous drive through the Heart of the Dolomites.

1 Trentino. This butterfly-shaped province is Italy with a German accent. Its principal city, history-rich Trento, is at the center. To the northwest are Madonna di Campiglio, one of Italy's most fashionable ski resorts, and Bormio, another notable skiing destination that doubles as a gateway to the Parco Nazionale dello Stelvio.

2 Bolzano. Alto Adige's capital is the Dolomites' most lively city. Look for high-gabled houses, wrought-iron signs, and centuries-old wine cellars.

3 Alto Adige. This region was a part of Austria until the end of World War I, and Austrian sensibilities still predominate over Italian. At the spa town of Merano you can soak in hot springs, take the "grape cure," and stroll along lovely walkways. To the southwest, Caldaro has an appealing wine-growing region.

4 Heart of the Dolomites. The spectacular Sella mountain range and the surrounding Val di Fassa and Val Gardena make up

this region. It's distinguished by great views and great mountain sports, both summer and winter. At the town of Canazei, the cable car 3,000 feet up to the Col Rodella lookout packages the vast panorama perfectly.

AUSTRIA

ALPS

Glorenza

Spondigna

40

41

38

SWITZERLAND

38

Parco Nazionale dello Stelvio

ORTLES-ORTLERGRUPPE

Bormio

38 PIEMONTE

VAL DI SOLE

42 Madonna di Campiglio

Pinzolo

1 TRENTINO

239

237 Tione

Arco

240

Trentino

Bolzano

Brenner Pass

A L P S

A22

49 Brunico

Bressanone

AUSTRIA

Dobbiaco

49

51

3

ALTO ADIGE

Merano

38

VAL GARDENA

SELLA MT. RANGE

5 Cortina d'Ampezzo

48

51

4

Grande Strada delle Dolomiti

2 Bolzano

Col Rodella

Canazei

Cles

A22

12

42

VAL DI FASSA

43

48

Predazzo

Mezzolombardo

Trento

Lago di Caldonazzo

12

47 Strigno

A22

Rovereto

46

0   10 mi

0   10 km

GETTING ORIENTED

8

Shadowed by the Dolomite Mountains—whose otherworldly pinnacles Leonardo depicted in the background of his *Mona Lisa*—the northeast Italian provinces of Trentino and Alto Adige are centered around the valleys of the Adige and Isarco rivers, which course from the Brenner Pass south to Bolzano.

Canazei

5 **Cortina d'Ampezzo.** A former hangout of the ultrahip, Cortina has aged gracefully into the grande dame of Italian ski resorts. But it's arguably at its best in summer, when there are countless options for hiking and mountain activities.

THE DOLOMITES PLANNER

Making the Most of Your Time

For a brief stay, your best choice for a base is vibrant Bolzano, where you can get a sense of the region's contrasts—Italian and German, medieval and ultramodern. After a day or two in town, venture an hour south to history-laden Trento, north to the lovely spa town of Merano, or southwest to Caldaro and its Strada di Vino; all are viable day trips from Bolzano, and Trento and Merano make good places to spend the night as well.

If you have more time, you'll want to get up into the mountains, which are the region's main attraction. The trip on the Grande Strada delle Dolomiti (Great Dolomites Road) through the Heart of the Dolomites to Cortina d'Ampezzo is one of Italy's most spectacular drives. Summer or winter, this is a great destination for mountain sports, with scores of trails for world-class hiking and skiing.

Hitting the Slopes

The Dolomites have some of the most spectacular downhill skiing in Europe, with the facilities to match. The most comprehensive centers are the upscale resorts of the massive Cortina d'Ampezzo and Madonna di Campiglio, which draw an international clientele with impressive terrain, expansive lift systems, and lively après-ski. For traditional Tirolean *Gemütlichkeit* (congeniality), try one of the more rustic resorts: in the Val di Fassa or Val Gardena your lift mate is more likely to be from a neighboring town than from Milan. Both major resorts and out-of-the-way villages have well-marked trails for *sci di fondo* (cross-country skiing). With the exception of the main bargain period known as *settimane bianche* (white weeks) in January and February, the slopes are seldom overcrowded.

Finding a Place to Stay

Classic Dolomite lodging options range from restored castles to chalets to stately 19th-century hotels. The small villages that pepper the Dolomites often have scores of flower-bedecked, Alpine-shuttered inns, many of them inexpensive. Hotel information offices at train stations and tourist offices can help if you've arrived without reservations. The Bolzano train station has a 24-hour hotel service, and tourist offices will give you a list of all the hotels in the area, arranged by location, stars, and price. Hotels at ski resorts cater to longer stays at full or half board: you should book ski vacations as packages well in advance. Most rural accommodations close from early November to mid- or late December, as well as for a month or two after Easter.

WHAT IT COSTS (IN EUROS)					
	¢	$	$$	$$$	$$$$
Restaurants	under €20	€20–€30	€30–€45	€45–€65	over €65
Hotels	under €75	€75–€125	€125–€200	€200–€300	over €300

Restaurant prices are for a first course (primo), second course (secondo), and dessert (dolce). Hotel prices are for two people in a standard double room in high season, including tax and service.

Getting Around by Car

Driving is easily the most convenient way to travel in the Dolomites; it can be difficult to reach the ski areas (or any town outside of Rovereto, Trento, Bolzano, and Merano) without a car. Driving is also the most exhilarating way to get around, as you rise from broad valleys into mountains with narrow, winding roads straight out of a sports-car ad. Caution is essential (tap your horn in advance of hairpin turns), as are chains in winter, when roads are often covered in snow. Sudden closures are common, especially on high mountain passes, and can occur as early as November and as late as May. Even under the best conditions, expect to negotiate mountain roads at speeds no greater than 50 KPH (30 MPH).

The most important route in the region is the A22, the main north–south highway linking Italy with central Europe by way of the Brenner Pass. It connects Innsbruck with Bressanone, Bolzano, Trento, and Rovereto, and near Verona joins autostrada A4 (which runs east–west across northern Italy, from Trieste to Turin). By car, Trento is 3 hours from Milan and 2½ hours from Venice. Bolzano is another hour's drive to the north, with Munich four hours farther on.

If you're planning a driving tour of the Dolomites, consider flying into Munich. Car rentals are less expensive in Germany, and it's easier to get automatic transmission (though manual is better suited to challenging mountain roads).

Getting Around by Train

The rail line following the course of the Isarco and Adige valleys—from Munich and Innsbruck, through the Brenner Pass, and southward past Bressanone, Bolzano, Trento, and Rovereto en route to Verona—is well trafficked, making trains a viable option for travel between these towns. Eurocity trains on the Dortmund–Venice and Munich–Innsbruck–Rome routes stop at these stations, and you can connect with other Italian lines at Verona. Although branch lines from Trento and Bolzano do extend into some of the smaller valleys (including hourly service between Bolzano and Merano), most of the mountain attractions are beyond the reach of trains. Check **Trenitalia** (☎ 892021 *within Italy* ⊕ *www.trenitalia.com*) for more information.

Getting Around by Bus

Regular bus service connects larger cities to the south (Verona, Venice, and Milan) with valley towns in Trentino–Alto Adige (Rovereto, Trento, Bolzano, and Merano). You'll need to change to less frequent local buses to reach resorts and smaller villages in the mountains beyond.

If you're equipped with current schedules and don't mind adapting your schedules to theirs, it's possible to visit even the remotest villages by bus. For information, contact **Trentino Trasporti** (☎ 0461/821000 ⊕ *www. ttesercizio.it*) or Alto Adige's **SIT** (*Servizio Integrato di Trasporto* ☎ 0471/415480 or 800/846047 ⊕ *www.sii.bz.it*).

Winter service with **CortinaExpress** (☎ 0436/867350 ⊕ *www.cortinaexpress.it*) connects the resort with Venice airport and nearby Mestre train station. **ATVO** (☎ 0421/383671 ⊕ *www.atvo.it*) provides year-round service to Cortina from Venice's Piazzale Roma bus park. **DolomitiBus** (☎ 0437/217111 ⊕ *www. dolomitibus.it*) covers the eastern Dolomites, including a number of small towns.

8

EATING AND DRINKING WELL IN THE DOLOMITES

Everything in Alto Adige (and, to a lesser extent, Trentino) has more than a tinge of the Teutonic—and the food is no exception. The rich and creamy food here, including fondues, polentas, and barley soups, reflects the Alpine climate and Austrian and Swiss influence.

The quintessential restaurant here is the wood-panel Tirolean *Stube* (pub) serving hearty meat-and-dumpling fare, and there's also a profusion of pastry shops and lively beer halls.

Although the early dining schedule you'll find in Germany or Austria is somewhat tempered here, your options for late-night meals are more limited than in southern Italy, where *la dolce vita* has a firmer grip.

Thankfully, the coffee is every bit as good as in parts south—just expect to hear "*danke, grazie*" when paying for your cappuccino.

BEST OF THE WURST

Not to be missed are the outdoor wurst carts, even (or perhaps especially) in colder weather. After placing your order you'll get a sheet of wax paper, followed by a dollop of mustard, a Kaiser roll, and your chosen sausage.

You can sometimes make your selection by pointing to whatever picture is most appealing; if not, pass on the familiar-sounding *Frankfurter* and try the local *Meraner*. Carts can reliably be found in Bolzano (try Piazza delle Erbe, or in front of the archaeological museum) and Merano (Piazza del Grano, or along the river).

POLENTA AND DUMPLINGS

Polenta is a staple in the region, in both its creamy and firm varieties, often topped with cheese or mushrooms (or both). Dumplings also appear on many menus; the most distinctive to the region are *canederli* (also known as *Knoedel*), pictured at right, made from seasoned bread in many variations, and served either in broth or with a sauce.

Other dumplings to look for are the dense *strangolapreti* (literally "priest-chokers") and *gnocchi di ricotta alla zucca* (ricotta and pumpkin dumplings).

CHEESE

Cheese from the Alpine dairy cows of Trentino–Alto Adige is a specialty, with each isolated mountain valley seeming to make its own variety, to be found nowhere else—it's often simply called *nostrano* (ours).

The best known of the cheeses are the mild Asiago and *fontal* and the more-pungent *puzzone di Moena* (literally, "stink-pot"). If your doctor permits it, try the *schiz*: fresh cheese that is sliced and fried in butter, sometimes with cream added.

PASTRIES AND BAKED GOODS

Bakeries turn out a wide selection of crusty dark rolls and caraway-studded rye breads—maybe not typical Italian bread, but full of flavor. Pastries are reminiscent of what you'd expect to find in Vienna. Apple strudel, pictured below, is everywhere, and for good reason: the best apples in Italy are grown here. There's other exceptional fruit as well, including pears, plums, and grapes that make its way into baked goods.

ALIMENTARI

If you're planning a picnic or getting provisions for a hike, you'll be well served by the fine *alimentari* (food shops) of Trentino and Alto Adige. They stock a bounty of regional specialties, including cheeses, pickles, salami, and smoked meats. These are good places to pick up a sample of *speck tirolese*, the salt-cured, cold-smoked, deboned ham hock usually cut in paper-thin slices, like prosciutto (though proud speck producers often bristle at the comparison). Don't discard the fat of the speck—it's considered the best part.

WINE

Though Trentino and Alto Adige aren't as esteemed for their wines as many other Italian regions, they produce a wide variety of crisp, dry, and aromatic whites—Kerner, Müller Thurgau, and Traminer, to name a few—not surprisingly, more like what you'd expect from German vineyards than Italian. Among the reds, look for Lagrein and the native Teroldego, a fruity, spicy variety produced only in the tiny valley north of Trento. The Trento D.O.C. is a marvelous sparkling wine in a class with Champagne.

8

Updated by
Nan McElroy

The vast, mountainous domain of northeastern Italy, unlike other celebrated Alpine regions, has remained relatively undeveloped. Strange, rocky pinnacles jut straight up like chimneys, looming over scattered, pristine mountain lakes. Below, rivers meander through valleys dotted with peaceful villages and protected by picture-book castles. In the most-secluded Dolomite vales, unique cultures have flourished: the Ladin language, an offshoot of Latin still spoken in the Val Gardena and Val di Fassa, owes its unlikely survival to centuries of topographic isolation.

The more-accessible parts of Trentino–Alto Adige, on the other hand, have a history of near-constant intermingling of cultures. The region's Adige and Isarco valleys make up the main access route between Italy and central Europe, and as a result, the language, cuisine, and architecture are a blend of north and south. Whereas the province of Trentino is largely Italian-speaking, Alto Adige is predominantly Germanic: until World War I, the area was Austria's south Tirol. As you move north toward the famed Brenner Pass—through the prosperous valley towns of Rovereto, Trento, and Bolzano—the Teutonic influence is increasingly dominant; by the time you reach Bressanone, it's hard to believe you're in Italy at all.

TRENTINO

Until the end of World War I, Trentino was Italy's frontier with the Austro-Hungarian Empire, and although this province remains unmistakably Italian, Germanic influences are tangible in all aspects of life here, including architecture, cuisine, culture, and language. Visitors are drawn by historical sights reflecting a strategic position at the intersection of southern and central Europe: Trento was the headquarters of the Catholic Counter-Reformation; Rovereto the site of an emblematically bloody battle during the Great War. Numerous year-round mountain resorts, including fashionable Madonna di Campiglio, are in the wings of the butterfly-shaped region.

TRENTO

51 km (32 mi) south of Bolzano, 24 km (15 mi) north of Rovereto.

VISITOR INFORMATION

Trento tourism office (✉ *Via Manci 2* ☎ *0461/216000* ⊕ *www.apt.trento.it*).

EXPLORING

Trento is a prosperous, cosmopolitan university town that retains an architectural charm befitting its historical importance. It was here, from 1545 to 1563, that the structure of the Catholic Church was redefined at the Council of Trent. This was the starting point of the Counter-Reformation, which brought half of Europe back to Catholicism. The word *consiglio* (council) appears everywhere in Trento—in hotel, restaurant, and street names, and even on wine labels.

Today the Piazza del Duomo remains splendid, and its enormous medieval palazzo dominates the city landscape in virtually its original form. The 24-hour Trento Card (€10) grants admission to all major town sights and can be purchased at the tourist office or any museum. A 48-hour card (€15) is also available, and includes entrance to the modern art museum in Rovereto. Both cards provide a number of other perks, including tours, free public transportation, wine tastings, and the cable car ride to Belvedere di Sardagna.

Guided tours of Trento depart Saturday from the Trento tourism office. You can meet at 10 AM for a visit to the Castello del Buonconsiglio (€6, including admission to the castle), or at 3 PM for a tour of the city center (€3). Reservations are not required; these tours and others are included in the Trento Card. ✉ *Via Manci 2* ☎ *0461/216000* ⊕ *www.apt.trento.it.*

The massive Romanesque **Duomo**, also known as the Cathedral of San Vigilio, forms the southern edge of the Piazza del Duomo. Locals refer to this square as the city's *salotto* (sitting room), as in fine weather it's always filled with students and residents drinking coffee, sipping an aperitif, or reading the newspaper. The baroque **Fontana del Nettuno** presides over it all. When skies are clear, pause here to savor the view of the mountaintops enveloping the city.

Within the Duomo, unusual arcaded stone stairways border the austere nave. Ahead is the *baldacchino* (altar canopy), a copy of Bernini's masterpiece in St. Peter's in Rome. To the left of the altar is a mournful 16th-century crucifixion, flanked by the Virgin Mary and John the Apostle. This crucifix, by German artist Sisto Frey, was a focal point of the Council of Trent: each decree agreed on during the two decades of deliberations was solemnly read out in front of it. Stairs on the left side of the altar lead down to the 4th-century Paleo-Christian burial vault. Outside, walk around to the back of the cathedral to see an exquisite display of 14th-century stonemason's art, from the small porch to the intriguing knotted columns on the graceful apse. ✉ *Piazza del Duomo* ☎ *0461/980132* ☉ *Daily 6:30–noon and 2–8.*

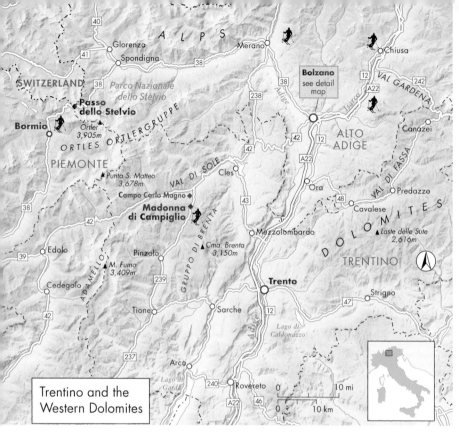

The crenellated **Palazzo Pretorio**, situated so as to seem like a wing of the Duomo, was built in the 13th century as the fortified residence of the prince-bishops, who enjoyed considerable power and autonomy within the medieval hierarchy. The remarkable palazzo has lost none of its original splendor. The crenellations are not merely decorative: the square pattern represents ancient allegiance to the Guelphs (the triangular crenellations seen elsewhere in town represent Ghibelline loyalty). The palazzo now houses the **Museo Diocesano Tridentino**, where you can see paintings showing the seating plan of the prelates during the Council of Trent; early-16th-century tapestries by Pieter van Aelst (1502–56), the Belgian artist who carried out Raphael's 15th-century designs for the Vatican tapestries; carved wood altars and statues; and an 11th-century sacramentary, or book of services. These and other precious objects all come from the cathedral's treasury. Accessible through the museum, a subterranean archaeological area reveals the 1st-century Roman Porta Veronensis, which marked the road to Verona. ⊠ *Piazza del Duomo 18* ☎ *0461/234419* ⊕ *www.museodiocesanotridentino.it* ⏍ *€4 includes archaeological area* ⏱ *June–Sept., Wed.–Mon. 9:30–12:30 and 2:30–6; Oct.–May, Wed.–Mon. 9:30–12:30 and 2–5:30.*

★ The ancient Roman city of **Tridentum** lies beneath much of Trento's city center. Centuries of Adige River flooding buried ruins that only recently have been unearthed on public and private land. Beneath this piazza lies the largest of the archaeological sites, revealing some marvels of Roman technology, such as under-floor home heating and under-street sewers complete with manhole covers. The Romans even used lead pipes for four centuries before recognizing it was hazardous to health. Other excavations you can visit lie beneath the Palazzo Pretoria and the Scrigno del Duomo restaurant. ⊠ *Piazza Cesare Battisti* ☎ *0461/230171* ≤ *€2* ⊘ *June–Sept., Tues.–Sun. 9:30–1 and 2–6; Oct.–May, Tues.–Sun. 9–1 and 2–5:30.*

QUICK BITES

Scrigno del Duomo. Upstairs, the Scrigno ("casket" in Italian) serves more than 30 wines by the glass, with an excellent selection of local cheeses to match, in a building with some of the oldest frescoes in town. Salads and regional specialties are also available; the *canederli* (seasoned bread dumplings) are especially flavorful here. In the upscale restaurant downstairs, Roman-era walls—this was the level of the ancient square that became Piazza del Duomo—now protect 750 different wines. ⊠ *Piazza del Duomo 30* ⊕ *www.scrignodelduomo.com* ☎ *0461/220030).*

Many sessions of the Council of Trent met at the Renaissance church **Santa Maria Maggiore.** Limited light enters through the simple rose window over the main door, so you have to strain to see the magnificent ceiling, an intricate combination of stucco and frescoes. The church is off the northwest side of the Piazza del Duomo, about 200 yards down Via Cavour. Note that at this writing, the church was closed for renovation, with reopening expected toward the end of 2011. ⊠ *Vicolo Orsoline 1* ☎ *0461/230037* ⊘ *Daily 8–noon and 2:30–6.*

Locals refer to **Via Belenzani** as Trento's outdoor gallery because of the frescoed facades of the hallmark Renaissance palazzi. It's an easy 50-yard walk up the lane behind the church of Santa Maria Maggiore.

The **Torre Vanga** is a 13th-century tower near the Adige River and one of the bridges that crosses it, the Ponte San Lorenzo.

You can take the Funivia Trento–Sardagna cable car up to the **Belvedere di Sardagna,** a lookout point 1,200 feet above medieval Trento. *Cable car* ⊠ *Ponte San Lorenzo* ☎ *0461/983627* ≤ *€2 round-trip; free with Trento Card* ⊘ *Daily 7–5.*

★ The **Castello del Buonconsiglio** *(Castle of Good Counsel)* was once the stronghold of the prince-bishops; its position and size made it easier to defend than the Palazzo Pretorio. Look for the evolution of architectural styles: the medieval fortifications of the Castelvecchio section (on the far left) were built in the 13th century; the fancier Renaissance Magno Palazzo section (on the far right) wasn't completed until 300 years later. Part of the Castello now houses the **Museo Provinciale d'Arte,** where permanent and visiting exhibits of art and archaeology hang in frescoed medieval halls or under Renaissance coffered ceilings. The 13th-century **Torre dell'Aquila** (Eagle's Tower) is home to the castle's artistic highlight, a 15th-century *ciclo dei mesi* (cycle of the months). The four-wall fresco is full of charming and detailed scenes of medieval life in both court and countryside. Reservations are required visit the tower; check

8

schedule at the ticket office. ⊠ *Via Bernardo Clesio 5* ☎ *0461/233770* ⊕ *www.buonconsiglio.it* ⌨ *Museo €7, Torre dell'Aquila €1 extra* ☉ *Apr.–mid-July, Tues.–Sun. 10–6; July–Mar., Tues.–Sun. 9:30–5.*

The **Torre Verde** (*Green Tower*) is part of Trento's 13th-century fortifications, standing alongside other fragments of the city walls. You can't go inside, but the exterior is worth a look. ⊠ *Piazza Raffaello Sanzio near castle.*

The **Museo d'Arte Moderna e Contemporanea di Trento e Rovereto** is installed in the Palazzo delle Albere, a Renaissance villa on the Adige River. Works in the permanent collection date from the 19th and 20th centuries, but the real focus here is the rotating exhibitions of contemporary artists. A €10 ticket allows you to visit this museum plus the two sister installations in the town of Rovereto, 24 km (15 mi) south of Trento. ⊠ *Via Roberto da Sanseverino 45* ☎ *800/397760 or 0424/600435* ⊕ *www.mart.trento.it* ⌨ *€6* ☉ *Tues.–Sun. 10–6.*

WHERE TO EAT

$ ✗ **Al Vò.** Trento's oldest trattoria (it's the descendant of a 14th-century
NORTHERN tavern) remains one of its most popular lunch spots. Locals crowd into
ITALIAN a simple, modern dining room to enjoy regional specialites like *crema di zucca e castagne* (squash and chestnut soup) and grilled meats served in copper skillets, such as the reliable *filetto di maialino* (pork fillet). An impressive (and inexpensive) selection of local wines is available; try the food-friendly red Teroldego, made in the valley north of Trento. ⊠ *Vicolo del Vò 11* ☎ *0461/985374* ⊕ *www.ristorantealvo.it* ▭ *AE, DC, MC, V* ☉ *Closed Sun. No dinner Sat. or Mon.–Wed.*

¢ ✗ **Antica Birreria Pedavena.** Come here for the beer—a half dozen varieties
NORTHERN are brewed in-house (as evidence by the big vats looming in front of you)
ITALIAN and served up in a cavernous old-fashioned-but-newly-renovated beer hall. Meals include wursts, meat and cheese platters, pizzas, and huge salads. It's open continuously from 9 AM to midnight (until 1 AM on Friday and Saturday). Smaller wood-paneled dining rooms and a summer terrace allow for more-peaceful dining. ⊠ *Piazza Fiera 13* ☎ *0461/986255* ⊕ *www.birreriapedavena.com* ▭ *MC, V* ☉ *Closed Tues.*

$–$$ ✗ **Chiesa.** Near the castle, a 15th-century building conceals a bright,
NORTHERN modern restaurant that attracts romancing couples and power lunchers
ITALIAN alike. Ubiquitous apple imagery and excellent risotto *alle mele* (with apples) celebrate the local produce—there's even a set meal featuring apples in every course. Otherwise, the food is traditional: specialties are *maccheroncini con salsiccia e verze* (short, narrow pasta tubes with sausage and cabbage) and *tonco de Pontesel* (a stew of mixed meat made according to a 15th-century recipe). ⊠ *Via San Marco 64* ☎ *0461/238766* ⊕ *www.ristorantechiesa.it* ▭ *AE, DC, MC, V* ☉ *Closed Sun. and Jan.*

$$$ ✗ **Le Due Spade.** This intimate restaurant, around the corner from the
NORTHERN Duomo, started out as a Tirolean tavern around the time of the Council of
ITALIAN Trent. Able servers deliver superb cuisine, both traditional and more inno-
★ vative, amid the coziness of wood paneling and an antique stove. You can sample *maialino* (suckling pig) wrapped in a crust of speck, or be more adventurous with *agnello in manto alle fave di cacao* (lamb coated with

cocoa beans) served with foie-gras sauce. Given the restaurant's deserved popularity with locals and the limited seating, reservations are a must. ✉ *Via Rizzi 11* ☎ *0461/234343* 🌐 *www.leduespade.com* ✍ *Reservations essential* 💳 *AE, DC, MC, V* ⏲ *Closed Sun. No lunch Mon.*

$$ NORTHERN ITALIAN ✕ **Trattoria Orso Grigio.** The family-run "gray bear," just off the main piazza, serves tasty fare in a congenial atmosphere. Choose from typical regional dishes—look for *rufioi* (homemade ravioli stuffed with savoy cabbage)—served in a bright garden courtyard when the weather it fine. The wine list is mostly regional and pairs well with the menu. ✉ *Via degli Orti 19* ☎ *0461/984400* 💳 *AE, MC, V* ⏲ *Closed Sun.*

WHERE TO STAY

$$ **Accademia.** This friendly hotel occupies an ancient, character-filled house in the historic center of Trento, close to Piazza del Duomo. Enter through a beautiful arched passage; the public rooms also retain the original vaulting. Bedrooms have comfortable beds and handsome lithographs of the town. In warm weather, you can enjoy a meal or a drink in the courtyard garden. **Pros:** central location; charming outdoor restaurant. **Cons:** some rooms are small; stark decor; basic breakfast. ✉ *Vicolo Colico 4* ☎ *0461/233600* 🌐 *www.accademiahotel.it* *35 rooms, 5 suites* *In-room: safe, refrigerator, Internet, Wi-Fi. In-hotel: bar, some pets allowed* 💳 *AE, DC, MC, V* ⏲ *Closed late Dec.–early Jan.* *BP.*

$–$$ **Castel Pergine.** A 13th-century castle, appropriated by Trento's prince-bishops in the 16th century, is now skillfully managed by Theo Schneider, an architect, and his charming wife, Verena Neff (a former translator), both from Switzerland. Amid the labyrinth of stone and brick chambers, prisons, and chapels are sparse, rustic rooms with carved-wood trim, lace curtains, and heavy wooden beds, some canopied. The grounds host a different modern-art installation each year. The popular candlelit restaurant serves ages-old seasonal recipes from Trento in lighter guises; guests can opt for half board for an additional €20. **Pros:** romantic setting; great restaurant. **Cons:** simple accommodations; need a car to get around. ✉ *Via al Castello 10, Pergine Val Sugana* ✣ *12 km (7½ mi) east of Trento* ☎ *0461/531158* 🌐 *www.castelpergine.it* *21 rooms, 14 with bath* *In-room: no a/c, no TV. In-hotel: restaurant, bar, parking (free)* 💳 *MC, V* ⏲ *Closed Nov.–Mar. No lunch Mon.* *BP.*

$$ **Grand Hotel Trento.** Its contemporary rounded facade amid ancient palaces makes this hotel on Piazza Dante an anomaly. Inside you'll find a handsome marble lobby, rich draperies in the restaurant, and ample rooms with clubby wood-trim furniture. Business travelers are drawn by the hotel's conveniences and efficient service. The sixth-floor terrace provides a great view of the surrounding mountains. **Pros:** near train station; professional service; great breakfast. **Cons:** not a quaint hotel; busy neighborhood. ✉ *Via Alfieri 1* ☎ *0461/271000* 🌐 *www.grandhoteltrento.com* *126 rooms, 10 suites* *In-room: safe, refrigerator, Internet. In-hotel: restaurant, bar, spa, laundry service, Internet terminal, parking (paid)* 💳 *AE, DC, MC, V* *EP.*

$$ **Hotel Garni Aquila d'Oro.** A prime location near Piazza del Duomo is a main selling point for the Aquila d'Oro. Each room has its own contemporary design; some have saunas and terraces with hot tubs and stunning views. The friendly owner gives good suggestions about

what to see, do, and eat in the area. **Pros:** excellent location; friendly service. **Cons:** common areas rather cramped. ⊠ *Via Belenzani 76* ☎ *0461/986282* ⊕ *www.aquiladoro.it* ↯ *16 rooms* ♿ *In-room: safe, refrigerator, Wi-Fi. In-hotel: bar* ⊟ *AE, DC, MC, V* ⊗ *Closed late Dec.– mid-Feb.* ⫶⊙⫶ *BP.*

¢ ⫶⊡⫶ **Hotel Garni Venezia.** For reasonably priced accommodations, it's hard to beat this *garni* (bed-and-breakfast) right on Piazza Duomo. Six of the rooms have wonderful views. Family run since 1912, it offers clean, simple lodging with free Wi-Fi and paid parking a 10-minute walk away. Some rooms share bathrooms, so be sure to ask. **Pros:** location; no TVs. **Cons:** piazza can be noisy; no TVs. ⊠ *Piazza Duomo 45* ☎ *0461/234114* ⊕ *www.hotelveneziatn.it* ↯ *50 rooms* ♿ *In-room: no TV, Wi-Fi. In-hotel: parking (paid), some pets allowed* ⊟ *MC, V* ⫶⊙⫶ *BP.*

$$$ ⫶⊡⫶ **Imperial Grand Hotel Terme.** If you're in the mood for some pampering, choose the graciously restored, golden yellow palace in the nearby spa town of Levico Terme. It's not hard to imagine yourself as Austrian nobility (for whom this was once home) while you idle in the beautiful swimming pool set in a restful garden or dine at one of the elegant restaurants. Your room may even have a frescoed ceiling. In summer a poolside bar and grill is open. **Pros:** beautiful park setting; pleasant indoor pool. **Cons:** standard rooms are small; use of thermal baths not included in rates. ⊠ *Via Silva Domini 1, Levico Terme* ⊹ *20 km (12 mi) east of Trento* ☎ *0461/706104* ⊕ *www.imperialhotel.it* ↯ *69 rooms, 12 suites* ♿ *In-room: safe, refrigerator, Wi-Fi. In-hotel: 4 restaurants, bars, pools, gym, spa, bicycles, laundry service, parking (paid), some pets allowed* ⊟ *AE, DC, MC, V* ⊗ *Closed Nov.–Mar.* ⫶⊙⫶ *MAP.*

SHOPPING

You can pick up meats, cheeses, produce, local truffles, and porcini mushrooms at the small morning market in **Piazza Alessandro Vittoria.** **Enoteca di Corso** (⊠ *Corso 3 Novembre 64* ☎ *0461/916424*), a bit outside the town center, is a delightful shop laden with local products, including wine and sweets. A picnic can be handily assembled with local salamis and cheeses from **La Salumeria Mattei** (⊠ *Via Mazzini 46* ☎ *0461/238053*). Whole grain breads and delicate pastries can be purchased at fragrant **Panificio Pulin** (⊠ *Via Cavour 23* ☎ *0461/234544*).

EN ROUTE

Traveling west and then north from Trento to Madonna di Campiglio, you zigzag through lovely mountain valleys, past small farming communities such as Tione. Outside the small mountain village of Pinzolo (on SS239), stop at the church of **San Vigilio** to see the remarkable 16th-century fresco on the exterior south wall. Painted in 1539 by the artist Simone Baschenis, the painting describes the Dance of Death: a macabre parade of 40 sinners from all walks of life (in roughly descending order of worldly importance), each guided to his end by a ghoulish escort. Unfortunately, the church's interior is closed to the public.

Madonna di Campiglio is one of the Dolomites' top ski resorts, with more than 75 miles of slopes.

MADONNA DI CAMPIGLIO

80 km (50 mi) northwest of Trento, 100 km (62 mi) southwest of Bolzano.

VISITOR INFORMATION

Madonna di Campiglio tourism office (✉ *Via Pradalago 4* ☎ *0465/447501* ⊕ *www.campiglio.it*).

EXPLORING

The chichi winter resort of Madonna di Campiglio vies with Cortina d'Ampezzo as the most fashionable place for young Italians to ski and be seen in the Dolomites. Madonna's popularity is well deserved, with 39 lifts connecting more than 120 km (75 mi) of well-groomed ski runs. The resort itself is a modest 5,000 feet above sea level, but the downhill runs, summer hiking paths, and mountain-biking trails venture high up into the surrounding peaks (including Pietra Grande at 9,700 feet). Madonna's cachet is evident in its well-organized lodging, skiing, and trekking facilities.

The stunning pass at **Campo Carlo Magno** (5,500 feet) is 3 km (2 mi) north of Madonna di Campiglio. This is where Charlemagne is said to have stopped in AD 800 on his way to Rome to be crowned emperor. Stop here to glance over the whole of northern Italy. If you continue north, take the descent with caution—in the space of a mile or so, hairpin turns and switchbacks deliver you down more than 2,000 feet.

WHERE TO EAT AND STAY

$$
NORTHERN
ITALIAN
★

✕ **Cascina Zeledria.** This remote, rustic mountain restaurant near Campo Carlo Magno is not accessible by car; in winter, you'll be collected on a motorized Sno-Cat and ferried up the slopes. After the 10-minute ride, sit down to grill your own meats and vegetables over stone griddles; the kitchen-prepared mushrooms and polenta are house specialties. Although the majority of meals in Madonna are taken in resort hotels, Italians consider an on-mountain dinner to be an indispensable part of a proper ski week. Call in advance to reserve a table—and arrange for transportation. ⌂ *Località Zeledria* ☎ *0465/440303* ⊕ *www.zeledria. it* ⌂ *Reservations essential* ▭ *AE, DC, MC, V* ⊘ *Closed May, June, Oct., and Nov.*

$$$–$$$$

🏨 **Golf Hotel.** You need to make your way north to the Campo Carlo Magno Pass to reach this grand hotel, the former summer residence of Habsburg emperor Franz Josef. A modern wing has been added, but there's still tons of Old World charm. Rooms 114 and 214 retain the lavish Imperial style, and the rest of the resort is replete with verandas, Persian rugs, and bay windows. In summer the golf course attracts a tony crowd. **Pros:** attractive indoor pool; elegant rooms. **Cons:** long walk into town; popular with business groups. ⌂ *Via Cima Tosa 3* ☎ *0465/441003* ⊕ *www.atahotels.it* ⤵ *109 rooms, 13 suites* ⌂ *In-room: no a/c, safe, refrigerator, Internet, Wi-Fi. In-hotel: restaurant, room service, bar, golf course, pool, gym, spa, laundry service, parking (free), some pets allowed (paid)* ▭ *AE, DC, MC, V* ⊘ *Closed mid-Apr.– June and Sept.–Nov.* ⏧ *MAP.*

$$$

🏨 **Grifone.** A comfortable lodge sits catching the sun with a distinctive wood facade and flower-bedecked balconies. Contemporary singles, doubles, and triples have views of the forested slopes. The restaurant serves home cooking as well as international dishes. The hotel is a bit out of town, but the Spinale cable car is nearby. **Pros:** convenient location; charming decor. **Cons:** half board is mandatory; lacks air-conditioning. ⌂ *Via Vallesinella 7* ☎ *0465/442002* ⊕ *www.hotelgrifone. it* ⤵ *38 rooms, 2 suites* ⌂ *In-room: no a/c, safe. In-hotel: restaurant, bar, spa, Internet terminal, Wi-Fi hotspot, parking (free)* ▭ *AE, DC, MC, V* ⊘ *Closed mid-Apr.–June and Sept.–Nov.* ⏧ *MAP.*

SPORTS AND THE OUTDOORS

HIKING AND CLIMBING

The Madonna di Campiglio tourism office has maps of a dozen trails leading to waterfalls, lakes, and stupefying views. The cable car to 6,900-foot **Punta Spinale** (*Spinale Peak* ⌂ *Off Via Monte Spinale* ☎ *0465/447744* 🚡 *Cable car €9 round-trip*) offers skiers magnificent views of the Brenta Dolomites in winter. It also runs during peak summer season.

SKIING

Miles of interconnecting ski runs—some of the best in the Dolomites— are linked by the cable cars and lifts of **Funivie Madonna di Campiglio** (⌂ *Via Presanella 12* ☎ *0465/447744* ⊕ *www.funiviecampiglio.it*). Advanced skiers will delight in the extremely difficult terrain found on certain mountain faces, but there are also many intermediate and beginner runs, all accessible from town. There are also plenty of off-piste opportunities. Ski passes (€35–€38 per day, discounts for multiple days) can be purchased at the main *funivia* (cable car) in town.

EN ROUTE

The route between Madonna di Campiglio and Bormio (2½ hours) takes you through a series of high mountain passes. After Campo Carlo Magno, turn left at Dimaro and continue 37 km (23 mi) west through Passo del Tonale (6,200 feet). At Ponte di Legno, turn north on SS300. You pass the *Lago Nero* (Black Lake) on your left just before the summit. Continue on to Bormio through the Passo di Gavia (8,600 feet).

THE WESTERN DOLOMITES

The Parco Nazionale dello Stelvio extends through western Trentino and the Altoaltesino area of Alto Adige, and even into eastern Lombardia. It's named for the famed Stelvio, Europe's highest road pass and the site of the highest battle fought during World War I. The town of Bormio is well preserved and merits a visit for its history and character, even if you don't want to ski or indulge in spa treatments, both of which it's renowned for.

BORMIO

97 km (60 mi) northwest of Madonna di Campiglio, 100 km (62 mi) southwest of Merano.

VISITOR INFORMATION
Bormio tourism office (✉ Via Roma 131/B ☎ 0342/903300 🖷 0342/904696 ⊕ www.bookbormio.com or www.valtellina.it).

8

EXPLORING
At the foot of Stelvio Pass, Bormio is the most famous ski resort on the western side of the Dolomites, with 38 km (24 mi) of long pistes and a 5,000-plus-foot vertical drop. In summer its cool temperatures and clean air entice Italians away from cities in the humid Lombard plain. This dual-season popularity supports the plentiful shops, restaurants, and hotels in town. Bormio has been known for the therapeutic qualities of its waters since the Roman era, and there are numerous spas.

Ancient Roman baths predate the wonderland of thermal springs, caves, and waterfalls now known as the **Bagni Vecchi** *(Old Baths)*; Leonardo da Vinci soaked here in 1493. ✉ *Strada Statale Stelvio* ☎ *0342/910131* ⊕ *www.bagnidibormio.it* 🖾 *Weekdays €41, weekends €45* ☉ *Daily 11–8, weekends 11–11.*

Modern facilities and comprehensive spa treatments are available at **Bormio Terme**. ✉ *Via Stelvio 14* ☎ *0342/901325* ⊕ *www.bormioterme.it* 🖾 *Weekdays €19, weekends €23* ☉ *Sat.–Tues., Thurs. 9–9; Wed., Fri. 9 AM–10:30 PM; closed 20 days in May.*

Bormio makes a good base for exploring the Alps' biggest national park, the **Parco Nazionale dello Stelvio** spread over 1,350 square km (520 square mi) and four provinces. Opened in 1935 to preserve flora and protect fauna, today it has more than 1,200 types of plants, 600 different mushrooms, and more than 160 species of animals, including the chamois, ibex, and roe deer. There are many entrances to the park, and

a dozen visitor centers; the closest entrance to Bormio is the year-round gateway at Torre Alberti. ⊠ *Via Roma 26* ☎ *0342/901654* ⊕ *www. parks.it/parco.nazionale.stelvio* 🔄 *Free.*

WHERE TO EAT AND STAY

$ ✕ **Caffe Kuerc.** This building was for centuries where justice was pub-
NORTHERN licly served to accused witches, among others. These days, things at the
ITALIAN restaurant are rather more refined: enjoy local specialties like *bresaola* (salted, air-dried beef) with lemon and olive oil, or *pizzoccheri* (buck-wheat pasta) with garlic and winter vegetables. ⊠ *Piazza Cavour 8* ☎ *0342/910787* ▭ *MC, V* ⊘ *Closed Tues.*

$–$$ ▦ **La Genzianella.** Here you get Alpine chic without expense or pretense.
★ Contemporary decor incorporates warm pine, ceramics, rich textiles, and beamed ceilings; all but three rooms have a balcony; "charme" suites include hydromassage. Genzianella is a bike-friendly hotel: there's safe storage, a sportswear laundry, mountain bike rental, maps, and even an instructor. Lifts to the Alta Valtellina are only 50 yards from the hotel entrance, and there are lockers for ski equipment. **Pros:** great for bikers; handy to slopes and town. **Cons:** no pool. ⊠ *Via Zandilla 6* ☎ *0342/904485* ⊕ *www.genzianella.com* 🔄 *40 rooms* ⚒ *In-room: no a/c, safe, Wi-Fi. In-hotel: restaurant, bar, gym, sauna, Wi-Fi hotspot, parking (free)* ▭ *AE, DC, MC, V* ⊘ *Closed May and Sept.–Dec.* ¶ *BP.*

$$ ▦ **Nazionale.** Bordering Stelvio National Park, the Nazionale caters to both the winter and summer crowds. Behind the Alpine exterior, rooms are small but have solid wood furniture and balconies on all floors except the top one. The hotel operates a shuttle bus to the cable cars and a garden play area for children. **Pros:** great location; winter and summer activities; family-friendly environment. **Cons:** no air-conditioning; may require a 20% supplement for stays of fewer than three nights. ⊠ *Via al Forte 28* ☎ *0342/903361* ⊕ *www.nazionalebormio.it* 🔄 *48 rooms* ⚒ *In-room: no a/c, safe, refrigerator, Wi-Fi. In-hotel: 2 restaurants, bar, gym, pool, parking (free), Wi-Fi hotspot* ▭ *AE, DC, MC, V* ¶ *MAP.*

SKIING

You can buy a ski pass (€34–€38 per day) and pick up a trail map at the base **funivia** (*Cable car* ⊠ *Via Battaglion Morbegno 25* ☎ *0342/902770* ⊕ *www.skipassaltavaltellina.it*) in the center of town to connect to the Bormio 2000 station (6,600 feet) on Vallecetta, the main resort mountain. From there, you can ski down intermediate trails (which comprise the majority of Bormio's runs), use the extensive lift network to explore secondary ski areas, or get another funivia up to the Bormio 3000 station at Cima Bianca (9,800 feet) for more challenging terrain. The cable car also runs July to mid-September, when it is used by mountain bikers to reach long trails through breathtaking Alpine terrain; less-ambitious visitors can wander around and then ride the cable car back down.

PASSO DELLO STELVIO

20 km (12 mi) north of Bormio, 80 km (48 mi) west of Merano.

★ At more than 9,000 feet, the Passo dello Stelvio is the second-highest pass in Europe, connecting the Valtellina in Lombardy with the Val Venosta in Alto Adige. The view from the top is well worth the drive;

looking north you can see Switzerland. The pass is open from May or June to October, depending on weather conditions. Stelvio itself is a year-round skiing center, with many of its runs open in summer.

EN ROUTE Between the Stelvio Pass and the town of Spondigna, 30 km (19 mi) of road wind down 48 hair-raising hairpin turns. The views are spectacular, but this descent is not for the faint of heart. In Spondigna keep to the right for the road to Naturno.

BOLZANO (BOZEN)

32 km (19 mi) south of Merano, 50 km (31 mi) north of Trento.

Bolzano (Bozen), capital of the autonomous province of Alto Adige, is tucked among craggy peaks in a Dolomite valley 77 km (48 mi) from the Brenner Pass and Austria. Tirolean culture dominates Bolzano's language, food, architecture, and people. It may be hard to remember that you're in Italy when walking the city's colorful cobblestone streets and visiting its lantern-lighted cafés, where you may enjoy sauerkraut and a beer among a lively crowd of blue-eyed German speakers. However, fine Italian espresso, fashionable boutiques, and reasonable prices will help remind you where you are. With castles and steeples topping the landscape, this quiet city at the confluence of the Isarco (Eisack) and Talvera rivers has retained a provincial appeal. Proximity to fabulous skiing and mountain climbing—not to mention the world's oldest preserved mummy—make it a worthwhile, and still undiscovered, tourist destination. And its streets are immaculate: with the highest per capita earnings of any city in Italy, Bolzano's residents enjoy a standard of living that is second to none.

VISITOR INFORMATION
Bolzano tourism office (✉ *Piazza Walther 8* ☎ *0471/307000* 🖷 *0471/980128* ⊕ *www.bolzano-bozen.it*).

EXPLORING BOLZANO

TOP ATTRACTIONS
Chiesa dei Domenicani. The 13th-century Dominican Church is renowned as Bolzano's main repository for paintings, especially frescoes. In the adjoining **Cappella di San Giovanni** you can see works from the Giotto school that show the birth of a pre-Renaissance sense of depth and individuality; come prepared with 50-cent coins for the lights. The church and chapel are closed to the public during religious ceremonies. ✉ *Piazza Domenicani* ☎ *0471/973133* ⊙ *Mon.–Sat. 9:30–5, Sun. noon–6.*

Duomo. A lacy spire looks down on the mosaic-like roof tiles of the city's Gothic cathedral, built between the 12th and 14th century. Inside are 14th- and 15th-century frescoes and an intricately carved stone pulpit dating from 1514. Outside, don't miss the **Porta del Vino** (Wine Gate) on the northeast side; decorative carvings of grapes and harvest workers attest to the long-standing importance of wine to this region. The church is closed to the public during religious ceremonies. ✉ *Piazza Walther* ☎ *0471/978676* ⊙ *Mon.–Sat. 10–noon and 2–5.*

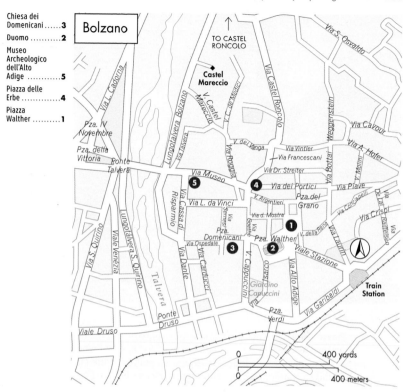

Bolzano

TO CASTEL
RONCOLO

Castel
Mareccio

Pza. IV
Novembre

Pza. della
Vittoria

Ponte
Talvera

Via S. Osvaldo

Via Cavour

Via A. Hofer

Via Piave

Via Crispi

Train
Station

0   400 yards

0   400 meters

8

Fodor's Choice
★   **Museo Archeologico dell'Alto Adige.** This museum has gained international
fame for Ötzi, its 5,300-year-old iceman, discovered in 1991 and the
world's oldest naturally preserved body. In 1998 Italy acquired it from
Austria after it was determined that the body lay 100 yards inside
Italy. The iceman's leathery remains are displayed in a freezer vault,
preserved along with his longbow, ax, and clothing. The rest of the
museum relies on models and artifacts from nearby archaeological sites
(an eloquent English audio guide is €2) to lead you not only through
Ötzi's Copper Age, but also into the preceding Mesolithic and Neolithic
eras, and the Bronze and Iron ages that followed. In July and August,
the museum's supervised play area keeps young children entertained
while adults experience the museum. ⊠ *Via Museo 43* ☎ *0471/320120*
⊕ *www.iceman.it* ☒ *€9* ⊙ *July, Aug., and Dec., daily 10–6; Jan.–June
and Sept.–Nov., Tues.–Sun. 10–6; last entry 5:30.*

Piazza delle Erbe. A bronze statue of Neptune, which dates to 1745,
presides over a bountiful fruit-and-vegetable market in this square. The
stalls spill over with colorful displays of local produce; bakeries and
grocery stores showcase hot breads, pastries, cheeses, and delicatessen
meats—a complete picnic. Try the *speck tirolese* (a thinly sliced smoked
ham) and the apple strudel.

Bolzano's Duomo, on Piazza Walther in the heart of the city.

Piazza Walther. This pedestrians-only square is Bolzano's heart; in warmer weather it serves as an open-air living room where locals and tourists alike can be found at all hours sipping a drink (such as a glass of chilled Riesling). In the center stands Heinrich Natter's white-marble, neo-Romanesque **Monument to Walther,** built in 1889. The piazza's namesake was the 12th-century German wandering minstrel Walther von der Vogelweide, whose songs lampooned the papacy and praised the Holy Roman Emperor.

WORTH NOTING

Castel Roncolo (*Schloss Runkelstein*). The green hills and farmhouses north of town surround the meticulously kept castle with a red roof. It was built in 1237, destroyed half a century later, and then rebuilt soon thereafter. There's a beautifully preserved cycle of medieval frescoes inside. A tavern in the courtyard serves excellent local food and wines. To get here from Piazza Walther, take the free shuttle (Tuesday–Sunday every half hour 10–5), or the number 12 bus. It's a 20-minute walk from Piazza delle Erbe: head north along Via Francescani, continue through Piazza Madonna, connecting to Via Castel Roncolo. ⊠ *Via San Antonio 1* ☎ *0471/329808 castle, 0471/324073 tavern* ⊕ *www.roncolo.info* 🖃 *€8* ⊙ *Tues.–Sun. 10–6; last entry 5:30.*

Messner Mountain Museum Firmian. Perched on a peak overlooking Bolzano, 10th-century Castle Sigmundskron is home to one of five Dolomite museums established by Reinhold Messner—the first climber to conquer Everest solo and the first to reach its summit without oxygen. The Tibetan tradition of *kora,* a circular pilgrimage around a sacred site, is an inspiration for the museum, where visitors contemplate the relationship between man and mountain, guided by images and objects Messner collected during his adventures. Guided tours begin every half hour. The museum is 3 km (2 mi) southwest of Bolzano, just off the Appiano exit on the highway to Merano. ⊠ *Via Castel Firmiano 53* ☎ *0471/631264* ⊕ *www.messner-mountain-museum.it* 🎫 *€8* ⊙ *Mar.– late-Nov., Tues.–Sun. 10–6.*

Passeggiata del Guncina. An 8-km (5-mi) botanical promenade dating from 1892 ends with a panoramic view of Bolzano. ⊠ *Entrance near Vecchia Parrocchiale, in Gries, across river and up Corso Libertà.*

Vecchia Parrocchiale *(Old Parish Church).* Visit this church, said to have been built in 1141, to see its two medieval treasures: an 11th-century Romanesque crucifix and an elaborately carved 15th-century wooden altar by Michael Pacher—a true masterpiece of the Gothic style. ⊠ *Via Martin Knoller, in Gries, across river and up Corso Libertà* ☎ *0471/283089* ⊙ *Apr.–Oct., weekdays 10:30–noon and 2:30–4.*

WHERE TO EAT

$–$$
NORTHERN
ITALIAN

✕ **Alexander.** Typical Tirolean dishes are served at this convivial restaurant. The venison ham and the lamb cutlets *al timo con salsa all'aglio* (with thyme and garlic sauce) are particularly good, but make sure to leave room for the rich chocolate cake. ⊠ *Via Aosta 37* ☎ *0471/918608* ⊟ *MC, V* ⊙ *Closed Sat.*

$
WINE BAR
★

✕ **Batzenhausl.** Locals hold animated conversations over glasses of regional wine in a modern take on the traditional Weinstube (wine tavern, often abbreviated to "stube"). Tasty south Tirolean specialties include speck tirolese and *mezzelune casarecce ripiene* (house-made stuffed half-moons of pasta). If you're seeking a quiet meal, ask for a table on the second floor, near the handsome stained-glass windows. This is a good spot for a late bite, as food is served until midnight. ⊠ *Via Andreas Hofer 30* ☎ *0471/050950* ⊕ *www.batzen.it* ⊟ *MC, V.*

$
NORTHERN
ITALIAN

✕ **Cavallino Bianco.** This restaurant near Via dei Portici is a dependable favorite with residents and visitors alike. A wide selection of Italian and German dishes is served in a spacious, comfortable dining room, where there are usually many extended families enjoying their meals together. ⊠ *Via Bottai 6* ☎ *0471/973267* ⊟ *MC, V* ⊙ *Closed Sun. No dinner Sat.*

$
NORTHERN
ITALIAN

✕ **Hopfen & Co.** Fried white *Würstel* (sausage), sauerkraut, and grilled ribs complement the excellent home-brewed Austrian-style pilsner and wheat beer at this lively pub-restaurant. There's live music on Thursday night, attracting Bolzano's students and young professionals. ⊠ *Piazza delle Erbe, Obstplatz 17* ☎ *0471/300788* ⊕ *www.boznerbier.it* ⊟ *MC, V.*

$$
NORTHERN
ITALIAN

✕ **Wirthaus Vögele.** Ask a resident of Bolzano where they like to dine out, and odds are good they'll tell you Vögele, one of the area's oldest inns. The classic wood-panel dining room on the ground level is often packed with diners, but don't despair, as the restaurant has two additional floors. The menu features Sud Tyrol standards, including canederli with speck and venison. ⊠ *Goethestr 3* ☎ *0471/973938* ⊕ *www. voegele.it* ⊟ *DC, MC, V* ⊙ *Closed Sun.*

8

WHERE TO STAY

$$$
Fodor's Choice
★

⛺ **Hotel Greif.** Even in a hospitable region, the Greif is a rare gem. This small central hotel has been a Bolzano landmark for centuries, and a beautiful renovation has set a standard for modernity in Alto Adige. In-room computers with high-speed Internet connections and private whirlpool baths are just a few of the perks. Public spaces are airy and immaculate; each guest room was designed by a different local artist—contemporary installations are thoughtfully paired with 19th-century paintings and sketches. The clean-line modern furnishings contrast with views of the Gothic cathedral across the square. **Pros:** elegant decor; helpful staff; central location. **Cons:** rooms vary in size; sometimes filled with tour groups. ⊠ *Piazza Walther 1* ☎ *0471/318000* ⊕ *www.greif.it* ⊷ *27 rooms, 6 suites* ⚴ *In-room: safe, refrigerator, Internet. In-hotel: laundry service, parking (paid)* ▭ *AE, DC, MC, V* ⏚❘❙ *BP.*

$$

⛺ **Luna-Mondschein.** This central yet secluded hotel in a tranquil garden dates from 1798. The comfortable rooms have wood paneling throughout; those overlooking the garden have balconies, others have good views of the mountains. First-rate dining is available in the art nouveau Ristorante Van Gogh, among the city's best in blending German traditions with Italian methods; the eclectic menu changes frequently. A convivial, traditional 17th-century Tirolean stube serves more-rustic fare. In summer the courtyard is filled with the scent of barbecue from the outdoor garden restaurant. **Pros:** central location; great buffet breakfast. **Cons:** rooms vary in size; rooms facing garage noisy. ⊠ *Via Piave 15* ☎ *0471/975642* ⊕ *www.hotel-luna.it* ⊷ *80 rooms* ⚴ *In-room: a/c (some), Wi-Fi (some). In-hotel: 3 restaurants, room service, bar, laundry service, parking (paid), some pets allowed* ▭ *AE, DC, MC, V* ⏚❘❙ *BP.*

$$–$$$
★

⛺ **Parkhotel Laurin.** An exercise in art nouveau opulence, Parkhotel Laurin ranks among the finest lodging in all of Alto Adige, with art-filled modern guest rooms and handsome public spaces. The sister hotel of the Greif presides over a large park in the middle of town. Its history is speckled with visits from Europe's grand nobility, including Archduke Franz Ferdinand (whose murder in Sarajevo sparked World War I). The bar is popular with locals, especially for Jazz Fridays. Restaurant Laurin is superb, using only local ingredients, and bringing a lighter sensibility to rustic regional dishes. **Pros:** convenient location; excellent restaurant. **Cons:** rooms facing park can be noisy; packed with business groups. ⊠ *Via Laurin 4* ☎ *0471/311000* ⊕ *www.laurin.it* ⊷ *93 rooms, 7 suites* ⚴ *In-room: safe, refrigerator, Internet. In-hotel: Internet terminal, restaurant, bar, pool, laundry service, parking (paid)* ▭ *AE, DC, MC, V* ⏚❘❙ *BP.*

$$–$$$
★

⛺ **Schloss Korb.** This romantic 13th-century castle with crenellations and a massive tower is perched in a park amid vine-covered hills. Much of the ancient character is preserved, and the public rooms are filled with antiques, elaborately carved wood, paintings, and attractive plants. The guest rooms have solid, rustic, pine beds with pillow-top mattresses; some in the tower have striking Romanesque arched windows. It's well worth the 5-km (3-mi) drive west from Bolzano to get here. **Pros:** romantic setting; charming traditional furnishings. **Cons:** not all rooms are in the castle; need a car to get around. ⊠ *Via Castel d'Appiano*

Enrosadira and the Dwarf King

The Dolomites, the inimitable craggy peaks Le Corbusier called "the most beautiful work of architecture ever seen," are never so arresting as at dusk, when the last rays of sun create a pink hue that languishes into purple. In the Ladin language, spoken only in the isolated valleys below, this magnificent transformation has its own word—the *enrosadira*. You can certainly enjoy this phenomenon from a distance, but one of the things that makes the Dolomites such an appealing year-round destination is the multitude of options for getting onto the mountains themselves. Whether you come for a pleasant stroll or a technical ascent in summer, to plunge down sheer faces or glide across peaceful valleys in winter, or to brave narrow switchbacks in a rented Fiat, your perspective, like the peaks around you, can only become more rose colored.

The enrosadira is so striking that it has prompted speculation about its origins. The French nobleman and geologist Déodat Guy Silvain Tancrède Gratet de Dolomieu (1750–1801) took the scientific approach: he got his name applied to the range after demonstrating that the peaks have a particular composition of stratified calcium magnesium carbonate that generates the evening glow. For those unconvinced that such a phenomenon can be explained by geology alone, Ladin legend offers a compelling alternative.

Laurin, King of the Dwarfs, became infatuated with the daughter of a neighboring (human) king, and captured her with the aid of a magic hood that made him invisible. As he spirited her back to the mountains, the dwarf king was pursued by many knights who were able to track the kidnapper after spotting his beloved rose garden. Laurin was captured and imprisoned, and when he finally managed to escape and return home, he cast a spell turning the betraying roses into rocks—so they could be seen neither by day nor by night. But Laurin forgot to include dusk in his spell, which is why the Dolomites take on a rosy glow just before nightfall. (This story is the subject of frescoes in the bar of Bolzano's Parkhotel Laurin.)

8

5, Missiano/Appiano ☎ *0471/636000* ⊕ *www.schlosskorb.com* ⇆ *35 rooms, 10 suites* ⌂ *In-room: Internet, no a/c. In-hotel: restaurant, bar, tennis courts, pools, gym, laundry service, Internet terminal, parking (paid)* ⊟ *V* ⊗ *Closed Nov.–Mar.* ⏃ *MAP.*

ALTO ADIGE

Prosperous valley towns (such as the famed spa center Merano) and mountain resorts entice those seeking both relaxation and adventure. Alto Adige (Südtirol) was for centuries part of the Austro-Hungarian Empire, only ceded to Italy at the end of World War I. Ethnic differences led to inevitable tensions in the 1960s and again in the '80s, though a large measure of provincial autonomy has, for the most part, kept the lid on nationalist ambitions. Today Germanic and Italian balance harmoniously, as do medieval and modern influences, with ancient castles regularly playing host to contemporary art exhibitions.

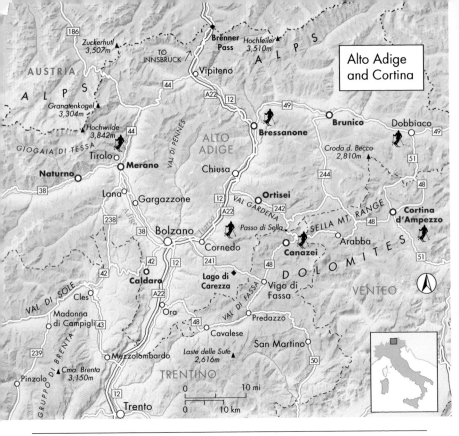

MERANO (MERAN)

★ *24 km (15 mi) north of Bolzano, 16 km (10 mi) east of Naturno.*

VISITOR INFORMATION
Merano tourism office (✉ *Corso Libertà 45* ☎ *0473/272000* ⊕ *www.meran.eu*).

EXPLORING

The second-largest town in Alto Adige, Merano (Meran) was once the capital of the Austrian region of Tirol. When the town and surrounding area were ceded to Italy as part of the 1919 Treaty of Versailles, Innsbruck became the capital. Merano, however, continued to be known as a spa town, attracting European nobility for its therapeutic waters and its grape cure, which consists simply of eating the grapes grown on the surrounding hillsides. Sheltered by mountains, Merano has an unusually mild climate, with summer temperatures rarely exceeding 80°F (27°C) and winters that usually stay above freezing, despite the skiing that is within easy reach. Along the narrow streets of Merano's old town, houses have little towers and huge wooden doors, and the pointed arches of the Gothic cathedral sit next to neoclassical and art nouveau buildings. Merano serves as a good respite from mountain adventures, or from the bustle of nearby Trento and Bolzano.

The 14th-century Gothic **Duomo**, with a crenellated facade and an ornate campanile, sits in the heart of the old town. The Capella di Santa Barbara, just behind the cathedral, is an octagonal church containing a 15th-century pietà. ⊠ *Piazza del Duomo* ☎ *0473/230174* ☉ *Easter–Sept., daily 8–noon and 2:30–8; Oct.–Easter, daily 8–noon and 2:30–7.*

The **Terme di Merano** is a sprawling spa complex with 25 pools (including a brine pool with underwater music) and eight saunas (with an indoor "snow room" available for cooling down). Along with the family-friendly options for bathing, personalized services for grown-ups include traditional cures using local products, such as grape-based applications and whey baths. An admission charge of €11 gets you two hours in thermal baths; €23 is for a full day's use of all baths and saunas. ⊠ *Piazza Terme 9* ☎ *0473/252000* ⊕ *www.termemerano. it* ☉ *Daily 9* AM–*10* PM.

Castel Trauttmansdorff, a Gothic castle 2 km (1 mi) southeast of town, was restored in the 19th century, and now serves as a museum, celebrating 200 years of tourism in south Tirol. Outside, a sprawling garden has an extensive display of exotic flora organized by country of origin. An English-language audio guide is available for €2.50. ⊠ *Via Valentino 51a* ☎ *0473/235730* ⊕ *www.trauttmansdorff.it* ✉ *€10.20* ☉ *Apr.–May 14 and Sept. 16–Nov. 15, daily 9–6; May 15–Sept. 15, daily 9–9.*

Overlooking the town atop Mt. Tappeinerweg is Castel Fontana, which was the home of poet Ezra Pound from 1958 to 1964. Still in the Pound family, the castle now houses the **Museo Agricolo di Brunnenburg,** devoted to Tirolean country life. Among its exhibits are a blacksmith's shop and, not surprisingly, a room with Pound memorabilia. To get here, take Bus 3, which departs every hour on the hour, from Merano to Dorf Tirol (20 minutes). ⊠ *Via Castello 17, Brunnenburg* ☎ *0473/923533* ✉ *€3* ☉ *Apr.–Oct., Sun.–Thurs. 10–5.*

Fodor's Choice ★ A stroll along one of Merano's well-marked, impossibly pleasant **promenades** may yield even better relaxation than a spa treatment. **Passeggiata Tappeiner** (Tappeiner's Promenade) is a 3-km (2-mi) path with panoramic views from the hills north of the Duomo and diverse botanical pleasures along the way. **Passeggiata d'Estate** (Summer Promenade) runs along the shaded south bank of the Passirio River, and the **Passeggiata d'Inverno** (Winter Promenade), on the exposed north bank, provides more warmth and the Wandelhalle—a sunny area decorated with idyllic paintings of surrounding villages. The popular Austrian empress Sissi (Elisabeth of Wittelsbach, 1837–98) put Merano on the map as a spa destination; a trail named in her honor, the **Sentiero di Sissi** (Sissi's Walk), follows a path from Castel Trauttmansdorff to the heart of Merano.

QUICK BITES

Cafe Saxifraga (⊠ *Passeggiata Tappeiner* ☎ *0473/239249* ⊕ *www. saxifraga.it*) occupies an enviable position overlooking Merano and the peaks enveloping the town; an extensive selection of teas and other beverages can be enjoyed on the patio, which has panoramic views.

8

WHERE TO EAT

$
NORTHERN
ITALIAN

✕ **Haisrainer.** Among the rustic wine taverns lining Via dei Portici, this one is most popular with locals and tourists alike; a menu in English is available for the latter. Warm wooden walls provide a comfortable setting for Tirolean and Italian standards: try the *zuppa al vino bianco* (stew with white wine) or the seasonal risottos (with asparagus in spring, or Barolo wine in chillier months). ⊠ *Via dei Portici 100* ☎ *0473/237944* ▭ *MC, V* ☻ *Closed Sun.*

$$
ITALIAN

✕ **Sieben.** Young Meraners crowd the hip bar on the ground floor of this modern bistro, in the town's central arcade. Upstairs, a more-mature crowd enjoys the contemporary cooking and attentive service in the jazz-themed dining room. Sieben occasionally hosts jazz concerts in summer. ⊠ *Via dei Portici 232* ☎ *0473/210636* ⊕ *www.bistrosieben.it* ▭ *MC, V* ☻ *Closed Tues. Nov.–Mar.*

$$$
NORTHERN
ITALIAN
★

✕ **Sissi.** In this relaxed, light-filled restaurant just off Via dei Portici, rustic regional dishes are prepared with the precision of haute Italian cooking. Menu choices may include gnocchi *di formaggio con salsa all' erba cipollina* (with cheese and chives) and *vitello alle castagne e tartufo nero* (veal with chestnuts and black truffles); a set menu (€60–€65) provides a complete four-course dinner. ⊠ *Via Galilei 44* ☎ *0473/231062* ⊕ *www.andreafenoglio.com* ⚐ *Reservations essential* ▭ *AE, MC, V* ☻ *Closed Mon. and last 2 wks Feb.*

$$
NORTHERN
ITALIAN

✕ **Vinoteca-Pizzeria Relax.** If you have difficulty choosing from the long list of appetizing pizzas here, ask the friendly English-speaking staff for help with the menu. You're unlikely to find a better selection of wine, or a more pleasant environment for sampling. You can also buy bottles of the locally produced vintage to take home. ⊠ *Via Cavour 31, opposite Palace Hotel* ☎ *0473/236735* ⊕ *www.weine-relax.it* ▭ *AE, MC, V* ☻ *Closed Sun. and 2 wks in late Feb.*

WHERE TO STAY

$$$–$$$$

⌂ **Castello Labers.** The red-tile gables, towers, and turrets give this castle its unmistakably Tirolean style, as it sits on a hilltop amid forested slopes. Ceiling beams, painted fresco decorations, and crossed halberds on the walls complete the look inside. The hospitable management includes dinner with the room price when guests book three nights or longer. The hotel is 3 km (2 mi) northeast of Merano's center. **Pros:** romantic setting; spectacular views. **Cons:** long walk into town; some bathrooms are small. ⊠ *Via Labers 25* ☎ *0473/234484* ⊕ *www.labers. it* ⚑ *32 rooms, 1 suite* ⚐ *In-room: no a/c, safe, Wi-Fi (some). In-hotel: restaurant, tennis court, pool, Internet terminal* ▭ *AE, DC, MC, V* ☻ *Closed early-Nov.–late-Apr.* ⵏⵔ *BP.*

$

⌂ **Conte di Merano.** If you don't feel like paying for one of Merano's resorts, this simple central hotel is a good alternative. Steps away from Via dei Portici and open year-round, it's an efficient base for exploring the town. Rooms have spartan furnishings, but are clean and comfortable. **Pros:** excellent base for exploring Merano; reasonable rates. **Cons:** basic decor; some street noise. ⊠ *Via delle Corse 78* ☎ *0473/490260* ⊕ *www.grafvonmeran.com* ⚑ *20 rooms* ⚐ *In-room: safe, refrigerator. In-hotel: restaurant, bar* ▭ *MC, V* ⵏⵔ *BP.*

NATURNO (NATURNS)

44 km (27 mi) northwest of Bolzano, 61 km (38 mi) east of Passo dello Stelvio.

VISITOR INFORMATION

Naturno tourism office (✉ *Piazza Municipio 1* ☎ *0473/666077* 🖷 *0473/666369* ⊕ *www.naturns.it*).

EXPLORING

Colorful houses covered with murals line the streets of Naturno (Naturns), a sunny horticultural center.

Art lovers will appreciate the church of **San Procolo** *(Prokolus)*. The frescoes inside are some of the oldest in the German-speaking world, dating from the 8th century. A small, modern museum offers multimedia installations (in Italian or German only) presenting four epochs in the region's history: ancient, medieval, Gothic, and the era of the Great Plague of 1636 (which claimed a quarter of Naturno's population, some of whom are buried in the church's cemetery). ✉ *Via San Procolo* ☎ *0473/667312* ⊕ *www.procolo.org* 🗝 *€5 church and museum* ☉ *2 wks before Easter–Oct., Tues.–Sun. 9:30–noon and 2:30–5:30; Nov.–2 wks before Easter, Tues.–Sun. 9:30–noon and 2:30–5.*

The 13th-century **Castel Juval** is in the hills above the hamlet of Stava, a five-minute shuttle ride from Naturno (there is no parking at the castle), or an hour hike on many local trails. Since 1983 it's been the home of the south Tirolese climber and polar adventurer Reinhold Messner—the first climber to conquer Everest solo. Part of the castle has been turned into one of five in Messner's chain of Dolomite museums, giving guided tours of his collection of Tibetan art and masks from around the world. ✉ *Viale Europa 2* ☎ *0473/631264, 0473/668058 shuttle* ⊕ *www.messner-mountain-museum.it* 🗝 *€7* ☉ *Apr.–mid-Nov., Tues.–Sun. 10–6.*

WHERE TO EAT

$–$$
NORTHERN
ITALIAN

✕ **Schlosswirt Juval.** Below Castel Juval, Reinhold Messner's restored farmhouse is home to an old-style restaurant serving Mediterranean standards and traditional local dishes. Not to be missed are the smoked hams and flavorful cheeses provisioned from the farm outside; they are well paired with the estate's Castel Juval wine. Dinner is often accompanied by live jazz. ✉ *Juval 2* ☎ *0473/668056* ⊕ *www.schlosswirtjuval.it* ▭ *No credit cards* ☉ *Closed Wed. and mid-Dec.–mid-Mar.*

CALDARO (KALTERN)

15 km (9 mi) south of Bolzano.

VISITOR INFORMATION

Caldaro tourism office (✉ *Piazza Mercato 8* ☎ *0471/963169* ⊕ *www.kaltern.com or www.suedtiroler-weinstrasse.it*).

EXPLORING

A vineyard village with clear views of castles high up on the surrounding mountains represents the centuries of division that forged the unique character of the area. Caldaro architecture is famous for the way it blends Italian Renaissance elements of balance and harmony with the soaring windows and peaked arches of the Germanic Gothic tradition. The church of Santa Caterina, on the main square, is a good example.

Close to Caldaro's main square is the **South Tyrolean Wine Museum**, with exhibits on how local wine has historically been made, stored, served, and worshipped. You can board the bus in front of the tourist office at 10 each Thursday for a museum tour and wine tasting in the cellar, or call ahead to reserve. ✉ *Via dell'Oro 1* ☎ *0471/963168* ⊕ *www. weinmuseum.it* ✆ *€3, wine tasting €4.60* ⊙ *Easter–Oct., Tues.–Sat. 10–5, Sun. 10–noon.*

BRESSANONE (BRIXEN)

40 km (25 mi) northeast of Bolzano.

VISITOR INFORMATION

Bressanone tourism office (✉ *Via Stazione 9* ☎ *0472/836401* ⊕ *www.brixen.org*).

EXPLORING

Bressanone (Brixen) is an important artistic center and was the seat of prince-bishops for centuries. Like their counterparts in Trento, these medieval administrators had the delicate task of serving two masters—the pope (the ultimate spiritual authority) and the Holy Roman Emperor (the civil and military power), who were virtually at war throughout the Middle Ages. Bressanone's prince-bishops became experts at tact and diplomacy.

The imposing **Duomo** was built in the 13th century but acquired a baroque facade 500 years later; its 14th-century cloister is decorated with medieval frescoes. Free guided tours (in German or Italian) are available April–October, Monday–Saturday at 10:30 and 3. ✉ *Piazza Duomo* ⊙ *Daily 6–noon and 3–6.*

The Bishop's Palace houses the **Museo Diocesano** *(Diocesan Museum)* and its abundance of local medieval art, particularly Gothic wood carvings. The wooden statues and liturgical objects were all collected from the cathedral treasury. During the Christmas season, curators arrange the museum's large collection of antique Nativity scenes; look for the shepherds wearing Tirolean hats. ✉ *Palazzo Vescovile 2* ☎ *0472/830505* ⊕ *www.dioezesanmuseum.bz.it* ✆ *€7* ⊙ *Museum: mid-Mar.–Oct. and Nov. 27–Jan. 6, Tues.–Sun. 10–5; closed Dec. 24 and 25.*

At **Abbazia di Novacella,** an Augustinian abbey founded in 1142, they've been making wine for at least nine centuries. In the tasting room you can sample varietals produced in the Isarco Valley; Novacella is most famous for the delicate stone-fruit character of its dry white Sylvaner. You can also wander the delightful grounds; note the progression of Romanesque, Gothic, and baroque building styles. Guided tours of the abbey (in Italian and German) depart daily at 10, 11, 2, 3, and 4, as well as at noon and 1 in summer; from January through March, tours are by reservation only. ✉ *Località Novacella 1, Varna* ⊹ *3 km (2 mi) north of Bressanone* ☎ *0472/836189* ⊕ *www.kloster-neustift.it* ✆ *Grounds and tasting room free, guided tours €5.50* ⊙ *Grounds: Mon.–Sat. 10–7. Tasting room: Mon.–Sat. 9:15–noon and 2–6.*

Cross-country skiing in the Dolomites.

WHERE TO EAT AND STAY

$$
NORTHERN
ITALIAN

✕**Fink.** The rustic wood-paneled dining room is upstairs in this restaurant under the arcades of the pedestrians-only town center. Try the *carré di maiale gratinato* (pork chops roasted with cheese and served with cabbage and potatoes) or the *castrato alla paesana,* a substantial lamb stew. In addition to hearty Tirolean specialties, there's an affordable daily set menu, as well as homemade pastries. ⊠ *Via Portici Minori 4* ☎ *0472/834883* ⊕ *www.restaurant-fink.it* ▤ *AE, MC, V* ⊘ *Closed Wed., 1 wk in Feb., 2 wks in May. No dinner Tues.*

$$$
★

⊞**Elephant.** This cozy inn, 550 years old and still one of the region's best, takes its name from the 1551 visit of King John III of Portugal, who stopped here while leading an elephant (a present for Austria's Emperor Ferdinand) over the Alps. Each room is unique, many filled with antiques and paintings. Housed on the park property is the separate Villa Marzari, with 14 rooms. A rustic three-room stube serves tasty fare. **Pros:** central location; good restaurant. **Cons:** rooms vary in size; often filled with groups. ⊠ *Via Rio Bianco 4* ☎ *0472/832750* ⊕ *www.hotelelephant.com* ⇆ *44 rooms* ⛁ *In-room: refrigerator, Internet. In-hotel: restaurant, bar, tennis courts, pool, gym, parking (paid)* ▤ *DC, MC, V* ⊘ *Closed early Jan.–late Mar.* ⋈ *BP.*

8

CLOSE UP

Hiking the Dolomites

For many overseas visitors, the Dolomites conjure images of downhill skiing at Cortina d'Ampezzo and Madonna di Campiglio. But summer, not winter, is high season here; Italians, German-speaking Europeans, and in-the-know travelers from farther afield come here for clear mountain air and world-class hiking. In 2009, UNESCO (the United Nations Educational, Scientific and Cultural Organization) named the Dolomites to its exclusive list of natural heritage sites. The dramatic terrain, inspiring vistas, an impossibly pleasant climate have are complemented by excellent facilities for enjoying the mountains.

On the trail, high in the Dolomites.

PICKING A TRAIL

The Dolomites boast a well-maintained network of trails for hiking and rock climbing. As long as you're in reasonably good shape, the number of appealing hiking options can be overwhelming.

Trails are well marked and designated by grades of difficulty: T for tourist path, H for hiking path, EE for expert hikers, and EEA for equipped expert hikers. On any of these paths you're likely to see carpets of mountain flowers between clutches of dense evergreens, with chamois and roe deer mulling about.

If you're just out for a day in the mountains, you can leave the particulars of your walk open until you're actually on the spot; local tourist offices (especially those in Cortina, Madonna, and the Heart of the Dolomites) can help you choose the right route based on trail conditions, weather, and desired exertion level. **Club Alpino Italiano,** the world's oldest organization of its kind, is an excellent resource for more-ambitious

adventures. Serious mountaineers might consider joining the group; their annual dues of €42 give you half-price rates when you reserve some mountain refuges and include insurance for air rescue. (Helicopters run €70 per minute!) It has offices in Bolzano and Trento. ⊠ *Piazza delle Erbe 46, Bolzano* ☎ *0471/978172* ⊕ *www.cai.it* ⊠ *Via Manci 57, Trento* ☎ *0461/982804.*

TRAVELING THE VIE FERRATE

If you're looking for an adventure somewhere between hiking and climbing, consider a guided trip along the Vie Ferrate (Iron Paths). These routes offer fixed climbing aids (steps, ladders, bridges, safety cables) left by Alpine divisions of the Italian and Austro-Hungarian armies and later converted for recreational use. Previous experience is generally not required, but vertigo-inducing heights do demand a strong stomach.

Detailed information about Vie Ferrate in the eastern Dolomites can be found at ⊕ *www.dolomiti.org.* Capable tour organizers include **Scuola di Alpinismo** (Mountaineering School) in Madonna di

Campiglio (📞 0465/442634 ⊕ www.guidealpinecampiglio.it) and Cortina d'Ampezzo (📞 0436/868505 ⊕ www.guidecortina.com).

BEDDING DOWN

One of the pleasures of an overnight adventure in the Dolomites is staying at a *rifugio,* one of the refuges that dot the mountainsides. There are hundreds of them, often in remote locations and ranging from spartan shelters to posh retreats. Most fall somewhere in between—they're cozy mountain lodges with dormitory-style accommodations. Pillows and blankets are provided (so there's no need to carry a sleeping bag), but you have to supply your own sheet. Bathrooms are usually shared, as is the experience of a cold shower in the morning.

The majority of rifugi are operated by the **Club Alpino Italiano** (⊕ www.cai.it). Contact information for both CAI-run and private rifugi is available from local tourist offices; most useful are those in Madonna di Campiglio (⊕ www.campiglio.to), Cortina d'Ampezzo (⊕ www.dolomiti.org), Val di Fassa (⊕ www.fassa.com), and Val Gardena (⊕ www.val-gardena.net). Reservations are a must, especially in August, although Italian law requires rifugi to accept travelers for the night if there is insufficient time to reach other accommodations before dark.

EATING WELL

Food is as much a draw at rifugi as location. Although the dishes served are the sort of rustic cuisine you might expect (salami, dumplings, hearty stews), the quality is uniformly excellent—an impressive feat, made all the more remarkable when you consider that supplies often have to arrive by helicopter. Your dinner may

cost as much as your bed for the night—about €20 per person—and it's difficult to determine which is the better bargain.

Snacks and packed lunches are available for purchase, but many opt to sit down for the midday meal. Serving as both holiday hiking destination and base camp for difficult ascents, the rifugi welcome walkers and climbers of all stripes from intersecting trails and nearby faces. Multilingual stories are swapped, food and wine shared, and new adventures launched.

STUMBLING ON ÖTZI

It was at the Similaun rifugio in September 1991 that a German couple arrived talking of a dead body they'd discovered near a "curious pickax." This was to be the world's introduction to Ötzi, the oldest mummy ever found.

The couple, underestimating the age of the corpse by about 5,300 years, thought it was a matter for the police. World-famous mountaineers Reinhold Messner and Hans Kammerlander happened to be passing through the same rifugio during a climbing tour, and a few days later they were on the scene, freeing the iceman from the ice. Ötzi's remarkable story was under way. You can see him on display, along with his longbow, ax, and clothes, at Bolzano's Museo Archeologico dell'Alto Adige, where he continues to be preserved at freezing temperatures.

8

BRUNICO (BRUNECK)

★ *33 km (20 mi) east of Bressanone, 65 km (40 mi) northwest of Cortina d'Ampezzo.*

VISITOR INFORMATION
Brunico tourism office (⊠ *Piazza Municipio 7* ☎ *0474/555722* ⊕ *www.bruneck. com*).

EXPLORING
With its medieval quarter nestling below the 13th-century bishop's castle, Brunico (Bruneck) is in the heart of the Val Pusteria. This quiet and quaint town is divided by the Rienza River, with the old quarter on one side and the modern town on the other.

The open-air **Museo Etnografico dell'Alto Adige** *(Alto Adige Ethnographic Museum)* recreates a Middle Ages farming village, built around a 300-year-old mansion. The wood-carving displays are most interesting. The museum is in the district of Teodone, northeast of the center. ⊠ *Herzog-Diet-Straße 24* ☎ *0474/552087* ⊕ *www.volkskundemuseum. it* 🎫 *€5* ⊙ *Tues.–Sat. 9:30–5:30, Sun. 2–6 (in Aug.: Tues.–Sat. 9:30– 6:30, Sun. 2–7).*

WHERE TO STAY
$$–$$$ 🏨 **Hotel Post.** The Von Grebmer family runs a homey hotel in a building dating from the 1880s. The efficient service is the hotel's trademark. This is the most central, appealing lodging choice in town, especially if you've got a sweet tooth: the attached pastry shop is as popular with locals as with international guests. The hotel has its own parking, an unusual perk in the pedestrians-only center. **Pros:** family-run friendliness; central location. **Cons:** no air-conditioning; deposit required to confirm reservations. ⊠ *Via Bastioni 9* ☎ *0474/555127* ⊕ *www. hotelpost-bruneck.com* 🛏 *33 rooms, 6 suites* 🔑 *In-room: no a/c, safe, refrigerator, Internet. In-hotel: restaurant, spa, laundry service, parking (free), some pets allowed* ⊟ *AE, MC, V* ⫛ *BP.*

SKIING
The **Alta Badia** (☎ *0471/836366 Corvara* ⊕ *www.altabadia.org*) ski area, which includes 52 ski lifts and 130 km (80 mi) of slopes, can be reached by heading 30 km (19 mi) south on SS244 from Brunico. It's less expensive (€30–€36)—and more Austrian in character—than other, more famous ski destinations in this region. Groomed trails for cross-country skiing (usually loops marked off by the kilometer) accommodate differing degrees of ability. Inquire at the local tourist office.

THE HEART OF THE DOLOMITES

The area between Bolzano and the mountain resort Cortina d'Ampezzo is dominated by two major valleys, Val di Fassa and Val Gardena. Both share the spectacular panorama of the Sella mountain range, known as the Heart of the Dolomites. Val di Fassa cradles the beginning of the Grande Strada delle Dolomiti (Great Dolomites Road—SS48 and SS241), which runs from Bolzano as far as Cortina. This route, opened in 1909, comprises 110 km (68 mi) of relatively easy grades and smooth driving between the two towns—a slower, more-scenic alternative to traveling by way of Brunico and Dobbiaco along SS49.

In both Val di Fassa and Val Gardena, recreational options are less expensive, though less comprehensive, than in better-known resorts like Cortina. The culture here is firmly Germanic. Val Gardena is freckled with well-equipped, photo-friendly towns with great views overlooked by the oblong *Sasso Lungo* (Long Rock), which is more than 10,000 feet above sea level. It's also home to the Ladins, descendants of soldiers sent by the Roman emperor Tiberius to conquer the Celtic population of the area in the 1st century AD. Forgotten in the narrow cul-de-sacs of isolated mountain valleys, the Ladins have developed their own folk traditions and speak an ancient dialect that is derived from Latin and similar to the Romansch spoken in some high valleys in Switzerland.

CANAZEI

60 km (37 mi) west of Cortina d'Ampezzo, 52 km (32 mi) east of Bolzano.

VISITOR INFORMATION

Canazei tourism office (⊠ Stréda de Pareda 63 ☎ 0462/608811 ⊕ www. canazei.org).

EXPLORING

Of the year-round resort towns in the Val di Fassa, Canazei is the most popular. The mountains around this small town are threaded with hiking trails and ski slopes, surrounded by large clutches of conifers.

About 4 km (2½ mi) west of Canazei, an excursion from Campitello di Fassa to the vantage point at **Col Rodella** is a must. A cable car (€13.50 round-trip) rises some 3,000 feet to a full-circle vista of the Heart of the Dolomites, including the Sasso Lungo and the rest of the Sella range.

WHERE TO STAY

$–$$　🏠 **Alla Rosa.** The view of the imposing Dolomites is the real attraction at this central hotel, so ask for a room with a balcony. The reception area is spacious and welcoming, and guest rooms pleasantly blend rustic and modern elements. There's a modest restaurant serving local and international cuisine, and a cozy bar. **Pros:** in the center of town; great views. **Cons:** half board mandatory in winter high season; busy neighborhood. ⊠ Stréda del Faure 18 ☎ 0462/601107 ⊕ www.hotelallarosa.com ➷ 49 rooms ♿ In-room: Wi-Fi, no a/c, refrigerator. In-hotel: restaurant, bar, gym, Internet terminal, parking (paid), Wi-Fi hotspot ⊟ MC, V ❀❁ BP.

LAGO DI CAREZZA

22 km (14 mi) west of Canazei, 29 km (18 mi) east of Bolzano.

Glacial Lake Carezza is some 5,000 feet above sea level. The crystal, almost florescent azure blue of the waters can at times change to magical greens and purples, reflections of the dense surrounding forest and rosy peaks of the Dolomites. You can hike down to this quintessential mountain lake from the nearby village of the same name; there's a fountain with two marmots in the center of town. If you're just driving by, there's

EN
ROUTE

free roadside parking before and after the lake; otherwise, look for the paid parking lot across from it. The **Passo di Sella** *(Sella Pass)* can be approached from SS48, affording some of the most spectacular mountain vistas in Europe before it descends into the Val Gardena. The road continues to Ortisei, passing the smaller resorts of Selva Gardena and Santa Cristina.

ORTISEI (ST. ULRICH)

28 km (17 mi) north of Canazei, 35 km (22 mi) northeast of Bolzano.

VISITOR INFORMATION

Ortisei (⊠ *Via Rezia 1* ☎ *0471/777600* ⊕ *www.valgardena.it).*

EXPLORING

Ortisei (St. Ulrich), the jewel in the crown of Val Gardena's resorts, is a hub of activity in both summer and winter; there are hundreds of miles of hiking trails and accessible ski slopes. Hotels and facilities are abundant—swimming pools, ice rinks, health spas, tennis courts, and bowling alleys. Most impressive of all is the location, a valley surrounded by formidable views in all directions.

For centuries Ortisei has also been famous for the expertise of its woodcarvers, and there are still numerous workshops. Apart from making religious sculptures—particularly the wayside calvaries you come upon everywhere in the Dolomites—Ortisei's carvers were long known for producing wooden dolls, horses, and other toys. As itinerant peddlers they traveled every spring on foot with their loaded packs as far as Paris, London, and St. Petersburg. Shops in town still sell woodcrafts.

Fine historic and contemporary examples of local woodworking can be seen at the **Museo della Val Gardena.** ⊠ *Via Rezia 83* ☎ *0471/797554* ⊕ *www.museumgherdeina.it* ⊡ *€5* ⊗ *Jan. 12–Mar., Thurs. and Fri. 10–noon and 2–5; May 15–Oct., weekdays 10–noon and 2–6 (July and Aug., also Sun. 3–6, Thurs. 8 AM–10 PM); Dec. 27–Jan. 9, daily 10–noon and 2–5.*

WHERE TO STAY

$$$–$$$$
★

⛱ **Adler.** This hotel has been under the same family management since 1810. The original building has been enlarged several times, yielding spacious guest rooms and an expansive spa complex but retaining much of the old turreted-castle appeal. Minimum stay is three nights, but most guests come for a full week, picking up the busy schedule of activities (such as guided ski tours and snowshoe walks) when they arrive on Saturday evening. The same activities, at a slower pace, are available for children. **Pros:** breathtaking views; superb staff; lots of family activities. **Cons:** standard rooms need redecorating; long walk to town center. ⊠ *Via Rezia 7* ☎ *0471/775000, 0471/775001 reservations* ⊕ *www. adler-dolomiti.com* ⊅ *123 rooms* ⚴ *In-room: safe, refrigerator, Internet, Wi-Fi. In-hotel: restaurant, bar, pool, gym, spa, children's programs*

8

(ages 4–12), Internet terminal, parking (free) ⊟ *MC, V* ⊗ *Closed mid-Apr.–mid-May* ⍥ *MAP.*

$$$–$$$$ ⬚ **Cavallino Bianco.** With delicate wooden balconies and an eye-catching wooden gable, the pink Cavallino Bianco (the Little White Horse) looks like a gigantic dollhouse, and it is in fact marketed especially toward families with children. Beyond this facade lies a sprawling, all-inclusive modern resort, but the cozy bar—with its large, handcrafted fireplace—retains some of the charm it had as the old postal hotel. Guest rooms have upholstered furniture with cheery, large-scale plaids and honey-tone wood accents. The hotel is only a five-minute walk from the main ski facilities; ski guides are available. **Pros:** family-friendly atmosphere; cheerful rooms. **Cons:** in the busy town center; a bit impersonal. ⊠ *Via Rezia 22* ☎ *0471/783333* ⊕ *www.cavallino-bianco.com* ⇰ *184 rooms* △ *In-room: safe, refrigerator, Internet. In-hotel: 2 restaurants, bar, pool, spa, bicycles, children's programs (ages 2–12), parking (paid)* ⊟ *AE, DC, MC, V* ⍥ *FAP.*

WORD OF MOUTH

"The drive from Cortina to Bolzano is spectacular—its only about 76 km but will take a full day. We also like the hiking and lakes around Cortina. The funicular takes you up the mountain where you can either hike or just enjoy the views." —cmeyer54

SKIING

With almost 600 km (370 mi) of accessible downhill slopes and more than 90 km (56 mi) of cross-country skiing trails, Ortisei is one of the most popular ski resorts in the Dolomites. Prices are good, and facilities are among the most modern in the region. In warmer weather, the slopes surrounding Ortisei are a popular hiking destination, as well as a playground for vehicular mountain adventures: biking, rafting, even paragliding.

An immensely popular ski route, the **Sella Ronda** relies on well-placed chairlifts to connect 26 km (16 mi) of downhill skiing around the colossal Sella massif, passing through several towns along the way. You can ski the loop, which requires intermediate ability and a full day's effort, either clockwise or counterclockwise. Going with a guide is recommended. Chairlifts here, as elsewhere in the Dolomites, are covered by the **Dolomiti Superski pass** (⊕ *www.dolomitisuperski.com*), available for varying prices and durations. The **Val Gardena tourism office** (⊠ *Via Dursan 81, Santa Cristina* ☎ *0471/777777* ⊕ *www.valgardena.it*) can provide detailed information about sport-equipment rental outfits and guided-tour operators. **Val Gardena Active** (☎ *335/6849031* ⊕ *www.selva-active.com*) outfits a particularly large choice of year-round mountain sport activities.

CORTINA D'AMPEZZO

The archetypal Dolimite resort, Cortina d'Ampezzo entices those seeking both relaxation and adventure. The town is the western gateway to the Strade Grande delle Dolomiti, and actually crowns the northern Veneto region and an area known as Cadore in the northernmost part of the province of Belluno. Like Alto Adige to the west, Cadore (birthplace to the Venetian Rennaisance painter Titian) was on the Alpine front during the First World War, and the scene of many battles commemorated in refuges and museums.

VISITOR INFORMATION

Cortina d'Ampezzo tourism office (⊠ *Piazzetta San Francesco 8* ☎ *0436/3231* ⊕ *www.infodolomiti.it*).

EXPLORING

Cortina d'Ampezzo has been the Dolomites' mountain resort of choice for more than 100 years; half a century before Turin, the Winter Olympics were held here in 1956. Although its glamorous appeal to younger Italians may have been eclipsed by steeper, sleeker Madonna di Campiglio, Cortina remains, for many, Italy's most idyllic incarnation of an Alpine ski town.

Surrounded by mountains and dense forests, the "Queen of the Dolomites" is in a lush meadow 4,000 feet above sea level. The town hugs the slopes beside a fast-moving stream, and a public park extends along one bank. Higher in the valley, luxury hotels and the villas of the rich are identifiable by their attempts to hide behind stands of firs and spruces. The bustling center of Cortina d'Ampezzo has little nostalgia, despite its Alpine appearance. The tone is set by smart shops and cafés as chic as their well-dressed patrons, whose corduroy knickerbockers may well have been tailored by Armani. Unlike neighboring resorts that have a strong Germanic flavor, Cortina d'Ampezzo is unapologetically Italian and distinctly fashionable.

On Via Cantore, a winding road heading up out of town to the northeast (becoming SS48), you can stop and see the **Pista Olimpica di Bob** *(Olympic Bobsled Course)* used in the 1956 Winter Games.

WHERE TO EAT

$$
NORTHERN
ITALIAN

✕ **Tavernetta.** Near the Olympic ice-skating rink, this popular restaurant has Tirolean-style wood-paneled dining rooms. Join the local clientele in sampling Cortina specialties such as *pasta with ragu bianco tartuffato* (white truffle sauce), and wild game. ⊠ *Via Castello 53* ☎ *0436/868102* ▭ *AE, DC, MC, V* ⊗ *Closed May, June, Nov., and Tues.*

WHERE TO STAY

$$

🏨 **Corona.** Noted ski instructor Luciano Rimoldi, who has coached such luminaries as Alberto Tomba, runs a cozy Alpine lodge. Modern art adorns small but comfortable pine-paneled rooms; the convivial bar is a pleasant place to relax. The hotel is a 10-minute walk—across the river—from the center of town, and a 10-minute ride from the lifts (a ski shuttle stops out front). **Pros:** cozy atmosphere; friendly staff; quiet location. **Cons:** small rooms; outside the town center. ⊠ *Via Val di Sotto 12* ☎ *0436/3251* ⊕ *www.hotelcoronacortina.it* ⟿ *44 rooms* ♨ *In-room: Wi-Fi, no a/c. In-hotel: restaurant, bar, Internet terminal, parking (free)* ▭ *AE, DC, MC, V* ⊗ *Closed Apr., May, and mid-Sept.–Nov.* ❢❂❙ *BP.*

8

$$$–$$$$ ★   ⊡ **De la Poste.** Loyal skiers return year after year to this classic old-school hotel; its main terrace bar is one of Cortina's social centers. De la Poste has been under the careful management of the Manaìgo family since 1936. Each unique room has antiques in characteristic Dolomite style; almost all have wooden balconies. A refined main dining room—with high ceilings and large chandeliers—serves nouvelle cuisine and superb soufflés; there's also a more-informal grill room with wood paneling and the family's pewter collection. **Pros:** professional service; romantic atmosphere. **Cons:** a bit stuffy; in a busy neighborhood. ⊠ *Piazza Roma 14* ☎ *0436/4271* ⊕ *www.delaposte.it* ⌨ *83 rooms* ⚹ *In-room: no a/c, Wi-Fi, safe, refrigerator. In-hotel: 2 restaurants, bar, parking (free)* ▭ *AE, DC, MC, V* ⊙ *Closed Apr.–mid-June and Oct.–mid-Dec.* ⑩ *BP.*

$$$$ ⊡ **Miramonti Majestic.** This imposing and luxe hotel, more than a century old, has a magnificent mountain-valley position about 1 km (½ mi) south of town. A touch of formality comes through in the imperial Austrian design. There's always a roaring fire in the splendid bar, and the hotel's recreation rooms are lined with windows overlooking mountain vistas. The history of Cortina is intricately tied to the Miramonti, and you can feel a part of it all here. **Pros:** magnificent location; old-world charm; splendid views. **Cons:** outside town center; minimum stay in high season. ⊠ *Località Peziè 103* ☎ *0436/4201* ⊕ *www. miramontimajestic.it* ⌨ *122 rooms* ⚹ *In-room: no a/c, refrigerator. In-hotel: restaurant, bar, golf course, tennis courts, pool, gym, laundry service, Internet terminal, parking (free)* ▭ *AE, DC, MC, V* ⊙ *Closed Apr.–June and Sept.–mid-Dec.* ⑩ *BP.*

SPORTS AND THE OUTDOORS

HIKING AND CLIMBING

Hiking information is available at the excellent local **tourism office** (⊠ *Piazzetta San Francesco 8* ☎ *0436/3231* ⊕ *www.infodolomiti.it*). The **Gruppo Guide Alpine Cortina Scuola di Alpinismo** (*Mountaineering School* ⊠ *Corso Italia 69* ☎ *0436/868505* ⊕ *www.guidecortina.com*) organizes climbing trips and trekking adventures.

SKIING

Cortina's long and picturesque ski runs will delight intermediates, but advanced skiers might lust for steeper terrain, which can be found only off-piste. Efficient ski bus service connects the town with the high-speed chairlifts and gondolas that ascend in all directions from the valley.

The **Dolomiti Superski pass** (⊠ *Via Marconi 15* ☎ *0471/795397* ⊕ *www. dolomitisuperski.com*) provides access to the surrounding Dolomites (€40–€45 per day)—with 450 lifts and gondolas serving 1,200 km (750 mi) of trails. Buy one at the ticket office next to the bus station. The **Faloria gondola** (⊠ *Via Ria de Zeta 10* ☎ *0436/2517*) runs from the center of town. From its top you can get up to most of the central mountains. Some of the most impressive views (and steepest slopes) are on **Monte Cristallo,** based at Misurina, 15 km (9 mi) northeast of Cortina by car or bus. The topography of the **Passo Falzarego** ski area, 16 km (10 mi) east of town, is quite dramatic.

Milan, Lombardy, and the Lakes

WORD OF MOUTH

"The towns around Lake Maggiore are beautiful, Isola Bella with its palace and garden is unique. Also the gardens of Villa Taranto are like a dream, full of floral arrangements, there are splendid views of the lake."

—Valtor

WELCOME TO MILAN, LOMBARDY, AND THE LAKES

Piazza del Duomo, Milan

TOP REASONS TO GO

★ **Lake Como:** Ferries crisscross the waters, taking you from stately villas to tiny towns.

★ **Leonardo Da Vinci's** *The Last Supper*: Behold one of the world's most famous works of art.

★ **Bergamo Alta:** A funicular ride takes you up to the magnificent medieval city.

★ **Window shopping in Milan:** Italians' refined fashion sense is on full display in the famed Quadrilatero shopping district.

★ **La Scala:** There's no better place to spend a night at the opera.

Lake Como

1 Milan. Italy lives in the present tense here. The country's leading city of commerce is also one of the world's fashion capitals, and there are cultural treasures here that rival those of Florence and Rome.

2 Pavia, Cremona, and Mantua. South of Milan are the walled cities where Renaissance dukes built towering palaces and intricate churches. They sit on the Po Plain, one of Italy's wealthiest regions.

3 Lake Garda. Italy's largest lake measures 16 km (10 mi) across at its widest point and 50 km (31 mi) from end to end. There are more tourists here than at the other lakes, but that means you can also find more opportunities for outdoor activities.

4 Lake Como. This relatively narrow lake is probably the country's best-known body of water. You can almost always see across to the other side, which lends a great sense of intimacy. Lake Lecco, to the southeast, is actually a branch of Lake Como.

5 Lake Maggiore. It may be smaller than Lake Garda and less famous than Lake Como, but Lake Maggiore is impressively picturesque with the Alps as a backdrop. One of the greatest pleasures here is exploring the lake's islands.

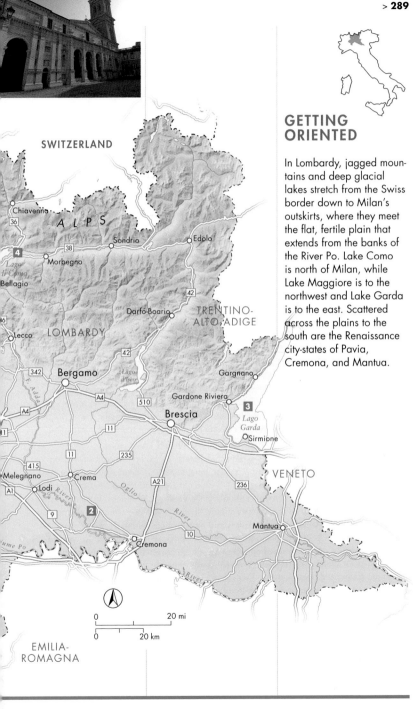

GETTING ORIENTED

In Lombardy, jagged mountains and deep glacial lakes stretch from the Swiss border down to Milan's outskirts, where they meet the flat, fertile plain that extends from the banks of the River Po. Lake Como is north of Milan, while Lake Maggiore is to the northwest and Lake Garda is to the east. Scattered across the plains to the south are the Renaissance city-states of Pavia, Cremona, and Mantua.

SWITZERLAND

Chiavenna
36
A L P S
Sondrio
Edolo
38
4
Lago
di Como
Morbegno
Bellagio
42
Darfo-Boario
TRENTINO-
ALTO ADIGE
6
Lecco
LOMBARDY
42
342
Bergamo
Lago
d'Iseo
Gargnano
A4
510
Gardone Riviera
A4
Brescia
3
1
11
Lago
Garda
Sirmione
11
235
9
415
11
A21
236
Melegnano
Crema
Oglio
VENETO
A1
Lodi
River
9
2
River
A21
10
Mantua
Fiume Po
Cremona
River

0   20 mi
0   20 km

EMILIA-
ROMAGNA

MILAN, LOMBARDY, AND THE LAKES PLANNER

Supper Reservations

Reservations are required to see Leonardo da Vinci's *The Last Supper*, housed in the refectory of Milan's Santa Maria delle Grazie church. You should call as far in advance as possible to make them, particularly if you're planning to go on a weekend. *For details, see the Santa Maria delle Grazie listing in this chapter.*

A Night at the Opera

Attending a performance at the world's most venerated opera house, La Scala, is an unforgettable experience, regardless of whether you're an opera buff. Tickets go on sale two months in advance, and they sell out quickly. Your best bet is to order online at ⊕ *www. teatroallascala.org* (phone orders aren't accepted). Once you're in Milan, you can check on ticket availability at the Scala box office, located in the Duomo metro station and open daily from noon to 6 PM. About 100 tickets for seats in the second gallery go on sale three hours before a performance—they're available at the ticket office of the theater itself.

Making the Most of Your Time

Italy's capital of commerce isn't a top priority for most leisure travelers, but the city has a sophisticated urban appeal: its fashionable shops rival New York and Paris, its soccer teams are Italy's answer to the Yankees and the Mets, its opera performances set the standard for the world, and its art treasures are considerable.

The biggest draw in the region, though, is the lake district. Lakes Como, Garda, Maggiore, and Orta all have long histories as travel destinations, and each has its own distinct character. If you have limited time, visit the lake you think best suits your style, but if you have more time, make the rounds to two or three to get a sense of their contrasts.

Finding a Place to Stay

The hotels in Italy's wealthiest region generally cater to a clientele willing to pay for extra comfort. Outside Milan, many are converted villas with well-landscaped grounds. Most of the famous lake resorts are expensive; more-reasonable rates can be found in the smaller towns. Local tourism offices can be an excellent source of information about affordable lodging.

Prices in almost all hotels can go up dramatically during Milan's big trade fairs, especially during the Furniture Fair in early April. Fashion, travel, and tech fairs also draw big crowds throughout the year, raising prices. In contrast to other cities in Italy, however, you can often find discounts on weekends and higher prices during the week. The three lake districts—Maggiore, Garda, and Como—have little to offer except quiet from November to March, when most gardens, hotels, and restaurants are closed.

WHAT IT COSTS (IN EUROS)					
	¢	$	$$	$$$	$$$$
Restaurants	under €20	€20–€30	€30–€45	€45–€65	over €65
Hotels	under €75	€75–€125	€125–€200	€200–€300	over €300

Restaurant prices are for a first course (primo), second course (secondo), and dessert (dolce). Hotel prices are for two people in a standard double room in high season, including tax and service.

Getting Around by Train

Milan's massive Central Station (Milano Centrale), 3 km (2 mi) northwest of the Duomo, is one of Italy's major passenger-train hubs, with frequent direct service within the region to Como, Bergamo, Brescia, Sirmione, Pavia, Cremona, and Mantua. Soaring domed glass ceilings and plenty of signage have significantly improved the renovated station's navigability, but its sheer size requires considerable walking and patience, so allow for some extra time here. For general information on trains and schedules, as well as online ticket purchase, visit the Web site of the Italian national railway, **FS** (⊕ *www.trenitalia.com*).

Tickets bought without a reservation need to be validated by stamping them in yellow machines on the train platforms. Tickets with reservations do not require validation. When in doubt, validate: it can't hurt.

Getting Around by Bus

Bus service isn't a good option for travel between cities here—it's not faster, cheaper, or more convenient than the train. For those determined to travel by bus, **Autostradale** (☎ *02/33910794* ⊕ *www.autostradale.it*) goes to Turin, Bergamo, and Brescia from its hub at Lampugnano (metro line 1), northwest of Milan's city center. Reservations are required.

Getting Around by Car

Outside Milan, driving is the best way to see the region. Getting almost anywhere is a snap, as several major highways intersect at Milan, all connected by the *tangenziale*, the road that rings the city. The A4 runs west to Turin and east to Venice; A1 leads south to Bologna, Florence, and Rome; A7 angles southwest down to Genoa. A8 goes northwest toward Lake Maggiore, and A9 north runs past Lake Como and over the St. Gotthard Pass into Switzerland.

Your car-rental company should be your first resource if you have a problem while driving in Italy, but it's also good to know that the **ACI** (☎ *803/116* ⊕ *www.aci.it*), the Italian auto club, offers 24-hour roadside assistance (free for members, for a fee for nonmembers). Regularly spaced roadside service phones are available on the autostrade.

9

EATING WELL IN MILAN, LOMBARDY, AND THE LAKES

Lombardy may well offer Italy's most varied cuisine. Local cooking is influenced by the neighboring regions of the north; foreign conquerors have left their mark; and today, well-traveled Milanese, business visitors, and industrious immigrants all appreciate exotic flavors not so eagerly embraced elsewhere in Italy.

Milan runs counter to many of the established Italian dining customs. A "real" traditional Milanese meal is a rarity; instead, Milan offers something for every taste, budget, and time of day, from expense-account elegance in fancy restaurants to all-day nibbles in wine bars. The city's cosmopolitan nature means trends arrive here first, and things move fast. Meals are not the drawn-out pastime they tend to be elsewhere in Italy. But food is still consistently good—competition among restaurants is fierce and the local clientele is demanding, which means you can be reasonably certain that if a place looks promising, it won't disappoint.

THE COTOLETTA QUESTION

Everyone has an opinion on *cotoletta*, photo upper right, the breaded veal cutlet known across Italy as *una Milanese*.

It's clearly related to Austria's Wiener schnitzel, but did the Austrians introduce it when they dominated Milan or take it home when they left? Should it be with bone or without? Some think it best with fresh tomato and arugula on top; others find this sacrilege.

Two things unite all camps: the meat must be well beaten until it is thin, and it must never leave a grease spot after it is fried.

REGIONAL SPECIALTIES

Ask an Italian what Lombards eat, and you're likely to hear *cotoletta, càsoeûla,* and *risotto giallo*—all dishes that reinforce Lombardy's status as the crossroads of Italy. *Cotoletta alla Milanese* has likely Austrian influences. *Càsoeûla* is a cabbage-and-pork stew that resembles French cassoulet, though some say it has Spanish origins. *Risotto giallo* (also known as *Milanese*), pictured at left, is colorful and perfumed with exotic saffron. With no tomatoes, olive oil, or pasta, these dishes hardly sound Italian.

BUTTER AND CHEESE

Agricultural traditions and geography mean that animal products are more common here than in southern Italy—and that means butter and cream take olive oil's place. A rare point of agreement about cotoletta is that it's cooked in butter. The first and last steps of risotto making—toasting the rice and letting it "repose" before serving—use ample amounts of butter. And the second-most-famous name in Italian cheese (after Parmesan) is likely Gorgonzola, named for a town near Milan. The best now comes from Novara.

RISOTTO

Novara is the center of Italian (and European) rice production. Introduced from the Orient and grown here since the 15th century, rice is Lombardy's answer to pasta. From Milan's risotto giallo with its costly saffron tint to Mantua's risotto with pumpkin or sausage, there's no end to the variety of rice dishes. Canonic risotto should be *all'onda,* or flow off the spoon like a wave. Keeping with the Italian tradition of nothing wasted, yesterday's risotto is flattened in a pan and fried in butter to produce *riso al salto,* which at its best has a crispy crust and a tender middle.

PANETTONE

Panettone, a sweet yeast bread with raisins and citron, pictured below left, is a national Christmastime treat invented in Milan. It's now so ubiquitous that its price is used as an economic indicator: is it up or down, compared to last year? Consumption begins on December 7, Milan's patron saint's day, and goes until supplies run out at January's end.

WINE

Lombardy is not one of Italy's most heralded wine regions, but its reputation is growing. Production is scattered throughout the province. The Valtellina area to the northeast of Milan produces two notable red DOCGs from the nebbiolo grape: Valtellina Superiore and the intense dessert wine Sforzato di Valtellina. The Franciacorta region around Brescia makes highly regarded sparkling wines. Lake breezes bring crisp, smooth whites from the shores around Lake Garda.

9

Updated by
Sara Rosso

It's tempting to describe Lombardy as a region that offers something for everyone. Milan is the country's business capital and the center for everything that's up to the minute. The great Renaissance cities of the Po Plain—Pavia, Cremona, and Mantua—are stately and serene, embracing their past with nostalgia while ever keeping an eye on the present. Topping any list of the region's attractions are the lakes—glacial waters stretching out below the Alps—which have been praised as the closest thing to paradise by writers throughout the ages, from Virgil to Hemingway.

Millions of travelers have concurred: for sheer beauty, the lakes of northern Italy—Como, Maggiore, Garda, and Orta—have few equals. Along their shores are 18th- and 19th-century villas, exotic formal gardens, sleepy villages, and dozens of resorts that were once Europe's most fashionable, and still retain a powerful allure.

Milan can be disappointingly modern—a little too much like the place you've come to Italy to escape—but its historic buildings and art collections in many ways rival those of Florence and Rome. And if you love to shop, Milan is a mecca. It truly offers a fashion experience for every taste, from Corso Buenos Aires, which has a higher ratio of stores per square foot than anywhere else in Europe, to upscale but affordable Corso Vercelli and elegant Via Montenapoleone, where there is no limit on what you can spend. Milan is home to global fashion giants such as Armani, Prada, and Trussardi; behind them stands a host of less-famous designers who help fill all those fabulous shops.

MILAN

Milan is Italy's business hub and crucible of chic. Between the Po's rich farms and the industrious mountain valleys, it has long been the country's capital of commerce, finance, fashion, and media. Rome may be bigger and have the political power, but Milan and the affluent north are what really make the country go. It's also Italy's transport hub, with the biggest international airport, the most rail connections, and the best subway system. Leonardo da Vinci's *The Last Supper* and other great works of art are here, as well as a spectacular Gothic Duomo, the finest of its kind. Milan even reigns supreme where it really counts (in the minds of many Italians), routinely trouncing the rest of the nation with its two premier soccer teams.

And yet, Milan hasn't won the battle for hearts and minds. Most tourists prefer Tuscany's hills and Venice's canals to Milan's hectic efficiency and wealthy indifference, and it's no surprise that in a country of medieval hilltop villages and skilled artisans, a city of grand boulevards and global corporations leaves visitors asking the real Italy to please stand up. They're right, of course. Milan is more European than Italian, a new buckle on an old boot, and although its old city can stand cobblestone for cobblestone against the best of them, seekers of Roman ruins and fairy-tale towns may pass. But Milan's secrets reveal themselves slowly to those who look. A side street conceals a garden complete with flamingos (Via dei Cappuccini, just off Corso Venezia), and a renowned 20th-century art collection hides modestly behind an unspectacular facade a block from Corso Buenos Aires (the Casa Museo Boschi-di Stefano). Visitors lured by the world-class shopping will appreciate Milan's European sophistication while discovering unexpected facets of a country they may have thought they knew.

Virtually every invader in European history—Gaul, Roman, Goth, Longobard, and Frank—as well as a long series of rulers from France, Spain, and Austria, took a turn at ruling the city. After being completely sacked by the Goths in AD 539 and by the Holy Roman Empire under Frederick Barbarossa in 1157, Milan became one of the first independent city-states of the Renaissance. Its heyday of self-rule proved comparatively brief. From 1277 until 1500 it was ruled by the Visconti and subsequently the Sforza dynasties. These families were known, justly or not, for a peculiarly aristocratic mixture of refinement, classical learning, and cruelty, and much of the surviving grandeur of Gothic and Renaissance art and architecture is their doing. Be on the lookout in your wanderings for the Visconti family emblem—a viper, its jaws straining wide, devouring a child.

VISITOR INFORMATION

The **tourism office** (⊠ *Piazza Duomo 19/A, Piazza Duomo* ☎ *02/77404343* ⊕ *www.visitamilano.it* ⊙ *Mon.–Sat. 8:45–1 and 2–6, Sun. 9–1 and 2–5*) in Piazza Duomo is the perfect place to begin your visit. It's accessible by elevator and down a deco stairway under the arches on the north side of Piazza Duomo; you can also enter from the Galleria in front of the Park Hyatt hotel. There are excellent maps, booklets with museum descriptions and itineraries on a variety of themes, and a selection of

LOMBARDY THROUGH THE AGES

Lombardy has had a tumultuous history. Control by outsiders dates back more than 3,000 years, to when the Etruscans of central Italy first wandered north of the River Po. They dominated the region for centuries, to be followed by the Cenomani Gauls, then the Romans in the later days of the Republic. The region was known as Cisalpine Gaul ("Gaul this side of the Alps"), and under the rule of Augustus became a Roman province.

The decline of the Roman Empire was followed by invasion by Attila of the Huns and Theodoric of the Goths. These conquerors gave way to the Lombards, who then ceded to Charlemagne their iron crown, which became the emblem of his vast, unstable empire. Even before the bonds of the empire had begun to snap, the cities of Lombardy were erecting walls in defense against the Hungarians, and against each other.

These city-states formed the Lombard League, which in the 12th century finally defeated the German ruler Frederick Barbarossa. With the northern invaders gone, new and even bloodier strife began. In each city the Guelphs (bourgeois supporters of the popes) and the Ghibellines (noblemen loyal to the Holy Roman Empire) clashed. The city-states declined, falling under the yoke of a few powerful regional rulers. The Republic of Venice dominated Brescia and Bergamo. Mantua was ruled by the Gonzaga family, and the Visconti and Sforza families took over Como, Cremona, Milan, and Pavia.

The Battle of Pavia in 1525, in which the generals of Holy Roman Emperor Charles V defeated the French, brought on 200 years of occupation by the Spanish—who proved generally less cruel than the local tyrants. The War of the Spanish Succession in the early years of the 18th century brought in the Austrians.

Napoléon and his generals defeated the Austrians at the turn of the 19th century. The Treaty of Campoformio resulted in the proclamation of the Cisalpine Republic, which soon became the Republic of Italy and then the Kingdom of Italy—which lasted only until Napoléon's defeat brought back the Austrians. In March of 1848, demonstrations in Milan took on surprising force: the Austrians were driven out of the city, and a provisional government of Milan soon became a provisional government of Lombardy. In June of the same year, Lombardy united with Sardinia—the first step toward Italian unification in 1870.

The spirit of 1848 was rekindled in 1943. Discontent with fascism provoked workers to strike in Turin and Milan, marking the beginning of the end of fascist dominance. The Lombardy-based partisan insurrection against Mussolini and the German regime was better organized and more successful than in many other parts of the country. Indeed, Milan was liberated from the Germans by its own partisan organization before the Allied troops entered the city.

Dissatisfaction with the federal government is practically a given among Lombardy residents, and the prevailing attitude has been to ignore Rome and get on with business. It's an approach that's proven successful: Lombardy accounts for one-fifth of Italy's economy.

brochures about smaller museums and cultural initiatives. Pick up a copy of the English-language *Hello Milano* (ask, if it is not on display, or see ⊕ *www.hellomilano.it*), a monthly publication with a day-to-day schedule of events of interest to visitors and a comprehensive map. The Autostradale bus operator, sightseeing companies, and a few theaters have desks in the tourism office where you can buy tickets.

THE DUOMO AND POINTS NORTH

Milan's main streets radiate out from the massive Duomo, a late-Gothic cathedral that was started in 1386. Leading north is the handsome Galleria Vittorio Emanuele, an enclosed walkway that takes you to the world-famous opera house known as La Scala. Beyond are the winding streets of the elegant Brera neighborhood, once the city's bohemian quarter. Here you'll find many art galleries, as well as the academy of fine arts. Heading northeast from La Scala is Via Manzoni, which leads to the *Quadrilatero della moda,* or fashion district. Its streets are lined with elegant window displays from the world's most celebrated designers—the Italians taking the lead, of course.

Leading northeast from the Duomo is Corso Vittorio Emanuele. Locals and visitors stroll along this pedestrians-only street, looking at the shop windows, buying ice cream, or stopping for a coffee at one of the sidewalk cafés. Northwest of the Duomo is Via Dante, at the top of which is the imposing outline of the Castello Sforzesco.

TOP ATTRACTIONS

★ **Castello Sforzesco.** For the serious student of Renaissance military engineering, the Castello must be something of a travesty, so often has it been remodeled or rebuilt since it was begun in 1450 by the *condottiere* (hired mercenary) who founded the city's second dynastic family, Francesco Sforza, fourth duke of Milan. Though today "mercenary" has a pejorative ring, during the Renaissance all Italy's great soldier-heroes were professionals hired by the cities and principalities that they served. Of them—and there were thousands—Francesco Sforza (1401–66) is considered one of the greatest, most honest, and most organized. It is said he could remember the names not only of all his men but of their horses as well. His rule signaled the enlightened age of the Renaissance but preceded the next foreign rule by a scant 50 years. The castle's crypts and battlements, including a tunnel that emerges well into the Parco Sempione behind, can be visited with privately reserved guides from **Ad Artem** (☏ *02/6596937* ⊕ *www.adartem.it*) or **Opera d'Arte** (☏ *02/45487400* ⊕ *www.operadartemilano.it/turismo-eng.html*). Since the turn of the 20th century, the Castello has been the depository of several city-owned collections of Egyptian and other antiquities, musical instruments, arms and armor, decorative arts and textiles, prints and photographs (on consultation), paintings, and sculpture. Highlights include the **Sala delle Asse,** a frescoed room still sometimes attributed to Leonardo da Vinci (1452–1519), which, at the time of writing, is closed for restoration (scheduled to reopen sometime before 2015). Michelangelo's unfinished *Rondanini Pietà* is believed to be his last work—an astounding achievement for a man nearly 90, and a moving

9

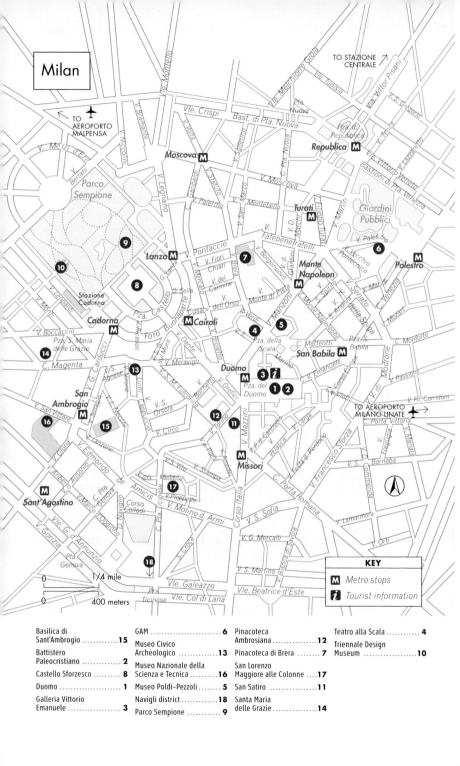

Milan

TO STAZIONE
CENTRALE

TO
AEROPORTO
MALPENSA

Parco
Sempione

Giardini
Pubblici

Pza. d.
Republica

Republica

Moscova

Turati

Palestro

Lanza

Monte
Napoleon

Stazione
Cadorna

Cadorna

Cairoli

San Babila

Pza. della
Scala

Duomo

Pza. del
Duomo

TO AEROPORTO
MILANO LINATE

San
Ambrogio

Missori

Sant'Agostino

Navigli district

coda to his life. The *pinacoteca* (picture gallery) features paintings from medieval times to the 18th century, including 230 works by Antonello da Messina, Canaletto, Andrea Mantegna, and Bernardo Bellotto. The **Museo dei Mobili** (furniture museum), which illustrates the development of Italian furniture from the Middle Ages to current design, includes a delightful collection of Renaissance treasure chests of exotic woods with tiny drawers and miniature architectural details. A single ticket purchased in the office in an inner courtyard admits visitors to these separate installations, which are dispersed around the castle's two immense courtyards. ⊠ *Piazza Castello, Brera* ☎ *02/88463700* ⊕ *www.milanocastello.it* ۞ *Castle: Apr.–Oct, daily 7–7; Nov.–Mar., daily 7–6. Museums: Tues.–Sun. 9–5:30; last entry at 5* ☟ *Museums: €3, free Fri. after 2 and daily after 4:30* Ⓜ *Cairoli; Tram 1, 3, 4, 7, 12, 14, or 27.*

★ **Duomo**. This intricate Gothic structure has been fascinating and exasperating visitors and conquerors alike since it was begun by Galeazzo Visconti III (1351–1402), first duke of Milan, in 1386. Consecrated in the 15th or 16th century, it was not completed until just before the coronation of Napoléon as king of Italy in 1809. Whether you concur with travel writer H.V. Morton's 1964 assessment that the cathedral is "one of the mightiest Gothic buildings ever created," there is no denying that for sheer size and complexity it is unrivaled. It is the second-largest church in the world—the largest being St. Peter's in Rome. The capacity is reckoned to be 40,000. Usually it is empty, a sanctuary from the frenetic pace of life outside and the perfect place for solitary contemplation.

The building is adorned with 135 marble spires and 2,245 marble statues. The oldest part is the apse. Its three colossal bays of curving and counter-curved tracery, especially the bay adorning the exterior of the stained-glass windows, should not be missed. At the end of the southern transept down the right aisle lies the **tomb of Gian Giacomo Medici**. The tomb owes some of its design to Michelangelo but was executed by Leone Leoni (1509–90) and is generally considered to be his masterpiece; it dates from the 1560s. Directly ahead is the Duomo's most famous sculpture, the gruesome but anatomically instructive figure of San Bartolomeo (St. Bartholomew), whose glorious martyrdom consisted of being flayed alive. It is usually said the saint stands "holding" his skin, but this is not quite accurate. It would appear more that he is luxuriating in it, much as a 1950s matron might have shown off a new fur stole.

As you enter the apse to admire those splendid windows, glance at the sacristy doors to the right and left of the altar. The lunette on the right dates from 1393 and was decorated by Hans von Fernach. The one on the left also dates from the 14th century and is ascribed jointly to Giacomo da Campione and Giovanni dei Grassi. Don't miss the view from the Duomo's roof; walk out the left (north) transept to the stairs and elevator. Sadly, air pollution drastically reduces the view on all but the rarest days. As you stand among the forest of marble pinnacles, remember that virtually every inch of this gargantuan edifice, including the roof itself, is decorated with precious white marble dragged from quarries near Lake Maggiore by Duke Visconti's team along road laid

GETTING AROUND MILAN

The city center is compact and walkable; trolleys and trams make it even more accessible, and the efficient Metropolitana (subway) and buses provide access to locations farther afield. Driving in Milan is difficult and parking miserable, so a car is a liability. In addition, drivers within the second ring of streets (the *bastioni*) must hold an Ecopass. (Ask your hotel about getting a pass.)

BY PUBLIC TRANSIT

A standard public transit ticket costs €1 and is valid for a 75-minute trip on a subway, bus, or tram. An all-inclusive subway, bus, and tram pass costs €3 for 24 hours or €5.50 for 48 hours. Individual tickets and passes can be purchased from news vendors and tobacconists, and at ticket counters and ticket machines at larger stops. Another option is a carnet (€9.20), good for 10 tram or subway rides. Once you have your ticket or pass, either stamp it or insert it into slots in station turnstiles or on poles inside trolleys and buses. (The electronic tickets will not function if bent or demagnetized. If you have a problem, contact a station manager, who can usually issue a new ticket.) Trains run from 6 AM to 12:20 AM (1:30 AM on Saturday). From 8 PM to 2 AM, **Radiobus** (☎ *02/48034803* ⊕ *www.atm-mi.it/en*) will pick you up and drop you off anywhere in Milan for a €1.50 supplement to a transit pass. Advance booking is required. For more information, check the Web site of **ATM** (*Azienda Trasporti Milanesi* ⊕ *www.atm-mi.it/en*) or visit information offices at the Duomo, Stazione Cadorna, Stazione Centrale, Garibaldi, and Loreto stops.

BY TAXI

Taxi fares in Milan are higher than in American cities. A short ride will run about €15. Taxis wait at stands marked by an orange "Taxi" sign, or you can call one of the city's taxi companies—**Amicotaxi** (☎ *02/4000*), **Autoradiotaxi** (☎ *02/8585*), **Radio-taxi–Yellow Taxi** (☎ *02/6969*), or **Taxiblu** (☎ *02/4040*). Dispatchers may speak some English; they'll ask for the phone number you're calling from, and they'll tell you the number of your taxi and how long it will take to arrive. If you're in a restaurant or bar, ask the staff to call a cab for you. For car service, contact **Autonoleggio Pini** (☎ *02/29400555* ⊕ *www.limousinepini.eu*). English-speaking drivers are available.

BY BICYCLE

The innovative BikeMI (⊕ *www.bikemi.com*) makes hop-on, drop-off bicycles available at designated spots around the city. There are more than 100 stations, and more than 300 stations are planned. Weekly and daily rates for tourists are available. Buy your subscription online; the site has a map showing stations and availability.

TOURS

A refurbished 1920s tramcar operates a hop-on/hop-off **Tram Turistico** (☎ *800/808181*) tour of the city. Tickets (€20) are valid all day and can be purchased on board. Departures are at 11 and 1 (also at 3, April–October) from Piazza Castello. **City Sightseeing Milano** (⊕ *www.milano.city-sightseeing.it*) has open-top double-decker buses running hop-on/hop-off tours on two routes departing from Piazza Castello. An all-inclusive day pass costs €20.

9

fresh for the purpose and through the newly dredged canals. Audio guides can be rented inside the Duomo from March to December and at Duomo Point in Piazza Duomo (just behind the cathedral) all year long. Exhibits at the **Museo del Duomo** shed light on the cathedral's history and include some of the treasures removed from the exterior for preservation purposes. At this writing, the museum is closed for restoration with no estimated date for completion. ☒ *Piazza del Duomo* ☏ *02/72023375* ⊕ *www.duomomilano.it* ☒ *Stairs to roof €5, elevator €8* ⊙ *Cathedral daily 8:30–6:45. Roof Nov.–Mar., daily 9–4:45; Apr.– Oct., daily 9–9. Museum closed for restoration* Ⓜ *Duomo.*

★ **Galleria Vittorio Emanuele.** This spectacular, late-19th-century glass-topped, belle epoque, barrel-vaulted tunnel is essentially one of the planet's earliest and most select shopping malls. Like its suburban American cousins, the Galleria Vittorio Emanuele fulfills numerous social functions. This is the city's heart, midway between the Duomo and La Scala. It teems with life, inviting people-watching from the tables that spill from the bars and restaurants, where you can enjoy an overpriced coffee. Books, records, clothing, food, pens, pipes, hats, and jewelry are all for sale. Known as Milan's "parlor," the Galleria is often viewed as a barometer of the city's well-being. By the 1990s, the quality of the stores (with the exception of the Prada flagship) and restaurants was uninspired. The city government, which owns the Galleria, and merchants' groups evicted some longtime tenants who had enjoyed anomalously low rents, in favor of Gucci, Tod's, and Louis Vuitton. The historic, if somewhat overpriced and inconsistent, Savini restaurant hosts the beautiful and powerful of the city, just across from McDonald's. Like the cathedral, the Galleria is cruciform in shape. Even in poor weather the great glass dome above the octagonal center is a splendid sight. Look up! The paintings at the base of the dome represent Europe, Asia, Africa, and America. Those at the entrance arch are devoted to science, industry, art, and agriculture. And the floor mosaics are a vastly underrated source of pleasure, even if they are not to be taken too seriously. Be sure to follow tradition and spin your heels once or twice on the more-"delicate" parts of the bull beneath your feet in the northern apse; the Milanese believe it brings good luck. ☒ *Piazza del Duomo* Ⓜ *Duomo.*

QUICK BITES

One thing has remained constant in the Galleria: the Caffè Zucca (⊕ *www.caffemiani.it*), known by the Milanese as Camparino. Its inlaid counter, mosaics, and wrought-iron fixtures have been welcoming tired shoppers since 1867. Enjoy a Campari or Zucca *aperitivo* (aperitif) as well as the entire range of Italian coffees, served either in the Galleria or in an elegant upstairs room where lunch is also served.

Museo Poldi-Pezzoli. This exceptional museum, opened in 1881, was once a private residence and collection, and contains not only pedigreed paintings but also porcelain, textiles, and a cabinet with scenes from Dante's life. The gem is undoubtedly the *Portrait of a Lady* by Antonio Pollaiuolo (1431–98), one of the city's most prized treasures and the source of the museum's logo. The collection also includes masterpieces

by Botticelli (1445–1510), Andrea Mantegna (1431–1506), Giovanni Bellini (1430–1516), and Fra Filippo Lippi (1406–69). Private guided tours are available by reservation. ⊠ *Via Manzoni 12, Quadrilatero* ☎ *02/794889* ⊕ *www. museopoldipezzoli.it* 🎟 *€8* ⊘ *Wed.– Mon. 10–6* Ⓜ *Montenapoleone.*

Parco Sempione. Originally the gardens and parade ground of the Castello Sforzesco, this open space was reorganized during the Napoleonic era, when the arena on its northeast side was constructed, and then turned into a park during the building boom at the end of the 19th century. It is still the lungs of the city's fashionable western neighborhoods, and the **Aquarium** (⊠ *Viale Gadio 2* ☎ *02/884957* ⊕ *www. acquariocivicomilano.eu* 🎟 *Free* ⊘ *Tues.–Sun. 9–1 and 2–5:30*) still attracts Milan's schoolchildren. The park became a bit of a design showcase in 1933 with the construction of the Triennale *(see below)*. The Fiat café offers outdoor dining in summer along with a view of De Chirico's sculpture-filled fountain *Bagni Misteriosi (Mysterious Baths)*.

Even if a walk in the park is not appealing, it is worth visiting to see the **Torre Branca** (⊠ *Parco Sempione* ☎ *02/3314120* 🎟 *€4* ⊘ *Irregular, seasonal hrs; check at* ⊕ *www.branca.it/torre/dati.asp*). Designed by architect Gio Ponti, who was behind so many of the projects that made Milan the design capital that it is, this steel tower rises 330 feet over the Triennale. Take the elevator up to get a nice view of the city, then have a drink at the glitzy Just Cavalli Café (Monday–Saturday, 8 PM–2 AM) at its base. *Parco Sempione:*⊠ *Piazza Castello, Sempione-Castello* ⊘ *Nov.–Feb., daily 6:30–8; Mar. and Apr., daily 6:30–9; May and Oct., daily 6:30–10; June–Sept., daily 6:30–11:30* Ⓜ *Cadorna; Bus 61.*

★ **Pinacoteca di Brera** *(Brera Gallery).* The collection here is star-studded even by Italian standards. The entrance hall (Room I) displays 20th-century sculpture and painting, including Carlo Carrà's (1881–1966) confident, stylish response to the schools of cubism and surrealism. The museum has nearly 40 other rooms, arranged in chronological order—pace yourself.

The somber, moving *Cristo Morto (Dead Christ)* by Mantegna dominates Room VI, with its sparse palette of umber and its foreshortened perspective. Mantegna's shocking, almost surgical precision—in the rendering of Christ's wounds, the face propped up on a pillow, the day's growth of beard—tells of an all-too-human agony. It is one of Renaissance painting's most quietly wondrous achievements, finding an unsuspected middle ground between the excesses of conventional gore and beauty in representing the Passion's saddest moment.

Room XXIV offers two additional highlights of the gallery. Raphael's (1483–1520) *Sposalizio della Vergine (Marriage of the Virgin)* with its mathematical composition and precise, alternating colors, portrays the betrothal of Mary and Joseph (who, though older than the other men gathered, wins her hand when the rod he is holding miraculously blossoms). *La Vergine con il Bambino e Santi* (*Madonna with Child and Saints*), by Piero della Francesca (1420–92), is an altarpiece commissioned by Federico da Montefeltro (shown kneeling, in full armor, before the Virgin); it was intended for a church to house the duke's tomb. The ostrich egg hanging from the apse, depending on whom you ask, either commemorates the miracle of his fertility—Federico's wife died months after giving birth to a long-awaited male heir—or alludes to his appeal for posthumous mercy, the egg symbolizing the saving power of grace. ☒ *Via Brera 28, Brera* ☎ *02/92800361* ⊕ *www.brera.beniculturali.it* ▨ *€11, higher during special exhibitions* ☉ *Tues.–Sun. 8:30–7:15; last admission 45 mins before closing* Ⓜ *Montenapoleone or Lanza.*

Teatro alla Scala. You need know nothing of opera to sense that, like Carnegie Hall, La Scala is closer to a cathedral than an auditorium. Here Verdi established his reputation and Maria Callas sang her way into opera lore. It looms as a symbol—both for the performer who dreams of singing here and for the opera buff who knows every note of *Rigoletto* by heart. Audiences are notoriously demanding and are apt to jeer performers who do not measure up. The opera house was closed after destruction by Allied bombs in 1943, and reopened at a performance led by Arturo Toscanini in 1946.

If you are lucky enough to be here during the opera season, which runs from December to June, do whatever is necessary to attend. Tickets go on sale two months before the first performance and are usually sold out the same day. Hearing opera sung in the magical setting of La Scala is an unparalleled experience.

At **Museo Teatrale alla Scala** you can admire an extensive collection of librettos, paintings of the famous names of Italian opera, posters, costumes, antique instruments, and design sketches for the theater. It is also possible to take a look at the theater, which was completely restored in 2004. Special exhibitions reflect current productions. ☒ *Piazza della Scala; museum Largo Ghiringhelli 1, Duomo* ☎ *02/72003744 theater, 02/88797473 museum* ⊕ *www.teatroallascala.org* ▨ *Museum €5* ☉ *Museum daily 9–12:30 and 1:30–5:30; last entry ½ hr prior to closing* Ⓜ *Duomo.*

Triennale Design Museum. After decades of false starts and controversy, Milan's Triennale is a museum that honors Italy's design talent, as well as offering a regular series of exhibitions on design from around the world. Originally the home of triennial decorative arts shows, a spectacular bridge entrance leads to a permanent collection, an exhibition space, and a stylish café (whose seating is an encyclopedia of design icons). The Triennale also manages the museum-studio of designer Achille Castiglione in nearby Piazza Castello. ☒ *Via Alemagna 6, Parco Sempione* ☎ *02/724341* ⊕ *www.triennaledesignmuseum.com* ▨ *€8* ☉ *Tues., Wed., and Fri.–Sun. 10:30–8:30, Thurs. 10:30 AM–11 PM; last entrance 1 hr before closing* Ⓜ *Cadorna.*

WORTH NOTING

Battistero Paleocristiano. Beneath the Duomo's piazza lies this baptistery ruin dating from the 4th century. Although opinion remains divided, it is widely believed to be where Ambrose, Milan's first bishop and patron saint, baptized Augustine. Tickets are available at the kiosk inside the cathedral. ⊠ *Piazza del Duomo, enter through Duomo* ☎ *02/72022656* 📠 *€4* ⊙ *Daily 9:30–5:30* Ⓜ *Duomo.*

Casa-Museo Boschi di Stefano *(Boschi di Stefano House and Museum).* To most of people, Italian art means Renaissance art. But the 20th century in Italy was a productive—if less well-known—era. Just a block behind the Corso Buenos Aires shopping area, the Casa-Museo Boschi di Stefano is a tribute to the enlightened private collectors who replaced popes and nobles as Italian patrons. An apartment on the second floor of a stunning art deco building designed by Milan architect Portaluppi houses this private collection, which was donated to the city of Milan in 2003. Its walls are lined with the works of postwar greats, such as Fontana, De Chirico, and Morandi. Along with the art, the museum holds distinctive postwar furniture and stunning Murano glass chandeliers. ⊠ *Via Jan 15, Corso Buenos Aires* ☎ *02/20240568* ⊕ *www. fondazioneboschidistefano.it* 📠 *Free* ⊙ *Tues.–Sun. 10–6; last entry at 5:30* Ⓜ *Lima; Tram 33; Bus 60.*

★ **GAM: Galleria d'Arte Moderna/Villa Reale.** One of the city's most beautiful buildings, this museum is an outstanding example of neoclassical architecture. It was built between 1790 and 1796 as a residence for a member of the Belgioioso family. It later became known as the Villa Reale (royal) when it was donated to Napoléon, who lived here briefly with Empress Josephine. Its origins as residence are reflected in the elegance of its proportions and its private garden behind.

Likewise, the collection of paintings is domestic rather than monumental. There are many portraits, as well as collections of miniatures on porcelain. Unusual for an Italian museum, this collection derives from private donations from Milan's hereditary and commercial aristocracies. On display are the collection left by prominent painter and sculptor Marino Marini and the immense *Quarto Stato* (*Fourth Estate*), which is at the top of the grand staircase. Completed in 1901 by Pellizza da Volpedo, this painting of striking workers is an icon of 20th-century Italian art and labor history, and as such it has been satirized almost as much as the *Mona Lisa.* This museum is a unique glimpse of the splendors hiding behind Milan's discreet and often stern facades. ⊠ *Via Palestro 16* ☎ *02/88445947* ⊕ *www.gam-milano.com* 📠 *Free* ⊙ *Tues.–Sun. 9–1 and 2–5:30; last entry 15 mins before closing* Ⓜ *Palestro or Turati.*

☾ The **Giardini Pubblici** *(Public Gardens)*, across Via Palestro from the Villa Reale, were laid out by Giuseppe Piermarini, architect of La Scala, in 1770. They were designed as public pleasure gardens, and today they still are popular with families who live in the city center. Generations of Milanese have taken pony rides and gone on the miniature train and merry-go-round. The park also contains a small planetarium and the **Museo Civico di Storia Naturale** (*Municipal Natural History Museum*). ⊠ *Corso Venezia 55* ☎ *02/88463337* ⊕ *www.assodidatticamuseale.it* 📠 *€5* ⊙ *Weekdays 9:30–1 and 2–4:30, weekends 9:30–1 and 2–5:30* Ⓜ *Palestro.*

SOUTH AND WEST OF THE DUOMO

If the part of the city to the north of the Duomo is dominated by its shops, the section to the south is famous for its works of art. The most famous is *Il Cenacolo*—known in English as *The Last Supper*. If you have time for nothing else, make sure you see this masterwork, which has now been definitively restored, after many, many years of work. Reservations will be needed to see this fresco, housed in the refectory of Santa Maria delle Grazie. Make these at least three weeks before you depart for Italy, so you can plan the rest of your time in Milan.

There are other gems as well. Via Torino, the ancient road for Turin, leads to a half-hidden treasure: Bramante's Renaissance masterpiece, the church of San Satiro. At the intersection of Via San Vittore and Via Carducci is the medieval Basilica di Sant'Ambrogio, named for Milan's patron saint. Another lovely church southeast of Sant'Ambrogio along Via de Amicis is San Lorenzo Maggiore. It's also known as San Lorenzo alle Colonne because of the 16 columns running across the facade.

TOP ATTRACTIONS

Basilica di Sant'Ambrogio *(Basilica of Saint Ambrose).* Noted for its medieval architecture, the church was consecrated by Milan's bishop, Saint Ambrose (one of the original Doctors of the Catholic Church), in AD 387. Saint Ambroeus, as he is known in Milanese dialect, is the city's patron saint, and his remains—dressed in elegant religious robes, a miter, and gloves—can be viewed inside a glass case in the crypt below the altar. Until the construction of the more imposing Duomo, this was Milan's most important church. Much restored and reworked over the centuries (the gold-and-gem-encrusted altar dates from the 9th century), Sant'Ambrogio still preserves its Romanesque characteristics (5th-century mosaics may be seen for €2). The church is often closed for weddings on Saturday. ✉ *Piazza Sant'Ambrogio 15, Corso Magenta* ☎ *02/86450895* ⊕ *www.santambrogio-basilica.it* ☉ *Mon.–Sat. 9:30–12:30 and 2:30–5:15; Sun. 3–5:15* Ⓜ *Sant'Ambrogio.*

9

QUICK BITES A bit overcrowded at night, when teenagers virtually block the sidewalk and traffic, the Bar Magenta (✉ *Via Carducci 13, at Corso Magenta, Sant'Ambrogio* ☎ *02/8053808* Ⓜ *Sant'Ambrogio or Cadorna*) can be a good stop en route during the day. Beyond coffee at all hours, lunch, and beer, the real attraction is its mix of old and new, trendy and aristocratic—a quintessentially Milanese ambience. It celebrated its 100th birthday in 2007 and is open weekdays 8 AM–2 AM and weekends 9 AM–2 AM. There's free Wi-Fi.

Pinacoteca Ambrosiana. Cardinal Federico Borromeo, one of Milan's native saints, founded this picture gallery in 1618 with the addition of his personal art collection to a bequest of books to Italy's first public library. More-recent renovations have reunited the core works of the collection, including such treasures as Caravaggio's *Basket of Fruit*; Raphael's monumental preparatory drawing (known as a "cartoon") for *The School of Athens*, which hangs in the Vatican; and the *Codice Atlantico*, the largest collection of designs by Leonardo da Vinci (on display through 2015). Heavy on Lombard artists, there are also paintings by Leonardo, Botticelli, Luini, Titian, and Jan Brueghel. Previous renovations done in the 1930s with their mosaics and stained-glass windows are worth a look, as are other odd items, including 18th-century scientific instruments and gloves worn by Napoléon at Waterloo. Access to the library, the Biblioteca Ambrosiana, is limited to researchers who apply for entrance tickets. ⊠ *Piazza Pio XI 2, near Duomo* 🕾 *02/806921* ⊕ *www.ambrosiana.it* 🖾 *€15* ⊙ *Tues.–Sun. 9–7* Ⓜ *Duomo.*

San Lorenzo Maggiore alle Colonne. Sixteen ancient Roman columns line the front of this sanctuary; 4th-century paleo-Christian mosaics survive in the Cappella di Sant'Aquilino (Chapel of Saint Aquilinus). ⊠ *Corso di Porta Ticinese 39* 🕾 *02/89404129* ⊕ *www.sanlorenzomaggiore. com* 🖾 *Mosaics €2* ⊙ *Weekdays 7:30–12:30 and 2:30–6:30; weekends 7:30–6:30.*

★ **San Satiro.** Just a few steps from the Duomo, this architectural gem was first built in 876 and later perfected by Bramante (1444–1514), demonstrating his command of proportion and perspective, keynotes of Renaissance architecture. Bramante tricks the eye with a famous optical illusion that makes a small interior seem extraordinarily spacious and airy, while accommodating a beloved 13th-century fresco. ⊠ *Via Speronari 3, near Duomo* 🕾 *02/874683* ⊙ *Weekdays 7:30–11:30 and 3:30–6:30, Sat. 3:30–7, Sun. 9:30–noon and 3:30–7* Ⓜ *Duomo.*

★ **Santa Maria delle Grazie.** Leonardo da Vinci's *The Last Supper,* housed in the church and former Dominican monastery of Santa Maria delle Grazie, has had an almost unbelievable history of bad luck and neglect—its near destruction in an American bombing raid in August 1943 was only the latest chapter in a series of misadventures, including, if one 19th-century source is to be believed, being whitewashed over by monks. Well-meant but disastrous attempts at restoration have done little to rectify the problem of the work's placement: it was executed on a wall unusually vulnerable to climatic dampness. Yet Leonardo chose to work slowly and patiently in oil pigments—which demand dry plaster—instead of proceeding hastily on wet plaster according to the conventional fresco technique. Novelist Aldous Huxley (1894–1963) called it "the saddest work of art in the world." After years of restorers' patiently shifting from one square centimeter to another, Leonardo's masterpiece is free of the shroud of scaffolding—and centuries of retouching, grime, and dust. Astonishing clarity and luminosity have been regained.

Despite Leonardo's carefully preserved preparatory sketches in which the apostles are clearly labeled by name, there still remains some small debate about a few identities in the final arrangement. But there can be no mistaking Judas, small and dark, his hand calmly reaching forward to the bread, isolated from the terrible confusion that has taken the hearts of the others. One critic, Frederick Hartt, offers an elegantly terse explanation for why the composition works: it combines "dramatic confusion" with "mathematical order." Certainly, the amazingly skillful and unobtrusive repetition of threes—in the windows, in the grouping of the figures, and in their placement—adds a mystical aspect to what at first seems simply the perfect observation of spontaneous human gesture.

Reservations are required to view the work. Viewings are in 15-minute, timed slots, and visitors must arrive 15 minutes before their assigned time in order not to lose their slot. Reservations can be made via phone (☎ *02/92800360*) or online (⊕ *www.cenacolovinciano.net*); it is worthwhile to make a call because tickets are set aside for phone reservations. Call at least three weeks if you want a Saturday slot, two weeks for a weekday slot. The telephone reservation office is open 9 AM to 6 PM weekdays and 9 AM to 2 PM on Saturday. Operators do speak English, though not fluently, and to reach one you must wait for the Italian introduction to finish and then press "2." However, you can sometimes get tickets from one day to the next. Some city bus tours include a visit in their regular circuit, which may be a good option. Guided tours in English are available for €3.50 and require a reservation.

The painting was executed in what was the order's refectory, which is now referred to as the **Cenacolo Vinciano.** Take a moment to visit Santa Maria delle Grazie itself. It's a handsome, completely restored church, with a fine dome, which Bramante added along with a cloister about the time that Leonardo was commissioned to paint *The Last Supper.* If you're wondering how two such giants came to be employed decorating and remodeling the refectory and church of a comparatively modest religious order, and not, say, the Duomo, the answer lies in the ambitious but largely unrealized plan to turn Santa Maria delle Grazie into a magnificent Sforza family mausoleum. Though Ludovico il Moro Sforza (1452–1508), seventh duke of Milan, was but one generation away from the founding of the Sforza dynasty, he was its last ruler. Two years after Leonardo finished *The Last Supper,* Ludovico was defeated by Louis XII and spent the remaining eight years of his life in a French dungeon. ⊠ *Piazza Santa Maria delle Grazie 2, off Corso Magenta, Sant'Ambrogio* ☎ *02/4987588 Last Supper; 02/4676111 church* ⊕ *www.cenacolovinciano.net* ☎ *Last Supper €6.50 plus €1.50 reservation fee; church free* ☉ *Last Supper: Tues.–Sun. 8:15–6:45; church: weekdays 10–noon and 3–5:30, Sun. 3:30–5:30* Ⓜ *Cadorna; Tram 16.*

9

WORTH NOTING

Museo Civico Archeologico *(Municipal Archaeological Museum).* Appropriately situated in the heart of Roman Milan, this museum's garden encloses the polygonal Ansperto tower, which was once part of the Roman walls. Housed in a former monastery, this museum has some everyday utensils, jewelry, an important silver plate from the last days of paganism, and several fine examples of mosaic pavement. Part of the early Middle Ages section is closed for restructuring. ⊠ *Corso Magenta 15, Sant'Ambrogio* ☎ *02/86450011* ☎ *€2* ☉ *Tues.–Sun. 9–1 and 2–5:30; last entry at 5* Ⓜ *Cadorna.*

ⓒ **Museo Nazionale della Scienza e Tecnica** *(National Museum of Science and Technology).* This converted cloister is best known for the collection of models based on Leonardo da Vinci's sketches (although these are not captioned in English, the labeling in many other exhibits is bilingual). On the ground level—in the hallway between the courtyards—is a room

Milan's Navigli district has some of the city's most vibrant street life.

featuring interactive, moving models of the famous *vita aerea* (aerial screw) and *ala battente* (beating wing), thought to be forerunners of the modern helicopter and airplane, respectively. The museum also houses a varied collection of industrial artifacts including trains, a celebrated Italian-built submarine, and several reconstructed workshops including a watchmaker's, a lute maker's, and an antique pharmacy. Displays also illustrate papermaking and metal founding, which were fundamental to Milan's—and the world's—economic growth. There's a bookshop and a bar. The 16th-century church in the same piazza is **San Vittore al Corpo** (🕑 *Sat.–Tues. and Thurs. 3–5:45*), which has one of the most beautiful interiors in Milan. ✉ *Via San Vittore 21, Sant'Ambrogio* ☎ *02/485551* ⊕ *www.museoscienza.org* 🎟 *€8* 🕑 *Wed.–Fri. 9:30–5, weekends 9:30–6:30* Ⓜ *Sant'Ambrogio; Bus 50, 58, or 94.*

Navigli District. In medieval times, a network of *navigli*, or canals, crisscrossed the city. Almost all have been covered over, but two—Naviglio Grande and Naviglio Pavese—are still navigable. Once a down-at-the-heels neighborhood, the Navigli district has undergone some gentrification over the last 20 years. Humble workshops have been replaced by boutiques, art galleries, cafés, bars, and restaurants. The Navigli at night is about as close as you will get to more-southern-style Italian street life in Milan. On weekend nights, it is difficult to walk (and impossible to park, although an underground parking area has been under construction for years) among the youthful crowds thronging the narrow streets along the canals. Check out the antiques fair on the last Sunday of the month. ✉ *South of Corso Porta Ticinese, Porta Genova* Ⓜ *Porta Genova; Tram 2, 3, 9, 14, 15, 29, or 30.*

WHERE TO EAT

CINQUE GIORNATE

$$$
ITALIAN

✕**Da Giacomo**. The fashion and publishing crowd, as well as international bankers and businessmen, favor this Tuscan/Ligurian restaurant. The emphasis is on fish; even the warm slice of pizza served while you study the menu has seafood in it. The specialty, *gnocchi Da Giacomo*, has a savory seafood-and-tomato sauce. Service is friendly and efficient; the wine list broad; and the dessert cart, with tarte tatin and Sicilian *cassata* (a concoction of sponge cake, ricotta, and candied fruit), rich and varied. With its tile floor and bank of fresh seafood, it has a refined neighborhood-bistro style. ⊠ *Via P. Sottocorno 6, entrance in Via Cellini, Cinque Giornate* ☎ *02/76023313* ⊕ *www.giacomomilano. com* ⌘ *Reservations essential* ▤ *AE, DC, MC, V* ☉ *Closed Christmas wk and last 2 wks of Aug.* Ⓜ *Tram 9, 12, 27, 29, or 30; Bus 54 or 60.*

DUOMO

$$$$
MODERN ITALIAN
★

✕**Cracco**. To international epicures, Carlo Cracco is on a similar plane as innovators Heston Blumenthal and Ferran Adrià. The tasting menus are a good way to savor many of the delicate inventions of Cracco's creative talent, though an à la carte menu is available. Delightful appetizers and desserts vary seasonally, but may include the scampi cream with freshwater shrimp, the disk of "caramelized Russian salad," and the mango cream with mint gelatin. Specialties include Milanese classics revisited—Cracco's take on saffron risotto and cotoletta (breaded veal cutlet) should not be missed. The elegant dining room favors cool earth tones and clean lines. ⊠ *Via Victor Hugo 4, Duomo* ☎ *02/876774* ⊕ *www.ristorantecracco.it* ⌘ *Reservations essential* ▤ *AE, MC, V* ☉ *Closed 3 wks in Aug. and last wk in Dec.; Sept.–June, closed Sun., no lunch Sat. and Mon.* Ⓜ *Duomo.*

$$$
MODERN ITALIAN
★

✕**Don Carlos**. One of the few restaurants open after La Scala lets out, Don Carlos, in the Grand Hotel et de Milan, is nothing like its indecisive operatic namesake (whose betrothed was stolen by his father). Flavors are bold, presentation is precise and full of flair, and service is attentive. The walls are blanketed with sketches of the theater, and the low-key opera recordings are every bit as well chosen as the wine list, setting the perfect stage for discreet business negotiation or, better yet, refined romance. A gourmet menu costs €85 for six courses (two-person minimum), excluding wine. ⊠ *Grand Hotel et de Milan, Via Manzoni 29, Duomo* ☎ *02/7234640* ⊕ *www.ristorantedoncarlos.it* ⌘ *Reservations essential* ▤ *AE, MC, V* ☉ *No lunch* Ⓜ *Montenapoleone; Tram 1 or 2.*

$–$$
ECLECTIC

✕**Rinascente Food & Restaurants**. The seventh floor of this famous Italian department store is a gourmet food market surrounded by several small restaurants that can be a good option for lunch, aperitivo, or dinner if you've been shopping or touring the Duomo. There are several places to eat, including the popular mozzarella bar Obika, My Sushi, De Santis for "slow food" sandwiches, and the sophisticated Maio restaurant. A terrace overlooking the Duomo is shared by three locations. It's best to get here early—it's popular, and there are often lines at mealtimes. ⊠ *Piazza Duomo* ☎ *02/8852471* ⊕ *www.rinascente. it* ▤ *AE, MC, V* Ⓜ *Duomo.*

9

GARIBALDI

$–$$ ✕ **Osteria Vecchi Sapori.** Simple but savory fare and a menu that varies
NORTHERN weekly characterize one osteria with two locations run by two broth-
ITALIAN ers, Paolo and Roberto. Specialties include their truffle tagliolini, and
primi of stuffed pasta like Gorgonzola-filled fiocchetti, or pear and
parmigiano-filled ravioli with a saffron butter sauce. Their extensive,
meat-rich second-course dishes are paired with creamy polenta *taragna*
(made with cornmeal and buckwheat flour) or their hand-cut fried potatoes. The dessert menu changes daily with in-house cakes, tiramisu, and
crostate (fruit tarts) reflecting traditional tastes and seasonal availability. ✉ *Via Carmagnola 3, Garbaldi* ☎ *02/6686148* ⊕ *www.vecchisapori.*
it ⌂ *Reservations essential* ▭ *AE, DC, MC, V* ⊘ *Closed Sun. No lunch*
Ⓜ *Garibaldi or Zara; Tram 3, 4, 7, or 31; Bus 82, 86, 90, or 91.*

$–$$ ✕ **Pizzeria La Fabbrica.** This lively pizzeria has two wood-burning ovens
PIZZA going full-steam every day of the week. Skip the appetizers and go
straight to the pizza. Pizzas vary from traditional (*quattro stagioni*) to
vegetable-based (with leeks and Gorgonzola) to in-house specialties
like the *tartufona* (with truffles). The menu also offers pasta like *pici*
with Tuscan sausage and main *secondi* dishes. Save room for a worthy
dessert like the *torta caprese al cioccolato* or tiramisu—though after
pizza, you might want to share. The Fabbrica is spacious enough to
handle groups; seek out a seat in the spacious garden area when the
weather's fine. ✉ *Viale Pasubio 2, Garbaldi* ☎ *02/6552771* ⊕ *www.*
lafabbricapizzeria.it ▭ *MC, V* ⊘ *No lunch Sun.* Ⓜ *Garibaldi.*

LORETO

$–$$ ✕ **Da Abele.** If you love risotto, then make a beeline for this neighbor-
MILANESE hood trattoria. The superb risotto dishes change with the season, and
★ there may be just two or three on the menu at any time. It is tempting
to try them all. The setting is relaxed, the service informal, the prices
strikingly reasonable. Outside the touristy center of town but quite convenient by subway, this trattoria is invariably packed with locals. ✉ *Via*
Temperanza 5, Loreto ☎ *02/2613855* ▭ *AE, DC, MC, V* ⊘ *Closed*
Mon., Aug., and Dec. 22–Jan. 7. No lunch Ⓜ *Pasteur.*

PORTA VENEZIA

$$$$ ✕ **Joia.** At this haute-cuisine vegetarian restaurant near Piazza della
VEGETARIAN Repubblica, delicious dishes are artistically prepared by chef Pietro
Leemann. Vegetarians, who often get short shrift in Italy, will marvel
at the variety of culinary traditions—Asian and European—and artistry
offered here. The ever-changing menu offers dishes in unusual formats:
tiny glasses of creamed cabbage with ginger, spheres of crunchy vegetables that roll across the plate. Fish also makes an appearance. Joia's
restful dining room has been refurbished, another room added, and its
kitchen enlarged. The fixed-price lunch "box" is a good value (€17 and
€35), but be sure to reserve ahead. Multicourse menus in the evening
range from €50 to €100, excluding wine. ✉ *Via Panfilo Castaldi 18,*
Porta Venezia ☎ *02/29522124* ⊕ *www.joia.it* ⌂ *Reservations essential*
▭ *AE, DC, MC, V* ⊘ *Closed Sun., 3 wks in Aug., and Dec. 24–Jan. 7.*
No lunch Sat. Ⓜ *Repubblica; Tram 1, 5, 11, 29, or 30.*

¢ ✕ **Pizza OK.** Pizza is almost the only item on the menu at this family-run
PIZZA pizzeria with three locations, the oldest near Corso Buenos Aires in the
Porta Venezia area. The pizza is extra thin and large, and possibili-
ties for toppings seem endless. A good choice for families, this dining
experience will be easy on your pocketbook. Other locations are on Via
San Siro 9 in Corso Vercelli, and Piazza Sempione 8. ⊠ *Via Lambro
15, Porta Venezia* ☎ *02/29401272* ▭ *MC, V* ⊗ *Closed Aug. 7–20 and
Dec. 24–Jan. 7* Ⓜ *Porta Venezia.*

PROCACCINI

$$ ✕ **Trattoria Montina.** Twin brothers Maurizio and Roberto Montina
MILANESE have turned this restaurant into a local favorite. Don't be fooled by
Fodor'sChoice the "trattoria" name. The sage-green paneling makes it airy and cozy
★ on a gray Milan day. Chef Roberto creates exquisite modern Italian
dishes such as warmed risotto with merlot and taleggio cheese, while
Maurizio chats with guests, regulars, and local families. Milan's famous
cotoletta (breaded veal cutlet) is light and tasty. Try fish or the *frittura
impazzita,* a wild-and-crazy mix of delicately fried seafood. There's a
fine selection of sweets on the dessert cart. ⊠ *Via Procaccini 54, Procac-
cini* ☎ *02/3490498* ▭ *AE, DC, MC, V* ⊗ *Closed Sun., Aug., and Dec.
25–Jan. 7. No lunch Mon.* Ⓜ *Tram/Bus 1, 7, 29, 43, or 57.*

QUADRILATERO

$$ ✕ **Paper Moon.** Hidden behind Via Montenapoleone and thus handy
ITALIAN to the restaurant-scarce Quadrilatero, Paper Moon is a cross between
a neighborhood restaurant and a celebrity hangout. Clients include
families from this well-heeled area, professionals, football players, and
television stars. What the menu lacks in originality it makes up for in
reliable consistency—pizza and cotoletta, to name just two. Like any
Italian restaurant, it's not child-friendly in an American sense—no high
chairs or children's menu—but children will find food they like. It's open
until 12:30 AM. ⊠ *Via Bagutta 1, Quadrilatero* ☎ *02/76022297* ▭ *AE,
MC, V* ⊗ *Closed Sun. and 2 wks in Aug.* Ⓜ *San Babila.*

SANT'AMBROGIO

$ ✕ **Taverna Moriggi.** This dusky, wood-panel wine bar near the stock
WINE BAR exchange, built in 1910, is the perfect spot to enjoy a glass of wine
with cheese and cold cuts. Pasta dishes and more-robust secondi like
cotoletta alla Milanese are available at both lunch and dinner; if you're
coming for a meal, a reservation is a good idea. ⊠ *Via Morigi 8, Duomo*
☎ *02/80582007* ⊕ *www.tavernamoriggi.it* ▭ *AE, MC, V* ⊗ *Closed
Sun., Dec. 25–Jan. 7, and Aug. No lunch Sat.* Ⓜ *Cairoli.*

BEYOND CITY CENTER

$$$$ ✕ **Antica Osteria del Ponte.** Rich, imaginative seasonal cuisine composed
ITALIAN according to the inspired whims of chef Ezio Santin is reason enough
Fodor'sChoice to make your way 20 km (12 mi) southwest of Milan to one of Italy's
★ finest restaurants. The setting is a traditional country inn, where a wood
fire warms the rustic interior in winter. The menu changes regularly; in
fall, wild porcini mushrooms are among the favored ingredients. Various fixed menus (€55 at lunch and €85 at dinner) offer broad samplings
of antipasti, primi, and meat or fish; some include appropriate wine

9

selections, too. ✉ *Piazza G. Negri 9, Beyond City Center, Cassinetta di Lugagnano* ✛ *3 km (2 mi) north of Abbiategrasso* ☎ *02/9420034* ⊕ *www.anticaosteriadelponte.it* ⌂ *Reservations essential* ▭ *AE, MC, V* ⊙ *Closed Sun. and Mon., Dec. 24–Jan. 10, and Aug.*

WHERE TO STAY

DUOMO

$$–$$$ ⊞ **Ariston.** This hotel claims it is designed around "bio-architectural" principles. Rooms are decorated in simple, minimalist style, and breakfast offers a selection of organic, unprocessed foods. The location is close to the lively Porta Ticinese shops and restaurants and the young people's fashion mecca, Via Torino. Although a longish walk from the nearest subway stop, the Duomo, it is well served by tram. **Pros:** good location; parking available. **Cons:** plain rooms. ✉ *Largo Carrobbio 2, Duomo* ☎ *02/72000556* ⊕ *www.aristonhotel.com* ⇱ *52 rooms* ⌂ *In-room: Wi-Fi. In-hotel: room service, bar, bicycles, laundry service, Internet terminal, Wi-Fi hotspot, parking (paid), some pets allowed* ▭ *AE, DC, MC, V* ⎟⊙⎟ *BP* Ⓜ *Duomo; Tram 2 or 14.*

$$–$$$ ⊞ **Hotel Gran Duca di York.** This small hotel has spare but classically elegant and efficient rooms—four with private terraces. Built around a courtyard, the 1890s building was originally a seminary and still belongs to a religious institution. With an ideal location a few steps west of the Duomo, it offers exceptional value for Milan and is managed by the same family that owns the Spadari. **Pros:** central; airy; well priced. **Cons:** rooms are simple. ✉ *Via Moneta 1/a, Duomo* ☎ *02/874863* ⊕ *www.ducadiyork.com* ⇱ *33 rooms* ⌂ *In-room: a/c, safe (some), Wi-Fi. In-hotel: room service, bar, laundry service, Internet terminal, Wi-Fi hotspot, parking (paid)* ▭ *AE, MC, V* ⊙ *Closed Aug.* ⎟⊙⎟ *EP* Ⓜ *Cordusio.*

$$$–$$$$ ⊞ **Hotel Spadari al Duomo.** That this hotel is owned by an architect's family shows in the details, including architect-designed furniture and a fine collection of contemporary art. The owner's idea of creating a hotel/gallery extends to the guest rooms, where paintings by young Milanese artists are on rotating display. For all the artistic accents, this is still a comfortable, homey hotel, with an inviting frescoed breakfast room and many rooms with private terraces. Personal touches, such as a collection of short stories on the turned-down beds, abound. **Pros:** good breakfast; good location; attentive staff. **Cons:** some rooms on the small side. ✉ *Via Spadari 11, Duomo* ☎ *02/72002371* ⊕ *www. spadarihotel.com* ⇱ *40 rooms, 3 suites* ⌂ *In-room: a/c, safe, Internet. In-hotel: bar, Internet terminal, Wi-Fi hotspot (free), parking (paid), laundry service, room service (limited), some pets allowed* ▭ *AE, DC, MC, V* ⎟⊙⎟ *BP* Ⓜ *Duomo.*

$$$$
Fodor's Choice
★

⊞ **Park Hyatt Milan.** Extensive use of warm travertine stone creates a sophisticated, yet inviting and tranquil backdrop for the Park Hyatt. Modern art embellishing the suites and the 30-foot-high glass-domed "Cupola." Rooms are spacious and opulent, with walk-in closets and bathrooms featuring double sinks, octagonal glass-enclosed rain showers, and separate soaking tubs; rooftop suites have terraces with city

A room in the Park Hyatt Milan.

views. The hotel seems determined to spoil its demanding clientele with a seemingly endless number of amenities. **Pros:** central; contemporary; refined. **Cons:** not particularly intimate. ✉ *Via Tommaso Grossi 1, Duomo* ☎ *02/88211234* ⊕ *milan.park.hyatt.com* ➧ *83 rooms, 29 suites* ⚲ *In-room: Wi-Fi, Internet, safe. In-hotel: restaurant, room service, bar, gym, spa, laundry service, bicycles, parking (paid), some pets allowed* ▭ *AE, DC, MC, V* †⊙| *EP* Ⓜ *Montenapoleone.*

$$$ 🏨 **UNA Maison Milano.** An understated entrance leads the visitor into what seems more like a sophisticated, upscale residence than a hotel—which is precisely the feeling the designers of Maison were striving for. This faithfully restored palazzo dates from the early 1900s; inside, spaciousness is accentuated with soft white interior, muted fabrics and marbles, and clean, contemporary lines. Massive mirrors don't hang, they lean; baths are almost as spacious as the living area. Two sets of windows separate you from any eventual street noise, and your personal butler will make sure your every need is met. **Pros:** the warmth of a residence and luxury of a design hotel. **Cons:** breakfast not included. ✉ *Via Mazzini 4, Duomo* ☎ *02/85605* ⊕ *www.unamaisonmilano. it* ➧ *13 rooms, 6 junior suites, 5 suites, penthouse* ⚲ *In-room: safe, Internet. In-hotel: restaurant, bar, Internet terminal, Wi-Fi hotspot, laundry service, some pets allowed* ▭ *AE, DC, MC, V* †⊙| *EP* Ⓜ *Duomo.*

PIAZZA REPUBBLICA

$–$$ 🏨 **Hotel Casa Mia Milan.** Easy to reach from the central train station (a few blocks away) and easy on the budget, this tiny hotel, up a flight of stairs, is family-run. Rooms are simple and clean with individual (small) baths, renovated in 2009. Although not in the center of things, it's two

CLOSE UP

'Appy Hour

The *aperitivo*, or prelunch or predinner drink, is part of life everywhere in Italy, and each town has its own rites and favorite drinks, but the Milanese aperitivo culture is particularly noteworthy—it's a must-try. Milan bar owners have enriched the usual nibbles of olives, nuts, and chips with full finger (and often fork) buffets serving cubes of pizza and cheese, fried vegetables, rice salad, sushi, and even pasta, and they baptized it 'Appy Hour—with the first "h" dropped and the second one pronounced. For the price of a drink (around €8), you can make a meal of hors d'oeuvres (though don't be a glutton; remember Italians value the quality of the food, not the quantity).

There are 'Appy Hours and *aperitivi* for all tastes and in all neighborhoods; you'll find the most options in Corso Sempione, Corso Como, and the Navigli areas. Changes happen fast, but these are reliable: Arthé (⊠ *Via Pisacane 57* ☎ *02/29528353*) is a chic *enoteca* (wine bar) with fresh and fried vegetables and pasta. The Capo Verde (⊠ *Via Leoncavallo 16*

☎ *02/26820430* ⊕ *www.capoverde. com*) is in a greenhouse/nursery and is especially popular for after-dinner drinks. G Lounge (⊠ *Via Larga 8* ☎ *02/8053042* ⊕ *www. glounge.it*) has rotating DJs and quality music. The elegant Hotel Sheraton Diana Majestic (⊠ *Viale Piave 42* ☎ *02/20581* ⊕ *www. sheratondianamajestic.com*) attracts a young professional crowd in good weather to its beautiful garden, which gets yearly thematic transformations. In the Brera neighborhood, the highly rated enoteca 'N Ombra de Vin (⊠ *Via S. Marco 2* ☎ *02/6599650* ⊕ *www.nombradevin.it*) serves wine by the glass and, in addition to the plates of sausage and cheese nibbles, has light food and not-so-light desserts. Check out the impressive vaulted basement where the bottled wine and spirits are sold. Peck (⊠ *Via Cesare Cantù 3* ☎ *02/8023161* ⊕ *www.peck.it*), the Milan gastronomical shrine near the Duomo, also has a bar that serves up traditional—and excellent—pizza pieces, olives, and toasted nuts in a refined setting.

---

short blocks from transport center Piazza Repubblica (tram and metro lines), which also hosts the doyenne of Milan's palace hotels, the Principe di Savoia. **Pros:** clean; good value; free Wi-Fi for guests. **Cons:** not the nicest neighborhood in Milan. ⊠ *Viale Vittorio Veneto 30, Piazza Repubblica* ☎ *02/6575249* ⊕ *www.hotelcasamiamilano.it* ⤴ *15 rooms* △ *In-hotel: room service, bar, laundry service, Internet terminal, Wi-Fi hotspot, parking (paid)* ☰ *AE, MC, V* ⦿| *BP* Ⓜ *Repubblica.*

$$$$ **Principe di Savoia.** Milan's grande dame has all the trappings of an ★ exquisite traditional hotel: lavish mirrors, drapes, and carpets, and Milan's largest guest rooms, outfitted with eclectic fin de siècle furnishings. Forty-eight Deluxe Mosaic rooms (named for the glass mosaic panels in their ample bathrooms) are even larger, and the three-bedroom Presidential Suite features its own marble pool. The Principe bar is an elegant aperitivo spot, and the Acanto restaurant ($$$) has garden seating and is open from breakfast to dinner. Lighter food is served in Il Salotto reception area. **Pros:** substantial spa/health club (considered chic by Milanese) in town; close to Central Station. **Cons:** overblown luxury in a not-very-central or attractive neighborhood. ✉ *Piazza della Repubblica 17, Piazza Repubblica* ☎ *02/62301* ⊕ *www. hotelprincipedisavoia.com* ⇨ *269 rooms, 132 suites* ☋ *In-room: safe, DVD, Wi-Fi. In-hotel: restaurant, room service, bar, pool, gym, spa, laundry service, Internet terminal, parking (paid), some pets allowed* ☰ *AE, DC, MC, V* ⑂ *EP* Ⓜ *Repubblica.*

QUADRILATERO

$$$$ ⛶ **Four Seasons.** The Four Seasons has been cited more than once by the Italian press as the country's best city hotel—perhaps because once you're inside, the feeling is anything but urban. Built in the 15th century as a convent, the hotel surrounds a colonnaded cloister, and some rooms have balconies looking onto a glassed-in courtyard. Parts of the original frescoes can still be seen in the lobby and lounge. Everything about the place is Four Seasons (high) style. The Theater restaurant has some of Milan's best hotel dining provided by chef Sergio Mei. There is a Sunday brunch that is well worth the €80 charge. Ask about the "Chocolate Room" when it is time for dessert. **Pros:** beautiful setting that feels like Tuscany rather than central Milan. **Cons:** expensive. ✉ *Via Gesù 6–8, Quadrilatero* ☎ *02/7708167* ⊕ *www.fourseasons.com* ⇨ *77 rooms, 41 suites* ☋ *In-room: safe, DVD, Internet, Wi-Fi. In-hotel: 2 restaurants, room service, bar, Wi-Fi hotspot, Internet terminal, laundry service, parking (paid)* ☰ *AE, DC, MC, V* ⑂ *EP* Ⓜ *Montenapoleone.*

SANT'AMBROGIO

$$$ ⛶ **Antica Locanda Leonardo.** Only a block from the church that houses *The Last Supper* and in one of Milan's most desired and historic neighborhoods with elegant shops and bars, this hotel has been family-run for more than 100 years. Half the rooms face a courtyard and the others a back garden. Many have balconies, and one ground-floor room has a private garden with table and chairs. The hotel has a relaxed feel, and the owners who live in the building are helpful. They have a special relationship with a car service that offers moderate-price airport pickups and tours to nearby factory outlets. **Pros:** very quiet and homey; breakfast is ample. **Cons:** more like a bed-and-breakfast than a hotel. ✉ *Corso Magenta 78, Sant'Ambrogio* ☎ *02/463317* ⊕ *www. anticalocandaleonardo.com* ⇨ *20 rooms* ☋ *In-room: safe, Wi-Fi. In-hotel: bar, Wi-Fi hotspot, laundry service, room service, parking (paid)* ☰ *AE, DC, MC, V* ☻ *Closed Dec. 31–Jan. 7 and 3 wks in Aug.* ⑂ *BP* Ⓜ *Sant'Ambrogio.*

"LET'S GO TO THE COLUMNS"

Andiamo al Le Colonne in Milanese youthspeak means to meet up at the sober Roman columns in front of the Basilica San Lorenzo Maggiore. Attracted by the bars and shops along Corso di Porta Ticinese, the young spill out on the street to chat and drink. Neighbors may complain about the noise and confusion, but students and nighthawks find it indispensable for socializing at all hours. It's a street—no closing time.

9

SCALA

$$$$ ⬛ **Grand Hotel et de Milan.** Only blocks from La Scala, this hotel, which opened in 1863, is sometimes called the Hotel Verdi because the composer lived here for 27 years. His apartment, complete with his desk, is now the Presidential Suite. It's everything you hope for in a traditional European hotel; dignified but not stuffy, elegant but not ostentatious. Moss-green and persimmon velvet enliven the 19th-century look without sacrificing dignity and luxury. The Don Carlos restaurant is one of Milan's best. **Pros:** traditional and elegant; great location. **Cons:** gilt decor may not suit those who like more modern design. ⊠ *Via Manzoni 29, Scala* ☎ *02/723141* ⊕ *www.grandhoteletdemilan.it* ↘ *72 rooms, 23 suites* ᗒ *In-room: Wi-Fi, safe. In-hotel: restaurant, room service, bar, gym, laundry service, Internet terminal, parking (paid), some pets allowed* ⊟ *AE, DC, MC, V* ⫟⃝*EP* Ⓜ *Montenapoleone.*

VIA SANTA SOFIA

$–$$ ⬛ **Hotel Canada.** In pricey Milan, the Hotel Canada is a relative bargain. It has recently renovated wood flooring, thorough sound-proofing, and contemporary furnishings that maximize space and bring in light. Flat-panel TVs with screens up to 32 inches bring in six Sky channels; Wi-Fi is available in every room, including the corner suite with outside terrace. **Pros:** services and decor make it a good value. **Cons:** although trams and buses are handy, it's a short walk to the nearest metro stop. ⊠ *Via San Sofia 16, Via San Sofia* ☎ *02/58304844* ⊕ *www. canadahotel. it* ↘ *37 rooms* ᗒ *In-room: safe, Wi-Fi. In-hotel: room service, bar, Internet terminal, Wi-Fi hotspot, laundry service, parking (paid), some pets allowed* ⊟ *AE, DC, MC, V* ⫟⃝*BP* Ⓜ *Repubblica.*

NIGHTLIFE AND THE ARTS

THE ARTS

For events likely to be of interest to non–Italian speakers, see *Hello Milano* (⊕ *www.hellomilano.it*), a monthly magazine available at the tourist office in Piazza Duomo, or *The American* (⊕ *www. theamericanmag.com*), which is available at international bookstores and newsstands, and which has a thorough cultural calendar. The tourist office publishes the monthly *Milano Mese*, which also includes some listings in English.

MUSIC

The modern **Auditorium di Milano** (⊠ *Largo Gustav Mahler [Corso San Gottardo, 39 at Via Torricelli], Conchetta, Navigli* ☎ *02/83389401 [also 402 and 403]* ⊕ *www.laverdi.org*), known for its excellent acoustics, is home to the **Orchestra Verdi,** founded by Milan-born conductor Richard Chailly. The season, which runs from September to June, includes many top international performers and rotating guest conductors.

The two halls belonging to the **Conservatorio** (⊠ *Via del Conservatorio 12, Duomo* ☎ *02/762110* ⊕ *www.consmilano.it* Ⓜ *San Babila*) host some of the leading names in classical music. Series are organized by several organizations, including the venerable chamber music society, the **Società del Quartetto** (☎ *02/76005500* ⊕ *www.quartettomilano.it*).

The **Teatro Dal Verme** ($\boxtimes$ *Via San Giovanni sul Muro 2, Castello* $\textcircled{\scriptsize{\cdots}}$ *02/87905* $\oplus$ *www.dalverme.org* $\boxed{M}$ *Cairoli*) stages frequent classical music concerts from October to May.

OPERA

Milan's hallowed **Teatro alla Scala** ($\boxtimes$ *Piazza della Scala* $\textcircled{\scriptsize{\cdots}}$ *02/72003744* $\oplus$ *www.teatroallascala.org* $\odot$ *Daily 9–noon* $\boxed{M}$ *Duomo*) underwent a complete renovation from 2002 to 2004, with everything refreshed, refurbished, or replaced except the building's exterior walls. Special attention was paid to the acoustics, which have always been excellent. The season runs from December 7, the feast day of Milan patron Saint Ambrose, through June. Plan well in advance, as tickets sell out quickly. For tickets, visit the **Biglietteria Centrale** ($\boxtimes$ *Galleria del Sagrato, Piazza Del Duomo* $\odot$ *Daily noon–6* $\boxed{M}$ *Duomo*), which is in the Duomo subway station. To pick up tickets for performances from two hours prior until 15 minutes after the start of a performance, go to the box office at the theater, which is around the corner in Via Filodrammatici 2. Although you might not get seats for the more popular operas with big stars, it is worth trying; ballets are easier. The theater is closed from the end of July through August and on national and local holidays.

NIGHTLIFE
BARS

Milan has a bar somewhere to suit any style; those in the better hotels are respectably chic and popular meeting places for Milanese as well as tourists. **Blue Note** ($\boxtimes$ *Via Borsieri 37, Garibaldi* $\textcircled{\scriptsize{\cdots}}$ *02/69016888* $\oplus$ *www.bluenotemilano.com*), the first European branch of the famous New York nightclub, features regular performances by some of the most famous names in jazz, as well as blues and rock concerts. Dinner is available, and there's a popular jazz brunch on Sunday. It's closed Monday. **Brellin Café** ($\boxtimes$ *Vicolo Lavandai at Alzaia Naviglio Grande* $\textcircled{\scriptsize{\cdots}}$ *02/58101351* $\oplus$ *www.brellin.com*) in the arty Navigli district has live music and serves late-night snacks. **Café Trussardi** ($\boxtimes$ *Piazza della Scala 5, Duomo* $\textcircled{\scriptsize{\cdots}}$ *02/80688295* $\oplus$ *www.trussardi.it*) has an enormous plasma screen that keeps hip barflies entertained with video art. Open throughout the day, it's a great place for coffee. In Brera, check out the **Giamaica** ($\boxtimes$ *Via Brera 32* $\textcircled{\scriptsize{\cdots}}$ *02/876723* $\oplus$ *www.jamaicabar.it*), a traditional hangout for students from the nearby Brera art school. On summer nights this neighborhood pulses with life; street vendors and fortune-tellers jostle for space alongside the outdoor tables. For an evening of live music—predominantly rock to jazz—head to perennial favorite **Le Scimmie** ($\boxtimes$ *Via Ascanio Sforza 49, Navigli* $\textcircled{\scriptsize{\cdots}}$ *02/89402874* $\oplus$ *www.scimmie.it*). It features international stars, some of whom jet in to play here, while others, including Ronnie Jones, are longtime residents in Milan. Dinner is an option. The bar of the **Sheraton Diana Majestic** ($\boxtimes$ *Viale Piave 42* $\textcircled{\scriptsize{\cdots}}$ *02/20581*), which has a splendid garden, is a prime meeting place for young professionals and the fashion people from the showrooms of the Porta Venezia neighborhood. For a break from the traditional, check out ultratrendy **SHU** ($\boxtimes$ *Via Molino delle Armi, Ticinese* $\textcircled{\scriptsize{\cdots}}$ *02/58315720*), whose gleaming interior looks like a cross between *Star Trek* and Cocteau's *Beauty and the Beast*.

9

Continued on page 324

THE FASHIONISTA'S MILAN

Opera buffs and lovers of Leonardo's *Last Supper,* skip ahead to the next section. No one else should be dismayed to learn that clothing is Milan's greatest cultural achievement. The city is one of the fashion capitals of the world and home base for practically every top Italian designer. The same way art aficionados walk the streets of Florence in a state of bliss, the style-conscious come here to be enraptured.

It all happens in the *quadrilatero della moda,* Milan's toniest shopping district, located just north of the Duomo. Along the cobblestone streets, Armani, Prada, and their fellow *stilisti* sell the latest designs from flagship stores that are as much museums of chic as retail establishments. Any purchase here qualifies as a splurge, but you can have fun without spending a euro—just browse, window-shop, and people-watch. Not into fashion? Think of the experience as art, design, and theater all rolled into one. If you wouldn't visit Florence without seeing the Uffizi, you shouldn't visit Milan without seeing the quadrilatero.

FLORENCE HAS THE *DAVID.*

ROME HAS THE PANTHEON.

MILAN HAS THE CLOTHES.

On these pages we give a selective, street-by-street list of stores in the area. Hours are from around 10 in the morning until 7 at night, Monday through Saturday.

VIA DELLA SPIGA (east to west)

Dolce & Gabbana (No. 2)
☎ 02/795747
www.dolcegabbana.it
women's accessories

Gio Moretti (No. 4)
☎ 02/76003186
women's and men's clothes: many labels, as well as books, CDs, flowers, and an art gallery

Bulgari Italia (No. 6)
☎ 02/777001
www.bulgari.com
jewelry, fragrances, accessories

Boutique Ferré (No. 6)
☎ 02/783050
www.gianfrancoferre. com
women's, men's, and children's sportswear

Malo (No. 7)
☎ 02/76016109
www.malo.it
everything cashmere

cross Via Sant'Andrea

Fay (No. 15)
☎ 02/76017597
www.fay.it
women's and men's clothes, accessories: a flagship store, designed by Philip Johnson

Prada (No. 18)
☎ 02/76394336
www.prada.com
accessories

Giorgio Armani (No. 19)
☎ 02/783511
www.giorgioarmani.com
accessories

Tod's (No. 22)
☎ 02/76002423
www.tods.com
shoes and handbags: the Tod's flagship store

Dolce & Gabbana (No. 26)
☎ 02 76001155
www.dolcegabbana.it
women's clothes, in a baroque setting

Moschino (No. 30)
☎ 02/76004320
www.moschino.it
women's, men's, and children's clothes: Chic and Cheap, so they say

✔ **Just Cavalli** (No. 30)
☎ 02/76390893
www.robertocavalli.net
women's and men's clothes, plus a café serving big salads and carpaccio. It's the offspring of the Just Cavalli Café in Parco Sempione, one of the hottest places in town for drinks (with or without dinner).

Roberto Cavalli (No. 42)
☎ 02/76020900
www.robertocavalli.net
women's and men's clothes, accessories: 3,200 square feet of Roberto Cavalli

I Pinco Pallino (No. 42) ☎ 02/781931
www.ipincopallino.it
extravagant children's clothing

Marni (No. 50)
☎ 02/76317327
www.marni.com
women's clothes

**VIA
MONTENAPO-
LEONE**
(east to west)

Fratelli Rossetti
(No. 1)
☎ 02/76021650
www.rossetti.it
shoes

Giorgio Armani
(No. 2)
☎ 02/76390068
www.
giorgioarmani.com
women's and
men's clothes

**Salvatore
Ferragamo Donna**
(No. 3)
☎ 02/76000054
www.ferragamo.com
women's clothes,
shoes, accessories

Bottega Veneta
(No. 5)
☎ 02/76024495
www.bottegaveneta.
com
leather goods:
signature woven-
leather bags

Etro (No. 5)
☎ 02/76005049
www.etro.it
women's and men's
clothes, leather goods,
accessories

Gucci (No. 5/7)
☎ 02/771271
www.gucci.com
women's and men's
clothes

Prada (No. 6)
☎ 02/76020273
www.prada.com
men's clothes

Prada (No. 8)
☎ 02/7771771
www.prada.com
women's clothes and
accessories

Agnona (No. 21)
☎ 02/76316530
www.agnona.com
women's clothes:
Ermenegildo excellence
for women

Ermenegildo Zegna
(No. 27A)
☎ 02/76006437
www.zegna.com.
men's clothes, in the

Versace in
Via Montenapoleone

finest fabrics

cross Via Sant'Andrea

Armani Junior (in
galleria) (No. 10)
☎ 02/783196
www.giorgioarmani.com

children's clothes: for
the under-14 fashionista

Versace (No. 11)
☎ 02/76008528
www.versace.com
everything Versace,
except Versus and
children's clothes

Corneliani (No. 12)
☎ 02/777361
www.corneliani.com
men's clothes: bespoke
tailoring excellence

REFUELING

If you want refreshments and aren't charmed by the quadrilatero's in-store cafés, try traditional **Cova** (Via Montenapoleone 8, ☎ 02/76000578) or more mod **Sant'Ambroeus** (Corso Matteotti 7, ☎ 02/76000540). Both serve coffee, aperitifs, and snacks in an ambience of starched tablecloths and chandeliers.

Cova's courtyard café

When the hurly-burly's done, head for the **Bulgari Hotel** (Via Fratelli Gabba 7b, ☎ 02/8058051), west of Via Manzoni, for a quiet (if pricey) drink. In summer, the bar extends into a beautiful, mature garden over an acre in size.

Aspesi (No. 13)
☎ 02/76022478
www.aspesi.it
low-key local design genius

Lorenzi (No. 9)
☎ 02/76022848
www.glorenzi.com
unique Milan—cutlery, razors, gifts

Valentino (No. 20)
corner Via Santo Spirito
☎ 02/76020285
www.valentino.it
women's clothes: elegant designs for special occasions

Salvatore Ferragamo Uomo (No. 20/4)
☎ 02/76006660
www.ferragamo.com
men's clothing and accessories

Loro Piana (No. 27c)
☎ 02/7772901
www.loropiana.it
women's and men's clothes, accessories: cashmere everything

VIA SAN PIETRO ALL'ORTO
(east to west)

Belfe-Postcard (No. 7)
☎ 02/781023
www.belfe.it
chic sport and skiwear

Pomellato (No. 17)
☎ 02/76006086
www.pomellato.it
classic Milan—style jewelry

Jimmy Choo (No. 17)
☎ 02/45481770
www.jimmychoo.com
women's and men's shoes

CORSO VENEZIA
(south to north)

Prada Linea Rossa (No. 3)
☎ 02/76001426
www.prada.com
Prada's sports line for men and women

D&G (No. 7)
☎ 02/76004095
www.dolcegabbana.it
swimwear, underwear, accessories: Dolce & Gabbana's younger line

Armani Collezioni (No. 9)
☎ 02/76390068
men's and women's clothing and accessories

✔ **Dolce & Gabbana** (No. 15)
☎ 02/76028485
www.dolcegabbana.it
Men's clothes, sold in a four-story, early 19th-century patrician home. An added feature is the Martini Bar, which also serves light lunches.

VIA VERRI
(south to north)

cross Via Bigli

D&G in Via della Spiga

Etro Profumi
corner Via Bigli
☎ 02/76005450
www.etro.it
fragrances

VIA SANT'ANDREA
(south to north)

✔ **Trussardi** (No. 5)
☎ 02/76020380
www.trussardi.com
Women's and men's clothes. The nearby flagship store (Piazza della Scala 5) includes the Trussardi Marino alla Scala Café (☎ 02/80688242), a fashion-forward bar done in stone, steel, slate, and glass. For a more substantial lunch, and views of Teatro alla Scala, head upstairs to the Marino alla Scala Ristorante (☎ 02/80688201), which serves creative Mediterranean cuisine.

Missoni (angolo via Bagutta)
☎ 02/76003555

BARGAIN-HUNTING AT THE OUTLETS

Milan may be Italy's richest city, but that doesn't mean all its well-dressed residents can afford to shop at the boutiques of the quadrilatero. Many pick up their designer clothes at outlet stores, where prices can be reduced by 50 percent or more.

Salvagente (Via Bronzetti 16 ☎ 02/76110328, www.salvagentemilano.it) is the top outlet for designer apparel and accessories from both large and small houses. There's a small men's department. To get there, take the 60 bus, which runs from the Duomo to the Stazione Centrale, to the intersection of Bronzetti and Archimede. Look for the green iron gate with the bronze sign, between the hairdressers and an apartment building. No credit cards.

DMagazine Outlet (Via Montenapoleone 26 ☎ 02/76006027, www.dmagazine.it) has bargains in the

women's and men's clothing

Banner (No. 8/A)
☎ 02/76004609
women's and men's clothes: a multibrand boutique

Moschino (No. 12)
☎ 02/76000832
www.moschino.it
women's clothes: world-renowned window displays

✔ **Gianfranco Ferré** (No. 15)
☎ 02/794864
www.gianfrancoferre.com
Everything Ferré, plus a spa providing facials, Jacuzzis, steam baths, and mud treatments. Reservations are essential (☎ 02/76017526), preferably a week in advance.

Miu Miu (No. 21)
☎ 02/76001799
www.prada.com
Prada's younger line

Armani in Via Manzoni

VIA MANZONI
(south to north)

Valextra (No. 3)
☎ 02/99786000
www.valextra.it
glamorous bags and luggage

✔ **Armani Megastore** (No. 31)
☎ 02/72318600
www.giorgioarmani.com
The quadrilatero's most conspicuous shopping complex. Along with many Armani fashions, you'll find a florist, a bookstore, a chocolate shop (offering Armani pralines), the Armani

CORSO COMO
✔ **10 Corso Como**
☎ 02/29000727
www.10corsocomo.com
Outside the quadrilatero, but it's a must see for fashion addicts. The bazaar-like 13,000-square-foot complex includes women's and men's boutiques, a bar and restaurant, a bookstore, a record shop, and an art gallery specializing in photography. You can even spend the night (if you can manage to get a reservation) at Milan's most exclusive B&B, Three Rooms (☎ 02/626163). The furnishings are a modern design-lover's dream.

Prada store in the Galleria

Caffè, and Nobu (of the upscale Japanese restaurant chain). The Armani Casa furniture collection is next door at number 37.

GALLERIA VITTORIO EMANUELE

(not technically part of the quadrilatero, but nearby)

✔ **Gucci**
☎ 02/8597991
www.gucci.com

Gucci accessories, plus the world's first Gucci café. Sit outside behind the elegant boxwood hedge and watch the world go by.

Prada (No. 63-65)

☎ 02/876979
www.prada.com
the original store: look for the murals downstairs.

Louis Vuitton
☎ 02/72147011
www.vuitton.com
accessories, women's and men's shoes, watches

Tod's
☎ 02/877997
www.tods.com
women's and men's shoes, leather goods, accessories

Borsalino (No. 92)
☎ 02/804337
www.borsalino.com
hats

Galleria Vittorio Emanuele

midst of the quadrilatero. Names on sale include Armani, Cavalli, Gucci, and Prada.

DT-Intrend (Galleria San Carlo 6 ☎ 02/76000829) sells last year's Max Mara, Max & Co, Sportmax, Marella, Penny Black, and Marina Rinaldi. It's just 300 meters from the Max Mara store located on Corso Vittorio Emanuele at the corner of Galleria de Cristoforis.

At the **10 CorsoComo** outlet (Via Tazzoli 3 ☎ 02/29015130, www.10corsocomo.com) you can find clothes, shoes, bags, and accessories. It's open Fri.–Sun. 11–7.

Fans of **Marni** who have a little time on their hands will want to check out the outlet (Via Tajani 1 ☎ 02/70009735 or 02/71040332, www.marni.com). Take the 61 bus to the terminus at Largo Murani, from which it's about 200 meters on foot.

Giorgio Armani has an outlet, but it's way out of town—off the A3, most of the way to Como. The address is Strada Provinciale per Bregnano 13, in the town of Vertemate (☎ 031 887373, www.giorgioarmani.com).

NIGHTCLUBS

For nightclubs, note that the cover charges can change depending on the day of the week. **Magazzini Generali** (✉ *Via Pietrasanta 14, Porta Vigentina* ☎ *02/5393948* ⊕ *www.magazzinigenerali.it*), in what was an abandoned warehouse, is a fun, futuristic venue for dancing and concerts. The €20 cover charge includes a drink. Its venerable age notwithstanding, **Plastic** (✉ *Viale Umbria 120* ☎ *02/733996* ⊕ *www. thisisplastic.com*), closed Monday through Wednesday and some Thursdays, is still considered Milan's most transgressive, avant-garde, and fun club, complete with drag-queen shows. The action starts late, even by Italian standards—don't bother going before midnight. Cover is €15 to €20. To its regular discotheque fare, **Tocqueville** (✉ *Via Alexis de Tocqueville, Corso Como* ☎ *02/29002973* ⊕ *www.tocqueville13.it* ⊘ *Closed Mon.*) has added two nights per week of live music, featuring young and emerging talent. The cover at this ever-popular Milan club is €10–€13.

SHOPPING

The heart of Milan's shopping reputation is the **Quadrilatero della moda** district north of the Duomo. Here the world's leading designers compete for shoppers' attention, showing off their ultrastylish clothes in stores that are works of high style themselves. You won't find any bargains, but regardless of whether you're making a purchase, the area is a great place for window-shopping and people-watching. But fashion is not limited to one neighborhood, and there is a huge and exciting selection of clothing that is affordable, well made, and often more interesting than what is offered by the international luxury brands with shops in the Quadrilatero.

Wander around the **Brera** to find smaller shops with some appealing offerings from lesser-known names that cater to the well-schooled taste of this upscale neighborhood. The densest concentration is along Via Brera, Via Solferino, and Corso Garibaldi. For inexpensive and trendy clothes—for the under-25 set—stroll **Via Torino**, which begins in Piazza Duomo. Stay away on Saturday afternoon if you don't like crowds. Milan has several shopping streets that serve nearby residential concentrations. In the Porta Venezia area, visit **Corso Buenos Aires**, which runs northeast from the Giardini Pubblici. The wide and busy street is lined with affordable shops. It has the highest concentration of clothing stores in Europe, so be prepared to give up halfway. Avoid Saturday after 3 PM, when it seems the entire city is here looking for bargains. Near the Corso Magenta area, walk a few blocks beyond *The Last Supper* to **Corso Vercelli**, where you will find everything from a branch of the Coin department store to the quintessentially Milanese **Gemelli** (✉ *Corso Vercelli 16* ☎ *02/48004689* ⊕ *www.gemelli.it*).

QUICK BITES   **Pasticceria Biffi** (✉ *Corso Magenta 87* ☎ *02/48006702* ⊕ *www. biffipasticceria.it*) is a Milan institution and the official pastry shop of this traditionally wealthy neighborhood. Have a coffee or a rich hot chocolate in its paneled room before facing the crowds in Corso Vercelli.

Milan's Furniture Fair

During the Salone del Mobile, Milan's furniture fair, in early April, the city is a scene—there are showroom openings, cocktail parties, and product launches, and design types dressed in black and wearing funny glasses fill the sidewalks and bars.

Except for a few free days, the Salone del Mobile is for professionals only, but you can still participate. Newspapers such as *Corriere della Sera* usually run an English supplement, and special design-week freebies list public events around Milan called "Fuorisalone" (⊕ *www.fuorisalone.it*). Major players such as bathroom and kitchen specialist Boffi (Via Solferino 11) and Capellini (Via Santa Cecilia 4) launch new products in their stores. Warning: Do not visit if you have not planned ahead. Hotel rooms and restaurant seating are impossible to find. See ⊕ *www.fieramilano.it* for dates.

MARKETS

Weekly open markets selling fruits and vegetables—and a great deal more—are still a regular sight in Milan. Many also sell clothing and shoes. Monday- and Thursday-morning markets in **Mercato di Via S. Marco** (✉ *Brera*) cater to the wealthy residents of this central neighborhood. In addition to food stands where you can get cheese, roast chicken, and dried beans and fruits, there are several clothing and shoe stalls that are important stops for some of Milan's most elegant women. Check out the knitwear at Valentino, about midway down on the street side. Muscle in on the students from the prestigious high school nearby who rush here for the french fries and potato croquettes at the chicken stand at the Via Montebello end.

Bargains in designer apparel can be found at the huge **Mercato Papiniano** (✉ *Porta Genova*) on Saturday all day and Tuesday from about 9 to 1. The stalls to look for are at the Piazza Sant'Agostino end of the market. It's very crowded and demanding—watch out for pickpockets.

PAVIA, CREMONA, AND MANTUA

Once proud medieval fortress towns rivaling Milan in power, these centers of industry and commerce on the Po Plain still play a key role in Italy's wealthiest, most populous region. Pavia is celebrated for its extraordinarily detailed Carthusian monastery, Cremona for its incomparable violin-making tradition. Mantua—the most picturesque of the three—was the home of the fantastically wealthy Gonzaga dynasty for almost 300 years.

PAVIA

41 km (25 mi) south of Milan.

GETTING HERE

By car from Milan, start out on the A7 autostrada and exit onto A53 as you near Pavia; the drive is 40 km (25 mi) and takes about 45 minutes. Pavia is 30 to 40 minutes by train from Milan and 1½ hours (by slower regional service) from Cremona. The Certosa is 30 minutes by train from several Milan stations.

VISITOR INFORMATION

Pavia tourism office (✉ *Palazzo del Broletto, Piazza della Vittoria* 🕾 *0382/597001* ⊕ *www.turismo.provincia.pv.it*).

EXPLORING

Pavia was once Milan's chief regional rival. The city dates from at least the Roman era and was the capital of the Lombard kings for two centuries (572–774). It was at one time known as "the city of a hundred towers," but only a handful have survived the passing of time. Its prestigious university was founded in 1361 on the site of a 10th-century law school, but it has roots that can be traced to antiquity.

The 14th-century **Castello Visconteo** now houses the local **Museo Civico** (Municipal Museum), with a Romanesque and Renaissance sculpture gallery, an archaeological collection, and a large picture gallery featuring works by Correggio, Bellini, Tiepolo, Hayez, Pelizza da Volpedo, and La Foppa, among others. ✉ *Viale XI Febbraio 35, near Piazza Castello* 🕾 *0382/33853* ⊕ *www.museicivici.pavia.it* 🎫 *€6* ⊙ *Feb.–June and Sept.–Nov., Tues.–Sun. 10–6; July, Aug., Dec., and Jan., Tues.–Sun. 9–1:30. Last entry 45 mins before closing.*

The main draw in Pavia is the **Certosa** *(Carthusian monastery)*, 9 km (5½ mi) north of the city center. Its elaborate facade shows the same relish for ornamentation as the Duomo in Milan. The Certosa's extravagant grandeur was due in part to the plan to have it house the tombs of the family of the first duke of Milan, Galeazzo Visconti III (who died during a plague, at age 49, in 1402). The best marble was used, taken undoubtedly by barge from the quarries of Carrara, roughly 240 km (150 mi) away. Though the floor plan may be Gothic—a cross shape divided into a series of squares—the gorgeous fabric that rises above it is triumphantly Renaissance. On the facade, in the lower frieze, are medallions of Roman emperors and Eastern monarchs; above them are low reliefs of scenes from the life of Christ and from the career of Galeazzo Visconti III.

The first duke was the only Visconti to be interred here, and not until some 75 years after his death, in a tomb designed by Gian Cristoforo Romano. Look for it in the right transept. In the left transept is a more appealing tomb—that of a rather stern middle-aged man and a beautiful young woman. The man is Ludovico il Moro Sforza, seventh duke of Milan, who commissioned Leonardo to paint *The Last Supper*. The woman is Ludovico's wife, Beatrice d'Este (1475–97), one of the most celebrated women of her day, the embodiment of brains, culture, birth, and beauty. Married when he was 40 and she was 16, they had

The Certosa di Pavia, north of the city center.

enjoyed six years together when she died while delivering a stillborn child. Ludovico commissioned the sculptor Cristoforo Solari to design a joint tomb for the high altar of Santa Maria delle Grazie in Milan. Originally much larger, the tomb for some years occupied the honored place as planned. Then, for reasons that are still mysterious, the Dominican monks sold the tomb to their Carthusian brothers to the south. Sadly, part of the tomb and its remains were lost. ✉ *Certosa, Località Monumento 4, 9 km (5½ mi) north of Pavia* ☎ *0382/925613* ⊕ *www. comune.pv.it/certosadipavia* ✉ *Donations accepted* ☾*May–Aug., Tues.–Sun. 9–11:30 and 2:30–6; Apr. and Sept., Tues.–Sun. 9–11:30 and 2:30–5:30; Mar. and Oct., Tues.–Sun. 9–11:30 and 2:30–5; Nov.– Feb., Tues.–Sun. 9–11 and 2:30–4:30.*

In the Romanesque church of **San Pietro in Ciel d'Oro** you can visit the tomb of Christianity's most celebrated convert, Saint Augustine, housed in an intricately carved, Gothic, white marble ark on the high altar. ✉ *San Pietro in Ciel d'Oro 2* ☎ *0382/303036* ⊕ *santagostinopavia.it* ☾ *Daily 7–noon and 3–7:30. Mass: Mon.–Sat. 9 and 6:30, Sun. 9, 11, and 6:30.*

WHERE TO EAT

$$$
NORTHERN
ITALIAN

✗ **Locanda Vecchia Pavia al Mulino.** At this sophisticated art nouveau restaurant 150 yards from the Certosa you can find creative versions of traditional regional cuisine, including *risotto alla certosina* (with sturgeon eggs, frogs' legs, and river shrimp). *Casoncelli* (stuffed pasta), *petto d'anatra* (duck breast), and veal cutlet alla Milanese are done with style, as are the imaginative seafood dishes. There's a veranda open in summer with a view of the Certosa. ✉ *Via al Monumento 5,*

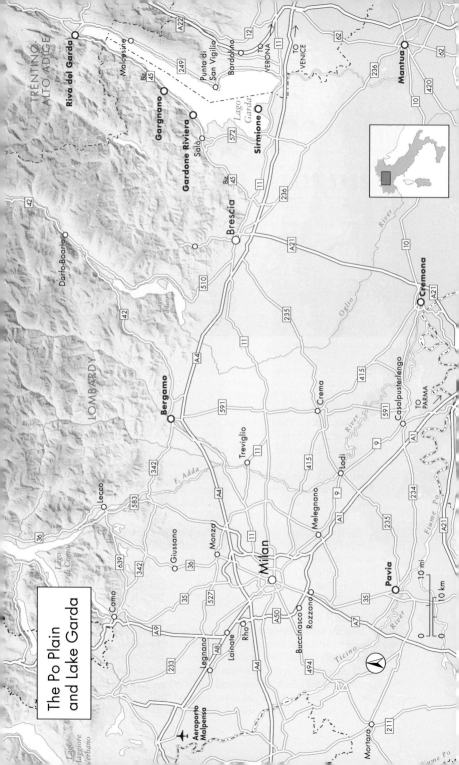

The Po Plain and Lake Garda

Certosa ☎ *0382/925894* ⊕ *www.vecchiapaviaalmulino.it* ⚞ *Reservations essential* ⊟ *AE, DC, MC, V* ☯ *Apr.–Oct., no lunch Mon. and Tues.; Nov.–Mar., no lunch Mon., closed Sun.*

CREMONA

104 km (65 mi) east of Pavia, 106 km (66 mi) southeast of Milan.

GETTING HERE

By car from Milan, start out on the A1 autostrada and switch to A21 at Piacenza; the drive is 100 km (62 mi) and lasts about 1½ hours. From Pavia, take SS617 to A21; the trip is 70 km (44 mi) and lasts about 1¼ hours. By train, Cremona is about an hour from Milan and 1½ hours from Desenzano, near Sirmione on Lake Garda.

VISITOR INFORMATION

Cremona tourism office (✉ *Piazza del Comune 5* ☎ *0372/23233* ⊕ turismo. provincia.cremona.it ☯ *Daily 9–1 and 2–5; July and Aug., closed Sun. afternoon*).

EXPLORING

Cremona is where the world's best violins are made. Andrea Amati (1510–80) invented the modern instrument here in the 16th century. Though cognoscenti continue to revere the Amati name, it was an apprentice of Amati's nephew for whom the fates had reserved wide and lasting fame. In a career that spanned an incredible 68 years, Antonio Stradivari (1644–1737) made more than 1,200 instruments—including violas, cellos, harps, guitars, and mandolins, in addition to his fabled violins. Labeled simply with a small printed slip reading ANTONIUS STRADIVARIUS CREMONENSIS. FACIEBAT ANNO, followed by the date inserted in a neat italic hand, they remain the most coveted, most expensive stringed instruments in the world.

Strolling about this quiet, medium-size city, you cannot help noting that violin making continues to flourish. There are, in fact, more than 50 *liutai*, many of them graduates of the Scuola Internazionale di Liuteria (International School of Violin Making). You are usually welcome to these ateliers, where traditional craftsmanship reigns supreme, especially if you are contemplating the acquisition of your own instrument; the tourist office can provide addresses.

Cremona's other claim to fame is *torrone* (nougat), which is said to have been created here in honor of the marriage of Bianca Maria Visconti and Francesco Sforza, which took place in October 1441. The new confection, originally prepared by heating almonds, egg whites, and honey over low heat and shaped and named after the city's tower, was created in symbolic celebration. The annual Festa del Torrone is held in the main piazza on the third Sunday in October.

QUICK BITES

Prepare to visit the sites of Cremona or wait for the next train at the Pasticceria Dondeo (✉ *Via Alghieri Dante 38* ☎ *0372/21224*), visible from and just to the right of the station. Dating back to 1912, this is one of Cremona's oldest and most beautiful art nouveau café and pastry shops. The fresh zabaglione and beignets are heaven.

9

The **Piazza del Comune**, surrounded by the Duomo, tower, baptistery, and city hall, is distinctive and harmonious: the combination of old brick, rose- and cream-color marble, terra-cotta, and old copper roofs brings Romanesque, Gothic, and Renaissance together with unusual success. The city's collection of stringed treasures are on display: a viola and five violins, including the golden-orange "Il Cremonese 1715" Stradivarius. ⊠ *Piazza del Comune 5* ☎ *0372/803618* ⊕ *www.musei.comune.cremona.it* ⌑ *Violin collection €6* ☉ *Tues.–Sat. 9–6, Sun. 10–6.*

Dominating Piazza del Comune is the **Torrazzo** *(Big Tower)*, the city's symbol and perhaps the tallest campanile in Italy, visible for a considerable distance across the Po Plain. It's open to visitors, but in winter, hours fluctuate depending on the weather. The tower's astronomical clock is the 1583 original. ⊠ *Piazza del Comune* ☎ *0372/495029* ⌑ *€6.50* ☉ *Tues.–Sun. 10–1 and 2:30–6.*

Cremona's Romanesque **Duomo** was consecrated in 1190. Here you can find the beautiful *Story of the Virgin Mary and the Passion of Christ,* the central fresco of an extraordinary cycle commissioned in 1514 and featuring the work of local artists, including Boccacio Boccancino, Giovan Francesco Bembo, and Altobello Melone. ⊠ *Piazza del Comune* ☎ *0372/495011* ☉ *Weekdays 8–noon and 3:30–7.*

Legendary violin maker Antonio Stradivari lived, worked, and died near the verdant square at **No. 1 Piazza Roma**. According to local lore, Stradivari kept each instrument in his bedroom for a month before varnishing it, imparting part of his soul before sealing and sending it out into the world. In the center of the park is **Stradivari's grave,** marked by a simple tombstone.

The **Museo Stradivariano** *(Stradivarius Museum)* in Palazzo Affaitati houses a collection of antique and modern instruments and informative exhibits of Stradivari's paper patterns, wooden models, and various tools. ⊠ *Via Ugolani Dati 4* ☎ *0372/803622* ⌑ *€7* ☉ *Tues.–Sat. 9–6, Sun. 10–6.*

WHERE TO EAT

$ ✗ **Centrale**. Close to the cathedral, this old-style trattoria is a favorite
NORTHERN   among locals for traditional regional fare, such as succulent *cotechino*
ITALIAN   (pork sausage) and *tortelli di zucca* (a small pasta with pumpkin filling),
★   at moderate prices. ⊠ *Vicolo Pertusio 4* ☎ *0372/28701* ▭ *AE, MC, V* ☉ *Closed Thurs. and July.*

$ ✗ **La Sosta**. This traditional restaurant looks to the 16th century for
NORTHERN   culinary inspiration, following a time-tested recipe for a favored first
ITALIAN   course, gnocchi *Vecchia Cremona*. The homemade salami is also excellent. To finish off the evening, try the *semifreddo al torroncino* (chilled almond cake) and a dessert wine. ⊠ *Via Sicardo 9* ☎ *0372/456656* ⊕ *www.osterialasosta.it* ▭ *AE, DC, MC, V* ☉ *Closed Mon. and 3 wks in Aug. No dinner Sun.*

WHERE TO STAY

$$ ⌂ **Delle Arti Design Hotel**. The name fits at this central hotel with elegant modern interiors and eclectic designer furniture. The contemporary feel provides a nice contrast to the surrounding historic center. **Pros:** ultramodern, industrial design; friendly staff; lots of amenities. **Cons:**

probably too contemporary for those seeking more traditional Italy. ✉ *Via Bonomelli 8* ☎ *0372/23131* ⊕ *www.dellearti.com* ⮡ *33 rooms, 3 suites* ⌂ *In-room: Internet, Wi-Fi. In-hotel: room service, bar, gym, Wi-Fi hotspot, parking (paid)* ▭ *AE, DC, MC, V* ⊗ *Closed Aug. 5–29 and late Dec.* ⦿ *BP.*

$ 🛏 **Hotel Impero.** This comfortable, modern hotel is well equipped to satisfy both leisure and business travelers. Some rooms overlook the piazza. The Impero makes a convenient base for those wisely disinclined to navigate old Cremona by car. **Pros:** highly professional staff; quiet rooms. **Cons:** rooms may seem a little out of style for some. ✉ *Piazza della Pace 21* ☎ *0372/413013* ⊕ *www.hotelimpero.cr.it* ⮡ *53 rooms* ⌂ *In-room: refrigerator, Wi-Fi. In-hotel: bar, Wi-Fi hotspot, parking (paid)* ▭ *AE, DC, MC, V* ⦿ *BP.*

SHOPPING

For Cremona's specialty nougat, visit famed **Sperlari** (✉ *Via Solferino 25* ☎ *0372/22346* ⊕ *www.fieschi1867.com*). In addition to nougat, Cremona's best *mostarda* (a condiment made from preserved fruit served with meat and cheese) has been sold from this handsome shop since 1836; Sperlari and parent company Fieschi have grown into a confectionary empire. Look for the historical product display in the back.

MANTUA

192 km (119 mi) southeast of Milan.

GETTING HERE

Mantua is 5 km (3 mi) west of the A22 autostrada. The drive from Milan, following A4 to A22, takes a little more than two hours. The drive from Cremona, along SS10, is 1¼ hours. Most trains arrive in just under 2 hours from Milan, depending on the type of service, and about 1½ hours from Desenzano, near Sirmione on Lake Garda, via Verona.

VISITOR INFORMATION

Mantua tourism office (✉ *Piazza A. Mantegna 6* ☎ *0376/432432* ⊕ *www. turismo.mantova.it* ⊗ *Daily 9–5*). Ask about the museum pass, which entitles you to reduced entrance fees at participating museums (not including the Palazzo Ducale or the Palazzo Te).

EXPLORING

Mantua stands tallest among the ancient walled cities of the Po Plain. Its fortifications are circled on three sides by the passing Mincio River, which long provided Mantua with protection, fish, and a steady stream of river tolls as it meandered from Lake Garda to join the Po. It may not be flashy or dramatic, but Mantua's beauty is subtle and deep, hiding a rich trove of artistic, architectural, and cultural gems beneath its slightly somber facade.

Although Mantua first came to prominence in Roman times as the home of Virgil, its grand monuments date from the glory years of the Gonzaga dynasty. From 1328 until the Austrian Habsburgs sacked the city in 1708, the dukes and marquesses of the Gonzaga clan reigned over a wealthy independent commune, and the arts thrived in the relative peace of that period. Raphael's star pupil Andrea Mantegna, who

9

served as court painter for 50 years, was the best known of a succession of artists and architects who served Mantua through the years, and some of his finest work, including his only surviving fresco cycle, can be seen here. Giulio Romano (circa 1499–1546), Mantegna's apprentice, built his masterpiece, Palazzo Te, on an island in the river. Leon Battista Alberti (1404–72), who designed two impressive churches in Mantua, was widely emulated later in the Renaissance.

★ The 500-room **Palazzo Ducale**, the palace that dominates the skyline, was built for the Gonzaga family. Unfortunately, as the Gonzaga dynasty waned in power and prestige, much of the art within the castle was sold or stolen. The highlight is the Camera Degli Sposi—literally, the "Chamber of the Wedded Couple"— where Duke Ludovico and his wife held court. Mantegna painted it over a nine-year period at the height of his power, finishing at age 44. He made a startling advance in painting by organizing the picture plane in a way that systematically mimics the experience of human vision. Even now, more than five centuries later, you can sense the excitement of a mature artist, fully aware of the great importance of his painting, expressing his vision with a masterly, joyous confidence. The circular trompe l'oeil around the vaulted ceiling is famous for the many details that attest to Mantegna's greatness: the three-dimensional quality of the seven Caesars (the Gonzagas saw themselves as successors to the Roman emperors and paid homage to classical culture throughout the palazzo); the self-portrait of Mantegna (in purple, on the right side of the western fresco); and the dwarf peering out from behind the dress of Ludovico's wife (on the northern fresco). Only 20 people at a time are allowed in the Camera Degli Sposi, and only for 10 minutes at a time. Read about the room before you enter so that you can spend your time looking up.

Walk-up visitors to Mantua's Palazzo Ducale may take a fast-paced guided tour conducted in Italian; signs in each room provide explanations in English. Audio guides are available for €4. Alternatively, call the **tourism office** (☎ 0376/432432) to arrange for English-language tours. ✉ *Piazza Sordello 40* ☎ *0376/224832* 🎫 *€6.50, additional €1 for reservation to see Camera Degli Sposi* ⊘ *Tues.–Sun. 8:30–7; last entry at 6:30.*

Serious Mantegna aficionados will want to visit the **Casa di Andrea Mantegna**, designed by the artist himself and built around an intriguing circular courtyard, which is usually open to view. The exterior is interesting for its unusual design, and the interior, with its hidden frescoes, can be seen by appointment or during occasional art exhibitions. Prices vary depending on the exhibition. ✉ *Via Acerbi 47* ☎ *0376/360506* ⊕ *www.casadelmantegna.it* ⊘ *Tues.–Fri. 10–1, weekends 10–1 and 3–6.*

Mantua's Palazzo della Ragione and its main clock tower.

Mantegna's tomb is in the first chapel to the left in the basilica of **Sant'Andrea**, most of which was built in 1472. The current structure, a masterwork by the architect Alberti, is the third built on this spot to house the relic of the Precious Blood. The crypt holds two reliquaries containing earth believed to be soaked in the blood of Christ, brought to Mantua by Longinus, the soldier who pierced his side. They are displayed only on Good Friday. ⊠ *Piazza di Mantegna* ☎ *0376/328504* 🖼 *Free, €1 to visit the crypt* ⊘ *Weekdays 8–noon and 3–7; Sat. 10:30– noon and 3–6; Sun. 11:45–12:15 and 3–6.*

★ **Palazzo Te** is one of the greatest of all Renaissance palaces, built between 1525 and 1535 by Federigo II Gonzaga. It is the mannerist masterpiece of artist-architect Giulio Romano, who created a pavilion where the strict rules of courtly behavior could be relaxed for libertine pastimes. Romano's purposeful breaks with classical tradition are lighthearted and unprecedented. For example, note the "slipping" triglyphs along the upper edge of the inside courtyard. Two highlights are the *Camera di Amore e Psiche* (Room of Cupid and Psyche) that depicts a wedding set among lounging nymphs, frolicking satyrs, and even a camel and an elephant; and the gasp-producing *Camera dei Giganti* (Room of the Giants) that shows Jupiter expelling the Titans from Mount Olympus. The scale of the work is overwhelming; the floor-to-ceiling work completely envelops the viewer. The room's rounded corners, and the river rock covering the original floor, were meant to give it a cavelike feeling. It is a "whisper chamber" in which words softly uttered in one corner can be heard in the opposite one. For fun, note the graffiti from as far back as the 17th century. ⊠ *Viale Te 13* ☏ *0376/323266* ⊕ *www. centropalazzote.it* ◿ *€8* ☉ *Tues.–Sun. 9–6; Mon. 1–6; last entry at 5:30.*

WHERE TO EAT

$$$$ ✕ **Ambasciata.** Heralded by food critics the world over as one of Italy's
NORTHERN finest restaurants, Ambasciata (Italian for "embassy") takes elegance
ITALIAN and service to new levels. Chef Romano Tamani, who is co-owner
★ with his brother Francesco, makes frequent appearances abroad but
is at home in tiny Quistello, 20 km (12 mi) southeast of Mantua. He
offers those willing to make the trek (and pay the bill) an ever-changing
array of superlative creations such as *timballo di lasagne verdi con
petto di piccione sauté alla crème de Cassis* (green lasagna with breast
of pigeon and red currant). ⊠ *Via Martiri di Belfiore 33, Quistello*
☏ *0376/619169* ⊕ *www.ristoranteambasciata.com* ⌕ *Reservations
essential* ═ *AE, DC, MC, V* ☉ *Closed Mon., Jan. 1–15, and Aug. No
dinner Sun.*

¢ ✕ **Ristorante Pavesi.** Locals have been coming to this central restaurant
ITALIAN for delicious food at reasonable prices since 1918. The menu changes
every other month; homemade pasta is always a good bet. In warmer
months you can dine on Mantua's handsome main square. ⊠ *Piazza
delle Erbe 13* ☏ *0376/323627* ⊕ *www.ristorantepavesi.com* ═ *AE, DC,
MC, V* ☉ *Closed Tues. from Jan. 6 to 14.*

WHERE TO STAY

$$ ⊡ **Casa Poli.** Refreshing, minimalist influences, creative touches (like
the room number projected onto the hall floor) and attention to detail
create a welcoming ambience in this contemporary hotel. Natural fab-
rics add to the relaxed feel; common areas include a reading room and
an indoor garden. **Pros:** attentive staff; tasteful, unusual decor; fami-
lies welcome. **Cons:** although convenient, not in the absolute center of
the city. ⊠ *Corso Garibaldi 32* ☏ *0376/288170* ⊕ *www.hotelcasapoli.
it* ◿ *27 rooms* ⌂ *In-room: a/c, safe, Wi-Fi. In-hotel: bar, elevator, laun-
dry service, bicycles, Internet terminal, Wi-Fi hotspot, parking (paid)*
═ *AE, MC, V* ⫧ *BP.*

$$ ⊡ **Hotel Rechigi.** With its white marble lobby and silver-and-taupe
lounge, this modern hotel and its collection of contemporary art offer
quiet refuge from the busy streets in the center of Mantua, only a block
away. Rooms are unpretentious and comfortable, and there's an outdoor garden for breakfast during the warmer months. Three of the
suites include spas. **Pros:** quiet and central with friendly service. **Cons:**
spare design might leave some guests cold. ⊠ *Via Pier Fortunato Calvi
30* ☏ *059/283600* ⊕ *www.rechigi.com* ◿ *50 rooms, 7 suites* ⌂ *In-room:
safe, Wi-Fi. In-hotel: bar, laundry service, Internet terminal, Wi-Fi hotspot, parking (paid), some pets allowed* ═ *AE, DC, MC, V* ⫧ *EP.*

LAKE GARDA

Lake Garda has had a perennial attraction for travelers and writers
alike; even essayist Michel de Montaigne (1533–92), whose 15 months
of travel journals contain not a single other reference to nature, paused

GETTING AROUND THE LAKES

Frequent daily ferry and hydrofoil services link the lakeside towns and villages. Residents take them to get to work and school, while visitors use them for exploring the area. There are also special round-trip excursions, some with (optional) dining service on board. Schedules and ticket price are available on the Web site of **Navigazione Laghi** (✉ *Via Ariosto 21, Milan* ☎ *02/4676101, 03/9149511 Lake Garda* ⊕ *www. navigazionelaghi.it*) and are posted at the landing docks.

To get around the lakes by car, you have to follow secondary roads—often of great beauty. S572 follows the southern and western shores of Lake Garda, SS45b edges the northernmost section of the western shore, and S249 runs along the eastern shore. Around Lake Como, follow S340 along the western shore, S36 on the eastern shore, and S583 on the lower arms. S33 and S34 trace the western shore of Lake Maggiore. Although the roads around the lake can be beautiful, they're full of harrowing twists and turns, making for a slow, challenging drive.

There's regular bus service between the small towns on the lakes. It's less convenient than going by boat or by car, and it's used primarily by locals (particularly schoolchildren), but sightseers can use it as well. The bus service around Lake Garda serves mostly towns on the western shore. Call the bus operator **SIA** (☎ *030/44061* ⊕ *www.sia-autoservizi.it*) for information.

to admire the view down the lake from Torbole, which he called "boundless."

Lake Garda is 50 km (31 mi) long, ranges roughly 1 km to 16 km (½ mi to 10 mi) wide, and is as much as 1,135 feet deep. The terrain is flat at the lake's southern base and mountainous at its northern tip. As a consequence, its character varies from stormy inland sea to crystal-line Nordic-style fjord. It's the biggest lake in the region and by most accounts the cleanest. Drivers should take care on the hazardous hairpin turns on the lake road.

GETTING HERE

The town of Sirmione, at the south end of the lake, is 10 km (6 mi) from Desenzano, which has regular train service; it's about an hour and 20 minutes by train from Milan and 25 minutes from Verona. The A4 autostrada passes to the south of the lake, and A22 runs north–south about 10 km (6 mi) from the eastern shore.

BERGAMO

52 km (32 mi) northeast of Milan.

GETTING HERE

Bergamo is along the A4 autostrada. By car from Milan, take A51 out of the city to pick up A4; the drive is 52 km (32 mi) and takes about 45 minutes. By train, Bergamo is about 1 hour from Milan and 1½ hours from Sirmione.

VISITOR INFORMATION

Bergamo tourism office (✉ Torre del Gombito, *Via Gombito 13, Bergamo Alta* ☎ *035/242226* ◷ *Daily 9–12:30 and 2–5:30* ✉ *Piazzale Marconi, Bergamo Bassa* ☎ *035/210204* ◷ *Closed holidays and winter weekends* ⊕ *www.comune.bergamo.it; summer events:* ⊕ *www.bergamoestate.com).*

EXPLORING

If you're driving from Milan to Lake Garda, the perfect deviation

from your autostrada journey is the lovely medieval town of Bergamo. Bergamo is also a wonderful side trip by train from Milan. In less than an hour, you will be whisked from the restless pace of city life to the medieval grandeur of Bergamo Alta, where the pace is a tranquil remnant of the past.

From behind a set of battered Venetian walls high on an Alpine hilltop, Bergamo majestically surveys the countryside. Behind are the snow-capped Bergamese Alps, and two funiculars connect the modern **Bergamo Bassa** (Lower Bergamo) to the ancient **Bergamo Alta** (Upper Bergamo). Bergamo Bassa's long arteries and ornate piazze speak to its centuries of prosperity, but it's nonetheless overshadowed by Bergamo Alta's magnificence.

The massive **Torre Civica** offers a great view of the two cities. ✉ *Piazza Vecchia* ☎ *035/247116* 🎫 *€3, minimum 5 people* ◷ *Mar.–Oct., Tues.–Fri. 9:30–7, weekends 9:30–9:30; Nov.–Feb., Tues.–Fri. by appointment, weekends 9:30–4:30.*

Bergamo's **Duomo** and **Battistero** are the most substantial buildings in Piazza Duomo. But the most impressive structure is the **Cappella Colleoni**, with stunning marble decoration. ✉ *Piazza Duomo* ☎ *Duomo 035/210223; cappella 035/210061* ◷ *Duomo, daily 7:30–11:45 and 3–5:30; cappella Mar.–Oct., daily 9–12:30 and 2:30–6; Nov.–Feb., Tues.–Sun. 9–12:30 and 2–4:30.*

In the **Accademia Carrara** you will find an art collection that is surprisingly rewarding given its size and remote location. Many of the Venetian masters are represented—Mantegna, Bellini, Carpaccio (circa 1460–1525/26), Tiepolo (1727–1804), Francesco Guardi (1712–93), Canaletto (1697–1768)—as well as Botticelli (1445–1510). At this writing the museum is undergoing remodeling, but a selection of works can be seen at Palazzo della Regione in Piazza Vecchia, Bergamo Alta. ✉ *Bergamo Bassa, Piazza Carrara 82* ☎ *035/270413* ⊕ *www.accademiacarrara.bergamo.it* 🎫 *€5* ◷ *Palazzo della Regione: June–Sept., Sun. and Tues.–Fri. 10–9, Sat. 10 AM–11 PM; Oct.–May, Sun. and Tues.–Fri. 9:30–5:30, Sat. 10–6.*

WHERE TO EAT

$
NORTHERN
ITALIAN

✕ **Agnello d'Oro.** A 17th-century tavern on the main street in Upper Bergamo, with wooden booths and walls hung with copper utensils and ceramic plates, Agnello d'Oro is a good place to imbibe the atmosphere as well as the good local wine. Specialties are Bergamo-style risotto and varieties of polenta served with game and mushrooms. ✉ *Via Gombito 22, Bergamo Alta* ☎ *035/249883* ▭ *AE, MC, V* ☯ *Closed Mon. and Jan. 7–Feb. 5. No dinner Sun.*

$
WINE BAR
Fodor's Choice
★

✕ **Al Donizetti.** Find a table in the back of this central, cheerful enoteca before choosing local hams and cheeses to accompany your wine (more than 800 bottles are available, many by the glass). Heartier meals are also available, such as eggplant stuffed with cheese and salami, but save room for the desserts, which are well paired with dessert wines. ✉ *Via Gombito 17/a, Bergamo Alta* ☎ *035/242661* ⊕ *www.donizetti. it* ▭ *AE, MC, V.*

$–$$
NORTHERN
ITALIAN

✕ **Da Ornella.** The vaulted ceilings of this popular trattoria on the main street in the upper town are marked with ancient graffiti, created by (patiently) holding candles to the stone overhead. Ornella herself is in the kitchen, turning out casoncelli in butter and sage and platters of assorted roast meats. Ask her to suggest the perfect wine pairing for your meal. Three prix-fixe menus are available during the week, two on the weekend. ✉ *Via Gombito 15, Bergamo Alta* ☎ *035/232736* ▭ *AE, DC, MC, V* ☯ *Closed Thurs.*

$$$
ITALIAN
★

✕ **Taverna Colleoni dell'Angelo.** Angelo Cornaro is the name behind the Taverna Colleoni, on the Piazza Vecchia right behind the Duomo. He serves imaginative fish and meat dishes, both regional and international, all expertly prepared. ✉ *Piazza Vecchia 7, Bergamo Alta* ☎ *035/232596* ⊕ *www.colleonidellangelo.com* ▭ *AE, DC, MC, V* ☯ *Closed Mon.*

WHERE TO STAY

$$–$$$

🏨 **Excelsior San Marco.** The most comfortable hotel in Lower Bergamo, the Excelsior San Marco is only a short walk from the walls of the upper town. The rooms are surprisingly quiet considering the central location; some have expansive views of the city. You can breakfast on the rooftop terrace. **Pros:** modern, plush, spectacular surroundings; lots of rooms means it's good for late reservations and groups. **Cons:** not for those seeking an intimate environment. ✉ *Piazza della Repubblica 6* ☎ *035/366111* ⊕ *www.hotelsanmarco.com* ⤷ *155 rooms* ♿ *In-room: safe (some), Wi-Fi. In-hotel: restaurant, bar, laundry service, Internet terminal, Wi-Fi hotspot, parking (paid)* ▭ *AE, MC, V* ⦿⦿ *BP.*

$–$$

🏨 **Mercure Bergamo Palazzo Dolci.** Opened in 2004, the hotel offers modern comfort in a restructured 19th-century palazzo in Lower Bergamo. A contemporary homage to Bergamasco artists in the form of paintings decorate hotel room walls. **Pros:** convenient to train station and some shopping. **Cons:** few luxury amenities; caters to business travelers. ✉ *Viale Papa Giovanni XXIII 100* ☎ *035/227411* ⊕ *www.mercure. com* ⤷ *88 rooms* ♿ *In-room: safe, Wi-Fi, Internet. In-hotel: bar, room service, Internet terminal, Wi-Fi hotspot, parking (paid)* ▭ *AE, MC, V* ⦿⦿ *EP.*

9

Sirmione on Lake Garda.

SIRMIONE

★ *138 km (86 mi) east of Milan.*

VISITOR INFORMATION
Sirmione tourism office (✉ *Viale Marconi 2* ☎ *030/916114* ⊕ *www.sirmione. com*).

EXPLORING

Dramatically rising out of Lake Garda is the enchanting town of Sirmione. *"Paene insularum, Sirmio, insularumque ocelle,"* sang Catullus in a homecoming poem: "It is the jewel of peninsulas and islands, both." The forbidding Castello Scaligero stands guard behind the small bridge connecting Sirmione to the mainland; beyond, cobbled streets wind their way through medieval arches past lush gardens, stunning lake views, and gawking crowds. Originally a Roman resort town, Sirmione served under the dukes of Verona and later Venice as Garda's main point of defense. It has now reclaimed its original function, bustling with visitors in summer. Cars aren't allowed into town; parking is available by the tourist office at the entrance.

Locals will almost certainly tell you that the so-called **Grotte di Catullo** *(Grottoes of Catullus)* was once the site of the villa of Catullus (87– 54 BC), one of the greatest pleasure-seeking poets of all time. Present archaeological wisdom, however, does not concur, and there is some consensus that this was the site of two villas of slightly different periods, dating from about the 1st century AD. But never mind—the view through the cypresses and olive trees is lovely, and even if Catullus didn't have a villa here, he is closely associated with the area and undoubtedly did have a villa nearby. The ruins are at the top of the isthmus and are poorly signposted: walk through the historic center and past the various villas to the top of the spit; the entrance is on the right. A small museum offers a brief overview of the ruins (on the far wall); for guided group tours in English, call ☏ 02/20421469. ⊠ *Piazzale Orti Manara* ☏ *030/916157* 🎟 *€4* ⊘ *Apr.–Oct., Tues.–Sat. 8:30–7, Sun. 8:30–6; Nov.–Feb., Tues.–Sat. 8:30–5, Sun. 8:30–1:30; Mar., Tues.–Sat. 8:30–7, Sun. 8:30–1:30.*

The **Castello Scaligero** was built, along with almost all the other castles on the lake, by the Della Scala family. As hereditary rulers of Verona for more than a century before control of the city was seized by the Visconti in 1402, they counted Garda among their possessions. You can go inside to take in the nice view of the lake from the tower, or you can swim at the nearby beach. ⊠ *Piazza Castello* ☏ *030/916468* 🎟 *€4* ⊘ *Tues.–Sun. 8:30–7.*

WHERE TO EAT

$$$
ITALIAN

✕ **La Rucola.** Next to Sirmione's castle, this elegant, intimate restaurant has a creative menu, with seafood and meat dishes accompanied by a good choice of wines. Three fixed-price menus are available. ⊠ *Via Strentelle 3* ☏ *030/916326* ⊕ *www.ristorantelarucola.it* ☰ *AE, DC, MC, V* ⊘ *Closed Thurs. and Jan.–mid-Feb. No lunch Fri.*

$
SEAFOOD

✕ **Ristorante Al Pescatore.** Lake fish is the specialty at this simple, popular restaurant in Sirmione's historical center. Try grilled trout with a bottle of local white wine and settle your meal with a walk in the nearby public park. ⊠ *Via Piana 20* ☏ *030/916216* ⊕ *ristorantealpescatore. com* ☰ *AE, DC, MC, V* ⊘ *Closed Wed. and Dec. 10–25.*

WHERE TO STAY

$$$$

🏨 **Hotel Sirmione.** Just inside the city walls, near the Castello, this hotel and spa sits amid lakeside gardens and terraces. Rooms are furnished with comfortable Scandinavian slat beds, matching floral draperies and wall coverings, and built-in white furniture. Many guests have been returning for years, due largely to the homey feel and the attentiveness of the staff. ⊠ *Piazza Castello 19* ☏ *030/916331* ⊕ *www.termedisirmione. com* ⇥ *101 rooms* ♿ *In-room: Internet. In-hotel: restaurant, bars, pool, spa, Wi-Fi hotspot, room service, laundry service, parking (paid), some pets allowed* ☰ *AE, DC, MC, V* � *BP.*

$$$$
★

🏨 **Villa Cortine.** This former private villa in a secluded park risks being just plain ostentatious, but it's saved by the sheer luxury of its setting and the extraordinary professionalism of its staff. The hotel dominates a low hill, and the grounds—a colorful mixture of lawns, trees, statues, and fountains—go down to the lake. The villa itself dates from the early part of the 19th century, although a wing was added in 1952: the trade-off is between the more-charming decor in the older rooms and the better lake views from the newer ones. **Pros:** an opulent experience. **Cons:** in summer a three-night minimum stay and half board are required. ⊠ *Via Grotte 6* ☏ *030/9905890* ⊕ *www.palacehotelvillacortine.com* ⇥ *40 rooms, 2 suites* ♿ *In-room: safe. In-hotel: 3 restaurants, bar, laundry service, room service, Wi-Fi hotspot, tennis court, pool, beachfront, parking (free)* ☰ *DC, MC, V* ⊘ *Closed mid-Oct.–Mar.* llll *BP.*

9

TOWNS ALONG LAKE GARDA'S EASTERN SHORE

VISITOR INFORMATION

Malcesine tourism office (✉ *Via Capitanato 6/8* ☎ *0457/400044* ⊕ *www. malcesineweb.it*).

Bardolino (⊕ *www.bardolinoweb.it*), famous for its red wine, hosts the Cura dell'Uva (Grape Cure Festival) in late September–early October. It's a great excuse to indulge in the local vino, which is light, dry, and often slightly sparkling. (Bring aspirin, just in case the cura turns out to be worse than the disease.) Bardolino is one of the most popular summer resorts on the lake. It stands on the eastern shore at the wider end of the lake. Here there are two handsome Romanesque churches: **San Severo,** from the 11th century, and **San Zeno,** from the 9th. Both are in the center of the small town.

Just about everyone agrees that **Punta San Vigilio** is the prettiest spot on Garda's eastern shore. The highlight is the cypress-filled gardens of the 15th-century **Villa Guarienti di Brenzone** (✉ *Frazione Punta San Vigilio 1*). The villa is closed to the public, but the nearby Locanda San Vigilio hotel ($$$$) is picturesque and has a private beach and restaurant.

Malcesine, about 30 km (20 mi) north of Punta San Vigilio, is one of the loveliest areas along the upper eastern shore of Lake Garda. It's principally known as a summer resort, with sailing and windsurfing schools. It tends to be crowded in season, but there are nice walks from the town toward the mountains. Six ski lifts and more than 11 km (7 mi) of runs of varying degrees of difficulty serve skiers. Dominating the town is the 12th-century **Castello Scaligero** (☎ *045/6570333* 🎫 *€6* ☉ *Apr.–Oct., daily 9:30–7; Nov.–Mar., Sun. 11–4*), built by Verona's dynastic Della Scala family.

The futuristic *funivia* (cable car) zipping visitors to the top of **Monte Baldo** (5,791 feet) is unique because it rotates. After a 10-minute ride you're high in the Veneto, where you can stroll while enjoying spectacular views of the lake. You can ride the cable car down or bring along a mountain bike (or hang glider) for the descent. ✉ *Via Navene Vecchia 12* ☎ *045/7400206* ⊕ *www.funiviamalcesine.com* 🎫 *Round-trip €18* ☉ *Daily 8–7. Closed Nov.–mid-Dec.*

RIVA DEL GARDA

18 km (11 mi) north of Malcesine, 180 km (112 mi) east of Milan.

VISITOR INFORMATION

Riva del Garda tourism office (✉ *Largo Medaglie d'Oro al Valor Militare 5* ☎ *0464/554444* ⊕ *www.gardatrentino.it*).

EXPLORING

Set on the northern tip of Lake Garda against a dramatic backdrop of jagged cliffs and miles of beaches, Riva del Garda is the lake's quintessential resort town. The old city, set around a pretty harbor, was built up during the 15th century, when it was a strategic outpost of the Venetian Republic.

A view from Riva del Garda.

The heart of Riva del Garda, the lakeside **Piazza 3 Novembre** is surrounded by medieval palazzi. Standing in the piazza and looking out onto the lake you can understand why Riva del Garda has become a windsurfing mecca: air currents ensure good breezes on even the most sultry midsummer days.

The **Torre Apponale**, predating the Venetian period by three centuries, looms above the medieval residences of the main square; its crenellations recall its defensive purpose. Thanks to a complete restoration in 2002, visitors can climb the 165 steps to see the view from the top. ☎0464/573869 ᎒€1 ᎗ *Late Mar.–June and Oct., Tues.–Sun. 10–12:30 and 1:30–6; July–Sept., daily 10–12:30 and 1:30–6.*

WHERE TO EAT

$$
NORTHERN ITALIAN
✕**Castel Toblino.** A lovely stop for a lakeside drink or a romantic dinner, this castle is right on a lake in Sarche, about 20 km (12 mi) north of Riva toward Trento. The compound is said to have been a prehistoric, then Roman, village, and was later associated with the Church of Trento. Bernardo Clesio had it rebuilt in the 16th century in the Renaissance style. It's now a sanctuary of fine food, serving such local specialties as lake fish and guinea fowl. ⊠ *Via Caffaro 1, Sarche* ☎ *0461/864036* ⊕ *www. casteltoblino.com* ▭ *AE, MC, V* ᎗ *Closed Tues. and Jan. and Feb.*

WHERE TO STAY

$$$
☖**Hotel du Lac et du Parc.** Riva's most splendid hotel has elegance befitting its cosmopolitan name, with personalized service rarely found on Lake Garda since its aristocratic heyday. The airy public spaces include a dining room, bar, and beautifully manicured private garden leading to the public beach. The rooms are well appointed and comfortable;

be sure to ask for air-conditioning if the season demands it. The outdoor pool has separate areas for adults and children. **Pros:** expansive and lush surroundings offering myriad lodging options; a pampering and indulgent staff. **Cons:** not a cozy atmosphere. ⊠ *Viale Rovereto 44* ☎ *0464/566600* ⊕ *www.dulacetduparc.com* ➟ *164 rooms, 5 suites* ♨ *In-room: a/c. In-hotel: 2 restaurants, bars, tennis courts, pools, spa, gym, beachfront, parking (free), some pets allowed* ⊟ *AE, DC, MC, V* ۞ *Closed Nov.–Mar.* ⵔ *BP.*

$$ ⊡ **Hotel Sole.** Within a lakeside 15th-century palazzo in the center of town, this lovely, understated hotel offers comfortable, affordable rooms. The terraced front rooms open to breathtaking views of the lake, and a secluded rooftop terrace is a perfect retreat from crowded beaches in summer. It was recently updated with modern amenities such as Wi-Fi availability. **Pros:** a classic lake resort updated with modern hotel conveniences. **Cons:** not for those looking for ultracontemporary design. ⊠ *Piazza 3 Novembre 35* ☎ *0464/552686* ⊕ *www.hotelsole. net* ➟ *52 rooms* ♨ *In-room: safe, refrigerator, Wi-Fi. In-room: safe. In-hotel: 2 restaurants, room service, bars, laundry service, bicycles, Wi-Fi hotspot, parking (free)* ⊟ *AE, DC, MC, V* ۞ *Closed Nov.–Dec. 19 and mid-Jan.–mid-Mar.* ⵔ *BP.*

$$ ⊡ **Luise.** This cozy, reasonably priced hotel has great amenities, including a big garden, a large swimming pool, and a welcome bowl of fresh fruit on arrival. The restaurant, La Limonaia, is recommended for its Trentino specialties. Look for their extensive luggage label collection from a bygone era. **Pros:** pleasant, reasonably priced option; great for kids. **Cons:** because it's popular with families, may not be the best choice if you want to avoid kids. ⊠ *Viale Rovereto 9* ☎ *0464/550858* ⊕ *www.feelinghotelluise.com* ➟ *68 rooms* ♨ *In-room: refrigerator, safe, no a/c (some), Wi-Fi. In-hotel: restaurant, room service, tennis court, pool, laundry facilities, bicycles, Internet terminal, parking (free), some pets allowed* ⊟ *AE, DC, MC, V* ⵔ *BP.*

EN ROUTE After passing the town of Limone—where it is said the first lemon trees in Europe were planted—take the fork to the right about 5 km (3 mi) north of Gargnano and head to Tignale. The view from the Madonna di Monte Castello church, some 2,000 feet above the lake, is spectacular. Adventurous travelers will want to follow this pretty inland mountain road to Tremosine; be warned that the road winds its way up the mountain through hairpin turns and blind corners that can test even the most experienced drivers.

GARGNANO

30 km (19 mi) south of Riva del Garda, 144 km (89 mi) east of Milan.

VISITOR INFORMATION

Gargnano tourism office (⊠ *Piazza Boldini 2* ☎ *0365/791243* ⊕ *www. gargnanosulgarda.it*).

EXPLORING

This small port town was an important Franciscan center in the 13th century, and now comes alive in the summer months when German tourists, many of whom have villas here, crowd the small pebble beach.

An Austrian flotilla bombarded the town in 1866, and some of the houses still bear marks of cannon fire. Mussolini owned two houses in Gargnano: one is now a language school and the other, Villa Feltrinelli, has been restored and reopened as a luxury hotel.

WHERE TO EAT AND STAY

$$$
NORTHERN
ITALIAN

✕ **La Tortuga.** This rustic trattoria is more sophisticated than it first appears, with an extensive wine cellar and nouvelle-style twists on local dishes. Specialties include *agnello con rosmarino e timo* (lamb with rosemary and thyme), *persico con rosmarino* (perch with rosemary), and *carpaccio d'anatra all'aceto balsamico* (duck carpaccio with balsamic vinegar). ⊠ *Via XXIV Maggio at small harbor* ☎ *0365/71251* ⊟ *AE, DC, MC, V* ⊘ *Closed Tues. and Dec.–Feb. No lunch.*

$ 🏠 **Garni Bartabel.** This cozy hotel on the main street offers comfortable accommodations at a reasonable price. Breakfast is served on an elegant terrace overlooking the lake. **Pros:** adorable; a bargain for this in area. **Cons:** not luxurious. ⊠ *Via Roma 35* ☎ *0365/71300* ⊕ *www.hotelbartabel.it* ⌇ *10 rooms* ⊖ *In-room: no a/c, Wi-Fi. In-hotel: bar, room service, Wi-Fi hotspot, some pets allowed* ⊟ *AE, DC, MC, V* ⊘ *Closed Nov.–mid-Mar.* ⦿ *EP.*

$$$$ 🏠 **Villa Feltrinelli.** This 1892 art nouveau villa hotel, named for the Italian publishing family that used to vacation here, is immersed in private gardens and overlooks the lake. The interior has been meticulously and opulently restored with frescoed ceilings, wood paneling, antique ceramics, and original tile floors. (The marble flooring is heated in the bathrooms.) The rooms are palatial and equipped with every luxury (as befits the final bill). If you can afford it, take the tower room, or one of the independent guesthouses if that's your style. There's an extensive library open to guests. **Pros:** first-class luxury hotel; like stepping into a bygone era. **Cons:** one of the most expensive hotels on the lake. ⊠ *Via Rimembranza 38/40* ☎ *0365/798000* ⊕ *www.villafeltrinelli.com* ⌇ *21 rooms* ⊖ *In-room: safe, refrigerator, Wi-Fi. In-hotel: restaurant, room service, bar, pool, laundry service, parking (free)* ⊟ *AE, DC, MC, V* ⊘ *Closed mid-Oct.–mid-Apr.* ⦿ *BP.*

SPORTS AND THE OUTDOORS

The **Upper Brescian Garda Park** stretches over nine municipalities on the western side of the lake, from Salò to Limone, covering 380 square km (147 square mi). Call the **Limone Hotel Owners Association** (⊠ *Via Quattro Novembre 2/c* ☎ *0365/954720*) for trail and bicycle-rental information. They're also the people to contact if you'd like to take part in one of the free treks led by the Gruppo Alpini Limone every Sunday from June to September.

9

GARDONE RIVIERA

12 km (7 mi) south of Gargnano, 139 km (86 mi) east of Milan.

EXPLORING

Gardone Riviera, a once-fashionable 19th-century resort now pleasantly faded, is the former home of the flamboyant Gabriele d'Annunzio (1863–1938), one of Italy's greatest modern poets. D'Annunzio's estate, **Il Vittoriale**, perched on the hills above the town, is an elaborate memorial to himself, filled with the trappings of conquests in art, love, and war (of which the largest is a ship's prow in the garden), and complete with an imposing mausoleum. ⊠ *Via Vittoriale 12* ☎ *0365/296511* ⊕ *www. vittoriale.it* 🎟 *€11 for house or museum, €16 for both* ⊗ *Grounds: Apr.–Sept., daily 8:30–8; Oct.–Mar., daily 9–5. House and museum: Apr.–Sept., Tues.–Sun. 9:30–7; Oct.–Mar., Tues.–Sun. 9–1 and 2–5.*

More than 2,000 Alpine, subtropical, and Mediterranean species thrive at the **Giardino Botanico Hruska**. ⊠ *Via Roma* ☎ *0366/410877* ⊕ *www. hellergarden.com* 🎟 *€9* ⊗ *Mar.–Oct., daily 9-7.*

OFF THE BEATEN PATH **Salò Market.** Four kilometers (2½ mi) south of Gardone Riviera is the enchanting lakeside town of Salò, which history buffs may recognize as the capital of the ill-fated Social Republic set up in 1943 by the Germans after they liberated Mussolini from the Gran Sasso. Every Saturday morning an enormous market is held in the Piazza dei Martiri della Libertà, with great bargains on everything from household goods to clothing to foodstuffs. In August or September a lone vendor often sells locally unearthed *tartufi neri* (black truffles) at affordable prices.

WHERE TO STAY

$$$ ★ 🏨 **Gran Hotel Gardone.** Directly facing the lake, this majestic 1800s palace is surrounded by an attractive landscaped garden. Nearly all the rooms look out over the water, and all bathrooms have been renovated in marble. The ground-floor Winnie's Bar, named after Winston Churchill, a frequent guest, envelopes you in charming art nouveau furniture and decorations. **Pros:** well-appointed; expansive gardens; lauded service. **Cons:** as of this writing, no Internet in the rooms. ⊠ *Via Zanardelli 84* ☎ *0365/20261* ⊕ *www.grangardone.it* 📞 *143 rooms, 25 suites* ⚷ *In-room: safe. In-hotel: 2 restaurants, bar, Wi-Fi hotspot, Internet terminal, pool, spa, room service, laundry service, parking (paid), some pets allowed* ═ *AE, DC, MC, V* ⊗ *Closed mid-Oct.–Mar.* ❑◗ *BP.*

$$$ 🏨 **Grand Hotel Fasano.** A former 19th-century hunting lodge between Gardone and Maderno, the Fasano has matured into a seasonal hotel of a high standard. To one side you face the deep waters of Lake Garda; on the others you're surrounded by a 31,080-square-km (12,000-square-mi) private park where the original Austrian owners no doubt spent their days chasing game. Besides myriad activities on the water, there are two golf courses in the vicinity. All the rooms have a lake view. **Pros:** every room has a view of the lake. **Cons:** not all rooms have Wi-Fi; no credit cards accepted. ⊠ *Corso Zanardelli 190* ☎ *0365/290220* ⊕ *www.ghf.it* 📞 *68 rooms* ⚷ *In-room: a/c, safe, refrigerator, Wi-Fi (some), Internet. In-hotel: 2 restaurants, bar, tennis court, pool, room service, laundry service, beachfront, gym, Wi-Fi hotspot, Internet ter-*

minal, parking (free), some pets allowed ⊟ *No credit cards* ⊘ *Closed mid-Oct.–Mar.* ⦿|*BP.*

$$$$ ⊞ **Villa del Sogno.** A narrow winding road takes you from town to this
★ imposing villa, which surveys the valley and the lake below it. The large hotel terrace and the quiet surrounding grounds create a sense of escape. You may think twice about a busy sightseeing itinerary once you've settled into position in the sun, cool drink in hand. **Pros:** endless amenities; individually decorated rooms; expansive terrace overlooking the lake. **Cons:** per-person prices can be confusing. ⊠ *Corso Zanardelli 107* ☎ *0365/290181* ⊕ *www.villadelsogno.it* ⇱ *35 rooms, 5 suites* ♿ *In-room: safe. In-hotel: 2 restaurants, bar, tennis court, pool, spa, room service, laundry service, parking (free)* ⊟ *AE, DC, MC, V* ⊘ *Closed Nov.–Mar.* ⦿|*BP.*

$$$$ ⊞ **Villa Fiordaliso.** The pink-and-white lakeside Villa Fiordaliso—once
★ home to Claretta Petacci, given to her by Benito Mussolini—is a high-quality restaurant, but it also has seven tastefully furnished rooms, some overlooking the lake. The Claretta Suite is where Mussolini and Petacci were said to have carried on an affair. The art nouveau restaurant ($$$–$$$$) features seasonal ingredients such as zucchini flowers and porcini mushrooms, paramount in salads and soups. **Pros:** has the charm of an intimate B&B. **Cons:** short on amenities given the price category. ⊠ *Corso Zanardelli 132* ☎ *0365/20158* ⊕ *www.villafiordaliso.it* ⇱ *6 rooms, 1 suite* ♿ *In-room: safe, refrigerator, Wi-Fi. In-hotel: 2 restaurants, Internet, Wi-Fi hotspot, room service, laundry service, parking (free)* ⊟ *AE, DC, MC, V* ⊘ *Closed Nov.–mid-Mar.* ⦿|*BP.*

¢ ⊞ **Villa Maria Elisabetta.** Many of the rooms in this charming hotel run by a group of hospitable nuns have views of Lago di Garda. You can sit in the hotel's garden or take one of the ground's trails down for a dip in the lake or a bask in the sun. **Pros:** a great bargain for a laid-back stay. **Cons:** no Internet; no a/c; some rooms have no TV. ⊠ *Corso Zanardelli 180* ☎ *0365/20206* ⊕ *www.monasterystays.com* ⇱ *42 rooms* ♿ *In-room: no a/c; TV (some). In-hotel: restaurant, bar, parking (free)* ⊟ *MC, V* ⊘ *Closed Oct. 15–Dec. 15* ⦿|*BP.*

LAKE COMO

If your idea of nirvana is palatial villas, rose-laden belvederes, hanging wisteria and bougainvillea, lanterns casting a glow over lakeshore restaurants, and majestic Alpine vistas, heaven is Lake Como. In his *Charterhouse of Parma*, Stendhal described it as an "enchanting spot, unequaled on earth in its loveliness." Virgil called it simply "our greatest" lake. Though summer crowds threaten to diminish the lake's dreamy mystery and slightly faded old-money gentility, the allure of this spectacular place endures. Como remains a consummate pairing of natural and man-made beauty. The villa gardens, like so many in Italy, are a union of two landscape traditions: that of Renaissance Italy, which values order, and that of Victorian England, which strives to create the illusion of natural wildness. Such gardens are often framed by vast areas of picturesque farmland—fruit trees, olive groves, and vineyards.

9

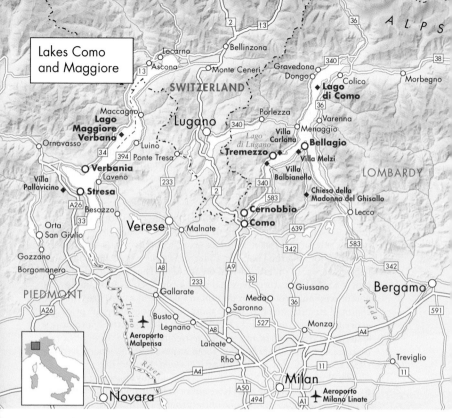

Lake Como is some 47 km (30 mi) long north to south and is Europe's deepest lake (almost 1,350 feet). Como itself is a leading textile center famous for its silks. Many travelers hasten to the vaporetti waiting to take them to Bellagio and the *centro di lago*, the center region of the lake's three branches, and its most beautiful section. The 2,000-year-old walled city of Como should not be missed, however. Car ferries traverse the lake in season, making it easy to get to the other main towns, Cernobbio, Tremezzo, and Varenna. Remember that Como is extremely seasonal: if you go to Bellagio, for example, from November through February, you will find nothing open—not a bar, restaurant, or shop.

GETTING HERE

Trains run regularly from Milan to the town of Como; the trip takes half an hour from the Central Station and an hour from the Cardorna Station. There's also service to the tiny town of Varenna, just across the lake from Bellagio; the trip from Milan takes 1¼ hours. Como is off the A9 autostrada. To get to the town from Milan, take A8 to A9; the drive takes about an hour. Ferries (mainly pedestrian) run regularly from Como and Varenna to different spots around the lake. Schedules can be consulted online at ⊕ *www.navigazionelaghi.it.*

BELLAGIO

Fodor's Choice
★

30 km (19 mi) northeast of Como, 56 km (35 mi) northwest of Bergamo.

VISITOR INFORMATION

Bellagio tourism office (✉ *Piazza Mazzini [Pontile Imbarcadero]* 📠 *031/950204* ⊕ *www.bellagiolakecomo.com*).

EXPLORING

Sometimes called the prettiest town in Europe, Bellagio always seems to be flag-bedecked, with geraniums ablaze in every window and bougainvillea veiling the staircases, or *montées,* that thread through the town. At dusk Bellagio's nightspots—including the wharf, where an orchestra serenades dancers under the stars—beckon you to come and make merry. It's an impossibly enchanting location, one that inspired French composer Gabriel Fauré to call Bellagio "a diamond contrasting brilliantly with the sapphires of the three lakes in which it is set."

Boats ply the lake to Tremezzo, where Napoléon's worst Italian enemy, Count Sommariva, resided at Villa Carlotta; and a bit farther south of Tremezzo, to Villa Balbianello. Check with the tourist office for the hours of the launch to Tremezzo.

★ **Villa Serbelloni,** a property of the Rockefeller Foundation, has celebrated gardens on the site of Pliny the Elder's villa overlooking Bellagio. There are only two 1½-hour-long guided visits per day, restricted to 30 people each, and in May these tend to be commandeered by group bookings. It's wise to arrive early to sign up. ✉ *Near Palazza della Chiesa* 📞 *031/951555* 💶 *€8.50* 🕙 *Guided visits Apr.–early Nov., Tues.–Sun. at 11 and 3:30; tours gather 15 mins before start.*

The famous gardens of the **Villa Melzi** were once a favorite picnic spot for Franz Lizst, who advised author Louis de Ronchaud in 1837: "When you write the story of two happy lovers, place them on the shores of Lake Como. I do not know of any land so conspicuously blessed by heaven." The gardens are open to the public, and though you can't get into the 19th-century villa, don't miss the lavish Empire-style family chapel. The Melzi were Napoléon's greatest allies in Italy (the family has passed down the name "Josephine" to the present day). ✉ *Via Melzi d'Eril 8* 📞 *3394573838* ⊕ *www.giardinidivillamelzi.it* 💶 *€6* 🕙 *Late Mar.–early Nov., daily 9:30–6:30.*

By ferry from Bellagio it's a quick trip across the lake to Varenna. The principal sight here is the spellbinding garden of the **Villa Monastero,** which, as its name suggests, was originally a monastery. Now it's an international science and convention center. Guided tours can be booked. ✉ *Viale Polvani 2, Varenna* 📞 *0341/295450* ⊕ *www. villamonastero.eu* 💶 *Garden €5, house and garden €8* 🕙 *Garden: mid-Mar.–Apr., weekdays 10–5, weekends 10–1 and 2–5; May–Sept., weekdays 9–7, weekends 10–7; Oct. 1–10, weekdays 10–6, weekends 10–1 and 2–6. House museum: mid-Mar.–Apr., weekends 10–1 and 2–5; May–Sept., Fri. 2–7, weekends 10–7; Oct. 1–10, weekends 10–1 and 2–6.*

9

A path in the gardens of Villa Serbelloni.

WHERE TO EAT

$–$$
NORTHERN
ITALIAN

✕ **La Pergola.** Try to reserve a table on the terrace at this popular lakeside restaurant a short walk (with many steps) from central Bellagio on the east side of the peninsula. The food is average, with the best option being the freshly caught fish; the view and the tranquility of the terrace are the main draws. You can also stay in one of the inn's 11 rooms ($$), all of which have baths. ⊠ *Piazza del Porto 4, Pescallo* 🕾 *031/950263* ⊕ *www.lapergolabellagio.it* ⊟ *AE, MC, V* ⊘ *Closed Tues. Mar.–Nov.*

$
NORTHERN
ITALIAN

✕ **Silvio.** At the edge of town, this family-owned trattoria with a lakeshore terrace specializes in fresh fish. Served cooked or marinated, with risotto or as a ravioli stuffing, the lake's bounty is caught by Silvio's family—it's local cooking at its best. There are also 17 modestly priced ($) guest rooms with balconies and lake views. ⊠ *Lòppia di Bellagio, Via Carcano 12* 🕾 *031/950322* ⊕ *www.bellagiosilvio.com* ⊟ *MC, V* ⊘ *Closed Jan. and Feb.*

WHERE TO STAY

$$–$$$

🖭 **Du Lac.** In the center of Bellagio, by the landing dock, this comfortable, medium-size hotel owned by an Anglo-Italian family has a relaxed and congenial feel. Most rooms have views of the lake and mountains, and there's a rooftop terrace garden for drinks or dozing. The hotel offers guests access to the Bellagio Sporting Club with restaurant, pool, and tennis at no charge. **Pros:** complimentary shuttle bus service. **Cons:** some decor a little worn at the edges. ⊠ *Piazza Mazzini 32* 🕾 *031/950320* ⊕ *www.bellagiohoteldulac.com* ⟋ *42 rooms* ⬝ *Inroom: safe. In-hotel: 2 restaurants, bar, Wi-Fi hotspot, parking (paid), some pets allowed* ⊟ *AE, MC, V* ⊘ *Closed Nov.–Mar.* ⍩⎪*BP.*

$$$$ ⊞ **Grand Hotel Villa Serbelloni.** Designed to cradle nobility in high style, this hotel is a refined haven for the discreetly wealthy, set within a pretty park down the road from the Punta di Bellagio. The sense of 19th-century luxury has not so much faded as mellowed: the rooms are immaculate and plush; public areas are gilt and marble with thick, colorful carpets, and breakfast is served inside the ballroom, Salone Reale. The staff is unobtrusive and very knowledgeable about lake transportation. **Pros:** historic lake hotel; great pool. **Cons:** high rates for yesteryear ambience but limited deluxe amenities. ⊠ *Via Roma 1* ☎ *031/950216* ⊕ *www.villaserbelloni.com* ⤴ *95 rooms* ⚇ *In-room: safe, Internet. In-hotel: 2 restaurants, room service, tennis court, pools, gym, spa, laundry service, Internet terminal, Wi-Fi hotspot, parking (free)* ⊟ *AE, DC, MC, V* ⊘ *Closed early Nov.–early Apr.* ⦿*BP.*

$$$–$$$$ ⊞ **Hotel Belvedere.** In Italian, belvedere means "beautiful view," and it's
★ an apt name for this enchanting spot. The hotel has been in the Martinelli-Manoni family since 1880, and the unbroken tradition of service makes it one of the best places to stay in town. Antique furniture and eye-catching rugs complement the modern rooms, many of which have balconies and views of the lake. The marble bathrooms are designed for comfort. Terraced gardens, a lovely pool, and a spa have replaced the vineyards that once surrounded the house. **Pros:** attention to detail; great views. **Cons:** breakfast is only so-so; a climb from the waterfront. ⊠ *Via Valassina 31* ☎ *031/950410* ⊕ *www.belvederebellagio.com* ⤴ *59 rooms, 5 suites* ⚇ *In-room: safe, Internet. In-hotel: restaurant, bar, pool, spa, parking (free), some pets allowed* ⊟ *AE, DC, MC, V* ⊘ *Closed Nov.–Mar.* ⦿*BP.*

$$ ⊞ **Hotel Florence.** This villa dating from the 1880s has an impressive lobby with vaulted ceiling and an imposing Florentine fireplace. Most of the rooms, furnished with interesting antiques, are large and comfortable and have splendid views of the lake. The restaurant and bar draw locals and visitors who appreciate the friendly and helpful staff. The hotel is across from the ferry stop. **Pros:** central location; appealing public spaces. **Cons:** location may feel too central if you're looking to get away from it all. ⊠ *Piazza Mazzini 46* ☎ *031/950342* ⊕ *www.hotelflorencebellagio.it* ⤴ *30 rooms* ⚇ *In-room: safe, Internet, no a/c (some). In-hotel: restaurant, room service, bar, spa, Wi-Fi hotspot* ⊟ *AE, MC, V* ⊘ *Closed Nov.–Mar.* ⦿*MAP.*

9

TREMEZZO

34 km (21 mi) north of Cernobbio, 78 km (48 mi) north of Milan.

VISITOR INFORMATION
Tremezzo tourism office (⊠ Via Regina 3 ☎ 0344/40493 ⊘ *Daily 9–noon and 3:30–6).*

EXPLORING
If you're lucky enough to visit the small lakeside town of Tremezzo in late spring or early summer, you will find the magnificent **Villa Carlotta** a riot of color, with more than 14 acres of azaleas and dozens of varieties of rhododendrons in full bloom. The height of the blossoms is late April to early May. The villa was built between 1690 and 1743

The waterfront promenade of Bellagio.

for the luxury-loving marquis Giorgio Clerici. The garden's collection is remarkable, particularly considering the difficulties of transporting delicate plants before the age of aircraft. Palms, banana trees, cacti, eucalyptus, a sequoia, orchids, and camellias are counted among the more than 500 species.

The villa's interior is worth a visit, particularly if you have a taste for the romantic sculptures of Antonio Canova (1757–1822). The best known is his *Cupid and Psyche*, which depicts the lovers locked in an odd but graceful embrace, with the young god above and behind, his wings extended, while Psyche awaits a kiss that will never come. The villa can be reached by boats from Bellagio and Como. ⊠ *Via Regina 2, Tremezzo* ☎ *0344/40405* ⊕ *www.villacarlotta.it* ✉ *€8.50* ⊙ *Mar. and Nov., daily 10–4; Apr.–Oct., daily 9–6.*

★ **Villa Balbianello** may be the most magical house in all of Italy. It sits on its own little promontory, Il Dosso d'Avedo—separating the bays of Venus and Diana—around the bend from the tiny fishing village of Ossuccio. Relentlessly picturesque, the villa is composed of loggias, terraces, and *palazzini* (tiny palaces), all spilling down verdant slopes to the lakeshore, where you'll find an old Franciscan church, a magnificent stone staircase, and a statue of San Carlo Borromeo blessing the waters. The villa is most frequently reached by launch from Como and Bellagio. Check with the **Como tourism office** (☎ *031/3300128* ⊕ *www.lakecomo.it*) for hours. Visits are usually restricted to the gardens, but if you plan in advance it's also possible to tour the villa itself. You pay €30 for a guide—regardless of how many are in your party—and an additional €5 entrance fee. ⊠ *Il Dosso d'Avedo; ferry* *stop Lenno* ☎ *0344/56110* ⌦ *Gardens €5* ⊗ *Mid-Mar.–mid-Nov., Tues. and Thurs.–Sun. 10–6; last entry to gardens 5:30. Nov. 4–mid-Nov., pedestrian entrance is open Tues. and Thurs.–Sun., otherwise access is only by boat.*

WHERE TO STAY

$$$$ ⌂ **Grand Hotel Tremezzo.** One hundred windows of this turn-of-the-20th-century building face the lake. The hotel, in the middle of a private park stretching over 12½ acres, has many creature comforts, from three heated swimming pools (one of them actually floats on pontoons on the lake) and private landing on the lake to a hillside bursting with flowers. The 18-hole Menaggio & Cadenabbia golf course is about five minutes away by car. **Pros:** lakeside location; beautiful views. **Cons:** not well situated if you're looking for shopping or nightlife. ⌧ *Via Regina 8* ☎ *0344/42491* ⊕ *www.grandhoteltremezzo.com* ⤴ *98 rooms, 2 suites* ⌃ *In-room: safe, Wi-Fi, DVD. In-hotel: 2 restaurants, room service, bars, tennis court, pools, gym, spa, beachfront, Internet terminal, Wi-Fi hotspot, parking (free), some pets allowed* ⊟ *AE, DC, MC, V* ⊗ *Closed mid-Nov.–Feb.* ⓞ *BP.*

$ ⌂ **Rusall.** On the hillside above Tremezzo in the midst of a large garden, this small, reasonably priced hotel offers quiet and privacy. You can lie out on the terrace and enjoy a nice view. Rooms are simple and comfortable. A shuttle for arrival/departure at the Tremezzo ferry stop can be arranged. **Pros:** lovely walks into town and in the countryside; more intimate than grander lake hotels. **Cons:** no pool; takes some effort to reach the hillside location. ⌧ *Via San Martino 2* ☎ *0344/40408* ⊕ *www.rusallhotel.com* ⤴ *23 rooms* ⌃ *In-room: some a/c, Wi-Fi. In-hotel: Wi-Fi hotspot, Internet terminal, restaurant, bar, tennis court* ⊟ *AE, DC, MC, V* ⓞ *EP.*

CERNOBBIO

5 km (3 mi) north of Como, 53 km (34 mi) north of Milan.

VISITOR INFORMATION

Cernobbio tourism office (⌧ *Via Regina 23* ☎ 031/349341).

EXPLORING

The legendary resort of Villa d'Este is reason enough to visit this jewel on the lake, but the town itself is worth a stroll. Despite the fact that George Clooney lunches here regularly, the place still has a neighborhood feel to it, especially on summer evenings and weekends when the piazza is full of families and couples taking their *passeggiata* (stroll).

Built on the site of a former nunnery, Cardinal Tolomeo Gallio's summer residence, **Villa d'Este,** has had a colorful and somewhat checkered history since its completion in 1568, swinging wildly between extremes of grandeur and dereliction. Its tenants have included the Jesuits, two generals, a ballerina, Caroline of Brunswick—the disgraced and estranged wife of the future king of England, George IV—a family of ordinary Italian nobles, and, finally, a czarina of Russia. Its life as a private summer residence ended in 1873, when it was turned into the fashionable hotel it has remained ever since.

WHERE TO EAT AND STAY

$–$$
NORTHERN
ITALIAN

✕ **Il Gatto Nero.** This restaurant in the hills above Cernobbio has a splendid view of the lake. Specialties include *filetto con aceto balsamico* (filet mignon with balsamic vinegar), *pappardelle al ragù di selvaggini* (pasta with wild game sauce), and lake fish. Save room for the warm chocolate torte with its delicious liquid chocolate center. Reservations are encouraged as this is a regular haunt of Italian soccer stars as well as the jet set. ✉ *Via Monte Santo 69, Rovenna* ☎ *031/512042* ⊕ *www. il-gatto-nero.it* ▭ *AE, DC, V* ⊘ *Closed Mon. No lunch Tues.*

$–$$
NORTHERN
ITALIAN, PIZZA

✕ **Il Giardino.** Aptly named "The Garden," this restaurant has an expansive shaded patio that's a welcome respite from the summer sun. With an extensive menu balanced between fish, meat, pizza, and salads, there's something for everyone. You can also stay the night in one of Il Giardino's 12 basic rooms ($). ✉ *Via Regina 73* ☎ *031/511154* ⊕ *www. giardinocernobbio.com* ▭ *AE, DC, V* ⊘ *Closed some days in Nov.*

¢–$
PIZZA

✕ **Pizzeria L'Ancora.** For the best pies in Como, and perhaps in the region, you won't want to miss this local haunt, run by a Neapolitan family that has been making pizza for three generations. Even Italians from out of town rave about the pizza here. Three sisters—Barbara, Grazie, and Linda—dish out hospitality as fine as the food. ✉ *Via Conciliazione 11, Tavernola* ☎ *031/340769* ▭ *No credit cards* ⊘ *Closed Wed.*

$$$$
Fodor's Choice
★

▥ **Villa d'Este.** One of the grandest hotels in Italy, the 16th-century Villa d'Este has long welcomed Europe's rich and famous, from Napoléon to the Duchess of Windsor. The chandeliers in the vast lobby illuminate marble staircases leading to guest rooms furnished in the Empire style: walnut paneling, sofas in striped silk, and gorgeous antiques. A broad veranda sweeps out to the lakefront, where a swimming pool extends above the water. The fanciful pavilions, temples, miniature forts, and mock ruins make for an afternoon's walk of whimsical surprises. **Pros:** fine service; world-renowned clientele. **Cons:** may seem too formal to some. ✉ *Via Regina 40* ☎ *031/3481* ⊕ *www.villadeste.it* ⟿ *152 rooms 7 suites, 2 private villas* ⚭ *In-room: safe, Internet. In-hotel: 2 restaurants, bar, room service, tennis courts, pools, laundry service, Wi-Fi hotspot, parking (free), some pets allowed* ▭ *AE, MC, V* ⊘ *Closed mid-Nov.–Feb.* ⬤| *FAP.*

COMO

5 km (3 mi) south of Cernobbio, 30 km (19 mi) southwest of Bellagio, 49 km (30 mi) north of Milan.

VISITOR INFORMATION

Como tourism office (✉ *Piazza Cavour 17* ☎ *031/269712* ⊕ *www.lakecomo.com* ⊘ *Mon.–Sat. 9–1 and 2:30–6* ✉ *Via Maestri Cumacini* ☎ *031/264215* ⊘ *Tues.–Fri. 10:30–12:30 and 2:30–6, weekends 10–8* ✉ *Piazza Matteotti* ☎ *0313/300128* ⊘ *Feb.–Dec., weekdays 10:30–12:30 and 2:30–6, weekends 10–6).*

EXPLORING

Como, on the south shore of the lake, is only part elegant resort, where cobbled pedestrian streets wind their way past parks and bustling cafés. The other part is an industrial town renowned for its fine silks. If you're

DID YOU KNOW?

Como, fed by runoff from the surrounding mountains, is the deepest lake in Europe.

traveling by car, leave it at the edge of the town center in the clean, well-lighted underground parking facility right on the lake.

The splendid 15th-century Renaissance-Gothic **Duomo** was begun in 1396. The facade was added in 1455, and the transepts were completed in the mid-18th century. The dome was designed by Filippo Juvara (1678–1736), chief architect of many of the sumptuous palaces of the royal house of Savoy. The facade has statues of two of Como's most famous sons, Pliny the Elder and Pliny the Younger, whose writings are among the most important documents from antiquity. Inside, the works of art include Luini's *Holy Conversation*, a fresco cycle by Morazzone, and the *Marriage of the Virgin Mary* by Ferrari. ⊠ *Piazza del Duomo* ☎ *031/265244* ⊗ *Daily 8–noon and 3–7.*

At the heart of Como's medieval quarter, the city's first cathedral, **San Fedele**, is worth a peek, if only because it is one of the oldest churches in the region. The apse walls and ceiling are completely frescoed as are the ceilings above the altar. ⊠ *Piazza San Fedele* ☎ *031/272334* ⊗ *Daily 7–noon and 3–7.*

If you brave Como's industrial quarter, you will find the beautiful church of **Sant'Abbondio**, a gem of Romanesque architecture begun by Benedictine monks in 1013 and consecrated by Pope Urban II in 1095. Inside, the five aisles of the church converge on a presbytery with a semicircular apse decorated with a cycle of 14th-century frescoes—now restored to their original magnificence—by Lombard artists heavily influenced by the Sienese school. To see them, turn right as you enter and put €0.50 in the mechanical box for a few minutes of lighting. In the nave, the cubical capitals are the earliest example of this style in Italy. ⊠ *Via Sant'Abbondio* ⊗ *Daily 8–5.*

Exhibiting the path of production from silkworm litters to moire-finishing machinery, the **Museo Didattico della Seta** *(Silk Museum)* is small but complete. The museum preserves the history of a manufacturing region that continues to supply almost three-fourths of Europe's silk. The friendly staffers will give you an overview of the museum; they are also happy to provide brochures and information about local retail shops. The museum's location isn't well marked: follow the textile school's driveway around to the low-rise concrete building on the left, and follow the shallow ramp down to the entrance. ⊠ *Via Castelnuovo 9* ☎ *031/303180* ⊕ *www.museosetacomo.com* ⊡ *€8* ⊗ *Tues.–Fri. 9–noon and 3–6. Guided tours, booked in advance, Mon. and weekends.*

WHERE TO STAY

$$–$$$ ⊡ **Terminus.** Commanding a panoramic view over Lake Como, this early-20th-century art nouveau building is the city's best hotel. The marbled public spaces have an understated elegance, and the guest rooms are done in floral patterns and furnished with large walnut wardrobes and silk-covered sofas. The 14 rooms added in 2007 are worth requesting—they're bright and fresh, while the remainder can feel dated by comparison. In summer the garden terrace is perfect for relaxing over a drink. Bar delle Terme ($), the candlelit restaurant (closed Tuesday), is worth a trip. The cranberry-hue space, filled with plush velvet sofas, resembles a large living room. The food and service are as fine as the

decor. Reservations are strongly advised, as there are only a few tables. **Pros:** old-world charm; right on the lake. **Cons:** limited number of rooms with lake views; decor in some rooms seems dated. ⊠ *Lungolario Trieste 14* ☎ *031/329111* ⊕ *www.albergoterminus.com* ⤳ *50 rooms* ♿ *In-room: safe, Internet, Wi-Fi. In-hotel: restaurant, room service, bar, gym, bicycles, laundry service, Wi-Fi hotspot, parking (paid), some pets allowed* ▭ *AE, DC, MC, V* ℃| *BP.*

$–$$ 🏠 **Tre Re.** This clean, spacious, welcoming hotel is a few steps west of the cathedral and convenient to the lake. Although the exterior gives away the age of this 16th-century former convent, the rooms are airy, comfortable, and modern. The moderately priced restaurant offers lunch and dinner. **Pros:** friendly staff; homey atmosphere. **Cons:** rooms are functional, not elegant—decor is spartan. ⊠ *Via Boldoni 20* ☎ *031/265374* ⊕ *www.hoteltrere.com* ⤳ *48 rooms* ♿ *In-room: Wi-Fi (some). In-hotel: Wi-Fi hotspot, Internet terminal, restaurant, bar, parking (free)* ▭ *MC, V* ☾ *Closed mid-Dec.–mid-Jan.* ℃| *BP.*

SPORTS AND THE OUTDOORS

Lake Como has many opportunities for sports enthusiasts, from windsurfing at the lake's northern end, to boating, sailing, and jet skiing at Como and Cernobbio. The lake is also quite swimmable in the summer months. For hikers there are lovely paths all around the lake. For an easy trek, take the funicular up to Brunate, and walk along the mountain to the lighthouse for a stunning view of the lake.

LAKE MAGGIORE

Magnificently scenic, Lake Maggiore has a unique geographical position: its mountainous western shore is in Piedmont, its lower eastern shore is in Lombardy, and its northern tip is in Switzerland. The lake stretches nearly 50 km (30 mi) and is up to 5 km (3 mi) wide. The better-known resorts are on the western shore.

GETTING HERE

Trains run regularly from Milan to the town of Stresa on Lake Maggiore; the trip takes from 1 to 1½ hours, depending on the type of train. By car from Milan to Stresa, take the A8 autostrada to A8dir, and from A8dir take A26; the drive is about 1¼ hours.

STRESA AND THE ISOLE BORROMEE

80 km (50 mi) northwest of Milan.

VISITOR INFORMATION

Stresa tourism office (⊠ *Piazza Marconi 16* ☎ *0323/30150* ⊕ *www. distrettolaghi.it or www.stresaturismo.it* ☾ *Weekdays 10–12:30 and 3–6:30, weekends 10–12:30.*

EXPLORING

One of the better-known resorts on the western shore, Stresa is a tourist town that provided one of the settings for Hemingway's *A Farewell to Arms*. It has capitalized on its central lakeside position and has to some extent become a victim of its own success. The luxurious elegance that distinguished its heyday has faded; the grand hotels are still grand, but traffic now encroaches upon their parks and gardens. Even the undeniable loveliness of the lakeshore drive has been threatened by the roar of diesel trucks and BMW traffic. The best way to escape is to head for the Isole Borromee (Borromean Islands) in Lake Maggiore. For amazing views, take the Funivia (⊕ *www.stresa-mottarone.it*), a cable car that takes you to heights from which you can see all seven lakes.

As you wander around the palms and semitropical shrubs of **Villa Pallavicino**, don't be surprised if you're followed by a peacock or even an ostrich: they're part of the zoological garden and are allowed to roam almost at will. From the top of the hill on which the villa stands you can see the gentle hills of the Lombardy shore of Lake Maggiore and, nearer and to the left, the jewel-like Borromean Islands. In addition to a bar and restaurant, the grounds also have picnic spots. ⊠ *Via Sempione 8* ☎ *0323/31533* ⊕ *www.parcozoopallavicino.it* ⬚ *€9* ⊙ *Early Mar.–Oct., daily 9–6.*

Boats to the **Isole Borromee** (⊕ *www.borromeoturismo.it*) depart every 15 to 30 minutes from the dock at Stresa's Piazza Marconi, as well as from Piazzale Lido at the northern end of the promenade. There is also a boat from Verbania; check locally for the seasonal schedule. Although you can hire a private boatman, it's cheaper and just as convenient to use the regular service. Make sure you buy a ticket allowing you to visit all the islands—Bella, Dei Pescatori, and Madre. The islands take their name from the Borromeo family, which has owned them since the 12th century.

Isola Bella *(Beautiful Island)* is the most famous of the three, and the first that you'll visit. It is named after Isabella, whose husband, Carlo III Borromeo (1538–84), built the palace and terraced gardens for her as a wedding present. Before Count Carlo began his project, the island was rocky and almost devoid of vegetation; the soil for the garden had to be transported from the mainland. Wander up the 10 terraces of the gardens, where peacocks roam among the scented shrubs, statues, and fountains, for a splendid view of the lake. Visit the palazzo to see the rooms where famous guests—including Napoléon and Mussolini—stayed in 18th-century splendor. Those three interlocked rings on walls and even streets represent the powerful Borromeo, Visconti, and Sforza families. ☎ *0323/30556* ⬚ *Garden and palazzo €12* ⊙ *Mid-Mar.–mid-Oct., daily 9–5:30. Painting gallery: daily 9–1 and 1:30–5.*

Stop for a while at the tiny **Isola dei Pescatori** *(Island of the Fishermen,* also known as Isola Superiore), less than 100 yards wide and only about ½ km (¼ mi) long. It's the perfect place for a seafood lunch before, after, or in between your visit to the other two islands. Of the 10 or so restaurants on this tiny island, the three worth visiting are **Ristorante Unione** (☎ *0323/933798*), **Ristorante Verbano** (☎ *0323/30408*), and **Ristorante Belvedere** (☎ *0323/32292*). The island's little lanes strung with fishing nets and dotted with shrines to the Madonna are the definition of picturesque; little wonder that in high season the village is crowded with postcard stands.

Isola Madre *(Mother Island)* is nicknamed the "Botanical Island." The entire island is a botanical garden, whose season stretches from late March to late October due to the climatic protection of the mighty Alps and the tepid waters of Lago Maggiore. The vision of cacti and palm trees on Isola Madre, its position so far north and so near the border of Switzerland, is a beautiful and unexpected surprise. Take time to see the profusion of exotic trees and shrubs running down to the shore in every direction. Two special times to visit are April (for the camellias) and May (for azaleas and rhododendrons). Also on the island is a 16th-century palazzo, where the Borromeo family still resides at different times throughout the year and where an antique puppet theater is on display, complete with string puppets, prompt books, and elaborate scenery designed by Alessandro Sanquirico, who was a scenographer at La Scala in Milan. ☎ *0323/31261* 💶 *€10* 🕙 *Late Mar.–Oct., daily 9–5:30.*

For more information about the islands, contact the tourism office or ask at the docks (look for Navigazione Lago Maggiore signs).

WHERE TO EAT AND STAY

$ ✕ **Da Cesare.** Off Piazza Cadorna and close to the embarcadero, this res-
PIEDMONTESE taurant serves tasty risotto *con filetti di persico* (with perch fillets) and typical Piedmontese meat dishes, such as beef braised in Barolo wine. Da Cesare also has hotel rooms ($). ✉ *Via Mazzini 14* ☎ *0323/31386* ⊕ *www.dacesare.com* ▭ *AE, DC, MC, V.*

$$$-$$$$ 🏨 **Grand Hotel des Iles Borromees.** This palatial, Liberty-style establishment has catered to a demanding European clientele since 1863. It still has the spacious salons and lavish furnishings of the turn of the 20th century, but there are signs of modernity as well, including a redesigned bar, a low-calorie menu at the restaurant, and extensive wellness treatments. The views and lakeside grounds are first-rate. **Pros:** the grace and style of a bygone era, with modern amenities. **Cons:** some might consider it isolated. ✉ *Corso Umberto I 67* ☎ *0323/938938* ⊕ *www. borromees.it* ⤙ *179 rooms, 11 suites* ⟁ *In-room: a/c, safe, Internet. In-hotel: restaurant, room service, bar, tennis court, pools, spa, laundry service, Wi-Fi hotspot, parking (free)* ▭ *AE, DC, MC, V* ⦿ *BP.*

$ 🏨 **Primavera.** A few blocks up from the lake, Primavera has compact, simply furnished rooms in a 1950s building hung with flower boxes. Most rooms have balconies overlooking the streets of Stresa's old center. **Pros:** good value; convenient location. **Cons:** no lake views; small, plainly furnished rooms. ✉ *Via Cavour 39* ☎ *0323/31286* ⊕ *www. hotelprimaverastresa.com* ⤙ *37 rooms* ⟁ *In-room: Wi-Fi, safe, refrigerator. In-hotel: bar, Internet terminal, parking (paid)* ▭ *AE, DC, MC, V* 🕙 *Closed mid-Nov.–mid-Mar.* ⦿ *BP.*

VERBANIA

16 km (10 mi) north of Stresa, 95 km (59 mi) northwest of Milan.

EXPLORING

Quaint Verbania is across the Gulf of Pallanza from its touristy neighbor Stresa. It is known for the **Villa Taranto**, which has magnificent botanical gardens. The villa was acquired in 1931 by Scottish captain

Neil McEachern, who expanded the gardens considerably, adding terraces, waterfalls, more than 3,000 plant species from all over the world, and broad meadows sloping gently to the lake. In 1938 McEachern donated the entire complex to the Italian people. ⊠ *Via Vittorio Veneto 111* ☎ *0323/404555* ⊕ *www.villataranto.it* ☒ *€9* ☉ *Late Mar.–Oct., daily 8:30–6:30; last entry 1 hr before closing.*

WHERE TO STAY

$ 📺 **Il Chiostro**. Originally a 17th-century convent, this hotel expanded into the adjoining 19th-century textile factory, adding some conference facilities. Rooms are very clean and functional. The rooms overlooking the *chiostro* offer a garden view, and the children's play area is on the other side of the hotel. Local residents are lunchtime regulars at the in-house restaurant, set in a simple room with attentive service, good value, and an emphasis on regional cuisine. Half- and full-board rates are available. **Pros:** friendly and efficient staff. **Cons:** rooms are fairly plain. ⊠ *Via Fratelli Cervi 14* ☎ *0323/404077* ⊕ *www.chiostrovb. it* ⊑ *100 rooms* ♦ *In-room: Internet, Wi-Fi. In-hotel: restaurant, bar, Internet terminal, Wi-Fi hotspot* ⊟ *AE, DC, MC, V* ❙⃝❙ *BP.*

$$$ 📺 **Il Sole di Ranco**. The same family has run this elegant lakeside inn,
Fodor's Choice   perched high on the banks of the lake opposite and below Stresa, for
★   more than 150 years. The latest addition is a stunning pool with views of the lake. The chefs, Davide Brovelli and his father, Carlo, do the family proud with their exceptional restaurant ($$–$$$). Lake trout and perch find their way onto the menu, as do artichoke dishes in spring and eggplant in summer. Guest rooms and suites are in two late-19th-century villas surrounded by a garden and overlooking the lake. Restaurant reservations are essential. **Pros:** classic lake setting; tranquil grounds, meticulously maintained. **Cons:** a bit distant from lake's tourist center (although hotel offers excursions with private driver). ⊠ *Piazza Venezia 5, Ranco* ✛ *near Angera* ☎ *0331/976507* ⊕ *www.ilsolediranco.it* ⊑ *2 rooms, 10 suites* ♦ *In-room: safe, a/c, Wi-Fi. In-hotel: restaurant, pool, laundry service, parking (free)* ⊟ *AE, DC, MC, V* ☉ *Closed Nov. 15–Jan. 21. Restaurant closed Tues. No lunch Mon.* ❙⃝❙ *BP.*

Piedmont and Valle d'Aosta

WORD OF MOUTH

"Piemonte is an absolutely gorgeous area, and each town is cuter than the next. The food is fantastic, has a bit of a French influence (while still being Italian) and it's very easy to go over the top in terms of consumption!"

—Lexma90

WELCOME TO PIEDMONT AND VALLE D'AOSTA

Landscape, Langhe

TOP REASONS TO GO

★ **Sacra di San Michele:** Explore one of the country's most spectacularly situated religious buildings.

★ **Castello Fénis:** This castle transports you back in time to the Middle Ages.

★ **Monte Bianco:** The cable car ride over the snowcapped mountain will take your breath away.

★ **Turin's Museo Egizio:** A surprising treasure—one of the world's richest collections of Egyptian art outside Cairo.

★ **Regal wines:** Some of Italy's most revered reds—led by Barolo, dubbed "the king wines"—come from the hills of southern Piedmont.

1 **Turin.** The region's main city isn't just the car capital of Italy and home to the Holy Shroud. Neoclassical piazzas, shops filled with chocolates and chic fashions, and elegant baroque palazzos have been restored in grand style.

2 **The Colline.** Gracing the "little hills" west of Turin are some opulent monuments of the 17th-century Piedmontese style, including the palace at Venaria Reale, designed by for the Savoy kings in the 16th and 17th centuries. Less worldly is the mesmerizingly medieval hilltop monastery of Sacra di San Michele.

3 **Monferrato and the Langhe.** These hills are famous among food and wine connoisseurs. Asti gave the world Asti Spumante, Alba is known for its truffles and mushrooms, and the Langhe hills produce some of Italy's finest wines.

4 **Valle d'Aosta.** The mountains and valleys of this region fairly cry out to be strolled, climbed, and skied. Here, the highest Alpine peaks—including Monte Bianco (aka Mont Blanc) and the Matterhorn—shelter resorts such as Breuil-Cervinia and Courmayeur and the great nature preserve known as the Gran Paradiso.

Castello Fénis

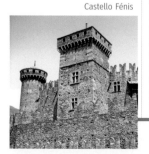

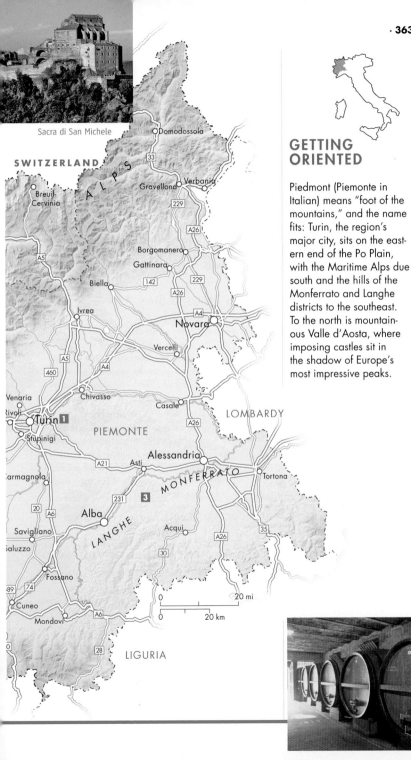

Sacra di San Michele

GETTING ORIENTED

Piedmont (Piemonte in Italian) means "foot of the mountains," and the name fits: Turin, the region's major city, sits on the eastern end of the Po Plain, with the Maritime Alps due south and the hills of the Monferrato and Langhe districts to the southeast. To the north is mountainous Valle d'Aosta, where imposing castles sit in the shadow of Europe's most impressive peaks.

SWITZERLAND

Domodossola

Breuil-
Cervinia

Gravellona

Verbania

Borgomanero

Gattinara

Biella

Ivrea

Novara

Vercelli

Venaria

Chivasso

Casale

LOMBARDY

Rivoli

Turin **1**

PIEMONTE

Stupinigi

Carmagnola

Asti

Alessandria

Tortona

3

MONFERRATO

Alba

Acqui

LANGHE

Savigliano

Saluzzo

Fossano

Cuneo

Mondovi

LIGURIA

0   20 mi

0   20 km

10

PIEDMONT AND VALLE D'AOSTA PLANNER

Making the Most of Your Time

Turin, the first capital of unified Italy and the fourth largest city in the country, is a commercial center once overlooked on tourist itineraries. But after hosting the Winter in Olympics in 2006, and getting a further polish for the 2011 celebration of the 150th anniversary of Italian unification, Turin is on the radar. There is good cause: the museum system is second to none, gourmet restaurants abound, the nightlife is hopping, and there are an unusual number of attractions for children. If you also like the idea of an Italian city with touches of Parisian sophistication, Turin will strike your fancy.

In the mountains that surround Turin the hiking, climbing, and skiing are exceptional. On the Piedmont–Valle d'Aosta border, the Gran Paradiso National Park has beautiful trails. Farther north is Monte Bianco, which should be a priority; you can ascend by cable car, or, if you're an experienced climber, make a go of it with professional guides. You'll find extensive ski slopes in Sestriere in Piedmont and in Breuil-Cervinia on the Matterhorn. Food and wine lovers should head for the hills of the Langhe, just south of Turin, home to world-class wines and the redolent white truffles.

The French Connection

Napoléon's regime controlled Piedmont and Valle d'Aosta in the 19th century, and French influence remains evident in everything from traditional recipes redolent of mountain cheeses, truffles, and cream to Versailles-style gardens and wide, tree-lined boulevards. Well-dressed women in the cafés of Turin are addressed more often as *madama* than *signora,* and French is often spoken in the more-remote mountain hamlets.

Finding a Place to Stay

High standards and opulence are characteristic of Turin's better hotels, and the same is true, translated into the Alpine idiom, at the top mountain resorts. Hotels in Turin and other major towns are generally geared to business travelers; make sure to ask whether lower weekend rates or special deals for two- or three-night stays are available.

Summer vacationers and winter skiers keep occupancy rates and prices high at the resorts during peak seasons. Many mountain hotels accept half- or full-board guests only and require that you stay for several nights; some have off-season rates that can reduce the cost by a full price category. If you're planning to ski, ask about package deals that give you a discount on lift tickets.

WHAT IT COSTS (IN EUROS)

	¢	$	$$	$$$	$$$$
Restaurants	under €20	€20–€30	€30–€45	€45–€65	over €65
Hotels	under €75	€75–€125	€125–€200	€200–€300	over €300

Restaurant prices are for a first course (primo), second course (secondo), and dessert (dolce). Hotel prices are for two people in a standard double room in high season, including tax and service.

Getting Around by Car

Like any rugged, mountainous region, the Italian Alps can be tricky to navigate by car. Roads that look like super-highways on the map can be narrow and twisting, with steep slopes and cliff-side drops. Generally, roads are well maintained, but the sheer distance covered by all of those curves tends to take longer than you might expect, so it's best to figure in extra time for getting around. This is especially true in winter, when weather conditions can cause slow traffic and road closings. Check with local tourist offices or, in a pinch, with the police, to make sure roads are passable and safe, and to find out whether you may need tire chains for snowy and icy roads.

For travel across the French, Swiss, and Italian borders in Piedmont and Valle d'Aosta, only a few routes are usable year-round: the 12-km (7-mi) Mont Blanc tunnel connecting Chamonix with Courmayeur; the Colle del Gran San Bernardo/Col du Grand St. Bernard (connecting Martigny with Aosta on Swiss highway E27 and Italian highway SS27, with 6 km [4 mi] of tunnel); and the Traforo del Fréjus (between Modane and Susa, with 13 km [8 mi] of tunnel). There are other passes, but they become increasingly unreliable between November and April.

Getting Around by Bus

Turin's main bus station is on the corner of Corso Inghilterra and Corso Vittorio Emanuele. Urban buses, trams, and the subway are operated by the agency **GTT** (☎ 800/019152 ⊕ www.comune.torino.it/gtt). Turin-based bus line **SADEM** (☎ 800/801600 ⊕ www.sadem.it) provides service throughout Piedmont and Valle d'Aosta. Aosta-based **SAVDA** (☎ 0165/262027 ⊕ www.savda.it) specializes in mountain service, providing frequent links between Aosta, Turin, and Courmayeur as well as Milan. There's also a major bus station at Aosta, across the street from the train station.

Getting Around by Train

Turin is on the main Paris–Rome TGV express line and is also connected with Milan, only 90 minutes away on the fast train. The fastest (Frecciarossa) trains cover the 667-km (414-mi) trip to Rome in just over four hours; other trains take between five and seven hours.

Services to the larger cities east of Turin are part of the extensive and reliable train network of the Lombard Plain. West of the region's capital, however, the train services soon peter out in the mountains. Continuing connections by bus serve these valleys; information about train-bus mountain services can be obtained from train stations and tourist information offices, or by contacting **FS–Trenitalia** (☎ 892021 ⊕ www. trenitalia.com), the Italian national train service.

10

EATING AND DRINKING WELL IN PIEDMONT AND VALLE D'AOSTA

In Piedmont and Valle d'Aosta you can find rustic specialties from farmhouse hearths, fine cuisine with a French accent, and everything in between. The Piedmontese take their food and wine very seriously.

There is a significant concentration of upscale restaurants in Piedmont, with refined cuisine designed to showcase the region's fine wines. Wine-oriented menus are prevalent both in cities and in the country, where even simply named trattorias may offer a *menu di degustazione* (a multicourse tasting menu) accompanied by wines paired to each dish.

In Turin the ritual of the *aperitivo* (aperitif) has been finely tuned, and most cafés from the early evening onward provide lavish buffets that are included in the price of a cocktail—a respectable substitute for dinner if you are traveling on a limited budget. As a result, restaurants in Turin tend to fill only after 9 PM.

GREAT GRISSINI

Throughout the region, though especially in Turin, you will find that most meals are accompanied by *grissini* (bread sticks), pictured above.

Invented in Turin in the 17th century to ease the digestive problems of little Prince Vittorio Amedeo II (1675–1730), these, when freshly made and hand-rolled, are a far cry from the thin and dry, plastic-wrapped versions available elsewhere.

Napoléon called them *petits batons* and was, according to legend, addicted to them.

TRUFFLES

The truffle (*tartufo* in Italian) is a peculiar delicacy—a gnarly clump of fungus that grows wild in forests a few inches underground. It's hunted down using truffle-sniffing dogs and can sell for a small fortune. The payoff is a powerful, perfume flavor that makes gourmets swoon. Though truffles are more abundant farther south in Umbria, the most coveted ones are the *tartufi bianchi* (white truffles), pictured at right, from Alba in Piedmont. A thin shaving of truffle often tops pasta dishes; they're also used to flavor soups and other dishes.

POLENTA AND PASTA

The area's best-known dish is probably polenta, creamy cornmeal served with *carbonada* (a meat stew), melted cheese, or wild mushrooms. *Agnolotti*—crescent-shaped pasta stuffed with meat filling, pictured below—is another specialty, often served with the pan juices of roast veal. *Agnolotti del Plin* is a smaller version topped with melted butter and shaved truffles.

CHEESE

In keeping with their northern character, a regional specialty in both Piedmont and Valle d'Aosta is *fonduta*, a version of fondue made with melted cheese, eggs, and sometimes grated truffles. Fontina and ham also often deck out

the ubiquitous French-style crepes *alla valdostana*, served casserole style.

MEAT

The locally raised beef of Piedmont is some of Italy's most highly prized; it's often braised or stewed with the region's hearty red wine. In winter, *bollito misto* (various meats, boiled and served with a rich sauce) shows up on many menus, and *fritto misto*, a combination of fried meats and vegetables, is another specialty.

DESSERTS AND SWEETS

Though desserts here are less sweet than in some other Italian regions, treats like *panna cotta* (a cooked milk custard), *torta di nocciole* (hazelnut torte), and *bonet* (a pudding made with hazelnuts, cocoa, milk, and macaroons) are delights. Turin is renowned for its delicate pastries and fine chocolates, especially for *gianduiotti*, made with hazelnuts.

WINE

Piedmont is one of Italy's most important wine regions, producing full-bodied reds, such as Barolo, Barbaresco, Freisa, Barbera, and the lighter Dolcetto. Asti Spumante, a sweet sparkling wine, comes from the region, while Valle d'Aosta is famous for schnapps-like brandies made from fruits or herbs.

10

Updated
by Peter
Blackman

A pair of contrasting characteristics define the appeal of northwest Italy's Piedmont and Valle d'Aosta regions: mountain splendor and bourgeois refinement. Two of Europe's most famous peaks—Monte Bianco (aka Mont Blanc) and Monte Cervino (the Matterhorn)—straddle Valle d'Aosta's borders with France and Switzerland, and the entire region is a magnet for skiers and hikers.

To the south, the mist-shrouded lowlands skirting the Po River are home to Turin, a city that may not have the artistic treasures of Rome or the cutting-edge style of Milan, but has developed a sense of urban sophistication that makes it a pleasure to visit. You also taste a mountain/city contrast in the cuisine: the hearty peasant cooking served in tiny stone villages and the French-accented delicacies found in the plain are both eminently satisfying. Meals are accompanied by Piedmontese wines commonly held to be Italy's finest.

TURIN

Turin—Torino, in Italian—is roughly in the center of Piedmont/Valle d'Aosta and 128 km (80 mi) west of Milan; it's on the Po River, on the edge of the Po Plain, which stretches eastward all the way to the Adriatic. Turin's flatness and wide, angular, tree-lined boulevards are a far cry from Italian *metropoli* to the south; the region's decidedly northern European bent is quite evident in its nerve center. Apart from its role as northwest Italy's major industrial, cultural, intellectual, and administrative hub, Turin also has a reputation as Italy's capital of black magic and the supernatural. This distinction is enhanced by the presence of Turin's most famous, and controversial, relic, the Sacra Sindone (Holy Shroud), still believed by many Catholics to be the cloth in which Christ's body was wrapped when he was taken down from the cross.

GETTING HERE

Turin is well served by the Italian highway system and can be reached easily by car from all directions: from Milan on the A4 highway (two hours); from Bologna (four hours) and Florence (five hours) on the A1 and A21 highways; from Genoa on the A6 highway (two hours).

Bus service to and from other major Italian cities is also plentiful, and Turin can be reached by fast train service from Paris in less than six hours. Fast train service also connects the city with Milan, Genova, Bologna, Florence, and Rome.

VISITOR INFORMATION

Turin's group and personally guided tours are organized by the city's tourist office. They also provide maps and details about a wide range of thematic self-guided walks through town. The Torino+Piemonte card, which provides discounts on transportation and museum entrances for two-, three-, five-, or seven-day visits can be purchased here, as well as Turin's unique Chocopass, which allows you to indulge in 10 tastings in as many chocolate shops.

Turin tourism office (✉ *Piazza Castello* ☏ *011/535181* ⊕ *www.turismotorino.org*).

DOWNTOWN TURIN

Many of Turin's major sights are clustered around Piazza Castello, and others are on or just off the portico-lined Via Roma, one of the city's main thoroughfares, which leads 1 km (½ mi) from Piazza Castello south to Piazza Carlo Felice, a landscaped park in front of the train station. First opened in 1615, Via Roma was largely rebuilt in the 1930s, during the Mussolini era.

TOP ATTRACTIONS

Duomo di San Giovanni. The most impressive part of Turin's 15th-century cathedral is the shadowy black marble–walled **Cappella della Sacra Sindone** (Chapel of the Holy Shroud), where the famous relic was housed before a fire in 1997. The chapel was designed by the priest and architect Guarino Guarini (1604–83), a genius of the baroque style who was official engineer and mathematician to the court of Duke Carlo Emanuele II of Savoy. The fire caused severe structural damage, and the chapel is closed indefinitely while restoration work proceeds.

10

The Sacra Sindone is a 4-yard-long sheet of linen, thought by millions to be the burial shroud of Christ, bearing the light imprint of his crucified body. The shroud first made an appearance around the middle of the 15th century, when it was presented to Ludovico of Savoy in Chambéry. In 1578 it was brought to Turin by another member of the Savoy royal family, Duke Emanuele Filiberto. It was only in the 1990s that the Catholic Church began allowing rigorous scientific study of the shroud. Not surprisingly, results have bolstered both sides of the argument. On the one hand, three separate university teams—in Switzerland, Britain, and the United States—have concluded, as a result of carbon 14 dating, that the cloth is a forgery dating from between 1260 and 1390. On the other hand, they are unable to explain how medieval forgers could have created the shroud's image, which resembles a

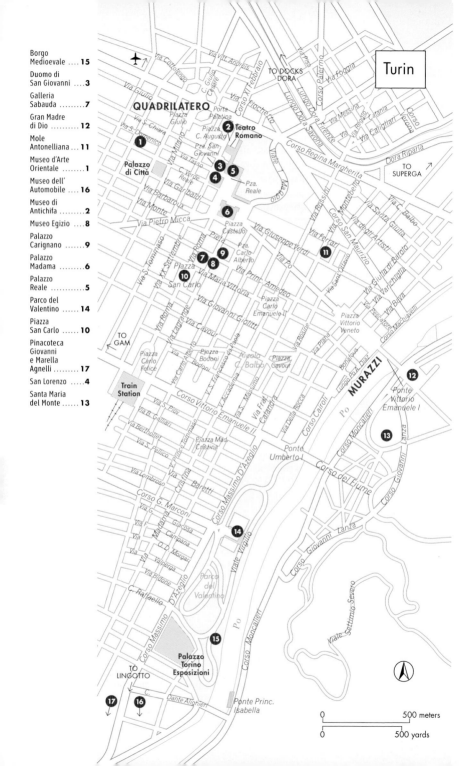

Turin

QUADRILATERO

MURAZZI

TO DOCKS
DORA

TO
SUPERGA

TO
SUPERGA

Palazzo
di Città

Teatro
Romano

Porta
Palatina

Piazza
Giulio

Piazza
C. Augusto

Pza. San
Giovanni

Pza.
Reale

Piazza
Castello

Pza.
Carlo
Alberto

Piazza
San Carlo

Piazza
Carlo
Emanuele II

Piazza
Vittorio
Veneto

Piazza
Bodoni

Piazza
Cavour

Piazza
Carlo
Felice

Piazza Mad.
Cristina

Train
Station

TO
GAM

Parco
del
Valentino

Palazzo
Torino
Esposizioni

TO
LINGOTTO

Ponte
Vittorio
Emanuele I

Ponte
Umberto I

Ponte Princ.
Isabella

Dora Riparia

Po

Corso Regina Margherita

Corso Vittorio Emanuele II

Corso del Fiume

Corso Moncalieri

0   500 meters

0   500 yards

NORTHWEST ITALY, PAST AND PRESENT

Ancient history. Piedmont and Valle d'Aosta were originally inhabited by Celtic tribes, who over time were absorbed by the conquering Romans. As allies of Rome, the Celts held off Hannibal when he came down through the Alpine passes with his elephants, but they were eventually defeated, and their capital—Taurasia, the present Turin—was destroyed. The Romans rebuilt the city, giving its streets the grid pattern that survives today. (Roman ruins can be found throughout both regions and are particularly conspicuous in the town of Aosta.)

The Middle Ages and the Savoy. With the fall of the Roman Empire, the region suffered the fate of the rest of Italy and was successively occupied and ravaged by barbarians from the east and the north. In the 11th century, the feudal French Savoy family ruled Turin briefly; toward the end of the 13th century it returned to the area, where it would remain, almost continuously, for 500 years. In 1798 the French republican armies invaded Italy, but when Napoléon's empire fell, the house of Savoy returned to power.

Risorgimento. Beginning in 1848, Piedmont was one of the principal centers of the Risorgimento, the movement for Italian unity. In 1861 the Chamber of Deputies of Turin declared Italy a united kingdom, with Turin as the new nation's capital. The capital moved to Florence in 1865, and then to Rome in 1870, effectively marking the end of Piedmont's prominence in national politics.

Industry and affluence. Piedmont became one of the first industrialized regions in Italy, and the automotive giant FIAT—the Fabbrica Italiana Automobili Torino—was established here in 1899. Today the region is the center of Italy's automobile, metalworking, chemical, and candy industries, having attracted thousands of workers from Italy's south. The FIAT company, led by the Agnelli family—roughly Italy's equivalent of the Kennedys—has been arguably the most important factor in the region's rise to affluence.

photographic negative, and how they could have had the knowledge or means to incorporate traces of Roman coins covering the eyelids and endemic Middle Eastern pollen woven into the cloth. Either way, the shroud continues to be revered as a holy relic, exhibited to the public on very rare occasions—the next official display is planned for 2025. In lieu of the real thing, a photocopy is on permanent display near the altar of the Duomo. ⊠ *Piazza San Giovanni, Centro* ☏ *011/4361540* ⊗ *Mon.–Sat. 6:30–noon and 3–7, Sun. 8–noon and 3–7.*

Galleria Sabauda. Some of the most important paintings from the vast collections of the house of Savoy are displayed here. The collection is particularly rich in 16th- and 17th-century Dutch and Flemish paintings: note the *Stigmate di San Francesco (St. Francis Receiving Stigmata)* by Jan Van Eyck (1395–1441), in which the saint receives the marks of Christ's wounds while a companion cringes beside him. Other Dutch masterpieces include paintings by Anthony Van Dyck (1599–1641) and Rembrandt (1606–69). *L'arcangelo Raffaele e Tobiolo (Tobias and the Angel)* by Piero del Pollaiuolo (circa 1443–96) is showcased, and other

10

featured Italian artists include Fra Angelico (circa 1400–55), Andrea Mantegna (1431–1506), and Paolo Veronese (1528–88). Along with the Egyptian Museum, the gallery is housed in the **Palazzo dell'Accademia delle Scienze,** a baroque tour de force designed by priest-architect Guarino Guarini. At this writing, there are plans to move the entire collection of paintings permanently to the Palazzo Reale in 2011. ⊠ *Via Accademia delle Scienze 6, Centro* ☎ *011/547440* ⊕ *www.museitorino. it* ⊠ *€7.50* ⊘ *Fri.–Sun. and Tues. 8:30–2, Wed. 2–7:30 and Thurs. 10–7:30.*

☾ **Mole Antonelliana.** You can't miss the unusual square dome and thin,
★ elaborate spire of this Turin landmark above the city's rooftops. This odd structure, built between 1863 and 1889, was originally intended to be a synagogue, but costs escalated and eventually it was bought by the city of Turin. In its time it was the tallest brick building in the world, and it is still the tallest building in Italy. You can take the crystal elevator to reach the terrace at the top of the dome for an excellent view of the city, the plain, and the Alps beyond. Also worth a visit is the Mole Antonelliana's **Museo Nazionale del Cinema** (National Cinema Museum), which covers more than 34,000 square feet and houses many items of film memorabilia as well as a film library with some 7,000 titles. ⊠ *Via Montebello 20, Centro* ☎ *011/8138560 museum* ⊕ *www.museocinema.it(museum)* ⊠ *Museum €7, elevator €5, combination ticket €9* ⊘ *Museum: Tues.–Fri. and Sun. 9–8, Sat. 9* AM*–11* PM*; ticket sales end 45 mins before closing. Elevator: Tues.–Fri. and Sun. 10–8, Sat. 10* AM*–11* PM.

★ **Museo d'Arte Orientale.** Housed in the magnificently renovated 17th-century Palazzo Mazzonis, this beautifully displayed collection of Southeast Asian, Chinese, Japanese, Himalayan, and Islamic art is a must-see for anyone interested in oriental sculpture, painting, and ceramics. Highlights include a towering 13th-century wooden statue of the Japanese temple guardian Kongo Rikishi and a sumptuous assortment of Islamic manuscripts. ⊠ *Via San Domenico 9/11, Centro* ☎ *011/4436927* ⊕ *www.maotorino.it* ⊠ *€7.50* ⊘ *Tues.–Sun. 10–6; ticket sales end 1 hr before closing.*

Fodor's Choice **Museo Egizio.** The Egyptian Museum's superb collection includes stat-
★ ues of pharaohs and mummies and entire frescoes taken from royal tombs—all in all, it's one of the world's finest and largest museums of its kind. Designed by Oscar-winner Dante Ferretti, the striking sculpture gallery is a veritable who's who of ancient Egypt. Look for the magnificent 13th-century BC statue of Ramses II and the fascinating Tomb of Kha. The latter was found intact with furniture, supplies of food and clothing, writing instruments, and a complete set of personal cosmetics and toiletries. Unfortunately, the museum's objects are not always displayed according to modern standards. Along with carefully constructed exhibits with detailed information in English and Italian you will also find rooms that resemble warehouses filled with objects, with little or no information provided. ⊠ *Via Accademia delle Scienze 6, Centro* ☎ *011/5617776* ⊕ *www.museoegizio.it* ⊠ *€7.50* ⊘ *Tues.–Sun. 8:30–7:30; ticket sales end 1 hr before closing.*

Palazzo Madama. In the center of Piazza Castello, this castle was named for the Savoy queen Maria Cristina, who made it her home in the 17th century. The building incorporates the remains of a Roman gate with later-medieval and Renaissance additions. The

castle's monumental baroque facade and grand entrance staircase were designed by Filippo Juvarra (1678–1736). The palace now houses the **Museo Civico d'Arte Antica,** whose collections comprise more than 30,000 items dating from the Middle Ages to the baroque era. The paintings, sculptures, illuminated manuscripts, and various decorative objects on display illustrate almost 10 centuries of Italian and European artistic production. Works by Jan van Eyck, Antonella da Messina (circa 1430–79), and Orazio Gentileschi (1563–1639) highlight the collection. ⊠ *Piazza Castello, Centro* ☎ *011/4433501* ⊕ *www. palazzomadamatorino.it* 🖾 *Grand staircase and medieval courtyard free, museum €7.50* ☉ *Grand staircase and medieval courtyard: Tues.– Sat. 9–6, Sun. 10–8. Museum: Tues.–Fri. 10–6, Sun. 10–8. Ticket sales end 1 hr before closing.*

Palazzo Reale. This 17th-century palace, a former Savoy royal residence, is an imposing work of brick, stone, and marble that stands on the site of one of Turin's ancient Roman city gates. In contrast to its sober exterior, the palace's interior is swathed in luxurious, mostly rococo trappings, including tapestries, gilt ceilings, and sumptuous 17th- to 19th-century furniture. You can head down to the basement and the old kitchens to see where food for the last kings of Italy was once dished up, and behind the palace you can relax in the royal gardens. At this writing, extensive restoration work is underway to allow the opening of all floors of the palace and for the permanent transfer here of the painting collection of the Galleria Sabauda in 2011.

The **Armeria Reale** *(Royal Armory)* ⊠ *Entrance at Piazza Castello 191, Centro* ☎ *011/543889* 🖾 *€4* ☉ *Tues.–Fri. 9–2, weekends 1–7),* in a wing of the Royal Palace, holds one of Europe's most extensive collections of arms and armor. It's a must-see for connoisseurs. ⊠ *Piazzetta Reale, Centro* ☎ *011/4361455* 🖾 *Gardens free, palace €6.50* ☉ *Palace: Tues.–Sun. 8:30–7:30; guided visits depart every 40 mins. Gardens: daily 9* AM*–1 hr before sunset.*

Piazza San Carlo. Surrounded by shops, arcades, fashionable cafés, and elegant baroque palaces, this is one of the most beautiful squares in Turin. In the center stands a statue of Duke Emanuele Filiberto of Savoy, victor at the battle of San Quintino in 1557. The melee heralded the peaceful resurgence of Turin under the Savoy after years of bloody dynastic fighting. The fine bronze statue erected in the 19th century is one of Turin's symbols. At the southern end of the square, framing the continuation of Via Roma, are the twin baroque churches of San Carlo and Santa Cristina.

A chocolate lover's pilgrimage to Turin inevitably leads to Al Bicerin (⊠ *Piazza della Consolata 5, Centro* ☎ *011/4369325* ⊕ *www.bicerin.it* ☉ *Closed Wed. and Aug.*), which first opened its doors in 1763. Cavour, Nietzsche, Puccini, and Dumas have all sipped here, and if you order the house specialty, the *bicerin* (a hot drink with layers of chocolate, coffee, and cream), you'll understand why. Don't be surprised if the friendly and energetic owner, Marité Costa, also tries to tempt you with one of her flavored *zabajoni* (warm eggnogs). Chocolate goodies, including chocolate-flavor pasta, are on sale in the café store. The historic **Caffè San Carlo** (⊠ *Piazza San Carlo 156, Centro* ☎ *011/532586*) is usually lively with locals gathered at the marble-top tables under the huge crystal chandelier. Breakfast and lunch, afternoon snacks, and evening aperitifs are all served in this particularly elegant neoclassical setting.

★ **San Lorenzo**. Architect Guarino Guarini was in his mid-sixties when he began this church in 1668. The masterful use of geometric forms and the theatrical control of light and shadow show him working at his mature and confident best. Stand in the center of the church and look up into the cupola to enjoy the full effect. ⊠ *Via Palazzo di Città 4, Centro* ☎ *011/4361527* ⊕ *www.sanlorenzo.torino.it* ☉ *Weekdays 7:30–noon and 4:30–7; weekends 9–1 and 3–7:30.*

Baratti e Milano (⊠ *Piazza Castello 27, Centro* ☎ *011/4407138* ⊕ *www.barattiemilano.it* ☉ *Closed Mon.*), in the glass-roofed Galleria Subalpina near Via Po, is one of Turin's charming old cafés. It's famous for its exquisite chocolates—indulge your sweet tooth or buy some *gianduiotti* (hazelnut chocolates) or candied chestnuts to take home to friends. Light lunches are served at the tables to the rear of the café. The tiny café **Mulassano** (⊠ *Piazza Castello 15, Centro* ☎ *011/547990*), decorated with marble and finely carved wood panels, is famous for its *tramezzini* (small triangular sandwiches made with white bread), invented here in the 1920s. Popular with the pre- and post-theater crowd, the café also offers a unique roulette system for clients trying to decide on who pays the bill—ask the cashier for an explanation.

10

WORTH NOTING

Museo di Antichità. A small but fascinating collection of artifacts found at archaeological sites in and around Turin is on display here. A spiral ramp winds through the subterranean museum, and like in a real archaeological site, the deeper you go the older the objects displayed. A life-size silver bust of the Roman Emperor Lucio Vero (AD 161–169) is one of the masterpieces of the collection. ⊠ *Via XX Settembre 88c, Centro* ☎ *011/5212251* ⊕ *www.museoantichita.it* ⊡ *€4* ☉ *Tues.–Sun. 8:30–7:30.*

Palazzo Carignano. A baroque triumph by Guarino Guarini (the priest who designed several of Turin's most noteworthy structures), this red-brick palace was built between 1679 and 1685 and played an important role in the 19th-century unification of Italy. Vittorio Emanuele II of Savoy (1820–78), united-Italy's first king, was born within these walls, and Italy's first parliament met here from 1860 to 1865. The palace now houses the **Museo del Risorgimento**, a museum honoring the 19th-century movement for Italian unity. At this writing, the palace is closed into 2011 for restoration. ⊠ *Via Accademia delle Scienze 5, Centro* ☎ *011/5621147* ⊕ *www.regione.piemonte.it/cultura/risorgimento* 🖃 *€5* ⊘ *Tues.–Sun. 9–7; ticket sales end 1 hr before closing.*

OFF THE BEATEN PATH

Galleria Civica d'Arte Moderna e Contemporanea (GAM). In 1863 Turin was the first Italian city to begin a public collection devoted to contemporary art. Housed in a modern building on the edge of downtown, a permanent display of more than 600 paintings, sculptures, and installation pieces provides an exceptional glimpse of how Italian contemporary art has evolved since the late 1800s. The futurist, pop, neo-Dada, and *arte povera* movements are particularly well represented, and the gallery has a fine video and art film collection. ⊠ *Via Magenta 31, Centro* ☎ *011/4429518* ⊕ *www.gamtorino.it* 🖃 *€7.50* ⊘ *Tues.–Sun. 10–6.*

ALONG THE PO

The Po River is narrow and unprepossessing here in Turin, only a hint of the broad waterway that it becomes as it flows eastward toward the Adriatic. It's flanked, however, by formidable edifices, a park, and a lovely pedestrian path. Public boats, operated by Turin's **public transport system** (☎ *800/019152 or 011/5764733* ⊕ *www.comune.torino.it/gtt*) make for a pleasant way to reach the Borgo Medioevale from the Murazzi dock at the northern end of the Parco del Valentino.

TOP ATTRACTIONS

Borgo Medioevale. Along the banks of the Po, this complex, built for a General Exhibition in 1884, is a faithful reproduction of a typical Piedmont village in the Middle Ages: crafts shops, houses, a church, and stores cluster the narrow lanes, and in the center of the village the **Rocca Medioevale**, a medieval castle, provides the town's main attraction. ⊠ *Southern end of Parco del Valentino, San Salvario* ☎ *011/4431701* ⊕ *www.borgomedioevaletorino.it* 🖃 *Village free, Rocca Medioevale €5* ⊘ *Village: Apr.–Oct., daily 9–8; Nov.–Mar., daily 9–7. Rocca Medioevale: Apr.–Oct., daily 9–7; Nov.–Mar., Tues.–Sun. 9–6; groups of no more than 25 enter castle every ½ hr. Ticket counter closes at 6:15.*

Museo dell'Automobile. No visit to car-manufacturing Turin would be ★ complete without a pilgrimage to see perfectly conserved Bugattis, Ferraris, and Isotta Fraschinis. Here you can get an idea of the importance of FIAT—and automobiles in general—to Turin's economy. There's a collection of antique cars from as early as 1896, and displays show how the city has changed over the years as a result of its premier industry. For the true automobile fan, there's even a section devoted to the history of car tires. At this writing, the museum was closed for renovations, but is expected to be open in 2012. ⊠ *Corso Unità d'Italia 40, Millefonti* ☎ *011/677666* ⊕ *www.museoauto.it* 🖃 *€7* ⊘ *Tues.–Sun. 10–6:30.*

A race car on exhibit at the Museo dell'Automobile.

Parco del Valentino. This pleasant riverside park is a great place to stroll, bike, or jog. Originally the grounds of a relatively simple hunting lodge, the park owes its present arrangement to Madama Maria Cristina of France, who received the land and lodge as a wedding present after her marriage to Vittorio Amedeo I of Savoy. With memories of 16th-century French châteaus in mind, she began work in 1620 and converted the lodge into a magnificent palace, the **Castello del Valentino.** The building, now home to the University of Turin's Faculty of Architecture, is not open to the general public. Next to the palace are botanical gardens, established in 1729, where local and exotic flora can be seen in a hothouse, herbarium, and arboretum. ⊠ *Parco del Valentino, San Salvario* ☎ *011/6612447 botanical gardens* ✉ *Gardens €3* ☉ *Gardens Apr.–Sept., weekends 9–1 and 3–7.*

10

Fodor's Choice
★ **Pinacoteca Giovanni e Marella Agnelli.** This gallery was opened in 2002 by Gianni Agnelli (1921–2003), the head of FIAT and patriarch of one of Italy's most powerful families, just four months before his death. The emphasis here is on quality rather than quantity: 25 works of art from the Agnelli private collection are on permanent display, along with temporary exhibitions. There are four magnificent scenes of Venice by Canaletto (1697–1768); two splendid views of Dresden by Canaletto's nephew, Bernardo Bellotto (1720–80); several works by Manet (1832–83), Renoir (1841–1919), Matisse (1869–1954), and Picasso (1881–1973); and fine examples of the work of Italian futurist painters Balla (1871–1958) and Severini (1883–1966). The gallery is on the top floor of the **Lingotto,** a former FIAT factory that was completely transformed between 1982 and 2002 by architect Renzo Piano.

The multilevel complex is now home to a shopping mall, several movie theaters, restaurants, two hotels, and an auditorium. ☒ *Via Nizza 230, Lingotto* 🕾 *011/0062713* ⊕ *www.pinacoteca-agnelli.it* 🎫 *€4* ☉ *Tues.– Sun. 10–7; last entrance at 6:15.*

WORTH NOTING

Gran Madre di Dio. On the east bank of the Po, this neoclassical church is modeled after the Pantheon in Rome. It was built between 1827 and 1831 to commemorate the return of the house of Savoy to Turin after the fall of Napoléon's empire. ☒ *Piazza Gran Madre di Dio, Borgo Po* 🕾 *011/8193572* ☉ *Mon.–Sat. 7:30–noon and 3:30–7, Sun. 7:30–1 and 3:30–7.*

Santa Maria del Monte. The church and convent standing on top of 150-foot Monte dei Cappuccini date from 1583. Don't be surprised if you find yourself in the middle of a wedding party, as couples often come here to be photographed. Next to the church is the tiny **Museo Nazionale della Montagna,** dedicated to mountains and mountaineers. ☒ *Piazzale Monte dei Cappuccini above Corso Moncalieri, Borgo Po* 🕾 *011/6604414 church, 011/6604104 museum* ⊕ *www. museomontagna.org* 🎫 *Church free, museum €6* ☉ *Church: daily 9– noon and 2:30–6. Museum: Tues.–Sun. 9–7; last entrance 6:30.*

OFF THE BEATEN PATH

Basilica di Superga. Since 1731, the Basilica di Superga has been the burial place of kings. Visible from miles around, the thoroughly baroque church was designed by Juvarra in the early 18th century, and no fewer than 58 members of the Savoy family are memorialized in the crypt. ☒ *Strada della Basilica di Superga 73, Sassi* 🕾 *011/8997456* ⊕ *www. basilicadisuperga.com* 🎫 *Basilica free, crypt €4* ☉ *Basilica: weekdays 9–noon and 3–5, weekends 9–noon and 3–6. Crypt: Mar.–Oct., daily 9–7:30; Nov.–Feb., weekends 9:30–6:30.*

🕄 **Sassi–Superga Cog Train.** The 18-minute ride from Sassi up the Superga hill is an absolute treat on a clear day. The view of the Alps is magnificent at the hilltop **Parco Naturale Collina Torinese,** a tranquil retreat from the bustle of the city. If you feel like a little exercise, you can walk back down to Sassi (about two hours) on one of the well-marked wooded trails that start from the upper station. Other circular trails lead through the park and back to Superga. ☒ *Piazza G. Modena, Sassi* 🕾 *011/5764733* ⊕ *www.comune.torino.it/gtt* 🎫 *Weekdays €2 one-way, weekends €3.50 one-way* ☉ *Hourly service Mon. and Wed.–Fri. 9–noon and 2–5, hourly service weekends 9–8; bus service replaces train on Tues.*

WHERE TO EAT

$$$

PIEDMONTESE

Fodor's Choice

★

✗ **Al Garamond.** The ocher-color walls and the ancient brick vaulting in this small, bright space set the stage for traditional meat and seafood dishes served with creative flair. Try the tantalizing *rombo in crosta di patate al barbera* (turbot wrapped in sliced potatoes and baked with Barbera wine). For dessert, the mousse *di liquirizia e salsa di cioccolato bianco* (licorice mousse with white-chocolate sauce) is a must, even if you don't usually like licorice. The level of service here is high, even by demanding Turin standards. ✉ *Via G. Pomba 14, Centro* ☎ *011/8122781* ▭ *AE, MC, V* ⊙ *Closed Sun., Jan. 1–6, and 3 wks in Aug. No lunch Sat.*

$$$$
PIEDMONTESE

✕ **Del Cambio.** Set in a palace dating from 1757, this is one of Europe's most beautiful and historic restaurants, with decorative moldings, mirrors, and hanging lamps that look just as they did when Italian national hero Cavour dined here more than a century ago. The cuisine draws heavily on Piedmontese tradition and is paired with fine wines of the region. Agnolotti pasta with *sugo d'arrosto* (roast veal sauce) is a recommended first course. ✉ *Piazza Carignano 2, Centro* ☎ *011/546690* ⌂ *Reservations essential* ▭ *AE, DC, MC, V* ⊙ *Closed Sun., Jan. 1–6, and 3 wks in Aug.*

$$
PIEDMONTESE

✕ **L'Agrifoglio.** This intimate local favorite has just 10 tables. Specialties change with the seasons, but you might find such delicacies as risotto *al Barbaresco* (with Barbaresco wine) and agnolotti *farciti di brasato* (crescent-shaped stuffed pasta) on the menu. L'Agrifoglio stays open late for the after-theater and after-cinema crowds. ✉ *Via Andrea Provana 7/E, Centro* ☎ *011/8136837* ▭ *MC, V* ⊙ *Closed Sun. and Mon.*

$$
PIEDMONTESE

✕ **Porta di Po.** They're vigilant about sticking to Piedmontese specialties at this elegant restaurant with minimalist decor. All the seasonal favorites are here: the *guanciale di vitello brasato* (braised veal cheek) melts in your mouth, and the fritto misto (mixed fried meats), which you must order in advance, is a treat. Desserts are all traditional, and the wine list, though limited, presents a reasonable collection of regional wines. ✉ *Piazza Vittorio Veneto 1, Centro* ☎ *011/8127642* ▭ *AE, MC, V* ⊙ *Closed Sun. and 2 wks in Sept. No lunch Mon.*

$$
PIEDMONTESE
★

✕ **Savoia.** The enthusiasm of chef and owner Mario Ferrero permeates three small rooms decorated with a few choice pictures and antique furniture. His kitchen turns out creative takes on Piedmontese specialties that change with the seasons. The bread and pasta are homemade, and the wine cellar is tended with equal care. ✉ *Via Corte d'Appello 13, Centro* ☎ *011/4362288* ▭ *AE, DC, MC, V* ⊙ *Closed Sun. No lunch Sat.*

$$
SEAFOOD

✕ **Trattoria Anna.** If you are hankering for something different from the usual meat-based Piedmontese cuisine, give this simple, extremely popular, family-run spot a try. They serve only seafood, and they do it well. The *tagliatelle Walter* (pasta with shellfish) and the grigliata di pesce (mixed grilled fish) are both excellent. ✉ *Via Bellezia 20, Centro* ☎ *011/4362134* ⌂ *Reservations essential* ▭ *MC, V* ⊙ *Closed Sun. and 2 wks in Aug. No lunch.*

$$$
NORTHERN
ITALIAN
★

✕ **Vintage 1997.** The first floor of an elegant town house in the center of Turin makes a fitting location for this sophisticated restaurant. You might try such specialties as *vitello tonnato alla nostra maniera* (roast veal with a light tuna sauce) or *filetto di pesce con asparagi purè dell'orto e foie gras* (fish filet with asparagus puree and foie gras). For the especially hungry gourmet there's the *menu del Vintage*, a 13-course feast that covers the full range of the restaurant's cuisine. There's an excellent wine list, with regional, national, and international vintages well represented. ✉ *Piazza Solferino 16/H, Centro* ☎ *011/535948* ▭ *AE, DC, MC, V* ⊙ *Closed Sun. and 3 wks in Aug. No lunch Sat.*

10

WHERE TO STAY

The **Turin Tourist Board** (⊠ *Via Bogino 8, Centro* ☎ *011/535181* ⊕ *www. turismotorino.org*) provides a booking service for hotels and bed-and-breakfast-style accommodations in the city and throughout the region. In order to use the service, you must book hotels 48 hours in advance and B&Bs seven days in advance.

$$ **Genio.** Though steps away from the main train station, spacious and tastefully decorated rooms provide a quiet haven from the bustle of the city. Best of all is the service, which resembles that of a friendly family-run inn rather than a big-city business hotel. **Pros:** recently refurbished property; close to the central train station; very friendly service. **Cons:** 15-minute walk to the center of town; area around the hotel is a little seedy. ⊠ *Corso Vittorio Emanuele II 47, Centro* ☎ *011/6505771* ⊕ *www.hotelgenio.it* ↘ *125 rooms, 3 suites* ☐ *In-room: safe, Wi-Fi. In-hotel: laundry service, Wi-Fi hotspot, parking (paid), some pets allowed* ⊟ *AE, DC, MC, V* ⏐◯⏐ *BP.*

$$$ ★ **Grand Hotel Sitea.** One of the city's finest hotels, the Sitea is in the historic center. Decorated in a warmly classical style, the public areas and guest rooms are elegant and comfortable. Top-notch service is provided by a courteous and efficient staff. Weekend rates are slightly lower. **Pros:** central location; well-appointed rooms; large bathrooms. **Cons:** some find the air-conditioning noisy; carpets are a little worn. ⊠ *Via Carlo Alberto 35, Centro* ☎ *011/5170171* ⊕ *www.sitea.thi-hotels.com* ↘ *118 rooms, 4 suites* ☐ *In-room: safe, Internet. In-hotel: restaurant, bar, spa, Wi-Fi hotspot, parking (paid), some pets allowed* ⊟ *AE, DC, MC, V* ⏐◯⏐ *BP.*

$$$$ **Le Meridien Turin Art+Tech.** Designed by architect Renzo Piano, this luxury hotel is part of the former Lingotto FIAT factory. The approach throughout is typically minimalist, with ultramodern fixtures and designer furniture decorating the rooms. The track on the roof, once used by FIAT to test its cars, is available to clients for jogging. **Pros:** interesting design and location; good ($$) weekend rates. **Cons:** outside the city center; some signs of wear and tear; services are a little limited for the price. ⊠ *Via Nizza 230, Lingotto* ☎ *011/6642000* ⊕ *www. lemeridien.com* ↘ *141 rooms, 1 suite* ☐ *In-room: safe. In-hotel: restaurant, bar, gym, Internet terminal, Wi-Fi hotspot* ⊟ *AE, DC, MC, V* ⏐◯⏐ *BP.*

$$$ Fodor's Choice ★ **Victoria.** Rare style, attention to detail, and comfort are the hallmarks of this boutique hotel furnished and managed to create the feeling of a refined English town house. The sitting room has deep-cushioned floral sofas, a library, a collection of bric-a-brac, and windows overlooking an enclosed garden. A newer wing has a grand marble staircase and individually decorated guest rooms in which fine prints and patterned fabrics abound. The same care is found in the refurbished rooms of the original wing, and the well-equipped spa area, an attractive addition. **Pros:** tranquil location in the center of town; excellent spa facilities; wonderful breakfast. **Cons:** entrance is a little run-down; hotel parking lot is a couple of blocks away and finding a spot on the street is difficult; no views from the rooms. ⊠ *Via Nino Costa 4, Centro* ☎ *011/5611909*

⊕ *www.hotelvictoria-torino.com* ⤶ *97 rooms, 9 suites* ⛾ *In-room: safe, Wi-Fi. In-hotel: bar, pool, spa, bicycles, Wi-Fi hotspot, parking (paid)* ⊟ *AE, DC, MC, V* ⭘⫯*BP.*

NIGHTLIFE AND THE ARTS

THE ARTS
MUSIC

Classical music concerts are held in the **Giovanni Agnelli Auditorium** (⊠ *Via Nizza 280, Lingotto* ☎ *011/6677415*), a space designed by Renzo Piano in the Lingotto district; internationally famous conductors and orchestras are frequent guests.

The **MITO Settembre Musica Festival** (☎ *011/4424703*), held for three weeks in September, highlights classical works. Traditional sacred music and some modern religious pieces are performed in the **Duomo** (⊠ *Via Montebello 20, Centro* ☎ *011/8154230*) on Sunday evening; performances are usually advertised in the vestibule or in the local edition of Turin's nationally distributed newspaper, *La Stampa*. The Friday edition comes with a supplement on music and other entertainment possibilities.

OPERA

The **Teatro Regio** (⊠ *Piazza Castello 215, Centro* ☎ *011/8815557* ⊕ *www. teatroregio.torino.it*), one of Italy's leading opera houses, has its season from October to June. You can buy tickets for most performances (premieres sell out well in advance) at the box office or on the Web site, where discounts are offered on the day of the show. In 2011, to celebrate the 150th anniversary of Italian unification, a program dedicated to Giuseppe Verdi is planned.

NIGHTLIFE

Two areas of Turin are enormously popular nightlife destinations: the Quadrilatero, to the north of the city center, and the Murazzi embankment, near the Ponte Vittorio Emanuele I.

On the Murazzi, near the Ponte Vittorio Emanuele I, is **Jammin's** (⊠ *Murazzi del Po 17, Centro* ☎ *011/882869* ⊗ *May–Sept., Mon.–Sat. 9 PM–4 AM*), a popular disco with a varied crowd; there's live music on Friday. The center of town is also popular, especially earlier in the evening. A trendy meeting place for an aperitif or a predisco drink in the piazza at the end of Via Po is the wine bar **Caffè Elena** (⊠ *Piazza Vittorio Veneto 5, Centro* ☎ *011/8123341*). South of the main train station is **Rockcity** (⊠ *Via Bertini 2, San Salvario* ☎ *011/3184737*), where you'll find a smart crowd in their mid-twenties to mid-thirties listening to rock, techno, and commercial music. The Quadrilatero Romano, which roughly corresponds to the grid pattern of Roman Turin and lies to the south of Piazza della Reppublica, is a hopping area filled with nightclubs and ethnic restaurants. Places open and close with startling frequency in the Quadrilateral, but **Pastis** (⊠ *Piazza Emanuele Filiberto 9b, Centro* ☎ *011/5211085*) has shown considerable staying power—several cultural groups hold their meetings in the bar.

10

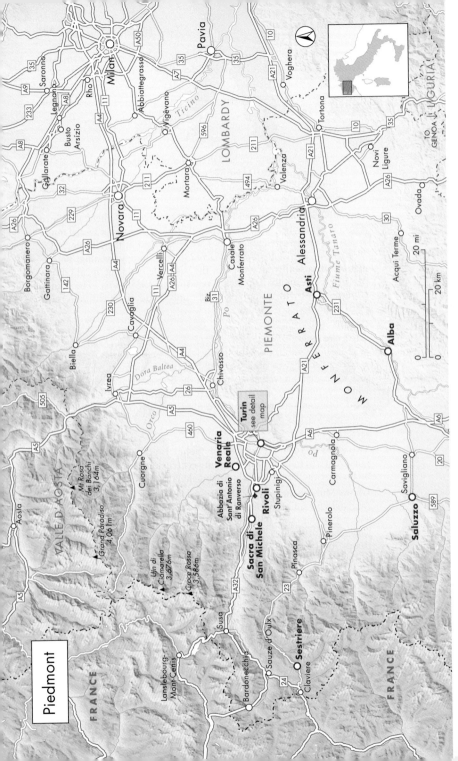

SPORTS

BIKE RENTALS

Turin has about 160 km (100 mi) of bike paths running through the city and its parks. From April to October, the **Ufficio Iniziative Ambientali** (✉ *Via Padova 29, Madonna di Campagna* ☎ *011/4020177* ⊕ *www.comune.torino.it/ambiente/bici/index.shtml*) provides bicycles for daily rental. Their Web site provides a detailed map of the bike paths and rental locations.

SHOPPING

CHOCOLATE

The tradition of making chocolate began in Turin in the early 17th century. Chocolate at that time was an aristocratic drink, but in the 19th century a Piedmontese invention made it possible to further refine cocoa, which could then be used to create solid bars and candies.

★ The most famous of all Turin chocolates is the *gianduiotto* (with cocoa, sugar, and hazelnuts), first concocted in 1867. The tradition of making these delicious treats has been continued at the small, family-run **Peyrano** (✉ *Corso Moncalieri 47, Centro* ☎ *011/6602202* ⊕ *www.peyrano.it*), where more than 80 types of chocolates are concocted. **Stratta** (✉ *Piazza San Carlo 191, Centro* ☎ *011/547920*), one of Turin's most famous chocolate shops, has been in business since 1836 and sells confections of all kinds—not just the chocolates in the lavish window displays but also fancy cookies, rum-laced fudges, and magnificent cakes.

MARKETS

Go to the famous **Balon Flea Market** (✉ *Piazza Repubblica, Centro*) on Saturday morning for excellent bargains on secondhand books and clothing and good browsing among stalls selling local specialties such as gianduiotti. (Be aware, however, that the market is also famous for its pickpockets.) The second Sunday of every month a special antiques market, appropriately called the **Gran Balon**, sets up shop in Piazza Repubblica.

SPECIALTY STORES

Most people know that Turin produces more than 75% of Italy's cars, but they are often unaware that it's also a hub for clothing manufacturing. Top-quality boutiques stocking local, national, and international lines are clustered along Via Roma and Via Garibaldi. Piazza San Carlo, Via Po, and Via Maria Vittoria are lined with antiques shops, some—but not all—specializing in 18th-century furniture and domestic items.

★ With branches in Milan, Bologna, and New York, **Eataly** (✉ *Via Nizza 230, Lingotto* ☎ *011/19506801* ⊕ *www.eatalytorino.it*) is perhaps Turin's most famous food emporium. As well as a food market, food-related bookstore, and wine bar, there are several different food counters and restaurants offering everything from hamburgers to haute cuisine.

Specialty food stores and delicatessens abound in central Turin. For a truly spectacular array of cheeses and other delicacies, try Turin's famous **Borgiattino** (✉ *Via Accademia Albertina 38/A, Centro* ☎ *011/8394686*).

10

Gianduiotti—hazelnut-filled chocolates—are one of Turin's sweetest pleasures.

THE COLLINE AND SAVOY PALACES

As you head west from Turin into the Colline ("little hills"), castles and medieval fortifications begin to pepper the former dominion of the house of Savoy, and the Alps come into better and better view. In the region lie the storybook medieval town of Rivoli; 12th-century abbeys; and, farther west in the mountains, the ski resort of Sestriere, one of the venues used during the 2006 Winter Olympics.

VENARIA REALE

10 km (6 mi) northwest of Turin.

GETTING HERE

Starting in Turin, from the north side of Piazza della Reppublica, take Bus 11 to reach Venaria; the trip takes approximately 40 minutes. By car, follow Corso Regina Margherita to the A55 highway. Head north and leave the highway at the Venaria exit, following signs for the Venaria Reale.

EXPLORING

★ The **Reggia di Venaria Reale** was built in the mid-16th century as a sumptuous hunting lodge for Carlo Emanuele II of Savoy. Extensive Italiante gardens surround the palace, and the Great Gallery inside is worthy of Versailles. The basements now house a historical exhibition that relates the story of the Savoy. The upper floors are given over to changing exhibitions. A sound-and-light show by Peter Greenaway enlivens rooms throughout the palace, and a permanent installation of works by arte povera artist Giuseppe Penone can be found in the Lower Park outside. At this writing, a major exhibition of Italian art from 1300 to 1861 is planned for 2011. ✉ *Piazza della Reppublica 4* ☎ *011/992333* 💰 *€12; €4 gardens only* ⏱ *Reggia: Tues.–Fri. 9–5; Sat. 9 AM–9:30 PM; Sun. 9–8; last entrance 1 hr before closing. Gardens: Tues.–Sun. 9–1 hr before sunset.*

RIVOLI

16 km (10 mi) west of Venaria, 13 km (8 mi) west of Turin.

GETTING HERE

GTT buses and trams regularly link central Turin with Rivoli. The journey takes just over one hour.

By car, follow Corso Francia from central Turin all the way to Rivoli. Unless there's a lot of traffic the trip should take a half hour.

EXPLORING

The Savoy court was based in Rivoli in the Middle Ages. The 14th- to 15th-century **Casa del Conte Verde** *(House of the Green Count)* sits right in the center of town, and the richness of its decorations hints at the wealth and importance of its owner, Amedeo VI of Savoy, during the period. Inside, a small gallery hosts temporary exhibitions. ✉ *Via Fratelli Piol 8* ☎ *011/9563020* 💰 *Admission varies with exhibits* ⏱ *Varies with exhibits.*

Fodor's Choice ★ The castle of Rivoli now houses the **Museo d'Arte Contemporanea** *(Museum of Contemporary Art).* The building was begun in the 17th century and then redesigned but never finished by Juvarra in the 18th century; it was finally completed in the late 20th century by minimalist Turin architect Andrea Bruno. On display are changing international exhibitions and a permanent collection of 20th-century Italian art. To get to Rivoli from downtown Turin, take Metro line 1 to Fermi and then the shuttle bus service to the museum. The schedule and cost of the shuttle bus can be found on the museum's Web site. ✉ *Piazzale Mafalda di Savoia* ☎ *011/9565222* ⊕ *www.castellodirivoli.org* 💰 *€6.50* ⏱ *Tues.–Thurs. 10–5, Fri.–Sun. 10–9.*

10

ABBAZIA DI SANT'ANTONIO DI RANVERSO

6 km (4 mi) west of Rivoli, 23 km (14 mi) west of Turin.

GETTING HERE

GTT offers twice-daily bus service to the abbey from Turin. By car, the abbey is 10 minutes from Rivoli on SS25.

EXPLORING

Abbazia di Sant'Antonio di Ranverso. This abbey was originally a hospital, founded in the 12th century by the Hospitallers of St. Anthony to care for victims of St. Anthony's Fire, a painful medical condition brought on by consuming contaminated rye. Pilgrims came here over the centuries for cures and to offer thanks for a miraculous recovery. The 15th-century frescoes with their lifelike depictions of pilgrims and saints retain their original colors. ✉ *Buttigliera Alta west of Rivoli, off*

SS25 ☎ 011/9367450 ⚟ €2.60 ⊙ Wed.–Sun. 9–12:30 and 3–5:30; last entrance ½ hr before closing.

SACRA DI SAN MICHELE

20 km (13 mi) west of Abbazia di Sant'Antonio di Ranverso, 43 km (27 mi) west of Turin.

GETTING HERE

Unless you want to do a 14-km (9-mi) uphill hike from the town of Avigliana, a car is essential for an excursion to the Abbey of Saint Michael—take the Avigliana Est exit from the Torino–Bardonecchia highway (A32).

EXPLORING

★ Perhaps best known as inspiration for the setting of Umberto Eco's novel *The Name of the Rose*, **Sacra di San Michele** was built on Monte Pirchiriano in the 11th century so it would stand out: it occupies the most prominent location for miles around, hanging over a 3,280-foot bluff. When monks came to enlarge the abbey they had to build part of the structure on supports more than 90 feet high—an engineering feat that was famous in medieval Europe and is still impressive today. By the 12th century this important abbey controlled 176 churches in Italy, France, and Spain; one of the abbeys under its influence was Mont-Saint-Michel in France. Because of its strategic position the Abbey of Saint Michael came under frequent attacks over the next five centuries and was eventually abandoned in 1622. It was restored, somewhat heavy-handedly, in the late 19th and early 20th centuries.

From **Porta dello Zodiaco,** a splendid Romanesque doorway decorated with the signs of the zodiac, you climb 150 steps, past 12th-century sculptures, to reach the church. On the left side of the interior are 16th-century frescoes representing New Testament themes; on the right are depictions of the founding of the church. In the crypt are some of the oldest parts of the structure, three small 9th- to 12th-century chapels. Note that some sections of the abbey are open only on weekends and, when particularly crowded, visits may be limited to hour-long tours. ⌧ *Via alla Sacra 4 Sant'Ambrogio di Torino ☎ 011/939130 ⊕ www. sacradisanmichele.com ⚟ €4 ⊙ Mid-Mar.–June and early Oct., Tues.– Sat. 9:30–12:30 and 4:30–6, Sun. 9:30–noon and 2:40–6:30; July–Sept., Mon.–Sat. 9:30–12:30 and 4:30–6, Sun. 9:30–noon and 2:40–6:30; mid-Oct.–mid-Mar., Tues.–Sat. 9:30–12:30 and 2:30–5, Sun. 9:30– noon and 2:40–5.*

SALUZZO

58 km (36 mi) southwest of Turin.

GETTING HERE

By car, follow the A6 south from Turin, exit at Marene, and then follow the SP662 west through Savigliano. You can also reach Saluzzo by train from Turin in just over an hour, though the trip requires that you change trains in Savigliano.

VISITOR INFORMATION

Saluzzo tourism office (⊠ *Piazzetta Mondagli 5* ☎ *0175/46710* ⊕ *www. comune.saluzzo.cn.it*).

EXPLORING

The russet-brick town of Saluzzo—a flourishing medieval center and later seat of a Renaissance ducal court—is a well-preserved gem with narrow, winding streets, frescoed houses, Gothic churches, and elegant Renaissance palaces. The tourism office can provide you with a map for a walking tour of the town's sights.

The older and more interesting part of the town hugs a hilltop in the Po Valley and is crowned by **La Castiglia**, a 13th-century castle that has served as a prison since the 1820s.

The exterior of the **Castello della Manta**, 4 km (2½ mi) south of Saluzzo, is austere, but inside are frescoes and other decorations of the period. Knights and damsels from an allegorical poem written by Marquis Tommaso III of Saluzzo, humanist lord of the castle, parade in full costume in the 15th-century frescoes of the **Sala del Barone**. The castle sometimes hosts exhibits, at which time higher admission is charged. ⊠ *Via al Castello 14, Manta* ☎ *0175/87822* 🎫 *€5* ⊘ *Mar.–Sept., Tues.–Sun. 10–6.*

SESTRIERE

32 km (20 mi) east of Briançon, 93 km (58 mi) west of Turin.

GETTING HERE

By car, follow the A32 west from Turin, exit at Oulx, and follow the SS24 to Sestriere. Train service is available from Turin as far as Oulx—regularly running SAPAV buses complete the journey to Sestriere.

VISITOR INFORMATION

Sestriere tourism office (⊠ *Via Louset 14* ☎ *0122/755444* ⊕ *www.comune. sestriere.to.it*).

EXPLORING

In the early 1930s, before skiing became a more egalitarian sport, the patriarch of the FIAT automobile dynasty had this resort built to cater to the elite. The resort has two distinctive tower hotels and ski facilities that have been developed into some of the best in the Alps. It lacks the charm of older Alpine centers, overdevelopment has added some eyesores, and the mountains don't have the striking beauty of those in Valle d'Aosta, but skiers have an excellent choice of trails, some of which cross the border into France.

WHERE TO STAY

$$$ 🏨 **Hotel Cristallo.** Half of the rooms at this hotel face the slopes of Sestriere, and the ski-lift station is just across the road. You can find all the facilities you need for a stay in the mountains either in the hotel or just steps away from the lobby entrance. Rooms are elegantly and warmly furnished in the style of a modern ski lodge; ask for one with a terrace facing the view. **Pros:** excellent location in the center of town; professional and helpful staff; good restaurant; pleasant

10

Skiing in Piedmont and Valle d'Aosta

Skiing is the major sport in both Piedmont and Valle d'Aosta. Excellent facilities abound at resort towns such as Courmayeur and Breuil-Cervinia. The so-called Via Lattea (Milky Way)—five skiing areas near Sestriere with 400 km (almost 250 mi) of linked runs and 90 ski lifts—provides practically unlimited skiing. Lift tickets, running around €35 for a day's pass, are significantly less expensive than at major U.S. resorts.

To Italian skiers, a weeklong holiday on the slopes is known as a *settimana*

bianca (white week). Ski resort hotels in Piedmont and Valle d'Aosta encourage these getaways by offering six- and seven-day packages, and though they're designed with the domestic market in mind, you can get a bargain by taking advantage of the offers. The packages usually, though not always, include half or full board.

You should have your passport with you if you plan a day trip into France or Switzerland—though odds are you won't be asked to show it.

decor. **Cons:** half-board and week stays may be required, not all rooms have views and terraces; standard rooms are small. ⊠ *Via Pinerolo 5* ☎ *0122/750707* ⊕ *www.newlinehotels.com* ⤳ *46 rooms* ⌂ *In-room: safe, Internet. In-hotel: restaurant, bar, gym, Internet terminal, parking (paid)* ⊟ *DC, MC, V* ⍥*BP.*

$$$ ⬚ **Roseo.** Large and elegant, this luxurious hotel sits on the slopes above the town, near the lifts and the town's golf course. Its secluded location heightens the sense of exclusivity, and though it's showing signs of age, the hotel still attracts a stylish clientele. The restaurant and a cozy bar invite après-ski relaxation. A minimum stay of one week is required during high season. **Pros:** secluded location; great service; outstanding views. **Cons:** outside the town center; pool area and rooms are a little run-down; half board is mandatory. ⊠ *Via Sauze 3/B* ☎ *0122/7941* ⊕ *www.roseohotelsestriere.com* ⤳ *96 rooms, 4 suites* ⌂ *In-room: safe. In-hotel: restaurant, bar, pool, spa, Wi-Fi hotspot, some pets allowed* ⊟ *AE, DC, MC, V* ⍥ *Closed early Apr.–June and Sept.–Nov.* ⍥*MAP.*

SPORTS AND THE OUTDOORS
SKIING
At 6,670 feet, the ski resort of **Sestriere** (☎ *0122/799411 for conditions* ⊕ *www.vialattea.it*) was built in the late 1920s under the auspices of Turin's Agnelli family. The slopes get good snow some years from November through May, other years from February through May. The **tourist office** (⊠ *Via Louset 14* ☎ *0122/755444* ⊕ *www.comune. sestriere.to.it*) in Sestriere provides complete information about lift tickets, ski runs, mountain guides, and equipment rentals, here and in neighboring towns such as Bardonecchia and Claviere. Its excellent Web site is also navigable in English. A quaint village with slate-roof houses, **Claviere** (⊠ *17 km [11 mi] west of Sestrie*) is one of Italy's oldest ski resorts. Its slopes overlap with those of the French resort of Montgenèvre.

Continued on page 392

ON THE TRAIL OF BAROLO

Picture yourself in the background of a grand medieval mural, and you won't be far off from what you experience driving through the idyllic wooded landscape south of Turin, in Piedmont's Langhe district.

10

The crests of the graceful hills are dotted with villages, each lorded over by an ancient castle. The gentle slopes of the valleys below are lined with row upon row of Nebbiolo grapes, the choicest of which are used to make Barolo wine. Dubbed "the king of wines and wine of kings" in the 19th century after finding favor with King Carlo Alberto, Barolo still wears the crown, despite stiff competition from all corners of Italy.

Above, Serralunga's castle
Right, bottles of old vintage Barolo

The Langhe district is smaller and surprisingly less visited by food-and-wine enthusiasts than Chianti and the surrounding areas of Tuscany, but it yields similar rewards. The best way to tour the Barolo-producing region is on day trips from the delightful truffle town of Alba—getting around is easy, the country roads are gorgeous, and the wine is fit for a king.

ALL ABOUT BAROLO

The Nebbiolo grapes that go into this famous wine come not just from Barolo proper (the area surrounding the tiny town of Barolo), but also from a small zone that encompasses the hill towns of Novello, Monforte d'Alba, Serralunga d'Alba, Castiglione Falletto, La Morra, and Verduno. All are connected by small but easy-to-navigate roads.

When wine lovers talk about Barolo, they talk about tannins—the quality that makes red wine dry out your mouth. Tannins come from the grape skins; red wine—which gets its color from the skins—has them, white wine doesn't. Tannins can be balanced out by acidity (the quality that makes your mouth water), but they also soften over time. As a good red wine matures, flavors emerge more clearly, achieving a harmonious balance of taste and texture.

A bottle of Barolo is often born so overwhelmingly tannic that many aficionados won't touch the stuff until it has aged 10 or 15 years. But a good Barolo ages beautifully, eventually spawning complex, intermingled tastes of tobacco, roses, and earth. It's not uncommon to see bottles for sale from the 1960s, 1950s, or even the 1930s.

WHERE TO DRINK IT

The word *enoteca* in Italian can mean a wine store, or a wine bar, or both. The words "wine bar," on the other hand—which are becoming increasingly trendy—mean just that. Either way, these are great places to sample and buy the wines of the Langhe.

An excellent enoteca in Alba is **Vincafé** (Via V. Emanuele, 12, Alba, 0173/364603). It specializes in tastes of Langhe wines, accompanied by *salumi* (cured meats), cheeses, and other regional products. More than 350 wines, as well as grappas and liqueurs, grace Vincafé's distinguished list. It's open from noon to midnight, and there's food until 9 pm.

In the fortfied hill town of Barolo, visit the **Castello di Barolo** (Piazza Falletti, 0173/56277, www.baroloworld.it) which has a little wine bar and a museum dedicated to Barolo.

HOW MUCH DOES IT COST?

The most reasonably priced, but still enjoyable Barolos will cost you €20 to €30. A very good but not top-of-the-line bottle will cost €40 to €60. For a top-of-the-line bottle you may spend anywhere from €80 to €200.

LABELS TO LOOK FOR

Barolo is a strictly controlled denomination, but that doesn't mean all Barolos are equal. Legendary producers include Prunotto, Aldo Conterno, Giacomo Conterno, Bruno Giacosa, Famiglia Anselma, Mascarello, Pio Cesare, and Michele Chiarlo.

WINE ESTATES TO VISIT

Right in the town of Barolo, an easy, if touristy, option for a visit is **Marchesi di Barolo** (Via Alba 12, Barolo, 0173/564400, www.marchesibarolo. com). In the estate's user-friendly enoteca you can taste wine, buy thousands of different bottles from vintages going way back, and look at display bottles, including an 1859 Barolo. Marchesi di Barolo's *cantine* (wine cellars, Via Roma 1, Barolo) are open daily 10:30–5:30. The staff here is used to catering to visitors, so you won't have to worry too much about endearing yourself to them.

From there you might want to graduate to **Famiglia Anselma** (Loc. Castello della Volta, Barolo, 0173/787217, www.anselma.it). Winemaker Maurizio Anselma, in his mid-20s, is something of a prodigy in the Barolo world, and he's quite open to visitors. He is known for his steadfast commitment to produce only Barolo—nothing else—and for his policy of holding his wines for several years before release.

A good, accessible example of the new school of Barolo winemaking is **Podere Rocche dei Manzoni** (3, Loc. Manzini Soprano, Monforte d'Alba, 0173/78421, www.barolobig.com). The facade of the cantina is like a Roman temple of brick, complete with imposing columns. Rocche dei Manzoni's reds include four Barolos, one Dolcetto, one Langhe Rosso, two Langhe DOCs, and two Barbera d'Albas.

WINE TOUR TIPS

Keep in mind that visiting wineries in Italy is different from what you might have experienced in the Napa Valley or in France. Wherever you go, reservations are most definitely required, and you'll usually be the only person or group on the tour—so be sure to show up when you say you will, and keep in mind that it's impolite not to buy something in the end.

Wine buyers and wine professionals are the expected audience for tours. While this attitude is slowly changing and many winemakers are beginning to welcome interested outsiders, it's important to be humble and enthusiastic. You'll be treated best if you come in with an open mind, respect that the winemaker probably knows more about wine than you do, and make it clear that you aren't just looking to drink for free. It helps to speak Italian, but if you don't, the international language of effusive compliments can still go a long way.

BEYOND BAROLO

Neive, in the Barbaresco region

By no means do the fruits of the Langhe end with Barolo. The region boasts Italy's highest concentration of DOC (denominazione di origine controllata) and DOCG (denominazione di origine controllata e garantita) wines, the two most prestigious categories of appellation in Italy. The other DOCG in the Langhe is Barbaresco, which, like Barolo, is made from the Nebbiolo grape. Barbaresco is not quite as tannic as Barolo, however, and can be drunk younger.

THE MONFERRATO AND THE LANGHE

Southeast of Turin, in the hilly wooded area around Asti known as the Monferrato and farther south in a similar area around Alba known as the Langhe, the rolling landscape is a patchwork of vineyards and dark woods dotted with hill towns and castles. This is wine country, producing some of Italy's most famous reds and sparkling whites. And hidden away in the woods are the secret places where hunters and their dogs unearth the precious, aromatic truffles worth their weight in gold at Alba's truffle fair.

ASTI

60 km (37 mi) southeast of Turin.

GETTING HERE

Asti is less than an hour away from Turin by car on the A21. GTT bus service connects the two towns, but is not direct. Train service to Asti, on the other hand, is frequent and fast.

VISITOR INFORMATION

Asti tourism office (✉ *Piazza Alfieri 29* ☎ *0141/530357* ⊕ *www.astiturismo.it*).

EXPLORING

Asti is best known outside Italy for its wines—excellent reds as well as the famous sparkling white spumante—but its strategic position on trade routes at Turin, Milan, and Genoa has given it a broad economic base. In the 12th century Asti began to develop as a republic, at a time when other Italian cities were also flexing their economic and military muscles. It flourished in the following century, when the inhabitants began erecting lofty **towers** (✉ *West end of Corso Vittorio Alfieri*) for its defense, giving rise to the medieval nickname "city of 100 towers." In the center of Asti some of these remain, among them the 13th-century **Torre Comentina** and the well-preserved **Torre Troyana**, a tall, slender tower attached to the **Palazzo Troya**. The 18th-century church of **Santa Caterina** has incorporated one of Asti's medieval towers, the **Torre Romana** (itself built on an ancient Roman base), as its bell tower. Corso Vittorio Alfieri is Asti's main thoroughfare, running west–east across the city. This road, known in medieval times as Contrada Maestra, was built by the Romans.

The **Duomo** is an object lesson in the evolution of Gothic architecture. Built in the early 14th century, it's decorated so as to emphasize geometry and verticality: pointed arches and narrow vaults contrast with the earlier, Romanesque attention to balance and symmetry. The porch on the south side of the cathedral facing the square was built in 1470 and represents Gothic at its most florid and excessive. ✉ *Piazza Cattedrale* ☎ *0141/592924* ⊙ *Daily 8:30–noon and 3:30–5:30.*

The Gothic church of **San Secondo** is dedicated to Asti's patron saint, reputedly decapitated on the spot where the church now stands. Secondo is also the patron of the city's favorite folklore and sporting event, the annual Palio di Asti, the colorful medieval-style horse race (similar to Siena's) held each year on the third Sunday of September in the vast Campo del Palio to the south of the church. ⊠ *Piazza San Secondo, south of Corso Vittorio Alfieri* ☎ *0141/530066* ⊗ *Mon.–Sat. 10:45–noon and 3:30–5:30, Sun. 3:30–5:30.*

WHERE TO EAT

$$$$
PIEDMONTESE
Fodor's Choice
★

✕ **Gener Neuv.** One of Italy's finest restaurants, the family-run Gener Neuv is known for its rustic elegance. The setting on the bank of the Tanaro River is splendid. The menu of regional specialties may include agnolotti *ai tre stufati* (with a filling of ground rabbit, veal, and pork), and to finish, *zabaione caldo al vino Vecchio Samperi* (warm eggnog flavored with a dessert wine). Fixed-price menus are available with or without the wine included. As you might expect, the wine list is first-rate. ⊠ *Lungo Tanaro 4* ☎ *0141/557270* ⊕ *www.generneuv.it* ✍ *Reservations essential* ⊟ *AE, DC, MC, V* ⊗ *Closed Aug. and Mon. No dinner Sun.*

$$$
PIEDMONTESE

✕ **L'Angolo del Beato.** Regional specialties such as *bagna cauda* (literally "hot bath," a dip for vegetables made with anchovies, garlic, butter, and olive oil) and *tagliolini al ragu di anatra* (pasta with a duck sauce) are the main attractions at this central Asti restaurant, housed in a building that dates to the 12th century. There's also a good wine list. ⊠ *Via Guttuari 12* ☎ *0141/531668* ⊕ *www.angolodelbeato.it* ⊟ *AE, DC, MC, V* ⊗ *Closed Sun., last wk of Dec., 1st wk of Jan., and 3 wks in Aug.*

WHERE TO STAY

$

⊡ **Reale.** This hotel in a 19th-century building is on Asti's main square. The spacious rooms are somewhat eclectically decorated, with a mix of contemporary and period furniture. Though this is one of the oldest hotels in Asti, all the bathrooms have been modernized and are spotlessly maintained. **Pros:** spacious rooms; central location. **Cons:** lobby area looking a little worn; rooms facing the main square can be noisy. ⊠ *Piazza Alfieri 6* ☎ *0141/530240* ⊕ *www.hotelristorantereale.it* ⤶ *24 rooms* ⌖ *In-room: Internet. In-hotel: parking (paid), Wi-Fi hotspot, some pets allowed* ⊟ *AE, DC, MC, V* ⊗| *BP.*

FESTIVALS

September is a month of fairs and celebrations in Asti, and the **Palio di Asti**, a horse race run through the streets of town, highlights the festivities. First mentioned in 1275, this annual event has been going strong ever since. After an elaborate procession in period costumes, nine horses and jockeys representing different sections of town vie for the honor of claiming the *palio*, a symbolic flag of victory. For 10 days in early September Asti is host to the **Douja d'Or National Wine Festival**—an opportunity to see Asti and celebrate the product that made it famous. During the course of the festival a competition is held to award "Oscars" to the best wine producers, and stands for wine tastings allow visitors to judge the winners for themselves. Musical events and other activities

10

accompany the festival. Contact the **tourist office** (☎ *0141/530357* ⊕ *www.astiturismo.it*) for the schedule of events.

SHOPPING

Tuit, a branch of Turin's Eataly food emporium, is a shop and café on a quiet street just off Piazza Alfieri. Open Tuesday-Saturday 10 AM–10 PM, it's a great place to shop for local and regional food specialties and have a light meal ($). *Via Carlo Grandi 3* ☎ *0141/095813* ⊗ *Closed Mon.*

ALBA

30 km (18 mi) southwest of Asti.

GETTING HERE

By car from Turin follow the A6 south to Marene and then take the A33 east. GTT offers frequent bus service between Alba and Turin—the journey takes approximately 1½ hours. There is no direct train service, but you can get to Alba from Turin by making one transfer in Asti, Bra, or Cavallermaggiore; the entire trip takes about 1½ hours.

VISITOR INFORMATION

Alba tourism office (✉ *Piazza Risorgimento 2* ☎ *0173/35833* ⊕ *www. langheroero.it*).

EXPLORING

This small town has a gracious atmosphere and a compact core studded with medieval towers and Gothic buildings. In addition to being a wine center of the region, Alba is known as the "City of the White Truffle" for the dirty little tubers that command a higher price per ounce than diamonds. For picking out your truffle and having a few wisps shaved on top of your food, expect to shell out an extra €16—which is well worth it.

WHERE TO EAT

$$$
PIEDMONTESE
★
✕ **Locanda del Pilone.** The elegant, formal dining room of the Locanda del Pilone hotel is one of the best restaurants in the region, serving refined variations of traditional dishes. The *carnaroli allo zafferano mantecato al Castelmagno con riduzione di Barbera d'Asti* (cheese and saffron risotto with wine sauce) is as delicious as it is unusual. ✉ *Località Madonna di Como 34* ☎ *0173/366616* ⊕ *www.locandadelpilone. com* ▤ *AE, DC, MC, V.*

$
PIEDMONTESE
★
✕ **Vigin Mudest.** Delicious regional specialties are served at this lively, family-run restaurant in the center of Alba. There's a sumptuous buffet spread of hot and cold antipasti, and their version of *carne cruda albese* (beef carpaccio in the style of Alba) is a favorite with the locals who flock here. All of the pasta (including the thin egg-yolk rich *tajarin* traditional to the region) is homemade, and the risotto *al Barolo* is particularly tasty. Outdoor seating is available in summer. ✉ *Via Vernazza 11* ☎ *0173/441701* ⚖ *Reservations essential* ▤ *MC, V* ⊗ *Closed Mon.*

WHERE TO STAY

$ 🏨 **La Meridiana.** If Alba strikes your fancy, consider a night at this reasonably priced belle epoque–style B&B, on a hill overlooking the historic center and surrounded by Dolcetto and Nebbiolo grapevines.

Pros: friendly, family atmosphere; in a secluded setting convenient for exploring the Langhe. **Cons:** long walk to nearest restaurants; no air-conditioning in some rooms. ⊠ *Località Altavilla 9* 🕿🖷 *0173/440112* ⊕ *www.villalameridiana.it* ↩ *9 rooms, 1 suite* ⚲ *In-room: no a/c (some), no phone. In-hotel: pool, gym* ⊟ *No credit cards* ⦶ *BP.*

WORD OF MOUTH

"I would recommend the area around Asti and Alba as the best and most central location to stay in Piedmont for visiting the wine country and sampling the fabulous cuisine (also, November is the best season for truffles). You really should rent a car as the best wineries and restaurants are located in little hilltop villages and there are the wonderful panaramic drives."   —Sampaguita

$$ 🝙 **Locanda del Pilone.** It would be
★ hard to imagine a more commanding position for this hotel above Alba. Ten minutes outside town, the inn sits on the top of a *langa* (one of hills that form the Langhe region) surrounded by vineyards. The rooms are simply but tastefully decorated with old prints, wooden furniture, and country-style patterned fabrics. An upstairs lounge with panorama windows and a fireplace is great place to unwind. **Pros:** spectacular location with 360-degree views; excellent restaurant. **Cons:** isolation makes own transportation a must; no air-conditioning. ⊠ *Località Madonna di Como 34* 🕿 *0173/366616* ⊕ *www.locandadelpilone.it* ↩ *7 rooms, 1 suite* ⚲ *In-room: no a/c* ⊟ *AE, DC, MC, V* ⦶ *BP.*

$$ 🝙 **Palazzo Finati.** This small boutique hotel in a carefully restored 19th-century town house has charm and character that set it apart from the other more business-oriented hotels in Alba. Rooms are individually decorated with modern furnishings, and changing exhibitions of contemporary art adorn the walls. The location, on a quiet backstreet but only steps away from the city center, can't be beat. A fine buffet breakfast is served in the vaulted basement of the building. **Pros:** quiet location in the center of town; rooms facing the courtyard have terraces. **Cons:** staff coverage is limited at night; breakfast room is a bit gloomy. ⊠ *Via Vernazza 8* 🕿 *0173/366324* ⊕ *www.palazzofinati.it* ↩ *4 rooms, 5 suites* ⚲ *In-room: Wi-Fi. In-hotel: Wi-Fi hotspot, parking (paid)* ⊟ *AE, DC, MC, V* ⊗ *Closed 2 wks in Aug., and Christmas–mid-Jan.* ⦶ *BP*

FESTIVALS

Alba's hilarious **Palio degli Asini** (donkey race), a lampoon of Asti's eminently serious horse race, is held on the first Sunday of October. Tickets to watch this competition between Alba's districts, with riders dressed in medieval garb astride their stubborn beasts, can be difficult to obtain; they go on sale at the beginning of July each year. Contact Alba's **tourist information office** (🕿 *0173/35833* ⊕ *www.langheroero.it*) for details.

On weekends every fall from the second Saturday in October to the second Sunday in November, Alba hosts the **Fiera Internazionale del Tartufo Bianco** (International White Truffle Fair) (⊠ *Cortile della Madalena* 🕿 *0173/361051* ⊕ *www.fieradeltartufo.org*). Merchants, chefs, and other aficionados of this pungent, yet delicious, fungus come from all over the world to buy and to taste white truffles at the height of their season. Though the affair has become increasingly commercialized, it

10

still makes Alba a great place to visit in fall. Note that hotel and restaurant reservations for October and November should be made well in advance.

VALLE D'AOSTA

The unspoiled beauty of the highest peaks in the Alps, the Matterhorn and Monte Bianco, competes with the magnificent scenery of Italy's oldest national park in Valle d'Aosta, a semiautonomous, bilingual region tucked away at the border with France and Switzerland. Luckily, you don't have to choose—the region is small, so you can fit skiing, après-ski, and wild ibex into one memorable trip. The main Aosta Valley, largely on an east–west axis, is hemmed in by high mountains where glaciers have gouged out 14 tributary valleys, 6 to the north and 8 to the south. A car is helpful here, but take care: though distances are relatively short as the crow flies, steep slopes and winding roads add to your mileage and travel time.

Coming up from Turin, beyond Ivrea the road takes you through countryside that becomes hillier and hillier, passing through steep ravines guarded by brooding, romantic castles. Pont St. Martin, about 18 km (11 mi) north of Ivrea, is the beginning of bilingual (Italian and French) territory.

BARD

65 km (40 mi) north of Turin.

GETTING HERE
Bard is just off the A5 highway that runs north from Turin into the Valle d'Aosta—by car the trip takes about an hour. Train service from Turin is infrequent, but Aosta has regular service. Traveling to Bard by bus is not a viable option.

EXPLORING
A few minutes beyond the French-speaking village of Pont St. Martin, you pass through the narrow Gorge de Bard and reach the **Forte di Bard**, a 19th-century reconstruction of a fort that stood for eight centuries, serving the Savoys for six of them. In 1800 Napoléon entered Italy through this valley and used the cover of darkness to get his artillery units past the castle unnoticed. Ten years later he remembered this inconvenience and had the fortress destroyed.

The rebuilt fort houses the high-tech and lavishly multimedia **Museo degli Alpi,** dedicated to the history and culture of the Alps and the Valle d'Aosta region. ⊠ *Forte di Bard* ☎ *0125/833811* ⊕ *www. fortedibard.it* ⊡ *€8* ⊙ *Tues.–Fri. 10–6, weekends 10–7; last entrance 1 hr before closing.*

EN ROUTE
Between Bard and the town of Donnas, 5 km (3 mi) south along the S26, you can walk on a short but fascinating section of a 1st-century Roman consular road that passed here on its way to France. Still showing the deeply worn tracks left by the passage of cart and chariot wheels, this section of road includes an archway carved through solid rock (used

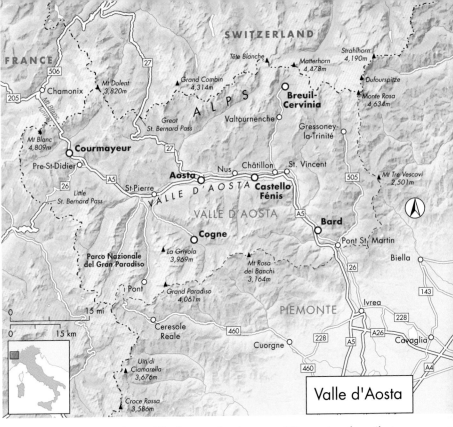

Valle d'Aosta

during the Middle Ages as the city gate of Donnas) and a milestone (XXXVI, to indicate 36 Roman miles from Aosta).

BREUIL-CERVINIA/THE MATTERHORN

50 km (30 mi) north of Bard, 116 km (72 mi) north of Turin.

GETTING HERE

From Aosta take the A5 and then the SR46 (one hour); from Turin take the A5 and then the SR46 (90 minutes). SADEM has regular bus service from Turin; SAVDA buses travel here from Milan. Breuil-Cervinia is not on a train line.

VISITOR INFORMATION

Breuil-Cervinia tourism office (✉ Piazzale Funivie ☎ 0166/944311 ⊕ www.cervinia.it).

EXPLORING

Breuil-Cervinia is a village at the base of the **Matterhorn** *(Monte Cervino in Italian; Mont Cervin in French)*. Like the village, the famous peak straddles the border between Italy and Switzerland, and all sightseeing and skiing facilities are operated jointly. Splendid views of the peak can be seen from **Plateau Rosa** and the **Cresta del Furggen,** both of which can be reached by cable car from the center of Breuil-Cervinia. Although

many locals complain that the tourist facilities and condominiums have changed the face of their beloved village, most would agree that the cable car has given them access to climbing and off-trail skiing in ridges that were once inaccessible.

WHERE TO STAY

$$ ⊞ Cime Bianche. This calm, quiet mountain lodge offers commanding views of the Matterhorn and surrounding peaks from the balconies of its guest rooms. Wood-paneled rooms are simply furnished with the trekker in mind. The restaurant (¢–$) is one of the few dining spots in town to offer regional Valdostana cuisine, serving *fonduta* (a local version of fondue, made with melted cheese, eggs, and sometimes grated truffles), polenta, and wild game in a rustic setting. The wood beams and tables are typical of a ski resort, but meals are produced with greater care than your average après-ski affairs. Reservations are highly recommended. **Pros:** next to the ski slopes; great restaurant; lovely views. **Cons:** lobby is showing wear; busy during the ski season; location is far from everything but slopes. ⊠ *Località La Vieille 44, near ski lift* ☎ *0166/949046* ⊕ *www.hotelcimebianche.com* ⤳ *13 rooms* ⌂ *In-room: no a/c. In-hotel: restaurant, bar, Wi-Fi hotspot* ☰ *MC, V* ⊗ *Closed Mon., and May, June, and Oct.* ⏃⊙⏃ *MAP.*

$$$$ ⊞ Hermitage. The entryway's marble relief of Saint Theodolus reminds you that this was the site of a hermitage, but asceticism has given way to comfort and elegance at what is now one of the most exclusive hotels in the region. It has the look of a relaxed but posh family chalet, with rustic antiques, petit-point upholstery, a fire always glowing in the enormous hearth, and a candlelit dining room. The bright bedrooms have balconies; suites have antique fireplaces and 18th-century furnishings. While here, you can make use of Hermitage's extensive health and beauty facilities and play golf (for half price) at the Cervinia Golf Club. **Pros:** superlative staff; refined atmosphere; frequent shuttle service into town and to ski lifts. **Cons:** located 2 km (1 mi) from the town center; half board is mandatory during the winter season. ⊠ *Via Piolet 1, Località Chapellette* ☎ *0166/948998* ⊕ *www.hotelhermitage. com* ⤳ *30 rooms, 6 suites* ⌂ *In-room: safe, Wi-Fi. In-hotel: restaurant, bar, pool, gym, Wi-Fi hotspot* ☰ *AE, DC, MC, V* ⊗ *Closed May, June, Sept., and Nov.* ⏃⊙⏃ *MAP.*

$$$ ⊞ ★ Les Neiges d'Antan. In an evergreen forest at Perrères, just outside Cervinia, this family-run inn is quiet and cozy, with three big fireplaces and a nice view of the Matterhorn. An excellent restaurant ($–$$) serves French dishes and local specialties such as *zuppa Valpellinentze* (a hearty soup of bread, cabbage, and fontina cheese) and an opulent antipasto (local salami, country *pâté*, *tomino* cheese, and much more). **Pros:** secluded and beautiful setting; excellent restaurant; well-designed spa facilities. **Cons:** 5 km (3 mi) outside Breuil-Cervinia (a car is essential); entrance and lobby areas are showing some wear. ⊠ *Località Perrères* ☎ *0166/948775* ⊕ *www.lesneigesdantan.it* ⤳ *21 rooms, 3 suites* ⌂ *In-room: no a/c, safe, DVD, Wi-Fi. In-hotel: restaurant, bar, spa, Wi-Fi hotspot, Internet terminal* ☰ *AE, MC, V* ⊗ *Closed May and June* ⏃⊙⏃ *BP.*

10

SPORTS AND THE OUTDOORS

CLIMBING

Serious climbers can make the ascent of the Matterhorn from Breuil-Cervinia after registering with the local mountaineering officials at the tourist office. This climb is for experienced climbers only. Before embarking on an excursion, contact the representative of the **Club Alpino Italiano** (✉ *Piazza E. Chanoux 8, Aosta* ☎ *0165/40194* ⊕ *www.cai.it*) for information about hikes and the risks. Guides from the **Società delle Guide Alpine** (✉ *Strada Villair 2, Courmayeur* ☎ *0165/842064* ⊕ *www. guidecourmayeur.com*) can accompany you on treks and also lead skiing, canyoning, and ice-climbing excursions. Less-demanding hikes follow the lower slopes of the valley of the River Marmore, to the south of town.

SKIING

Because its slopes border the Cervino glacier, this resort at the foot of the Matterhorn offers year-round skiing. Sixty lifts and a few hundred miles of ski runs ranging from beginner to expert make the area one of the best and most popular in Italy. Contact the tourist office for information.

CASTELLO FÉNIS

34 km (22 mi) northwest of Bard, 104 km (65 mi) north of Turin.

GETTING HERE

To reach the castle by car, take the Nus exit from the main A5 highway. SAVDA buses provide infrequent service between Aosta and Fénis. The closest train station, in Nus, is a 5-km (3-mi) walk from the castle.

EXPLORING

☺ **Castello Fénis.** The best-preserved medieval fortress in Valle d'Aosta, Fodor'sChoice the many-turreted Castello Fénis was built in the mid-14th century ★ by Aimone di Challant, a member of a prolific family related to the Savoys. The castle, which used a double ring of walls for its defense, is the sort imagined by schoolchildren, with pointed towers, portcullises, and spiral staircases. The 15th-century courtyard surrounded by wooden balconies is elegantly decorated with well-preserved frescoes. Inside you can see the kitchen, with an enormous fireplace that provided central heat in winter; the armory; and the spacious, well-lighted rooms used by the lord and lady of the manor. If you have time to visit only one castle in Valle d'Aosta, this should be it. ✉ *Frazione Chez Croiset 22* ☎ *0165/764263* 🎫 *€5* ⊙ *Mar.–June and Sept., daily 9–6:30; July and Aug., daily 9–7:30; Oct.–Feb., Mon. and Wed.–Sat. 10–noon and 1:30–4:30; Sun. 10–noon and 1:30–5:30. Maximum of 25 people allowed to enter every ½ hr.*

EN ROUTE The highway continues climbing through Valle d'Aosta to the town of Aosta itself. The road at this point is heading almost due west, with rivulets from the wilderness reserve Parco Nazionale del Gran Paradiso streaming down from the left to join the Dora Baltea River, one of the major tributaries of the Po and an increasingly popular spot for rafting. Be careful driving here in late spring, when melting snow can turn some of these streams into torrents.

The exceptionally well-preserved Castello Fénis.

AOSTA

12 km (7 mi) west of Castello Fénis, 113 km (70 mi) north of Turin.

GETTING HERE

Aosta can easily be reached by car or bus from Milan and Turin. The town is off the main A5 highway. SAVDA buses regularly travel to and from Milan, Turin, and Chamonix in France. Direct train service (two hours) is also available from Turin, but a change of trains is required if traveling here from Milan (three hours).

VISITOR INFORMATION

Aosta tourism office (✉ *Piazza E. Chanoux 2* ☎ *0165/236627* ⊕ *www.lovevda.it*).

EXPLORING

Aosta stands at the junction of two of the important trade routes that connect France and Italy—the valleys of the Rhône and the Isère. Its significance as a trading post was recognized by the Romans, who built a garrison here in the 1st century BC. At the eastern entrance to town, in the Piazza Arco d'Augusto and commanding a fine view over Aosta and the mountains, is the **Arco di Augusto** *(Arch of Augustus)*, built in 25 BC to mark Rome's victory over the Celtic Salassi tribe. (The sloping roof was added in 1716 in an attempt to keep rain from seeping between the stones.) The present-day layout of streets in this small city tucked away in the Alps more than 644 km (400 mi) from Rome is the clearest example of Roman urban planning in Italy. Well-preserved Roman walls form a perfect rectangle around the center of Aosta, and the regular pattern of streets reflects its role as a military stronghold. Saint Anselm, born in Aosta, later became archbishop of Canterbury in England.

The **Collegiata di Sant'Orso** is the sort of church that has layers of history in its architecture. Originally there was a 6th-century chapel on this site founded by the Archdeacon Orso, a local saint. Most of this structure was destroyed or hidden when an 11th-century church was erected over it. This church, in turn, was encrusted with Gothic, and later baroque, features, resulting in a jigsaw puzzle of styles, but, surprisingly, not a chaotic jumble. The 11th-century features are almost untouched in the crypt, and if you go up the stairs on the left from the main church you can see the 11th-century frescoes (ask the sacristan who let you in). These restored frescoes depict the life of Christ and the apostles. Although only the tops are visible, you can see the expressions on the faces of the disciples. Take the outside doorway to the right of the main entrance to see the church's crowning glory, its 12th-century cloister. Next to the church, it's enclosed by some 40 stone columns with masterfully carved capitals depicting scenes from the Old and New Testaments and the life of Saint Orso. The turrets and spires of Aosta peek out above. ⊠ *Via Sant'Orso* ☎ *0165/40614* ⊙ *Apr.–Sept., daily 9–5; Oct.–Mar., daily 10–5.*

The huge **Roman Porta Pretoria**, regally guarding the city, is a remarkable relic from the Roman era. The area between the massive inner and outer gates was used as a small parade ground for the changing of the guard. ⊠ *West end of Via Sant'Anselmo.*

The 72-foot-high ruin of the facade of the **Teatro Romano** guards the remains of the 1st-century BC amphitheater, which once held 20,000 spectators. Only a bit of the outside wall and seven of the amphitheater's original 60 arches remain. The latter, once incorporated into medieval buildings, are being brought to light by ongoing archaeological excavations. ⊠ *Via Anfiteatro 4.*

Aosta's **Duomo** dates from the 10th century, but all that remains from that period are the bell towers. The decoration inside is primarily Gothic, but the main attraction of the cathedral predates that era by 1,000 years: a carved ivory diptych portraying the Roman Emperor Honorius and dating from AD 406 is among the many ornate objects housed in the treasury. ⊠ *Via Monsignor de Sales* ☎ *0165/40251* ⊙ *Duomo: Easter–Sept. 7, Mon.–Sat. 6:30 PM–8 PM, Sun. 7 AM–8 PM; Sept. 8–Easter, Mon.–Sat. 6:30–noon and 3–7, Sun. 7–noon and 3–7. Treasury: Apr.–Sept., Tues.–Sun. 9–11:30 and 3–5:30; Oct.–Mar., Sun. 3–5:30.*

WHERE TO EAT

$$ ✕ **La Brasserie du Commerce.** In the heart of Aosta, this small and lively
ITALIAN eatery specializing in grilled meat dishes sits near the Piazza Emile Chanoux. On a sunny summer day try to snag a table in the restaurant's courtyard garden. Typical valley dishes such as fonduta are on the menu, as well as many vegetable dishes and chef's salads. Pizza is also served, but only on the ground floor. ⊠ *Via de Tillier 10* ☎ *0165/35613* ⊕ *www.brasserieducommerce.com* ▭ *AE, DC, MC, V* ⊙ *Closed Sun.*

$–$$ ✕ **Praetoria.** Just outside the Porta Pretoria, this simple and unpreten-
NORTHERN tious restaurant serves hearty local dishes such as *crespelle alla valdo-*
ITALIAN *stana* (crepes with cheese and ham). The pasta is made on the premises,

and all of the menu offerings are prepared from traditional recipes. ⊠ *Via Sant'Anselmo 9* ☎ *0165/44356* ⊟ *AE, MC, V* ☾ *Closed Thurs. No dinner Wed.*

$$$

NORTHERN

ITALIAN

✕ **Vecchio Ristoro**. Housed in a converted mill, the intimate spaces of this elegant restaurant are furnished with antiques, and a traditional ceramic stove provides additional warmth in cool weather. The chef-proprietor takes pride in creative versions of regional recipes, including *gnocchetti di castagnesu crema di zucca* (chestnut gnocchi with pumpkin cream) and *quaglietto disossata farcita alle castagne fatta al forno* (roast quail with chestnut stuffing). ⊠ *Via Tourneuve 4* ☎ *0165/33238* ⊕ *www.ristorantevecchioristoro.it* ⊟ *AE, DC, MC, V* ☾ *Closed Sun., June, and 1 wk in Nov. No lunch Mon.*

WHERE TO STAY

$ 🏠 **Casa Ospitaliera del Gran San Bernardo**. Here's your chance to sleep in a 12th-century castle without emptying your wallet. In a monastery that Amedeo of Savoy gave to the Order of Saint Bernard in 1137, this bargain-price lodging is still run by monks. Only 15 km (8 mi) north of Aosta, this simple pension is a good base for hikers and cross-country skiers. Hearty food is included in the full meal plan. **Pros:** good base for budget-conscious skiers and hikers; secluded atmosphere. **Cons:** isolated location (no towns or restaurants nearby); extremely simple accommodations. ⊠ *Rue de Flassin 3, Saint-Oyen* ☎ *0165/78247* ⊕ *www.gsbernard.net* ⤳ *15 rooms* ♿ *In-room: no a/c, no phone, no TV* ⊟ *No credit cards* ☾ *Closed May* ⦿ *FAP.*

$$$

★

🏠 **Le Miramonti**. On the road leading up to the Little Saint Bernard Pass and only 20 minutes by car from the French border, this delightful Alpine inn is perfectly situated for those who wish to participate in the area's enormous variety of year-round outdoor activities. Built on the banks of a branch of the Dora Baltea River, the small family-run establishment offers all the comforts needed for a relaxing evening after a day of hiking, skiing, mountain biking, or river rafting. Wood and traditional regional furnishings abound and the terrace of the bar affords magnificent views of the surrounding mountains. **Pros:** Friendly, efficient service; excellent location for outdoor sports. **Cons:** isolated location in a small village; rooms facing the mountain river can be noisy. ⊠ *Via Piccolo San Bernardo 3, La Thuile* ☎ *0165/883084* ⊕ *www.lemiramonti.it* ⤳ *35 rooms, 5 suites* ♿ *In-room: no a/c, safe, Wi-Fi. In-hotel: restaurant, spa, Wi-Fi hotspot, parking (free), bicycles* ⊟ *AE, DC, MC, V* ☾ *Closed May, Oct., and Nov.* ⦿ *BP.*

$$

Fodor's Choice

★

🏠 **Milleluci**. This small and inviting family-run hotel sits in an enviable position overlooking Aosta, 1 km (½ mi) north of town. A huge brick hearth and rustic wooden beams highlight the lounge. Bedrooms, some with balconies, are bright and charmingly decorated; all with splendid views of the city and mountains. The same great views are available in summer months from the pool. **Pros:** panoramic views; great spa facilities; cozy and traditionally decorated rooms. **Cons:** need a car to get around; no air-conditioning. ⊠ *Località Porossan Roppoz 15* ☎ *0165/235278* ⊕ *www.hotelmilleluci.com* ⤳ *31 rooms* ♿ *In-room: no a/c, safe, Wi-Fi. In-hotel: bar, pool, spa, Wi-Fi hotspot* ⊟ *AE, DC, MC, V* ⦿ *BP.*

10

FESTIVALS

The streets of Aosta are brightened each year on last weekend of January by the **Sant'Orso Fair**, an arts-and-crafts market that brings artisans from all over the Valle d'Aosta to display and sell their work. All the traditional techniques are featured: wood carving and sculpture, soapstone work, wrought iron, leather, wool, lace, and household items of all kinds. Food and wine are sold at outdoor stands and wandering minstrels enliven the whole event. Contact the tourist office (☎ *0165/236627* ⊕ *www.lovevda.it*) for details.

COURMAYEUR/MONTE BIANCO

★   *35 km (21 mi) northwest of Aosta, 150 km (93 mi) northwest of Turin.*

GETTING HERE

Courmayeur is on the main A5 highway and can easily be reached by car from both Turin and Milan via Aosta. SAVDA buses run regularly from both Turin and Milan. Train service is not available.

VISITOR INFORMATION

Courmayeur tourism office (✉ *Piazzale Monte Bianco 13* ☎ *0165/842060* ⊕ *www.aiat-monte-bianco.com*).

EXPLORING

The main attraction of Courmayeur is a knock-'em-dead view of Europe's tallest peak, **Monte Bianco** *(Mont Blanc)*. Jet-set celebrities flock here, following a tradition that dates from the late 17th century, when Courmayeur's natural springs first began to draw visitors. The spectacle of the Alps gradually surpassed the springs as the biggest draw (the Alpine letters of the English poet Percy Bysshe Shelley were almost advertisements for the region), but the biggest change came in 1965 with the opening of the Mont Blanc tunnel. Since then, ever-increasing numbers of travelers have passed through the area.

Luckily, planners have managed to keep some restrictions on wholesale development within the town, and its angled rooftops and immaculate cobblestone streets maintain a cozy (if prepackaged) feeling.

From La Palud, a small town 4 km (2½ mi) north of Courmayeur, you can catch the cable car up to the top of Monte Bianco. In summer, if you get the inclination, you can then switch cable cars and descend into Chamonix, in France. In winter you can ski parts of the route off-piste. The Funivie La Palud whisks you up first to the Pavillon du Mont Fréty—a starting point for many beautiful hikes—and then to the Rifugio di Torino, before arriving at the viewing platform at **Punta Helbronner** (more than 11,000 feet), which is also the border post with France. Monte Bianco's attraction is not so much its shape (much less distinctive than that of the Matterhorn) as its expanse and the vistas from the top.

The next stage up—only in summer—is on the **Télépherique de L'Aiguille du Midi,** as you pass into French territory. The trip is particularly impressive: you dangle over a huge glacial snowfield (more than 2,000 feet below) and make your way slowly to the viewing station above Chamonix. It's one of the most dramatic rides in Europe.

From this point you're looking down into France, and if you change cable cars at the Aiguille du Midi station you can make your way down to Chamonix itself. The return trip, through the Monte Bianco tunnel, is made by bus. Schedules are unpredictable, depending on weather conditions and demand; contact the **Funivie Monte Bianco** for information. ⊠ *Frazione La Palud 22* ☎ *0165/89925 Italian side, 0450/532275 French side* ⊕ *www.montebianco.com* ✉ *€16 round-trip to Pavillon du Mont Fréty, €38 round-trip to Helbronner, €62 round-trip to Aiguille du Midi, €96 round-trip to Chamonix with return by bus* ☉ *Call for hrs. Closed mid-Oct.–mid-Dec., depending on demand and weather.*

WHERE TO EAT

$$ ✕ **Cadran Solaire**. The Garin family made over the oldest tavern in Cour-
NORTHERN mayeur to create a warm and inviting restaurant that has a 17th-century
ITALIAN stone vault, old wooden floor, and huge stone fireplace. The menu offers
★ seasonal specialties and innovative interpretations of regional dishes: when available, the ravioli maison (filled with ricotta cheese flavored with walnuts and bathed with butter and sage) are particularly delicious. The cozy bar is a popular place for a before-dinner drink. ⊠ *Via Roma 122* ☎ *0165/844609* ⚑ *Reservations essential* ▭ *AE, MC, V* ☉ *Closed Tues., May, and Oct.*

$$ ✕ **Maison de Filippo**. Here you'll find country-style home cooking in
NORTHERN a mountain house with lots of atmosphere, furnished with antiques,
ITALIAN farm tools, and bric-a-brac of all kinds. There's a set menu only, which
★ includes an abundance of antipasti, a tempting choice of local soups and pasta dishes, and an equally impressive array of traditional second courses, including fonduta *valdostana* (cheese fondue), and an equally hearty *carbonada* (beef stew and polenta). Cheese, dessert, and fresh fruit complete the meal. Don't head here if you are looking for something light to eat, and make sure to reserve in advance—it's one of the most popular restaurants in Valle d'Aosta. ⊠ *Via Passerin d'Entrèves 8* ☎ *0165/869797* ⊕ *www.lamaison.com* ⚑ *Reservations essential* ▭ *MC, V* ☉ *Closed Tues., mid-May–June, Oct., and Nov.*

WHERE TO STAY

$$–$$$ ⊞ **Auberge de la Maison**. This modern hotel's stone-and-wood construction, typical of this region, gives it the feeling of a country inn. Most of the cozy rooms have views of Monte Bianco. Alpine prints on the walls, plush fabrics, and wood-burning stoves make the accommodations very comfortable. A massage here can be the perfect ending to a day of hiking or skiing. **Pros:** secluded location in the center of Entrèves; nice spa; charming decor. **Cons:** isolated location (a car is essential); not all standard rooms have views of Monte Bianco. ⊠ *Via Passerin d'Entrèves 16* ☎ *0165/869811* ⊕ *www.aubergemaison.it* ⟿ *30 rooms, 3 suites* ♿ *In-room: no a/c, safe, Wi-Fi. In-hotel: restaurant, spa, Wi-Fi hotspot, parking (free)* ▭ *AE, DC, MC, V* ☉ *Closed May and 15 days in Nov.* ⑩ *BP.*

$$ ⊞ **Croux**. This bright, comfortable hotel is near the town center on the road leading to Monte Bianco. Half the rooms have balconies, the other half have great views of the mountains. The friendly staff goes out of its way to make you feel welcome. **Pros:** central location; great views; B&B rates are available. **Cons:** only half the rooms have views; on a

10

The off-piste skiing options around Monte Bianco are among the best in Europe.

busy road in the town center. ⊠ *Via Croux 8* ☎ *0165/846735* ⊕ *www.hotelcroux.it* ⇄ *31 rooms* ⚇ *In-room: no a/c. In-hotel: bar, Wi-Fi hotspot* ⊟ *AE, DC, MC, V* ⊘ *Closed mid-Apr.–mid-June, Oct., and Nov.* ⊧○⊧ *BP.*

$$$$ ⊡ **Royal e Golf.** A longtime landmark in the center of Courmayeur, the Royal rises high above the surrounding town. With wide terraces and wood paneling, it is the most elegant spot in town. The cheery rooms have plenty of amenities. The hotel's restaurant ($$$–$$$$) is renowned for its regional and national cuisine—the *scaloppina alla valdostana* (fillet of veal with cheese, wine, and nutmeg sauce) is excellent. Light lunches are served in the hotel bar. The heated outdoor pool, with its panoramic view, is a great place to relax after a day on the slopes. The hotel caters to longer stays with half- or full-board service. **Pros:** central location on Courmayeur's main pedestrian street; panoramic views; heated outdoor pool. **Cons:** standard rooms can be small; meal plan required; town center can be busy. ⊠ *Via Roma 87* ☎ *0165/831611* ⊕ *www.hotelroyalegolf.com* ⇄ *80 rooms, 6 suites* ⚇ *In-room: no a/c, safe, Internet. In-hotel: restaurant, bar, pool, gym, some pets allowed, Wi-Fi hotspot* ⊟ *AE, DC, MC, V* ⊘ *Closed wk after Easter–mid-June and mid-Sept.–Nov.* ⊧○⊧ *MAP.*

$$$–$$$$
Fodor's Choice
★
⊡ **Villa Novecento.** Run with the friendly charm and efficiency of Franco Cavaliere and his son Stefano, the Novecento is a peaceful haven near Courmayeur's otherwise busy center. In keeping with the style of a comfortable mountain lodge, the lounge is warmed by a log fire in winter. Traditional fabrics, wooden furnishings, and early-19th-century prints

The Parco Nazionale del Gran Paradiso is one of the few European habitats of the ibex.

lend a soothing quality to the rooms. The restaurant, with only a few extra tables for nonguests, serves creative adaptations of traditional cuisine; it's a good choice for a relaxed evening meal after an active day on the slopes. **Pros:** charming and cozy accommodations; good restaurant; close to town center but away from the hubbub. **Cons:** parking is limited; no air-conditioning. ⊠ *Viale Monte Bianco 64* ☎ *0165/843000* ⊕ *www.villanovecento.it* ↵ *26 rooms* ⌂ *In-room: no a/c, safe, Wi-Fi. In-hotel: restaurant, bar, gym, some pets allowed, Wi-Fi hotspot* ⊟ *AE, DC, MC, V* ⊙ *BP.*

SKIING

Courmayeur pales in comparison to its French neighbor, Chamonix, in both the number (it has only 24) and the quality of its trails. But with good natural snow cover, the trails and vistas are spectacular. A huge gondola leads from the center of Courmayeur to Plan Checrouit, where gondolas and lifts lead to the slopes. The skiing around Monte Bianco is particularly good, and the off-piste options are among the best in Europe. The off-piste routes from Cresta d'Arp (the local peak) to Dolonne, and from La Palud area into France, should be done with a guide. Contact the **Funivie Courmayeur/Mont Blanc** (☎ *0165/89925* ⊕ *www.montebianco.com*) for complete information about lift tickets, ski runs, and weather conditions. For Alpine guide services contact the **Società delle Guide Alpine** (⊠ *Strada Villair 2* ☎ *0165/842064* ⊕ *www. guidecourmayeur.com*).

COGNE AND THE PARCO NAZIONALE DEL GRAN PARADISO

52 km (32 mi) southeast of Courmayeur, 134 km (83 mi) northwest of Turin.

GETTING HERE

Cogne is easily reached by car from the A5—take the Aosta Ovest–St. Pierre exit and follow the SR47 for 20 km (12 mi). SAVDA buses arrive here frequently from Aosta, but no train service is available.

VISITOR INFORMATION

Cogne tourism office (⊠ *Via Bourgeois 34* ☎ *0165/74040* ⊕ *www.cogne.org*).

EXPLORING

Cogne is the gateway to the **Parco Nazionale del Gran Paradiso.** This huge park, once the domain of King Vittorio Emanuele II (1820–78) and bequeathed to the nation after World War I, is one of Europe's most rugged and unspoiled wilderness areas, with wildlife and many plant species protected by law. This is one of the few places in Europe where you can see the ibex (a mountain goat with horns up to 3 feet long) and the chamois (a small antelope). The park is open free of charge throughout the year and is managed by a park board, the **Ente Parco Nazionale Gran Paradiso** (⊠ *Via della Rocca 47, Turin* ☎ *011/8606211 park board, 0165/749264 visitor information center* ⊕ *www.grandparadis.it*). Try to visit in May, when spring flowers are in bloom and most of the meadows are clear of snow.

HIKING

There's wonderful hiking to be done here, both on daylong excursions and longer journeys with overnight stops in the park's mountain refuges. The **Cogne tourism office** (⊠ *Via Bourgeois 34* ☎ *0165/74040* ⊕ *www.cogne.org*) has a wealth of information and trail maps to help.

The Italian Riviera

WORD OF MOUTH

"Somewhat against my will, I stumbled into the Riviera the first time, picking a town almost by accident, didn't do ANYTHING for 3 days despite my plans to be a good tourist, and ended up living here. It's just BELLA, so come enjoy, no worries."

—zeppole

WELCOME TO THE ITALIAN RIVIERA

TOP REASONS TO GO

★ **Walking the Cinque Terre:** Hike the famous Cinque Terre trails past gravity-defying vineyards, rock-perched villages, and the deep blue sea.

★ **Portofino:** See the world through rose-tinted sunglasses at this glamorous little harbor village.

★ **Genoa's historical center and port:** From the palaces of Via Garibaldi to the labyrinthine backstreets of the old city to the world-class aquarium, the city is full of surprising delights.

★ **Giardini Botanici Hanbury:** A spectacular natural setting harbors one of Italy's largest, most exotic botanical gardens.

★ **Pesto:** The basil-rich sauce was invented in Liguria, and it's never been equaled elsewhere.

Portovenere

1 Riviera di Levante. East of Genoa, the Riviera of the Rising Sun has tiny bays and inlets, set among dramatic cliffs, making for some of the most beautiful coastline in Italy. The pastel-hue town of Portofino has charmed generations of the rich and famous.

2 Cinque Terre. Five isolated seaside villages seem removed from the modern world—despite the many hikers who populate the trails between them.

3 Genoa. Birthplace of Christopher Columbus, this city is an urban anomaly among Liguria's charming villages. At its heart is Italy's largest historic district, filled with beautiful architecture.

11

4 **Riviera di Ponente.**
The Riviera of the Setting
Sun, reaching from the
French border to Genoa, has
protected bays and sandy
beaches. The seaside resorts
of Bordighera and San Remo
share some of the glitter of
their French cousins to the
west.

GETTING ORIENTED

A thin crescent of rug-
ged and verdant land
between France, Piedmont,
Tuscany, the Alps, and
the Mediterranean Sea,
Liguria is best known as the
Italian Riviera. Genoa, the
region's largest city and
one of Italy's most important ports, lies directly in
the middle, with the Riviera
di Ponente to the west
and the Riviera di Levante
to the east. It is here that
the Italians perfected *il
dolce far niente*—the
sweet art of idleness.

0   20 mi
0   20 km

EMILIA-
ROMAGNA

35

Busalla

45

Rosso

A26

A10

3 Genoa

A12

225

Nervi

Camogli

Portofino Santa
Margherita
Ligure

Rapallo

Chiavari

Lavagna

TUSCANY

*Golfo di
Genova*

Sestri Levante

1

Moneglia

Monterosso
al Mare

Vernazza
Manarola
Riomaggiore

CINQUE TERRE

1

A12

2

La
Spezia

RIVIERA DI LEVANTE

THE ITALIAN RIVIERA PLANNER

Hiking

Walking Liguria's extensive network of trails, and taking in the gorgeous views, is a major outdoor activity. The mild climate and laid-back state of mind can lull you into underestimating just how strenuous such walks can be. Wear good shoes, use sunscreen, and carry water—you'll be glad you did. Trail maps are available from tourist information offices, or upon entry to the Cinque Terre National Park.

Other walks to consider: On Portofino promontory, the relatively easy walk to the Abbazia di San Fruttuoso is popular, and there's a more challenging hike from Ruta to the top of Monte Portofino. From Genoa, you can take the Zecca–Righi funicular up to Righi and walk along the ring of fortresses that used to defend the city, or ride the Genova–Casella railroad to one of the trailheads near the station stops.

Walking tours can introduce you to lesser-known aspects of the region. For the Cinque Terre and the rest of the Province of La Spezia, the **Cooperativa Arte e Natura** (⊠ *Viale Amendola 172, La Spezia* ☎ *0187/739410* ✍ *coop.arte@ tin.it*) is a good source for English-speaking guides. A half day costs around €150.

Making the Most of Your Time

Your first decision, particularly with limited time, is between the two Rivieras. The Riviera di Levante, east of Genoa, is quieter and has a more distinct personality with the rustic Cinque Terre, ritzy Portofino, and the panoramic Gulf of Poets. The Riviera di Ponente, west of Genoa, is a classic European resort experience with many white-sand beaches and more nightlife—similar to, but not as glamorous as, the French Riviera across the border.

In either case, your second choice is whether to visit Genoa. Despite its rough exterior and (diminishing) reputation as a seamy port town, Genoa's artistic and cultural treasures are significant—you won't find anything remotely comparable elsewhere in the region. Unless your goal is to avoid urban life entirely, consider a night or two in the city.

Season is everything. Shops, cafés, clubs, and restaurants stay open late in resorts during high season (at Easter and from June through August), but during the rest of the year they close early, if they're open at all.

Finding a Place to Stay

Liguria's lodging options may be a step behind such resort areas as Positano and Taormina, so reservations for its better accommodations, and limited ones in the Cinque Terre, should be made far in advance. Lodging tends to be pricey in high season, particularly June to August. At other times of year, ask for a *sconto bassa stagione* (low-season discount).

WHAT IT COSTS IN EUROS

	¢	$	$$	$$$	$$$$
Restaurants	under €20	€20–€30	€30–€45	€45–€65	over €65
Hotels	under €75	€75–€125	€125–€200	€200–€300	over €300

Restaurant prices are for a first course (primo), second course (secondo), and dessert (dolce). Hotel prices are for two people in a standard double room in high season, including tax and service.

11

Getting Around by Boat

With so much coastline—350 km (217 mi)—and so many pretty little harbors, Liguria is a great place to get around by boat. A busy network of local ferry lines, such as **Servizio Marittimo del Tigullio** (☎ *0185/284670* ⊕ *www.traghettiportofino.it*) and **Alimar** (☎ *010/256775*), connects many of the resorts. **Golfo Paradiso** (☎ *0185/772091* ⊕ *www.golfoparadiso.it*) lines run between Camogli, San Fruttuoso (on the Portofino promontory), and Recco, and in summer from the port of Genoa and Nervi to Portofino, the Cinque Terre, and Portovenere, stopping in Recco and Camogli. **Navigazione Golfo dei Poeti** (☎ *0187/732987* ⊕ *www.navigazionegolfodeipoeti.it*) runs regular ferry services between Lerici, Portovenere, the Cinque Terre, Santa Margherita, and Genoa.

But you can have as much fun (or more) negotiating a price with a boat owner at one of the smaller ports such as Camogli, Portovenere, and Lerici. You're likely to deal with someone who has a rudimentary command of English at best, but that's all you need to discuss price, time, and destination. For smaller groups (eight or fewer) interested in seeing the Cinque Terre by sea, local fisherman **Angelo Benvenuto** (✉ *Monterosso* ☎ *333/3182967* ✎ *angelosboattours@yahoo.com*) offers a variety of boating excursions. A private half day costs approximately €300.

Getting Around by Bus

Generally speaking, buses are a difficult way to come and go in Liguria. **Diana Tours** (☎ *800/651931*) provides service from the airport in Nice, but there's no bus service between Genoa and other major Italian cities. There's no regular service connecting Genoa with the towns along the Riviera di Ponente. Things are somewhat easier along the Riviera di Levante where **Tigullio Trasporti** (☎ *0185/373234* ⊕ *www.tigulliotrasporti.it*) runs regular service.

Getting Around by Car

With the freedom of a car, you could drive from one end of the Riviera to the other on the autostrada in less than three hours. Two good roads run parallel to each other along the coast of Liguria. Closer to shore and passing through all the towns and villages is SS1, the Via Aurelia, which was laid out by the ancient Romans and has excellent views at almost every turn but gets crowded in July and August.

More direct and higher up than SS1 are the autostrade, A10 west of Genoa and A12 to the south—engineering wonders with literally hundreds of long tunnels and towering viaducts. These routes save time on weekends, in summer, and on days when festivals slow traffic in some resorts to a standstill.

Getting Around by Train

Train travel is convenient throughout the region. It takes three hours for an express train to cover the entire Liguria coast. Local trains take upward of five hours to get from one end of the coast to the other, stopping in or near all the towns along the way. For schedules, check the Web site of the national railway, **FS** (☎ *892021* ⊕ *www.trenitalia.com*).

EATING AND DRINKING WELL IN THE ITALIAN RIVIERA

Ligurian cuisine might surprise you. As you'd expect given the long coastline, it employs all sorts of seafood, but the real claim to fame is the exemplary use of vegetables and herbs.

Basil is practically revered in Genoa (the word is derived from the Greek *basileus*, meaning "king"), and the city is considered the birthplace of pesto, the basil-rich pasta sauce. This and other herbs—laurel, fennel, and marjoram—are cultivated but also grow wild on the sun-kissed hillsides. Seafood also plays a prominent role on the menu, appearing in soups, salads, and pasta dishes. Especially bountiful are anchovies, sea bass, squid, and octopus. Vegetables—particularly artichokes, eggplant, and zucchini—are abundant, usually prepared with liberal amounts of olive oil and garlic.

Like much of Italy, Liguria has a full range of eating establishments from cafeteria-like *tavole calde* to family-run trattorias to sophisticated *ristoranti*. Lunch is served between 12:30 and 2:30 and dinner between 7:30 and 11. Also popular, especially in Genoa, are *enoteche* (wine bars), which serve simply prepared light meals late into the night.

FABULOUS FOCACCIA

When you're hankering for a snack, turn to bakeries and small eateries serving focaccia *(pictured above)*. The flat bread here is more dense and flavorful than what's sold as focaccia in American restaurants; it's the region's answer to pizza, usually eaten on the go.

It comes simply salted and dribbled with olive oil; flavored with rosemary and olives; covered with cheese or anchovies; and even *ripiena* (filled), usually with cheese or vegetables and herbs. Another local delicacy is *farinata*, a chickpea pancake baked like a pizza.

ANTIPASTI

Seafood antipasti are served in abundance at most Ligurian restaurants. These usually include marinated anchovies from Monterosso, *cozze ripiene* (mussel shells stuffed with minced mussel meat, prosciutto, Parmesan, herbs, and bread crumbs), and *sopressato di polpo* (flattened octopus in olive oil and lemon sauce).

PASTA

Liguria's classic pasta sauce is pesto, made from basil, garlic, olive oil, pine nuts, and hard cheese. It's usually served with *trenette* (similar to spaghetti) or the slightly sweet *testaroli* (a flat pasta made from chestnut flour).

You can also find *pansotti* (triangular pockets of pasta filled with a cheese mixture (*pictured below*), and *trofie* (doughy, short pasta twists) with *salsa di noci*, a rich sauce of garlic, walnuts, and cream that, as with pesto, is ideally pounded with a mortar and pestle.

Spaghetti *allo scoglio* is an olive oil, tomato, and white wine–based sauce containing an assortment of local *frutti di mare* (seafood) including shrimp, clams, mussels, and cuttlefish.

FISH AND MEAT

Fish is the best bet for a second course: the classic preparation is a whole grilled or baked whitefish—*branzino* (sea bass) and *orata* (dorado) are good choices—served with olives, potatoes, Ligurian

spices, and a drizzle of olive oil. A popular meat dish is *cima alla Genovese*, a veal roll stuffed with a mixture of eggs and vegetables, served as a cold cut.

PANIGACCI

One of the real treats of the region is *panigacci* from the Lunigiana area, the valley extending inland along the border between Liguria and Tuscany. Balls of dough are laid in a small, terra-cotta dishes known as *testine* and stacked one on top of the other in order to flatten the dough. Then they are placed over hot coals (or in a pizza oven), and what emerges is flat, firm, almost pitalike bread. Panigacci is usually served with *stracchino* cheese (similar to cream cheese), pesto, or nut sauce and cold cuts—a delicious, hearty meal.

WINE

Local vineyards produce mostly light and refreshing whites such as Pigato, Vermentino, and Cinque Terre. Rossese di Dolceacqua, from near the French border, is the best red wine the region has to offer, but for a more robust accompaniment to meats opt for the more full-bodied reds of the neighboring Piedmont region.

Updated
by Megan
McCaffrey-
Guerrera

Like the family jewels that bedeck its habitual visitors, the Italian Riviera is glamorous, but in the old-fashioned way. The resort towns and coastal villages that stake intermittent claim on the rocky shores of the Ligurian Sea are the long-lost cousins of newer seaside paradises found elsewhere.

Here the grandest palazzi share space with frescoed, angular, late-19th-century apartment buildings. The rustic and elegant, the provincial and chic, the small-town and cosmopolitan all collide here in a sun-drenched blend that defines the Italian side of the Riviera. There is the glamour of its chic resorts such as San Remo and Portofino, the tranquil beauty and outdoor adventures of the Cinque Terre, plus the history and architectural charm of Genoa. Mellowed by the balmy breezes blowing off the sea, travelers bask in the sun, explore the picturesque fishing villages, and pamper themselves at the resorts that dot this ruggedly beautiful landscape.

RIVIERA DI LEVANTE

East of Genoa lies the Riviera di Levante (Riviera of the Rising Sun). It has a more raw, unpolished side to it than the Riviera di Ponente, and its stretches of rugged coastline are dotted with fishing villages. Around every turn of this area's twisting roads the hills plummet sharply to the sea, forming deep, hidden bays and coves. Beaches on this coast tend to be rocky, backed by spectacular sheer cliffs. (Yet there are some rather lovely sandy beaches in Lerici, Monterosso, Levanto, and Paraggi.) It is also home to one of Europe's well-known playgrounds for the rich and famous, the inlet of Portofino.

LERICI

106 km (66 mi) southeast of Genoa, 65 km (40 mi) west of Lucca.

GETTING HERE

By car, Lerici is less than a 10-minute drive west from the A12 with plenty of blue signs indicating the way. There is a large pay-parking lot about a 10-minute walk along the seaside promenade from the center. By train, the closest station is either Sarzana (10-minute drive) or La Spezia Centrale (20-minute drive) on the main north–south line between Genoa and Pisa.

VISITOR INFORMATION

Lerici tourism office (⊠ *Via Biaggini 6* ☎ *0187/967346* ⊕ *www.aptcinqueterre. sp.it*).

EXPLORING

Near Liguria's border with Tuscany, this colorful village dates to the 1200s. It is set on a magnificent coastline of gray cliffs and surrounded by a national park of pine forests and olive trees. The waterfront piazza is filled with deceiving trompe l'oeil frescoes, and seaside cafés line its charming little harbor that holds boats of all sizes.

There are several white beaches and bathing establishments dotting the 2-km (1-mi) walk along the bay from the village center to nearby San Terenzo. It was here that the writer and poet Percy Shelley spent some of his happiest days. After his death in 1822, the bay was renamed the *Golfo dei Poeti* (Gulf of Poets) in his and Lord Byron's honor.

With its proximity to the autostrada, Lerici makes a great base for exploring not only the more famous attractions of the area but also the tiny hill towns and walled villages that dot the hinterlands.

Its promontory is dominated by the 13th-century **Castello di Lerici.** The Pisan castle now houses a museum of paleontology. ⊠ *Piazza S. Giorgio 1* ☎ *0187/969042* ⊕ *www.castellodilerici.it* ⌑ *€5* ⊙ *Mar. 16– June, Sept.–Oct. 19, and Dec. 26–Jan. 6, Tues.–Sun. 10:30–12:30 and 2:30–5:30; July and Aug., daily 10:30–12:30 and 6:30–midnight; Oct. 20–Dec. 23 and Jan. 7–Mar. 15, Tues.–Fri. 10:30–12:30, weekends 10:30–12:30 and 2:30–5:30.*

WHERE TO EAT

$
PIZZA
✕ **Bonta Nascoste.** In the local dialect, *bonta nascoste* means "hidden goodness," a reference to this restaurant's back-alleyway location and consistently good food. Some of the best pizza and farinata in the Gulf of Poets is served here, but the pasta, fish, and meat dishes are also all noteworthy. There are only eight tables (and a couple more outside in summer), so reserve ahead. ⊠ *Via Cavour 52* ☎ *0187/965500* ⊕ *www. bontanascoste.it* ⌑ *Reservations essential* ▭ *AE, MC, V* ⊙ *Closed Wed. and 2 wks in Nov. and June.*

$$
LIGURIAN
✕ **Golfo dei Poeti.** Owners Claudio and Annalisa have taken this grotto-like space on the waterfront and created a fun restaurant specializing in delicious homemade pasta dishes and seafood. Their tagliatelle with *gamberi* (shrimp) and zucchini in an olive oil and white wine sauce is mouthwateringly good. Very good pizza is served in the evening. ⊠ *Ca-*

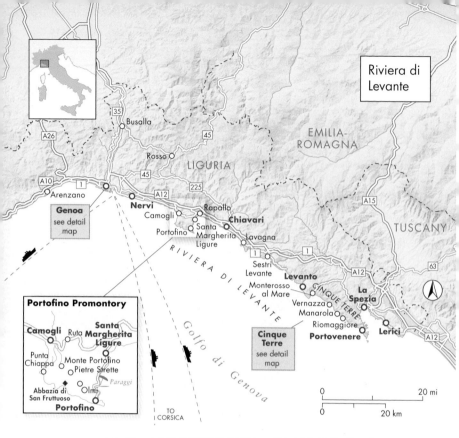

Riviera di Levante

Portofino Promontory

lata Mazzini 52 ☎ *0187/966414* ▬ *AE, MC, V* ☺ *Closed Tues. and 2 wks in Nov. No lunch Mon. and Wed.*

$$$
LIGURIAN

✕ **Miranda.** Perched amid the clustered old houses in seaside Tellaro, 4 km 2½ mi) southeast of Lerici, this small family-run restaurant has become a gourmet's destination because of chef Angelo Cabani's imaginative Ligurian cooking. His seafood menu changes daily, but might include shrimp and lobster salad with fennel, or risotto with asparagus and shrimp. This pretty building is also a small inn with seven charming and comfortable rooms ($$). ⊠ *Via Fiascherino 92, Tellaro* ☎ *0187/964012* ⊕ *www.miranda1959.com* ▬ *AE, DC, MC, V* ☺ *Closed Mon. and Nov. and Jan.*

$$–$$$
LIGURIAN

✕ **Osteria di Redarca.** Within the pine forest of the Montemarcello National Park, this *osteria* (a simple, informal restaurant) serves some of the best homemade pastas in the area. It also offers a "surf-and-turf"–type menu, with abundant cooked-to-perfection fish platters and succulent meat dishes. The location may not be seaside, but the setting and the food are both a treat. ⊠ *Rocchetta Località Redarca 6, Lerici* ☎ *0187/966140* ▬ *AE, MC, V* ☺ *Closed Wed. and 2 wks in Jan.*

Lerici, the easternmost of Liguria's charming seaside villages.

WHERE TO STAY

$$–$$$ **Doria Park.** Nestled between olive-tree hills and the village center, with views over the harbor and bay beyond, the Doria has the best location in Lerici. Erminio and Claudia Beghé have created a welcoming and relaxing atmosphere for their guests. The junior suites have larger terraces and Jacuzzi tubs, but the sea-view rooms are a real value. A bountiful and delicious breakfast is served until noon. The first-rate restaurant specializes in fresh seafood. **Pros:** sea views; comfortable beds; not far from the main piazza and harbor. **Cons:** many stairs, including several sets that can be challenging for people with weak knees or heavy bags. ⊠ *Via Doria 2* ☎ *0187/967124* ⊕ *www.doriaparkhotel.it* ⤴ *48 rooms, 5 suites* ⌖ *In-room: safe, Wi-Fi. In-hotel: restaurant, bar, laundry service, Wi-Fi hotspot, parking (free), some pets allowed* ⊟ *AE, DC, MC, V* ⏐◎⏐ *BP.*

$$ **Florida.** This seafront, family-run establishment has a sunny, welcoming facade and a friendly staff inside. Extras such as Wi-Fi and sea-view balconies make this reasonably priced hotel well worth the euros. Lounge in one of the deck chairs on the rooftop solarium or enjoy the nearby tennis courts, public outdoor pool, and golf course. **Pros:** beachfront location; bay views. **Cons:** small rooms; beach across the street can be noisy, especially on Thursday and Saturday nights in summer. ⊠ *Lungomare Biaggini 35* ☎ *0187/967332* ⊕ *www.hotelflorida.it* ⤴ *40 rooms* ⌖ *In-room: safe, refrigerator. In-hotel: bar, beachfront, Wi-Fi hotspot* ⊟ *AE, DC, MC, V* ☒ *Closed approximately Dec.–Feb.* ⏐◎⏐ *BP.*

$$$ **Piccolo Hotel del Lido.** Although the 12 waterfront rooms at this boutique hotel are not large, they are well equipped and tastefully decorated. Bathrooms are large by Italian standards, and each room has a private rooftop terrace where you can sunbathe or sip a glass of local wine while watching the sunset. **Pros:** beachfront; great views; large bathrooms. **Cons:** limited parking; adjacent beach club can get noisy by day during high season. ✉ *Lungomare Biaggini 24* 🕾 *0187/968159* ⊕ *www.locandadellido.it* ⇄ *12 rooms* ⚬ *In-room: safe, refrigerator* ⊟ *AE, DC, MC, V* ⊘ *Closed late Oct.–Easter* ⦅⦆ *BP.*

EN ROUTE   Ten minutes inland from Lerici is the medieval village of **Sarzana**, designed by the military leader Castruccio Castracani, who also designed Lucca. Here you will find some of the most authentic and well-restored palazzos in Liguria. Its pedestrians-only cobblestone streets bustling with people, fine boutiques, and packed cafés are perfect for a *passeggiata* (late-afternoon stroll).

LA SPEZIA

11 km (7 mi) northwest of Lerici, 103 km (64 mi) southeast of Genoa.

GETTING HERE

By car, take La Spezia exit off the A12. La Spezia Centrale train station is on the main north–south railway line between Genoa and Pisa.

VISITOR INFORMATION

La Spezia tourism office (✉ *Via Mazzini 45* 🕾 *0187/770900* ⊕ *www.aptcinqueterre.sp.it*).

EXPLORING

La Spezia is sometimes thought of as nothing but a large, industrialized naval port en route to the Cinque Terre and Portovenere, but it does possess some charm, and it gives you a look at a less tourist-focused part of the Riviera. Its palm-lined promenade, fertile citrus parks, renovated Liberty-style palazzos, and colorful balcony-lined streets make parts of La Spezia surprisingly beautiful. On mornings Monday through Saturday, you can stroll through the fresh fish, produce, and local-cheese stalls at the outdoor market on Piazza Cavour, and on Friday take part in the lively flea market on Via Garibaldo.

The remains of the massive 13th-century **Castel San Giorgio** now house a small museum dedicated to local archaeology. ✉ *Via XX Settembre* 🕾 *0187/751142* ⊡ *€5* ⊘ *June–Aug., Wed.–Mon. 9:30–12:30 and 5–8; Apr., May, and Sept., Wed.–Mon. 9:30–12:30 and 3–8; Oct.–Mar., Wed.–Mon. 9:30–12:30 and 2–5.*

WHERE TO EAT

¢ ✕ **La Pia.** Considered an institution in La Spezia, this *farinateria* and pizzeria dates back to 1887. During the lunch hour, you will find a line out the door while inside—and on the patio in summer—locals munch on *farinata*, a chickpea pancake that's a Ligurian delicacy, and on thick-crust pizzas served hot out of the wood-burning oven. ✉ *Via Magenta 12* 🕾 *0187/739999* ⊟ *AE, MC, V* ⊘ *Closed Wed. and 2 wks in Nov. and Aug.*

A view from Portovenere.

PORTOVENERE

★ *12 km (7 mi) south of La Spezia, 114 km (70 mi) southeast of Genoa.*

GETTING HERE

By car from the port city of La Spezia, follow the blue signs for Portovenere. It is about a 20-minute winding drive along the sea through small fishing villages. From the La Spezia train station you can hire a taxi for about €30. By bus from Via Garibaldi in La Spezia (a 10-minute walk from the train station), it takes 20 minutes.

VISITOR INFORMATION

Portovenere doesn't have a tourist office; you get information at the Commune (Town Hall) or at the tourist office in La Spezia Centrale train station.

EXPLORING

The colorful facades and pedestrians-only *calata* (promenade) make Portovenere a quintessential Ligurian seaside village. Its tall, thin *terratetto* (houses) date from as far back as the 11th century and are connected in a wall-like formation to protect against attacks by the Pisans and local pirates. At the tip of the peninsula, with a dramatic position over the sea, stands the commanding San Pietro church. The *caruggi* (alleylike passageways) lead to an array of charming shops, homes, and gardens.

Lord Byron (1788–1824) is said to have written *Childe Harold's Pilgrimage* in Portovenere. Near the entrance to the huge, strange **Grotto Arpaia**, at the base of the sea-swept cliff, is a plaque recounting the poet's strength and courage as he swam across the gulf to the village of San Terenzo, near Lerici, to visit his friend Shelley (1792–1822).

San Pietro, a 13th-century Gothic church, is built on the site of an ancient pagan shrine, on a formidable solid mass of rock above the Grotto Arpaia. With its black-and-white-striped exterior, it is a landmark recognizable from far out at sea. There's a spectacular view of the Cinque Terre coastline from the front porch of the church. ⊠ *Waterfront promenade* 🕾 *No phone* ☉ *Apr.–Oct., daily 7* AM*–8* PM*; Nov.–Mar., daily 7* AM*–6* PM.

WHERE TO EAT

¢   ✕ **Bacicio.** Tucked away on Portovenere's main *caruggio*, this *enoteca*
WINE BAR   (wine bar) and antipasto bar is popular with locals and slowly being discovered by tourists looking for good, local dishes. The owner whips up some wonderful finger food—including *crostini* (grilled bread) with fresh anchovies, and smoked herring with spicy orange salsa—and offers a robust list of local wines. He also designed the entire place, right down to the tables and chairs made from anchors and pieces of old boats. ⊠ *Via Cappellini 17* 🕾 *0187/792054* ⌦ *Reservations not accepted* ▭ *No credit cards* ☉ *Closed Wed., Nov., and Jan.*

$$–$$$ ✕ **Da Iseo.** Try to get one of the tables outside at this waterfront restau-
LIGURIAN   rant with bistro accents and paintings of Portovenere. Seafood here is fresh and plentiful, and the pasta courses are inventive. Try spaghetti *alla Giuseppe* (with shellfish and fresh tomato) or *alla Iseo* (with a seafood curry sauce). ⊠ *Calata Doria 9* 🕾 *0187/790610* ▭ *AE, DC, MC, V* ☉ *Closed Wed., Dec. 1–15, and Jan. 15–Feb. 1.*

$$$$ ✕ **Le Bocche.** At the end of the Portovenere promontory in the shadow
LIGURIAN   of San Pietro, this is the village's most exclusive and possibly most delicious restaurant. The menu consists of only the freshest in-season fish, prepared with a creative touch, such as marinated tuna encrusted with pistachios or asparagus soup with small fillets of sole. The setting is romantic and unique, as you feel almost immersed in the Mediterranean. The dinner menu is quite expensive (as is the lengthy wine list), but you can get a real deal at lunch with a limited but equally good menu at lower prices. ⊠ *Calata Doria 102* 🕾 *0187/790622* ⊕ *www.lebocche.it* ▭ *AE, DC, MC, V* ☉ *Closed Nov.–Feb.*

$$–$$$ ✕ **Locanda Lorena.** Across the small bay of Portovenere lies the rugged
LIGURIAN   island of Palmaria. There is only one restaurant on the island, the sister establishment to Da Iseo, and here Iseo (aka Giuseppe), an accomplished chef, actually still does the cooking. Fresh pasta and local fish such as *branzino* (sea bass) are headliners at this fun dining spot with lovely views looking back toward Portovenere. To get here, take the restaurant's free speedboat from the dock just outside Da Iseo. ⊠ *Palmaria Island* 🕾 *0187/792370* ⊕ *www.locandalorena.com* ▭ *AE, DC, MC, V* ☉ *Closed Nov.*

WHERE TO STAY

$$–$$$ 🛏 **Grand Hotel Portovenere.** Built in the 13th century as a Franciscan convent, this pale pink building with arches and frescoes is now the best hotel in the village. Rooms are fairly basic, but the views of the historic center and sea are magnificent. The hotel also has a fine restaurant and serves a robust breakfast on the terrace. **Pros:** nice location; many extra

Continued on page 434

THE CINQUE TERRE

FIVE REMOTE VILLAGES MAKE ONE MUST-SEE DESTINATION

"Charming" and "breathtaking" are adjectives that get a workout when you're traveling in Italy, but it's rare that both apply to a single location. The Cinque Terre is such a place, and this combination of characteristics goes a long way toward explaining its tremendous appeal.

The area is made up of five tiny villages (Cinque Terre literally means "Five Lands") clinging to the cliffs along a gorgeous stretch of the Ligurian coast. The terrain is so steep that for centuries footpaths were the only way to get from place to place. It just so happens that these paths provide beautiful views of the rocky coast tumbling into the sea, as well as access to secluded beaches and grottoes.

Backpackers "discovered" the Cinque Terre in the 1970s, and its popularity has been growing ever since. Despite summer crowds, much of the original appeal is intact. Each town has maintained its own distinct charm, and views from the trails in between are as breathtaking as ever.

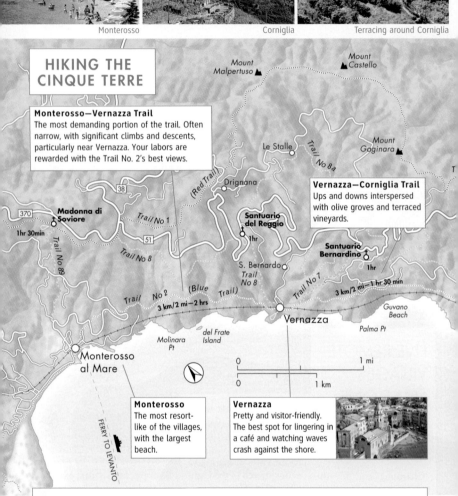

Monterosso

Corniglia

Terracing around Corniglia

HIKING THE CINQUE TERRE

Mount Malpertuso

Mount Castello

Monterosso–Vernazza Trail
The most demanding portion of the trail. Often narrow, with significant climbs and descents, particularly near Vernazza. Your labors are rewarded with the Trail No. 2's best views.

Le Stalle

Mount Gaginara

Trail No 8a

(Red Trail)

Drignana

38

Vernazza–Corniglia Trail
Ups and downs interspersed with olive groves and terraced vineyards.

370

Madonna di Soviore

Trail No 1

Santuario del Reggio

1hr 30min

51

Trail No 8

Trail No 89

Santuario Bernardino

1hr

S. Bernardo
Trail No 8

Trail No 7

3 km/2 mi–1 hr 30 min

Trail No 2 (Blue Trail)
3 km/2 mi–2 hrs

Vernazza

Guvano Beach

Molinara Pt

del Frate Island

Palma Pt

Monterosso al Mare

0   1 mi

0   1 km

Monterosso
The most resort-like of the villages, with the largest beach.

Vernazza
Pretty and visitor-friendly. The best spot for lingering in a café and watching waves crash against the shore.

FERRY TO LEVANTO

THE CLASSIC HIKE

Hiking is the most popular way to experience the Cinque Terre, and Trail No. 2, the Sentiero Azzurro (Blue Trail), is the most traveled path. To cover the entire trail is a full day: it's approximately 13 km (8 mi) in length, takes you to all five villages, and requires about five hours, not including stops, to complete. The best approach is to start at the eastern-most town of Riomaggiore and warm up your legs on the easiest segment of the trail. As you work your way west, the hike gets progressively more demanding. For a less strenuous experience, you can choose to skip a leg or two and take the ferry (which provides its own beautiful views) or the inland train running between the towns instead.

Manarola

Along Trail No.2

Via dell'Amore

Corniglia–Manarola Trail
Runs through the hills near Manarola, descends to rocky beach near Corniglia.

Manarola–Riomaggiore Trail
Known as the Via dell'Amore (Lovers' Lane). A wide, paved, flat path with fine views.

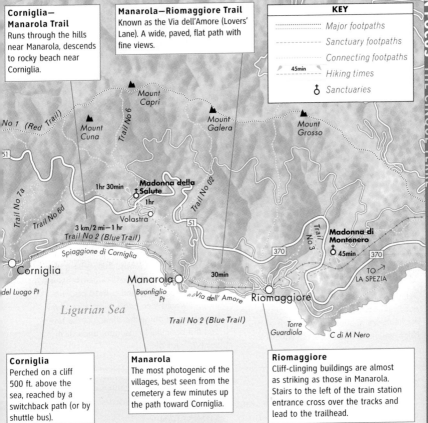

KEY

············ Major footpaths
- - - - - - - Sanctuary footpaths
–––––––– Connecting footpaths
45min ⚐ Hiking times
♀ Sanctuaries

Mount Capri
Mount Galera
Mount Grosso
Mount Cuna
No 1 (Red Trail)
Trail No 6
Trail No 7a
Trail No 6d
51
1hr 30min
Madonna della Salute †
1hr
Volastra
3 km/2 mi – 1 hr
Trail No 2 (Blue Trail)
Trail No 02
51
Trail No 3
Madonna di Montenero ♀ 45min
370
370
TO → LA SPEZIA
Spiaggione di Corniglia
Corniglia
del Luogo Pt
Manarola
Buonfiglio Pt
30min
Via dell' Amore
Riomaggiore
Ligurian Sea
Trail No 2 (Blue Trail)
Torre Guardiola
C di M Nero

Corniglia
Perched on a cliff 500 ft. above the sea, reached by a switchback path (or by shuttle bus).

Manarola
The most photogenic of the villages, best seen from the cemetery a few minutes up the path toward Corniglia.

Riomaggiore
Cliff-clinging buildings are almost as striking as those in Manarola. Stairs to the left of the train station entrance cross over the tracks and lead to the trailhead.

BEYOND TRAIL NO.2

Trail No. 2 is just one of a network of trails crisscrossing the hills. If you're a dedicated hiker, spend a few nights and try some of the other routes. Trail No. 1, the Sentiero Rosso (Red Trail), climbs from Portovenere (east of Riomaggiore) and returns to the sea at Levanto (west of Monterosso al Mare). To hike its length takes from 9 to 12 hours; the ridge-top trail provides spectacular views from high above the villages, each of which can be reached via a steep path. Other shorter trails go from the villages up into the hills, some leading to religious sanctuaries. Trail No. 9, for example, starts from the old section of Monterosso and ends at the Madonna di Soviore Sanctuary.

FODOR'S FIRST PERSON

Angelo Benvenuto
Fisherman,
Monterosso al Mare

Angelo Benvenuto is a 10th-generation fisherman from Monterosso who organizes special boating excursions along the Cinque Terre in his *lampara* (wooden anchovy fishing boat).

Q: Although hiking the Cinque Terre has become a favorite with travelers, you and others maintain that the "way of life" in the Cinque Terre is really that of the sea....

A: For nearly one thousand years Monterosso has been a fishing village. We eat, live, and breathe the sea. In fact, when the barbarians invaded Italy during the middle ages, they did not come down to Monterosso because they were afraid of the sea. Because of this Monterosso as well as the other villages were protected and untouched. Everyday life is always connected to the sea.

Yet, the *sentiri* (trails) were also essential to our livelihood. They provided access to the elements we needed on land such as produce, animals, and of course wine! Now they are a source of entertainment and beauty for our visitors.

Q: How has the Cinque Terre changed over the past 20 years?

A: There are obviously more people visiting, but everyday life has remained the same. I still go out to fish for the majority of our meals, and my wife works in the garden to provide us with fresh vegetables, fruit, even eggs. It is this way for most of the Cinque Terre.

Of course, many of us have gone into the tourism business—hotels, restaurants, cafes. The tourists have brought us opportunity and some financial stability which is very good for us, for all of the villages.

Q: What is your perfect day in the Cinque Terre?

A: Take a hike up to the garden (located on the slopes above town) or maybe even to Vernazza to visit friends. Then after a nice fresh seafood lunch, glass of *Sciacchetra'* (local dessert wine) and a short *pisolino* (nap), I would then head out to sea on my lampara and enjoy the silence of the sea and the beautiful landscape, and catch some fish for dinner!

PRECAUTIONS

If you're hitting the trails, you'll want to carry water with you, wear sturdy shoes (hiking boots are best), and have a hat and sunscreen handy. ⚠ Check weather reports before you start out; especially in late fall and winter, thunderstorms can send townspeople running for cover and make the shelterless trails slippery and dangerous. Rain in October and November can cause landslides and close the trails. Note that the lesser-used trails aren't as well maintained as Trail No. 2. If you're undertaking the full Trail No. 1 hike, bring something to snack on as well as your water bottle.

ADMISSION

Entrance tickets for use of the trails are available at ticket booths located at the start of each section of Trail No. 2, and at information offices in the Levanto, Monterosso, Vernazza, Corniglia, Manarola, Riomaggiore, and La Spezia train stations.

A one-day pass costs €5, which includes a trail map and a general information leaflet. Information about local train and boat schedules is also available from the information offices.

Working Cinque Terre's vertical vineyards

GETTING HERE AND AROUND

The local train on the Genoa–La Spezia line stops at each of the Cinque Terre, and runs approximately every 30 minutes. Tickets for each leg of the journey (€1.30) are available at the five train stations. In Corniglia, the only one of the Cinque Terre that isn't at sea level, a shuttle service (€1) is provided for those who don't wish to climb (or descend) the hundred-or-so steps that link the train station with the cliff-top town.

Along the Cinque Terre coast two ferry lines operate. From June to September, Golfo Paradiso runs from Genoa and Camogli to Monterosso al Mare and Vernazza. The smaller, but more frequent, Golfo dei Poeti stops at each village from Lerici (east of Riomaggiore) to Monterosso, with the exception of Corniglia, four times a day. A one-day ticket costs €22.

WHEN TO GO

The ideal times to see the Cinque Terre are September and May, when the weather is mild and the summer tourist season isn't in full swing.

SWIMMING & BEACHES

Each town has something that passes for a beach, but there are only two options where you'll find both sand and decent swimming. The more accessible is in Monterosso, opposite the train station; it's equipped with chairs, umbrellas, and snack bars. The other is the secluded, swimwear-optional Guvano Beach, between Corniglia and Vernazza. To reach it from the Corniglia train station, bypass the steps leading up to the village, instead following signs to an abandoned train tunnel. Ring a bell at the tunnel's entrance, and the gate will automatically open; after a dimly lit 10-minute walk, you'll emerge at the beach. Both beaches have a nominal admission fee.

Monterosso al Mare

THE TOWNS

Riomaggiore

At the eastern end of the Cinque Terre, Riomaggiore is built into a river gorge (thus the name, which means "river major") and is easily accessible from La Spezia by train or car. It has a tiny harbor protected by large slabs of alabaster and marble, which serve as as tanning beds for sunbathers, as well as being the site of several outdoor cafes with fine views. According to legend, settlement of Riomaggiore dates far back to the 8th century, when Greek religious refugees came here to escape persecution by the Byzantine emperor.

Manarola

The enchanting pastel houses of Manarola spill down a steep hill overlooking a spectacular turquoise swimming cove and a bustling harbor. The whole town is built on black rock. Above the town, ancient terraces still protect abundant vineyards and olive trees. This village is the center of the wine and olive oil production of the region, and its streets are lined with shops selling local products.

Corniglia

The buildings, narrow lanes, and stairways of Corniglia are strung together amid vineyards high on the cliffs; on a clear day views of the entire coastal strip are excellent. The high perch and lack of harbor make this farming community the most remote of the Cinque Terre. On a pretty pastel square sits the 14th-century church of **San Pietro.** The rose window of marble imported from Carrara is impressive, particularly considering the work required to get it here. ⊠ *Main Sq.* ☎ *0187/3235582* ⊙ *Wed. 4–6, Sun. 10–noon.*

Vernazza

With its narrow streets and small squares, Vernazza is arguably the most charming of the five towns. Because it has the best access to the sea, it became wealthier than its neighbors—as evidenced by the elaborate arcades, loggias, and marblework. The village's pink, slate-roof houses and colorful squares contrast with the remains of the medieval fort and castle, including two towers, in the old town. The Romans first inhabited this rocky spit of land in the 1st century.

Today Vernazza has a fairly lively social scene. It's a great place to refuel with a hearty seafood lunch or linger in a café between links of the hike on Trail No. 2.

Monterosso al Mare

Beautiful beaches, rugged cliffs, crystal-clear turquoise waters, and plentiful small hotels and restaurants make Monterosso al Mare, the largest of the Cinque Terre villages (population 1,730), the busiest in midsummer. The village center bustles high on a hillside. Below, connected by stone steps, are the port and seaside promenade, where there are boats for hire. The medieval tower, Aurora, on the hills of the Cappuccini, separates the ancient part of the village from the more modern part. The village is encircled by hills covered with vineyards and olive groves, and by a forest of scrubby bushes and small trees.

Monterosso has the most festivals of the five villages, starting with the Lemon Feast on the Saturday preceding Ascension Sunday, followed by the Flower Festival of Corpus Christi, celebrated yearly on the second Sunday after Pentecost. During the afternoon, the streets and alleyways of the *centro storico* (historic center) are decorated with thousands of colorful flower petals set in beautiful designs that the evening procession passes over. Finally, the Salted Anchovy and Olive Oil Festival takes place each year during the second weekend of September.

Thursday, the **market** attracts mingled crowds of tourists and villagers from along the coast to shop for everything from pots and pans and underwear to fruits, vegetables, and fish. Often a few stands sell local art and crafts as well as olive oil and wine. ⊠ *Old town center* ⊙ *Thurs. 8–1.*

The **Chiesa di San Francesco,** was built in the 12th century in the Ligurian Gothic style. Its distinctive black stripes and marble rose window make it one of the most photographed sites in the Cinque Terre. ⊠ *Piazza Garibaldi* ☎ *No phone* ✉ *Free* ⊙ *Daily 9–1 and 4–7.*

Main Square, Vernazza

WHERE TO EAT AND STAY

From June through September, reservations are essential if you plan to stay in a hotel or B&B here. *Affitacamere* (rooms for rent in private homes) are a more modest alternative, often indicated by a simple sign on the front door. At agencies in Riomaggiore and Monterosso you can book officially licensed affitacamere. Rooms run the gamut; arrive early for a good selection.

Riomaggiore

$$–$$$ ✕ **La Lanterna.** Chalkboards in front of this small trattoria by the harbor list the day's selection of fresh fish; the set-up seems modest, but this is arguably the finest restaurant in the Cinque Terre. In winter, Chef Massimo teaches at the Culinary Academy in Switzerland; he always returns with new ideas for his menu. When available, *cozze ripiene* (stuffed mussels) shouldn't be missed. Other offerings may be a touch exotic, such sting ray with ligurian herbs. ✉ *Via San Giacomo 10* ☎ *0187/920589* ▭ *AE, DC, MC, VC* ⊗ *Closed Jan and 2 wks in Nov.*

Manarola

$$$ ⛱ **La Torretta.** A welcome retreat after a day of exploring, this boutique accommodation has well-appointed rooms, most with sea views. The hotel has many nice touches such as a free aperitivo (aperitif) at sunset, a solarium, and iPod docking stations. **Pros:** head and shoulders above most accommodations in the area; lovely views. **Cons:** five- to ten-minute walk to the reception. ✉ *Via Volto 20, 19017* ☎ *0187/920327* 🖷 *0187/920678* ⊕ *www.torrettas. com* 🛏 *4 rooms, 5 suites* ⚗ *In-room: a/c (some), safe, refrigerator, Wi-Fi. In-hotel: bar* ▭ *AE, DC, MC, V* ⊗ *Closed Nov.–mid-Mar.* ⭑⊙⭑ *BP.*

Corniglia

$–$$ ✕⛱ **Cecio.** On the outskirts of Corniglia, many of the spotless rooms at the family-run Cecio have spectacular views of the town. The same memorable vista can be enjoyed from the hotel's restaurant, which serves inexpensive and well-prepared local seafood dishes. Try the delicious lasagna with pesto sauce as a first course. ✉ *Via Serra 58, 19010, toward Vernazza* ☎ *0187/812043* 🖷 *0187/812138* 🛏 *12 rooms* ⚗ *Restaurant; no a/c, no room phones, no TV in some rooms* ▭ *DC, MC, V* ⭑⊙⭑ *BP.*

Vernazza

$$$ ✕ **Bel Forte.** High above the sea in one of Vernazza's remaining stone towers is this unique restaurant serving typical Cinque Terre dishes. The prices are high, but it's worth it. People come from all over Liguria for Bel Forte's famous stuffed mussels and insalata di polpo (octopus salad). The setting is magnificent. ✉ *Via Guidoni 42* ☎ *0187/812222* ▭ *AE, DC, MC, V* ⊗ *Closed Tues. and Nov.–Easter.*

$$–$$$ ✕ **Gambero Rosso.** Relax on Vernazza's main square at this fine trattoria looking out at a church. Enjoy such delectable dishes as shrimp salad, vegetable torte, and squid-ink risotto. The creamy pesto, served atop spaghetti, is some of the best in the area. End your meal with Cinque Terre's own *sciacchetrà*, a dessert wine served with semisweet biscotti. Don't drink it out of the glass—dip the biscotti in the wine instead. ✉ *Piazza Marconi 7* ☎ *0187/812265* ▭ *AE, DC, MC, V* ☺ *Closed Mon. Jan. and Feb.*

$$$ ✕▭ **La Malà.** A cut above other lodging options in the Cinque Terre, this family-run B&B has only four rooms, and they fill up quickly. The rooms are small but well equipped, with flat screen TVs, a/c, marble showers, and comfortable bedding. Two of the rooms have sea views; the other two face the port of Vernazza. There's a shared terrace literally suspended over the Mediterranean. Book early! ✉ *Giovanni Battista 29, 19018* ☎ *334/2875718* ⊕ *www.lamala. it* ▭ *4 rooms* ☺ *In-room: safe, refrigerator, satellite TV, hairdryer, tea & coffee maker.* ▭ *AE, DC, MC, V* ☺ *Closed Jan. 10–Mar.*

Monterosso al Mare

★ **$$$** ✕ **Miky.** Specialties here are anything involving seafood. The *insalata di mare* (seafood salad), with squid and fish, is more than tasty; so are the grilled fish and any pasta with seafood. Miky has a beautiful little garden in the back, perfect for lunch on a sunny day. ✉ *Via Fegina 104* ☎ *0187/817608* ▭ *AE, DC, MC, V* ☺ *Closed Nov. and Dec., and Tues. Sept.–July.*

$ ✕ **Enoteca Internazionale.** Located on the main street in centro, this wine bar offers a large variety of vintages, both local from further afield, plus delicious light fare; its umbrella-covered patio is a perfect spot to recuperate after a day of hiking. The owner, Susanna, is a certified sommelier who's always forthcoming with helpful suggestions on local wines. ✉ *Via Roma 62* ☎ *0187/817278* ▭ *AE, MC, V* ☺ *Closed Tues., Jan–Mar.*

$$ ✕▭ **Il Giardino Incantato.** This small B&B in the historic center of Monterosso oozes comfort and old-world charm. The building dates back to the 16th century and still maintains its wood beam ceiling and stone walls. Each room has been impeccably restored with modern amenities. Breakfast is served either in your room on request or in their lovely private garden under the lemon trees. The owner, Maria Pia, goes out of her way to make you feel at home and whips up a fabulous frittata for breakfast. ✉ *Via Mazzini 18, 19016* ☎ *0185/818315* ⊕ *www.ilgiardinoincantato.net* ▭ *3 rooms, 1 junior suite* ☺ *In-room: safe, refrigerator, satellite TV, hairdryer, tea & coffee maker. In-hotel: private garden.* ▭ *AE, DC, MC.*

$$ ▭ **Porto Roca.** The Cinque Terre's only "high-end" hotel is perched on the famous terraced cliffs, hovering over the magnificent sea below, and thankfully removed from the crowds. The hotel has an old-fashioned feel but the large balconies and panoramic views make it all worth it. There is also a nice restaurant serving very good Ligurian cuisine. Avoid the back rooms as they are dark and have no view. Pros: unobstructed sea views; tranquil position. Cons: some of the rooms could use updating; back-facing rooms can be a bit dark. ✉ *Via Volto 20, 19017* ☎ *0187/920327* ▭ *0187/920678* ⊕ *www.torrettas.com* ▭ *4 rooms, 5 suites* ☺ *In-room: a/c (some), safe, refrigerator, Wi-Fi. In-hotel: bar* ▭ *AE, DC, MC, V* ☺ *Closed Nov.–mid-Mar.* ⦿ *BP.*

amenities such as the spa; cooking lessons. **Cons:** lobby and rooms could use a revamping. ⊠ *Via Garibaldi 5* ☏ *0187/792610* ⊕ *www. portovenerehotel.it* ↰ *44 rooms, 10 suites* ⚇ *In-room: refrigerator. In-hotel: restaurant, bar, spa, Internet terminal* ▭ *AE, DC, MC, V* ⍟*BP.*

$$ ⊡ **Hotel Belvedere.** This sunny Liberty-style building has simply furnished guest rooms that don't break the bank in what can be an expensive destination. The location faces the bay of Portovenere, and front rooms have lovely views of Palmaria Island and the Gulf of Poets. **Pros:** reasonably priced rooms with water views. **Cons:** parts of the hotel could use a makeover; limited parking. ⊠ *Via G. Garibaldi 26* ☏ *0187/790608* ⊕ *www.belvedereportovenere.it* ↰ *19 rooms* ⚇ *In-room: safe. In-hotel: beachfront, Internet terminal, parking (free), some pets allowed* ▭ *AE, DC, MC, V* ⊗ *Closed Nov.–mid-Mar.* ⍟*BP.*

LEVANTO

8 km (5 mi) northwest of Monterosso al Mare, 60 km (36 mi) southeast of Genoa.

GETTING HERE

By car, take the Carodanno/Levanto exit off the A12 for 25 minutes to the town center. By train, Levanto is on the main north–south railway, one stop north of Monterosso.

VISITOR INFORMATION

Levanto tourism office (⊠ *Piazza Mazzini 1* ☏ *0187/808125* ⊕ *www. aptcinqueterre.sp.it*).

EXPLORING

Tucked nicely between two promontories, Levanto offers an alternative and usually less-expensive base to explore the Cinque Terre and the Riviera di Levante. This town retains much of the typical Ligurian character with trompe l'oeil frescoed villas and the olive tree–covered hills of the national park. Monterosso, one of the Cinque Terre villages, is a four-minute train ride away.

WHERE TO STAY

$$ ⊡ **La Giada del Mesco.** On Punto Mesco headland, this stone bed-and-breakfast has unobstructed vistas of the Mediterranean and Riviera coastline. Rooms are tastefully decorated and bright—all with sea views. **Pros:** great position; nice pool and sunning area. **Cons:** shuttle service is not always available; the 3½ km (1½ mi) into town is quite a walk, so you'll want a car. ⊠ *Via Doria 2* ☏ *0187/967124* ⊕ *www. lagiadadelmesco.it* ↰ *12 rooms* ⚇ *In-room: safe, refrigerator. In-hotel: pool, Wi-Fi hotspot, parking (free)* ▭ *AE, DC, MC, V* ⊗ *Closed mid-Nov.–Feb.* ⍟*BP.*

CHIAVARI

46 km (29 mi) northwest of Levanto, 38 km (23 mi) southeast of Genoa.

GETTING HERE

By car, take the Chiavari exit off the A12. The Chiavari train station is located on the main north–south train line between Genoa and Pisa.

VISITOR INFORMATION

Chiavari tourism office (⊠ *Via Remolari 9* ☎ *0185/365216* ⊕ *www.apttigullio. liguria.it*).

EXPLORING

Chiavari is a fishing town (rather than village) of considerable character, with narrow, twisting streets and a good harbor. Chiavari's citizens were intrepid explorers, and many emigrated to South America in the 19th century. The town boomed, thanks to the wealth of the returning voyagers, but Chiavari retains many medieval traces in its buildings.

In the town center, the **Museo Archeologico** displays objects from an 8th-century BC necropolis, or ancient cemetery, excavated nearby. The museum closes the first and third Sunday of the month. ⊠ *Palazzo Costaguta, Via Costaguta 4, Piazza Matteotti* ☎ *0185/320829* ⊟ *Free* ☉ *Tues.–Sat. and 2nd and 4th Sun. of month 9–1:30.*

SANTA MARGHERITA LIGURE

60 km (37 mi) northwest of Levanto, 31 km (19 mi) southeast of Genoa.

GETTING HERE

By car, take the Rapallo exit off the A12 and follow the blue signs, about a 10-minute drive. The Santa Margherita Ligure train station is on the main north–south line between Genoa and Pisa.

VISITOR INFORMATION

Santa Margherita Ligure tourism office (⊠ *Via XXV Aprile 2/B* ☎ *0185/287485* ⊕ *www.apttigullio.liguria.it*).

EXPLORING

A beautiful old resort town favored by well-to-do Italians, Santa Margherita Ligure has everything a Riviera playground should have—plenty of palm trees and attractive hotels, cafés, and a marina packed with yachts. Some of the older buildings here are still decorated on the outside with the trompe l'oeil frescoes typical of this part of the Riviera. This is a pleasant, convenient base, which for many represents a perfect balance on the Italian Riviera: more spacious than the Cinque Terre; less glitzy than San Remo; more relaxing than Genoa and environs; and ideally situated for day trips, such as an excursion to Portofino.

WHERE TO EAT

$$–$$$ ✕ **La Paranza.** From the piles of tiny *bianchetti* (young sardines) in oil and
LIGURIAN lemon that are part of the antipasto *di mare* (of the sea) to the simple, perfectly grilled whole sole, fresh seafood in every shape and form is the specialty here. Mussels, clams, octopus, salmon, or whatever else is

fresh that day is what's on the menu. Locals say this is the town's best restaurant, but if you're looking for a stylish evening out, look elsewhere—La Paranza is about food, not fashion. It's just off Santa Margherita's port. ⊠ *Via Jacopo Ruffini 46* ☎ *0185/283686* ⊴ *Reservations essential* ☰ *AE, DC, MC, V* ⊘ *Closed Mon. and Nov.*

WORD OF MOUTH

"Portofino is a beautiful site. I wouldn't miss a hike to Castello Brown or the scenic path to the lighthouse at Punta da Capo. Both offer lovely and very photogenic views."   —waggis

$$$
LIGURIAN
Fodor'sChoice
★

✕ **La Stalla dei Frati.** The breathtaking, hilltop views of Santa Margherita from this villa-turned-restaurant are worth the harrowing 3-km (2-mi) drive northwest to get here from Santa Margherita's port. Cesare Frati, your congenial host, is likely to tempt you with his homemade fettuccine *ai frutti di mare* (with seafood) followed by the *pescato del giorno alla moda ligure* (catch of the day baked Ligurian style, with potatoes, olives, and pine nuts) and a delightfully fresh lemon sorbet to complete the feast. ⊠ *Via G. Pino 27, Nozarego* ☎ *0185/289447* ☰ *AE, DC, MC, V* ⊘ *Closed Mon. and Nov.*

$$$-$$$$
INTERNATIONAL
★

✕ **Oca Bianca.** The menu at this small, excellent restaurant breaks away from the local norm—there is no seafood on the offer. Meat dishes are the specialty, and choices may include mouthwatering preparations of lamb from France or New Zealand, steak from Ireland or Brazil, South African ostrich, and Italian pork. Delicious antipasti, an extensive wine list, and the attentive service add to the experience. Dinner is served until 1 AM. ⊠ *Via XXV Aprile 21* ☎ *0185/288411* ⊴ *Reservations essential* ☰ *AE, DC, MC, V* ⊘ *Closed Mon. and Jan.–mid-Feb. No lunch Tues.–Thurs. Sept.–Dec.*

$$-$$$
LIGURIAN
Fodor'sChoice
★

✕ **U' Giancu.** Owner Fausto Oneto is a man of many hats. Though original cartoons cover the walls of his restaurant and a playground is the main feature of the outdoor seating area, Fausto is completely serious about his cooking. Lamb dishes are particularly delicious, his own garden provides the freshest possible vegetables, and the wine list (ask to visit the cantina) is excellent. For those who want to learn the secrets of Ligurian cuisine, Fausto provides lively morning cooking lessons. U' Giancu is 8 km (5 mi) northwest of Santa Margherita Ligure. ⊠ *Via San Massimo 78, Località San Massimo, Rapallo* ☎ *0185/261212* ⊕ *www.ugiancu.it* ☰ *DC, MC, V* ⊘ *Closed Wed. and mid-Dec.–early Jan. No lunch.*

WHERE TO STAY

$$-$$$

▥ **Continental.** Built in the early 1900s, this stately seaside mansion with a columned portico stands in a lush garden shaded by tall palms and pine trees. The style is a blend of classic furnishings, mostly inspired by the 19th century. The hotel's cabanas and swimming area are at the bottom of the garden. **Pros:** lovely location; private beach. **Cons:** rooms in the annex are not as nice as those in the main building; breakfast is unimaginative. ⊠ *Via Pagana 8* ☎ *0185/286512* ⊕ *www.hotel-continental.it* ⇱ *70 rooms, 4 suites* �� *In-room: safe, refrigerator, Wi-Fi. In-hotel: restaurant, bar, Wi-Fi hotspot, parking (paid), some pets allowed* ☰ *AE, DC, MC, V* ⏍ *BP.*

11

$$$$ ★ 🏨 **Grand Hotel Miramare.** Classic Riviera elegance prevails at this palatial hotel overlooking the bay south of the town center. Stroll through the lush garden, then take a dip in the curvaceous heated swimming pool or at the private swimming area on the sea. Antique furniture, such as crystal chandeliers and Louis XV chairs, fills the high-ceiling rooms, and there are marble bathrooms. **Pros:** top-notch service; private beach; well-maintained rooms. **Cons:** unfinished parking structure can be an eyesore from some rooms and create some noise in low- and mid-season (construction stops May to September); traffic in summer from the road in front of the hotel. ⊠ *Via Milite Ignoto 30* ☎ *0185/287013* ⊕ *www.grandhotelmiramare.it* ⇥ *75 rooms, 9 suites* ⚭ *In-room: safe, refrigerator, Internet. In-hotel: 2 restaurants, bars, pool, beachfront, Internet terminal, some pets allowed* ⊟ *AE, DC, MC, V* ⦿| *BP.*

$$ 🏨 **Hotel Jolanda.** It may not have a sea view, but the Jolanda is stylish and comfortable. The spacious rooms are tastefully decorated. Some rooms have large balconies and all bathrooms have been remodeled. There is also a modestly priced in-house restaurant with a menu that changes daily. **Pros:** reasonable rates in a high-price area. **Cons:** no sea view; parking is limited and expensive. ⊠ *Via Luisito Costa 6* ☎ *0185/287512* ⊕ *www.hoteljolanda.it* ⇥ *47 rooms, 3 suites* ⚭ *In-room: safe, refrigerator, Wi-Fi. In-hotel: restaurant, bar, gym, Wi-Fi hotspot, parking (paid)* ⊟ *AE, DC, MC, V* ⦿| *BP.*

PORTOFINO

★ *5 km (3 mi) south of Santa Margherita Ligure, 36 km (22 mi) east of Genoa.*

GETTING HERE

By car, exit at Rapallo off the A12 and follow the blue signs (about a 20-minute drive mostly along the coast). The nearest train station is Santa Margherita Ligure.

Trying to reach Portofino by bus or car on the single narrow road can be a nightmare in summer and on holiday weekends. No trains go directly to Portofino: you must stop at Santa Margherita and take the Number 82 public bus from there (€1). An alternative is to take a boat from Santa Margherita.

Portofino can also be reached from Santa Margherita on foot: it's about a 40-minute (very nice) walk along the sea.

VISITOR INFORMATION

Portofino tourism office (⊠ *Via Roma 35* ☎ *0185/269024* ⊕ *www.apttigullio.liguria.it*).

EXPLORING

One of the most photographed villages along the coast, with a decidedly romantic and affluent aura, Portofino has long been a popular destination for the rich and famous. Once an ancient Roman colony and taken by the Republic of Genoa in 1229, it has also been ruled by the French, English, Spanish, and Austrians, as well as by marauding bands of 16th-century pirates. Elite British tourists first flocked to the lush harbor in the mid-1800s. Some of Europe's wealthiest lay anchor in Portofino in summer, but they stay out of sight by day, appearing in the evening after buses and boats have carried off the day-trippers.

There's not actually much to *do* in Portofino other than stroll around the wee harbor, see the castle, walk to Punta del Capo, browse at the pricey boutiques, and sip a coffee while people-watching. However, weaving through picture-perfect cliff-side gardens and gazing at yachts framed by the turquoise Ligurian Sea and the cliffs of Santa Margherita can make for quite a relaxing afternoon. There are also several tame, photo-friendly hikes into the hills to nearby villages.

Unless you're traveling on a deluxe budget, you may want to stay in Camogli or Santa Margherita Ligure rather than at one of Portofino's few very expensive hotels. Restaurants and cafés are good but also pricey (don't expect to have a beer here for much under €10).

From the harbor, follow the signs for the climb to the **Castello di San Giorgio,** the most worthwhile sight in Portofino, with its medieval relics, impeccable gardens, and sweeping views. The castle was founded in the Middle Ages but restored in the 16th through 18th century. In true Portofino form, it was owned by Genoa's English consul from 1870 until it opened to the public in 1961. ⊠ *Above harbor* ☎ *0185/269046* 🕙 *€3* 🕙 *Apr.–Sept., Wed.–Mon. 10–6; Oct.–Mar., Wed.–Mon. 10–5.*

The small church **San Giorgio,** sitting on a ridge, was rebuilt four times during World War II. It is said to contain the relics of its namesake, brought back from the Holy Land by the Crusaders. Portofino enthusiastically celebrates Saint George's Day every April 23. ⊠ *Above harbor* ☎ *0185/269337* 🕙 *Daily 7–6.*

Pristine views can be had from the deteriorating *faro* (lighthouse) at **Punta Portofino,** a 15-minute walk along the point that begins at the southern end of the port. Along the seaside path you can see numerous impressive, sprawling private residences behind high iron gates.

The only sand beach near Portofino is at **Paraggi,** a cove on the road between Santa Margherita and Portofino. The bus will stop here on request.

On the sea at the foot of Monte Portofino, the medieval **Abbazia di San Fruttuoso** *(Abbey of San Fruttuoso),* built by the Benedictines of Monte Cassino, protects a minuscule fishing village that can be reached only on foot or by water—a 20-minute boat ride from Portofino and also reachable from Camogli, Santa Margherita Ligure, and Rapallo. The restored abbey is now the property of a national conservation fund (FAI) and occasionally hosts temporary exhibitions. The church contains the tombs of some illustrious members of the Doria family. The old abbey and its grounds are delightful places to spend a few hours, perhaps lunching at one of the modest beachfront trattorias nearby (open only in summer). Boatloads of visitors can make it very crowded very fast; you might appreciate it most off-season. ⊠ *15-min boat ride or 2-hr walk northwest of Portofino* ☎ *0185/772703* 🕙 *€7 Apr.–Sept., €5 Oct.–Mar.* 🕙 *Mar., Apr., and Oct., Tues.–Sun. 10–3:45; May–Sept., daily 10:45–6; Nov.–Feb., Tues.–Sun. 10–3:45. Last entry 45 mins before closing.*

11

WHERE TO EAT

¢ ✕ **Canale.** If the staggering prices of virtually all of Portofino's restau-

BAKERY rants put you off, the long line outside this family-run bakery indicates that you're not alone and that something special is in store. Here all the focaccia is baked on the spot and served fresh from the oven, along with all kinds of sandwiches, pastries, and other refreshments. The only problem is there's nowhere to sit—time for a picnic! ⊠ *Via Roma 30* ☎ *0185/269248* ⊟ *No credit cards* ⊘ *Closed Nov.–Feb.*

$$$ ✕ **Ristorante Puny.** A table at this tiny restaurant is difficult to come by in

LIGURIAN summer, as the manager caters mostly to friends and regulars. If you are lucky enough to get in, however, the food will not disappoint you, nor will the cozy but elegant yellow interior. The unforgettable *pappardelle* (large, flat noodles) *al portofino* delicately blends two of Liguria's tastes: tomato and pesto. Ligurian seafood specialties include baked fish with bay leaves, potatoes, and olives as well as the inventive *moscardini al forno* (baked mini-octopus with lemon and rosemary in tomato sauce). ⊠ *Piazza Martiri dell'Olivetta 4–5, on harbor* ☎ *0185/269037* ⚓ *Reservations essential* ⊟ *AE, DC, MC, V* ⊘ *Closed Thurs. and Jan. and Feb.*

WHERE TO STAY

$$$$ ⊞ **San Giorgio.** If you decide to stay in Portofino, this is perhaps your best choice. Tucked away on a quiet backstreet with no views of the harbor, the San Giorgio offers rooms that are immaculate, comfortable, and soothingly designed with canopy beds, pastel walls, and ultramodern bathrooms. Two small 19th-century town houses were joined to form the hotel, making the hallways seem like a labyrinth, but the level of service is high. **Pros:** luxurious accommodations in the middle of the village; secluded garden at the back. **Cons:** some of the lower -level rooms do not receive much light. ⊠ *Via Del Fondaco 11* ☎ *0185/26991* ⊕ *www.portofinohsg.it* ⇶ *17 rooms, 1 suite* ♿ *In-room: safe, refrigerator, Internet. In-hotel: bar, Internet terminal, some pets allowed* ⊟ *AE, DC, MC, V* ⊘ *Closed Dec.–Feb.* ⏀ *BP.*

$$$$ ⊞ **Splendido.** Arriving at this 1920s luxury hotel is so much like entering a Jazz Age film set that you'd almost expect to see a Bugatti or Daimler roll up the winding drive from the seaside below. There's a particular attention to color, from the coordinated floral linens in corals and gold to the fresh flowers in the reception rooms and on the large terrace. Even grander than the hotel are its prices (more than €800). A half-board plan is mandatory during high season. Rooms have garden or sea views. **Pros:** gorgeous rooms; caring staff; lovely views. **Cons:** be prepared to spend upward of €100 for a simple lunch for two (it's not just the rooms that are pricey). ⊠ *Salita Baratta 16* ☎ *0185/267801* ⊕ *www.hotelsplendido.com* ⇶ *31 rooms, 34 suites* ♿ *In-room: safe, refrigerator, Wi-Fi. In-hotel: restaurant, bars, tennis court, pool, gym, Wi-Fi hotspot, parking (paid), some pets allowed* ⊟ *AE, DC, MC, V* ⊘ *Closed mid-Nov.–late Mar.* ⏀ *MAP.*

Camogli seen from above.

SPORTS AND THE OUTDOORS
HIKING

If you have the stamina, you can hike to the Abbazia di San Fruttuoso from Portofino. It's a steep climb at first, and the walk takes about 2½ hours one-way. If you're extremely ambitious and want to make a day of it, you can hike another 2½ hours all the way to Camogli. Much more modest hikes from Portofino include a 1-hour uphill walk to Cappella delle Gave, a bit inland in the hills, from where you can continue downhill to Santa Margherita Ligure (another 1½ hours) and a gently undulating paved trail leading to the beach at Paraggi (½ hour). Finally, there's a 2½-hour hike from Portofino that heads farther inland to Ruta, through Olmi and Pietre Strette. The trails are well marked and maps are available at the tourist information offices in Rapallo, Santa Margherita, Portofino, and Camogli.

CAMOGLI

★ *15 km (9 mi) northwest of Portofino, 20 km (12 mi) east of Genoa.*

GETTING HERE

By car, exit the A12 at Recco and follow the blue signs. There are several pay-parking lots near the village center. Camogli is on the main north–south railway line between Genoa and La Spezia.

VISITOR INFORMATION

Camogli tourism office (⊠ *Via XX Settembre 33/R* ☎ *0185/771066* ⊕ *www. camogli.it*).

11

EXPLORING

Camogli, at the edge of the large promontory and nature reserve known as the Portofino Peninsula, has always been a town of sailors. By the 19th century it was leasing its ships throughout the continent. Today, multicolor houses, remarkably deceptive trompe l'oeil frescoes, and a massive 17th-century seawall mark this appealing harbor community, perhaps as beautiful as Portofino but without the glamour. When exploring on foot, don't miss the boat-filled second harbor, which is reached by ducking under a narrow archway at the northern end of the first one.

The Castello Dragone, built onto the sheer rock face near the harbor, is home to the **Acquario** *(Aquarium)*, which has tanks filled with local marine life built into the ramparts. ☒ *Via Isola* ☎ *0185/773375* 🖭 *€3* ⊘ *May–Sept., daily 10–noon and 3–7; Oct.–Apr., Fri.–Sun. 10–noon and 2:30–6, Tues.–Thurs. 10–noon.*

OFF THE BEATEN PATH

Ruta. The footpaths that leave from Ruta, 4 km (2½ mi) east of Camogli, thread through rugged terrain and contain a multitude of plant species. Weary hikers are sustained by stunning views of the Riviera di Levante from the various vantage points along the way.

WHERE TO EAT AND STAY

$$

LIGURIAN

✗**Vento Ariel.** This small, friendly restaurant serves some of the best seafood in town. Dine on the shaded terrace in summer months and watch the bustling activity in the nearby port. Only the freshest of seafood is served; try the spaghetti *alle vongole* (with clams) or the mixed grilled fish. ☒ *Calata Porto* ☎ *0185/771080* ▭ *AE, DC, MC, V* ⊘ *Closed Wed., 1st half of Dec., and Jan.*

$$$–$$$$

★

🏨**Cenobio dei Dogi.** Perched majestically a step above Camogli, over-looking harbor, peninsula, and sea, this is indisputably the best address in town. Genoa's doges once summered here. Ask for one of the rooms with expansive balconies and commanding vistas of Camogli's cozy port. You can relax in the well-kept park or enjoy a game of tennis. **Pros:** location and setting are wonderful. **Cons:** crowds make it seem overbooked in summer; decor is a bit old-fashioned. ☒ *Via Cuneo 34* ☎ *0185/7241* ⊕ *www.cenobio.it* ⤳ *102 rooms, 4 suites* ⚭ *In-room: safe, refrigerator, Wi-Fi. In-hotel: restaurant, bar, tennis court, pool, gym, beachfront, Wi-Fi hotspot* ▭ *AE, DC, MC, V* ⅋*BP.*

$$–$$$

🏨**Villa Rosmarino.** This small boutique hotel is a recent addition to the beautiful Camogliese hillside. A 10-minute walk from the seaside village, you can enjoy the tranquility of its well-manicured gardens and welcoming pool. The villa retains its typical Ligurian style with an exterior of rose paint, green shutters, and trompe l'oeil decorations, yet the interior is chic, contemporary, and comfortable. **Pros:** large beds; well-equipped bathrooms; total sense of relaxation. **Cons:** rooms are small and may not have enough amenities for everyone's taste. ☒ *Via Figari 38* ☎ *0185/771580* ⊕ *www.villarosmarino.com* ⤳ *6 rooms* ⚭ *In-room: no a/c, no TV, Wi-Fi. In-hotel: Wi-Fi hotspot, parking (free), no kids under 8* ▭ *MC, V* ⅋*BP.*

GETTING AROUND GENOA

The best way by far to get around Genoa is on foot, with the occasional assistance of public transportation. Many of the more interesting districts are either entirely closed to traffic, have roads so narrow that no car could fit, or are, even at the best of times, blocked by gridlock. Although it might seem a daunting task, exploring the city is made simple by its geography. The historical center of Genoa occupies a relatively narrow strip of land running between the mountains and the sea. You can easily visit the most important monuments in one or two days.

The main bus station in Genoa is at Piazza Principe. Local buses, operated by the municipal transport company AMT (⊠ *Piazza Acquaverde* ☎ *010/5582414* ⊕ *www.amt. genova.it*), serve the steep valleys that run to some of the towns along the western coast. Tickets may be bought at local bus stations or at newsstands. (You must have a ticket before you board.) AMT also operates the funicular railways and the elevators that service the steeper sections of the city.

NIGHTLIFE AND THE ARTS

★ **Sagra del Pesce**, the highlight of the festival of San Fortunato, is held on the second Sunday of May each year. It's a crowded, festive, and free-to-the-public feast of freshly caught fish, cooked outside at the port in a frying pan 12 feet wide.

GENOA

GETTING HERE

By car, take the Genoa Ovest exit off the A12 and take the upper bridge (*sopralevata*) to the second exit, Genova Centro–Piazza Corvetto. But be forewarned: driving in Genoa is harrowing and is best avoided whenever possible—if you want to see the city on a day trip, go by train; if you're staying in the city, park in a garage or by valet and go by foot and by taxi throughout your stay.

Regular train service operates from Genoa's two stations. Departures from **Stazione Principe** (⊠ *Piazza del Principe, San Teodoro*) travel to points west. Departures from **Stazione Brignole** (⊠ *Piazza Giuseppe Verdi, Foce* ☎ *892021*) go to points east and south. All the coastal resorts are on this line.

VISITOR INFORMATION

The Terminal Crociere tourist office is closed October–April.

Genoa tourism offices (⊠ *Palazzo delle Torrette, Via Garibaldi 12r, Maddalena* ☎ *010/5572903* ⊠ *Aeroporto Internazionale Cristoforo Colombo, Ponente* ☎ *010/6015247* ⊠ *Via Roma 11* ☎ *010/576791* ⊠ *Terminale Crociere, Ponte dei Mille* ☎ *No phone* ⊕ *www.apt.genova.it*).

The harbor of Genoa.

EXPLORING

Genoa (Genova in Italian) was the birthplace of Christopher Columbus, but the city's proud history predates that explorer by hundreds of years. Genoa was already an important trading station by the 3rd century BC, when the Romans conquered Liguria. The Middle Ages and the Renaissance saw it rise into a jumping-off place for the Crusaders, a commercial center of tremendous wealth and prestige, and a strategic bone of international contention. A network of fortresses defending the city connected by a wall second only in length to the Great Wall of China was constructed in the hills above, and Genoa's bankers, merchants, and princes adorned the city with palaces, churches, and impressive art collections.

Known as *La Superba* (The Proud), Genoa was a great maritime power in the 13th century, rivaling Venice and Pisa in strength and splendor. But its luster eventually diminished, and it was outshined by these and other formidable cities. By the 17th century it was no longer a great sea power. It has, however, continued to be a profitable port. Modern container ships now unload at docks that centuries ago served galleons and vessels bound for the spice routes. Genoa is now a busy, sprawling, and cosmopolitan city, apt to break the spell of the coastal towns in a hurry.

Crammed into a thin crescent of land between sea and mountains, Genoa expanded up rather than out, taking on the form of a multilayer wedding cake, with churches, streets, and entire residential neighborhoods built on others' rooftops. Public elevators and funiculars are as common as buses and trains.

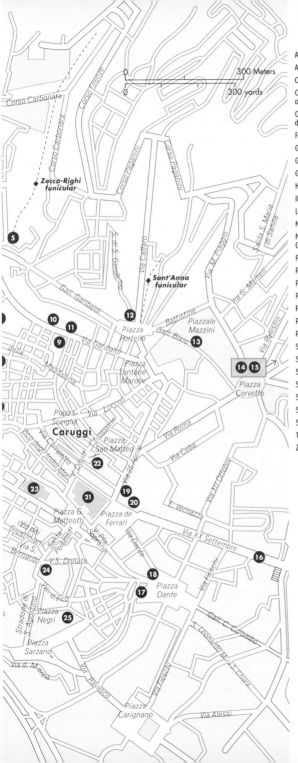

But with its impressive palaces and museums, the largest medieval city center in Europe, and an elaborate network of ancient hilltop fortresses, Genoa may be just the dose of culture you are looking for. Europe's biggest boat show, the annual Salone Nautico Internazionale, is held here. Fine restaurants are abundant, and classical dance and music are richly represented; the Teatro Carlo Felice is the local opera venue, and where the internationally renowned annual Niccolò Paganini Violin Contest takes place.

THE MEDIEVAL CORE AND POINTS ABOVE

The medieval center of Genoa, threaded with tiny streets flanked by 11th-century portals, is roughly the area between the port and Piazza de Ferrari. This mazelike pedestrian zone is officially called the Caruggi District, but the Genovese, in their matter-of-fact way, simply refer to the area as the place of the *vicoli* (alleys). In this warren of narrow, cobbled streets extending north from Piazza Caricamento, the city's oldest churches sit among tiny shops selling antique furniture, coffee, cheese, rifles, wine, gilt picture frames, camping gear, and even live fish. The 500-year-old apartment buildings lean so precariously that penthouse balconies nearly touch those across the street, blocking what little sunlight would have shone down onto the cobblestones. Wealthy Genovese built their homes in this quarter in the 16th century, and prosperous guilds, such as the goldsmiths for whom Vico degli Indoratori and Via degli Orefici were named, set up shop here.

TOP ATTRACTIONS

★ **Cimitero Monumentale di Staglieno.** One of the most famous of Genovese landmarks is this bizarrely beautiful cemetery; its fanciful marble and bronze sculptures sprawl haphazardly across a hillside on the outskirts of town. A pantheon holds indoor tombs and some remarkable works like an 1878 *Eve* by Villa. Don't miss Rovelli's 1896 **Tomba Raggio,** which shoots Gothic spires out of the hillside forest. The cemetery began operation in 1851 and has been lauded by such visitors as Mark Twain and Evelyn Waugh. It covers a good deal of ground; allow at least half a day to explore. It's difficult to locate; reach it via Bus 480 or 482 from the Stazione Genova Brignole, Bus 34 from Stazione Principe, or a taxi. ⊠ *Piazzale Resasco, Piazza Manin* ☎ *010/870184* 🖃 *Free* ⊗ *Daily 7:30–5; last entry at 4:30.*

Galleria Nazionale. This gallery, housed in the richly adorned **Palazzo Spinola** north of Piazza Soziglia, contains masterpieces by Luca Giordano and Guido Reni. The *Ecce Homo,* by Antonello da Messina, is a hauntingly beautiful painting, of historical interest because it was the Sicilian da Messina who first brought Flemish oil paints and techniques to Italy from his sojourns in the Low Countries. ⊠ *Piazza Pellicceria 1, Maddalena* ☎ *010/2705300* ⊕ *www.palazzospinola.it* 🖃 *€4, €6.50 with Palazzo Reale* ⊗ *Tues.–Sat. 8:30–7:30, Sun. 1:30–7:30.*

Palazzo Bianco. It's difficult to miss the splendid white facade of this town palace as you walk down Via Garibaldi, once one of Genoa's most important streets. The building houses a fine collection of 17th-century art, with the Spanish and Flemish schools well represented. ⊠ *Via*

A courtyard of Palazzo Reale.

Garibaldi 11, Maddalena ☎ 010/2759185 ⊕ www.museopalazzobianco.
it ⌨ €7, includes Palazzo Rosso and Palazzo Doria Tursi ⊗ Tues.–Fri
9–7, weekends 10–7.

Palazzo Reale. Lavish rococo rooms provide sumptuous display space for
paintings, sculptures, tapestries, and Asian ceramics. The 17th-century
palace—also known as Palazzo Balbi Durazzo—was built by the Balbi
family, enormously wealthy Genovese merchants. Its regal pretensions
were not lost on the Savoy, who bought the palace and turned it into
a royal residence in the early 19th century. The gallery of mirrors and
the ballroom on the upper floor are particularly decadent. Look for
works by Sir Anthony Van Dyck, who lived in Genoa for six years,
beginning in 1621, and painted many portraits of the Genovese nobility. The formal gardens, which you can visit for €1, provide a welcome
respite from the bustle of the city beyond the palace walls, as well as
great views of the harbor. ⊠ Via Balbi 10, Pré ☎ 010/2710236 ⊕ www.
palazzorealegenova.it ⌨ €6 including Galleria Nazionale ⊗ Tues. and
Wed. 9–1:30, Thurs.–Sun. 9–7.

Palazzo Rosso. This 17th-century baroque palace was named for the
red stone used in its construction. It now contains, apart from a number of lavishly frescoed suites, works by Titian, Veronese, Reni, and
Van Dyck. ⊠ Via Garibaldi 18, Maddalena ☎ 010/2759185 ⊕ www.
museopalazzorosso.it ⌨ €7 including Palazzo Bianco and Palazzo
Doria Tursi ⊗ Tues.–Fri 9–7, weekends 10–7.

Zecca-Righi funicular. This is a seven-stop commuter funicular beginning
at Piazza della Nunziata and ending at a high lookout on the fortified
gates in the 17th-century city walls. Ringed around the circumference

of the city are a number of huge fortresses; this gate was part of the city's system of defenses. From Righi you can undertake scenic all-day hikes from one fortress to the next. ⊠ *Piazza della Nunziata, Pré* ☎ *010/5582414* ⊕ *www. amt.genova.it* 🎫 *€2* ⊘ *Daily 6* AM–*11:45* PM.

WORTH NOTING

WORD OF MOUTH

"Be sure to wander around the maze of narrow lanes in the ancient part of (Genoa) by the port—all scrubbed up recently—this warren of tiny lanes is the epitome of old-world charm—once a dicey area now all gussied up for tourists." —PalenQ

Castelletto. To reach this charming neighborhood high above the city center, you take one of Genoa's handy municipal elevators that whisk you skyward from Piazza Portello, at the end of Galleria Garibaldi, for a good view of the old city. ⊠ *Piazza Portello, Castelletto* 🎫 *€1.20* ⊘ *Daily 6:40* AM–*midnight.*

🎠 **Ferrovia Genova–Casella.** In continuous operation since 1929, the Genova–Casella Railroad runs from Piazza Manin in Genoa (follow Via Montaldo from the center of town, or take Bus 33 or 34 to Piazza Manin) through the beautiful countryside above the city, finally arriving in the rural hill town of Casella. On the way, the tiny train traverses a series of precarious switchbacks that afford sweeping views of the forested Ligurian hills. In Casella Paese (the last stop) you can hike, eat lunch, or just check out the view and ride back. There are two restaurants and two pizzerias near the Casella station; try local cuisine at Trattoria Teresin in Località Avosso. **Canova** (two stops from the end of the line) is the start of two possible hikes through the hills: one a two-hour, one-way trek to a small sanctuary, **Santuario della Vittoria,** and the other a more grueling four-hour hike to the hill town of **Creto.** Another worthwhile stop along the rail line is **Sant'Olcese Tullo,** where you can take a half-hour (one-way) walk along a river and through the **Sentiero Botanico di Ciaé,** a botanical garden and forest refuge with labeled specimens of Ligurian flora and a tiny medieval castle. For Canova and Sant'Olcese, inform your conductor that you want him to stop. The Genova–Casella Railroad is a good way to get a sense of the rugged landscape around Genoa, and you may have it to yourself. The train departs about every hour. ⊠ *Piazza Manin* ☎ *010/837321* ⊕ *www. ferroviagenovacasella.it* 🎫 *€3.20 round-trip* ⊘ *Mon.–Sat. 7:30–7:30, Sun. 9–8:15.*

🎠 **Granarolo funicular.** Take a cog railway up the steeply rising terrain to another part of the city's fortified walls. It takes 15 minutes to hoist you from Stazione Principe, on Piazza Acquaverde, to **Porta Granarolo,** 1,000 feet above, where the sweeping view gives you a sense of Genoa's size. The funicular departs about every half hour. ⊠ *Piazza del Principe, San Teodoro* ☎ *010/5582414* ⊕ *www.amt.genova.it* 🎫 *€2* ⊘ *Daily 6* AM–*11:45* PM.

Loggia dei Mercanti. This merchants' row dating from the 16th century is lined with shops selling local foods and gifts as well as raincoats, rubber boots, and fishing line. ⊠ *Piazza Banchi, Maddalena.*

Museo d'Arte Orientale Chiossone. In the Villetta di Negro park on the hillside above Piazza Portello, the Chiossone Oriental Art Museum has one of Europe's most noteworthy collections of Japanese, Chinese, and Thai objects. There's a fine view of the city from the museum's terrace. ✉ *Piazzale Mazzini 4, Maddalena* ☎ *010/542285* ⊕ *www. museochiossonegenova.it* ▣ *€4* ☾ *Tues.–Fri. 9–7, weekends 10–7.*

Palazzo dell'Università. Built in the 1630s as a Jesuit college, this has been Genoa's university since 1803. The exterior is unassuming, but climb the stairway flanked by lions to visit the handsome courtyard, with its portico of double Doric columns. ✉ *Via Balbi 5, Pré* ☎ *01020991* ⊕ *www.unige.it.*

Palazzo Doria Tursi. In the 16th century, wealthy resident Nicolò Grimaldi had a palace built of pink stone quarried in the region. It's been reincarnated as Genoa's Palazzo Municipale (Municipal Building), and so most of the goings-on inside are the stuff of local politics and quickie weddings. You can visit the richly decorated **Sala Paganini,** where the famous Guarnerius violin that belonged to Niccolò Paganini (1782–1840) is displayed, along with the gardens that connect the palace with the neighboring Palazzo Bianco. ✉ *Via Garibaldi 9, Maddalena* ☎ *010/2759185* ⊕ *www.stradanuova.it* ▣ *€7, includes Palazzo Bianco and Palazzo Rosso* ☾ *Tues.–Fri. 9–7, weekends 10–7.*

San Siro. Genoa's oldest church was the city's cathedral from the 4th to the 9th century. Rebuilt in the 16th and 17th centuries, it now feels a bit like a haunted house—imposing frescoes line dank hallways, and chandeliers hold crooked candles flickering in the darkness. ✉ *Via San Luca, Maddalena* ☎ *010/22461468* ☾ *Daily 7:30–noon and 4–7.*

Santissima Annunziata. Exuberantly frescoed vaults decorate the 16th- to 17th-century church, which is an excellent example of Genovese baroque architecture. ✉ *Piazza della Nunziata, Pré* ☎ *010/297662* ☾ *Daily 9–noon and 3–7.*

SOUTHERN DISTRICTS AND THE AQUARIUM

Inhabited since the 6th century BC, the oldest section of Genoa lies on a hill to the southwest of the Caruggi District. Today, apart from a section of 9th-century wall near Porta Soprana, there is little to show that an imposing castle once stood here. Though the neighborhood is considerably run-down, some of Genoa's oldest churches make it a worthwhile excursion. No visit to Genoa is complete, however, without at least a stroll along the harbor front. Once a squalid and unsafe neighborhood, the port was given a complete overhaul during Genoa's preparations for the Columbus quincentennial celebrations of 1992, and additional restorations in 2003 and 2004 have done much to revitalize the waterfront. You can easily reach the port on foot by following Via San Lorenzo downhill from Genoa's cathedral, Via delle Fontane from Piazza della Nunziata, or any of the narrow vicoli that lead down from Via Balbi and Via Pré.

A tank in Acquario di Genova, Europe's biggest aquarium.

TOP ATTRACTIONS

Acquario di Genova. Europe's biggest aquarium, second in the world only to Osaka's in Japan, is the third-most-visited museum in Italy and a must for children. Fifty tanks of marine species, including sea turtles, dolphins, seals, eels, penguins, and sharks, share space with educational displays and re-creations of marine ecosystems, including a tank of coral from the Red Sea. If arriving by car, take the Genova Ovest exit from the autostrada. ⌧ *Ponte Spinola, Porto Vecchio* ☎ *0101/23451* ⊕ *www.acquario.ge.it* ✉ *€14* ⊗ *Mar.–June, weekdays 9–7:30, weekends 8:45–8:30; July and Aug., daily 8:30 AM–10 PM; Nov.–Feb., weekdays 9:30–7:30, weekends 9:30–8:30. Entry permitted every ½ hr; last entry 1½ hrs before closing.*

Galata Museo del Mare. Devoted entirely to the city's seafaring history, this museum is probably the best way, at least on dry land, to get an idea of the changing shape of Genoa's busy port. Highlighting the displays is a full-size replica of a 17th-century Genovese galleon. ⌧ *Calata de Mari 1, Ponte dei Mille* ☎ *010/2345655* ⊕ *www.galatamuseodelmare.it* ✉ *€10* ⊗ *Mar.–Oct., daily 10–7:30; Nov.–Feb., Tues.–Fri. 10–6, weekends 10–7:30. Last entry 1½ hrs before closing.*

The Harbor. A boat tour gives you a good perspective on the layout of the harbor, which dates to Roman times. The Genoa inlet, the largest along the Italian Riviera, was also used by the Phoenicians and Greeks as a harbor and a staging area from which they could penetrate inland to form settlements and to trade. The port is guarded by the Diga Foranea, a striking wall 5 km (3 mi) long built into the ocean. The **Lanterna,** a lighthouse more than 360 feet high, was built in 1544; it's one of Italy's oldest lighthouses and a traditional emblem of Genoa. Boat tours of the harbor, operated by the **Consorzio Liguria Viamare** (⊠ *Via Sottoripa 7/8, Porto Vecchio* ☎ *010/265712* ⊕ *www.liguriaviamare. it* ☒ *€10* ☽ *Daily; departure times vary*), launch from the aquarium pier and run about an hour. The tour includes a visit to the breakwater outside the harbor, the Bacino delle Grazie, and the Molo Vecchio (Old Port). Reservations aren't necessary.

Palazzo Ducale. This palace was built in the 16th century over a medieval hall, and its facade was rebuilt in the late 18th century and later restored. It now houses temporary exhibitions and a restaurant-bar serving fusion cuisine. Reservations are necessary to visit the dungeons and tower. Guided tours (€4) of the palace and its exhibitions are sometimes available. ⊠ *Piazza Matteotti 9, Portoria* ☎ *010/5574004* ⊕ *www. palazzoducale.genova.it* ☒ *Free* ☽ *Tues.–Sun. 9–9.*

San Lorenzo. Contrasting black slate and white marble, so common in Liguria, embellishes the cathedral at the heart of medieval Genoa—inside and out. Consecrated in 1118, the church honors Saint Lawrence, who passed through the city on his way to Rome in the 3rd century. For hundreds of years the building was used for religious and state purposes such as civic elections. Note the 13th-century Gothic portal, the fascinating twisted barbershop columns, and the 15th- to 17th-century frescoes inside. The last campanile dates from the early 16th century. The **Museo del Tesoro di San Lorenzo** (San Lorenzo Treasury Museum) housed inside has some stunning pieces from medieval goldsmiths and silversmiths, for which medieval Genoa was renowned. ⊠ *Piazza San Lorenzo, Molo* ☎ *010/2471831* ☒ *Cathedral free, museum €5.50* ☽ *Cathedral daily 8–11:45 and 3–6:45. Museum Mon.–Sat. 9–11:30 and 3–5:30.*

Sant'Agostino. This 13th-century Gothic church was damaged during World War II, but it still has a fine campanile and two well-preserved cloisters that house an excellent museum displaying pieces of medieval architecture and fresco paintings. Highlighting the collection are the enigmatic fragments of a tomb sculpture by Giovanni Pisano (circa 1250–1315). ⊠ *Piazza Sarzano 35/R, Molo* ☎ *010/2511263* ⊕ *www. museosantagostino.it* ☒ *€4* ☽ *Tues.–Fri. 9–7, weekends 10–7.*

Santa Maria di Castello. One of Genoa's most significant religious buildings, an early Christian church, was rebuilt in the 12th century and finally completed in 1513. You can visit the adjacent cloisters and see the fine artwork contained in the museum. Museum hours vary during religious services. ⊠ *Salita di Santa Maria di Castello 15, Molo* ☎ *010/2549511* ☒ *Free* ☽ *Daily 9–noon and 3:30–6.*

WORTH NOTING

Accademia delle Belle Arti. Founded in 1751, the Academy of Fine Arts, as well as being a school, houses a collection of paintings from the 16th to the 19th century. Genovese artists of the baroque period are particularly well represented. ⊠ *Largo Pertini 4, Portoria* ☎ *010/581957* ⊕ *www. accademialigustica.it* ☒ *Free* ☽ *Mon.–Sat. 9–1.*

Childhood home of Christopher Columbus. The ivy-covered remains of this fabled medieval house stand in the gardens below the Porta Soprana.

The Art of the Pesto Pestle

Pesto made the traditional way.

You may have known Genoa primarily for its salami or its brash explorer, but the city's most direct effect on your life away from Italy may be through its cultivation of one of the world's best pasta sauces. The sublime blend of basil, extra-virgin olive oil, garlic, pine nuts, and grated pecorino and Parmigiano Reggiano cheeses that forms *pesto alla Genovese* is one of Italy's crowning culinary achievements, a concoction that Italian food guru Marcella Hazan has called "the most seductive of all sauces for pasta." Ligurian pesto is served only over spaghetti, gnocchi, lasagna, or—most authentically—*trenette* (a flat, spaghetti-like pasta) or *trofie* (short,

doughy pasta twists), and then typically mixed with boiled potatoes and green beans. Pesto is also occasionally used to flavor minestrone. The small-leaf basil grown in the region's sunny seaside hills is considered by many to be the best in the world, and pesto sauce was invented primarily as a showcase for that singular flavor. The simplicity and rawness of pesto is one of its virtues, as cooking (or even heating) basil ruins its delicate flavor. In fact, pesto aficionados refuse even to subject the basil leaves to an electric blender; Genovese (and other) foodies insist that true pesto can be made only with mortar and pestle.

A small and rather disappointing collection of objects and reproductions relating to the life and travels of Columbus are on display inside. ⊠ *Piazza Dante, Molo* ☎ *010/2465346* 🖾 *€4* ⊙ *Tues.–Sun. 9–5.*

☽ **Il Bigo.** This spiderlike white structure, designed by world-renowned architect Renzo Piano, was erected in 1992 to celebrate the Columbus quincentenary. You can take its **Ascensore Panoramico Bigo** (Bigo Panoramic Elevator) up 650 feet for a 360-degree view of the harbor, city, and sea. In winter there's an ice-skating rink next to the elevator, in an area covered by sail-like awnings. ⊠ *Ponte Spinola, Porto Vecchio* ☎ *010/2345278 skating rink* 🖾 *Elevator €4, skating rink €8*

⊗ *Elevator: Jan. 7–Feb. and Nov.–Dec. 25, weekends 10–5; Mar.–May, Sept., and Oct., Mon. 2–6, Tues.–Sun. 10–6; June–Aug., Mon. 4–11 PM, Tues.–Sun. 10 AM–11 PM; Dec. 26–Jan. 6, daily 10–5. Skating rink: Nov. or Dec.–Mar., weekdays 8 AM–9:30 PM, Sat. 10 AM–2 AM, Sun. 10 AM–midnight.*

Mercato Orientale. In the old cloister of a church along Via XX Settembre, this bustling produce, fish, and meat market is a wonderful sensory overload. Get a glimpse of colorful everyday Genovese life watching the merchants and buyers banter over prices. ⊠ *Via XX Settembre, Portoria* ⊗ *Weekdays 7–1.*

Porta Soprana. A striking 12th-century twin-tower structure, this medieval gateway stands on the spot where a road from ancient Rome entered the city. It is just steps uphill from Columbus's boyhood home, and legend has it that the explorer's father was employed here as a gatekeeper. ⊠ *Piazza Dante, Molo.*

San Donato. Although somewhat marred by 19th- and 20th-century restorations, the 12th-century San Donato—with its original portal and octagonal campanile—is a fine example of Genovese Romanesque architecture. Inside, an altarpiece by the Flemish artist Joos Van Cleve (circa 1485–1540) depicts the Adoration of the Magi. ⊠ *Piazza San Donato, Portoria* ☎ *010/2468869* ⊗ *Mon.–Sat. 8–noon and 3–7, Sun. 9–12:30 and 3–7.*

San Matteo. This typically Genovese black-and-white-striped church dates from the 12th century; its crypt contains the tomb of Andrea Doria (1466–1560), the Genovese admiral who maintained the independence of his native city. The well-preserved Piazza San Matteo was, for 500 years, the seat of the Doria family, which ruled Genoa and much of Liguria from the 16th to the 18th century. The square is bounded by 13th- to 15th-century houses decorated with portals and loggias. ⊠ *Piazza San Matteo, Maddalena* ☎ *010/2474361* ⊗ *Mon.–Sat. 8–noon and 4–7, Sun. 9:30–10:30 and 4–5.*

Teatro Carlo Felice. The World War II–ravaged opera house in Genoa's modern center, Piazza de Ferrari, was rebuilt and reopened in 1991 to host the fine Genovese opera company; its massive tower has been the subject of much criticism. ⊠ *Passo Eugenio Montale 4, Piazza de Ferrari, Portoria* ☎ *010/53811* ⊕ *www.carlofelice.it.*

WHERE TO EAT

$$$–$$$$
LIGURIAN

✕**Antica Osteria del Bai.** Look out from a large dark wood–paneled room over the Ligurian Sea from this romantic upscale restaurant perched high on a cliff. A seaside theme pervades the art and menu, which might include black gnocchi with lobster sauce or ravioli ai frutti di mare. The restaurant's traditional elegance is reflected in its white tablecloths, dress code, and prices. ⊠ *Via Quarto 16, Quarto* ☎ *010/387478*

⊕ *www.osteriadelbai.it* ⋔ *Jacket and tie* ⊟ *AE, DC, MC, V* ⊙ *Closed Mon., Jan. 10–20, and Aug. 1–20.*

$ ✕ **Bakari.** Hip styling and ambient lighting hint at this eatery's creative,
LIGURIAN even daring, takes on Ligurian classics. Sure bets are the spinach-and-cheese gnocchi, any of several carpaccios, and the delicate beef dishes. Reserve ahead, requesting a table on the more imaginative ground floor or just stop by for an aperitivo and people-watching. ⊠ *Vico del Fieno 16/R, northwest of Piazza San Matteo, Maddalena* ☎ *010/291936* ⊟ *AE, MC, V* ⊙ *No lunch weekends.*

$–$$ ✕ **Da Domenico.** Don't be dismayed by the labyrinth of rooms and wood
LIGURIAN passages that lead to your table at this restaurant in a quiet square near Piazza Dante—you've found one of those hidden corners that only the Genovese know. Traditional seafood and meat dishes make up most of the menu. ⊠ *Piazza Leonardo 3, Molo* ☎ *010/540289* ⌕ *Reservations essential* ⊟ *AE, DC, MC, V* ⊙ *Closed Mon.*

$$ ✕ **Enoteca Sola.** Menus are chosen specifically to complement wines at
WINE BAR Pino Sola's airy, casually elegant enoteca in the heart of the modern town. The short menu emphasizes seafood and varies daily but might include stuffed artichokes or baked stockfish. The real draw, though, is the wine list, which includes some of the winners of the prestigious Italian Tre Bicchieri (Three Glasses) Award, denoting only the very best. ⊠ *Via C. Barabino 120/R, Foce* ☎ *010/594513* ⊟ *AE, DC, MC, V* ⊙ *Closed Sun. and Aug.*

$ ✕ **Exultate.** When the weather permits, umbrella-shaded tables spread
LIGURIAN out from this tiny eatery into the nearby square. Popular with locals, the restaurant's inexpensive daily menu is presented on a chalkboard for all to see; excellent pizza, meal-size salads, and homemade delicious desserts highlight the list. ⊠ *Piazza Lavagna 15/R, Maddalena* ☎ *010/2512605* ⊟ *MC, V* ⊙ *Closed Sun.*

$$ ✕ **Le Rune.** The intimate setting, creative Ligurian dishes, and fine service
LIGURIAN make this a favorite with local businessmen and the after-opera crowd from nearby Teatro Carlo Felice. Standouts from the menu include the *tagliata di tonno* served with fresh fennel and a grapefruit sauce, and for an antipasto, the wonderful *timballo di robiola*, which is similar to a cheese soufflé served with a pear and cinnamon sauce. It's so good you could almost have it again for dessert. ⊠ *Vico Domoculta 14/R, just off Via XXV Aprile, Portoria* ☎ *010/594951* ⊟ *AE, DC, MC, V* ⊙ *No lunch weekends.*

$$ ✕ **Maxela.** Beef is king at this upscale but casual trattoria. The building
ITALIAN dates to a restaurant started in 1790. The owners have retained most of its original design, including wood benches and slabs of marble for tables. Daily specials are listed on chalkboards, or you can just walk up to the butcher counter and pick your cut of choice. ⊠ *Vico Inferiore del Ferro 9/R, Maddalena* ☎ *010/2474209* ⊕ *www.maxela.it* ⊟ *AE, DC, MC, V* ⊙ *Closed Sun.*

$$$$ ✕ **Zeffirino.** The five Belloni brothers share chef duties at this well-known
LIGURIAN restaurant full of odd combinations, including decor that has both rustic wood and modern metallic pieces. Try the *passutelli* (ravioli stuffed with ricotta cheese, herbs, and fruit) or any of the homemade pasta dishes. With a Zeffirino restaurant in Las Vegas and another in Hong Kong, the

enterprising Bellonis have gone international, yet their Ligurian location remains an institution among the Genovese. ⊠ *Via XX Settembre 20, Portoria* ☎ *010/591990* ⊕ *www.zeffirino.com* ⌕ *Reservations essential* ⋔ *Jacket required* ⊟ *AE, DC, MC, V.*

WHERE TO STAY

¢–$ ▦ **Agnello d'Oro.** The friendly owner at Agnello d'Oro does double duty as a travel agent: he's happy to help you with plane reservations and travel plans. Only a few of the simple, modern rooms have balconies, but a surprisingly varied Continental breakfast awaits you in the morning. **Pros:** 100 yards from Stazione Principe; near the Palazzo Reale. **Cons:** few amenities. ⊠ *Vico delle Monachette 6, Pré* ☎ *010/2462084* ⊕ *www.hotelagnellodoro.it* ⇆ *25 rooms* ⌕ *In-room: no a/c (some). In-hotel: restaurant, bar, parking (paid), some pets allowed* ⊟ *AE, DC, MC, V* ⦿ *BP.*

$$$$ ▦ **The Bentley Hotel.** Glamour has returned to Genoa with this luxury hotel on the wide, tree-lined road leading down to the port. The rooms are bright and sleekly decorated in muted tones with a wide variety of modern amenities such as plasma TVs and some with Jacuzzi tubs. The in-house "Genovese-gourmet" restaurant is frequented by local celebrities and soccer players. **Pros:** for top-of-the-line style and amenities, this is Genoa's best bet. **Cons:** it's a bit of a walk to the port and centro. ⊠ *Via Corsica 4, Carignano* ☎ *010/5315111* ⊕ *www.bentley.thi.it* ⇆ *85 rooms, 14 suites* ⌕ *In-room: safe, Internet. In-hotel: restaurant, bar, gym, spa, laundry service, Wi-Fi hotspot, parking (paid)* ⊟ *AE, DC, MC, V* ⦿ *BP.*

$$ ▦ **Best Western City.** In the heart of the city, near Via Roma, the grand shopping street, and one block from Piazza de Ferrari, which divides new Genoa from old Genoa, a bland apartment-building exterior gives way to a polished lobby and light, modern rooms. Suites, on the top floor, have spectacular views, as do many of the standard rooms on the upper floors. A choice of pillows—firm and low, or fluffy and soft—and coffeemakers in all the rooms are pleasant added touches. **Pros:** location can't be beat. **Cons:** regular rooms are small. ⊠ *Via San Sebastiano 6, Portoria* ☎ *010/584707* ⎙ *010/586301* ⊕ *www.bwcityhotel-ge.it* ⇆ *63 rooms, 3 suites* ⌕ *In-room: safe, Internet, Wi-Fi. In-hotel: restaurant, bar, Wi-Fi hotspot, parking (paid)* ⊟ *AE, DC, MC, V* ⦿ *BP.*

$ ▦ **Best Western Metropoli.** This welcoming hotel is on the border of the historic district and Via Garibaldi. Rooms and bathrooms both are bright and spacious with high ceilings. The staff is more than happy to offer you local advice, especially on dining options. Breakfast is abundant and the price is reasonable. **Pros:** guest rooms and bathrooms are large. **Cons:** parking lot is a bit of a hike; can be confusing to find if you are driving. ⊠ *Piazza Fontane Marose, Portoria* ☎ *010/2468888* ⊕ *www.bestwestern.it* ⇆ *48 rooms* ⌕ *In-room: refrigerator, Wi-Fi. In-hotel: bar, laundry service, Wi-Fi hotspot, parking (paid), some pets allowed* ⊟ *AE, DC, MC, V* ⦿ *BP.*

$$$–$$$$ ▦ **Bristol Palace.** The 19th-century grand hotel carefully guards its reputation for courtesy and service. Spacious guest rooms all have high
★ ceilings and elegant wood wardrobes or headboards. Public spaces, all

connected to the hotel's central oval staircase, are comfortable, small, and pleasantly discreet with panel walls and soft lighting. **Pros:** in the heart of the shopping district. **Cons:** busy street outside can sometimes be noisy. ⊠ *Via XX Settembre 35, Portoria* ☎ *010/592541* ⊕ *www.hotelbristolpalace.com* ⌁ *128 rooms, 5 suites* ⎰ *In-room: safe, refrigerator. In-hotel: restaurant, bar, Wi-Fi hotspot, parking (paid), some pets allowed* ⊟ *AE, DC, MC, V* ⧖*BP.*

NERVI: A SIDE TRIP FROM GENOA

★ *11 km (7 mi) east of Genoa.*

GETTING HERE

By car, exit the A12 at Genova Nervi and follow the CENTRO signs. The Nervi train station is located on the main north–south line, and you can also take the local commuter trains from Genova Principe and Brignole. It can also be reached on Bus 15 from Genoa's Piazza Cavour.

EXPLORING

The identity of this stately late-19th-century resort, famous for its 1½-km-long (1-mi-long) seaside promenade—the **Passeggiata Anita Garibaldi**—its palm-lined roads, and its 300 acres of parks rich in orange trees, is given away only by the sign on the sleepy train station. Although Nervi is technically part of the city, its peace and quiet are as different from Genoa's hustle and bustle as its clear blue water is from Genoa's crowded port. From the centrally located train station, walk east along the seaside promenade to reach the beaches, a cliff-hanging restaurant, and the 2,000 varieties of roses in the public **Parco Villa Grimaldi**, all the while enjoying one of the most breathtaking views on the Riviera. Nervi, and the road between it and Genoa, is known for its nightlife in summer.

WHERE TO EAT AND STAY

$$ ✕ **Marinella.** Here you can have a casual but sophisticated dining expe-
LIGURIAN rience while overlooking the Ligurian Sea. Try the *zuppa di pesce* (fish soup) and freshly baked focaccia; main dishes change according to the day's catch. The restaurant perches on seaside shoals: be sure to ask for one of the tables on the terrace, where you are suspended above the sea. There's a nice, inexpensive hotel on-site as well. ⊠ *Passeggiata Anita Garibaldi 18/R, Nervi* ☎ *010/3728343* ⊟ *MC, V* ⧖ *Closed Mon. and Nov.*

$$$ 🛏 **Romantik Hotel Villa Pagoda.** In a 19th-century merchant's mansion
Fodor'sChoice modeled after a Chinese temple, this luxury hotel has a private park,
★ access to the famed cliff-top walk, and magnificent ocean views. Request a tower room for the best vantage point. Villa Pagoda is the best of both worlds, as you can enjoy peace and quiet or be in bustling Genoa in 15 minutes. **Pros:** lovely guest and common rooms; everything has a touch of class. **Cons:** nearby train can be softly heard. ⊠ *Via Capolungo 15, Nervi* ☎ *010/3726161* ⊕ *www.villapagoda.it* ⌁ *13 rooms, 4 suites* ⎰ *In-room: safe, refrigerator. In-hotel: restaurant, bar, tennis court, pool, some pets allowed* ⊟ *AE, DC, MC, V* ⧖*BP* ⧖ *Closed Nov.–Mar.*

RIVIERA DI PONENTE

The Riviera di Ponente (Riviera of the Setting Sun) covers the narrow strip of northwest Liguria from Genoa to the French border. The sapphire-color Mediterranean Sea to one side and the verdant foothills of the Alps on the other allow for temperate weather and a long growing season—hence its nickname Riviera dei Fiori (Riviera of the Flowers). Once filled with charming seaside villages, elegant structures, and sophisticated visitors, this area now struggles to maintain a balance between its natural beauty and development. Highly populated resort areas and some overly industrialized areas are jammed into the thin stretch of white-sand and pebble beaches. Yet, while its sister Riviera (di Levante) may retain more of its natural beauty, the Ponente remains a popular and well-organized retreat for visitors looking for sunshine, nightlife, and relaxation.

ALBISOLA MARINA

43 km (27 mi) west of Genoa.

GETTING HERE

By car, take the Albisola exit off the A10 and follow the signs for the Albisola marina center. Albisola is on the main railway line between Genoa and France.

EXPLORING

Albisola Marina has a centuries-old tradition of ceramics making. Numerous shops here sell the distinctive wares, and a whole sidewalk, **Lungomare degli Artisti**, which runs along the beachfront, has been transformed by the colorful ceramic works of well-known artists.

The 18th-century **Villa Faraggiana**, near the parish church, has exhibits on the history of pottery and hosts an array of events from concerts to weddings. ⊠ *Via dell'Oratorio* ☎ *019/480622* ⌑ *Free* ☉ *Apr.–Sept., Wed.–Mon. 3–7.*

SHOPPING

Ceramiche San Giorgio (⊠ *Corso Matteotti 5* ☎ *019/482747*) has been producing ceramics since the 17th century, and is known for both classic and modern designs. **Ernan** (⊠ *Corso Mazzini 77, Albisola Superiore* ☎ *019/489916*) sells blue-and-white patterned ceramics typical of the 18th century. **Mazzotti** (⊠ *Corso Matteotti 25* ☎ *019/481626*) has an exclusive ceramics selection and a small museum.

FINALE LIGURE

30 km (19 mi) southwest of Albisola Marina, 72 km (44 mi) southwest of Genoa.

GETTING HERE

By car, take the Finale Ligure exit off the A10 and follow the CENTRO signs. Finale Ligure is on the main train line between Genoa and France.

Riviera di Ponente

VISITOR INFORMATION

Finale Ligure tourism office (✉ *Via San Pietro 13* ☎ *019/681019* ⊕ *www. inforiviera.it*).

EXPLORING

Finale Ligure is actually made up of three small villages: Finalmarina, Finalpia, and Finalborgo. The former two have fine sandy beaches and modern resort amenities. The most attractive of the villages is Finalborgo, less than 1 km (½ mi) inland. It's a hauntingly preserved medieval settlement, planned to a rigid blueprint, with 15th-century walls. The surrounding countryside is pierced by deep, narrow valleys and caves; the limestone outcroppings provide the warm pinkish stone found in many buildings in Genoa. Rare reptiles lurk among the exotic flora.

OFF THE BEATEN PATH

Noli. Just 9 km (5½ mi) northeast of Finale Ligure, the ruins of a castle loom benevolently over the tiny medieval gem of Noli. It's hard to imagine that this charming seaside village was—like Genoa, Venice, Pisa, and Amalfi—a prosperous maritime republic in the Middle Ages. If you don't have a car, get a bus for Noli at Spotorno, where local trains stop.

WHERE TO EAT AND STAY

$$$–$$$$ ✕ **Ai Torchi.** You could easily become a homemade-pesto snob at this
LIGURIAN Finalborgo eatery. The high prices are justified by excellent inventive
seafood and meat dishes and by the setting—a restored 5th-century
olive-oil refinery. ✉ *Via dell'Annunziata 12, Finalborgo* ☎ *019/690531*
☐ *AE, DC, MC, V* ✆ *Closed Jan. 7–Feb. 10 and Tues. Sept.–July.*

$$$ ⊡ **Punta Est.** This lovely small resort hotel is perched above the white-
sand beaches of Finale Ligure. Several buildings surrounded by lush gar-
dens, beautiful views, and a natural grotto with Jacuzzi and bar make
this a wonderful retreat from the crowds down at the water's edge.
Pros: nice pool and garden areas. **Cons:** rooms are a bit outdated. ✉ *Via
Aurelia 1* ☎ *39/019600611* ⊕ *www.puntaest.com* ↪ *40 rooms* ⌂ *In-
room: safe, refrigerator, Wi-Fi. In-hotel: restaurant, bars, pool, gym,
beachfront, laundry service, Internet terminal, Wi-Fi hotspot, parking
(free)* ☐ *AE, DC, MC, V* ✆ *Closed Nov.–Apr.* ⊙l *BP.*

ALBENGA

*20 km (12 mi) southwest of Finale Ligure, 90 km (55 mi) southwest
of Genoa.*

GETTING HERE

By car, take the Albenga exit off the A10 and follow the CENTRO signs.
Albenga is on the main train line between Genoa and France.

VISITOR INFORMATION

Albenga tourism office (✉ *Lungocento Croce Bianca 12* ☎ *0182/558444*
⊕ *www.inforiviera.it*).

EXPLORING

Albenga has a medieval core, with narrow streets laid out by the ancient
Romans. A network of alleys is punctuated by centuries-old towers
surrounding the 18th-century Romanesque cathedral, with a late-14th-
century campanile and a baptistery dating to the 5th century. It's a nice
place to take an afternoon stroll and explore it many quaint shops
and cafés.

**OFF THE
BEATEN
PATH**
Bardineto. For a look at some of the Riviera's mountain scenery, make
an excursion by car to this attractive village in the middle of an area
rich in mushrooms, chestnuts, and raspberries, as well as local cheeses.
A ruined castle stands above the village. From Borghetto Santo Spirito
(between Albenga and Finale Ligure), drive inland 25 km (15 mi).

WHERE TO STAY

$$$ ⊡ **La Meridiana.** An oasis of hospitality and refinement occupies a hand-
some farmhouse compound surrounded by a garden. The interiors feel
like a comfortable home, with brightly colored prints, fresh flowers,
and a mix of traditional and period-style furniture in the common and
guest rooms. The restaurant, Il Rosmarino ($$$$), serves fine wines
and seafood. You can enjoy privileges at the golf, tennis, and equestrian
clubs nearby. **Pros:** nice in-house restaurant. **Cons:** high cost for ameni-
ties available on-site. ✉ *Via ai Castelli (off A10), Garlenda* ⊹ *8 km (5
mi) north of Albenga* ☎ *0182/580271* ⊕ *www.lameridianaresort.com*
↪ *10 rooms, 18 suites* ⌂ *In-room: safe, refrigerator, Internet. In-hotel:*

3 restaurants, bar, pool, bicycles, Internet terminal, some pets allowed ☐ *AE, DC, MC, V* ☺ *Closed Nov.–Mar.* ⦿ *BP.*

ALASSIO

100 km (62 mi) southwest of Genoa.

GETTING HERE
By car, take the Albenga exit off the A10 and follow the blue signs for Alassio. Alassio is on the main train line between Genoa and France.

VISITOR INFORMATION
Alassio tourism office (✉ *Palazzo Commune, Piazza della Libertà* ☎ *0182/6021* ⊕ *www.comune.alassio.sv.it*).

EXPLORING
Although Alassio is no longer a sleepy fishing village, the centro still possesses some Old World charm, colorful buildings, a great beachfront promenade, and white-sand beaches. Spend the day soaking up some sun, grab a seafood lunch or pizza along the boardwalk, and then finish off with a passeggiata and shopping on its caruggi.

CERVO

23 km (14 mi) southwest of Albenga, 106 km (65 mi) southwest of Genoa.

GETTING HERE
By car, take the Diano Marina exit off the A10 and follow the signs for Cervo located just east of Diano Marina. Diano Marina is on the main train line between Genoa and France.

EXPLORING
Cervo is the quintessential sleepy Ligurian coastal village, nicely polished for the tourists who come to explore its narrow byways and street staircases. It's a remarkably well-preserved medieval town, crowned with a big baroque church. In July and August the square in front of the church is the site of chamber music concerts.

IMPERIA

12 km (7 mi) west of Cervo, 116 km (71 mi) southwest of Genoa.

GETTING HERE
By car, take the Imperia Est exit off the A10 and follow the signs for CENTRO or PORTO MAURIZIO. Both Imperia and Porto Maurizio are on the main rail line between Genoa and France.

VISITOR INFORMATION
Imperia tourism office (✉ *Viale Matteotti 37* ☎ *0183/660140* ⊕ *www.rivieradeifiori.org*).

EXPLORING
Imperia actually consists of two towns: Porto Maurizio, a medieval town built on a promontory, and Oneglia, now an industrial center for oil refining and pharmaceuticals. Porto Maurizio has a virtually intact

medieval center, an intricate spiral of narrow streets and stone portals, and some imposing 17th- and 18th-century palaces. There's little of interest in modern Oneglia, except for a visit to the olive-oil museum.

Imperia is king when it comes to olive oil, and the story of the olive is the theme of the small **Museo dell'Olivo**. Displays of the history of the olive tree, farm implements, presses, and utensils show how olive oil has been made in many countries throughout history. ✉ *Via Garessio 11, Oneglia* ☎ *0183/720000* 🌐 *www.museodellolivo.com* 🎫 *Free* ⏲ *Wed.–Mon. 9–12:30 and 3–6:30.*

WHERE TO STAY

$$ **Relais San Damian.** At this charming bed-and-breakfast, set among the olive trees high above Porto Maurizio, all the rooms are suites, and you can take in the views from an inviting infinity pool. The owners, Roberto and Pamela, are more than happy to assist you in planning your days in the area, but the best part about the Relais is relaxing and just enjoying the views. **Pros:** large suites and plenty of outdoor space; gorgeous pool area. **Cons:** limited amenities (no TVs or phones). ✉ *Strada Vasia 47* ☎ *0183/280309* 🌐 *www.san-damian.com* *9 suites* *In-room: no phone, no TV, safe, kitchenettes, refrigerator. In-hotel: pool, laundry service, Wi-Fi hotspot, parking (free), some pets allowed, no kids under 14* ▭ *AE, DC, MC, V* ⏲ *Closed Nov.–Mar.* 🍴 *BP.*

TAGGIA

20 km (12 mi) west of Imperia, 135 km (84 mi) southwest of Genoa.

GETTING HERE

By car, take the Arma di Taggia exit off the A10 and follow the signs for CENTRO. The closest train station is San Remo. From the train station it is a 20-minute taxi ride.

EXPLORING

The town of Taggia has a medieval core and one of the most imposing medieval bridges in the area.

The church of **San Domenico,** with a small museum, was once part of a monastery founded in the 15th century that remained a beacon of faith and learning in Liguria for 300 years. An antiques market is held here, just south of Taggia, on the fourth weekend of the month. ✉ *Piazzale San Domenico, Arma di Taggia* ☎ *No phone* 🎫 *Free* ⏲ *Fri.–Wed. 9–5.*

SAN REMO

50 km (31 mi) southwest of Cervo, 146 km (90 mi) southwest of Genoa.

GETTING HERE

By car, take the San Remo exit off the A10 and follow the CENTRO signs. San Remo is on the main train line between Genoa and France.

VISITOR INFORMATION

San Remo tourism office (✉ *Palazzo Riviera, Largo Nuvoloni 1* ☎ *0184/59059* 🌐 *www.sanremonet.com*).

11

EXPLORING

Once the crown jewel of the Riviera di Ponente, San Remo is still the area's largest resort, lined with polished hotels, exotic gardens, and seaside promenades. Renowned for its VIPs, glittering casino, and romantic setting, San Remo maintains remnants of its glamorous past from the late 19th century to World War II, but it also suffers from the same epidemic of overbuilding that has changed so much of the western Riviera for the worse. Still, it continues to be a lively town, even in the off-season.

The Mercato dei Fiori, Italy's most important wholesale flower market, is held here in a market hall between Piazza Colombo and Corso Garibaldi and open to dealers only. More than 20,000 tons of carnations, roses, mimosa flowers, and innumerable other cut flowers are dispatched from here each year. As the center of northern Italy's flower-growing industry, the town is surrounded by hills where verdant terraces are now blanketed with plastic to form immense greenhouses.

Explore the warren of alleyways in the old part of San Remo, **La Pigna** *(The Pinecone)*, which climbs upward to Piazza Castello and offers a splendid view of the town.

In addition to gaming, the art nouveau **San Remo Casinò** has a restaurant, a nightclub, and a theater that hosts concerts and the annual San Remo Music Festival. If you want to try your luck at the gaming tables, there's a €7.50 cover charge on weekends. Dress is elegant, with jacket and tie requested at the French gaming tables. ⊠ *Corso Inglesi 18* ☎ *0184/5951* ⊘ *Slot machines: Sun.–Fri. 10 AM–2:30 AM, Sat. 10 AM–3:30 AM. Tables: Sun.–Fri. 2:30 PM–2:30 AM, Sat. 2:30 PM–3:30 AM.*

The onion-dome Russian Orthodox church of **Cristo Salvatore, Santa Caterina d'Alessandria, e San Serafino di Sarov** testifies to a long Russian presence on the Italian Riviera. Russian empress Maria Alexandrovna, wife of Czar Alexander I, built a summerhouse here, and in winter San Remo was a popular destination for other royal Romanovs. The church was consecrated in 1913. ⊠ *Via Nuvoloni 2* ☎ *0184/531807* ⊑ *€1 donation* ⊘ *Daily 9:30–noon and 3–6.*

OFF THE BEATEN PATH

Bussana Vecchia. In the hills where flowers are cultivated for export sits Bussana Vecchia, a self-consciously picturesque former ghost town largely destroyed by an earthquake in 1877. The inhabitants packed up and left en masse after the quake, and for almost a century the houses, church, and crumbling bell tower were empty shells, overgrown by weeds and wildflowers. Since the 1960s an artists' colony has evolved among the ruins. Painters, sculptors, artisans, and bric-a-brac dealers have restored dwellings. ⊠ *8 km (5 mi) east of San Remo.*

WHERE TO EAT AND STAY

$ ✕ **Nuovo Piccolo Mondo.** Old wooden chairs dating from the 1920s, when the place opened, evoke the homey charm of this small, family-run trattoria. The place has a faithful clientele, so get here early to grab a table and order Ligurian specialties such as *sciancui* (a roughly cut flat pasta with a mixture of beans, tomatoes, zucchini, and pesto) and *polpo e patate* (stewed octopus with potatoes). ⊠ *Via Piave 7* ☎ *0184/509012* ⊟ *No credit cards* ⊘ *Closed Mon. No dinner Sun.*

LIGURIAN

$$-$$$ 🛏 **Paradiso.** A quiet palm-fringed garden gives the Paradiso an air of seclusion in this sometimes hectic resort city. Rooms are well equipped and bright; sea-facing rooms have nice-size balconies. The hotel restaurant has a good fixed-price menu. This small central hotel is adjacent to a lush public park. **Pros:** friendly service; comfortable accommodations. **Cons:** a steep walk up some stairs and a hill from town. ⊠ *Via Roccasterone 12* 🕾 *0184/571211* ⊕ *www.paradisohotel.it* ⤴ *41 rooms* △ *In-room: safe, refrigerator. In-hotel: restaurant, bar, pool, Wi-Fi hotspot* ⊟ *AE, DC, MC, V* ⊺◯⦚ *BP.*

$$$-$$$$ 🛏 **Royal.** This is arguably Liguria's second-most-luxurious resort after the Splendido in Portofino. Rooms are beautifully decorated, have modern amenities, and most have views of the sea. The heated seawater swimming pool, open April through October, is in a large tropical garden. On the terrace, candlelight dining and music are offered each night in warm weather. Keep your eyes open for off-season discounts. The Royal is only a few moments from the world-famous Casino. **Pros:** the glamour of yesteryear with all the expected high-end amenities. **Cons:** some of the property seems outdated (though at this writing renovations are planned); on-site meals and beverages are expensive. ⊠ *Corso Imperatrice 80* 🕾 *0184/5391* ⊕ *www.royalhotelsanremo.com* ⤴ *114 rooms, 13 suites* △ *In-room: safe, Wi-Fi. In-hotel: 3 restaurants, room service, bars, tennis court, pool, gym, spa, beachfront, laundry service* ⊟ *AE, DC, MC, V* ⊗ *Closed Nov.–mid-Feb.* ⊺◯⦚ *BP.*

BORDIGHERA

12 km (7 mi) west of San Remo, 155 km (96 mi) southwest of Genoa.

GETTING HERE

By car, take the Bordighera exit off the A10 and follow the signs for CENTRO, about a 10-minute drive. Bordighera is on the main railway line between Genoa and France.

VISITOR INFORMATION

Bordighera tourism office (⊠ *Via Vittorio Emanuele II 172* 🕾 *0184/262322* ⊕ *www.rivieradeifiori.org*).

EXPLORING

On a lush promontory, Bordighera sits as a charming seaside resort with panoramas from Genoa (on a clear day) to Monte Carlo. A large English colony, attracted by the mild climate, settled here in the second half of the 19th century and is still very much in evidence today; you regularly find people taking afternoon tea in the cafés, and streets are named after Queen Victoria and Shakespeare. This garden spot was the first town in Europe to grow date palms, and its citizens still have the exclusive right to provide the Vatican with palm fronds for Easter celebrations.

Thanks partly to its many year-round English residents, Bordighera does not close down entirely in the off-season like some Riviera resorts but rather serves as a quiet winter haven for all ages. With plenty of hotels and restaurants, Bordighera makes a good base for exploring the region and is quieter and less commercial than San Remo.

A view from the Hanbury Botanical Gardens.

Running parallel to the ocean, **Lungomare Argentina** is a pleasant promenade, 1½ km (1 mi) long, which begins at the western end of the town and provides good views westward to the French Côte d'Azur.

WHERE TO EAT AND STAY

$
LIGURIAN

✕**Bagni Sant'Ampeglio.** This combination beach club and seafront restaurant has wonderful choices for both lunch and dinner. Try the house-specialty *branzino in carciofi* (sea bass with artichokes) and homemade desserts. ⊠ *Lungomare Argentina 3* ☎ *0184/262106* ▭ *AE, DC, MC, V* ⊙ *Closed Wed. in Sept.–Nov., 1st half of Jan., and Feb.–May.*

$
WINE BAR

✕**Il Tempo Ritrovato.** A small wine bar and restaurant combine forces here on Bordighera's seaside promenade. Simple pasta dishes and a spectacular wine list make this a great choice. ⊠ *Bagni Amarea on Lungomare Argentina* ☎ *0184/261207* ▭ *AE, DC, MC, V* ⊙ *Closed Sun. and Mon.*

$$$
LIGURIAN
Fodor's Choice
★

✕**Magiargè.** A mix of great charm and great food make this small osteria in the historic center an absolute dining delight. Dishes are Ligurian with a creative twist, such as the *stoccafisso sopra panizza* (salt cod served over a chickpea polenta) and *fritteline di bianchetti* (small frittatas made with tiny white fish). The selection of local wines is excellent. ⊠ *Via della Loggia 6* ☎ *0184/262946* ⊕ *www.magiarge.it* ▭ *DC, MC, V* ⊙ *Closed 2 wks in Feb. and Oct. No lunch June–Aug.*

$$

🛏**Hotel Piccolo Lido.** This quaint hotel along the promenade provides clean and simple rooms at reasonable prices year-round. Sea-view rooms have nice little balconies, and there is a terrace perfect for enjoying the sunset and vistas of France. **Pros:** a good value. **Cons:** few amenities. ⊠ *Lungomare Argentina 2* ☎ *0184/261297* ⊕ *www.hotelpiccololido.*

it ⮑ *33 rooms* ⌂ *In-room: safe, refrigerator. In-hotel: restaurant, beach-front, parking (paid)* ⊟ *AE, DC, MC, V* ⊙l *BP.*

$$ ⊡ **Hotel Villa Elisa.** On a street filled with beautiful old villas, this Victorian-style hotel has a relaxed and friendly atmosphere, beautiful gardens, and well-equipped rooms at reasonable prices. In the back garden there are two swimming pools (one for adults and one for children) plus a playground, making it a good choice for families. **Pros:** helpful staff; a good value. **Cons:** only partial views in sea-view rooms; limited parking; covered parking costs extra. ⊠ *Via Romana 70* ☎ *0184/261313* ⊕ *www. villaelisa.com* ⮑ *33 rooms, 2 suites, 1 apartment for up to 6 people* ⌂ *In-room: safe, refrigerator. In-hotel: restaurant, bar, pools, laundry service, Wi-Fi hotspot, parking (free), some pets allowed* ⊟ *AE, DC, MC, V* ⊙l *BP, MAP.*

EN
ROUTE

From Ventimiglia, a provincial road swings 10 km (6 mi) up the Nervi River valley to a lovely sounding medieval town, **Dolceacqua** (its name translates as Sweetwater), with a ruined castle. Liguria's best-known red wine is the local Rossese di Dolceacqua. A farther 6 km (4 mi) along the road lies Pigna, a fascinating medieval village built in concentric circles on its hilltop.

GIARDINI BOTANICI HANBURY

6 km (4 mi) west of Ventimiglia, 10 km (6 mi) west of Bordighera.

GETTING HERE

Take the S1 along the coast west from Bordighera, through the town of Ventimiglia, and toward the French border. The gardens are about 1 km (½ mi) beyond the tunnel.

Fodor'sChoice
★

Giardini Botanici Hanbury. Mortola Inferiore, only 2 km (1 mi) from the French border, is the site of the world-famous Giardini Botanici Hanbury (Hanbury Botanical Gardens), one of the largest and most beautiful in Italy. Planned and planted in 1867 by a wealthy English merchant, Sir Thomas Hanbury, and his botanist brother, Daniel, the terraced gardens contain species from five continents, including many palms and succulents. There are panoramic views of the sea from the gardens. ⊠ *Corso Montecarlo 43, Località Mortola Inferiore* ☎ *0184/229507* ⊡ *€7.50 July–Mar. 19, €9 Mar. 20–June* ☉ *Mar.–June 15, daily 9:30–6; June 16–Sept. 15, daily 9:30–7; Sept. 16–last Sat. in Oct., daily 9:30–6; last Sun. in Oct.–Feb., Tues.–Sun. 10–6. Last entry 1 hr before closing.*

ITALIAN VOCABULARY

ENGLISH	ITALIAN	PRONOUNCIATION

BASICS

Yes/no	Sí/no	see/no
Please	Per favore	pear fa-**vo**-ray
Yes, please	Sí grazie	see **grah**-tsee-ay
Thank you	Grazie	**grah**-tsee-ay
You're welcome	Prego	**pray**-go
Excuse me, sorry	Scusi	**skoo**-zee
Sorry!	Mi dispiace!	mee dis-spee-**ah**-chay
Good morning/ afternoon	Buongiorno	bwohn-**jor**-no
Good evening	Buona sera	**bwoh**-na **say**-ra
Good-bye	Arrivederci	a-ree-vah-**dare**-chee
Mr. (Sir)	Signore	see-**nyo**-ray
Mrs. (Ma'am)	Signora	see-**nyo**-ra
Miss	Signorina	see-nyo-**ree**-na
Pleased to meet you	Piacere	pee-ah-**chair**-ray
How are you?	Come sta?	**ko**-may **stah**
Very well, thanks	Bene, grazie	**ben**-ay **grah**-tsee-ay
Hello (phone)	Pronto?	**proan**-to

NUMBERS

one	uno	**oo**-no
two	due	**doo**-ay
three	tre	tray
four	quattro	**kwah**-tro
five	cinque	**cheen**-kway
six	sei	say
seven	sette	**set**-ay
eight	otto	**oh**-to
nine	nove	**no**-vay
ten	dieci	dee-**eh**-chee
eleven	undici	**oon**-dee-chee
twelve	dodici	**doe**-dee-cee

thirteen	tredici	**tray**-dee-chee
fourteen	quattordici	kwa-**tore**-dee-chee
fifteen	quindici	**kwin**-dee-chee
sixteen	sedici	**say**-dee-chee
seventeen	diciassete	dee-cha-**set**-ay
eighteen	diciotto	dee-**cho**-to
nineteen	diciannove	dee-cha-**no**-vay
twenty	venti	**vain**-tee
twenty-one	ventuno	vain-**too**-no
twenty-two	ventidue	vain-tee-**doo**-ay
thirty	trenta	**train**-ta
forty	quaranta	kwa-**rahn**-ta
fifty	cinquanta	cheen-**kwahn**-ta
sixty	sessanta	seh-**sahn**-ta
seventy	settanta	seh-**tahn**-ta
eighty	ottanta	o-**tahn**-ta
ninety	novanta	no-**vahn**-ta
one hundred	cento	**chen**-to
one thousand	mille	**mee**-lay
ten thousand	diecimila	dee-eh-chee-**mee**-la

USEFUL PHRASES

Do you speak English?	Parla inglese?	**par**-la een-**glay**-zay
I don't speak Italian	Non parlo italiano	non **par**-lo ee-tal-**yah**-no
I don't understand	Non capisco	non ka-**peess**-ko
Can you please repeat?	Può ripetere?	pwo ree-**pet**-ay-ray
Slowly!	Lentamente!	**len**-ta-men-tay
I don't know	Non lo so	non lo **so**
I'm American	Sono americano(a)	**so**-no a-may-ree-**kah**-no(a)
I'm British	Sono inglese	so-no een-**glay**-zay
What's your name?	Come si chiama?	**ko**-may see kee-**ah**-ma

My name is . . .	Mi chiamo . . .	mee kee-**ah**-mo
What time is it?	Che ore sono?	kay **o**-ray **so**-no
How?	Come?	**ko**-may
When?	Quando?	**kwan**-doe
Yesterday/today/tomorrow	Ieri/oggi/domani	**yer**-ee/**o**-jee/do-**mah**-nee
This morning	Stamattina	sta-ma-**tee**-na
This afternoon	Oggi pomeriggio	**o**-jee po-mer-**ee**-jo
Tonight	Stasera	sta-**ser**-a
What?	Che cosa?	kay **ko**-za
What is it?	Chee cos'é?	kay ko-**zay**
Why?	Perché?	pear-**kay**
Who?	Chi?	kee
Where is . . .	Dov'è . . .	doe-**veh**
the bus stop?	la fermata dell'autobus?	la fer-**mah**-tadel ow-toe-**booss**
the train station?	la stazione?	la sta-tsee-**oh**-nay
the subway	la metropolitana?	la may-tro-po-lee-**tah**-na
the terminal?	il terminale?	eel ter-mee-**nah**-lay
the post office?	l'ufficio postale?	loo-**fee**-cho po-**stah**-lay
the bank?	la banca?	la **bahn**-ka
the . . . hotel?	l'hotel . . .?	lo-**tel**
the store?	il negozio?	eel nay-**go**-tsee-o
the cashier?	la cassa?	la **kah**-sa
the . . . museum?	il museo . . .?	eel moo-**zay**-o
the hospital?	l'ospedale?	lo-spay-**dah**-lay
the first-aid station?	il pronto soccorso?	Eel **pron**-to so-**kor**-so
the elevator?	l'ascensore?	la-shen-**so**-ray
a telephone?	un telefono?	oon tay-**lay**-fo-no
the restrooms?	il bagno?	eel **bahn**-yo
Here/there	Qui/là	kwee/la
Left/right	A sinistra/a destra	a see-**neess**-tra/a **des**-tra
Straight ahead	Avanti dritto	a-**vahn**-tee dree-to
Is it near/far?	È vicino/lontano?	ay vee-**chee**-no/lon-**tah**-no
I'd like . . .	Vorrei . . .	vo-**ray**
a room	una camera	**oo**-na **kah**-may-ra
the key	la chiave	la kee-**ah**-vay
a newspaper	un giornale	oon jor-**nah**-lay
a stamp	un francobollo	oon frahn-ko-**bo**-lo

I'd like to buy . . .	Vorrei comprare . . .	vo-**ray** kom-**prah**-ray
How much is it?	Quanto costa?	**kwahn**-toe **coast**-a
It's expensive/cheap	È caro/economico	ay **car**-o/ ay-ko-**no**-mee-ko
A little/a lot	Poco/tanto	**po**-ko/**tahn**-to
More/less	Più/meno	pee-**oo**/**may**-no
Enough/too (much)	Abbastanza/troppo	a-bas-**tahn**-sa/**tro**-po
I am sick	Sto male	sto **mah**-lay
Call a doctor	Chiama un dottore	kee-**ah**-mah oon doe-**toe**-ray
Help!	Aiuto!	a-**yoo**-toe
Stop!	Alt!	ahlt
Fire!	Al fuoco!	ahl **fwo**-ko
Caution/Look out!	Attenzione!	a-ten-**syon**-ay

DINING OUT

A bottle of . . .	Una bottiglia di . . .	**oo**-na bo-**tee**-lee-ahdee
A cup of . . .	Una tazza di . . .	**oo**-na **tah**-tsa dee
A glass of . . .	Un bicchiere di . . .	oon bee-key-**air**-ay dee
Bill/check	Il conto	eel **cone**-toe
Bread	Il pane	eel **pah**-nay
Breakfast	La prima colazione	la **pree**-ma ko-la-**tsee**-oh-nay
Cocktail/aperitif	L'aperitivo	la-pay-ree-**tee**-vo
Dinner	La cena	la **chen**-a
Fixed-price menu	Menù a prezzo fisso	may-**noo** a **pret**-so **fee**-so
Fork	La forchetta	la for-**ket**-a
I am diabetic	Ho il diabete	o eel dee-a-**bay**-tay
I am vegetarian	Sono vegetariano/a	**so**-no vay-jay-ta-ree-**ah**-no/a
I'd like . . .	Vorrei . . .	vo-**ray**
I'd like to order	Vorrei ordinare	vo-**ray** or-dee-**nah**-ray
Is service included?	Il servizio è incluso?	eel ser-**vee**-tzee-o ay een-**kloo**-zo
It's good/bad	È buono/cattivo	ay **bwo**-no/ka-**tee**-vo

It's hot/cold	È caldo/freddo	ay **kahl**-doe/**fred**-o
Knife	Il coltello	eel kol-**tel**-o
Lunch	Il pranzo	eel **prahnt**-so
Menu	Il menù	eel may-**noo**
Napkin	Il tovagliolo	eel toe-va-lee-**oh**-lo
Please give me . . .	Mi dia . . .	mee **dee**-a
Salt	Il sale	eel **sah**-lay
Spoon	Il cucchiaio	eel koo-kee-**ah**-yo
Sugar	Lo zucchero	lo **tsoo**-ker-o
Waiter/waitress	Cameriere/cameriera	ka-mare-**yer**-ay/ ka-mare-**yer**-a
Wine list	La lista dei vini	la **lee**-sta **day**-ee **vee**-nee

Travel Smart Venice and Northern Italy

GETTING HERE AND AROUND

■ AIR TRAVEL

Air travel to Italy is frequent and virtually problem-free, except for airport- or airline-related union strikes that may cause delays. Although most nonstop flights are to Rome and Milan, many travelers find it more convenient to connect through a European hub to Florence, Pisa, Venice, Bologna, or another smaller airport. The airport in Venice also caters to international carriers.

Flying time to Milan or Rome is approximately 8–8½ hours from New York, 10–11 hours from Chicago, and 11½ hours from Los Angeles.

Labor strikes are frequent and can affect not only air travel, but also local transit that serves airports (private transit is not affected by strikes, however). Confirm flights within Italy the day before travel. Your airline will have information about strikes directly affecting its flight schedule. If you are taking a train to the airport, check with the local tourist agency or rail station about upcoming strikes. Be aware it's not unusual for strikes to be canceled at the last minute.

Airline Security Issues Transportation Security Administration (⊕ www.tsa.gov) has answers for almost every question that might come up.

Contact A helpful Web site for information (location, phone numbers, local transportation, etc.) about all of the airports in Italy is ⊕ www.travel-library.com.

AIRPORTS

The major gateways to Italy include Rome's Aeroporto Leonardo da Vinci (FCO), better known as Fiumicino, and Milan's Aeroporto Malpensa (MPX). Most flights to Venice, Florence, and Pisa make connections at Fiumicino and Malpensa or another European airport hub. You can take the FS airport train to Rome's Termini station, or an express motor coach to Milan's central train station (Centrale) and catch a train to any other location in Italy. It will take about 30 minutes to get from Fiumicino to Roma Termini, about an hour to Milano Centrale.

Many carriers fly into the smaller airports. Venice is served by Aeroporto Marco Polo (VCE), Naples by Aeroporto Capodichino (NAP), and Palermo by Aeroporto Punta Raisi (PMO). Florence is serviced by Aeroporto A. Vespucci (FLR), which is also called Peretola, and by Aeroporto Galileo Galilei (PSA), which is about 2 km (1 mi) outside the center of Pisa and about one hour from Florence. The train to Florence stops within 100 feet of the entrance to the Pisa airport terminal. Bologna's airport (BLQ) is a 20-minute direct Aerobus-ride away from Bologna Centrale, which is about 40 minutes from Florence by train.

Italy's major airports are not known for being new, fun, or efficient. Security measures include random baggage inspection and bomb-detection dogs. All of the airports have restaurants and snack bars, and there is Wi-Fi Internet access.

When you take a connecting flight from a European airline hub (Frankfurt or Paris, for example) to a local Italian airport (Florence or Venice), be aware that your luggage might not make it onto the second plane with you. The airlines' lost-luggage service is efficient, however, and your delayed luggage is usually delivered to your hotel or holiday rental within 12 to 24 hours.

Airport Information Aeroporto A. Vespucci (*FLR, also called Peretola*✚ 6 km [4 mi] northwest of Florence ☎ 055/3061300 ⊕ www.aeroporto.firenze.it). **Aeroporto di Bologna** (*BLQ, also called Guglielmo Marconi*✚ 6 km [4 mi] northwest of Bologna ☎ 051/6479615 ⊕ www.bologna-airport.it). **Aeroporto di Venezia** (*VCE, also called Marco Polo*✚ 6 km [4 mi] north of Venice ☎ 041/2609260 ⊕ www.

veniceairport.it). **Aeroporto Galileo Galilei** (PSA✈ 2 km [1 mi] south of Pisa, 80 km [50 mi] west of Florence ☎ 050/849300 ⊕ www.pisa-airport.com). **Aeroporto Leonardo da Vinci** (FCO, also called Fiumicino✈ 35 km [20 mi] southwest of Rome ☎ 06/65951 ⊕ www.adr.it). **Aeroporto Malpensa** (MPX✈ 45 km [28 mi] north of Milan ☎ 02/74852200 ⊕ www.sea-aeroportimilano.it). **Naples International Airport** (NAP, also called Capodichino✈ 7 km [4 mi] northeast of Naples ☎ 081/7896111 ⊕ www.naples-airport.com). **Palermo International Airport** (PMO, also called Punta Raisi✈ 32 km [19 mi] northwest of Palermo ☎ 091/7020272 ⊕ www.gesap.it).

FLIGHTS

On flights from the United States, Alitalia and Delta Air Lines serve Rome, Milan, Pisa, and Venice. The major international hubs in Italy, Milan, and Rome are also served by Continental Airlines and American Airlines, and US Airways serves Rome. From April through October, the Italy-based Meridiana EuroFly has non-stop flights from New York to Naples and Palermo.

Alitalia and British Airways have direct flights from London to Milan, Venice, Rome, and 10 other locations in Italy. Smaller, no-frills airlines also provide service between Great Britain and Italy. EasyJet connects Gatwick with Milan, Venice, Rome, and Bologna. British Midland connects Heathrow and Milan (Linate), Naples, and Venice. Ryanair, departing from London's Stansted airport, flies to Milan, Rome, Pisa, and Venice. Meridiana has flights between Gatwick and Olbia on Sardinia in summer, and flights to Rome and Florence throughout the year.

Tickets for flights within Italy, on Alitalia and small carriers, such as EuroFly, Meridiana, and Air One, cost less when purchased from agents within Italy. Tickets are frequently sold at discounted prices, so check the cost of flights, even one-way, as an alternative to train travel.

Airline Contacts Alitalia (☎ 800/223–5730 in U.S., 06/2222 in Rome, 800/650055 elsewhere in Italy ⊕ www.alitalia.it). **American Airlines** (☎ 800/433–7300, 02/69682464 in Milan ⊕ www.aa.com). **British Airways** (☎ 800/247–9297 in U.S., 119/712266 in Italy ⊕ www.britishairways.com). **British Midland** (☎ 0807/6070–555 for U.K. reservations, 1332/64–8181 callers outside U.K. ⊕ www.flybmi.com). **Continental Airlines** (☎ 800/523–3273 for U.S. reservations, 800/231–0856 for international reservations, 02/69633256 in Milan, 800/555580000 elsewhere in Italy ⊕ www.continental.com). **Delta Air Lines** (☎ 800/221–1212 for U.S. reservations, 800/241–4141 for international reservations, 848/780376 in Italy ⊕ www.delta.com). **EasyJet** (☎ 0905/821–0905 in U.K., 899/234589 in Italy ⊕ www.easyjet.com). **Northwest Airlines** (☎ 800/225–2525 ⊕ www.nwa.com). **Ryanair** (☎ 08701/24–60000 in U.K., 899/678910 in Italy ⊕ www.ryanair.com). **US Airways** (☎ 800/428–4322 for U.S. reservations, 800/622–1015 for international reservations, 848/8813177 in Italy ⊕ www.usairways.com).

Domestic Carriers Air One (☎ 06/48880069 in Rome, 800/650055 elsewhere in Italy ⊕ www.flyairone.it). **Meridiana EuroFly** (☎ 866/387–6359 in U.S., 892928 in Italy ⊕ www.euroflyusa.com).

▌ BUS TRAVEL

Italy's regional bus network, often operated by private companies with motorcoach fleets, is extensive, although not as attractive an option as in other European countries, partly due to convenient train travel. Schedules are often drawn up with commuters and students in mind and may be sketchy on weekends. Regional bus companies often provide the only means (not including car travel) of getting to out-of-the-way places. Even when this isn't the case, buses can be faster and more direct than local trains, so it's a good idea to compare bus and train schedules. SITA operates throughout Italy; Lazzi

Eurolines operates in Tuscany and central Italy. DolomitiBus serves the Dolomites.

All major cities in Italy have urban bus service. It's inexpensive, and tickets may be purchased in blocks or as passes. Buses can become jammed during busy travel periods and rush hours.

Smoking is not permitted, and both public and private buses offer only one class of service. Cleanliness and comfort levels are high on private motor coaches, which have plenty of legroom and comfortable seats, but no toilets. Private bus lines usually have a ticket office in town or allow you to pay when you board. When traveling on city buses, you must buy your ticket from a machine, newsstand, or tobacco shop and stamp it on board (although some city buses have ticket machines on board).

Bus Information ATAC (✉ *Rome* ☎ *800/431784 or 06/46952027* ⊕ *www.atac. roma.it [no English version]*). **ATAF** (✉ *Stazione Centrale di Santa Maria Novella, Florence* ☎ *800/424500* ⊕ *www.ataf.net*). **DolomitiBus** (✉ *Via Col da Ren 14, Belluno* ☎ *0437/217111* ⊕ *www.dolomitibus.it*). **Lazzi Eurolines** (✉ *Via Mercadante 2, Florence* ☎ *055/363041* ⊕ *www.lazzi.it*). **SITA** (✉ *Via Santa Caterina da Siena 17/r, Florence* ☎ *055/47821* ⊕ *www. sitabus.it*).

▮ CAR TRAVEL

Italy has an extensive network of autostrade (toll highways), complemented by equally well-maintained but free *superstrade* (expressways). Save the ticket you are issued at an autostrada entrance, as you need it to exit; on some shorter autostrade, you pay the toll when you enter. Viacards, on sale for €25 and up at many autostrada locations, allow you to pay for tolls in advance, exiting at special lanes where you simply slip the card into a designated slot.

An *uscita* is an "exit." A *raccordo annulare* is a ring road surrounding a city, while a *tangenziale* bypasses a city entirely. *Strade*

regionale and *strade provinciale* (regional and provincial highways, denoted by *S, SS, SR,* or *SP* numbers) may be two-lane roads, as are all secondary roads; directions and turnoffs aren't always clearly marked.

GASOLINE

Gas stations are along the main highways. Those on autostrade are open 24 hours. Otherwise, gas stations generally are open Monday–Saturday 7–7, with a break at lunchtime. At self-service gas stations the pumps are operated by a central machine for payment, which doesn't take credit cards; it accepts only bills in denominations of 5, 10, 20, and 50 euros, and does not give change. Those with attendants accept cash and credit cards. It's not customary to tip the attendant.

At this writing, gasoline (*benzina*) costs about €1.33 per liter and is available in unleaded (*verde*) and superunleaded (*super*). Many rental cars in Italy use diesel (*gasolio*), which costs about €1.18 per liter (ask about the fuel type for your rental car before you leave the agency).

PARKING

Parking is at a premium in most towns, especially in the *centri storici* (historic centers). Fines for parking violations are high, and towing is common. Don't think about tearing up a ticket, as car-rental companies can use your credit card to be reimbursed for any fines you incur. It's a good idea to park in a designated (and preferably attended) lot. And don't leave valuables in your car, as thieves often target rental cars.

In congested cities, indoor parking costs €25–€30 for 12–24 hours; outdoor parking costs about €10–€20. Parking in an area signposted *zona disco* (disk zone) is allowed for short periods (from 30 minutes to two hours or more—the time is posted); if you don't have a cardboard disk (check in the glove box of your rental car) to show what time you parked, you can use a piece of paper. In most metropolitan areas you can find the curbside *parcometro:* once you insert change, it prints a ticket that you then leave on your dashboard.

RENTALS

Fiats, Fords, and Alfa Romeos in a variety of sizes are the most typical rental cars. Note that most Italian cars have standard transmission, so if you need to rent an automatic, be specific when you reserve the car. Significantly higher rates will apply.

Most American chains have affiliates in Italy, but the rates are usually lower if you book a car before you leave home. A company's rates are the standard throughout the country: rates are the same for airport and city pickup; airport offices are open later. An auto broker such as AutoEurope.com can allow you to compare rates among companies while guaranteeing lowest rates.

Most rental companies will not rent to someone under age 21 and also refuse to rent any car larger than an economy or subcompact car to anyone under age 23, and, further, require customers under age 23 to pay by credit card. Additional drivers must be identified in the contract and must qualify with the age limits. There is likely a supplementary daily fee for additional drivers. Upon rental, all companies require credit cards as a warranty; to rent bigger cars (2,000 cc or more), you must often show two credit cards. There are no special restrictions on senior citizen drivers. Book car seats, required for children under age 3, in advance (the cost is generally about €36 for the duration of the rental).

Hiring a car with a driver can come in handy, particularly if you plan to do some wine tasting or drive along the Amalfi Coast. Search online (the travel forums at fodors.com are a good resource) or ask at your hotel for recommended drivers. Drivers are paid by the day, and are usually rewarded with a tip of about 15% upon completion of the journey.

All rental agencies operating in Italy require that you buy a collision-damage waiver (CDW) and a theft-protection policy, but those costs will already be included in the rates you are quoted. Be aware that coverage may be denied if the named driver on the rental contract is not the driver at the time of the incident. In Sicily there are some roads for which rental agencies deny coverage; ask in advance if you plan to travel in remote regions. Also ask your rental company about other included coverage when you reserve the car and/or pick it up.

ROAD CONDITIONS

Autostrade are well maintained, as are most interregional highways. Most autostrade have two lanes in both directions; the left lane is used only for passing. Italians drive fast and are impatient with those who don't, so tailgating (and flashing with bright beams to signal an intent to pass) is the norm if you dawdle in the left lane; the only way to avoid it is to stay to the right.

The condition of provincial (county) roads varies, but road maintenance at this level is generally good in Italy. In many small hill towns the streets are winding and extremely narrow; consider parking at the edge of town and exploring on foot.

Driving on the back roads of Italy isn't difficult as long as you're on the alert for bicycles and passing cars. In addition, street and road signs are often missing or placed in awkward spots, so a good map or GPS and lots of patience are essential.

Be aware that some maps may not use the *SR* or *SP* (*strade regionale* and *strade provinciale*) highway designations, which took the place of the old *SS* designations in 2004. They may use the old *SS* designation or no numbering at all.

ROADSIDE EMERGENCIES

Automobile Club Italiano offers 24-hour road service; English-speaking operators are available. Your rental-car company may also have an emergency tow service with a toll-free call; keep that number handy. Be prepared to report which road you're on, the *verso* (direction) you're headed, and your *targa* (license plate number). Also, in an emergency, call the police (113).

When you're on the road, always carry a good road map and a flashlight; a cell phone is highly recommended. There are also emergency phones on the autostrade and superstrade; to locate them, look on the pavement for painted arrows and the term "SOS."

Emergency Services Automobile Club Italiano (*ACI* ☎ *803/116 emergency service* ⊕ *www.aci.it*).

RULES OF THE ROAD

Driving is on the right. Speed limits are 130 KPH (80 MPH) on autostrade, reduced to 110 KPH (70 MPH) when it rains, 90 KPH (55 MPH) on state and provincial roads, unless otherwise marked. In towns, the speed limit is 50 KPH (30 MPH), which may drop as low as 10 KPH (6 MPH) near schools, hospitals, and other designated areas. Note that right turns on red lights are forbidden. Headlights are required to be on while driving on all roads (large or small) outside municipalities. You must wear seat belts and strap young children into car seats at all times. Using hand-held mobile phones while driving is illegal; fines can exceed €100. In most Italian towns the use of the horn is forbidden in many areas; a large sign, *zona di silenzio*, indicates a no-honking zone.

In Italy you must be 18 years old to drive a car. A U.S. driver's license is acceptable to rent a car, but by law Italy requires non-Europeans also to carry an International Driver's Permit (IDP), which essentially translates your license into Italian (and a dozen other languages). In practice, it depends on the police officer who pulls you over whether you will be penalized for not carrying the IDP. Obtaining an IDP is simple and costs only $15; check the AAA Web site for more information.

The blood-alcohol content limit for driving is 0.5 (stricter than U.S. limits) with fines up to €5,000 for surpassing the limit and the possibility of six months' imprisonment. Although enforcement of laws varies depending on the region, fines for speeding are uniformly stiff: 10 KPH over the speed limit can warrant a fine of up to €500; greater than 10 KPH, and your license could be taken away from you. The police have the power to levy on-the-spot fines.

∎ TRAIN TRAVEL

In Italy, traveling by train is simple and efficient. Service between major cities is frequent, and trains usually arrive on schedule. The fastest trains on the Ferrovie dello Stato (FS), the Italian State Railways, are the Eurostar express trains, and the fastest Eurostar lines are designated as Alta Velocità; they run between all major cities from Venice, Milan, and Turin down through Florence and Rome to Naples. Seat reservations are mandatory on all Eurostar trains. You will be assigned a specific seat in a specific coach; to avoid having to squeeze through narrow aisles, board only at your designated coach (the number on your ticket matches the one near the door of each coach). Reservations are also required for the next-fastest, and less-frequent *Intercity* (IC) trains, tickets for which are about half the price of Eurostar. If you miss your reserved train, go to the ticket counter within the hour and you will be able to move your reservation to a later train (check these rules at booking).

Reservations are available but not required on *Interregionale* trains, which are slower and make more stops, and are less expensive still. *Regionale* and *Espresso* trains make the most stops and are the most economical; many serve commuters. There are refreshments on long-distance trains, purchased from a mobile cart or a dining car, but not on the commuter trains.

All but commuter trains have first and second classes. On local trains a first-class fare ensures you a little more space and a likely emptier coach. On long-distance trains you also get wider seats (three across as opposed to four) and a bit more legroom, but the difference is minimal. At peak travel times, a first-class fare may be worth the additional cost as the coaches may be less crowded. In Italian, *prima classe* is first class; second is *seconda classe*.

Many cities—Milan, Turin, Genoa, Naples, Florence, Rome, and even Verona included—have more than one train station, **so be sure you get off at the right place.** When buying train tickets be particularly aware that in Rome and Florence some trains do not stop at all of the cities' train stations and may not stop at the main, central station. This is a common occurrence with regional and some Intercity trains. When scheduling train travel on the Internet or through a travel agent, be sure to request to arrive at the station closest to your destination in Rome and Florence.

Except for Pisa, Milan, and Rome, none of the major cities have trains that go directly to the airports, but there are always commuter (frequently direct) bus lines connecting train stations and airports.

You can pay for your train tickets in cash or with a major credit card such as MasterCard, Visa, American Express, and Diners Club at travel agencies, and at the train station ticket counters and automatic ticketing machines. If you would like to board a train and do not have a ticket, seek out the conductor prior to boarding; he or she will tell you if you may board and what the surcharge will be (usually €8). If you board a train without a ticket you will be fined €50 plus the price of the ticket. Trains can be crowded, so it's always a good idea to make a reservation when that's possible. You can review schedules at the FS Web site and reserve seats up to three months in advance at the train station or at an Italian travel agency displaying the FS emblem. You will need to reserve seats even if you are using a rail pass.

Even though it's not required for high-speed travel, for other trains **you must validate your ticket before boarding** by punching it at a yellow box in the waiting area of smaller train stations or at the end of the track in larger stations. If you forget, tell the conductor immediately to avoid a hefty fine.

Train strikes of various kinds are common, so it's a good idea to make sure your train is running. During a strike, minimum service is guaranteed, but what exactly that service consists of is difficult to predict.

Traveling by night can be a good deal (if somewhat of an adventure), as you will pass a night without having to have a hotel room. More-comfortable trains run on the longer routes (Sicily–Rome, Sicily–Milan, Sicily–Venice, Rome–Turin, Lecce–Milan); ask for the good-value T3 (three single beds), Intercity Notte, and Carrozza Comfort. The Vagone Letto Excelsior has private bathrooms and single-, double-, or twin-bed suites.

Information FS–Trenitalia (☎ *892021 in Italy* ⊕ *www.trenitalia.com*).

TRAIN PASSES

Rail passes may offer the possibility to save on train travel. Compare rail-pass cost with actual fares to determine whether you truly save, as fares can vary considerably. Generally, the more often you plan to travel long distances on high-speed trains, the more likely a rail pass would make sense.

A Eurail Italy Pass allows a certain number of travel days within Italy over the course of two months. Three to 10 days of travel cost from $277 to $510 (first class) or $225 to $413 (second class). If you're in a group of from two to five people, consider the discounted **Eurail Italy Pass Saver:** a pass for 3 to 10 travel days costs from $236 to $434 (first class) or $192 to $351 (second class); children's passes are further discounted. **Eurail Italy Youth** (for those under 26) is second-class only and costs from \$183 to \$337 for 1 to 10 days of travel.

Italy is one of 17 countries that accept the Eurail Pass, which allows unlimited first- and second-class travel. If you plan to rack up the miles, get a Global Eurail Pass. The Eurail Select Pass allows for travel in three to five contiguous countries. In addition to standard Eurail Passes, there are the Eurail Youth Pass (for those under 26), the Eurail Flexipass (which allows a certain number of travel days within a set period), the Eurail Saver (which gives a discount for two or more people traveling together), and the Eurail Drive Pass (which combines travel by train and rental car).

All passes must be purchased before you leave for Europe. Keep in mind that even with a rail pass, you still need to reserve seats on the trains you plan to take.

Contacts Europe on Rail (☎ *866/858-6854* ⊕ *www.europeonrail.com*). **Rail Europe** (☎ *800/622-8600* ⊕ *www.raileurope.com*). **Rail-Pass** (☎ *877/724-5727* ⊕ *www.railpass.com*).

Travel Times by Train

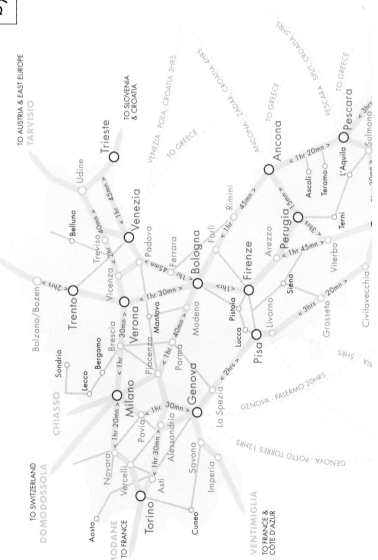

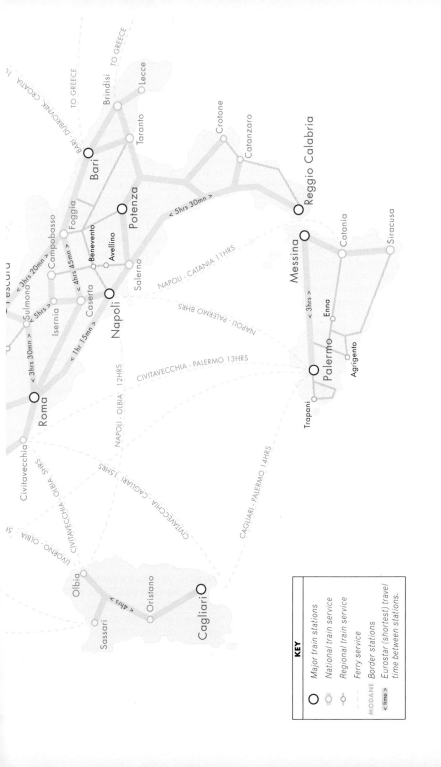

KEY

- ○ Major train stations
- ○ National train service
- ○ Regional train service
- ----- Ferry service
- **MODANE** Border stations
- < time > Eurostar (shortest) travel time between stations.

ESSENTIALS

▌ACCOMMODATIONS

Italy has a varied and abundant number of hotels, bed-and-breakfasts, *agriturismi (farm stays)*, and rental properties. Throughout the cities and the countryside you can find sophisticated, luxurious palaces and villas as well as rustic farmhouses and small hotels. Six-hundred-year-old palazzi and converted monasteries have been restored as luxurious hotels, while retaining the original atmosphere. At the other end of the spectrum, boutique hotels inhabit historic buildings using chic Italian design for the interiors. Increasingly, the famed Italian wineries are creating rooms and apartments for three-day to weeklong stays.

The lodgings we list are the cream of the crop in each price category. We always list the facilities that are available, but we don't specify whether they cost extra; when pricing accommodations, always ask what's included and what costs extra. Properties are assigned price categories based on the range between their least and most expensive standard double room at high season (excluding holidays).

Hotels with the designation **BP** (for Breakfast Plan) at the end of their listing include breakfast in their rate; offerings can vary from coffee and a roll to an elaborate buffet. Those designated **EP** (European Plan) have no meals included; **MAP** (Modified American Plan) means you get breakfast and dinner; **FAP** (Full American Plan) includes all meals.

APARTMENT AND HOUSE RENTALS

More and more travelers are turning away from the three-countries-in-two-weeks style of touring and choosing to spend a week in one city or a month in the countryside. Renting an apartment, a farmhouse, or a villa can be economical depending on the number of people in your group and your budget. All are readily available throughout Italy. Most are owned by individuals and managed by rental agents who advertise available properties on the Internet. Many properties are represented by more than one rental agent, and thus the same property is frequently renamed ("Chianti Bella Vista," "Tuscan Sun Home," and "Casa Toscana Sole" are all names of the same farmhouse) on the various Internet rental sites. The rental agent may meet you at the property for the initial check-in or the owner may be present, while the rental agent handles only the online reservation and financial arrangements.

Issues to keep in mind when renting an apartment in a city or town are the neighborhood (street noise and ambience), the availability of an elevator or number of stairs, the furnishings (including pots and pans and linens), what's supplied on arrival (dishwashing liquid, coffee or tea), and the cost of utilities (are they included in the rental rate?). Inquiries about countryside properties should also include how isolated the property is. (Do you have to drive 45 minutes to reach the nearest town?) If you're arriving too late in the day to grocery shop, request that provisions for the next day's breakfast be supplied.

Contacts At Home Abroad (☎ 212/421–9165 ⊕ www.athomeabroadinc.com). **Barclay International Group** (☎ 800/845–6636 or 516/364–0064 ⊕ www.barclayweb.com). **Drawbridge to Europe** (☎ 888/268–1148 or 541/482–7778 ⊕ www.drawbridgetoeurope. com). **Hosted Villas** (☎ 800/374–6637 or 416/920–1873 ⊕ www.hostedvillas.com). **Italy Rents** (☎ 202/821–4273 ⊕ www. italyrents.com). **Rent A Villa** (☎ 877/250– 4366 or 206/417–3444 ⊕ www.rentavilla. com). **Suzanne B. Cohen & Associates** (☎ 207/622–0743 ⊕ www.villaeurope.com). **Tuscan House** (☎ 800/844–6939 ⊕ www. tuscanhouse.com). **Villas & Apartments Abroad** (☎ 212/213–6435 ⊕ www.vaanyc.

com). **Villas International** (☎ *800/221–2260 or 415/499–9490* ⊕ *www.villasintl.com*). **Villas of Distinction** (☎ *800/289–0900* ⊕ *www. villasofdistinction.com*). **Wimco** (☎ *866/850– 6140* ⊕ *www.wimco.com*).

CONVENTS AND MONASTERIES

Throughout Italy, tourists can find reasonably priced lodging at convents, monasteries, and religious houses. Religious orders usually charge from €30 to €60 per person per night for rooms that are clean, comfortable, and convenient. Many have private bathrooms; spacious lounge areas and secluded gardens or terraces are standard features. A Continental breakfast ordinarily comes with the room, but be sure to ask. Sometimes, for an extra fee, family-style lunches and dinners are available.

Be aware of two issues when considering a convent or monastery stay: most have a curfew of 11 PM or midnight, and you need to book in advance, because they fill up quickly.

Contacts Hospites.it (⊕ *www.hospites. it*) has listings of convents throughout Italy. **Monastery Stays** (⊕ *www.monasterystays. com*) is an online booking service, with photos and descriptions, for many religious houses throughout Italy.

FARM HOLIDAYS AND AGRITOURISM

Rural accommodations in the *agriturismo* (agricultural tourism) category are increasingly popular with both Italians and visitors to Italy; you stay on a working farm or vineyard. Accommodations vary in size and range from luxury apartments, farmhouses, and villas to basic facilities. Agriturist has compiled *Agriturism,* which is available only in Italian, but includes more than 1,600 farms in Italy; pictures and the use of international symbols to describe facilities make the guide a good tool. Local APT tourist offices also have information.

Information Agriturismo.net (⊕ *www. agriturismo.net*). **Agriturist** (☎ *06/6852342*

⊕ *www.agriturist.it*). **Italy Tourist: Farm Holiday** (⊕ *www.italytourist.it*).

HOME EXCHANGES

With a direct home exchange you stay in someone else's home while they stay in yours. Some outfits also deal with vacation homes, so you're not actually staying in someone's full-time residence, just their vacant weekend place.

Italians have historically not been as enthusiastic about home exchanges as others have been; however, there are many great villas and apartments in Italy owned by foreigners, such as Americans, who use the home-exchange services.

Exchange Clubs Home Exchange.com (☎ *800/877–8723* ⊕ *www.homeexchange. com*) ; membership is $9.95 monthly or $15.95 for three months. **HomeLink International** (☎ *800/638–3841* ⊕ *www.homelink.org*) ; $115 for one year, $118 for two. Additional listings, $18 each. **Intervac U.S.** (☎ *800/756–4663* ⊕ *www.intervacus.com*) ; $99 for one-year membership.

HOSTELS

Hostels offer bare-bones lodging at low, low prices—often in shared dorm rooms with shared baths—to people of all ages, though the primary market is young travelers, especially students (some have an upper age limit, in fact). Most hostels serve breakfast; dinner and/or shared cooking facilities may also be available. In some hostels you aren't allowed to be in your room during the day, and there may be a curfew at night. Nevertheless, hostels provide a sense of community, with public rooms where travelers often gather to share stories. Many hostels are affiliated with Hostelling International (HI), an umbrella group of hostel associations with some 4,500 member properties in more than 70 countries. Other hostels are independent and may be nothing more than a really cheap hotel.

Membership in any HI association, open to travelers of all ages, allows you to stay in HI-affiliated hostels at member rates.

One-year membership is about $28 for adults; hostels charge about $20–$40 per night. Members have priority if the hostel is full; they're also eligible for discounts around the world, even on rail and bus travel in some countries.

Hostels in Italy run the gamut from low-end hotels to beautiful villas. In Florence, the campground and hostel near Piazzale Michelangelo has a better view of the city than any luxury hotel in town.

Information HiHostels (☎ +44–0–1707–324170 ⊕ www.hihostels.com). **Hostelling International—USA** (☎ 301/495–1240 national office; check online for phone number of office in your state ⊕ www.hiusa.org). **Hostel World** (⊕ www.hostelworld.com). **Hostelz** (⊕ www.hostelz.com).

∎ COMMUNICATIONS

INTERNET

Getting online in Italian cities isn't difficult: public Internet stations and Internet cafés, some open 24 hours, are common. Prices differ from place to place, so spend some time to find the best deal. Chains like Internet Train can be handy if you're moving about the country, as you can simply prepay your time, and then use the nearest location to connect without staff intervention. You can even use your own laptop if you prefer.

Wi-Fi hot spots can be found in lodgings from high-end hotels to B&Bs, major airports and train stations, cafés, and shopping centers, but are rarely free.

Broadband and Wi-Fi connections are becoming increasingly common in lodging. Some hotels have in-room modem lines, but, as with phones, using the hotel's line is relatively expensive. Always check modem rates before plugging in. You may need a plug adapter for your computer for the European-style electric socket (a converter will likely not be necessary). If you are traveling with a laptop, carry a spare battery and an adapter. Never plug your computer into any socket before asking about surge protection. IBM sells a tiny modem tester that plugs into a telephone jack to check whether the line is safe to use.

Contacts Internet Cafes in Italy (⊕ cafe.ecs. net) has an extensive list of Italian Internet cafés. **Jiwire** (⊕ www.jiwire.com) has a fairly complete, comprehensible list of Italian Wi-Fi locations, including maps.

PHONES

The good news is that you can now make a direct-dial telephone call from virtually any point on Earth. The bad news? You can't always do so cheaply. Calling from a hotel is almost always the most expensive option; hotels usually add huge surcharges to all calls, particularly international ones. Calling cards can keep costs to a minimum, but only if you purchase them locally. And then there are mobile phones; as expensive as mobile phone calls can be, they are still usually a much cheaper option than calling from your hotel. With a little effort, you can manage to reduce the call expense, though.

CALL ITALY FROM ABROAD

When calling Italy from North America, dial 011 (which gets you an international line), followed by Italy's country code, 39, and the phone number, including any leading 0. Note that Italian cell numbers have 10 digits and always begin with a 3; Italian landline numbers will contain from 4 to 10 digits, and will always begin with a 0. So for example, when calling Rome, whose numbers begin with 06, you dial 011 + 39 + 06 + phone number; for a cell phone, dial 011 + 39 + cell number.

CALLING WITHIN ITALY

With the advent of mobile phones, public pay phones are becoming increasingly scarce, although they can be found at train and subway stations, main post offices, and in some bars. In rural areas, town squares usually have a pay phone. Pay phones require a *scheda telefonica* (phone card ⇨ *below*).

For all calls within Italy, whether local or long-distance, you'll dial the entire phone

LOCAL DO'S AND TABOOS

GREETINGS

Upon meeting and leave-taking, both friends and strangers wish each other good day or good evening (*buongiorno, buonasera*); *ciao* isn't used between strangers. Italians who are friends greet each other with a kiss, usually first on the left cheek, then on the right. When you meet a new person, shake hands.

SIGHTSEEING

Italy is full of churches, and many of them contain significant works of art. They are also places of worship, however, so be sure to dress appropriately.

Shorts, tank tops, and sleeveless garments are taboo in most churches throughout the country. In summer carry a sweater or other item of clothing to wrap around your bare shoulders to avoid being denied entrance.

You should never bring food into a church, and do not sip from your water bottle while inside. If you have a cell phone, turn it off before entering. Ask if photographs are allowed; never use a flash. And never enter a church when a service is in progress, especially if it is a private affair such as a wedding or baptism.

OUT ON THE TOWN

Table manners in Italy are formal; rarely do Italians share food from their plates. In a restaurant, be formal and polite with your waiter—no calling across the room for attention.

When you've finished your meal and are ready to go, ask for the check (*il conto*); unless it's well past closing time, no waiter will put a bill on your table until you've requested it.

Italians do not have a culture of sipping cocktails or chugging pitchers of beer. Wine, beer, and other alcoholic drinks are almost always consumed as part of a meal. Public drunkenness is abhorred.

Smoking has been banned in all public establishments, much like in the United States.

Flowers, chocolates, or a bottle of wine are appropriate hostess gifts when invited to dinner at the home of an Italian.

DOING BUSINESS

Showing up on time for business appointments is the norm and expected in Italy. There are more business lunches than business dinners, and even business lunches aren't common, as Italians view mealtimes as periods of pleasure and relaxation.

Business cards are used throughout Italy, and business attire is the norm for both men and women. To be on the safe side, it is best not to use first names or a familiar form of address until invited to do so.

Business gifts are not the norm, but if one is given it is usually small and symbolic of your home location or type of business.

LANGUAGE

One of the best ways to connect with Italians is to learn a little of the local language. You need not strive for fluency; just mastering a few basic words and terms is bound to make interactions more rewarding.

"Please" is *per favore*, "thank you" is *grazie*, "you're welcome" is *prego*, and "excuse me" is *scusi*.

In larger cities such as Venice, Rome, and Florence, language is not a big problem. Most hotels have English speakers at their reception desks, and, if not, they can always find someone who speaks at least a little English. You may have trouble communicating in the countryside, but a phrase book and expressive gestures will go a long way. A phrase book and language-tape set can help get you started before you go. *Fodor's Italian for Travelers* (available at bookstores everywhere) is excellent.

number that starts with 0, or 3 for cell phone numbers. Rates from landlines vary according to the time of day; it's cheaper to call before 9 AM and after 7 or 8 PM; calling a cell phone will cost significantly more. Italy uses the prefix "800" for toll-free or "green" numbers.

MAKING INTERNATIONAL CALLS

Because of the high rates charged by most hotels for long-distance and international calls, you're better off making such calls from public phones or your mobile phone (⇨ *below*), using an international calling card (⇨ *below*). If you prefer to use the hotel phone to make an international call, you can still save money by using an international calling card.

Although not advised because of the exorbitant cost, you can place international calls or collect calls through an operator by dialing 170. Rates to the United States are lowest on Sunday around the clock and between 10 PM and 8 AM (Italian time) on weekdays and Saturday. You can also place a direct call to the United States using your U.S. phone calling-card number. You automatically reach a U.S. operator and thereby avoid all language difficulties.

The country code for the United States and Canada is 1 (dial 00 + 1 + area code and number).

Access Codes AT&T Direct (☏ *800/172–444*). **MCI WorldPhone** (☏ *800/905–825*). **Sprint International Access** (☏ *800/172–405*).

CALLING CARDS

Prepaid *schede telefoniche* (phone cards) are available throughout Italy and are best for calls within the country. Cards in different denominations are sold at post offices, newsstands, tobacco shops, and some bars. When using with pay phones, tear off the corner of the card and insert it into the phone's slot. When you dial, the card's value appears in a display window. After you hang up, the card is returned (so don't walk off without it).

International calling cards are different; you call a toll-free number from any

phone, entering the code found on the back of the card followed by the destination number. The best card for calling North America and elsewhere in Europe is the Europa card, which comes in two denominations, €5 for 180 minutes and €10 for 360 minutes, available at tobacco shops. Just ask for a card for calling the United States (or the country you prefer).

MOBILE PHONES

If you have a multiband phone (Europe and North America use different calling frequencies) and your service provider uses the world-standard GSM network (as do T-Mobile, AT&T, and Verizon), you can probably use your own phone and provider abroad. Roaming fees can be steep, however: 99¢ a minute is considered reasonable. And overseas you normally pay the toll charges for incoming calls. It's almost always cheaper to send a text message than to make a call, since text messages have a low set fee (often less than 15¢).

To further reduce calling expenses, consider buying an Italian SIM card (making sure your service provider first unlocks your phone for use with a different SIM) and a prepaid service plan once at your destination. You then have a local number and can make calls at local rates (which also means you pay only for calls made, not received).

■**TIP**➜ If you travel internationally frequently, save one of your old mobile phones (ask your cell phone company to unlock it for you) or buy an unlocked, multiband phone online; take it with you as a travel phone, buying a new SIM card with pay-as-you-go service in each destination.

The cost of cell phones is dropping; you can purchase a dual band (Europe only) cell phone with a prepaid call credit (no monthly service plan) in Italy for less than €50, then top off the credit as you go if necessary. This plan will not allow you to call the United States, but using an international calling card with the cell phone solves that problem in an inexpensive manner. Most medium-size to large towns have stores dedicated to selling cell phones. The purchase of a multiband phone means it will also function once you return home, European phones are not "locked" to their provider's SIM (which is also why they cost more). You will need to present your passport to purchase any SIM card.

Rental cell phones are available online prior to departure ($\Rightarrow$ *below*) and in Italy in cities and larger towns. Many Internet cafés offer them, but shop around for the best deal. Most rental contracts require a refundable deposit that covers the cost of the cell phone (€75–€150) and then set up a monthly service plan that is automatically charged to your credit card. Frequently, rental cell phones will be triple band with a plan that allows you to call North America. Be sure to check the rate schedule to avoid a nasty surprise when you receive your credit-card bill two or three months later. Often the prepaid option will be the more cost-effective one.

■**TIP→** Beware of cell phone (and PDA) thieves. Keep your phone or PDA in a secure pocket or purse. Do not lay it on the bar when you stop for an espresso. Do not zip it into the outside pocket of your backpack in crowded cities. Do not leave it in your hotel room. If you are using a phone with a monthly service plan, notify your provider immediately if it is lost or stolen.

Contacts Cellular Abroad (☎ *800/287–5072* ⊕ *www.cellularabroad.com*) rents and sells GMS phones and sells SIM cards that work in many countries. **Mobal** (☎ *888/888–9162* ⊕ *www.mobal.com*) rents mobiles and sells GSM phones (starting at $49) that will operate in 140 countries. Per-call rates vary throughout the world. **Planet Fone** (☎ *888/988–4777* ⊕ *www.planetfone.com*) rents cell phones, but the per-minute rates are expensive.

■ CUSTOMS AND DUTIES

You're always allowed to bring goods of a certain value back home without having to pay any duty or import tax. But there's a limit on the amount of tobacco and liquor you can bring back duty-free, and some countries have separate limits for perfumes; for exact figures, check with your customs department. The values of so-called duty-free goods are included in these amounts. When you shop abroad, save all your receipts, as customs inspectors may ask to see them as well as the items you purchased. If the total value of your goods is more than the duty-free limit, you'll have to pay a tax (most often a flat percentage) on the value of everything beyond that limit.

Travelers from the United States should experience little difficulty clearing customs at any airport in Italy.

Italy requires documentation of the background of all antiques and antiquities before the item is taken out of the country. Under Italian law, all antiquities found on Italian soil are considered state property, and there are other restrictions on antique artwork. Even if purchased from a business in Italy, legal ownership of such artifacts may be in question if brought into the United States. Therefore, although they do not necessarily confer ownership, documents such as export permits and receipts are required when importing such items into the United States.

For returning to the United States, clearing customs is sometimes more difficult. U.S. residents are normally entitled to a duty-free exemption of $800 on items accompanying them. Although there is no problem with aged cheese (vacuum-sealed works best), you cannot bring back any of that delicious prosciutto or salami or any other meat product. Fresh mushrooms, truffles, or fresh fruits and vegetables are also forbidden. There are also restrictions on the amount of alcohol allowed in duty-free. Generally, you are allowed to bring in one liter of wine, beer, or other alcohol without paying a customs duty.

Information in Italy Dogana Sezione Viaggiatori (☎ *06/65954343* ⊕ *www. agenziadogane.it*). **Ministero delle Finanze,**

Direzione Centrale dei Servizi Doganali, Divisione I (☎ 06/50242117 ⊕ www.finanze.it).

U.S. Information U.S. Customs and Border Protection (⊕ www.cbp.gov).

∎ EATING OUT

Italian cuisine is still largely regional. Ask what the local specialties are: by all means, have spaghetti *alla carbonara* (with bacon and egg) in Rome, pizza in Rome or Naples, *bistecca alla fiorentina* (steak) in Florence, *cinghiale* (wild boar) in Tuscany, truffles in Piedmont, and risotto *alla milanese* in Milan. Although most restaurants in Italy serve traditional local cuisine, you can find Asian and Middle Eastern alternatives in Rome, Venice, and other cities.

The restaurants we list are the cream of the crop in each price category.

MEALS AND MEALTIMES

What's the difference between a ristorante and a trattoria? Can you order food at an *enoteca* (wine bar)? Can you go to a restaurant just for a snack, or order just a salad at a pizzeria? The following definitions should help.

Not too long ago, *ristoranti* tended to be more elegant and expensive than trattorias and *osterie,* which serve traditional, home-style fare in an atmosphere to match. But the distinction has blurred considerably, and an osteria in the center of town might be far fancier (and pricier) than a ristorante across the street. In any sit-down establishment, be it a ristorante, osteria, or trattoria, you are generally expected to order at least a two-course meal, such as: a *primo* (first course) and a *secondo* (main course) or a *contorno* (vegetable side dish); an *antipasto* (starter) followed by either a primo or secondo; or a secondo and a *dolce* (dessert).

In an enoteca (wine bar) or pizzeria it's common to order just one dish. An enoteca menu is often limited to a selection of cheese, cured meats, salads, and desserts, but if there's a kitchen you can also find soups, pastas, and main courses. The typical pizzeria fare includes *affettati misti* (a selection of cured pork), simple salads, various kinds of bruschetta, *crostini* (similar to bruschetta, with a variety of toppings), and, in Rome, *fritti* (deep-fried finger food) such as *olive ascolane* (green olives with a meat stuffing) and *suppli* (rice balls stuffed with mozzarella).

The handiest and least expensive places for a quick snack between sights are probably bars, cafés, and pizza *al taglio* (by the slice) spots. Pizza al taglio shops are easy to negotiate but few have seats. They sell pizza by weight: just point out which kind you want and how much.

Bars in Italy resemble what we think of as cafés, and are primarily places to get a coffee and a bite to eat, rather than drinking establishments. Most bars have a selection of *panini* (sandwiches) warmed up on the griddle (*piastra*) and *tramezzini* (sandwiches made of untoasted white bread triangles). In larger cities, bars also serve vegetable and fruit salads, cold pasta dishes, and gelato. Most bars offer beer and a variety of alcohol as well as wines by the glass (sometimes good but more often mediocre). A café is like a bar but usually with more tables. Pizza at a café should be avoided—it's usually heated in a microwave.

If you place your order at the counter, ask if you can sit down: some places charge for table service (especially in tourist centers); others do not. In self-service bars and cafés it's good manners to clean your table before you leave. Note that in some places (such as train stations and stops along the highway) you first pay a cashier, then show your *scontrino* (receipt) at the counter to place your order. Menus are posted outside most restaurants (in English in tourist areas); if not, you might step inside and ask to take a look at the menu (but don't ask for a table unless you intend to stay). Italians take their food as it is listed on the menu, seldom if ever making special requests such as "dressing on the side" or "hold the olive oil." If you have special dietary needs, however, make them known; they can usually be accommodated. Although mineral water makes its way to almost every table, you can order a carafe of tap water (*acqua di rubinetto* or *acqua semplice*) instead, but keep in mind that such water can be highly chlorinated.

Wiping your bowl clean with a (small) piece of bread is usually considered a sign of appreciation, not bad manners. Spaghetti should be eaten with a fork only, although a little help from a spoon won't horrify locals the way cutting spaghetti into little pieces might. Order your caffè (Italians drink cappuccino only in the morning) after dessert, not with it. Don't ask for a doggy bag.

Breakfast (*la colazione*) is usually served from 7 to 10:30, lunch (*il pranzo*) from 12:30 to 2:30, dinner (*la cena*) from 7:30 to 10; outside those hours, best head for a bar. Peak times are usually 1:30 for lunch and 9 for dinner. *Enoteche* and *bacari* (wine bars) are open also in the morning and late afternoon for a snack at the counter. Most pizzerias open at 8 PM and close around midnight—later in summer and on weekends. Most bars and cafés are open from 7 AM until 8 or 9 PM; a few stay open until midnight.

Unless otherwise noted, the restaurants listed in this guide are open daily for lunch and dinner.

PAYING

Most restaurants have a cover charge per person, usually listed at the top of the check as *coperto* or *pane e coperto*. It should be a modest charge (€1–€2.50 per person) except at the most expensive restaurants. Whenever in doubt, ask before you order to avoid unpleasant discussions later. It is customary to leave a small tip (around 10%) in appreciation of good service. If *servizio* is included at the bottom of the check, no tip is necessary. Tips are always given in cash.

The price of fish dishes is often given by weight (before cooking), so the price you see on the menu is for 100 grams of fish, not for the whole dish. (An average fish portion is about 350 grams.) In Tuscany, *bistecca alla fiorentina* (Florentine steak) is also often priced by weight (€4 for 100 grams or €40 for 1 kilogram [2.2 pounds]).

Major credit cards are widely accepted in Italy, though cash is always preferred. More restaurants take Visa and MasterCard than American Express.

When you leave a dining establishment, take your meal bill or receipt with you; although not a common experience, the Italian finance (tax) police can approach you within 100 yards of the establishment at which you've eaten and ask for a receipt. If you don't have one, they can fine you and will fine the business owner for not providing the receipt. The measure is intended to prevent tax evasion; it's not necessary to show receipts when leaving Italy.

RESERVATIONS AND DRESS

Regardless of where you are, it's a good idea to make a reservation. We only mention them specifically when reservations are essential (there's no other way you'll ever get a table) or when they are not accepted. For popular restaurants, book as far ahead as you can (often 30 days), and reconfirm as soon as you arrive. (Large parties should always call ahead to check the reservations policy.) If you change your mind, be sure to cancel, even at the last minute.

We mention dress only when men are required to wear a jacket or a jacket and tie. But unless they're dining outside or at an oceanfront resort, Italian men never wear shorts or running shoes in a restaurant. The same applies to women: no casual shorts, running shoes, or plastic sandals when going out to dinner. Shorts are acceptable in pizzerias and cafés.

WINES, BEER, AND SPIRITS

The grape has been cultivated in Italy since the time of the Etruscans, and Italians justifiably take pride in their local vintages. Though almost every region produces good-quality wine, Tuscany, Piedmont, the Veneto, Puglia, Calabria, and Sicily are some of the more-renowned areas. Wine in Italy is less expensive than almost anywhere else, so it's often affordable to order a bottle of wine at a restaurant rather than to stick with the house wine (which, nevertheless, is sometimes quite good). Many bars have their own *aperitivo della casa* (house aperitif); Italians are imaginative with their mixed drinks, so you may want to try one.

You can purchase beer, wine, and spirits in any bar, grocery store, or enoteca, any day of the week, any time of the day. Italian and German beer is readily available, but it can be more expensive than wine.

There's no minimum drinking age in Italy. Italian children begin drinking wine mixed with water at mealtimes when they are teens (or thereabouts). Italians are rarely seen drunk in public, and public drinking, except in a bar or eating establishment, isn't considered acceptable behavior. Bars usually close by 9 PM; hotel and restaurant bars stay open until midnight. Brewpubs and discos serve until about 2 AM.

▮ ELECTRICITY

The electrical current in Italy is 220 volts, 50 cycles alternating current (AC); wall outlets take Continental-type plugs, with two or three round prongs.

Consider the purchase of a universal adapter, which has several types of plugs in one lightweight, compact unit, available at travel specialty stores and online. You can pick up plug adapters in Italy in any electric supply store for about €2 each. You'll likely not need a converter, however: most portable devices are dual voltage (i.e., they operate equally well on 110 and 220 volts), so require only an adapter; just check label specifications and manufacturer instructions to be sure. Don't use 110-volt outlets marked FOR SHAVERS ONLY for high-wattage appliances such as hair dryers.

Contacts Steve Kropla's Help for World Travelers (⊕ *www.kropla.com*) has information on electrical and telephone plugs around the world. **Walkabout Travel Gear** (⊕ *www.walkabouttravelgear.com*) has a good coverage of electricity under "adapters."

▮ EMERGENCIES

No matter where you are in Italy, you can dial 113 in case of emergency: the call will be directed to the local police. Not all 113 operators speak English, so you may want to ask a local person to place the call. Asking the operator for *"pronto soccorso"* (first aid and also the emergency room of a hospital) should get you an *ambulanza* (ambulance). If you just need a doctor, ask for *"un medico."*

Italy has the *carabinieri* (national police force, their emergency number is 112 from anywhere in Italy) as well as the *polizia* (local police force). Both are armed and have the power to arrest and investigate crimes. Always report the loss of your passport to the police as well as to your embassy. When reporting a crime, you'll be asked to fill out *una denuncia* (official report); keep a copy for your insurance company. You should also contact the police any time you have a car accident of any sort.

Local traffic officers, known as *vigili*, are responsible for, among other things, giving out parking tickets. They wear white (in summer) or black uniforms. Should you find yourself involved in a minor car accident in town, contact the vigili.

Pharmacies are generally open weekdays 8:30–1 and 4–8, and Saturday 9–1. Local pharmacies rotate covering the off-hours in shifts: on the door of every pharmacy is a list of which pharmacies in the vicinity will be open late.

Foreign Embassies U.S. Consulate Florence (✉ *Via Lungarno Vespucci 38, Florence* ☎ *055/266951*). **U.S. Consulate Milan** (✉ *Via Principe Amedeo 2/10, Milan* ☎ *02/290351*). **U.S. Consulate Naples** (✉ *Piazza della Repubblica, Naples* ☎ *081/5838111*). **U.S.**

Embassy (✉ *Via Veneto 119/A, Rome* ☎ *06/46741* ⊕ *www.usembassy.it*).

General Emergency Contacts Emergencies (☎ *113*). **National police** (☎ *112*).

▌ HOURS OF OPERATION

Religious and civic holidays are frequent in Italy. Depending on the holiday's local importance, businesses may close for the day. Businesses do not close Friday or Monday when the holiday falls on the weekend.

Banks are open weekdays 8:30–1:30 and for one or two hours in the afternoon, depending on the bank. Most post offices are open Monday–Saturday 9–12:30; central post offices are open 9–6:30 weekdays, 9–12:30 or 9–6:30 on Saturday. On the last day of the month all post offices close at midday.

Most churches are open from early morning until noon or 12:30, when they close for three hours or more; they open again in the afternoon, closing at about 6 PM. A few major churches, such as St. Peter's in Rome and San Marco in Venice, remain open all day. Walking around during services is discouraged. Many museums are closed one day a week, often Monday. During low season, museums often close early; during high season, many stay open until late at night.

Pharmacies are generally open weekdays 8:30–1 and 4–8, and Saturday 9–1. Local pharmacies rotate covering the off-hours in shifts: on the door of every pharmacy is a list of which pharmacies in the vicinity will be open late or available in emergency.

Most shops are open Monday–Saturday 9–1 and 3:30 or 4–7:30. Clothing shops are generally closed Monday mornings. Barbers and hairdressers, with some exceptions, are closed Sunday and Monday. Some bookstores and fashion- and tourist-oriented shops in places such as Rome and Venice are open all day, as well as Sunday. Large chain supermarkets such as Standa, COOP, and Esselunga do not close for lunch and are usually open Sunday; smaller *alimentari* (delicatessens) and other food shops are usually closed one evening during the week (it varies according to the town) and are almost always closed Sunday.

HOLIDAYS

Traveling through Italy in August can be an odd experience. Although there are some deals to be had, the heat can be oppressive, and much of the population is on vacation. Most cities are deserted (except for foreign tourists) and many restaurants and shops are closed. The national holidays in 2011 include January 1 (New Year's Day); January 6 (Epiphany); April 24 and April 25 (Easter Sunday and Monday); April 25 (Liberation Day); May 1 (Labor Day or May Day); June 2 (Festival of the Republic); August 15 (Ferragosto); November 1 (All Saints' Day); December 8 (Immaculate Conception); and December 25 and 26 (Christmas Day and the feast of Saint Stephen).

In addition, feast days of patron saints are observed locally. Many businesses and shops may be closed in Florence, Genoa, and Turin on June 24 (Saint John the Baptist); in Rome on June 29 (Saints Peter and Paul); in Palermo on July 15 (Santa Rosalia); in Naples on September 19 (San Gennaro); in Bologna on October 4 (San Petronio); in Trieste on November 3 (San Giusto); and in Milan on December 7 (Saint Ambrose). Venice's feast of Saint Mark is April 25, the same as Liberation Day, so the Madonna della Salute on November 21 makes up for the lost holiday.

▌ MAIL

The Italian mail system has a bad reputation but has become noticeably more efficient in recent times with some privatization. Allow from 7 to 15 days for mail to get to the United States. Receiving mail in Italy, especially packages, can take weeks, usually due to customs (not postal) delays.

Most post offices are open Monday–Saturday 9–12:30; central post offices are open weekdays 9–6:30, Saturday 9–12:30 (some until 6:30). On the last day of the month, post offices close at midday. You can buy stamps at tobacco shops as well as post offices.

Posta Prioritaria (for regular letters and packages) is the name for standard postage. It guarantees delivery within Italy in three to five business days and abroad in five to six working days. The more expensive express delivery, *Postacelere* (for larger letters and packages), guarantees one-day delivery to most places in Italy and three- to five-day delivery abroad. The postal service has no control over customs, however, which makes international delivery estimates meaningless.

Mail sent as Posta Prioritaria to the United States costs €0.85 for up to 20 grams, €1.50 for 21–50 grams, and €1.85 for 51–100 grams. Mail sent as Postacelere to the United States costs €43–€50 for up to 500 grams.

Other package services to check are Quick Pack Europe, for delivery within Europe; and EMS Express Mail Service, a global three- to five-day service for letters and packages that can be less expensive than Postacelere.

Two-day mail is generally available during the week in all major cities and at popular resorts via UPS and Federal Express. Service is reliable; a Federal Express letter to the United States costs about €35. If your hotel can't assist you, try an Internet café, many of which also offer two-day mail services using major carriers.

SHIPPING PACKAGES

You can ship parcels only via air, which takes about two weeks. If you have purchased antiques, ceramics, or other objects, ask if the vendor will do the shipping for you; in most cases this is a possibility, and preferable, because they have experience with these kinds of shipments.

If so, ask if the article will be insured against breakage. When shipping a package out of Italy, it is virtually impossible to find an overnight delivery option—the fastest delivery time is 48 to 72 hours, though this will not include any time your shipment might spend in customs.

▍MONEY

Prices vary from region to region and are substantially lower in the country than in the cities. Of Italy's major cities, Venice and Milan are by far the most expensive. Resorts such as Portofino and Cortina d'Ampezzo cater to wealthy people and charge top prices. Good values can be had in the scenic Trentino–Alto Adige region of the Dolomites and in Umbria and the Marches. With a few exceptions, southern Italy and Sicily also offer bargains for those who do their homework before they leave home.

Prices throughout this guide are given for adults. Substantially reduced fees are almost always available for children, students, and senior citizens from the EU; citizens of non-EU countries rarely get discounts, but be sure to inquire before you purchase your tickets because this situation is constantly changing.

■**TIP**➔ Banks never have every foreign currency on hand, and it may take as long as a week to order. If you're planning to exchange funds before leaving home, don't wait until the last minute.

ATMS AND BANKS

An ATM (*bancomat* in Italian) is the easiest way to get euros in Italy. There are numerous ATMs in large cities and small towns, as well as in airports and train stations. They are not common in places such as grocery stores. Be sure to **memorize your PIN in numbers,** as ATM keypads in Italy don't usually display letters. Check with your bank to confirm that you have an international PIN (*codice segreto*) that will be recognized in the countries you are visiting, to find out your maximum daily withdrawal allowance, and to learn what your bank's fee is for withdrawing money.

■ **TIP→** Be aware that PINs beginning with a 0 (zero) tend to be rejected in Italy.

Your own bank may charge a fee for using ATMs abroad or charge for the cost of conversion from euros to dollars. Nevertheless, you can usually get a better rate of exchange at an ATM than you will at a currency-exchange office or even when changing money inside a bank with a teller. Extracting funds as you need them is a safer option than carrying around a large amount of cash. Finally, it's a good idea to obtain more than one card that can be used for cash withdrawal, in case something happens to your main one.

CREDIT CARDS

Throughout this guide, the following abbreviations are used: **AE**, American Express; **DC**, Diners Club; **MC**, Master-Card; and **V**, Visa.

It's a good idea to **inform your credit-card company before you travel**, especially if you're going abroad and don't travel internationally often. Otherwise, the credit-card company might put a hold on your card owing to unusual activity—not a good thing halfway through your trip. Record all your credit-card numbers—as well as the phone numbers to call if your cards are lost or stolen—in a safe place, so you're prepared should something go wrong. MasterCard and Visa have general numbers you can call (collect if you're abroad) if your card is lost, but you're better off calling the number of your issuing bank, because MasterCard and Visa generally just transfer you to your bank; your bank's number is usually printed on your card.

Although it's usually cheaper (and safer) to use a credit card abroad for large purchases (so you can cancel payments or be reimbursed if there's a problem), note that some credit-card companies *and* the banks that issue them add substantial percentages to all foreign transactions, whether they're in a foreign currency or not. Check on these fees before leaving home, so there won't be any surprises when you get the bill. Because of the exorbitant fees, avoid using your credit card for ATM withdrawals or cash advances (use a debit or cash card instead).

■ **TIP→** Before you charge something, ask the merchant whether or not he or she plans to do a dynamic currency conversion (DCC). In such a transaction the credit-card processor (shop, restaurant, or hotel, not Visa or MasterCard) converts the currency and charges you in dollars. In most cases you'll pay the merchant a 3% fee for this service in addition to any credit-card company and issuing-bank foreign-transaction surcharges.

Dynamic currency conversion programs are becoming increasingly widespread. Merchants who participate in them are supposed to ask whether you want to be charged in dollars or the local currency, but they don't always do so. And even if they do offer you a choice, they may well avoid mentioning the additional surcharges. The good news is that you *do* have a choice. And if this practice really gets your goat, you can avoid it entirely thanks to American Express; with its cards, DCC simply isn't an option.

MasterCard and Visa are preferred by Italian merchants, but American Express is usually accepted in popular tourist destinations. Credit cards aren't accepted everywhere, though; if you want to pay with a credit card in a small shop, hotel, or restaurant, it's a good idea to make your intentions known early on.

Reporting Lost Cards American Express (☏ 800/268–9824 in U.S., 336/393–1111 collect from abroad ⊕ www.americanexpress. com). **Diners Club** (☏ 800/234–6377 in U.S., 303/799–1504 collect from abroad ⊕ www. dinersclub.com). **MasterCard** (☏ 800/627–8372 in U.S., 636/722–7111 collect from abroad ⊕ www.mastercard.com). **Visa** (☏ 800/847–2911 in U.S., 410/581–9994 collect from abroad, 800/819014 in Italy ⊕ www. visa.com).

CURRENCY AND EXCHANGE

The euro is the main unit of currency in Italy, as well as in 12 other European countries. Under the euro system there are 100 *centesimi* (cents) to the euro. There are coins valued at 1, 2, 5, 10, 20, and 50 centesimi as well as 1 and 2 euros. There are seven notes: 5, 10, 20, 50, 100, 200, and 500 euros.

At this writing, 1 euro was worth was about 1.39 U.S. dollars.

Post offices exchange currency at good rates, but you will rarely find an employee who speaks English, so be prepared. (Writing your request can help in these cases.)

■TIP→ Even if a currency-exchange booth has a sign promising no commission, rest assured that there's some kind of huge, hidden fee. You're almost always better off getting foreign currency at an ATM or exchanging money at a bank.

■ PASSPORTS AND VISAS

U.S. citizens need only a valid passport to enter Italy for stays of up to 90 days.

PASSPORTS

Although somewhat costly, a U.S. passport is relatively simple to obtain and is valid for 10 years. You must apply in person if you're getting a passport for the first time; if your previous passport was lost, stolen, or damaged; or if your previous passport has expired and was issued more than 15 years ago or when you were under 16. All children under 18 must appear in person to apply for or renew a passport. Both parents must accompany any child under 14 (or send a notarized statement with their permission) and provide proof of their relationship to the child.

There are 13 regional passport offices, as well as 7,000 passport acceptance facilities in post offices, public libraries, and other governmental offices. If you're renewing a passport, you can do so by mail. Forms are available at passport acceptance facilities and online.

The cost to apply for a new passport is $100 for adults, $85 for children under 16; renewals are $75. Allow six weeks for processing, both for first-time passports and renewals. For an expediting fee of $60 you can reduce this time to about two weeks. If your trip is less than two weeks away, you can get a passport even more rapidly by going to a passport office with the necessary documentation. Private expediters can get things done in as little as 48 hours, but charge hefty fees for their services.

■TIP→ Before your trip, make two copies of your passport's data page (one for someone at home and another for you to carry separately). Or scan the page and e-mail it to someone at home and/or yourself.

VISAS

When staying for 90 days or less, U.S. citizens are not required to obtain a visa prior to traveling to Italy. If you plan to travel or live in Italy or the European Union for longer than 90 days, you must acquire a valid visa from the Italian consulate serving your state *before you leave the United States*. Plan ahead because the process of obtaining a visa will take at least 30 days, and the Italian government does not accept visa applications submitted by visa expediters.

U.S. Passport Information U.S. Department of State (☎ 877/487–2778 ⊕ www.travel.state. gov/passport).

U.S. Passport Expediters A. Briggs Passport & Visa Expeditors (☎ 800/806–0581 or 202/338–0111 ⊕ www.abriggs.com). **American Passport Express** (☎ 800/455–5166 ⊕ www.americanpassport.com). **Passport Express** (☎ 800/362–8196 ⊕ www. passportexpress.com). **Travel Document Systems** (☎ 800/874–5100 or 202/638–3800 *[additional offices in New York and San Francisco]* ⊕ www.traveldocs.com). **Travel the World Visas** (☎ 866/886–8472 or 202/223–8822 ⊕ www.world-visa.com).

▌TAXES

A 10% V.A.T. (value-added tax) is included in the rate at all hotels except those at the upper end of the range.

No tax is added to the bill in restaurants. A service charge of approximately 10%–15% is often added to your check; in some cases a service charge is included in the prices.

The V.A.T. is 20% on clothing, wine, and luxury goods. On consumer goods it's already included in the amount shown on the price tag (look for the phrase "IVA inclusa"), whereas on services it may not be; feel free to confirm. Because you are not a European citizen, if your purchases in a single transaction total more than €155, you may be entitled to a refund of the V.A.T.

When making a purchase, ask whether the merchant gives refunds—not all stores do, nor are they required to. If they do, they'll help you fill out the V.A.T. refund form, which you'll submit to a company that will issue you the refund in the form of cash, check, or credit-card adjustment.

As you leave the country (or, if you're visiting several European Union countries, on leaving the EU), present your merchandise and the form to customs officials, who will stamp it. After you're through passport control, take the stamped form to a refund-service counter for an on-the-spot refund (the quickest and easiest option). You may also mail it to the address on the form (or on the envelope with it) after you arrive home, but processing time can be long, especially if you request a credit-card adjustment. Note that in larger cities the cash refund can be obtained at in-town offices prior to departure; just ask the merchant or check the envelope for local office addresses.

Global Refund is the largest V.A.T.-refund service with 225,000 affiliated stores and more than 700 refund counters at major airports and border crossings. Its refund form, called a Tax Free Check, is the most common across the European continent.

Premier Tax Free is another company that represents more than 70,000 merchants worldwide. Look for their logos in store windows.

V.A.T. Refunds Global Refund (☎ 800/566–9828 ⊕ www.globalrefund.com). **Premier Tax Free** (☎ 905/542-1710 ⊕ www.premiertaxfree. com).

▌TIME

Italy is in the Central European Time Zone (CET). From March to October it institutes Daylight Saving Time. Italy is 6 hours ahead of U.S. Eastern Standard Time, 1 hour ahead of Great Britain, 10 hours behind Sydney, and 12 hours behind Auckland. Like the rest of Europe, Italy uses the 24-hour (or "military") clock, which means that after noon you continue counting forward: 13:00 is 1 PM, 23:30 is 11:30 PM.

▌TIPPING

In restaurants a service charge of 10% to 15% may appear on your check. If so, it's not necessary to leave an additional tip. If service is not included, leave a tip of up to 10%. Always leave your tip in cash, even if there's a line item on your credit-card slip for a tip (otherwise the server will never see it). Tip checkroom attendants €1 per person and restroom attendants €0.50 (more in expensive hotels and restaurants). In major cities, tip €0.50 or more for table service in cafés. At a hotel bar, tip €1 and up for a round or two of drinks.

Italians rarely tip taxi drivers, which is not to say that you shouldn't. A euro or two is appreciated, particularly if the driver helps with luggage. Service-station attendants are tipped only for special services; give them €1 for checking your tires. Railway and airport porters charge a fixed rate per bag. Tip an additional €0.25 per person, more if the porter is helpful. Give a barber €1–€1.50 and a hairdresser's assistant €1.50–€4 for a shampoo or cut, depending on the type of establishment.

On sightseeing tours, tip guides about €1.50 per person for a half-day group tour, more if they are especially knowledgeable. In monasteries and other sights where admission is free, a contribution (€0.50–€1) is expected.

In hotels, give the *portiere* (concierge) about 10% of the bill for services, or €2.50–€5 for help with dinner reservations and such. Leave the chambermaid about €0.75 per day, or about €4.50–€5 a week in a moderately priced hotel; tip a minimum of €1 for valet or room service. In an expensive hotel, double these amounts; tip doormen €0.50 for calling a cab and €1.50 for carrying bags to the check-in desk and bellhops €1.50–€2.50 for carrying your bags to the room.

▮ TOURS

Guided tours are a good option when you don't want to do it all yourself. You travel along with a group (sometimes large, sometimes small), stay in prebooked hotels, eat with your fellow travelers (the cost of meals may or may not be included in the price of your tour), and follow a schedule. Not all guided tours are an if-it's-Tuesday-this-must-be-Belgium experience, however. A knowledgeable guide can take you places that you might never discover on your own, and you may be pushed to see more than you would have otherwise. Tours aren't for everyone, but they can be just the thing for trips to places where making travel arrangements is difficult or time-consuming, particularly when you don't speak the language.

Whenever you book a guided tour, find out what's included and what isn't. A "land-only" tour includes all your travel (by bus, in most cases) in the destination, but not necessarily your flights to and from or even within it. Also, in most cases prices in tour brochures don't include fees and taxes. You'll also want to review how much free as opposed to organized time

you'll have, and see if that meets with your personal preferences. Remember, too, that you'll be expected to tip your guide (in cash) at the end of the tour.

Even when planning independent travel, keep in mind that every province and city in Italy has tour guides licensed by the government. Some are eminently qualified in relevant fields such as architecture and art history and are a pleasure to spend time with; others have simply managed to pass the test and have weaker interpersonal skills. Lots of private guides have Web sites: check online and in travel forums for recommendations. Best to book before you leave home, especially for popular destinations. Tourist offices and hotel concierges can also provide the names of knowledgeable local guides and the rates for certain services. When hiring on the spot, ask about their background and qualifications and make sure you can understand each other. Tipping is always appreciated, but never obligatory, for local guides.

Recommended Generalists Abercrombie & Kent (☎ 800/554–7016 ⊕ www.abercrombiekent.com). **CIE Tours International** (☎ 800/243–8687, +353 1/703–0888 in Ireland ⊕ www.cietours.com). **Maupin Tour** (☎ 800/255–4266 ⊕ www.maupintour.com). **Perillo Tours** (☎ 800/431–1515 ⊕ www.perillotours.com). **Travcoa** (☎ 800/992–2005 ⊕ www.travcoa.com).

Biking and Hiking Tour Contacts Backroads (☎ 800/462–2848 ⊕ www.backroads.com). **Butterfield & Robinson** (☎ 866/551–9090 ⊕ www.butterfield.com). **Ciclismo Classico** (☎ 800/866–7314 ⊕ www.ciclismoclassico.com). **Genius Loci Travel** (☎ +39–089–791–896 ⊕ www.genius-loci.it). **Italian Connection** (☎ 800/462–7911 ⊕ www.italian-connection.com).

Culinary Tour Contact Epiculinary (☎ 888/380–9010 ⊕ www.epiculinary.com).

Golf Tour Contact Rosso Soave (☎ +39–055–2305210 ⊕ www.rossosoave.com/GolfETuscany.html).

Volunteer Programs Elderhostel (☎ 800/454–5768 ⊕ www.elderhostel.com).

Wine Tour Contacts Cellar Tours (☎ 310/928–7559 ⊕ www.cellartours.com). **Food & Wine Trails** (☎ 800/367–5348 ⊕ www.foodandwinetrails.com).

▌TRIP INSURANCE

Comprehensive trip insurance is valuable if you're booking an expensive or complicated trip (particularly to an isolated region) or if you're booking far in advance. Comprehensive policies typically cover trip cancellation and interruption, letting you cancel or cut your trip short because of illness, or, in some cases, acts of terrorism in your destination. Such policies usually also cover evacuation and medical care. (For trips abroad you should have at least medical and medical evacuation coverage. With a few exceptions, Medicare does not provide coverage abroad, nor does regular health insurance.) Some also cover you for trip delays because of bad weather or mechanical problems as well as for lost or delayed luggage.

Another type of coverage to consider is financial default—that is, when your trip is disrupted because a tour operator, airline, or cruise line goes out of business. Generally you must buy this when you book your trip or shortly thereafter, and it's available to you only if your operator isn't on a list of excluded companies.

Many travel insurance policies have exclusions for preexisting conditions as a cause for cancellation. Most companies waive those exclusions, however, if you take out your policy within a short period (which varies by company) after the first payment toward your trip.

Always read the fine print of your policy to make sure that you're covered for the risks that most concern you. Compare several policies to be sure you're getting the best price and range of coverage available.

Insurance Comparison Info Insure My Trip (☎ 800/487–4722 ⊕ www.insuremytrip.com). **Square Mouth** (☎ 800/240–0369 or 727/564–9203 ⊕ www.squaremouth.com).

Comprehensive Insurers Access America (☎ 800/284–8300 ⊕ www.accessamerica.com). **CSA Travel Protection** (☎ 800/711–1197 ⊕ www.csatravelprotection.com). **HTH Worldwide** (☎ 610/254–8700 ⊕ www.hthworldwide.com). **Travel Guard** (☎ 800/826–4919 ⊕ www.travelguard.com). **Travelex Insurance** (☎ 800/228–9792 ⊕ www.travelexinsurance.com). **Travel Insured International** (☎ 800/243–3174 ⊕ www.travelinsured.com).

INDEX

PHOTO CREDITS

ABOUT OUR WRITERS

After completing his master's degree in art history, Peter Blackman, updater of the Piedmont chapter, settled permanently in Italy in 1986. Since then he's worked as a biking and walking tour guide. When he's not leading a trip, you'll find Peter at home in Florence.

Bruce Leimsidor studied Renaissance literature and art history at Swarthmore College and Princeton University, and in addition to his scholarly works, he has published articles on political and social issues in the *International Herald Tribune* and the *Frankfurter Allgemeine Zeitung*. He lives in Venice, where he teaches at the university, works for the municipality, collects 17th- and 18th-century drawings, and is rumored to make the best *pasta e fagioli* in town. He updated the chapters on Venice Exploring and the Veneto and Friuli–Venezia Giulia.

After a dozen trips to and a two-decade-long love affair with Liguria, Italian Riviera updater Megan McCaffrey-Guerrera moved to the seaside village of Lerici in 2004. Soon after, she started a personal travel concierge service. When not organizing tailor-made vacations of the area, Megan can be found hiking the trails of the Cinque Terre, sailing the Gulf of Poets, or searching for the freshest anchovies in the Mediterranean.

Nan McElroy is the author of the palm-size, purely practical *Italy: Instructions for Use*. (The series also includes France and Greece.) She traveled throughout Italy before relocating to Venice in 2004, where she writes *www.livingveniceblog.com* and publishes the Vap Map downloadable vaporetto guide. Nan is also an AIS sommelier who conducts wine tastings and an avid practitioner of the *voga alla veneta*—traditional Venetian rowing. She updated the Venice dining, lodging, arts, and shopping chapters.

Writer, photographer, and digital strategist Sara Rosso moved to Italy in July 2003 and has lived in Rome and Pavia as well as her current home, Milan. In her blog *www.msadventuresinitaly.com* she writes about cooking and her travels in Italy and beyond (24 countries and counting). She udpated the Milan, Lombardy, and the Lakes chapter.